Multiskilling for Television Production

Multiskilling for Television Production

Peter Ward
Alan Bermingham
Chris Wherry

Focal Press

OXFORD   AUCKLAND   BOSTON   JOHANNESBURG   MELBOURNE   NEW DELHI

Focal Press
An imprint of Butterworth-Heinemann
Linacre House, Jordan Hill, Oxford OX2 8DP
225 Wildwood Avenue, Woburn, MA 01801-2041
A division of Reed Educational and Professional Publishing Ltd

 A member of the Reed Elsevier Group

First published 2000

British Library Cataloguing in Publication Data
Ward, Peter, 1936–
   Multiskilling for television production
   1. Television – Production and direction
   I. Title   II. Bermingham, Alan   III. Wherry, Chris
   791.4'5'0232

Library of Congress Cataloguing in Publication Data
A catalogue record for this book is available from the Library of Congress

ISBN 0 240 51557 9

Printed and bound in Great Britain

FOR EVERY VOLUME THAT WE PUBLISH, BUTTERWORTH-HEINEMANN
WILL PAY FOR BTCV TO PLANT AND CARE FOR A TREE.

Contents

Acknowledgements

The authors wish to acknowledge the help and assistance in compiling this manual from many television colleagues and equipment manufacturers. In particular, Arthur Attenborough, Alison Chapman, Pat Morris, Andrew Parr, Ian Lewis, Gill Wherry, John Lisney, John Treays, Ken MacGregor, Dave Evans, Chris Watts, Chris Woolf, Hugh Snape and Carlton Television, Paul Roberts of Paul Roberts Sound, AMS Neve, Anton/Bauer Inc., Audio Developments Ltd, Audio Ltd, Dorrough Electronics, Avid Technology, Cannon (UK) Ltd, JVC, OpTex, Panasonic, Sony Corporation, Thomson Broadcast Systems, Peter Tunnah, Vinten Broadcast Ltd, Ultimatte.

Various figures have been reproduced courtesy of: Anton/Bauer Inc.; Avid Technology; Alan Bermingham, Michael Talbot-Smith, Ken Angold-Stephens and Ed Boyce *The Video Studio*, Focal Press Media Manual, Oxford; Cannon (UK) Ltd; JVC Japan; Andrew F. Inglis and Arch C. Luther; HHB Communications Ltd; Rycote Microphone Windshields Ltd; *Satellite Technology*, Focal Press, Oxford; Alec Nisbett *The Use of Microphones*, Focal Press Media Manual, Oxford; Brian Fitt and Joe Thornley *Lighting Technology*, Focal Press, Oxford; Society of TV Lighting Directors; Panasonic Broadcast; Sony Corporation; and Thomson Broadcast Systems.

Introduction

Broadcasting is always in the process of change. New technology, new production techniques and new methods of delivering the programme to the viewer are constantly evolving. Continuous innovation has been the stimulus to an industry created less than seventy years ago.

For many technicians, one of the biggest challenges in the last ten years has been the transition from a career working in a solo core skill such as camerawork, audio, etc. to acquiring the experience and expertise of a range of production jobs. Multiskilling is not a new concept. There are many technical operators who have always been able to work in any one of a number of programme-making roles, but the number of multiskillers has considerably increased due to the emphasis on lower budgets, casualization and the economics of job flexibility. Many people who find employment in the broadcast industry are expected to work in a number of crafts and to equip themselves with a much wider range of television techniques than has been customary in the past.

What are the qualities and abilities needed to operate each day in a different job? There is obviously a need for an understanding of television technology. Television programme-making is not possible without technology, even though there is a constant quest for user-friendly equipment loaded with auto facilities supposedly avoiding the need to understand what happens when each auto button is selected.

But if the technology of television programme-making equipment is understood, if each control and usage is mastered, there is still the need to assimilate programme-making technique.

Pressing buttons is not enough

Simply understanding how to operate equipment will not make you production competent. When learning to play the piano, the student can eventually understand and name each note on the piano, they can understand the function and purpose of the foot pedals, they may even have perfect pitch and correctly identify any note that is played, but this only prepares them to become a musician; they have still to learn how to apply this basic information.

Programme formats

To an understanding of technique and how technology influences technique must be added the knowledge of programme-making formats. Any competent technician, for example, will automatically apply the appropriate production methods to a news broadcast, and then be able to switch on the following day to the appropriate production methods of a pop concert. Often the two techniques are not compatible.

A production team will expect each member of the unit to be fully familiar with the customary techniques of the programme format in production. Nobody, for example, will have the time to explain the rules of a sport that is being transmitted live. They will assume that the technical operator knows the standard TV response to different phases of the event.

To an understanding of technology, technique and programme formats is added the essential skill and ability to work in a team. TV programmes are made by groups of people working together as a production unit. There are a number of professional attitudes and responsibilities commonly shared by everyone in the industry. To gain your colleagues' respect and cooperation, make certain that you adequately prepare for a production and can anticipate the technique required and, above all, you can concentrate. Viewers will often notice a small mistake whilst being completely oblivious to the competence and skills being exercised throughout a production because most television skills aim to be anonymous to the viewer. The fingerprint of skilled technicians on a production is a seamless flow of vision and sound reaching the audience with no trace (to the uninitiated) of the mechanics, planning and technique that was required.

Which standard to work to?

Multiskilling need not be de-skilling – a shallow knowledge of a wide range of skills leading to lower standards. As a technical operator, aim to work to the highest possible expertise. At some time, one of the skills that you practise may become a specialist core skill that can be developed when all your working time is concentrated on that activity. At the very least, with a greater understanding of the crafts of your fellow production team colleagues, you can improve your contribution and add to the overall programme finish.

This book will concentrate on techniques associated with news and magazine programme production where most technical operators are usually employed, but most techniques are shared across the whole spectrum of television and film-making. This may lead to the same topic being repeated in different chapters sometimes from a different perspective.

1 Television engineering

1.1 Introduction

This section introduces the basic engineering concepts necessary for operational competence in television operations. The depth of treatment is restricted to include only that which is relevant to the role of a multiskilled operator. It is essential that all such operators have an awareness of the basic television system as it affects their operational roles.

The bibliography at the end of this book provides excellent titles for further reading in the engineering aspects of television.

1.2 The video system

The basic television system is shown in Fig. 1.1.

The 'heart' of the operational system is the vision mixing console, vision mixer or switcher. All the video sources making up the programme resources are connected to the input of the vision mixer. The vision mixer (operator) selects the appropriate source as required by the Director, and on cue will initiate the necessary transition between sources, i.e. cut, mix, wipe, etc. Normal practice is to include a **distribution amplifier** (DA) in the feed of each source to enable several **isolated** feeds to be derived. The extra feeds can be used for monitoring purposes, providing isolated feeds for recording purposes (ISO feeds), etc.

The output of the vision mixing console is also fed to a distribution amplifier to enable 'programme feeds' to be available for:

- recording
- feeding to transmission suite for 'live' transmission
- monitoring.

Note the abundance of 'monitoring' – this is vital so that the video sources can be identified (for remote sources), and checked for picture content and quality. In addition to providing picture monitoring on suitable television screens, there is also a need to check the video signal levels on a waveform monitor (oscilloscope).

The sources available on the vision mixing console may include:

- studio cameras
- caption generator (cap. gen.)
- videotape replays
- electronic slide library
- video server
- graphics
- computer-generated backgrounds
- remote cameras, i.e. remote to studios but within the studio centre complex
- remote contributing source, i.e. outside broadcast or remote studio.

1.3 The television signal

From the above overview, it can be seen that there is a need to be familiar with the television signal, so that routing procedures and monitoring of the signal can be handled with ease.

The best way to approach an understanding of the television signal is first to look at the needs of a monochrome system and then develop this to look at the colour system, i.e. in the way in which the systems have evolved.

Television is the process of transmitting moving pictures. In practice a series of still pictures is transmitted, but at a rapid enough rate to see the change from one picture to the next picture as 'continuous' movement. The persistence of vision (a form of image retention) of the eye/brain means that this is possible.

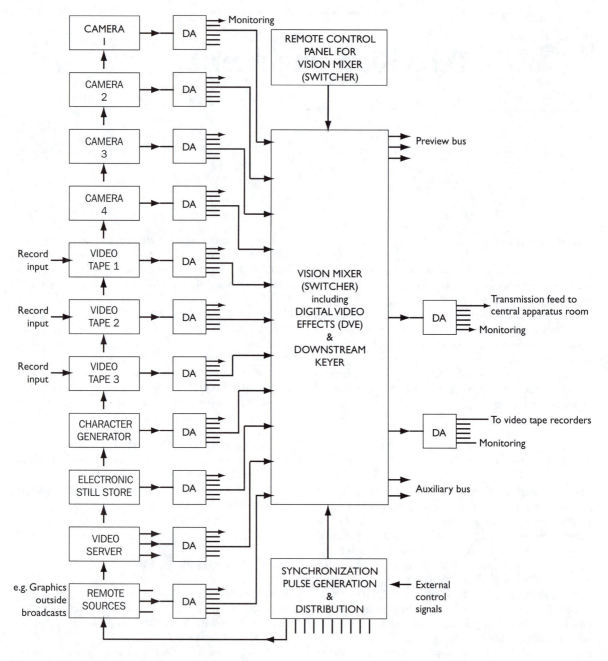

Figure 1.1 Basic television system.

This has a parallel in the film world with film shot at 24 pictures/second. Unfortunately, although a picture rate of 24 Hz is sufficient for conveying movement without 'jerky' transitions, the perceived picture suffers from **flicker**. To overcome this the picture rate needs to be above about 42 Hz. In the film world it would be expensive to shoot at 48 Hz – one would need twice as much film! The solution is a simple one: in the cinema the film projector simply displays each picture or frame twice, resulting in an effective picture rate of 48 Hz. In television the expense of a high picture rate is also prohibitive (see later note on bandwidth) – basically the more information to be transmitted in a second, the more expensive it becomes!

Having defined what is required to be done, we need to establish the basic parameters:

- aspect ratio
- scanning system
- number of lines/picture
- number of pictures/second
- interlace
- synchronization
- television signal
- bandwidth.

Aspect ratio is the ratio of picture width to picture height, the current standard of 4:3 dating back to the 1930s when early high-definition systems were developed. 4:3 was chosen as a compromise on film formats and the availability of suitable display tubes. The trend is towards 16:9 widescreen, with 14:9 as an interim measure.

The first function of the television camera is to produce an optical image of the scene to be televised and convert this to an electrical charge pattern, where the magnitude of the electrical charge is proportional to the 'brightness' (more strictly correct 'luminance') of the scene. This electrical charge pattern needs to be 'read-off' in a regular manner for transmission to the viewer. This is known as a **scanning** process and involves dividing the 'picture' into a number of horizontal lines, then 'reading' the electrical charge on each line in sequence, starting at the top left of the picture (rather like reading a page of type in a book) – see Fig. 1.2.

The **number of lines/picture** is an important parameter: too few and the line structure becomes visible; too many and information is transmitted which the viewer will not see! The limit of the acuity of the eye (ability to see fine detail) occurs when the structure of one television line subtends an angle of 1 second (1/60 of one degree); when viewing from the

Figure 1.3 Limit of visual acuity and lines/picture.

normal viewing distance (6–8 times screen diagonal), the total angle subtended at the eye is about 10°. This indicates the need for about 600 lines/picture (Fig. 1.3).

In the earlier discussion on film frame rates, an effective frame rate of 48 Hz was required to overcome 'flicker' effects. In television an 'effective' picture rate linked to mains frequency was considered desirable, i.e. 60 Hz in the USA, 50 Hz in Europe. Unfortunately, to transmit fine detail at these rates is too expensive, so a system of **interlace** scanning was adopted to halve the picture rate while still maintaining an effective flicker rate of 60 Hz and 50 Hz respectively.

Fig. 1.4 illustrates the basic principle of interlace scanning where each picture is divided into a number of lines, but having initially numbered the lines in sequence they are scanned as two separate fields, one field scanning the odd-numbered lines and the second field made up of the even-numbered lines. These are known as the odd and even fields. Note that a basic requirement for interlace work is the need for an odd number of lines/picture, e.g. 625, 525, 819.

From Fig 1.4 can be seen the need for **synchronization**, i.e. that the display scanning system (television receiver or picture monitor) must be in absolute synchronization with the camera scanning system. Synchronization is achieved by transmitting appropriate synchronizing pulses (sync pulses) at the end of each

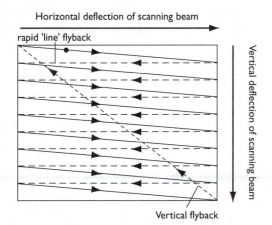

Figure 1.2 Basic sequential scanning, illustrating deflection of scanning beam.

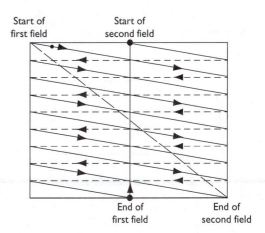

Figure 1.4 Illustrating the principle of interlace scanning.

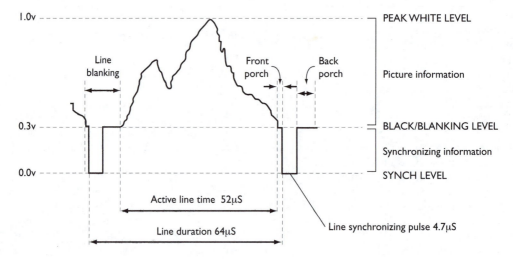

Figure 1.5 Typical television line waveform (625 line system).

line to initiate 'flyback' in the line direction and at the end of each field, to initiate field flyback.

The **television signal** therefore needs to have two components, namely:

- picture information indicating the point-by-point picture 'brightness'
- synchronizing information to synchronize the displayed picture with the camera scanning process.

These components must be readily detected at the receiver/monitor. This is achieved by separating the two lots of information:

- by voltage level
- in time.

Fig. 1.5 illustrates a typical waveform for one line of information.

The basic television waveform is a one volt signal with defined voltage levels for peak white (100% video signal), black level, blanking level and synchronizing level (sync level). Note the space between adjacent lines, called **blanking** – this is longer than the sync pulse duration to ensure that the sync pulse is not affected by picture information at the end of a line (front porch), and to allow a reference blank signal (back porch), to be transmitted. The back porch is used to re-establish the true black level of the signal; the +0.3 V black level voltage is 'lost' when the television signal is a.c. coupled in the transmission path.

A field synchronizing pulse (field sync) is included at the end of each field. This is made much longer in duration (2.5 lines) than the line sync pulse to enable the receiver to recognize it and initiate the field flyback of the scanning system. Fig. 1.6 illustrates the basic field sync pulse, including field blanking.

Unfortunately, the line scanning system also needs to be kept operational and in synchronism during the

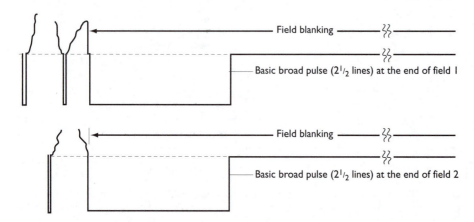

Figure 1.6 Basic field synchronizing pulses.

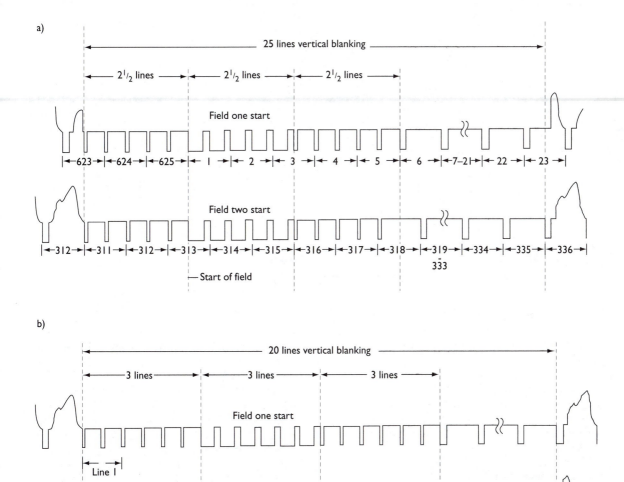

Figure 1.7 (a) 625/50 signal – vertical (field) signal timings; (b) 525/60 signal – vertical (field) signal timings.

period of field blanking, so these are included in the waveform (Fig. 1.7). This results in an inequality of signal prior to the broad pulses, so five equalizing pulses are included to make the 'run in' to and run out from the broad pulses to be identical. This is essential for good interlace.

The field blanking period enables the flyback of the scanning system to be completed before displaying picture information. In practice, this duration is more than adequate, so the blank lines are used to include text signals known as vertical interval text signals

(VITS). These can be extracted and viewed on special oscilloscopes.

In the USA a system of IRE units is used for waveform measurement (Fig. 1.8). Note that the USA system uses a pedestal of 7.5 IRE units of lift to blank level, i.e. blanking level and black level are not coincident.

The final concept to examine is that of **bandwidth**. Bandwidth relates to the ability of a system to transmit fine detail without distortion and is often referred to as the resolution or definition of a system or device (CCD).

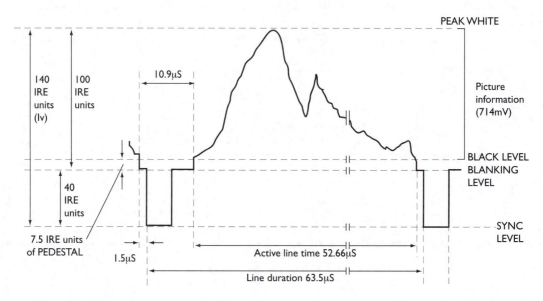

Figure 1.8 525 line waveform.

From our previous discussions we have established:

Picture aspect ratio	4:3
Lines/picture	625 (lines/field 312½)
Picture rate	25 Hz interlaced to give a 50 Hz field rate
Period of 1 line	= 64 μS
Line blanking	= 12 μS
Active picture time/line	= 52 μS
Field blanking	= 25 lines/field (50 lines/picture)

So, the active number of lines/picture = 625 – 50 = 575, i.e. the maximum resolution in the vertical direction is 575 pieces of information.

However, if you did frame a chart with 575 pieces of information, alternating black and white in a vertical direction, the probability of aligning the television line structure exactly with the pattern is very low, i.e. it would be difficult to resolve this fine detail. Usually, a factor called the Kell factor is introduced to take account of the probability of resolving fine detail, typically 0.7. This means the practical vertical resolution is $0.7 \times 575 \simeq 400$ lines/picture height.

Assuming equal horizontal and vertical resolution the number of pieces of information along one line will be ⅘ × 400 = 533.

If we consider this as alternate black/white information, we have the number of cycles of information/line = 533/2 = 266.5, and this takes place in a period of 52 μS. So the frequency represented by this information is 266.5/52 ≃ 5.2 MHz.

This figure of 5.2 MHz represents the bandwidth requirements for the system, i.e. the ability to transmit a range of frequencies from field frequency to 5.2 MHz. 5.5 MHz is adopted in the UK, with 5.0 MHz for much of Europe.

Often, to avoid confusion with different scanning rates, the resolution is quoted in lines/picture height, e.g. 575 × 0.7 = 402.5, so 400 lines/picture height corresponds with 5.2 MHz (625 line system).

Note: Often manufacturers will quote resolution as 700 lines. This usually means that the horizontal resolution is such that one can just discern a pattern of 700 lines/picture height along a line. To be

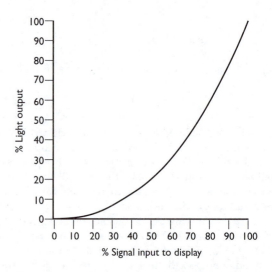

Figure 1.9 Television display tube transfer characteristic.

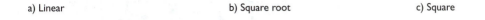

a) Linear   b) Square root   c) Square

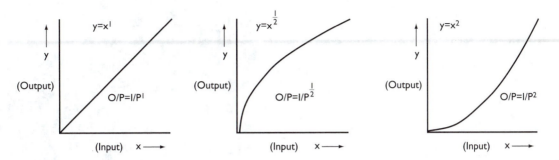

Figure 1.10 Basic mathematical laws.

meaningful, any figure quoting resolution should also indicate the depth of modulation as well, e.g. 20% at 700 lines.

Assume 10% depth of modulation (just discernible) if no qualifying percentage is indicated.

1.4 Tonal reproduction and gamma

Faithful reproduction of the tonal values in a televised scene is one of the main objectives of any television system, i.e. no stretching or crushing of tonal information. If all parts of the television system had a linear transfer characteristic between input and output, there would be no need to discuss this any further. Unfortunately, one part of the system, the television display tube, is non-linear, so there is a need to discuss the implications of this for the remaining parts of the system. The transfer characteristic of a television display tube can be described with a graph (Fig. 1.9).

Another way to describe this characteristic is to express the curve as a mathematical law, for example:

Fig. 1.10(a) illustrates a linear law $y = x$
Fig. 1.10(b) illustrates a square-root law $y = \sqrt{x} = x^{1/2}$
Fig. 1.10(c) illustrates a square law $y = x^2$

In each of these examples, the law is described by the index associated with x. Use is made of this concept in television to describe the relationship between the input and output of any part of the system. The term gamma (γ) is used to indicate the transfer characteristic, for example:

CCD camera chip $\gamma = 1$
TV display tube $\gamma = 2.4$ (colour)

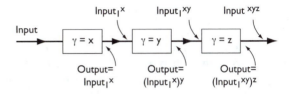

Figure 1.11 Derivation of overall gamma.

Note that individual gammas are multiplied to derive the overall gamma (Fig. 1.11).

So, in the case of the television system, if the signal derived from a CCD is applied directly to the display tube, severe black 'crushing' will occur, together with 'stretching' of the highlight information, i.e. $\gamma = 1 \times 2.4 = 2.4$ (Fig. 1.12).

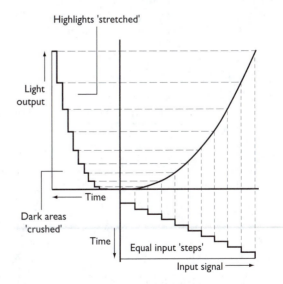

Figure 1.12 Illustrating black crush/white stretch of CRT display.

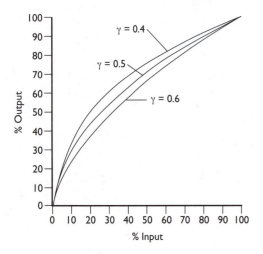

Figure 1.13 Typical camera gamma laws.

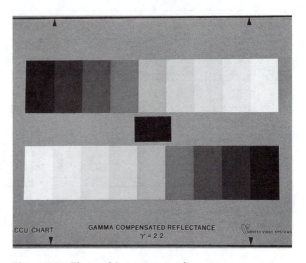

Figure 1.14 Photo of 9-step grey scale.

Clearly, this indicates the need for some form of **gamma correction** to provide an overall gamma of approximately 1. Typically, a gamma corrector with a 0.45 law is used to give an overall gamma of 1.08:

$$1 \times 0.45 \times 2.4 = 1.08$$

This slightly enhanced gamma is desirable to compensate for the effect of ambient lighting conditions of the viewer.

The gamma corrector law is selectable in the camera (Fig. 1.13).

The curves shown in Fig. 1.13 represent the ideal condition of a full gamma correction. In practice, correction is not applied fully to the darker tones. A quick examination of the correction needed for a 1% signal to a 0.5 gamma reveals the reason why:

Output = (input)$^\gamma$
Output = $0.01^{0.5}$ = 0.1

i.e. the extra gain required is ×10, which is clearly undesirable if an acceptable signal-to-noise ratio is to be maintained. Usually, a compromise is made where the gamma correction applied to the 0–5% signal area is a fixed gain of ×5. It is worth checking that your camera has the recommended correction; in practice, some manufacturers operate with a reduced fixed gain to preserve the signal-to-noise ratio. The consequences of undercorrection are black crushing of dark tones, for example the detail seen in dark hair. Gamma correction, because it adds noise, is completed where the signal-to-noise ratio is at its best, i.e. at the camera.

Often, a 9-step step-wedge chart is used to check the transfer characteristic of cameras (Table 1.1 and Fig. 1.14). The basic test is to observe the difference between step 9 (2% reflectivity) and the black patch (0.5% reflectivity), i.e. expect about a 10% difference.

Note: Typical European face tones are approximately half the reflectivity of a white (60% reflectivity), resulting in a television signal of about 50%

Table 1.1 Typical video levels for 9-step grey scale and various gamma levels.

Step	% Reflectivity	As % of Step 1 $\gamma = 1$	% TV signal $\gamma = 0.4$	% TV signal $\gamma = 0.5$
1	60	100	100	100
2	49	81	92	90
3	36	60	81	77
4	26	43	70	65
5	16	26	56	50
6	13	21	51	44
7	8	13	41	35
8	5	8	32	26
9	2	3	14	14
Background	16	26	56	50
Black patch	<0.5	<0.5	≅3	≅3

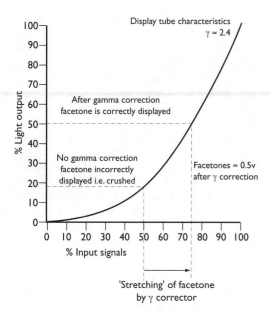

Figure 1.15 Typical face tone video levels after gamma correction.

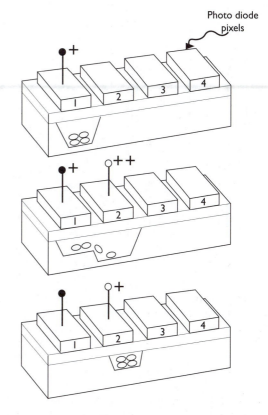

Figure 1.16 Basic CCD action.

(before gamma correction); after gamma correction this becomes a 70–75% television signal, i.e. about 0.5 V (Fig. 1.15). (Hence some ENG cameras set zebra patterns to onset at a 75% signal.)

The need for gamma correction caused by the high gamma of the display tube is not all bad news. The 'crushing' of the signal at the display tube means that the 'noise' received at the receiver is also crushed, i.e. made less visible – this is clearly a bonus!

LCD and plasma screens have an inherent gamma of one, so they have to be fitted with a 2.4 gamma law to ensure correct display of the television signal.

1.5 Camera sensors

Camera tubes have rapidly been replaced by **charge coupled devices** (CCDs) in most television cameras. The CCD is a solid state device using special integrated circuitry technology, hence it is often referred to as a **chip camera**. The complete CCD sensor or chip has at least 450 000 picture elements or **pixels**, each pixel being basically an isolated (insulated) photodiode. The action of the light on each pixel is to cause electrons to be released which are held by the action of a positive voltage. Fig. 1.16 illustrates how this charge may be moved, i.e. how scanning may be achieved.

The charge held under electrode 1 can be moved to electrode 2 by changing the potential on the electrodes as shown. The electrons (negative charges)

follow the most positive attraction. A repeat of this process would move the charges to electrode 3, hence the term charge coupled device. A system of transfer clock pulses is used to move the charges in CCDs to achieve scanning.

There are three types of CCD device:

- frame transfer (FT)
- interline transfer (IT)
- frame interline transfer (FIT).

Frame transfer was the first of the CCDs to be developed. It consists of two identical areas, an imaging area and a storage area (Fig. 1.17).

The imaging area is the image plane for the focused optical image, the storage area being masked from any light. The electrical charge image is built up during one field period but during field blanking this charge is moved rapidly into the storage area. A mechanical shutter is used during field blanking to avoid contamination of the electrical charges during their transfer to the storage area. The storage area is 'emptied' line by line into a read-out register where, during line-time, one line of pixel information is

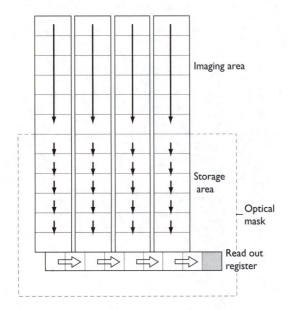

Figure 1.17 Basic frame transfer (FT) CCD principle.

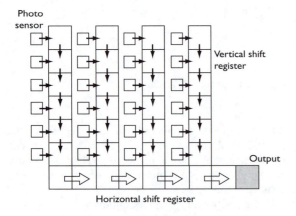

Figure 1.18 Basic interline transfer (IT) CCD principle.

'clocked' through the register to produce the video signal.

Interline transfer CCDs were developed to avoid the need for a mechanical shutter (Fig. 1.18). The storage cell is placed adjacent to the pick-up pixel, and during field blanking the charge generated by the pixel is shifted sideways into the storage cell.

The read-out process is similar to the frame transfer device, with the storage elements being 'clocked' through the vertical shift register at field rate into the horizontal shift register, then the charges read out at line rate. Earlier forms of IT devices suffered from severe vertical smear which produced a vertical line running through a highlight. This was caused by excessive highlights penetrating deeply into the

semiconductor material, leaking directly into the vertical shift register. Later IT devices have improved the technology to make this a far less objectionable effect.

Frame interline transfer CCDs are a further development of the interline transfer device to overcome the problem of vertical smear. As its name suggests, it is a combination of both types (Fig. 1.19).

The FIT sensor has a short-term storage element adjacent to each pixel (as IT) and a duplicated storage area (as FT). During field blanking the charges are moved from the pixels into the adjacent short-term storage element and then moved at 60 times field frequency into the storage area. This rapid moving of the charge away from the vulnerable imaging area overcomes the vertical smear problem.

Development in CCD technology has seen the introduction of:

- the hole accumulated diode (HAD) sensor which enabled up to 750 pixels/line, with increased sensitivity and a reduction in vertical smear
- the hyper HAD sensor which included a microlens on each pixel to collect the light more efficiently. This gave a one-stop increase in sensitivity over the HAD sensor
- the power HAD sensor with improved signal-to-noise ratio which resulted in at least half a stop gain in sensitivity
- CCD output integration.

The two interlaced fields may be obtained in one of two ways:

(1) **Field integration** in which the signals from adjacent lines are averaged, i.e.:

   Field 1 – (line 1 and line 2), (line 3 and line 4), etc.
   Field 2 – (line 2 and line 3), (line 4 and line 5), etc.

   This gives less motion blur than frame integration, but the vertical resolution is reduced. The effective exposure is 1/50 second.

(2) **Frame integration** reads out once every frame or picture period, 1/25 second, resulting in more motion blur due to the larger integration time but should give better vertical resolution on static subjects.

Normally, cameras are operated in the field integration mode.

Electronic shutters

The integration time of CCDs can be shortened electronically by draining unwanted charges on each pixel during the 1/50 second exposure time, that is:

1/60, 1/125, 1/250, 1/500, 1/1000, etc.

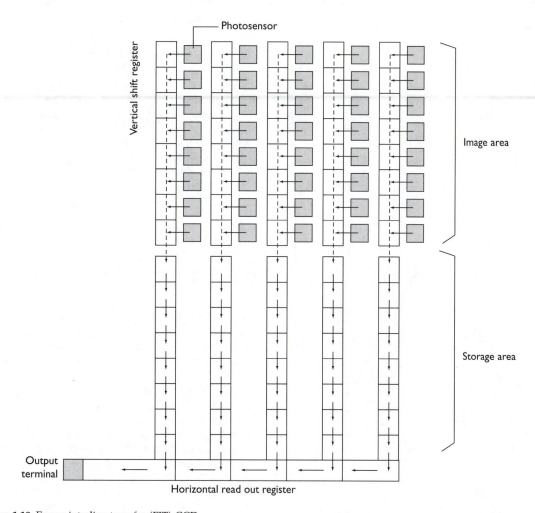

Figure 1.19 Frame interline transfer (FIT) CCD.

This is particularly useful for 'still' shots of fast moving objects (less blur), or simply reducing the camera sensitivity. Note, however, that live fast moving action and short exposure times result in 'jerky' action, not to be recommended.

Enhanced Vertical Definition System (EVS) refers to the technique of blanking out one field with the electronic shutter when in the field integration mode. This results in improved vertical resolution, no averaging of lines, and a reduction in sensitivity of one stop.

Resolution of sensors, the ability to resolve fine detail, has increased as the technology has improved, for example:

Sony BVP 50 – approx. 500 pixels/line
Sony BVP 70 – approx. 700 pixels/line
Sony BVP 90 – approx. 900 pixels/line (1000 pixels/line).

1.6 Colour television – principles

Colour television is based on the principle of additive colour mixing in which three suitable primaries (red, green and blue) can be mixed together to produce (synthesize) white and a wide range of colours. The colour seen is dependent on the relative amounts of red, green and blue light. This is illustrated in Fig. 1.20.

Mixtures between two of the primary colours can be plotted as points on the line joining the two primaries, e.g. a mixture of Red and Green produces Yellow. When the three primary colours are mixed together the resultant colour 'mix' can be plotted inside the triangle. In colorimetry (the measurement of colour) it is a useful concept to consider White being made up of equal amounts of Red, Green and Blue (see later), and hence White plots at the centre of the triangle.

a) Colour triangle

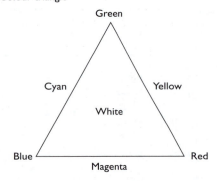

b) Illustrating hue and saturation

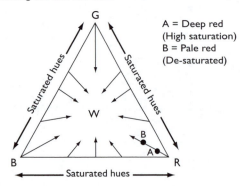

A = Deep red
(High saturation)
B = Pale red
(De-saturated)

Figure 1.20 Additive colour mixing.

Hue is the term given to the dominant wavelength of any object and literally means the colour we see. **Saturation** is a measure of the purity of the colour, and is an indication of how diluted the hue is with the other wavelengths. The following important results should be noted:

Red and Green
 and Blue   ≡ White

Red and Green   ≡ Yellow ⎫ Secondary or
Green and Blue ≡ Cyan   ⎬ complementary
Blue and Red   ≡ Magenta ⎭ colours
i.e. Primary colour plus its complementary colour
    produces white.

Red and Cyan   ≡ White
Green and Magenta ≡ White
Blue and Yellow   ≡ White

When additive colour mixing, a colour may be desaturated by adding 'white' light or a suitable amount of the complementary colour.

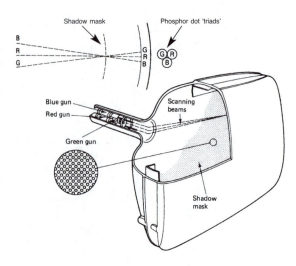

Figure 1.21 Shadow mask tube principle.

In colour television the display tube in the colour monitor or receiver generates three separate Red, Green and Blue pictures, the viewer seeing the appropriate 'mixture' colour, e.g. **shadow mask tube** (Fig. 1.21).

The principle of the shadow mask tube relies on accurate positioning of the shadow mask, a metallic screen with about one-third of a million holes in it. With the mask in place, appropriate phosphors are photographically deposited from the position of the Red, Green and Blue electron guns on the screen face. The shadow mask ensures that the electrons from the gun controlled by the Red signal only strike the Red phosphors, and similarly with the Green and Blue guns. The naked eye cannot resolve the dots at normal viewing distances; the eye/brain therefore integrates the colour mixture according to the relative excitation of the three phosphors.

Having established how colours may be synthesized with suitable mixtures of Red/Green/Blue light we need to turn our attention to the analysis of the scene to be televised to see how the appropriate Red/Green/Blue signals may be derived.

The inherent colour of an object is fundamental to the pigmentation of the surface of the object. For example an object painted blue will have pigments which absorb all wavelengths except the blue ones. Note that this will be a band of wavelengths not a single wavelength. The process of light absorption gives rise to subtractive colour mixing which applies to paint pigments, and colour filters used in combination. Fig. 1.22 illustrates the principle of subtractive mixing.

Note the reversal of colour roles, i.e. primaries are Cyan, Magenta and Yellow and complementaries are

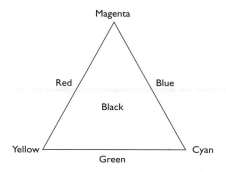

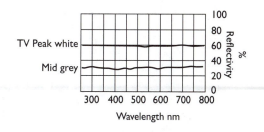

Figure 1.24 Reflectivity of neutral surfaces.

Magenta filter stops Green wavelengths, Cyan filter stops
Red wavelengths so a combined Magenta/Cyan filter
will only transmit Blue.

Figure 1.22 Subtractive colour mixing triangle.

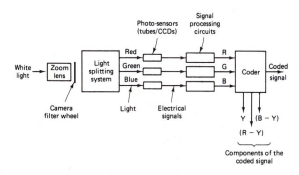

Figure 1.25 Basic camera system.

Red, Green and Blue; all three absorbent pigments present results in Black. Remember when using water colours how all the colours when mixed gave Black, or the brush cleaning water eventually became black! If three different red surfaces are examined, say, bright red, dull red and pale red, they can be illustrated as reflectance against wavelength to give the graphs shown in Fig. 1.23.

If we are going to reproduce three colours we need to know three things about the 'colour':

- hue — the dominant wavelength, the colour perceived
- saturation — the purity of the colour
- luminance value — the total amount of light reflected from the colour.

Note: 'light' here means visible light measured with a meter which has a photopic response (eye response).

Note that if the surface is White or a neutral Grey there will be no colour present, i.e. no hue, and therefore no saturation measurement (Fig. 1.24).

Camera overview

The basic camera system is shown in Fig. 1.25.

The optical image of the scene to be televised is focused by the zoom lens onto the appropriate light sensor (CCD) via a light-splitting block. The light-splitting block splits the light into a red image, a green image and a blue image. Dichroic layers are used in the light-splitting prism which reflect a band of wavelengths (red or blue). Fig. 1.26 illustrates the principle.

The action of the light sensor is to turn the optical image into an electrical charge pattern corresponding to the point-by-point scene luminance. The charge image is scanned to produce the appropriate Red, Green and Blue video signals; these are processed in

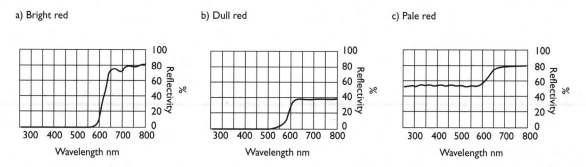

Figure 1.23 Reflectivity of three different red surfaces.

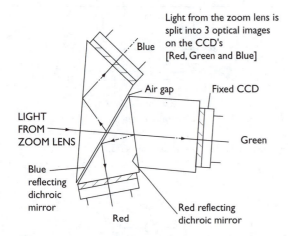

Light from the zoom lens is split into 3 optical images on the CCD's [Red, Green and Blue]

Figure 1.26 Light-splitting block.

the camera to produce standard Red, Green and Blue signals of 0–0.7 V. A fundamental requirement in colour television is that the Red, Green and Blue signals are equal when focused on a White or Neutral Grey object (i.e. no hue and no saturation).

This relationship is maintained throughout the television system, and only at the display tube are the proportions of Red, Green and Blue corrected for display (30% Red, 59% Green and 11% Blue) for a White or Neutral area.

1.7 Coding principles

The television system requires several criteria to be met, namely that the transmitted signal must:

(1) Satisfy the needs of the colour television receiver, i.e. display a colour picture satisfactorily.
(2) Satisfy the needs of the monochrome television receiver, i.e. display a compatible black and white picture. This means that the grey scale of the tonal values must be correct.
(3) Satisfy the needs of the colour television receiver for reverse compatibility, i.e. correctly display a black and white picture.
(4) Occupy the same available bandwidth for colour transmission as a black/white transmission.

This is achieved by deriving suitable signals from the camera RGB signals, namely luminance and chrominance signals. These are then transmitted using one of three coding systems: NTSC, PAL or SECAM.

The luminance signal is derived by taking suitable proportions of the Red, Green and Blue signals and is given the symbol Y:

$$Y = 30\% \times \text{Red} + 59\% \times \text{Green} + 11\% \times \text{Blue}$$

or

$$Y = 0.3R + 0.59G + 0.11B$$

Note that the above proportions would be obtained if the light from each colour was measured at the display tube, when displaying White.

Note also that for a neutral scene, i.e. no colour present, then since $R = G = B$ it follows that $Y = R = G = B$, i.e. $Y = 0.3R + 0.59R + 0.11R = R$ ($= G = B$).

This has satisfied the compatibility problem; the luminance signal represents the point-by-point luminance of the televised signal.

Reverse compatibility can be achieved by transmitting colour difference signals, namely $(R - Y)$, $(G - Y)$ and $(B - Y)$. At the receiver the addition of Y to each of these signals will give R, G and B again.

For neutral scenes (or monochrome transmission) $R = G = B = Y$ so the colour difference signals will be zero. The only signal transmitted will be the luminance signal giving correct reverse compatibility.

Note that the colour difference signals can have both positive and negative values.

Fortunately, only two of the colour difference signals need to be transmitted. The mathematical relationship between the R, G, B and Y enable the missing colour difference signal to be derived at the receiver!

In a typical scene the Green signal is the largest, which means that $(G - Y)$ will be the smallest signal and therefore vulnerable to noise, distortion and interference. Consequently this signal is not transmitted. It can be shown that:

$$(G - Y) = -0.51(R - Y) - 0.19(B - Y)$$

This results in three signals for transmission, each of 5.5 Mhz bandwidth! Fortunately, the acuity of the eye is such that we do not perceive fine detail in colour as much as we perceive changes in luminance. Consequently the bandwidth of the colour difference signals can be reduced to about one-quarter of the luminance signal (Fig. 1.27).

The three signals Y, $(R - Y)$ and $(B - Y)$ are the **components** of the colour signal which need to be coded for transmission to the viewer. Y is the luminance signal and $(R - Y)$ and $(B - Y)$ are referred to as the chrominance signals.

The colour difference signals $(R - Y)$ and $(B - Y)$ may be plotted graphically to represent the chrominance information (Table 1.2 and Fig. 1.28).

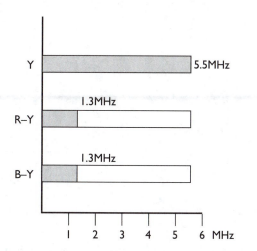

Figure 1.27 Bandwidth of component signals.

Table 1.2 Colour difference signals.

Colour	R	G	B	Y	(R – Y)	(B – Y)
Red	1	0	0	0.3	0.70	–0.30
Green	0	0	1	0.59	–0.59	–0.59
Blue	0	0	1	0.11	0.11	0.89
Cyan	0	1	1	0.70	–0.70	0.30
Magenta	1	0	1	0.41	0.59	0.59
Yellow	1	1	0	0.89	0.11	–0.89

Two observations from this chart are:

- The angle displacement from the $(B - Y)$ axis indicates the hue.
- The length of the line from the origin represents the saturation of the colour.

Note: the combined amplitude of the luminance and chrominance exceed the amplitude limits of transmission systems. To overcome this the chrominance signals are reduced by weighting factors and designated U and V:

$$U = 0.493 \; (B - Y) \text{ and } V = 0.877 \; (R - Y)$$

The problem outstanding is that of transmitting the luminance and chrominance signals within the prescribed bandwidth. This is achieved with one of three coding systems: NTSC, PAL and SECAM. The PAL system is a derivation of the NTSC system, providing greater immunity to distortion. The main feature of these two systems will be discussed before outlining the characteristics of the SECAM system.

In the NTSC system the solution was to use the chrominance signals to modulate a high frequency subsidiary carrier signal (**sub-carrier**) within the luminance bandwidth. The frequency of the sub-carrier was carefully chosen to minimize interference with the luminance signal and a modulation system known as **suppressed carrier** was used to ensure minimum visibility of this signal on the monochrome receiver (Fig. 1.29).

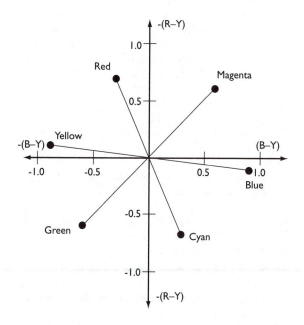

Figure 1.28 Display of graphical representation of $(R - Y)$ and $(B - Y)$ for RGB and complementary colours.

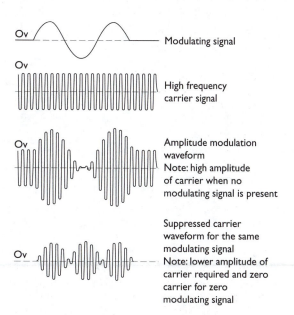

Figure 1.29 Illustrating the advantage of a suppressed carrier system.

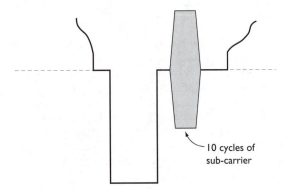

Figure 1.30 Reference 'colour burst'.

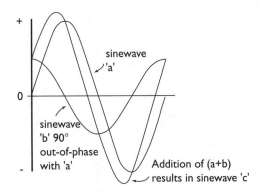

Figure 1.32 Addition of two sine waves in quadrature.

To detect (decode) a suppressed carrier signal requires the re-insertion of the carrier at the receiver. In the receiver a phase-locked oscillator operating at sub-carrier frequency is kept in perfect phase lock with the studio by using a few cycles of reference sub-carrier (**colour burst**) transmitted on the TV signal back porch (Fig. 1.30).

But how can two signals, $(R - Y)$ and $(B - Y)$, be transmitted simultaneously on this single sub-carrier? The principle is based on the observation that two sine waves out of phase (out of step) by 90° have their maximum and zero values exactly opposite (Fig. 1.31).

This means that if two feeds of sub-carrier are used, one out of phase by 90° (in quadrative phase), the $(R - Y)$ sub-carrier has its maximum value when the $(B - Y)$ sub-carrier is at zero, and vice versa for the $(B - Y)$ sub-carrier. So by detecting (sampling) the

combined sub-carrier signal at the receiver at the right moment one can derive the $(R - Y)$ signal and the $(B - Y)$ signal, and hence derive the appropriate signals needed at the receiver.

When the two sub-carrier signals are combined at the coder the resultant single sub-carrier signal can be shown as Fig. 1.32. The amplitude of the sub-carrier represents the saturation and the phase angle of reference to the colour burst indicates the hue.

Unfortunately, this signal is vulnerable to any phase errors in the transmission path. The PAL system (Phase Alternate Line) overcomes this by reversing the phase of the $(R - Y)$ signal on alternate lines. Use is made of a one-line store in the receiver to make possible an electronic averaging of the two lines of chrominance to cancel out any phase errors. The PAL system uses a 'swinging' burst ±45° on the $(B - Y)$ axis to enable the receiver to follow the PAL switching sequence.

Fig. 1.33 illustrates the 'plot' of chrominance data for NTSC and PAL systems for saturated colour bars.

The SECAM (SEquential Couleur Avec Memoire) system uses the same chrominance signals as NTSC and PAL but differs in that:

- the colour difference information is transmitted in line sequence with $(R - Y)$ on one line, $(B - Y)$ on the next line, etc.
- the chrominance information uses a frequency modulation system.

In the receiver a one-line memory is used to make available both colour difference signals, i.e. each colour difference signal is used for two lines.

1.8 Colour camera – processing and line-up

Television cameras can be divided into two categories, namely full facility studio cameras and

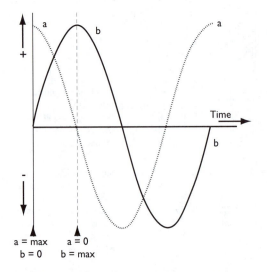

Figure 1.31 Two sine waves out-of-phase by 90° (in quadrature).

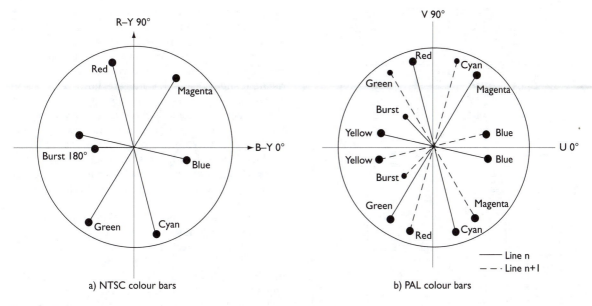

a) NTSC colour bars

b) PAL colour bars

Figure 1.33 Chrominance 'plot': (a) NTSC colour bars; (b)PAL colour bars.

lightweight cameras. The lightweight cameras are available as a basic camera, camera plus dockable recorder or as an integral camcorder. The full facility cameras have a better specification and obviously offer more facilities than the lightweight versions; however, many studios, especially robotic camera studios, use lightweight cameras.

All television cameras require signal processing to ensure that the Red, Green and Blue signals are correct, prior to recording or coding. Lightweight cameras house all of the electronics, including the coder. Studio cameras usually include a camera control unit (CCU) for remotely controlling the pre-set conditions of the camera, together with an operational control panel (OCP).

The basic block diagram of a colour camera channel is shown in Fig. 1.34.

The Operational Control Panel (OCP), Fig. 1.35, includes the remote controls for Black level and iris together with camera pre-set controls and camera line-up facilities.

The video signals from the sensors are processed in the head amplifier to produce equal Red, Green and Blue signals when the camera is viewing a White or neutral scene. This is known as a White balance, and is an automatic adjustment.

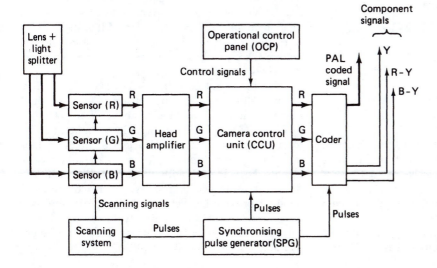

Figure 1.34 Basic block diagram of a colour camera channel.

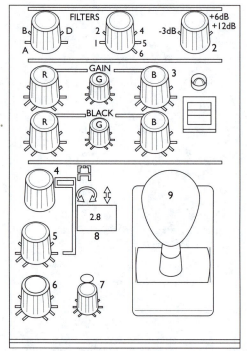

OPERATIONAL CONTROL PANEL

Typical operational control panel (OCP) for a full facilities camera

1. Remote control of filter wheels located between lens and light-splitting system (colour correction, neutral density and other effects filters).
2. Master gain control; extra gain is used when operating in low light.
3. Gain and black trims, used for minor adjustment of colour gain and black level when matching pictures.
4. Auto/manual iris control.
5. Detail enhancement.
6. Contrast control, used to modify the 'law', i.e. to stretch/ crush appropriate parts of the grey scale.
7. Range control, adjusts the range over which the joystick will operate, and selects the mean aperture.
8. Readout of lens aperture.
9. Joystick, the main operational control has three functions:
   Twist to adjust master black level.
   Forward/back to open/close iris.
   Depress to switch channel to preview monitor.

Figure 1.35 Operational control panel (OCP).

The OCP has a 'paint' facility which, when enabled, allows for the individual adjustment of the Red, Green and Blue gain. These controls are used operationally to help with colour matching, removing unwanted colour casts in highlights or deliberately introducing a colour shift, i.e. warm or cool the picture. Extra gain can be selected for conditions of low light levels, but of course introduces extra noise

to the signal. With the increase in camera sensitivity some cameras provide a reduction in gain, i.e. –3 dB, –6 dB, with consequent reduction in noise.

Detail enhancement provides special high-frequency correction to improve the rendition of fine detail. It should be used with care, however – if over-corrected the pictures will look 'edgy' and artificially sharp. Faces will look leathery in appearance due to the enhancement of spots and blemishes, skin pores, etc. Noise is increased by detail enhancement.

Black level (lift) adjustment is used to establish the Black level in a picture by 'fixing' (clamping) the level of picture signal with reference to the back porch level (Black level).

Black balance refers to the setting of the individual black levels for the Red, Green and Blue signals to be identical and unaffected by picture content. This is an automatic alignment usually carried out at the same time as the White balance. The OCP has individual adjustments of Red, Green and Blue Black levels for picture matching, removing unwanted colour casts in dark areas of the picture or to deliberately introduce a colour shift in the 'blacks'.

The adjustment of Black level is very critical and relies on the appropriate colour monitor being aligned accurately! A few per cent change in the Black level can have a major impact on the picture quality:

- Black level control adjusted so that picture information is 'sat up' or 'lifted' relative to true black will lack 'punch'; colours will be desaturated.
- Black level control adjusted so that the picture information is below true black level ('sat' too hard) produces pictures which are 'black crushed', i.e. over-contrasted and over-saturated.

Peak White clippers provide a pre-set 'limit' to the excursion of the RGB signals just above Peak White level. Typically the Peak White clippers are set to operate at about 105%. It is essential that they are set correctly to ensure that the picture information is within the prescribed voltage limits. Picture monitors have good 'head room' for input signal levels so a 20% overload may not be noticed – however, Peak White clippers situated later in the transmission chain would simply remove all information above about 100%!

Linear Matrix improves the colour rendition of the camera by correcting for deficiencies in the colour analysis system. Some basic analysis characteristics cannot be achieved with the light splitting block; however, using a circuit (matrix) which allows a small amount of coupling between RGB signals improves the saturation of the colours. Note that the Linear Matrix usually operates on linear signals, i.e. before gamma correction, hence its name.

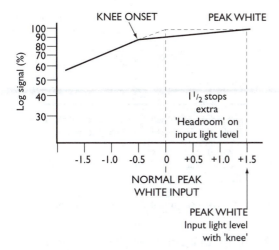

Figure 1.36 Basic 'knee' facility.

Gamma correction has been discussed in a previous section. The OCP has a selection of gamma laws available, typically 0.4, 0.45, 0.5, together with Black Stretch which can be used to reveal detail in the darker areas of the picture. Modern digital cameras have made excellent progress in extending the contrast range over which full gamma correction is possible without severely affecting the noise in the picture. Incidentally, noise is most noticeable in the darker parts of the picture.

Associated with the gamma correction is a 'knee' facility which enables the signal to be compressed above a pre-set value known as the knee (Fig. 1.36).

Use of the knee facility extends the dynamic range of the camera, i.e. increases the 'headroom' to accommodate excessive highlights; however, above the knee the tonal values will obviously be compressed. This is preferable to the signal limiting, resulting in distracting burn-out of picture information.

Clearly the knee has to be 'located' above the level of face tones to avoid loss of tonal gradation in these areas.

Some cameras enable a 'smart card' to be used to set up the characteristics of a camera, i.e. gamma law, White balance, etc. This is a miniature credit card sized memory card which can be inserted into the camera to pre-set the above parameters.

The RGB signals, after processing, are fed to a **coder** which provides outputs of the components {Y, (R − Y) and B − Y} and the coded PAL signal.

The electronic 'heart' of a television station is the **synchronizing pulse generator** (SPG). This generates the necessary synchronizing pulses, clocking pulses and colour sub-carrier signals to ensure complete synchronization of the station pictures. The SPG also provides test signals.

A signal called Black and Burst is usually sent to the cameras – this is a feed of synchronizing pulses, plus colour burst and Black level. This is enough information for the cameras to 'lock' their own SPG in synchronism with the station SPG. The camera timing can be adjusted (to ensure perfect synchronism at the vision mixer). For sources to be synchronous (in complete synchronism) the leading edge of line sync pulses must be within 20 nanoseconds, and colour burst phase within (1.5°) 2 nanoseconds. (Note that at 3×10^8 m/sec speed of electrons a few feet of extra cable can introduce a significant timing change.)

Camera line-up

With the advent of CCDs, camera line-up procedures have become simplified. The CCDs are permanently mounted on the light-splitting block at the factory and should arrive with all three electrical images exactly the same size and in perfect register with each other. Consequently, after initial acceptance testing, the CCD chips should not require any further checking of registration.

Modern cameras are very stable and require little alignment except for **Black and White balance**.

White balance can be achieved by simply pointing the camera at a suitably lit white card and pressing the Auto White Balance switch. This is the method adopted by cameramen on location operating single cameras. Black balance is also achieved electronically on depressing the appropriate switch. This is completed in the camera and requires no external input; the lens is stopped down and 'capped up' during an Auto Black Balance.

In studios it is usual practice to use a grey scale, typically 9 steps, which indicates tonal values from Black to Peak White (60% reflectance). This is lit with a luminaire, the 'line-up lamp' which has been set to give the correct illuminance, say 500 lux, and the correct colour temperature 2960 K (see later notes on colour temperature).

The advantage of using this step wedge is that the assessment of correct black and white balance is made more critical. After completing an auto-white and auto-black balance the 'painting' controls can be used to reduce any residual errors and ensure that cameras 'match'. Matching of cameras is best observed by a horizontal split screen display of two of the cameras, while shooting identical shots of the grey scale. The side-by-side comparison of the grey-scale steps is a very critical test for matching.

Some engineers use the waveform monitor to assess colour balance, i.e. lack of sub-carrier on the waveform 'steps'; others use the vectorscope and adjust for minimum chrominance information.

1.9 Picture and waveform monitoring

1.9.1 Picture monitoring

To assess picture **quality** critically it is essential that a good picture monitoring facility is provided in all lighting and vision control areas, i.e. the facility should be comprehensive and user-friendly. Picture monitors are graded according to their specification: Grade 1 monitors have the highest specification in terms of stability, picture geometry, colour rendition, convergence, picture sharpness, stabilized black level, and ability to operate in simple PAL mode.

Grade 2 monitors have a reduced specification but are of a much better performance than the average domestic receiver. Many manufacturers have Grade 1½, a monitor which is superior to a Grade 2 but not quite up to Grade 1 performance.

An important aspect of monitoring is that the signal must be at the correct level, i.e. 1 V peak-to-peak. Coaxial cable is used to distribute video signals and it is an essential requirement that this is correctly terminated in 75 Ω.

Video systems must not have any tee-ing of cables (Fig. 1.37).

75 Ω is the **characteristic impedance** of the coaxial cable used for video signals. The characteristic impedance of a cable is the impedance measured 'looking into' an infinitely long length of the cable. A video signal connected to such a cable would simply decay to zero at infinity, i.e. no reflections of energy (Fig. 1.38)!

Terminating the monitor in 75 Ω makes the cable look like an infinite length of cable – hence the need to terminate in 75 Ω.

a) Correct termination of monitors

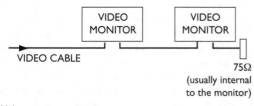

b) Incorrect connection

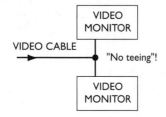

Figure 1.37 Termination of monitors.

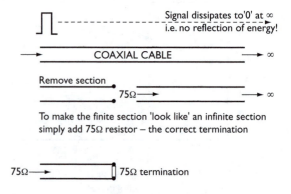

Figure 1.38 Making a coaxial cable look like an 'infinite' cable.

The correct alignment of the colour monitors in the lighting and vision control area should be considered to be the most important studio complex adjustment!

Colour monitor line-up should be checked regularly. Test signals used are:

- *PLUGE* to set brightness and contrast.
- *Grille* to check accuracy of the convergence of the scanning electron beams, i.e. accurate overlaying of the three colour pictures.
- *Neutral step wedge* to check the grey scale of the monitor, i.e. no colour casts on the neutral tones from black to white.
- *Colour bars* to check for saturation of the colour display.
- *Purity* – the ability of the Red electron gun to only 'see' red phosphors is easily assessed by feeding the monitor with a 'lifted' black level then switching off the Green and Blue guns. Lack of purity will show immediately as an impure red colour, i.e. yellow or magenta.

The white point of the colour television display should be 6500 K (illuminated D_{65}); modern monitors use an external probe fixed to the monitor face to set this up automatically.

Note: Control room lighting should be at 6500 K from high frequency, dimmable, fluorescent lights fitted with louvres to ensure that only the control panels are lit. Control room walls and desks should be neutral grey in colour. (Colour monitor line-up is covered later in Section 4.19).

1.9.2 Waveform monitoring

In addition to being able to assess picture quality there is a need to measure the levels of the television signal. Two aspects need to be measured:

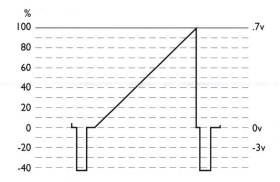

Figure 1.39 Typical television waveform monitor.

- composite television signal/components of the television signal
- hue and saturation.

The first aspect can be measured by using an oscilloscope with a suitably calibrated graticule to indicate sync level, Black level and Peak White, plus percentage signal levels (Fig. 1.39).

The time base, horizontal display is normally preset to give:

1 line display
2 line display
1 field display
2 field display

It will also include a filter to enable the luminance signal to be measured without the presence of the chrominance signal.

The vectorscope is a special oscilloscope which can be used to display the hue and saturation of a composite colour signal (Fig. 1.40). The graticule has an engraving which indicates the 'boxes' in which the colour bar signals should 'lie'.

1.9.3 Colour bars

Colour bars are a special text signal used in studios and in location cameras as a check of transmission/recording performance. They are easily generated by suitable frequency square waves as shown in Fig. 1.41.

After 'weighting', the colour bars are known as 100% bars. These were used in many studio complexes as the standard test signal and exist on many archive recordings. Current practice is to generate bars known as 75% or EBU bars. These are used extensively in cable and satellite operations. Both these standards are shown in Fig. 1.42, for reference. It is important that operators can distinguish between the two.

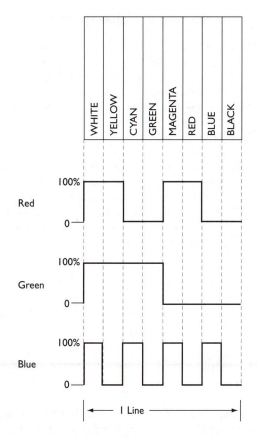

Figure 1.41 Colour bar generation.

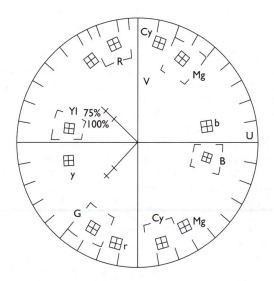

Figure 1.40 Vectorscope graticule.

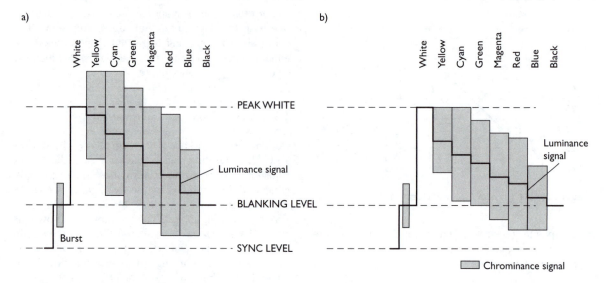

Note: In Fig (b) upper level of Yellow/Cyan bars equal to peak white; lower level of Red/Blue bars equal; level of lower Green signal coincident with Blanking level

Figure 1.42 Colour bar signals: (a) 100% saturation; (b) 75% saturation (EBU bars).

1.10 Introduction to digital systems

An analogue signal is one which is continually varying, e.g. a television signal or an audio signal. The disadvantage of an analogue signal is that it is susceptible to distortion when transmitted over long distances or when recorded and replayed. The distortion may be simply loss of signal level, at all or selected frequencies, plus the addition of 'noise'. Noise is the engineer's enemy!

Digital systems offer the facility of converting the signal to a series of numbers for transmission or storage. The nature of the digital signal is such that it is very robust and immune to the distortions encountered with analogue signals, i.e. the decoded number is identical to the coded number.

1.10.1 Digital principles

Three processes are involved with converting an analogue signal into a digital signal:

- sampling
- quantizing
- coding.

Sampling is the process of measuring the analogue signal to produce a series of voltages which are representative of the signal. Paramount to sampling is the sampling frequency, e.g. a man living in the depths of a cave, sampling the outside world at midnight every day, would conclude that the outside world is always dark. Clearly there were not enough samples within a day to gain a true picture of the outside world!

Sampling theory states that the sampling frequency should be at least 2.2 times the highest frequency for representative sampling to take place, i.e. to produce an identical waveshape on decoding.

Quantizing is the process of deciding how precisely we need to define the voltage sample, i.e. how many discrete signal levels have to be used to accurately transmit or record the sample. For example, in defining an address one could just say England but, of course, this is not precise enough – one needs to give more data, e.g. county, town, street, home number, in order to ensure no errors in the transmission of post!

Fig. 1.43 illustrates the principle of quantizing using just eight quantizing levels. This is very coarse quantizing with errors introduced, because the increment between quantizing levels is too large.

The basic digital vision system used 256 quantizing levels, resulting in a signal-to noise ratio of about 50 dB (decibels); a later system using 1024 possible quantizing levels results in a signal-to-noise ratio of about 62 dB.

Basic audio systems use 65 536 possible quantizing levels!

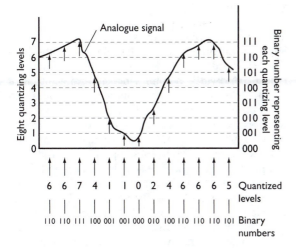

Figure 1.43 The basic principle of quantizing.

Coding is the process of converting the sample into digital form, i.e. a number.

The basic video signal referred to above was quantized in 256 levels. Using the decimal or denary system this is really:

Hundreds		Tens		Units	
10^2		10^1		10^1	
2×100	$+$	5×10	$+$	6×1	
200	$+$	50	$+$	6	$= 256$

Note that each column has a possibility of 10 different values, i.e. 0, 1, 2, 3, 4, 5, 6, 7, 8, 9. So if a simple device existed with 10 separate, recognizable states we could use three of these devices to represent the hundreds, tens and units columns. Unfortunately, such a device does not exist.

The simplest multistate device is a switch, either ON or OFF. So if one counted in a system requiring only two identifiable states, a simple switch could be used to represent the ON/OFF information. Such a system uses 2 as its base (not 10) and is known as the **binary system**:

Value in decimal notation	2^2 (4)	2^1 (2)	2^0 (1)	Binary notation
0	0	0	0	000
1	0	0	1	001
2	0	1	0	010
3	0	1	1	011
4	1	0	0	100
5	1	0	1	101
6	1	1	0	110
7	1	1	1	111

Decimal 6 for example is $1 \times 2^2 + 1 \times 2^1 + 0 \times 2^0$. Or: $4 + 1 + 0 = 6$.

In this simple example three binary digits (bits) have been used to represent eight possible states, i.e. 2^3.

In basic digital video 8 bits are used to represent $2^8 = 256$ signal levels. When 10 bits are used, this represents $2^{10} = 1024$ signal levels (Serial Digital Interface, SDI).

In basic audio digital systems, 16 bits are used to represent $2^{16} = 65\ 536$ signal levels.

The digit with the lowest value (2^0) is known as the **least significant digit**, LSD, and the one with the highest value is known as the **most significant digit**, MSD.

A single sample expressed as an 8 bit number is known as a byte.

The robustness of this system relies on only one of two possible states being recognized after transmission or storage, i.e. V or 0 V, and of course if it is not one of the states it must be the other!

1.10.2 Digital television

The use of equipment using digital television has evolved from using **digital islands** within a television studio complex to complete **digital systems**. Initially the individual items using digital television were:

- caption generators
- frame synchronizers
- picture manipulation devices
- video recorders
- computer graphics.

These operated in television complexes which were either composite (PAL/NTSC) or component. Current practice is to consider a fully integrated **component** digital system for all new installations, i.e. using a digital highway between each of the parts of the video system, known as a Serial Digital Interface (SDI).

Digital television divides into two basic categories:

- Component $\{Y, (B - Y), \text{and } (R - Y)\}$.
- Composite (PAL or NTSC signals).

Component digital systems have a common sampling rate for 525/60 Hz and 625/50 Hz which is locked to the horizontal line rate, i.e. 13.5 MHz, 720 samples/active line.

(Remember that the 525 and 625 line durations are almost identical; also that in digital systems full bandwidth signals are available.)

The sampling rate, defined by ITU 601, uses the lowest practical video sampling rate (one-quarter of the luminance sampling rate) of 3.375 MHz as '1'; 6.75 MHz is therefore 2 and 13.5 MHz is 4.

Note: $(R - Y)$ and $(B - Y)$ are known as Cr and Cb when in the digital domain. Most component production equipment uses 4.2.2 sampling. 4.4.4 systems are sometimes used for computer graphics. 4.4.4.4 means that a high definition signal (for chroma key operation) is also included.

Connection between the various parts of a television station may be as a parallel interface or as a special digital interface SDI. Parallel interfaces require a multiway connection limited to about 50 metres, and are usually used within a particular area, e.g. graphics/post-production. The serial digital interface using standard coaxial cable can be used for up to about 230 m. With SDI each coded sample is sent in sequence down the single cable. Using a 10 bit system and 4.2.2 sampling this requires a bandwidth of 270 MHz! That is, $\{(13.5 + 6.75 + 6.75) \times 10\}$ MHz = 270 MHz. The standard SDI includes 16 channels of **embedded** digital audio when using component digital and four when using composite digital signals.

1.10.3 Compression

Most digital studios operate with full bandwidth SDI; however, the high frequency bit rate of 270 Mbs illustrates the need for some form of bit rate reduction, i.e. reduce bandwidth requirements, for transmitting a digital television signal. Compression techniques have been developed which recognize information which is redundant and exclude it from the transmitted information, e.g. only send changes to information. For recording purposes typically 2:1 and 3.3:1 compression ratios have been developed and these can be used with only minimal image degradation, while for Digital Video Broadcasting (DVB) using techniques developed by MPEG 2 compression ratios of about 40:1 are employed!

Composite digital systems usually sample at four times the sub-carrier frequency ($4f_{sc}$). This gives a sampling frequency for PAL of 17.72 MHz and 14.3 MHz for NTSC.

Eventually, all transmission systems will be based on a compressed SDI system, thus replacing the NTSC, PAL and SECAM systems completely.

2 Production methods

2.1 Planning a production

A video camera produces an electronic picture which can be transmitted and displayed on a TV set instantaneously; it requires no 'processing'. This is called live television. As an event happens so it can be seen.

Live multicamera production technique uses a number of cameras which are switched to in turn to show different viewpoints of an event. This production method allows the material to be transmitted as it occurs or to be recorded for future transmission. If it is recorded then the material can be edited before transmission.

Single-camera coverage is usually recorded and the material receives extensive editing before transmission. This is similar to the film technique where one shot is recorded and then the single camera moved to another position or location to record another shot. The shots can be recorded out of sequence from their subsequent edited order. This type of production method is very flexible but does require more time in acquiring the material and in editing.

Pictures are nearly always accompanied by audio, either actuality speech, music, or effects of the subject in shot, or sound is added in post-production. The old cliché that television is a visual medium is a half-truth. In nearly every circumstance the viewer wants to hear, as well as see, what is transmitted. Pictures may have a greater initial impact, but sound frequently adds atmosphere, emotion and space to the image.

2.1.1 Advance planning

Every programme involves some type of advance planning. A two-minute news bulletin, broadcast four or five times a day, with a newsreader reading straight to camera, will need scheduling of resources and people. It will require the news to be collected

Single- and multicamera production compared

live multicamera production
- allows the event to be transmitted as it occurs
- follows the timescale of the event (e.g. music)
- on-screen production errors are transmitted
- can use pre-recorded inserts

recorded multicamera production
- discontinuous recording allows production flexibility
- post-production allows greater production flexibility
- can be more economic in time and budget than single-camera

single-camera recording
- greater flexibility in location and production style
- requires extensive post-production
- can achieve greater precision in technique and performance.

Figure 2.1

and scripted, for the presenter to have access to make-up, the studio facility to be booked and technicians to be scheduled to control the studio facilities. More complex programmes require a longer planning period, and a standard procedure to inform and involve all the diverse crafts and skills needed to mount the programme.

2.1.2 Two types of programming

Programmes can be roughly divided into those that have a content that has been conceived and devised for television and those programmes with a content that cannot be pre-planned, or are events that take place independently of television coverage. Many programmes have a mixture of both types of content.

If it is scripted for television, then the production is under the direct control of the production team who can arrange the content as they wish. The timescale of what happens on the screen is under their supervision and can be started and stopped as required. If it is an event that would happen independently of TV, such as a sports event, then the production team will have to make arrangements to cover the event as it unfolds in its own timescale.

There are some made-for-television programmes which are not normally interrupted by production requirements such as discussion or live news broadcasts. Their method of production is similar to following, for example, a football match or a concert. These require continuous camera coverage which follows the timescale of the event.

CONTENT COMMISSIONED BY TV can control time and location of the event to be transmitted

ACTUALITY EVENT COVERAGE is controlled by the duration and location of the event to be transmitted.

Three types of programme

1　**commissioned for television allows**
   - control of content
   - control of production timetable
   - choice of production methods

2　**independent event**
   - content is decided by the nature of the event
   - timescale dictated by the nature of the event
   - production method less flexible

3　**actuality – news, documentaries and discussion**
   - content based on 'real' events
   - shaped and structured by editoral decisions
   - dependent on access to relevant material.

Figure 2.2

2.1.3 Planning for the unpredictable

There are many events covered by TV that contain unpredictable action which cannot be rehearsed, such as sport, discussion programmes and other ad-lib activities. No one knows when a goal is going to be scored in a football match, or how the run of play will develop, but the TV camera deployment must provide for any of the normal occurrences during a game. Planning for this requires predicting potential incidents and having cameras assigned to capture such eventualities.

From the initial commissioned idea some form of script or, possibly to begin with, a rough 'running order' of the contents of the programme will be structured. The running order identifies individual sequences in the programme, what the sequences will contain, the vision and sound sources utilized and the duration of each item.

The next stage of the planning involves preparing a script and deciding on design requirements. The flow chart of decisions to be made before recording or transmission day depends on the programme format. Scenery needs to be built, scripts written, artistes contracted or programme guests contacted, technical facilities booked and pre-recorded inserts arranged and edited. A regular weekly series will have a production planning formula which fits the turnaround time between each programme. It will also have some advanced projects in the planning stage.

Depending on the complexity of the programme, there will be planning meetings and/or recces if it is a location production with engineering managers, lighting directors, camera supervisors, sound supervisors and all other members of the production team who need advance information in order to plan for the programme.

2.2 Shot number system

For many programmes, a camera script will be prepared which breaks down the programme into sections or scenes, and then further subdivides any significant action into separately numbered shots which are assigned to specific cameras. This camera script is usually modified in rehearsal, but allows a reference point for all concerned in the production. Each camera operator has his/her own camera cards detailing the shots they will be taking.

The production assistant calls each shot number as they are taken during rehearsal and transmission/recording, and the director reminds everyone on talkback of any significant action/event that will occur. The shot number system binds together a whole range of different production activities from lighting changes to equipment repositioning, scenery changes and vision mixing. It is not simply a structure for camera operators.

The shot number system provides for the most detailed planning and production precision in, for example, the camera coverage of an orchestral concert where the shots are directly linked to the orchestral score. The score is followed by the director, vision mixer and production assistant and each shot is cut to at a predetermined point in the score. But multi-camera coverage can use a mixture of other techniques including:

- Some sequences of the production are shot numbered but other sequences are 'as-directed' (i.e. they are not pre-rehearsed). In this method of camera coverage, the director will identify what shots are required on each camera during the transmission or recording combined with appropriate shots being offered by the camera crew.
- Cameras are assigned a role in a structured sequence of shots. For example, a game show where each sequence of the quiz or game will have a defined structure, but the order of the shots will depend on the progress of the game. For example, if competitor 'A' answers Camera 2 will be used. If 'B' answers then Camera 3 will be used, etc. This is the most common technique in covering group discussions.
- Cameras are assigned a role (e.g. football coverage – one camera holds a wide shot, one camera is close, one camera picks up 'personality' shots, one camera for slo-mo replay, etc). With this system, cameras stick to their 'role' and do not attempt to offer additional shots unless directed.
- Cameras are assigned a role for part of the event. For example, a state occasion where a camera position allows unique coverage of a location – perhaps a section of a street through which the procession will pass – but is subsequently available to pick up other shots to reflect the atmosphere of the event.
- An as-directed shoot such as a pop concert where some cameras concentrate on lead singers, instrumentalist, etc., and other cameras are on wide shots and audience.
- All cameras are isoed (i.e. they are individually recorded) and then edited together in post-production. This technique is more likely to occur using PSC (portable single cameras).

Programme planning – flow chart
- programme idea
- idea is commissioned/budget agreed
- research and script
- contract technical staff/performers
- detailed planning/design/rehearsals
- camera script/running order
- planning meetings/recces
- book facilities
- schedules and call sheets
- set and light studio or location
- record or transmit
- post-production
- transmission
- audience research and feedback.

Figure 2.3

2.3 Invisible technique

2.3.1 The creation of 'invisible' technique

The ability to record an event on film was achieved in the latter part of the nineteenth century. During the next two decades, there was the transition from the practice of running the camera continuously to record an event, to the stop/start technique of separate shots where the camera was repositioned between each shot in order to film new material. The genesis of film narrative was established.

The screen was conceived as an acting area similar to the stage as seen by an audience in a theatre. The action moved within the screen space without either the camera moving or the size of shot changing. Many of the techniques that we are familiar with now had to be learnt in the first two decades of the twentieth century. The first film-makers had to experiment and invent the grammar of editing, shot-size, and the variety of camera movements that are now standard.

As well as camera movement came the problems involved in stopping the camera, moving to a new position and starting the camera again. The ability to find ways of shooting subjects and then editing the shots together without distracting the audience was learnt by the commercial cinema over a number of years.

The guiding concept that connected all these developing techniques of camera movement and shot-change was the need to persuade the audience that they were watching continuous action in real time. This required the mechanics of film-making to be hidden from the audience – i.e. to be invisible.

2.3.2 'Invisible' cuts

There was a need for unobtrusive shot transition and camera movement in order to achieve a seamless flow of images in the story-telling. A number of 'invisible' techniques were discovered and became the standard conventions of film-making and later television camerawork.

In essence, this convention directs the audience's attention to the action rather than to the mechanics of production. Methods are employed to cut between shots, to keep attention on what is contained within the frame rather than beyond its enclosing area, and to move the camera smoothly to a new viewpoint without distracting the audience.

There are alternative conventions of presentation which intentionally draw attention to the means of production. Camera movement in this alternative technique is often restlessly on the move, panning abruptly from subject to subject, making no effort to disguise the transitions and deliberately drawing attention to the means by which the images are brought to the viewer. This breaking down or subverting the Hollywood convention of an 'invisible' seamless flow of images has a number of different forms or styles. In general, television production adopted the 'Hollywood' model of invisible technique.

'Invisible' technique

- Shots are structured to enable the audience to understand the space, time and logic of the action.

- Each shot follows the line of action to maintain consistent screen direction so that the geography of the action is completely intelligible. (e.g. camera positions on a football match direct the audience to the content of the production rather than the mechanics of television production.)

- Invisible technique creates the illusion that distinct, separate shots (possibly recorded out of sequence and at different times) form part of a *continuous* event witnessed by the audience.

Figure 2.4

Most of the above 'invisible technique' examples concern camerawork, but every craft involved in television production attempts to disguise their contribution. For example, audio is faded-up and faded-down unobtrusively, exposure changes usually take place 'off-shot', the cutting point between two shots is carefully chosen to avoid a visual 'jump' that may be obvious to the viewer. Invisible technique emphasizes the content of the production, not the mechanics of production.

2.4 Production staff and facilities

A television studio equipped to mount live and recorded multicamera productions usually contains three main areas: the studio floor area, the control rooms and a series of production rooms.

2.4.1 The studio floor area

The studio floor surface needs to be absolutely level and free from bumps, cracks or unevenness. One of the basic needs of multicamera work is to move the camera 'on-shot' smoothly and quietly without the use of tracks or boards. If the floor surface cannot accommodate camera movement 'on-shot' then it is unsuitable for the production of continuous multicamera programme making.

Access for scenery is through large double doors. There must be sufficient grid height overhead to accommodate a cyclorama, a 16'+ cloth that is stretched taut in an arc around one, two or three sides of the studio to provide a lit backing. Suspended from the grid are lighting hoists that can be lowered for rigging lamps and individually routed to a numbered input into the lighting console. Access to the grid area is often required for rigging lamps, monitors, speakers and suspended scenery. Electrically driven hoists are used to suspend scenery and for flying in scenery pieces. Other hoists may be available for audience monitors and speakers or simply to liberate more floor space.

The studio walls are usually acoustically treated to improve the sound handling qualities. Installed at strategic positions along the studio walls are the technical facilities commonly called wall boxes. Monitors, microphones, foldback-loudspeakers, technical mains and talkback can be plugged into these boxes to provide flexibility in technical rigging depending on the production layout. Positioned on the studio wall may be outlets for water, gas, etc. for production purposes.

Studios require air-conditioning to extract the heat generated by the lamps and a 'house' lighting system (plus emergency lights), when studio lamps are not switched on, for rigging and de-rigging. Fire alarms and fire lanes are required to provide an unimpeded route for audiences and production staff to the fire exits.

2.4.2 Control rooms

Away from the studio floor area are the production control rooms. If they are sited above the floor level, there is often quick access via stairs straight on to the studio floor. The main studio production control room contains a vision mixing panel, a talkback system and communications to other technical areas, possibly a caption generator for in-vision text and possibly the control system of the prompter device. All the equipment is housed in a long customized desk facing a bank of preview picture monitors displaying each video source used in the production.

Some of the preview monitors may be switchable depending on the number of video sources used in the production. These will include each camera's

Figure 2.5 Studio control room.

output, VTR, telecine and frame store outputs, any input from an outside broadcast that may be used or other studio inserts, caption generator and electronic graphics output, electronic VTR clock, a special effects output and a 'studio out' monitor displaying the visual source that is selected at the vision mixing panel. Other monitors may provide feeds of programmes currently being transmitted. Prominent on the monitor bank wall will be a large clock plus an indication of the studio status (e.g. blue light: 'rehearsal'; red light: 'transmission').

2.4.3 Sound, lighting and vision control

Adjacent to the production control room (commonly called the 'gallery') is the sound control room where the audio inputs to a programme are mixed. Opposite a bank of preview picture monitors and monitoring loudspeakers is a sound desk used to control the level and quality of all audio outputs. There will also be audio record and replay equipment.

Lighting and vision control usually share the same room and are equipped with preview monitors, a lighting console to control lamp intensity and for grouping lamps for coordinated lighting changes. A diagram of the lamps in use (mimic board) helps the console operator during rehearsal and transmission. Alongside the lighting area is the vision control panel which houses the controls for altering the exposure, Black level, colour balance, gain and the gamma of each camera. From this position, the vision control engineer matches each camera's output so that, for example, the skin tones of a face that is in shot on several cameras is the same. If the studio is equipped with robotic cameras, the remote controls may be located on the vision control panel.

Each studio camera has its associated bay of equipment housed in the vision control room or in a technical area adjacent to the control rooms. Vision control also needs communications to other technical areas. Other production facilities used in multicamera programming are a graphics area which feeds electronic graphics, animations and electronic text to the studio and a technical area where VTRs, frame stores, etc. are centrally available and allocated according to production requirements. Half-inch VTRs are often located in the production control area.

Two other rooms connected with programme making are the production office, which is the base for the planning and preparation of a programme, and a green room or hospitality room which is used for the reception of programme guests before and after the programme.

2.4.4 Control room staff

Walk into a control room which is engaged in making a programme and there will usually be a programme director with a script or running order on the desk, talking into a microphone to a number of other production personnel. Talkback – the information from the director and the responses from other members of the crew – is the lifeblood of any multi-camera production. On one side of the director sits the production assistant who works with the director in the preparation of the programme. He or she times the show, calls the shot numbers and in some broadcast organizations will cue video machines to replay pre-recorded inserts. On the other side of the director is the vision mixer working from a script and under direction, operating the vision mixing panel switching between cameras and all other vision sources.

Figure 2.6 Control room staff.

Also in the control room there may be a technical coordinator, who deals with planning and communications, and a producer or editor who, depending on programme formats, will oversee content and running order of items. There may also be a caption generator operator who adds text to the pictures (e.g. name superimpositions abbreviated to 'supers' or sometimes referred to as 'Astons').

In the sound control room, the sound supervisor controls the audio and can talk to sound assistants on the studio floor. Possibly there is also a sound assistant playing-in music and effects. In the lighting and

vision control room, the lighting director sits with his lighting plot and a console operator at the lighting console and balances the intensity of each lamp in the studio according to the shot and the requirements of the production, and groups the lamps for lighting changes and effects if needed.

A vision control operator, responsible for the exposure and matching the cameras, sits alongside, and may also control robotic cameras. There are usually four adjustable pre-sets on a robotic camera. The variable lens angle can be selected and the pan and tilt head adjusted to frame up a specific shot. These positions, plus an elevation unit on the camera mount to adjust camera height, are stored in a memory bank to be recalled when that specific shot is required.

2.4.5 Studio floor staff

On the studio floor the floor manager (FM) relays information from the director during rehearsal and recording/transmission to the front-of-camera artistes, and liaises and coordinates all other technicians working on the studio floor. The FM may have an assistant floor manager (AFM) and/or a floor assistant (FA) working alongside, depending on the nature and complexity of the programme.

Camera operators wear headsets and can hear the director's instructions and provide shots of the production according to a pre-rehearsed sequence or, in an as-directed production, according to the role allocated to them.

There may be sound technicians on booms positioning a microphone in relation to artiste movement and the lighting design, or they may be rigging and adjusting personal microphones worn by the programme presenters.

A prompter operator controls the script text displayed on a television screen attached to the front of the camera. This allows presenters to look straight at the lens while reading scripted links via a mirror reflection of the text monitor. Depending on the studio, the prompt may be controlled from the control room, the studio floor, or another production area.

Scene-hands may be needed to reposition furniture and/or scenery during rehearsal and recording/transmission. Electricians working with the lighting director pre-rig and adjust lamps and electrical equipment according to the lighting plot.

Other members of the production team such as the designer, make-up supervisor, costume design and wardrobe may be on the studio floor, in the control rooms or working in their own specific areas (e.g. make-up). Additional crafts will augment the basic production team depending on the demands of the programme (e.g. a special effects designer).

2.4.6 Technical areas

Usually in a central technical area, engineers operate film and video machines to provide pre-recorded and pre-filmed inserts into the programme (although VTRs may be run by control room staff), and also to record the programme if required. Often a studio or maintenance engineer will be responsible for the serviceability and line-up of all studio equipment.

These are the basic crafts involved with everyday programme making. Depending on the type of programme, there may be many other specialist staff on the production team such as property master, special effects, unit managers, painters, carpenters, etc. On OB units, riggers drive the OB vehicles, rig cables, lay tracks and track cameras.

There is often an overlap of job functions, and a multiskiller may be required to work in any of these production skills.

2.5 Outside broadcasting

An outside broadcast (OB) is any multicamera video format programme or programme insert that is transmitted or recorded outside the studio complex. Most of the equipment permanently installed in a studio complex is required for an outside broadcast. Production, sound, engineering and recording facilities are usually housed in customized vehicles (often referred to as 'scanners') or as a travelling kit of lightweight, portable vision mixing panels, video tape recorders and associated engineering equipment, sound mixers, etc. housed in cases and reassembled in a suitable area at the location (e.g. for drama production).

In general terms, studio productions have more control of setting, staging and programme content than an OB. There is a logistic difficulty in duplicating all these facilities outside the studio, but location recording offers the advantage of complex and actual settings plus the ability to cover a huge range of events that are not specifically staged for television.

2.5.1 OB vehicles

The main OB vehicle houses the control room which serves the same function as a studio control but the equipment and operating areas are designed and compressed to fit a much smaller space.

Figure 2.7

Technical support vehicles are used for transporting cable, sound and camera equipment, monitors, lighting gear and other production facilities that may be required. In addition there may be a separate VTR vehicle equipped with recording and slow motion machines, etc. For a live transmission there will be a radio links vehicle or portable equipment – which may be a terrestrial or a satellite link or, alternatively, a land line that carries the programme back to a base station or transmitter. The number of vehicles on site will increase with the complexity of the programme and the rig. There may be props, scenery and furniture to be delivered to the site. Dressing rooms, make-up and catering may be required.

2.5.2 PSC units

The first generation of colour cameras were large pieces of electronic equipment which were immobile unless mounted on pedestals, cranes or dollies running on smooth surfaces. With the evolution of new technology, cameras light enough to be hand-held and portable were developed. These lightweight cameras were combined with a video recorder to allow the same flexibility in location production previously enjoyed by film cameras. The techniques developed with this type of video camera and recorder were a mixture of TV and film method. It could be edited or it could be used live. It required the technology of video but could use the discontinuous recording methods of film. Whereas live multicamera television broadcasts often require the separation of operational responsibility, the one-piece camera and recorder can be controlled by one person. To employ this video/film hybrid technique competently, a basic knowledge of camerawork, video recording, sound, lighting, video editing and TV journalism needs to be developed (see Chapter 7).

2.5.3 Post-production

Planning and acquiring the video and audio material is the first stage of programme production. There is often a second stage of post-production when the material is edited and audio dubbed. These activities are covered in Chapters 11 and 12.

2.5.4 Graphics area

Graphic designers provide electronically generated visual material for the programme as well as two-dimensional graphics.

Figure 2.8

2.6 Production methods

Having looked at the standard facilities provided by a studio and a location facility we can now examine how a multicamera programme production uses these resources. There are many types of production formats such as, for example, the studio situation comedy which is usually three or four sets facing an audience rostrum; or sports coverage, where six or more cameras will be positioned to cover all aspects of the contest. All programme formats require planning, the dissemination of information to the production team before the event, and a method of communicating and coordinating everyone's contribution on the transmission or recording.

Multicamera programme-making is a team effort and over the years a production procedure has been evolved which maximizes the efficiency of the production group.

2.6.1 Working as a team

The individual skills of many crafts combine to work together under the guidance of the director to transmit or record a programme. Sometimes the programme format requires a planned and precise camera script which is followed from opening titles to closing credits (e.g. a concert). Other programmes require the ad-lib technique of jazz where each camera is allocated a role but may shift and modify the shots they offer according to circumstances (e.g. sports coverage, public events, pop concerts).

Once a transmission (and sometimes a recording) has started there is no opportunity to stop and sort out production problems or make substantial alterations to the camera coverage of the programme. The basic requirement of live multicamera camerawork is to get it right first time – there are no retakes.

2.6.2 Preparation and anticipation

The rehearsal period is the time to discover what the contribution from each craft group will be. Each member of the crew has to establish what their role in the production is via a two-way exchange of information with the director and by talking to other technicians. In many rehearsals, all the information may be supplied on scripts and even a floor plan marked with camera positions. The feasibility of the planning is then tested by a rehearsal of every shot.

With other programme formats, the barest information on a running order is supplied and the technical operator has to seek details of the production that may affect him/her. Experience enables the right questions to be asked as this is the only opportunity to discover what is required before the crew is faced with a 'live' performance.

Each member of the crew has to work in the real time of the programme and all decisions are governed by the timescale of the event. Whilst the planning may have taken months or weeks, and the rehearsal days or hours, transmission is governed by the timescale of the event covered. Shot decisions have to be made in seconds with no time-out to consider the best way of tackling a particular situation. Preparation and anticipation are essential in order to create the time for fast, effective technique.

2.7 Customary technique

The nature of many programmes (e.g. sport, discussion programmes) does not allow precise information about shots either to be rehearsed or confirmed. What should be clear in the mind of each camera operator is the range of shots they will be involved with.

Multicamera production technique relies on the assumption that every member of the production crew is equipped with a knowledge of the conventions of the specific programme format and has a thorough mastery of the basic skills in their particular craft. Information about shots will be supplied during rehearsal and/or during transmission/recording but it will be assumed by the director that the crew will respond with customary technique to the specific programme requirements (e.g. matched shots for interviews – see Chapter 6).

2.8 Camera rehearsal

The rehearsal period is structured in a variety of ways, depending on the programme.

Blocking or looking at shots allows the whole production team to make the necessary adjustments section by section. The programme is rehearsed shot by shot, stopping each time there is a problem (unsatisfactory framing, unacceptable sound, unflattering lighting, etc.). During this phase of the rehearsal, shots are established and lighting and sound adjusted. A solution is found or will be found before continuing with the rehearsal.

This may be followed by a run-through of a particular sequence adding pre-recorded inserts, and this gives an indication of the time needed for camera moves, pace of movement and change of shot.

Finally, depending on the programme, there may be a full dress run-through from opening titles to end credits. This final rehearsal is an attempt to run the programme exactly as it will be transmitted or recorded with no stoppages. The dress run may

reveal logistical problems of moving cameras, presenters, scenery, etc. between sequences and all the other craft adjustments that need to be made in continuous camera coverage. Any significant alterations to the production as the result of this rehearsal may be rehearsed again (time permitting) or the production crew will be made aware of any unrehearsed material or shots before the recording or transmission.

The rehearsal period should be used to check the production requirements for the whole programme. There is no point in having a perfectly rehearsed third of a programme if the remaining two-thirds could not be rehearsed because of lack of time.

2.9 Rehearse/record

There are two main methods for recording a programme using multicameras:

- Rehearse a section of the programme and record that section.
- Rehearse the whole of the programme and then record or transmit the programme 'live'.

To some extent the first method of rehearse/record is efficient in that only small sections are rehearsed and remembered, but it does require a high level of concentration throughout the shooting day because the production is periodically in 'Transmission' conditions and sometimes allows insufficient time for all disciplines to get it right.

The second method requires extended rehearsal unless production content is so flexible that coverage is arranged by assigning a role for each camera during the programme (e.g. Camera One on a wide shot, Camera Two on close-ups). If content is precisely known (e.g. drama serials/soaps, sitcoms), then the camera rehearsal will involve working through the programme shot by shot so that every one associated with the production is aware of what is required.

3 Safety

3.1 Individual responsibility

While others working on the programme (e.g. the producer) may have a contractual or insurance obligation for the overall safety of the production, health and safety legislation obliges everyone to take reasonable care of their own health and safety and that of others who may be affected by what they do or fail to do. Everyone also has a responsibility to cooperate, as necessary, to ensure satisfactory safety standards.

If you comply with the requirements for safety and something goes wrong, then your employer will be held to account. If you fail to comply, you may lose any claim for compensation for injury and could even be prosecuted individually.

What you must do:

- Follow the safety requirements and any instructions that are given, especially in relation to emergencies (e.g. know the location of fire exits).
- Ask for further information if you need it.
- Report accidents (and 'near misses'), dangerous situations and defects in safety arrangements.
- Do not interfere with or misuse safety systems or equipment, or engage in horseplay that could be dangerous.
- Work within the limits of competence, which means a knowledge of best practice and an awareness of the limitations of one's own experience and knowledge.

Assessing risk

The key to good, safe working practices is to assess any significant risk and to take action to eliminate or minimize such risks. The procedure is as follows:

- Identify precisely what is required in the production.

Lifting
- Posture:
  keep the back straight
  use the leg muscles to lift
  keep the load close to the body
  use a firm palm grip
  keep the elbows tucked into the body
  position feet to provide a stable base.
- Review the task, the load, the working environment and individual capacity.
- When loading vehicles, place heavy and most used items in the most convenient position for lifting into and out of the vehicle.
- Get help from another person if loads are particularly heavy, bulky, or have to be carried a long way.
- Use mechanical aids wherever possible.

Figure 3.1

- Identify any potential hazards in that activity.
- Identify the means by which those risks can be controlled.

The key terms in risk assessment are:

- *Hazard* – the inherent ability to cause harm.
- *Risk* – the likelihood that harm will occur in particular circumstances.
- *Reasonably practicable* – the potential improvement in safety balanced against the cost and inconvenience of the measures that would be required. If the costs and inconvenience do not heavily outweigh the benefits, then the thing is reasonably practicable and should be done.
- *Residual risk* – the risk remaining after precautions have been taken.

An example of the above four terms in action might be when it is proposed to rig a camera hoist near overhead power lines because it is claimed that this is the best position for the required shot. The power lines are a hazard. Touching them could result in death. What is the likelihood (risk) that harm will occur in particular circumstances? There may be the risk of a high wind blowing the hoist onto the power lines. Is the weather changeable? Could a high wind arise? What is reasonable and practical to improve safety? The obvious action is to reposition the hoist to provide a usable shot but eliminate all risk of it touching the power lines. As weather is often unpredictable, the hoist should be repositioned as the costs and inconvenience do not heavily outweigh the benefits. There remains the residual risk of operating a camera on a hoist, which can only be partially reduced by wearing a safety harness.

3.2 The importance of safety

Nearly all television production environments are temporary rigs and therefore potentially hazardous. One of the most dangerous times is during rigging and de-rigging. Apart from the risks of lifting heavy equipment, hoisting, climbing and cabling, there is, when de-rigging, the universal tendency to want to get the job done as fast as possible, coupled on location with a de-rig that is often carried out at night. It is in such situations that a couple of minutes of thought could prevent a lifetime of backache.

Make yourself aware of the fire procedure and alarms in studios and on location. A staff member of an organization is usually familiar with every corridor, exit and shortcut in a studio complex. A freelance may need to read signs when finding their way around. Make certain that you could find your way through smoke-filled corridors to the nearest exit. Location work means continuously operating in new or unfamiliar buildings or stadiums filled with spectators. When rigging, walk the quickest route you can find to an outside exit in the case of fire.

3.3 Studio safety and rigging

Allocated rigging time may be shared by many different craft groups. The simultaneous activities of rigging lights, setting, set dressing and sound and camera rigging can lead to a potentially dangerous situation. Ensure that all precautions are taken to ensure the safety of yourself and others. In particular, observe the following:

• Check when pulling cables that they will not trip or unsettle other colleagues carrying weights.

• Do not continue to pull a cable that is out of sight and snagged. Apart from the possible damage to the cable end, it may be snagged on a ladder in use, etc.

• Get help when lifting heavy weights and use the advised procedure of bending at the knees and keeping the back straight when lifting. Lift in two stages – up to chair height, then up to required height.

• Do not go into the studio grid area without observing the proper procedure (see Section 3.3.5).

3.3.1 Cable routing

Camera cable routing should ensure that access routes are not obstructed.

Where necessary (e.g. crossing fire lanes, audience or performer entrances and exits), cables must be flown or ramped. Take special precautions in unlit areas of the location or studio (behind sets, etc.) which may be used by performers and crew in a hurry during a production. Ask for working lights to be rigged.

Where possible, camera cable runs should take the safest and shortest route to the cable point avoiding floor areas that are access points on to the set or to production rooms (e.g. make-up, wardrobe, etc.). If a safety rail is fitted around the base of the studio wall, the camera cable should pass under the rail before being plugged into the cable point.

A cable eight (see Fig. 3.2) is a convenient way of storing camera cable that is not immediately needed.

Figure 3.2 A cable 'eight'.

3.3.2 Cable clearing

Be particularly vigilant when clearing cables behind large cranes. Often the cable will be bound with a power cable and possibly a camera headlamp cable. These additional cables require very careful lashing with gaffer tape to prevent small loops of cable developing which can easily catch under the cable guards. Do not allow the back or front of the crane to push large loops of cable when moving. Keep all cable away from the guards to prevent the speed and weight of the crane overriding the cable.

3.3.3 Electricity

Rigging camera cables, monitors and dolly power supplies is a daily occurrence but, however familiar, an electrical supply is a potential hazard unless safe handling procedures are observed.

No one should carry out electrical work unless they have sufficient knowledge to prevent danger to themselves or others. The electrical safety of plugs and connectors should be inspected before plugging into a supply and a periodic check should be made on earthing and the condition of cables for signs of cuts or worn insulation.

On location, water (rain, sea, rivers, swimming pools, etc.) in contact with electricity poses a special

---

Electrical safety checklist:
- Carry out regular visual checks of cables, plugs and equipment.
- Know how to check fuse ratings, earth and wiring connections inside a plug.
- Look for evident faults, e.g. overheated, discoloured or worn cables.
- Withdraw defective equipment from service, report it and clearly mark item as faulty.
- Check portable equipment subject to constant and heavy use more frequently. A combined inspection/test should be carried out at least once every 3 months.
- Keep records of inspections and tests.
- Use a protective device such as a residual current device (RCD).

Note: RCDs need to be 'exercised' regularly; trip them using the test button on each occasion before taking the equipment they are protecting into use and install them as close as possible to the supply socket. Ensure RCDs are tested on a regular basis to ensure their tripping characteristics are satisfactory.

Health and Safety Executive publication
Camera Operations on Location

Figure 3.3

---

hazard. When more than one power source is used at a location dangerous voltage differences can occur. There should be segregation between different power supplies.

Only open the side of the camera and alter controls if you can see what you are touching and are competent to carry out the adjustment. Never feel around for a control while looking in the viewfinder.

3.3.4 Working in the grid

Sometimes it is necessary to enter the grid area in order to sling a monitor above the studio floor. Extreme care should be taken that nothing taken on to the grid falls through on to the studio floor below. Access to the grid must be strictly controlled while people are working on the studio floor and the following procedures enforced:

- Remove any loose item either worn or pocketed when entering the grid, e.g. coins, keys, screwdrivers, spanners, and especially video barrels.
- If tools are essential for the rig, then they must be kept secure when working overhead.
- Do not allow video or mains cable ends to fall though the grid – lower them to the floor.
- If possible, clear the floor; but if this is not practical, have an 'exclusion zone' with someone 'policing' it.
- Only suspend monitors from agreed suspension points (hoists etc.).

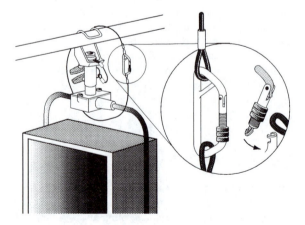

Figure 3.4 A safety bond is used to protect every overhead rigged linkage in case of failure of the means of attachment to the suspension component. A safety bond is a flexible steel wire rope fitted with a quick-release fastener. It is looped between a suspended item and a firm support and is a safeguard against the accidental release of a rigged connection. It is entirely separate from the primary means of support and normally carries no load.

3.3.5 Slung video/sound monitors

- Check that the safe working load (SWL) of the hoist or support is suitable for the slung monitor and cradle.
- Check that the monitor cradle is safe and all adjustable struts are tight and hold the monitor securely.
- Use two people to lift and present the monitor/cradle to the suspension arm and have another to attach the monitor to the spigot or whatever method is used to attach the monitor cradle to the hoist.
- Attach a steel safety bond (see Fig. 3.4) to prevent the monitor falling if the primary means of attachment to the hoist should fail.
- Video/sound cable and main cables should be tied off at the grid and also tied to the monitor cradle. Always check there is a sufficient amount of slack cable before lowering a hoist.
- When the mains/video cable is plugged to the monitor, switch on and check the monitor is functioning with the correct feed and termination, before hoisting.
- Do not manually assist the hoist.
- The hoist must be under surveillance when being raised or lowered.
- There must be nobody under the load.
- Check that the hoist movement does not foul adjacent suspended items and sufficient slack cable is available when lowering.

3.4 Rigging cameras

Basic checks need to be carried out before rigging or de-rigging a full facility television camera on to a wedge plate pan/tilt head attached to a mounting:

- Check the stability of the mounting and the head is secured to the mounting (e.g. on a four-bolt fixing, all bolts are in place and tight).
- Check that the tripod is level and the base and legs are secure and locked.
- Check that the pedestal column is locked down with safety locks and the head is locked off with the safety fitment in place.
- Check that the crane or jib arm is locked or restrained with a security strap or someone is securing the boom. *Note*: Do not stand on the crane platform when rigging or de-rigging a camera. The crane arm will require weights to be added at the rear of the boom arm to balance out the combined weight of cameraman, camera and lens.

- Know the route you are carrying the camera and check that the route is clear and free from obstructions (e.g. closed doors can be pushed open in the direction of movement).
- Check that the safety locking pin on the wedge plate on the pan/tilt head is removed and the retaining spigot is clear of the shoe of the wedge plate and is in a condition to accept the wedge on the base of the camera.
- Check that the back of the pan/tilt head (i.e. the widest part of the wedge plate) is facing the direction in which the camera will be slid on to the head.
- Check that the camera is seated in the wedge plate before sliding in the securing spigot and replacing the locking pin.
- When rigging a lens, protect the back element and keep the pedestal/crane or arm locked off at minimum height to facilitate hanging the lens on the camera. Remove the back element lens cap (if fitted) and the cap/protection for the camera prism block. When rigging most box lenses, present the top of the lens to the hinge at the top of the camera and then lower the lens down to engage the securing spigots. Slide the retaining clamp and tighten.
- Connect lens cables and zoom controls, checking that they are routed correctly and that there are no excessive loops of cable that could snag the pan/tilt head in operation.
- When connecting a multicore camera cable, check the position of the key ring configuration inside the cable connector and match this to the cable connector on the camera.
- Remove the security bar or locking pins on the pedestal column, unlock any column brake and check that the pedestal is balanced.

3.4.1 Rigging a lightweight camera

- Check that the fitting on the base of the camera matches the tripod adaptor plate on the pan/tilt head fitting.
- Check the cam size of the pan/tilt head if fitting a lightweight camera and box lens combination.
- When fitting a lightweight camera into a harness equipped with a box lens, take care to protect the back element of the lens as the camera is presented to the lens.
- Make sure the height adjustment of the camera plate is correct so that no weight or pressure is applied to the lens to camera flange.
- When fitting a lightweight camera/lens on to a lightweight head, check that the holding pin is not in the centre of the wedge. Move the lever to reseat the holding pin in its inoperative position. Slide

the camera into the tripod adaptor plate until a click is heard. Check that the camera is locked by testing if the camera can be slid out of the adaptor plate. The method of securing the base of a light-weight camera to the tripod adaptor varies with the make of camera. Adjust balance, CoG and required friction.

• Cable up zoom, viewfinder, cue lights, mixed viewfinder and check if the lens can be powered from the camera cable or if it is to be battery-driven.

• Check that the connecting cable between the lens and the camera will supply the correct voltage on the correct pins.

3.4.2 De-rigging a camera

• Check that the pedestal column is locked down and the safety chains are secured on the pan/tilt head and that, ideally, the pedestal wheels are oriented 90° to the wedge plate sliding section.

• Check that the crane or jib arm is locked or restrained with a security strap or someone is securing the boom.

• Fit the front lens cap and switch the camera off before disconnecting the camera cable and all lens cables.

• Recheck that no cables remain connected before removing the lens and refitting the back element lens cap.

• Pan the camera so that both people sliding the camera out of the wedge plate are comfortably positioned and are able to move the camera away from the mounting without obstruction.

• Remove the locking pin on the head and slide the restraining spigot out of the wedge plate channel.

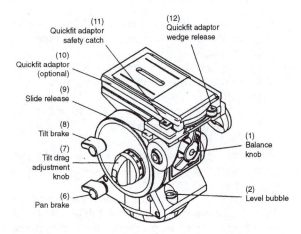

Figure 3.5 A lightweight camera pan/tilt head.

• Slide the camera back on the head and lift clear.

• Leave the pedestal/crane/jib arm in a secure and balanced condition.

3.4.3 Rigging a crane/jib arm

• Route the camera cable and any other cable required to provide sufficient loop at any point on the mounting which moves. Check that there is sufficient cable slack by positioning the arm throughout its complete operational range.

• If the dolly is motorized, check that the correct power supply is available before connecting. Secure the power cable to the camera cable with gaffer tape along the length of cable in use.

• Always leave an unattended crane in a secure and locked condition.

3.5 Outside broadcast rigging

An outside broadcast is a programme that is recorded or transmitted away from normal studio facilities and therefore every item of equipment required by the production needs to be transported to the location.

At a location, camera mountings often have to be positioned on scaffolding, in stadiums or inside build-ings inaccessible to wheeled transport. Every item has to be manhandled, for example up stairs or to a remote part of the stadium, before being rigged. Mountings need to be broken down into manageable sections that can be carried. In general, OB mountings are smaller and lighter than their studio equivalent although sharing the same operational range of height and manoeuvrability.

Once the camera and mounting have been carried to their operating position, a cable or a radio link is required to allow for the return signal, picture control and communications. Power may be supplied to the camera via cable, battery or from a local mains supply via an adaptor. If possible, avoid rigging in isolation on location as this increases the risk of being hurt while lifting heavy weights without assistance or the risk of electrocution without immediate help.

3.5.1 OB rigging hazards

As well as the general details of rigging previously discussed, rigging cameras and mountings at a location involves solving problems caused by:

• lifting and carrying heavy weights when rigging;
• working among the public;

- working at heights (see Section 3.6);
- personal and equipment protection against adverse weather.

3.5.2 Hoisting and lifting equipment

Although instruction is available on lifting heavy weights to avoid back injury, the nature of access to some stadiums, public buildings, etc. makes recommended procedure impossible. Always attempt to maintain the advised body posture of chin in, straight arms and back when lifting heavy weights.

When hoisting equipment up to a height, use a block and tackle if available and double-check anchor points and securing arrangements on the equipment. Have someone policing the area below the hoisting position and whenever possible use an approved and tested lifting bag. Make certain tripods and bases are secure, stable and level before rigging the camera and lens. In an exposed position or on uneven ground, use additional ropes to anchor the mounting to prevent damage by high winds. Always leave the camera weather-protected and with the smallest area of camera/lens facing the prevailing wind.

3.6 Working at heights

A significant proportion of serious accidents arise from work carried out at heights. There is always a risk of a person or object falling from a height.

When a person has to work at a height, a safe working environment should be provided if at all possible. The camera operating height at risk is any distance likely to cause injury and certainly any drop in excess of 2 m. Safety barriers (at least 1.1 m high) plus toe boards and intermediate rails or equivalent protection must be erected. If the edge cannot be protected, then people must be kept at least 3 m from the edge or wear a harness attached to a securely anchored safety line.

Harnesses and lifelines should not be considered as the primary safety requirement unless there are no reasonably practicable reasonable alternatives. *Note*: Harnesses and lifelines will only limit the danger if a person falls.

Any object that could fall or be blown off the structure (e.g. a lens cap) should be removed or anchored. Equipment in exposed positions must be adequately secured to withstand the foreseeable wind force. Check when a camera cable is connected to an elevated camera that it is tied off so that the weight of the cable does not stretch the cable or pull on the camera.

High vantage points are often required for shoots, particularly at sports events. Improvised vantage points, such as drums or pallets, create additional risks to health and safety.

The practice of using fork lift trucks to provide an elevated platform is especially dangerous and should not be carried out without a properly built cage for containment and proper control of any movement of the vehicle.

3.6.1 Scaffolding

Scaffolding should be erected by an approved contractor and certified for its intended use before being rigged with camera/lens/mounting. There should be the normal 'edge protection' of a 1.1 m barrier and a 'kick' or toe board to indicate to the cameraman whilst operating the camera that he or she is approaching the edge of the platform.

Sometimes the base of the scaffolding is sheeted with blockboard for cosmetic or security reasons (e.g. it prevents unauthorized personnel clambering up the scaffolding). Sheeted scaffold structures may suffer considerable strain at high wind speeds.

Be especially vigilant in the use of zip-up towers built from 'snap-together' components. The height to least-base ratio must not be more than 3:1 in *light winds* and 3.5:1 when used inside. Guy ropes and ground anchor/ballasting may be used to improve stability.

Tips on the use of scaffolding
- The scaff tag labelling system will give:
  the contact name and number of the scaffold contractor
  when the scaffold was erected and by whom
  when the scaffold is due for re-inspection.
- A scaff tag showing a green label clipped to the side of the scaffold normally means that it is complete. If there is a red scaff tag label this means that the scaffold is incomplete and no unauthorized persons are allowed on the structure.
- The absence of a scaff tag does not necessarily mean that scaffolding is unsafe but it should be treated with caution. Check with the owner or person in charge. Where a number of crews are to use a scaffold the owner/person in control should be advised of the combined weight of equipment and numbers of persons in advance of the work. A 'hand-over certificate' should then be available which will declare whether the scaffold is fit for use and specify the design loading.

Health and Safety Executive publication
Camera Operations on Location

Figure 3.6

3.6.2 Ladders

Check that access ladders are securely attached to the scaffolding, and that rungs are free from mud, grease, etc. If a free-standing ladder is used for rigging, check that the foot of the ladder is on a firm and level surface and someone is using their weight to stabilize the ladder when in use.

3.6.3 Hydraulic platforms

- Check that a competent person is operating the hoist and will be in continuous attendance while the hoist is in use.
- Check the safety inspection cards and date of last inspection.
- Check the arrangements for communication between the cage and the ground.
- Check the emergency procedure if the camera operator is trapped aloft (e.g. bleeding down the system, rescue by another hoist, etc.).
- Check the operation of any self-lowering system.
- Check that the base of the hoist will be continuously supervised to prevent unauthorized operation.
- Check the condition of the hoist and look for hydraulic oil leaks, cracks in the welding of the cage, etc.
- Check that the legs are positioned for adequate load spreading of the rig and are not positioned on or near drain covers.
- Have a system for measuring wind speed and know the maximum wind speed for safe working on the specific rig and height to be worked.
- Use a harness and properly attached lifeline.

3.6.4 Height and overhead power cables

Be careful when using mast scaffold poles, mike booms, etc. when close to overhead power lines. Operating positions should be no closer than 15 m from wire suspended from a metal structure and no closer than 11 m from wire suspended from a wooden structure.

3.7 Working amongst the public

Most people watch television and therefore most people have an interest in how programmes are made. On location there will often be an interchange between the production crew and the public. Try to accommodate their genuine interest while safeguarding their safety.

Where work is taking place at a height:
- the means of getting up to and down from the place of work must be safe;
- ladders must either be footed or secured;
- equipment should be transferred safely, i.e. slung, over the shoulder or hoisted up separately;
- leave both hands free to hold on to ladders;
- use safety harnesses and equipment safety lines when working from articulated or telescopic hoists, or cherry pickers.

Health and Safety Executive publication
Camera Operations on Location

Figure 3.7

Never rig or de-rig camera equipment above an audience unless a safe area has been cleared and is being continuously 'policed'. If a camera is positioned among the public (e.g. in an audience), make certain that there is someone in addition to the camera operator who can assist with organizing and controlling an operational area. Check that the condition of the camera, lens and mounting cannot cause harm if there is accidental contact in a crowd.

Organize additional help if the camera is cabled and requires repositioning among the public. The rigger should ensure that sufficient slack cable is available at all times and be ready to pay it out as and when the camera moves. To a large extent, roving cameras are now equipped with radio links and therefore cable-bashing for a mobile camera is redundant (e.g. running the touch line at a rugby or football match).

Cameras mounted above an audience must be rigged before the audience is seated and checked for any loose or movable items that could be displaced when operating. Cranes manoeuvring above an audience should be no lower than the height of a person suddenly standing up and with no trailing loops of cable. There should always be an observer of the camera's physical position when manoeuvring a remotely controlled camera. On location, clearance to work a crane above an audience may be required from the local authority.

Camera crews working in front of audiences or spectators at public events or performances should wear the appropriate clothing to integrate with the event (e.g. avoid very casual clothes at a church service).

3.7.1 Security

Precautions must always be taken against the loss or damage to equipment. When working in a public place, avoid leaving equipment unattended.

Overnight security of equipment is necessary unless the camera position is secure and inaccessible. If there is a risk of someone scaling a scaffold tower then blockboard can be used to clad the base and the access ladder removed.

Public disorder
- Meet at the edge of the disorder.
- Make a further assessment of the situation.
- Remain as inconspicuous as possible.
- Avoid conspicuous use of cameras or equipment.
- Withdraw if presence appears to be prolonging or intensifying a dangerous situation.
- Cease if subjects start to behave abnormally.
- Do not attempt an immediate reconstruction of an event or incident.
- Consider the advantages and disadvantages of using unmarked cars.
- Vehicles should meet at secure sites in close proximity to the location. They should not proceed without clearance from a person responsible for the assignment or by the authority in control.

Health and Safety Executive publication
Camera Operations on Location

Figure 3.8

3.7.2 Hostile crowds

No story is worth a life. During public disorder or a civil disturbance, stay together as a crew and avoid conspicuous display of cameras, etc. Withdraw immediately if the presence of TV cameras intensifies a dangerous situation.

3.8 Outside broadcast hazards

A checklist of potential OB safety hazards includes the following:

- Boats – it is essential to wear life-lines and life-jackets when operating on a boat or near water such as on a harbour wall.
- Confined spaces – check the quality of air and ventilation when working in confined spaces such as trenches, pipes, sewers, ducts, mines, caves, etc.
- Children are a hazard to themselves. When working in schools or on a children's programme, check that someone is available and responsible to prevent them touching or tripping over cables, floor lamps, camera mountings, etc.

- Explosive effects and fire effects must be regulated by a properly trained effects operator and especial care should be taken with those effects that cannot be rehearsed.
- Excessive fatigue is a safety problem when operating equipment that could cause damage to yourself or others and when driving a vehicle on a long journey home after a production has finished.
- Fork-lift trucks must have a properly constructed cage if they are to carry a camera operator and camera.
- Lamps – all lamps should have a safety glass/safety mesh as protection against exploding bulbs. Compact source discharge lamps must always be used with a UV radiation protective lens. Lamps rigged overhead must be fitted with a safety bond. Check that lamp stands are secured and cabled to avoid being tripped over and that they are securely weighted at the base to prevent them being blown over.
- Location safety – in old buildings, check for weak floors, unsafe overhead windows, derelict water systems and that the electrical supply is suitable for the use it is put to. Check the means of escape in case of fire and the local methods of dealing with a fire. Check for the impact of adverse weather and, in remote locations, the access to and time of response of emergency services.
- Level floor – every OB vehicle should be earthed and vehicles that require people to work inside should be parked and levelled with adequate ventilation. If operating a camera on the roof of a vehicle, it should either have a fully guarded edge or a safety harness and safety line should be worn by the camera operator. Check the risk from radio frequency radiation if there are aerials mounted on the same roof.
- Noise – high levels of location noise (machinery etc.), effects (gunshots, explosions) as well as close working to foldback speakers can damage hearing. Stress will be experienced when attempting to listen to talkback with a very high ambient noise. Wear noise-cancelling headsets. If wearing single-sided cans, use an ear plug in the unprotected ear.
- Stunt vehicles – motor vehicles travelling at speed involved in a stunt are likely to go out of control. Leave the camera locked-off on the shot and stand well away from the action area in a safe position agreed with the stunt coordinator.
- Filming from a moving vehicle – the camera must be either securely mounted or independently secured on safety lanyards. Operators should be fitted with seat belts or safety harnesses attached to safety lines securely anchored.

- Roadside working – wear high-visibility clothing and have the police direct traffic if required. Police may give permission for a member of the crew to direct traffic but motorists are not obliged to obey such instructions.

3.9 Adverse weather

Often the most unpredictable factor in an outside broadcast is the weather. The positions of the cameras are usually controlled by the nature of the event but they are often sited to avoid looking into the sun. Extreme weather changes may be experienced during the period of rig, rehearsal and transmission, and therefore adequate precautions must be made to protect:

- equipment against adverse weather;
- personnel against adverse weather.

3.9.1 Planning for adverse weather conditions

The standard advice in weather protection for equipment or people is to prepare for the worst.

This means checking weather forecasts and assessing if scaffold towers or hoists in exposed positions can withstand any anticipated high winds and whether equipment requires additional anchorage. Often, long before the structure is at risk, the winds may be too high to hold a camera steady on anything other than a fairly wide angle.

A weather cover should always be fitted to a camera before use as it offers protection from rain and heat. Water and electricity do not mix and there should be precautions taken to protect all electrical connections such as headsets, zoom controls, cable plugs, etc. Often the simplest but most satisfactory method is covering hand controls with small plastic bags. In driving rain, keep the camera panned away from the wind whenever possible and use the front lens cap during any extended break in coverage. Check that there is adequate ventilation if the camera is covered and left switched on overnight.

Rain building up on the front element of the lens will be more obvious on a wide angle shot and lens cloths will be needed to periodically clean the lens. In rainy conditions, the lens shade, if adjustable, should be positioned to provide the greatest protection with gaffer tape stuck along the top and bottom of the hood to reduce rain penetration or flare. Check that it does not vignette (e.g. appear in shot) when the widest angle of the lens is selected.

Extremes of cold or heat can have an adverse effect on the performance of cameras. Use additional thermal linings inside camera covers and/or shade from direct sun if feasible.

3.9.2 Personal weather protection

Large-scale events (e.g. golf) involve cameras being scattered a long way from the scanner. They also involve long transmissions. A camera operator setting out for the day therefore needs to be equipped with a choice of clothing to match any changing weather conditions.

Those who work regularly out of doors must make themselves aware of the risks involved and how to protect themselves against sunburn, skin cancer, heat stress and heat stroke, hypothermia, white finger and frostbite.

3.9.3 Risk assessment during a thunderstorm

A check on the effects of any extreme weather forecast must be assessed each day on exposed camera positions. Individual safety requires a personal assessment and only the individual on a scaffold tower or hoist can judge when it is time to call it a day and retreat from the threat of lightning.

3.9.4 Single-person working

Single-person crews should not be deployed in areas of civil unrest or public disorder. These 'high risk' assignments include coverage of high crime areas, sports events or court proceedings where violence might be anticipated.

Walking backwards on shot with a hand-held camera is a common occurrence with a two-man crew, but highly dangerous for the single-person operator who has no opportunity to check where they are going. Single-person operators should not be assigned to cover, for example, marches or arrivals and departures of people in the news, where tracking back on shot is the standard technique for this type of story.

Carrying a large amount of lighting and camera equipment from a camera car into a building where stairs have to be used, is dangerous to the heath of the single camera operator, and the security of the equipment.

3.10 Location lighting and safety

Location recording is often a scramble to rig, record, wrap and move on to the next set up. There is always

Location lighting questions
- Who is to provide the lighting?
- Has sufficient time been allowed for setting up and cooling down?
- Have arrangements been made to prevent lighting from accidentally overturning?
- Has sufficient information been given about the job, the facilities available, and backup (technical or otherwise)?
- Is the lighting required complex?
- Should a lighting specialist or other person be 'on call' or part of the team?
- Is additional help needed to move the equipment?
- Will environmental conditions dictate special arrangements, e.g. flammable, explosive or wet conditions?
- Do you need to coordinate work with other persons present?
- Will members of the public be present?

Health and Safety Executive publication
Camera Operations on Location

Figure 3.9

Placement of lamps
- Adequate time should be allowed for the selection of suitable sites for the safe placement of lamps and for their setting up.
- Lamps should be placed so that they do not obstruct entrances, exits or passageways. They should be placed in such a way that there is no risk of them being knocked over.
- Stands should be sited on firm, level ground and set at a height to ensure maximum stability. Use portable sand bags to weigh stands down.
- Particular care should be taken when placing lamps so that any heat generated can do no danger nor cause a risk of fire.
- Cables should not run across thoroughfares unless they do not cause a tripping hazard or they are at a suitable height. Any cables which are flown (unsupported) must be securely tied off at a suitable height.
- If a lamp is knocked over it should be switched off, allowed to cool and not used again until it has been examined.

Health and Safety Executive publication
Camera Operations on Location

Figure 3.10

the urgency to get the job done but, as pressurized as this may be, it is never expedient to cut corners on safety. A couple of minutes saved by not making safe a cable crossing the top of a flight of stairs may result in injury and many hours of lost time. You have a responsibility to ensure that the condition and the method of rigging lamps and cables at a location is safe to yourself and to members of the public.

Periodically check the earthing and safety of your lamps. Make certain the safety glass or wire is fitted and not damaged in any way. Check the condition of cables for frayed or worn insulation and that they are earthed correctly.

3.10.1 HMIs

Discharge light sources such as HMI lamps produce light by ionizing a gas contained in the bulb. Because of a high bulb pressure they are liable to explode and they also produce a harmful level of ultraviolet radiation. Therefore all discharge sources must be fitted with a glass filter as a safety glass. Usually an interlock will prevent the supply of EHT if the safety glass is broken or missing.

Check that any HMI you are using has a safety glass fitted.

3.10.2 Location electrical supplies

It is important to check the power supply fuse rating and the condition of the wiring before using a domestic supply. Blown fuses can waste time but burnt-out wiring could start a fire. Also check cable runs, especially around doors and tops of stairs. Check where you place lamps. They get hot and so will anything touching them.

3.10.3 Care and consideration

If you need to attach any material to windows, use masking tape or lowtack tape so that you leave the paintwork as you found it. Remember, you may want to return to that location. If you have ever followed a TV crew that caused problems on a site, you will appreciate that loss of goodwill from the public makes for a very hard day's shoot.

People appearing on television for the first time may be nervous or excited. You may be under pressure to get the job done and onto the next set up. When working with the public, their safety and your safety are equally important.

3.10.4 Filming from the air

Use a reputable aircraft operator who has experience of filming with single operators. Private pilot licence holders are not allowed to fly for reward.

Flight safety

- Shoot lists need to be pre-planned and agreed with the pilot.
- The person responsible for the shoot should ensure that the permission of the CAA has been obtained where necessary.
- Pilots need to be thoroughly briefed before take-off. All manoeuvres should be agreed before take-off. Prior to the flight, single words of communication and simple signals need to be agreed between the pilot and camera operator or producer. The advice of the pilot about the safety of the shoot or any part of it is critical.
- The camera operators may need a suitable safety harness.
- Ensure that all equipment is properly secured.

Health and Safety Executive publication
Camera Operations on Location

Figure 3.11

The Civil Aviation Authority (CAA) normally invoke an air exclusion zone around any major news incident.

3.10.5 Work-related stress

Occupational stress in television can pose a significant risk to health.

Stress factors

- Working long and unsociable hours.
- Assignment communications.
- Workload time and pressure.

Stresses to be avoided

- Frequent shift changes.
- Changing from night to day shifts without adequate time to recover.
- Poor communications leading to increased risks or unnecessary work.
- Inadequate provision for refreshment and toilet breaks.
- Driving long distances after lengthy periods of work.
- The length of the working day.
- The number of days scheduled along with the need for time off.
- Insufficient information about the work and the right equipment for the location.
- The need for complex or detailed information.
- The spoken word, what is said and how it is said.

Health and Safety Executive publication
Camera Operations on Location

Figure 3.12

News gathering may involve assignments where crews experience distressing events. Avoid adopting a 'macho' tendency to shrug this off if the event continues to cause psychological trauma. Seek professional help and support.

Working in television involves long, unpredictable, and unsociable hours of work. If this is coupled with tight deadlines, workload pressure and driving long distances after lengthy periods of work without adequate rests and recuperation, stress will increase until the health of the person is at risk.

Further reading

Essentials of Health and Safety at Work. HSE Books 1994. ISBN 0 7176 0716 X.

A Guide to the Health and Safety at Work etc. Act 1974 (5th edition). L1. HSE Books 1993. ISBN 0 7176 0441 1.

5 Steps to Risk Assessment. IND(G)163L. HSE Books 1994. (Priced packs also available, ISBN 0 7176 0904 9.)

Management of Health and Safety at Work. Management of Health and Safety at Work Regulations 1992 Approved Code of Practice. L21. HSE Books 1992. ISBN 0 7176 041 8.

Workplace Heath, Safety and Welfare. Workplace Regulations 1992 Approved Code of Practice and Guidance. L4. HSE Books 1992. ISBN 0 7176 0413 6.

Workplace Health, Safety and Welfare – A Short Guide. IND(G)P44L. HSE Books 1997. ISBN 0 7176 11328 3.

A Guide to the Reporting of Injuries, Diseases and Dangerous Occurrences Regulations. L73. HSE Books 1996. ISBN 0 7176 1012 8.

Electrical Safety and You. IND(G)231L. HSE Books 1996. (Priced packs also available. ISBN 0 7176 1207 4.)

Electrical Safety at Places of Entertainment. GS 50. HSE Books 1991. ISBN 0 11 885598 0.

Electrical Safety for Entertainers. IND(G)247L. HSE Books.

Electricity at Work: Safe Working Practices. HS(G)85. HSE Books 1993. ISBN 0 7176 0442 X.

Maintaining Portable and Transportable Electrical Equipment. HS(G)107. HSE Books 1994. ISBN 0 7176 0715 1.

HSE Video Live Wires: What to Look For When Inspecting Portable Electrical Equipment. Obtainable from CFL Vision, PO Box 35, Wetherby, West Yorkshire LS23 7EX. Tel: 01937 541010.

Diving Operations at Work. Diving Operations at Work Regulations 1981 as amended by the Diving Operations at Work (Amendment) Regulations 1990. L6 HSE Books 1981. ISBN 0 11 885599 9.

Safety Representatives and Safety Committees (3rd edition). L87. HSE Books 1996. ISBN 0 7176 1220 1.

4 Lighting and vision control

4.1 Lighting overview

Effective lighting is essential to the production of good television pictures, that is pictures which are technically and artistically 'pleasing'. The criterion for good lighting can be summed up by 'when it looks right – it is!'.

Lighting is very much a mixture of art and craft. One has to visualize the final result and then realize it by using the appropriate hardware. The lighting process is dictated by **time**, **technology** and **technique**; with the technique to be applied being influenced by the time and the technology (hardware) available. This section will discuss the basic lighting principles in terms of the technology and the techniques that may be used. Very few lighting problems have a unique solution – what works one day may not be as effective on another day for a variety of reasons. There is a need for a flexible approach, constantly looking for new solutions to old problems. Often, some of the best results are obtained by 'breaking the rules'; however, the 'rules' need to be known before they can be broken, deliberately! The basic techniques offered in this section should form a good basis on which to build and develop your own particular style of lighting.

4.1.1 Lighting aims

The **lighting aims** can be expanded as follows.

Artistic requirements
- To produce pictures which look three-dimensional; the pictures will ultimately be viewed on a two-dimensional screen so it is an essential requirement to create the illusion of depth.
- To create the right lighting condition as indicated by the script – day/night/dawn, etc. – the **explicit** requirement.

- To create the right atmosphere or mood as interpreted from the script – dramatic/cheerful/documentary, etc. – the **implicit** requirement. The lighting director must ensure that his or her interpretation of the script is exactly in tune with the director's!
- To produce a good compatible picture (monochrome picture). Generally, if the monochrome picture looks good, the colour picture should also look good.

Technical requirements
- To provide the right amount of light so that the cameras are correctly exposed – **illuminance**.
- To provide the correct colour of light – **colour temperature**.
- To reproduce a full range of tonal values from black though to white without any apparent distortion – **contrast ratio**.

The artistic and technical requirements will be discussed fully later.

4.1.2 The lighting process

The **lighting process** can be summarized as:

- **Planning** – information gathering so that a lighting strategy can be evolved.
- **Plotting** – using the planning information to produce a **lighting plot**. This is usually a 1:50 scale drawing of the studio on which the lighting director will plot luminaire positions, indicate colour filters, practical lamps and any special lighting requirements.
- **Rigging** – the electricians use a copy of the lighting plot to rig all the appropriate lighting equipment.
- **Setting** – the lighting director, together with the electricians, will set each luminaire to the correct height and adjust it to light the required area.

- **Balance** – the lighting director, console operator and vision control operator will work together to achieve a satisfactory **lighting balance** of all the required luminaires. A rough lighting balance may be achieved during the setting process, but usually the rehearsal is used to achieve a satisfactory balance.
- **Recording/transmission** – repeat of lighting conditions/lighting cues set up during the rehearsals.

4.1.3 The lighting team

Lighting is very much a team activity, headed by the lighting director:

- *Lighting Director
- *Lighting Console Operator, or Vision Control Supervisor, or Lighting Assistant
- *Vision Control Operator, or Engineer, or CCU Operator
- Foreman or Chargehand Electrician – depending on the scale of the production
- Electricians – numbers depend on the scale of the production.

The trio responsible for the picture-making process, marked *, ideally operate together in the same control room, the **lighting and vision control room**. In some organizations, they will form part of a career progression, e.g. in the UK (BBC) from vision operator to lighting assistant to lighting director. This always seems to be a logical progression and is a well-tried arrangement, which works well in practice. Other organizations use an engineer (or the technical director) for vision control, and an electrician for the console operator. Whatever system is used, an important aspect is that of close liaison to ensure that the best possible result is achieved.

Lighting directors in the BBC usually move through the above progression, having first worked on the studio floor, probably as a camera operator, although anyone showing potential and flair for the work would be considered for training. In other organizations, the lighting director may have had various backgrounds; however, the common interest in lighting will have emerged. To anyone aspiring towards lighting it is recommended to develop your interest by:

- learning about the job of lighting director – know what is required of you;
- learning to see what you are looking at – become more observant;
- observing nature and how people are lit in different environments;

- observing artificially lit environments and how people are lit;
- observing lighting directors at work;
- sharpening your powers of observation, for example taking up photography or by taking up watercolour painting in a 'serious' way;
- building up a library of information on the hardware of lighting;
- learning about the technology of lighting;
- learning about lighting techniques by watching others and reading as many different viewpoints as possible to get a 'well-rounded' knowledge;
- developing a critical attitude to picture quality;
- analysing your own qualities – be aware of any shortcomings you feel you may have and try to improve your performance, e.g. be more flexible, improve your communication skills.

4.1.4 The role of the lighting director

Typically, the lighting process involves the lighting director being responsible for:

- identifying the lighting needs of a production, including budget restraints;
- planning the lighting treatment for a production, within the given budget;
- producing a suitable lighting plot for the electricians to rig;
- setting the appropriate lighting equipment, safely and within the given timescale;
- using the rehearsal to obtain a satisfactory lighting balance, rehearse lighting changes (cues) and identify lighting problems;
- carrying out remedial lighting adjustments as needed;
- reproducing rehearsed conditions for transmission/recording.

4.1.5 What must a lighting director know?

To cope with this important aspect of television production the lighting director needs to have a knowledge of:

- production techniques (know what is required!);
- human perception, behaviour of the eye/brain;
- lighting techniques;
- associated techniques, i.e. camera, sound, chroma key, etc.;
- lighting hardware, e.g. luminaires, control systems, rigging systems, special effects;
- lighting costs;

- the basic television system as it applies to lighting;
- safety;
- standards, i.e. good lighting/bad lighting.

4.1.6 What qualities should the lighting director possess?

The lighting director should possess the following qualities:

- enthusiasm towards programme making;
- enthusiasm towards team colleagues – a team person;
- willingness to compromise;
- planning skills;
- communication skills;
- good imagination and aptitude for lighting;
- good powers of observation;
- person-management skills;
- ability to cope with the unexpected, i.e. last minute changes;
- ability to recognize lighting/vision faults and be able to fix them;
- ability to apply lighting techniques effectively within the given timescale and budget;
- ability to work under pressure;
- decisiveness, ability to decide quickly what is needed;
- good sense of humour.

4.1.7 Planning

The lighting process starts with **planning**. As with all team operations the absolute essential is:

> **KNOW WHAT IS REQUIRED OF YOU!**

The programme director has the responsibility of briefing the team of people helping to make a particular programme. Depending on the nature of a programme, there may be several planning meetings prior to the studio operations, or for a simple programme just a single meeting.

The planning meeting is essential for the lighting director to gather information in order to visualize the production and plan the lighting treatment accordingly.

The planning meeting should have a two-way flow with the director explaining his or her concepts and ideas and the production team trying to anticipate problems and find alternatives. Ideally, this is the time to identify problems, not on the studio floor with the complete crew at a standstill because something was overlooked at the planning stage.

The seven 'C's' at the planning meeting summarize the planning needs:

- **Consultation** – what can be done? Problems?
- **Communication** – the need to know, gather information.
- **Compromise** – the need to give and take, i.e. display a willingness to accept a less than perfect result to enable colleagues to do their job.
- **Commitment** – decisions need to be made, not left open-ended until the studio day – clarifies thinking!
- **Co-operation** – teamwork is vital.
- **Creativity** – raises the standards from mediocrity (95% perspiration, 5% inspiration).
- **Contribution** – everyone in the team wants/needs to make their contribution to the final result.

4.2 Basics of light, its measurement and perception

Light is part of the electromagnetic spectrum of radio waves which, over a limited range of wavelengths, is visible to the human eye/brain. The position of the visible spectrum within the electromagnetic radiation spectrum is shown in Fig. 4.1.

It is common practice to refer to light in terms of its wavelength expressed in nanometres (nm), where a nanometre is 10^{-9} m. Visible light extends from approximately 400 nm (blue) through to approximately 700 nm (red). The response of the eye/brain is not uniform, falling to zero either side of a peak sensitivity of 555 nm. The average response of the eye/brain is known as the **photopic curve** (Fig. 4.2).

For any light measurement to be meaningful, it is important that it relates directly with how we see, i.e. all light measuring instruments should have a **photopic response**. Light units have evolved based

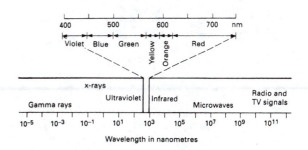

Figure 4.1 The position of the visible spectrum.

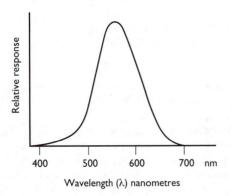

Figure 4.2 The photopic curve – average eye response.

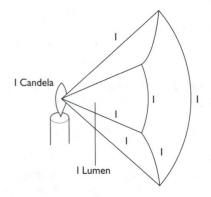

Figure 4.4 Definition of the lumen.

on comparison with a known visual standard. Fig. 4.3 illustrates the different lighting parameters that need to be defined and measured.

Luminous intensity (*I*) is a measure of a light source's ability to radiate light. In principle, this requires a visual comparison with a known standard, originally a standard candle from which the term **candlepower** evolved, e.g. 100 000 candlepower for a 5 kW Fresnel spotlight in full flood mode. The modern standard is the **candela**, which is a more scientifically defined unit. However, for most practical purposes candelas and candlepower can be regarded as similar.

Luminous flux (*F*) is the term used to indicate that we are measuring electromagnetic radiation (light) weighted by the **photopic curve**, i.e. we are taking into account how the eye/brain 'sees' the radiation. Luminous flux, measured in **lumens**, is an indication of quantity of light flow. One lumen is simply defined as: 'the luminous flux emitted into a unit solid angle from a point source of one candela'.

Illuminance (*E*) or illumination is a measure of the total luminous flux incident onto a surface. It is measured in terms of lumens per unit area, i.e. lumens/m^2 or lumens/ft^2.

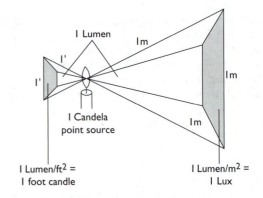

Figure 4.5 Definition of the units of illuminance.

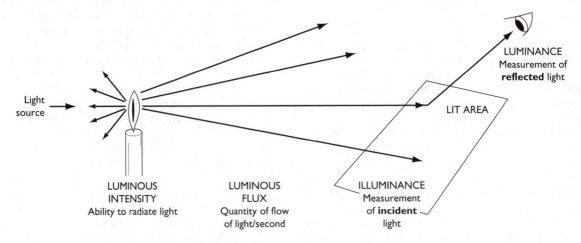

Figure 4.3 Light measurement parameters.

Lumens/m^2 are known as **lux** and lumens/ft^2 are known as **foot-candles**. The lux is the preferred term in television (except for the USA); however the foot-candle has been around since the origins of film and is still used by most cinematographers. Many incident light meters still use scales calibrated in foot-candles. The conversion is 10.76 lux = 1 foot candle (the factor relating a square metre to a square foot), though for most practical purposes this is approximated to ×10, e.g. 300 lux ≈ 30 foot candles.

Incident light meters usually have a very wide angle of acceptance. To measure incident light one usually uses a diffusing disc over the photocell; however, when using the meter as an exposure meter it is more usual to use a diffusing hemisphere over the photocell. This integrates all of the light hitting the subject and gives a better indication of the total light onto the subject.

The fourth unit is that of **luminance** (*L*), a measure of the reflected light from a surface. When a surface reflects a total luminous flux of 1 lumen/m^2 it is said to have a luminance of 1 **Apostilb**. This is a term not in general use because usually the point-by-point luminance of a scene is 'measured' by the television camera.

The amount of light reflected from a surface depends on its reflectivity or reflectance (ρ):

Luminance = ρ × Illuminance Apostilbs.

For example, if the scene illuminance is 600 lux, what is the luminance of a television peak white surface of 60% reflectance?

Luminance = ρ × Illuminance = 0.6 × 600
= 360 Apostilbs.

(*Note*: A surface which reflects a total of 1 lumen/ft^2 has a luminance of 1 foot lambert.)

Luminance meters are normally a very narrow angle of acceptance, typically 1°, e.g. Pentax spotmeter or Minolta spotmeter. Most spotmeters are calibrated in **exposure values** (EV) where the exposure value increases by a factor of one when the luminance is doubled. Often, exposure values are thought of in terms of f_{stops}.

For example, **peak white** gives a reading of 9 EV. **Black** gives a reading of 4 EV. This represents a contrast of 5 EV or 5 f_{stops}, that is, a ratio of $2^5{:}1$ = 32:1.

Note: The term '**brightness**' strictly speaking refers to human perception. How bright we see something depends on a number of physiological factors. Nevertheless, the term 'brightness' is often used, incorrectly, in everyday usage when really it should be '**luminance**'.

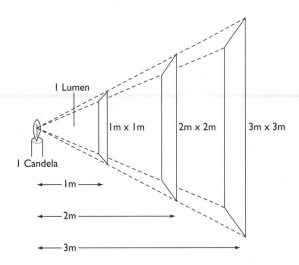

Figure 4.6 The inverse square law.

The **inverse square law** is a fundamental law of nature, and is met in sound as well as in lighting. Light from a point source will diverge (spread out), and consequently the further away from the light source the greater the area illuminated (Fig. 4.6).

At 1 m from the light source, 1 lumen is spread over 1 m^2, so illuminance = 1 lux.
At 2 m from the light source, 1 lumen is spread over 4 m^2, so illuminance = ¼ lux.
At 3 m from the light source, 1 lumen is spread over 9 m^2, so illuminance = ⅑ lux.

$$\text{illuminance } (E) \propto \frac{1}{\text{distance}^2}$$

If we had doubled the candlepower in the above example the illuminance would have doubled, so the equation becomes:

$$\text{illuminance } (E) = \frac{\text{candlepower}}{\text{distance}^2} \text{ lux}$$

Example

What illuminance would you expect at 5 m from a 1.2 kW HMI Fresnel spotlight which has an effective candlepower of 50 000 candelas?

$$\text{illuminance } (E) = \frac{\text{candlepower}}{\text{distance}^2} = \frac{50\,000}{5 \times 5} = 2000 \text{ lux}$$

Incidentally, this illustrates how easy it is to estimate the illuminance at any given 'throw', provided the effective candlepower is known. Note the **effective**

candlepower is normally quoted for 'centre beam' performance.

4.2.1 Cosine law

In the above discussion it has been assumed that the incident light is landing 'normal' to the surface, i.e. at right angles to it. This is rarely the case in practice, and with light beams landing obliquely the illuminance is reduced by a factor determined from the cosine law (Fig. 4.7):

Illuminance ∝ cosine (angle of incidence)

At 60° angle of incidence
the area covered is doubled!

Illuminance is halved
compared to illuminance at
90° to the surface

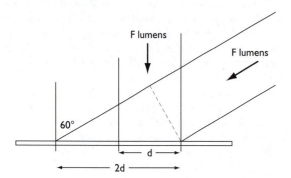

Figure 4.7 Illustrating the cosine law.

So, the complete inverse square law becomes:

$$\text{illuminance} = \frac{\text{candlepower}}{(\text{distance})^2} \cos\theta \text{ lux}$$

However, for angles less than about 25°, the effect of the cosine law is minimal:

cos 25° = 0.9, only 10% reduction

However:

cos 45° = 0.7, a 30% reduction
cos 60° = 0.5, a 50% reduction

When measuring illuminance on a surface, say a camera line-up chart, it is important to hold the light meter parallel to the surface being measured, to ensure that the reading is correct – do not point meter directly towards the light source or the camera.

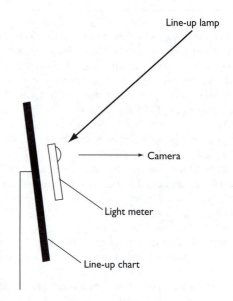

Figure 4.8 Correct way to measure illuminance.

4.2.2 Reflection of light

Clearly, lighting is very much to do with the reflection of light; it is therefore important that the three types of reflection encountered are understood and can be recognized. These are:

- direct or specular reflection;
- diffuse reflection;
- glare reflection.

Direct or specular reflection usually occurs when light is reflected from metallic surfaces, i.e. conductors. Light is reflected according to the laws of optics such that the angle of incidence equals the angle of reflection, in the same plane (Fig. 4.9).

Diffuse reflection is scattered light reflected from a diffuse surface. Most everyday objects are diffuse reflectors, although some may exhibit a combination of direct and diffuse reflection (Fig. 4.10).

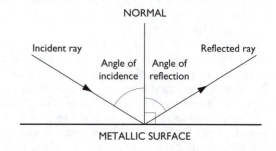

Figure 4.9 Direct or specular reflection.

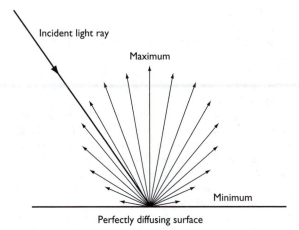

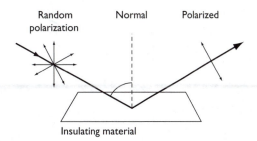

Figure 4.12 Glare reflection (polarization of electric field only shown).

direction of propagation. Normal light sources produce light that is polarized randomly; however, when reflected from insulators it becomes polarized, i.e. all the electric fields become aligned. Glare reflection can be controlled by using a polarizing filter on the camera; this is most effective when the angle of incidence of the light on the insulator is approximately 57°. Note, however, 2 stop loss of the filter! See later comments on glare reflection with the use of kickers and in chroma key set-ups.

If wishing to control direct reflection as well as glare reflection the light source also needs to be fitted with a polarizing filter.

Figure 4.10 Diffuse reflection, illustrating the Cosine Law of Reflection.

Note: Maximum light is reflected at right angles to a surface, reducing proportionally by cosine θ to zero parallel to the surface.

Note that a perfectly diffuse surface will appear equally bright when viewed from any angle (Fig. 4.11)! This statement is so important and so fundamental to vision control – but why is this so?

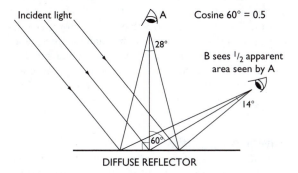

Figure 4.11 The principle of 'equal brightness' for diffuse reflectors.

Area seen reduces in proportion to cosine θ.
Luminous flux also reduces in proportion to cosine θ.
So luminance appears to be the same!

Glare reflection occurs when light is reflected from the surface of an insulator, e.g. polished wood, leather, plastics, glass. It has the appearance of a direct reflection, that is a reflection of the light source. It is the result of light being polarized when reflected off an insulator.

Light occurs as **photons**, small packets of energy. These have an associated magnetic field and electric field at a fixed 90° to each other and at 90° to the

4.2.3 The psychology of seeing

Several important aspects of how we see should be appreciated when lighting for television, film or a theatre, namely:

- logarithmic nature of the eye/brain;
- colour adaptation;
- brightness adaptation;
- revelation of shape, form and texture;
- psychological power of colour, light and darkness;
- perception of depth.

Logarithmic perception

Most human judgement operates in a logarithmic manner, e.g. change in pitch, loudness, and also our perception of changes in brightness. What do we mean by logarithmic law? This is where each succeeding term of a series of numbers is a common multiple of the previous one, for example:

Number	1	2	4	8	16	32	64	(i.e. ×2)
Logarithm	0.0	0.3	0.6	0.9	1.2	1.5	1.8	(i.e. +0.3)

The logarithmic scale of the changes produces a fixed increment scale, i.e. equal changes. Another example is:

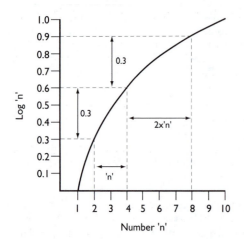

Note: Linear change by a factor of x2 results in the **same** change in logarithmic values

Figure 4.13 Basic logarithmic law.

Number	1	10	100	1000	(i.e. $\times 10$)
Logarithm	0.0	1.0	2.0	3.0	(i.e. $+1$)

Probably the most common 'log' scale is that of f_{no}, i.e. f1.4, 2.0, 2.8, 4.0, 5.6, 8.0, 11.0, ... where the common factor is $\times 1.4$.

In this case a change of f_{no} by one f_{stop} f4.0 to f2.8 will increase the diameter of the lens aperture by factor of $\sqrt{2}$, resulting in an increase in the area of the aperture by a factor of $\sqrt{2} \times \sqrt{2} = 2$, and in the exposure being doubled. Remember:

$$f_{no} = \frac{\text{focal length}}{\text{diameter of lens aperture}} = \frac{f}{d}$$

This perception of changes in brightness in a logarithmic manner is reflected in the design of grey scale charts. For the eye/brain to see the change in grey scale step brightness in equal amounts, the actual reflectivities of the different steps need to follow a logarithmic law. For example, starting at 100% and decreasing by $\sqrt{\frac{1}{2}}$ ($\frac{1}{2}$ of one f_{stop}) we get:

100.0%	White
70.0%	
50.0%	
35.0%	
25.0%	
17.5%	Mid-Grey (Average Scene Brightness)
12.5%	
9.0%	
6.0%	
4.5%	
3.5%	Black

Note that the mid-grey of 17.5% is the **average** reflectivity of nature; however, this is normally rounded off to 18% and is the figure used for exposure meters and auto-iris systems.

Colour adaptation

The eye and the brain are continually adapting to make 'sense' of what we see. In many cases, we see things as a certain colour because the eye/brain know the colour an object should be. White is a particularly good example – we accept as white many colours which are in fact very different, for example tungsten light, daylight, fluorescent light. Colour vision theory is based on the concept of the eye having three basic types of receptor, which respond to red, green and blue light. When the eye is exposed, for example, to a scene lit with a warm light (amber), the eye/brain removes the warm bias to some extent so that if we replace the warm scene with one of no colour bias it will look 'cold', i.e. complementary colour to the warm amber. This is called **local colour adaptation** where we get a complementary colour image in areas of strong colour.

Lateral colour adaptation

Lateral colour adaption occurs when a strong colour area induces a complementary hue in the background colour. This is most noticeable when strong colours are used on backgrounds to presenters. The colour perception of the presenter's face will be affected by the use of strong background colour. For example, a strong magenta background will induce green into the foreground – the presenter's face!

Brightness adaptation

In a similar way, we judge the brightness of an object relative to the brightness of the object's surrounding. For example, when seen against a daytime window a face will look dark. With the same illumination on the face against a night-time window, the face will look very bright. So remember:

- colours appear lighter against a dark background;
- colours appear darker against a light background.

Revelation of form and texture

The eye/brain interprets the shape of objects by the shadows they cast and the patterns of light and shade introduced by the source of illumination. The degree of modelling produced is basically determined by the angle between the keylight and camera, and the type of light source used, i.e. hard or soft.

In a similar way the nature of a surface, its texture, whether rough or smooth, is revealed to a maximum when the angle between the keylight and camera is large and when a hard light is used. Conversely, to avoid revealing texture, i.e. ageing lines or eye-bags, one should use a soft source with little angle between keylight and camera.

Psychological power of colour etc.

This concerns the effect that light and colour have on us. Basically, we can use light, colour and shade to help to create a particular mood.

Generally, lightness is associated with good; darkness and heavy shadows are associated with bad. Red/orange colours are associated with warmth. Blue colours are associated with cold and night-time.

Green is a 'funny' colour; pastel shades can be used to create a cool environment. However, more saturated shades are often used to suggest evil. Some lighting directors avoid the use of green in variety shows preferring to keep a 'palette' of orange, red, magenta, lavender and blue.

The term 'key' is often used to describe the mood of a picture:

- **High key picture** – one which has a predominance of light tomes and 'thin' shadows, an almost two-dimensional lightweight picture.
- **Low key picture** – one which has a predominance of dark tones and heavy shadows, resulting in a very solid dramatic looking picture.
- **Medium key picture** – one which has a 'normal' distribution of tones.

Perception of depth

Generally, the eye is drawn towards the areas containing highlights or the areas which contain the greatest contrast. This, in fact, is one of the principles of theatre lighting where lighting emphasis is used to direct the audience's attention to the appropriate part of the stage. In nature, saturation of colours decreases with distance so that a distant horizon appears lightest and most desaturated. Immediate foreground areas are most saturated. In addition, the blue colours enhance depth, i.e. appear further away, while red colours reduce the illusion of depth. So, to create depth, consider the lighting of the foreground, mid-ground and background planes. Avoid overlighting the foreground; adding highlights to the background will help create depth; deeply saturated red cycloramas will lack depth.

For good depth and good separation of planes put light tones against dark tones and dark tones against light tones.

4.3 The technical parameters of lighting

There are three main technical parameters which have to be acknowledged if one is to avoid pictures which are not technically correct. These are:

- enough light – illuminance of the correct level;
- colour temperature – light of the correct white-ness';
- contrast ratio – scene contrast within the limits of the system.

4.3.1 Enough light (illuminance)

Camera sensitivity is usually quoted in terms which link three interrelated parameters, namely lens aperture (f_{no}), illuminance (lux) and signal-to-noise ratio (dB), when correctly exposing a particular reflectance peak white (Fig. 4.14).

A typical CCD camera sensitivity would be:

$f8.0$ with illuminance of 2000 lux and 89.9% reflectance Peak White, 60 dB signal-to-noise ratio

This is an engineering definition, which enables direct camera-to-camera sensitivity to be compared. It is not an instruction on how much light to use!

The above definition is based on the Japanese standard for peak white reflectivity of 89.9%. The rest of the world usually uses a 60% reflectance peak white, based on the need to correctly expose face tones without overloading (over-exposing) on a peak white area. Clearly, this surface will only be

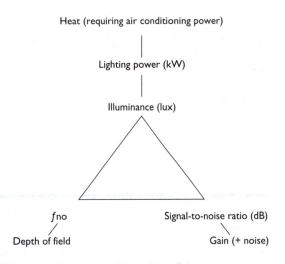

Figure 4.14 Camera sensitivity 'triangle'.

two-thirds exposed with 2000 lux, so the illuminance has to be increased to 3000 lux, i.e.:

f8.0 with 3000 lux and 60% reflectance Peak White, 60 dB signal-to-noise ratio

The operating lens aperture is clearly going to be the deciding factor in determining the illuminance required, unless gain adjustment is made which will increase the noise, thus reducing the signal-to-noise ratio. Opening up the lens aperture results in a significant drop in illuminance requirements (Table 4.1).

Table 4.1 Camera sensitivity and illuminance requirements.

Lens aperture	Scene illuminance (60% Peak White reflectance)
f8.0	3000 lux
f5.6	1500 lux
f4.0	750 lux
f2.8	375 lux
f2.0	187.5 lux

Depth-of-field is proportional to f_{no}, and, in fact, is usually the deciding factor. Custom and practice over the years has led to the concept of 'nominal' lens apertures based on camera sensor format (Table 4.2).

Table 4.2 Nominal lens aperture and camera formats.

Camera format	Image size	Nominal f_{no}
30 mm (1¼″)	17.1 mm × 12.8 mm	f4.0
25 mm (1″)	12.8 mm × 9.6 mm	f2.8
18 mm (⅔″)	8.8 mm × 6.6 mm	f2.0
12.5 mm (½″)	6.4 mm × 4.8 mm	f1.4

Using cameras at the nominal aperture results in similar depths-of-field for a given shot size and camera distance.

Lens sharpness decreases as the lens is opened up. This would appear to be a conflict in operating at an f2.0 aperture. Fortunately, with the evolution of the high resolution CCD camera with an excess of 700 pixels/line (within the 8.8 mm format) lenses have to be capable of superior resolution compared with lenses for tube cameras. Consequently, good quality modern lenses produce good optical sharpness even at f2.0. This means that lenses can be used in the f2.0–f2.8 region – this results in pictures with good 'optical separation' of the subject and background. Unless other criteria exist, one should aim to be in this 'ball park'.

In news studios, the use of teleprompters reduces the camera sensitivity by at least half of an f_{stop} (70%

transmission) and with robotic cameras (no constant monitoring of the shot by a camera operator) an aperture of about f2.8 is generally satisfactory – i.e. aim for about 500–600 lux.

Variety programmes need to have a 'lit' look with lighting levels much higher than corridor lighting. This has the effect of 'lifting' the actor's performance. Typically, 800 lux is acceptable; however, close-ups may lack the optical separation previously discussed. This can be remedied by operating with a 0.3 neutral density filter in the camera or reducing the camera gain. (See also the note on the use of electronic shutter later in this section.)

Other factors which affect illuminance requirements are:

- use of range-extenders;
- zoom ramping;
- camera minus blue filter;
- camera ND filters;
- electronic gain;
- electronic shutter.

Use of range-extenders

When a ×2 range-extender is used it will double the focal length of the lens and hence double the f_{no}. So a lens operating at f2.0 becomes effectively f4.0, requiring an increase in illuminance to compensate for the loss of two f_{stops}, i.e. sensitivity reduced by 75%.

Zoom ramping

This may occur when using large lens apertures at the long focal length end of the zoom, causing a reduction in effective f_{no}.

Lens aperture or f_{no} is given by:

$$f_{no} = \frac{\text{focal length}}{\text{diameter of lens aperture}} = \frac{f}{(d)}$$

However, it is not the physical iris diameter which is important, but 'the diameter of the lens aperture seen from the object space' which determines the exposure (Fig. 4.15).

The action of a zoom lens is such that when zooming in (increasing f), the size of the aperture optically increases (iris is magnified). Thus, the f_{no} remains constant. However, when a large ratio zoom lens at its maximum sensitivity is zoomed in, a point is reached where the diameter of the lens front element is not large enough to give the required d. Any subsequent zooming in results in a change in f but no change in d. The effective f_{no} gradually

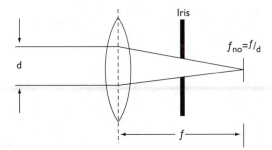

Figure 4.15 Illustrating f_{no}.

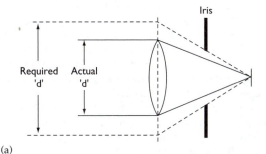

(a)

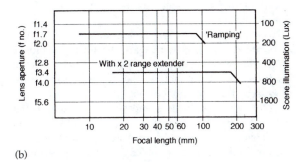

(b)

Figure 4.16 (a) Zoom ramping; (b) camera sensitivity, zoom ramping and range extenders (14 × 9 zoom lens).

increases, resulting in a decrease in sensitivity – this is known as zoom ramping (Fig. 4.16).

Zoom ramping occurs because of the practical compromises which have to be made in the design of a zoom lens, i.e. size of front element, weight and cost.

Camera minus blue filter

Colour cameras are designed to operate in a tungsten lit environment. Consequently, when exposed to daylight there is a significant increase in light at the blue end of the spectrum. The minus blue filter (¾ CTO) in the camera filter wheel (position 3) removes the excess of blue light to equalize the daylight to tungsten values. The loss introduced by this filter is

almost one stop. Historically, the minus blue filter was needed on tube cameras to avoid the overloading of the blue tube (tubes became overloaded very easily), and to reduce the significant changes in red and blue gain required when white balancing to daylight.

It should be noted that most CCD cameras can cope with white balancing to daylight even on filter 1. In conditions of low daylight this can be useful to maintain a good f_{no}, i.e. $f2.0$–$f2.8$ instead of $f1.4$.

CCD cameras have excellent highlight handling capabilities. CCDs overload at approximately 600% of normal input lighting level. Consequently, the need for a minus blue filter has diminished and many of the latest CCD cameras do not have this facility, all adjustments for white balance being achieved electronically.

Camera ND filters

Usually a combination of minus blue filter and neutral density filters are included in the camera filter wheel – typically as shown in Table 4.3.

Table 4.3 Camera filter wheel.

Filter wheel position	Colour temperature	Loss
1	3200 K	0
2	5600 K + ¼ND	as filter 3 + 2 stops
3	5600 K	approx. 1 stop
4	5600 K + ¹⁄₁₆ND	as filter 3 + 4 stops

Note: Preset White Balance follows position of the filter wheel. ¼ND means ¼ transmission, i.e. 25% transmission, not 0.25ND ¹⁄₁₆ND means ¹⁄₁₆ transmission, i.e. 6.25% transmission, not 0.0625ND

Electronic gain

Electronic gain may be used to maintain signal levels when operating in difficult circumstances. Usually, this is switched to give discrete increments in gain (Table 4.4).

Table 4.4 Camera gain/sensitivity.

Selection	Change in gain	Equivalent change in sensitivity
−6 dB	×0.5	$-1f_{stops}$
−3 dB	×0.7	$-\frac{1}{2}f_{stops}$
0 dB	×1.0	0
+3 dB	×1.4	$+\frac{1}{2}f_{stops}$
+6 dB	×2.0	$+1f_{stops}$
+9 dB	×2.8	$+1\frac{1}{2}f_{stops}$
+12 dB	×4.0	$+2f_{stops}$
+15 dB	×5.6	$+2\frac{1}{2}f_{stops}$
+18 dB	×8.0	$+3f_{stops}$

The precise amounts of switched gain available differ from camera to camera. Sony, for example, use +6 dB and +12 dB on single-sensor cameras and +9 dB and +18 dB on three-sensor cameras.

Remember that extra gain will result in an increase in noise and a consequent reduction in signal-to-noise ratio.

Electronic shutter

Most CCD cameras have the facility of an electronic shutter which enables the exposure time to be reduced. For example:

1/60, 1/125, 1/250, 1/500, 1/1000 sec

Obviously, there will be a need to adjust illuminance levels as appropriate when using a shutter speed less than 1/50 second. Note that when using short exposure times fast subject movement will appear 'jerky'.

ASA rating and video cameras

It can sometimes be useful to think of video camera sensitivity in terms of film speeds, i.e. give the video camera an ASA rating:

$$\text{ASA rating} = \frac{1250 \times f_{no}^2}{\text{illuminance}}$$

where illuminance is in foot-candles, and exposure is 1/50 second. So for a Hyper Had camera ($f8$, 2000 lux for 89.9% P.W., 60 dB) such as the Sony BVW 400AP, operating with 60% peak white, we have a need for 187.5 lux at $f2$ (or 17.4 foot candles). So, ASA rating is:

$$\frac{1250 \times 2 \times 2}{17.4} = 287$$

$$= 280 \text{ ASA}$$

With this, gain becomes as shown in Table 4.5.

4.3.2 Colour temperature

In colour television we are more concerned with the reproduction of white than any other colour. Prior to making any recordings or transmission, it is essential that the cameras have been properly white balanced, in which the camera is calibrated to an appropriate 'white light'. To do this, expose the camera to a white card or line-up chart which has been suitably illuminated, then

Table 4.5 Gain/ASA ratings.

Gain	ASA rating
0	280
+ 3 dB	400
+ 6 dB	560
+ 9 dB	800
+ 12 dB	1120
+ 15 dB	1600
+ 18 dB	2240

operate the camera's auto-white balance so that the camera RGB signals are equalized, resulting in the white card looking white on a TV monitor, or the grey scale looking neutral. So, how can we define what we mean by white? One convenient way is to use the concept of colour temperature. The colour temperature of a light source is that temperature at which the colour of light from a black body radiator (e.g. a poker or furnace) is identical to that of the light source. When an iron poker is cold it will look black, i.e. no light is reflected from it; as it is heated up it will glow first red, then amber, yellow, white and then blue, where the colour of the light relates to the temperature of the poker.

Note an important psychological difference. We associate red colours with warmth and blue colours with cold, but with colour temperature, as the source becomes physically hotter, the colour temperature increases and it becomes bluer!

Colour temperature is measured in Kelvin (K) where 0 Kelvin corresponds to –273°C or 0° Absolute. A tungsten halogen light source, at full mains voltage, has a colour temperature of 3200 K. Average summer sunlight is quoted as 5500 K. Strictly speaking this term colour temperature should only be used for incandescent sources, i.e. those which are glowing because they are hot – e.g. tungsten, carbon, candle, gas mantle, the sun.

However, it is useful to quote a correlated colour temperature for discharge sources. The correlated colour temperature of a discharge source is the colour temperature which best matches the discharge source.

Tolerances

Having defined our white point by using the concept of colour temperature, what deviations, if any, can be tolerated? Typical tolerances are ±150 K when white balanced to tungsten sources (3200 K), and ±400 K when white balanced to daylight sources (5500 K). These tolerances apply to lighting face tones; on scenery a greater deviation can usually be tolerated since the viewer is not aware of the true colour of the scenery but of course is very aware of face tones and very critical of the way in which they are reproduced.

4.3.3 Contrast ratio

The contrast ratio of a scene is the ratio of the luminance of the darkest part of the scene to the luminance of the brightest part of the scene. The average out-of-doors contrast is about 150:1, although it can be as high as 1000:1. Television and film cameras have a limited range of contrast handling capability, typically 32:1 for television cameras, and 128:1 or higher for film cameras. This places an operational constraint on lighting, especially in television, where the major objectives will be:

- The scene contrast should be within the 32:1 contrast ratio handling of the television camera (or 128:1 for film) if 'over-exposure' or 'crushing' are to be avoided.
- The face tones must be correctly exposed.

This latter point is extremely important – television consists mainly of facial close-up shots rather than wide-angle shots. We are very critical about the way in which faces look, both in terms of colour and exposure. The reflectivity of average European skin tones is about 30%.

Choice of scene peak white

If a scene peak white has a reflectivity of 100%, the face tones at 30% reflectivity would look rather dark. Consequently, for most applications in the western world a scene peak white of 60% reflectivity is chosen. This puts the face tone at approximately half this value or one stop down on the peak white. If faces are over-exposed they will lose significant tonal detail.

So now we have established not only the need for the scene contrast to be within 32:1, but also that the face tone is approximately one stop down on the peak white luminance. Incidentally, if a grey scale with a 32:1 contrast is correctly exposed, a reduction in exposure by 5 stops will reduce the signal to almost zero, i.e. the dynamic range of the camera can also be thought of as 5 stops. This is a useful concept, especially when working on location (see Section 4.16). Table 4.6 illustrates reflectivities of some typical surfaces.

Note the obvious problems if one has to cope with an excessive range of scene contrast:

- Black velvet – this is outside the 32:1 range, consequently any subtle details in the velvet will be

Table 4.6 Typical surface reflectances.

Surface	% Reflectivity	TV Grey scale
Polished silver	100	
White nylon shirts	90	
White cartridge paper	80	
Chrome plate	70	
White cloth	60	TV WHITE
Newspaper	50	
	40	LIGHT GREY
European face tones		
Light oak wood	30	
Green leaves		
Concrete	20	MEDIUM GREY
Dark skin		
Dark oak wood	10	
	9	
	8	
Dark hair	7	DARK GREY
	6	
Black paper	5	
	4	
	3	TV BLACK
	2	
Black cloth	1	
Black velvet 0.4%		

hidden. To reveal this, the camera iris has to open-up resulting in over-exposure of the facial tones
- White nylon shirt – this will look over-exposed unless the camera iris is stopped-down, resulting in under-exposure of the face tones.

Clearly there is a need for the costume department to ensure that artistes' costumes are within the desired contrast ratio (see Section 4.19).

As we have seen earlier, it is possible to introduce a form of compression (knee) or black stretch to help with these problems; however, the knee facility will, of course, compress or crush the tonal values. The black stretch facility will help to reveal detail in the black areas, but will also introduce some extra noise.

Note: Because of the gamma correction in the camera, the face tone video level is stretched from approximately 50% to 70%, i.e. 70% of 0.7 V ≃ 0.5 V. This is a useful reference, or 'ballpark' value (see Section 4.19).

4.4 Light sources

The light sources used in television include:

Tungsten
Tungsten Halogen } Incandescent

Compact Source Iodide   CSI ⎫
Compact Source Daylight   CID ⎪ High
Hg (Mercury), Medium Arc, Iodides HMI ⎬ Pressure
Medium Arc, Source Rare-Earth MSR ⎪ Discharge
Xenon   ⎭

Fluorescent   Low Pressure Discharge

Tungsten halogen is the most commonly used light source in television. However, the others have merits which make them more appropriate for use in certain applications.

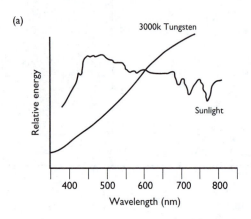

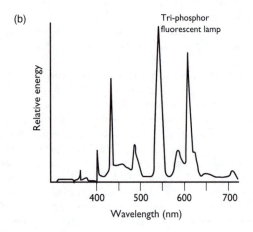

Figure 4.17 Relative spectral energy distribution: (a) incandescent sources; (b) discharge sources.

4.4.1 Choice of light source

The decision on choice of light source is mainly influenced by:

- efficacy or lumens/watt;
- lumens package;
- colour temperature;
- colour rendition index, R_a.

Other considerations are:

- ability to dim the source electronically (or mechanically);
- lack of auxiliary equipment, e.g. ballasts, starting gear, etc.;
- stability of light source colour – with dimming and with lamp life;
- lamp life;
- compactness of light source – ability to collect the light and project it;
- cost.

Lamp efficacy

This is a measure of the ability of the light source to convert electrical energy into visible light. It is expressed simply as lumens/watt. One watt of electrical power converted into light of a single wavelength at 555 nm would provide 683 lumens/watt (this is an alternative definition of the lumen). This, however, is not particularly useful for comparisons because the light is of a single wavelength. A more realistic comparison can be achieved with 240 lumens/watt, an efficacy achieved if 1 watt of electrical power is converted totally into an equal energy visible spectrum.

Domestic tungsten lamps have an efficacy of 12 lumens/watt, tungsten halogen about 25 lumens/watt and HMIs in the region of 100 lumens/watt for the higher wattage lamps.

Lumens package

This indicates the total lumens available from a light source and is the product of lamp wattage and efficacy. For example, a 4 kW HMI would produce a total lumens package of 4000 × 100 = 400 000 lumens whereas a 55 W high frequency PL-L fluorescent lamp only produces 55 × 87.5 = 4812 lumens.

Clearly, the PL-L lamp has to be used in multiples to produce a luminaire capable of delivering a useful light output.

Colour temperature

This is a convenient way of expressing the 'whiteness' of a light and is a vital parameter of any light source.

Colour rendition index R_a

Faithful reproduction of scene colour is obviously important in television. It is therefore essential that the colour rendition or colour fidelity of light sources used in television is acceptable. Tungsten sources and daylight are regarded as excellent. The visible spectrum from these sources is continuous (Fig. 4.17(a)), and a smooth transition of light output between adjacent wavelengths results in the source being totally acceptable. All discharge sources have 'spiky' spectrums (Fig. 4.17(b)) – it is therefore necessary to give an indication of the colour fidelity achieved by such sources.

The colour rendition index, R_a, uses an arbitrary scale of 0 to 100, which gave the original warm white fluorescent tube an R_a of 50. Generally, an R_a of 70 is regarded as the lower limit of acceptability for colour television.

The R_a for a light source is calculated by equating the colour errors when illuminating eight test colours, compared with the colours measured when the eight test colours are illuminated with a tungsten light of the same colour temperature. If the lamp under test is of a colour temperature greater than 5000 K, then a reconstituted daylight source of the same colour temperature is used, using computer data.

It should be noted that R_a is only a guide. The R_a gives no indication of the direction of error so two different sources of identical R_a and at the same colour temperature may not look identical. When considering the colour rendition of each colour test individually, a shift in the index of 5 is just discernible.

4.4.2 Tungsten and tungsten halogen sources

These are the most commonly used light sources and are very simple in operation. They are based on the principle of using the heating effect of an electric current to heat a tungsten filament to incandescence,

Table 4.7(a) Table of R_a for television sources.

Television light sources	Colour temperature (K)	Colour rendition index R_a	Efficacy (lumens/W)
Tungsten, domestic	2760	100	12
Tungsten, studio	3200	100	25
Tungsten halogen	3200	100	25–29
CSI	4000 ± 400	80	90
HMI	5600 ± 400	95	70–105
CID	5500 ± 400	70	70–80
MSR	5600 ± 400	90	95
XENON	6200	98	15–50
Fluorescent – Warm White	3000	58	78
HF fluorescent – 55 W PL-L (Colour 80)	3200	85	87
HF fluorescent – 55 W PL-L (Colour 90)	3200	95	55

Table 4.7(b) Table of R_a for non-television sources.

Non-TV sources	Colour temperature (K)	Colour rendition index R_a	Efficacy (lumens/W)
Low pressure sodium sox	–	–	200
High pressure sodium son	2000	20	120
High pressure sodium son/d/l	2000	60	92
High pressure sodium son comfort	2000	70	80
High pressure sodium sdw-t	2500	85	50
High pressure mercury hpl-n	4000	50	63
High pressure mercury hpl-Comfort	3500	55–60	60
Metal halide HPI	4000	68	76
Metal halide HPI – T	4000	65	94

i.e. until it glows. Fundamental to its operation is the fact that when it is dimmed the colour of light changes; however, if the changes are restricted to about ±150 K they are not normally perceived on skin tones. Unfortunately, operation of a tungsten source results in the filament gradually evaporating and condensing on the envelope. This darkens the envelope and reduces the lamp life. Tungsten halogen sources overcome this by introducing a halogen into the envelope (Fig. 4.18); they are characterized by small, tough quartz glass envelopes, which have led to the development of many new small luminaires, i.e. compact ranges.

At normal operating temperatures
Tungsten evaporates from the
lamp filament – this combines
with halogen at the envelope
(250°C - 800°C) to give Tungsten
Halide, at temperatures in
excess of 1250°C this 'dissociates'
to give halogen released and Tungsten
deposited on the cooler parts of the filament

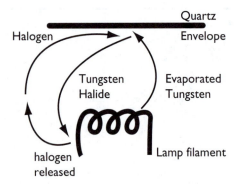

Figure 4.18 Halogen cycle to keep quartz envelope clean.

Operating notes

Tungsten halogen sources should be burnt within the range of tilt angles recommended by the manufacturer, otherwise the lamp life will be reduced significantly. The plastic glove or sleeve supplied by the manufacturer should always be used when handling quartz glass envelopes. Touching the envelope of a tungsten halogen lamp results in harmful body acids being deposited. When heated, the acids attack the quartz glass envelope causing it to become opaque. Light and heat are then not transmitted, so the lamp over-heats and destroys itself.

Typical operational practices

It is normal practice in television studios to feed each tungsten source via a dimmer so that the intensity of the light source may be varied (dimmed). The dimmer is usually controlled via a fader calibrated with a 0–10 scale or 0% to 100% scale. A fader setting of 7 is usually adopted as a 'nominal' setting; this corresponds to 50% light output (see Section 4.18.1) and a theoretical colour temperature of 2960 K. i.e. cameras are white balanced to 2960 K.

The value of working in this way is that the light output may be increased or decreased about this nominal value, within the accepted tolerances (±150 K), providing a useful range of intensity change. This is illustrated in Fig. 4.19.

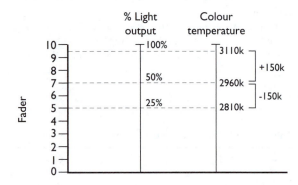

Figure 4.19 Fader setting versus percentage light output and colour temperature.

It should be noted that because of cable and dimmer losses it is usually not possible to reach 3200 K; consequently, moving the fader to 10 provides light within the specified colour temperature tolerance.

Operating at fader 7 results in a significant increase in lamp life, i.e. ×10. Running cooler results in less filament evaporation thus prolonging the life of the lamp. Typically, a lamp rated at 150 hrs life at full mains voltage would last approximately 1500 hours at fader 7!

4.4.3 Dual filament lamps

Some studios employ a saturation rig of luminaires to reduce rigging time. This may mean that a rigged luminaire is too powerful for the particular 'throw' and consequently it has to be dimmed below fader 5. Twin-filament lamps reduce this problem. Each lamp has two filaments and a four-pin base; each filament may be switched separately to be on or off.

Typical ranges are:

2 × 2.5 kW	giving 2.5 kW or 5 kW
2 × 1.25 kW	giving 1.25 kW or 2.5 kW
1 × 1.25 kW	
1 × 2.5 kW	giving 1.25 kW, 2.5 kW or 3.75 kW

Clearly, the twin filament lamp offers operational flexibility over the single filament lamp. The disadvantages are:

- high cost;
- failure of one filament means a complete lamp change;
- performance is less than a single-filament lamp, due to mutual shadowing of filaments;
- when operating with 1¼/2½ kW filaments in the 1¼ kW mode the luminaire is very large for such a source.

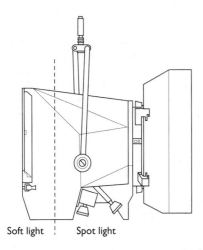

Soft light   Spot light

Figure 4.20
Dual source
luminaire.

4.4.4 Discharge sources

These are either low pressure or high pressure discharge sources. They produce light as a by-product of an electrical discharge (current) through a gas. The colour of the light is characterized by the particular mixture of gas present in the quartz glass envelope or the nature of the tubular phosphor coating with the fluorescent lamp.

Discharge light sources used in television are:

Compact Source Iodide (CSI)
Mercury (Hg), Medium Arc Gap,
    Iodides (HMI) } High Pressure
Compact Iodide Daylight (CID)
Medium Source Rare-Earth (MSR)
Xenon

Fluorescent   Low Pressure

CSI, HMI, CID and MSR 24 W–18 kW

The first four sources are basically mercury vapour discharge sources with added iodides to give the

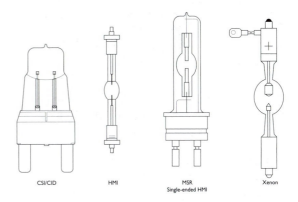

CSI/CID   HMI   MSR
Single-ended HMI   Xenon

Figure 4.21 Discharge light sources.

correct colour temperature and colour rendition. Their merit lies in:

- greater efficacy than tungsten, approximately 3 to 4 times, thus less power required;
- compact light source, easy to collect (condense) and project the light;
- depending on type, can produce light which approximates to daylight;
- produce less infrared radiation than tungsten, i.e. cooler in operation;
- available from 24 W through to 18 kW.

Their disadvantages are that they:

- require an EHT supply, typically 27 kV, to ionize the gas and so produce an electric current;
- require a current limiting device, which may be a wire-wound choke or an electronic ballast. The electronic ballast is associated with 'flicker-free' operation, resulting in a constant light output, i.e. it is operated with, typically, a 166 Hz square wave voltage so the light does not extinguish on each half-cycle;
- require a warm-up period of 1–2 minutes before full output and correct colour is reached;
- may not have a hot re-strike facility;
- in many cases, may not be dimmed electronically. However, some of the later sources using an electronic ballast do have a dimming capacity down to approximately 30% maximum light output;

Table 4.8 Discharge sources, comparison of features.

	Range of wattages	Correlated colour temperature (K)	Lumens/ watt	R_a	Harmful UV	Liable to explode
CSI	400–1000 W	4000 ± 400	80–90	80	✓	✓
CID	200–2500 W	5500 ± 400	70–80	85	✓	✓
HMI*	24 W–18 kW	5600 ± 400	80–96	>90	✓	✓
MSR	125 W–6 kW	5600 ± 400	75–95	>90	✓	✓
Xenon	75 W–10 kW	6200	15–50	98	✓	✓
High frequency fluorescent	11–55 W	2700–6500	55–88	>80	–	–

*Notes:
(i) HMI also available as single-ended option – HMI(SE).
(ii) HTI and HSR are compact versions. HSR is single-ended version of HTI.

• operate at a high bulb pressure and are liable to explode;
• produce an output which is rich in harmful ultraviolet radiation. This is transmitted by the quartz envelope, therefore all discharge sources must be operated with a glass filter, i.e. lens or safety glass.

High pressure discharge sources – operating practices

These sources are not as flexible in use as tungsten sources, and need to be fitted with mechanical shutters if they are required to fade-up from a black-out condition.

Operators of high pressure discharge sources must be aware of the safety aspects and potential hazards:

(1) Extra high tension (EHT) starting voltage 27 kV (dangerous electric shock hazard)
    – correct earthing of all metalwork
(2) Harmful ultraviolet radiation (severe sunburn, headache and blindness hazard)
    – correct optical filter in place and undamaged, i.e. lens or protective glass. No leakage of light directly from the light source
(3) High operating pressure (lamp exploding hazard)
    – restrict mechanical movement to a minimum when lamp is hot
    – use safety goggles when changing lamps
    – avoid changing hot lamp
(4) Mercury vapour (inhalation of mercury vapour hazard)
    – if lamp explodes harmful mercury vapour will be released

The colour of the light from these sources is not stable – it is affected by temperature and lamp life. Typically, the correlated colour temperature reduces by 1 K for each hour of life, and, in addition, the colour of the light shifts along the green/magenta colour axis. Consequently, operators should be prepared to apply colour correction when using several HMIs together. There may be a need to apply correction in the blue-orange direction and in the green-magenta direction – use ⅛ CTO and ⅛ CTB filters and ⅛ plus green and ⅛ minus green filters.

These sources have been designed to match average summer sunlight of 5500 K. However, there will be occasions when daylight is not 'average' so be prepared to use ¼ CTO or ¼ CTB filters to correct these sources.

When it looks right, it is!

When operating with daylight sources, typically they need to be within ±400 K to look 'matched'.

Operating notes

(1) The operating current for these sources is larger than indicated by the lamp wattage, e.g. a 4 kW HMI operates at 21 A, and its starting current is 35 A! However, discharge sources using electronic ballasts have a controlled starting current and, consequently, do not have this characteristic of high initial current.
(2) Non-flicker-free HMIs should *not* be used with CCD cameras when a shutter speed of less than 1/50 second is required. This is because the output signal suffers a 'breathing' effect – the shorter the exposure time the greater is the effect.
(3) Generators supplying to a mainly discharge source load should be under-rated by a factor of

0.7 to take account of the effect of the ballast chokes, i.e. a 100 kVA generator should be rated as 70 kVA. Recent developments have produced a unity power factor ballast which, when used, removes the need to down-rate generators.

Xenon (100 W–10 kW)

Xenon produces an excellent 'white' light, with a colour rendition index of 98 and a stable colour output; this compact light source is ideal for long-throw follow-spotlights. Note that the xenon lamp, even when cold, has an internal gas pressure greater than atmospheric pressure, and is likely to explode if disturbed mechanically. Special safety precautions should be taken when handling xenon lamps, e.g. face mask, gauntlets and body protection.

Fluorescent sources (6–60 W)

Fluorescent lights (coldlights) have recently become a viable option in television lighting: with similar efficacies to the high pressure discharge lights, they offer good savings in power requirements, especially in small/medium studios. The wide range of colour temperatures available makes them particularly useful when on location, or when there is a need for light sources to match a given environment. The merits of the fluorescent light sources are:

- good efficacy (3–4 times better than tungsten);
- consequently there are significant power savings in lighting power and air-conditioning power;
- no radiant heat (tungsten sources have 55% of the electrical power as radiant heat in the light beam), hence the term 'coldlight';
- large area source means kinder modelling and less glare for artistes (more comfortable);
- long life (approximately 10 000 hours);
- high frequency operation at greater than 40 kHz, no flicker;
- dimmable 100%–1% with little colour change;
- choice of colour temperature available: 2700 K/3000 K/3200 K/4100 K/5500 K.

Basic principle of the fluorescent light source (low pressure mercury vapour)

The fluorescent light source relies on the principle of luminescence, whereby visible light is produced when phosphors are exposed to ultraviolet radiation. An electrical discharge is set up in the fluorescent tube, producing mainly harmless long wavelength ultraviolet radiation (60% of the input power), plus a single wavelength of green light (3% of the input power). The ultraviolet radiation (energy) is absorbed by the phosphors and re-radiated at a lower, visible wavelength (40% of the UV energy). Hence the colour of the light (colour temperature) and colour fidelity (R_a) are very much dictated to by the chemical make-up of the phosphors.

Note: The above description shows that the overall efficacy is about 27% (input power × 60% × 40% + 3%); this is improved by 10% on light output and a reduction on ballast losses of 10%, when operating at high frequency (40 kHz). That is, light output is approximately 32% of input power (compare tungsten at approximately 8%).

Safety

- These are low pressure mercury vapour sources and, as such, do not have the safety hazards of the high pressure sources. However, care should be taken in disposing of old or broken tubes to ensure that none of the chemicals inside get into any cuts or damaged skin areas.

Control

- The integrated high frequency ballast is easily controlled with a 0–10 V analogue signal for dimming purposes.
- The digital data signal, known as DMX 512 (Section 4.18.2), from modern lighting consoles needs to be converted to 0–10 V. This is done either with an integral DMX de-multiplexer or a separate multi-channel DMX de-multiplexer.
- Special ballasts are available for direct mains dimming, i.e. fed from thyristor dimmers.

Note: As with all discharge lights, these sources require a few minutes warm-up time before full light output is achieved.

Colour

- The colour temperature and colour rendition properties of these sources are dictated by the phosphors used for the tube coating. They are indicated by the manufacturer's coding (Table 4.9).

Table 4.9 Typical manufacturer's coding to indicate R_a and K for fluorescent lamps.

Colour 830	≡	Colour rendition >80; 3000 K
Colour 930	≡	Colour rendition >90; 3000 K

Note: Lamps of 2700 K, 3000 K, 3500 K, 4000 K, 5000 K and 6500 K may be available in various types.

- Colour 83 lamps, with R_a better than 80, at 3000 K have an efficacy of 87.5 lumens/watt. Consequently, these are recommended for all studios, using an 'all' coldlight solution to take advantage of the high light output. If tungsten sources are used for set lighting they should not pose any colour matching problems.
- Colour 93 lamps, with R_a better than 90, at 3000 K have a reduced efficacy of 55 lumens/watt. These are recommended for 'hybrid' installations where mixing of cold light and tungsten light is required on faces, i.e. where cold light is being used for fill-lights and tungsten sources are being used as keylights, and studios using Philips cameras.

4.5 Luminaires

Over the years many different types of luminaire have been developed to satisfy specific needs of lighting:

- Fresnel spotlights (soft-edged projectors);
- softlights, including fluorescent lights;
- dual source;
- hard-edged projectors, including follow-spotlights;
- cyclorama top lights;
- ground row;
- PAR lights;
- intelligent lights (moving lights);
- open-faced luminaires.

Luminaires are often referred to as 'hard' or 'soft' depending on the type of shadow they produce, i.e. hard-edged or soft-edged.

Hard sources are point sources, i.e. small area sources (Fig. 4.22). Hard sources:

- produce a single hard-edged shadow;
- are usually a point source or of a small area;
- reveal surface texture to a maximum;

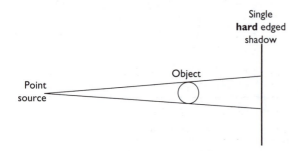

Figure 4.22 Definition of a hard source.

- can either be a focused source or an open-faced luminaire;
- have their beam shape controlled with barndoors.

The sun and moon are examples of natural hard sources.

All the light sources discussed earlier, except for fluorescent lights, can be considered as point sources. The tungsten/tungsten halogen source obviously gets larger as the wattage is increased, but at the normal lamp throws it is viable to think of it as a hard source. The fluorescent lamp is *not* a point source and never will be. It is an **extended** light source, usually used in groups to obtain a large area and a practical level of illuminance.

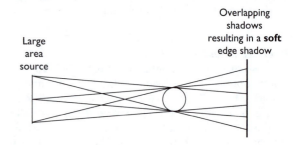

Figure 4.23 Definition of a soft source.

Soft sources are effectively large area sources, which can be thought of as many point sources (Fig. 4.23). Soft sources:

- produce multiple overlapping shadows which result in a soft-edged shadow;
- need to be of a large area to be truly soft;
- tend to destroy texture;
- produce light which cannot be controlled as easily as a hard source (it usually goes everywhere!);
- can be created by **bouncing** a hard source off a suitable large area reflector.

A completely overcast sky is an example of a very good soft source, producing almost shadowless lighting.

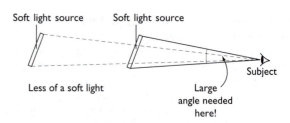

Figure 4.24 Requirements of a soft source.

Fundamentally, it is the angle which the light source subtends at the subject which determines whether it will behave as a hard or soft source, i.e. it is a function of area of light source and luminaire throw (Fig. 4.24).

4.5.1 Luminaire performance

Manufacturers usually publish data which gives the illuminance and width of coverage at various distances from the luminaire. While these are useful in determining performance, reference to the beam angle and the effective luminous intensity in candelas (candlepower) is all that is needed to work out the illuminance and coverage at any distance. The beam angle is the angle between the 'half intensity' points (Fig. 4. 25). This is an angle which can be measured easily, and does of course indicate where the light has dropped to 50%. In order to get a more useful figure which gives uniform coverage, the beam angle should be reduced by 10°, e.g. a typical beam angle for a Fresnel spotlight is 55°, so a useful beam width would be 45° (Fig. 4.25).

The inverse square law can be used to estimate the illuminance:

$$\text{Illuminance} = \frac{\text{candlepower (candelas)}}{\text{(distance)}^2} \text{ lux}$$

where the distance is expressed in metres.

Taking a 2 kW Fresnel spotlight, with a candlepower of 30 000 candelas, the illuminance at 5 metres would be:

$$\frac{30\ 000}{5 \times 5} = 1200 \text{ lux}$$

This is the illuminance at full mains voltage; at fader 7 it would be 50%, i.e. 600 lux.

Manufacturers will publish data based on a new clean luminaire, a new lamp and full mains voltage. To take account of lamp ageing, tarnished optics and possible reduced mains it is recommended to reduce manufacturers' data by approximately 15–20%.

4.5.2 Fresnel spotlight or soft-edged spotlight 100 W–24 kW

The Fresnel spotlight is generally recognized as the main 'work-horse' of luminaires. It is a good modelling light and may be used as a keylight, backlight, set light or hard fill-light. It is a general purpose luminaire with a wide range of operating wattages: 100 W; 300 W; 500 W; 650 W; 1 kW; 2 kW; 5 kW; 10 kW; 20 kW; 24 kW; also there are twin filament versions giving 1¼/2½/3¾ kW, 1¼/2½ kW, and 2½/5 kW. Fresnel spotlights are also available with HMI/MSR sources from 200 W to 18 kW. The construction of the Fresnel spotlight is illustrated in Fig. 4.26.

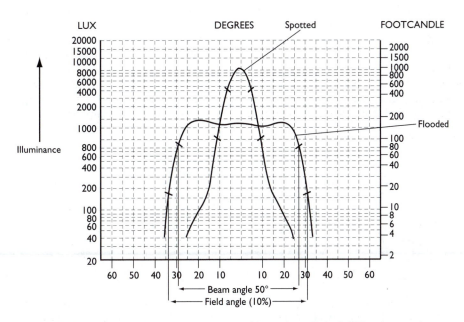

Figure 4.25 Polar diagram showing performance of Fresnel spotlight (1 kW at 3 metres).

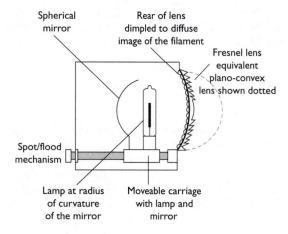

Figure 4.26 Fresnel spotlight construction.

Use of the Fresnel lens (cut-away lens) results in:

- a thin lens compared with a plano-convex lens;
- less weight than a plano-convex lens;
- a lens which is less likely to crack than a plano-convex lens.

The reflector/lamp assembly can be moved to alter the beam angle from wide angle (full flood) to narrow angle (full spot). When fully flooded it behaves like a point source producing hard-edged shadows. When spotted, the lens acts as a magnifying glass so that the light source appears larger, i.e. a softer source (Fig. 4.27).

All Fresnel spotlights should be fitted with **barndoors** which are essential in controlling the beam shape. They should be captive, i.e. not fall out easily, and rotate freely, even when hot.

To 'set' a luminaire it is necessary to be able to adjust easily the pan, tilt and spot/flood mechanism. All of these functions can be made 'pole-operated' so that they may be operated from the studio floor with the aid of a lighting stick or operating pole. It is recommended to include pole-operation on Fresnel spotlights and all other appropriate luminaires.

4.5.3 Softlights

Softlights may be produced by:

(a) 'bouncing' **linear** lamps (strip lamps), tungsten halogen/HMI/MSR off a suitable reflector. The reflector may be matt white or dimpled polished metal (Fig. 4.28(a));
(b) reflecting **point** sources (tungsten or discharge) off a special dimpled polished reflector;
(c) 'bouncing' a hard source off a suitable matt white reflector, e.g. polystyrene board (Fig. 4.28(b));
(d) punching a hard source through diffusion material to create a second light source of large area (Fig. 4.28(c));
(e) creating the effect of a large 'gas mantle' by diffusing several **linear** sources through a silk skirt (Fig. 4.28(d));
(f) grouping together a number of light sources to produce a large area, e.g. fluorescent lights (Fig. 4.28(e)).

Often, soft luminaires are grouped together to maintain a large effective area.

A good soft source is one which:

- looks evenly bright over the complete area of the source;
- does not change its effective area when power switching, i.e. when some of the sources are switched off to achieve a reduced light output, without a change in colour temperature (rather than dimming excessively resulting in a significant change in colour temperature);

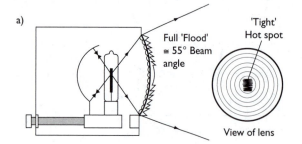

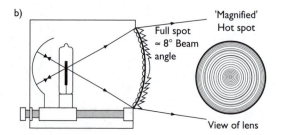

Figure 4.27 (a) Fresnel spotlight in full flood mode, lamp close to lens, approximately 32% efficient at collecting and projecting the lamp light; (b) Fresnel spotlight in full spot mode, lamp furthest from lens, approximately 8% efficient at collecting and projecting the lamp light.

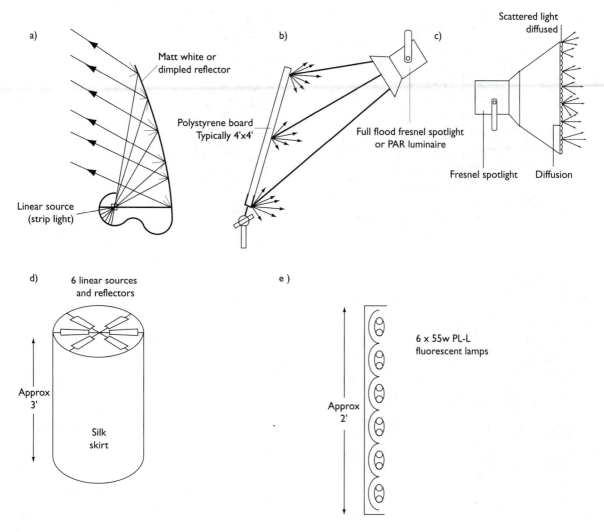

Figure 4.28 Methods of devising a soft light: (a) linear source 'bounced' off a reflector; (b) use of a reflector board; (c) use of diffusion; (d) spacelight; (e) use of fluorescent lamps.

- includes an eggcrate (louvre system) or honeycomb screen to give some degree of control of the sideways spill of light (Fig. 4.29).

Note that barndoors have a limited effect on soft sources (Fig. 4.30).

Some manufacturers use the term 'broad' source to indicate that it has a wide spread of light. Generally these are small area sources and produce hard-edged shadows.

Softlights are usually used:

- to provide the 'fill-light' to control the density of shadows;
- as keylights where a softlight is appropriate;

- to light audiences;
- to provide a shadowless backlight when required.

The techniques which have evolved for deriving suitable softlights are often very ingenious, as is the application of the sources in providing the filler which does not intrude by:

- creating a second shadow – use of a large enough **area** source;
- overlighting the foreground – use of eggcrate/ honeycomb control screen plus **flag** or **veil**;
- washing out the background – use of eggcrate/ honeycomb control screens plus **cutter**.

(a)

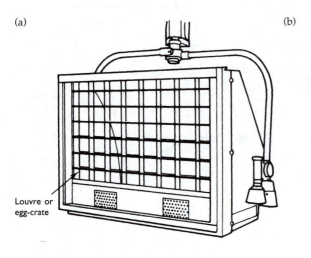

Louvre or
egg-crate

(b) Control of light beam spread is by
means of a honeycomb type screen
over the front of the fixture. The degree
of control depends on the depth of the
honeycomb or the area of the apertures,
typically 90°, 60° or 30°.

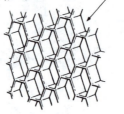

Alternatives to using
control screens are
egg-crates, barn-
doors or flags

Figure 4.29
(a) Egg-crate; (b) honeycomb
control screen.

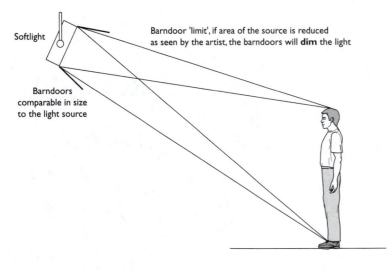

Softlight

Barndoor 'limit', if area of the source is reduced
as seen by the artist, the barndoors will **dim** the light

Barndoors
comparable in size
to the light source

Figure 4.30 The limit for barndooring
a softlight.

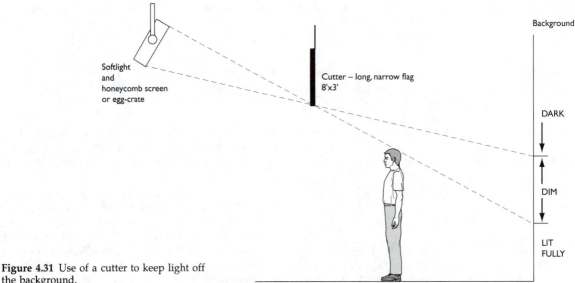

Softlight
and
honeycomb screen
or egg-crate

Cutter – long, narrow flag
8'x3'

Background

DARK

DIM

LIT
FULLY

Figure 4.31 Use of a cutter to keep light off
the background.

Conventional softlight

To be a good 'soft' source a luminaire should be of a large area. This means that such a source will be bulky and to some extent impractical, especially when transporting these sources to location shoots. Hence the use of several softlights grouped together to produce a better 'softlight'.

Bounced softlight

By using a 4' × 4' or 4' × 8' white polystyrene reflector with a 'bounced' Fresnel spotlight a large area softlight is created.

Note, when using 'bounce' techniques:

- The effective candlepower is reduced to about one-fifth of the original candlepower.
- A Fresnel spotlight should *always* be used in its **full flood** condition when 'bounced'. About 32% of the generated light leaves the luminaire in the full flood mode, but only 8% in the full spot mode!
- The need to control where the light goes using suitable size of 'flags' and 'cutters'.
- Often PAR cans are used as bounce-lights because of their better efficiency, i.e. less power is needed to achieve a particular lighting level.

Use of diffusion

The use of diffusion clipped to the extreme edges of the barndoors on a Fresnel spotlight is a quick way of deriving a softlight. A quick browse through the filter swatch book will reveal many different varieties of diffusion, so which one should we use?

Taking as an example white diffusion, this is available as:

White diffusion	¾ White diffusion
¾ White diffusion	⅛ White diffusion
½ White diffusion	⅟₁₆ White diffusion
⅜ White diffusion	

Each filter will provide a different degree of diffusion or scattering of the light, i.e. there will be reflection, absorption, direct transmission and diffuse transmission according to the properties of the filter.

A useful compromise is that of **half white diffusion**. This has a transmission of about 50% and provides a good level of diffusion. White diffusion has a transmission of less than 30%, but provides more diffusion.

To check which diffusion to use it is useful to set up a test using a luminaire on a stand as the test object, positioned about 0.15 m (6") from a wall. Observe the quality of shadow achieved for the luminaire head, the cable and the lamp stand when

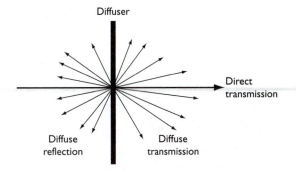

Figure 4.32 The action of a diffuser on a single light ray.

a) Diffusion clipped to 'boxed' doors

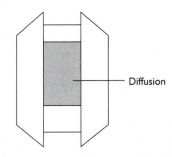

b) Diffusion clipped to wide open barndoors

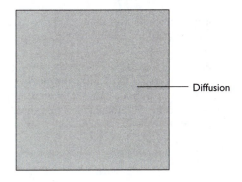

Figure 4.33 (a) 'Strangled' diffuse source; (b) using maximum possible area.

the test object is illuminated with a Fresnel spotlight, plus the various diffusion media. This simple test will quickly reveal the amount of direct/diffuse transmission.

Whatever you decide to do with diffusion, remember that the **area** of diffusion filter used determines the maximum **softness** possible from a given luminaire position. Consequently, avoid 'strangling' diffused sources, i.e. not using maximum possible area of diffusion.

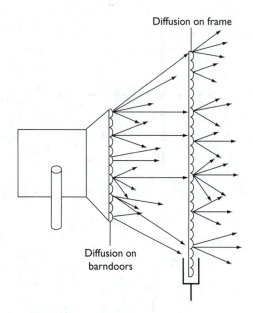

Figure 4.34 Double diffusion technique.

Where space is at a premium (small studio or small location), one can reduce the space required for a large diffuser by using a double diffusion technique (Fig. 4.34).

Two other diffusion-related factors not discussed above are:

- Noise factor – is the filter likely to cause noise problems in a windy environment, i.e. on location?
- Evenness of diffusion – some of the light 'spun' type of diffusers may give rise to a pattern of directly transmitted light. If this is a problem, consider using a double layer – this should help to even out the transmission as well as improving the diffusion.

Chimera

A special type of very popular diffuser is the **chimera**, which is basically a collapsible conical **snoot** which can be fitted to almost any light source using an appropriate **speed-ring**; the speed-ring is mounted on the luminaire after first removing the barndoors.

The front of the chimera is made of diffusion material, and the inside of the snoot has a metal-based reflective coating. The major benefits in using the chimera are:

- it is simple and quick to use;
- it collapses into an easily transportable package;
- it enables large area softlight to be achieved easily;

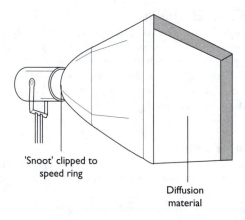

Figure 4.35 Chimera.

- little or no spill light is emitted from the rear of the chimera, unlike when using simple diffusion on a frame.

A collapsible eggcrate is also available, which can be attached to the front of the 'snoot' with Velcro.

Large chimeras should be used on suitably robust stands to ensure that the luminaire plus chimera does not overbalance.

Rifa-light

The rifa-light is a very simple collapsible softlight, but it contains its own light source.

It operates on the umbrella principle to produce a snoot with a diffuser; the light source (1 kW lamp) is suitably protected from coming into contact with the snoot when closed.

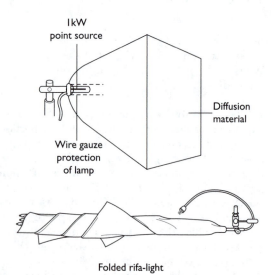

Figure 4.36 Rifa-light.

Aurosoft

This is an innovative development which converts point sources into a softlight. Based on the principle that a softlight, i.e. shadowless lighting, can be obtained by using many point sources, the Aurosoft has a special reflector consisting basically of many polished hemispheres. Each hemisphere reflects the light source to produce an excellent softsource.

a)

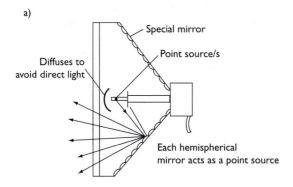

b)

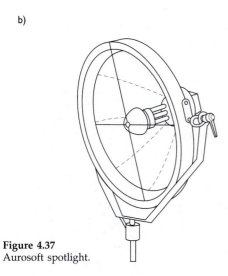

Figure 4.37
Aurosoft spotlight.

This light source is unique in that it can operate with either tungsten sources or discharge sources by changing the light source unit.

Two versions exist:

Approx. diameter 0.7 m	1 kW/2 kW/3 kW tungsten or 575 W/1200 W HMI/MSR
Approx. diameter 1.0 m	2 kW/4 kW tungsten or 1.2 kW/2.5 kW HMI/MSR

Switching the tungsten sources does not change the effective area of the soft source.

The deep eggcrate has an asymmetric construction so, by rotating it, the sideways spread/upstage spread can be varied.

Spacelight

This is yet another way of deriving a softlight, this time using six linear sources to illuminate a large silk 'skirt'. Fig. 4.38 illustrates the principle.

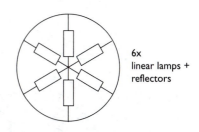

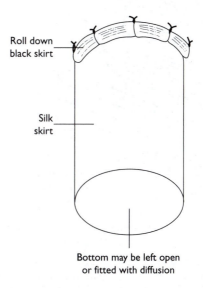

Figure 4.38 Spacelight.

The bottom of the spacelight may be left open or fitted with suitable diffusion. An additional black 'skirt' on the outside of the white skirt may be lowered to give control to the sideways spread of the light.

The spacelight is particularly effective for large sets, when it is used to simulate sky-light or for large chroma key set-ups when shadowless lighting is required.

Note: The six linear sources may be switched to provide half-power.

Fluorescent luminaires (coldlights)

Most fluorescent luminaires consist of several lamps in order to make a suitable luminaire, i.e. sufficient light output. Although they can never be regarded as point sources they are of finite area, not infinite area. Consequently, they can be controlled to some extent by using suitable honeycomb control screens, 'eggcrates, barndoors or flags/cutters. The honeycomb control screen is particularly effective and is usually available in wide, medium and narrow angle (90°, 60° and 30°) (Fig. 4.39).

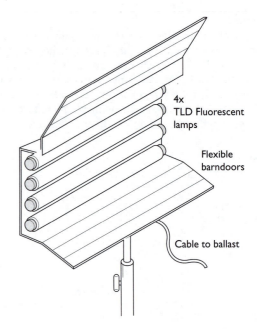

Figure 4.40 Example of a lightweight fluorescent luminaire.

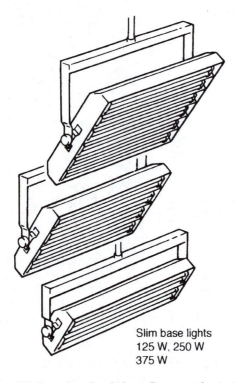

Figure 4.39 Examples of multi-lamp fluorescent luminaires.

There are two basic types of fluorescent luminaire, one using the conventional tubular lamps (TL-D) and the other using the compact fluorescent lamps (PL-L and PL-C). Like all discharge lights the fluorescent luminaire includes a current limiting ballast in addition to auxiliary electronics for starting. The ballast also includes the necessary electronics to drive the lamps at high frequency (>40 kHz). The luminaires using the TL-D lamps were designed for use mainly on location. They are made with a separate ballast, usually dimmable, to provide an extremely lightweight and thin softlight, ideal for use in cramped conditions (Fig. 4.40).

The luminaires using the PL-L lamps were initially designed for studio use; however, derivatives of the designs are available for location use. These are especially useful on location where a compact source is needed (Fig. 4.41).

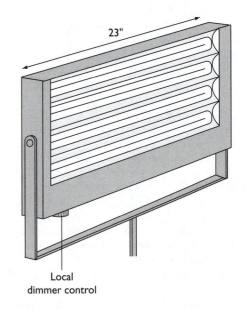

Figure 4.41 Compact location luminaire.

Initially, the PL-C lamp was used in conjunction with a V-shaped mirror system; however, most studio luminaires use the PL-L lamps, each with its own mirror to reflect the light forward (Fig. 4.42).

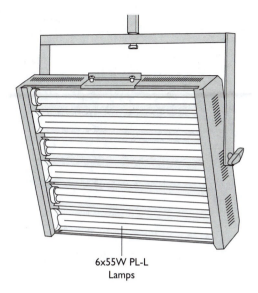

Figure 4.42 Typical 6 × 55 W baselight fluorescent luminaire.

The **baselight** type of construction results in a luminaire with a very wide beam angle. Consequently, when a control screen is used the sideways spreading light is lost. An **intensifier**, basically mirrored barndoors, can be fitted to these luminaires which redirects the sideways spreading light onto the main acting area. Use of an intensifier can double the on-axis illuminance for most luminaires. Control screens are available for use with intensifiers (Fig. 4.43).

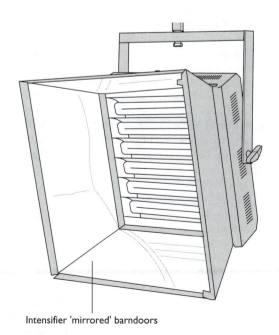

Intensifier 'mirrored' barndoors

Figure 4.43 6 × 55 W fluorescent luminaire and intensifier.

A modular luminaire is very useful for lighting the cyclorama of a virtual reality set. These luminaires can be slotted together to produce a larger lumens package or used individually to light a vertical surface (Fig. 4.44).

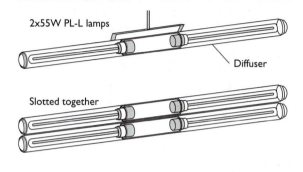

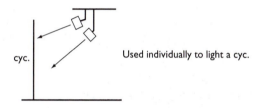

Figure 4.44 Modular fluorescent luminaires.

Individual fluorescent lights (6 W) are available for use in car kits, i.e. for night lighting in cars at night. These are dimmable and can be powered from the car battery (cigarette lighter connection), or from mains.

Soft sources and the inverse square law
The inverse square law is only strictly true for point sources; however, when considering soft sources one can still use this law to estimate the illuminance. For large area sources the illuminance follows an inverse law up to distances comparable with the size of the source. Thereafter, it becomes an inverse square law. When making calculations at a distance of three times the largest dimension of the light source the 'error' in using the inverse square law is 10%; at five times the distance it is approximately 2%.

Dual source luminaires
The BBC pioneered the use of dual source luminaires in studios by using a saturation rig of these luminaires to reduce the turn-around time between productions and set changes. It is basically a hard source and a soft source bolted together with pole-operation of pan, tilt,

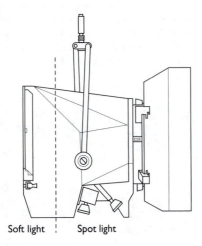

Soft light | Spot light

Figure 4.45 Dual source luminaire.

spot/flood, hard/soft and power switching. Its disadvantages are the compromise on the area of the soft end and its physical size, e.g. when used as a 1¼ kW hard source it occupies about ten times the space of a single-ended 1 kW spotlight.

4.5.4 Hard-edged projectors (100 W–2 kW)

This luminaire may be known alternatively as an effects, profile, ellipsoidal, mirror spotlight or gobo projector. It is a luminaire which has a lens system that can produce a sharply focused disc of light, hence its name, or project the shape of a metal profile (gobo). The projector includes metal shutters within it to shape the beam with precision. It may have a single lens system or have twin lens optics. The latter have the advantage of providing a variable beam angle (zoom lens) usually over about a 2:1 ratio, i.e. variable image size, and also provide variable image focus at any image size, unlike the single lens projector which will only have one focused size of image from a given position.

An invaluable recent development has been the introduction of a rotatable gobo holder which makes it very easy to correct gobo tilt errors.

Hard-edged projectors are used:

- to light artistes in complete isolation – the shaping shutters are more precise than the barndoors on a Fresnel spotlight. Hamburgh Frost or Hampshire Frost can be used to soften the edge of the shaping shutters. This avoids the need to de-focus the projector, which changes the projected image size;
- to add interest or effects to background or floors, usually using gobos, in combination or singly.

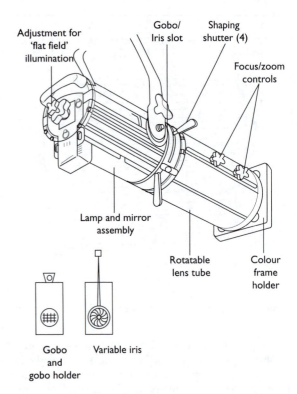

Figure 4.46 600 W profile projector with variable beam angle 15–32°.

It should be noted that gobos get very hot, consequently when changing hot gobos it is recommended to use appropriate gloves.

Often the best results are obtained with de-focused gobo images, usually moving towards the larger image size. This is an important point when de-focusing gobos – there is a difference in the 'de-focused' look either side of the in-focus position. If there is a need for a really sharp image with no flare, a 'doughnut' made from black wrap can be inserted on the front of the projector. This will dim the light to some extent. An alternative is to use projectors which have condenser optics. There are usually three ranges of zoom lens projectors providing, typically:

Wide angle	28°	to	58°
Medium angle	15°	to	30°
Narrow angle	7°	to	17°

A recently developed single lens projector offers six beam angles by using six interchangeable snoots (lens tubes), i.e. 5°, 10°, 19°, 26°, 36° and 50°. This projector incorporates a new axially mounted 575 W lamp which has resulted in on-light output performance comparable to a 1 kW projector.

Although profile projectors use mainly tungsten halogen sources there is a range of projectors available which use HMI/MSR sources, for long throw applications.

Tungsten halogen	–	up to 2.5 kW
CSI	–	up to 1.2 kW
HMI	–	up to 2.5 kW
Xenon	–	up to 3 kW

For many studio applications it is worth considering using the 2.5 kW tungsten follow spot (or lower wattage spotlight if capable of providing the correct illuminance). The advantages of using a tungsten follow spot are:

Following spotlights (follow-spots)

The follow-spot is used to light artistes at long throws in complete isolation, and to follow any artiste movement (Fig. 4.47).

- no colour matching problems (all discharge lights require colour correction when matching to tungsten is required);
- can be dimmed electronically;
- no auxiliary equipment;
- no warm-up needed.

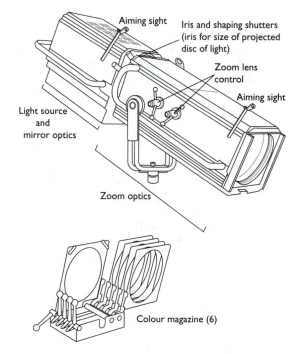

Xenon follow-spots have the advantage of compact light source (easily focused) and very stable colour with excellent colour rendition. Other discharge sources (CSI, CID and HMI) do not have such a stable light source. Consequently, there is a need to check and match the colour of the light using appropriate filters.

All follow-spots should be fitted with:

- colour changers – colour magazine;
- variable iris – to change size of the lit area;
- black-out facility;
- ergonomically useful controls for pan and tilt.

Essential to good follow-spot operation are:

Figure 4.47 Follow spotlight – typical tungsten version.

- a good pan and tilt mechanism on a sturdy luminaire stand;
- talkback to the lighting director;
- production talkback;
- an operator with a steady hand and good anticipation.

It is a narrow angle version of a twin-lens hard-edged projector, designed to use a tungsten halogen or discharge light source depending on the lamp throw required:

Table 4.10 Follow-spot data.

Description	Beam angles	Peak candelas	
		Wide angle	Narrow angle
1200 W tungsten	10°–22°	17 600 cd	77 000 cd
2000 W tungsten	8°–13½°	285 000 cd	650 000 cd
2500 W tungsten	8°–14°	320 000 cd	500 000 cd
1200 W HMI	10°–15°	680 000 cd	1 500 000 cd
2500 W HMI	5.5°–9.2°	1 300 000 cd	5 300 000 cd
1000–2000 W xenon (Super Trouper)	6.8°–11.5°	325 000 cd	3 100 000 cd
2500 W xenon Gladiator II	6.5°–9.5°	2 000 000 cd	15 000 000 cd
3000 W xenon Gladiator III	5.5°–9.2°	1 300 000 cd	5 300 000 cd

Transparency projectors (2 kW tungsten halogen, HMI)

Transparency projectors are available to project still or moving effects, e.g. clouds, water ripple, flames. These are luminaires with condenser optics and a high definition projection lens, to ensure that the projected image is a good quality.

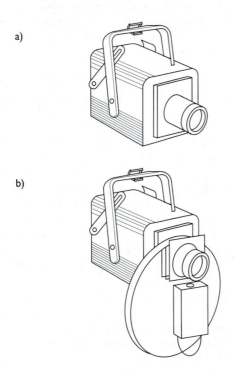

Figure 4.48 Transparency projectors: (a) still slide; (b) moving effects, e.g. clouds, fire.

Different focal length projection lenses provide flexibility in throw and image size. The HMI projectors are especially useful for large-scale projection at location events.

4.5.5 The cyclorama lights

The studio cyclorama is a large vertical off-white cloth, used as a general purpose background. Nature provides a 'cyclorama', the sky, with a natural reduction in saturation and an increase in luminance as one looks towards the horizon, i.e. the deepest blue is immediately overhead. In television, the aim is either to mimic nature with a shaded cyclorama, or to light the cyclorama evenly from top to bottom and provide a wide range of colour options. It is not usual to light the cyclorama to be bright at the top – the eye/brain would be led out of the picture. There are two basic ways to light a cyclorama:

- from floor level using a ground row;
- from above the cyclorama cloth with top cyc luminaires.

A combination of both methods may be used.

A third method exists, although not very common, whereby a plastic cyclorama is rear-lit using Red/Green/Blue fluorescent lights.

Note: The term ground row is also used to describe free-standing scenery pieces such as cut-outs of distant hills, etc.

Ground row

Ground row units provide the most natural look when lighting the cyclorama. They are available as single units or four separate units slotted together to make a 4-unit (rigid) or 4-unit (hinged) (Fig. 4.49).

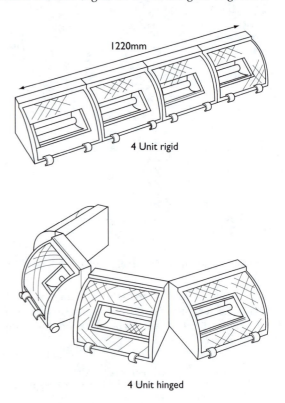

1220mm

4 Unit rigid

4 Unit hinged

Figure 4.49 Ground row units.

Each unit uses a frosted 625 W or 500 W linear tungsten halogen lamp. The 4-unit ground rows are interconnected with a special 9-way connector, i.e. 4 separate circuits, plus earth. They have been designed to have a very soft-edged beam in the sideways direction, enabling them to overlap with adjacent units and so provide an even horizontal illuminance. The illuminance in the vertical direction will reduce in a natural way with distance from the light source. When placed 1.2 metres from the cyclorama the units have to be repeated every 1.2 metres to ensure even coverage. The 4-unit ground row at 1.2 metres long means that 8 such units placed 1.2 m from the cyclorama can light over 9 metres of cyclorama (32 feet), with just $8 \times 625\,W = 5\,kW$ of power.

Each component in a 4-unit ground row is fitted with a different colour filter, enabling **colour mixing** on the cyclorama (Fig. 4.50).

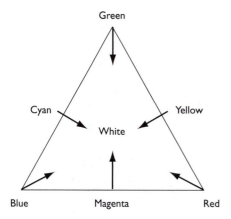

Colours are de-saturated by:
1) adding complementary colour
2) adding white light

Figure 4.50 Additive colour mixing.

At first, it may seem that primary red, primary green and primary blue filters plus white (clear) are all that is required to obtain a wide range of hues, saturation and luminance. Unfortunately, the low transmission of the primary colour filters, especially the primary blue filter, means that the luminance of such colour mixes is low. Consequently, lighting directors often supplement a dark blue filter with a bright blue to enable high luminance cycloramas to be achieved. Similarly, light red and moss green may be used in preference to the primary colours. Note, however, that if a deeply saturated blue cyclorama is required then one must use a deeply saturated blue filter, and it may be necessary to double-up on using this filter, i.e. circuit A and C being fitted with deep blue or congo blue filter.

Use of a ground row is a very economic way to light a cyclorama. However, it has the disadvantages of:

- requiring at least 1.2 m of space between it and the cyc cloth;
- requiring **coving** to hide the units if they are not obscured by scenery (Fig. 4.51).

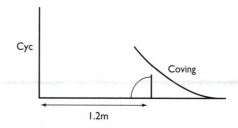

Figure 4.51 The use of coving.

Note the use of **frosted** lamps in all cyclorama luminaires. This is to ensure that shadows of the lamp filament supports are not seen on the cyclorama.

If the ground row has to be used closer to the cyclorama than 1.2 m it will be necessary to use alternate units with identical colours or, if very close, every unit with the same colour to ensure that a smooth horizontal spread of light is achieved. The closer the units are to the cyc the more the vertical spread of light will be reduced.

Top cyc lights

These are special cyclorama lights which have been developed to provide:

(i) a very soft edge to the light beam which enables sources to be overlapped easily;

(ii) an asymmetric reflector enabling the cyclorama to be evenly illuminated from top to bottom (Fig. 4.52).

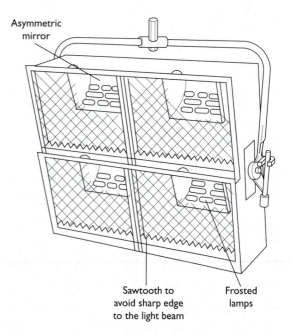

Figure 4.52 Four-unit top cyclorama lighting unit.

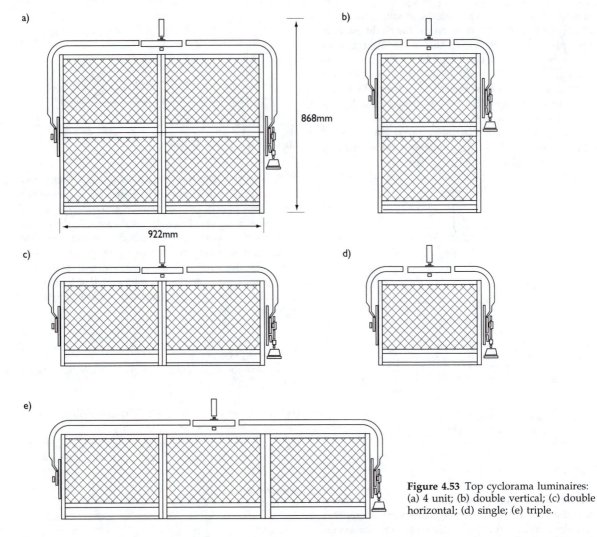

Figure 4.53 Top cyclorama luminaires: (a) 4 unit; (b) double vertical; (c) double horizontal; (d) single; (e) triple.

These luminaires are available singly or in groups of 2, 3 or 4 (Fig. 4.53).

For most medium to large studios (>200 m²) the 4-unit cyclorama luminaire is used. It may be fitted with 1.2 kW lamps or 625 W lamps as appropriate to the camera sensitivity needs of the studio. Each compartment may be fitted with a different colour filter, enabling colour mixing on the cyclorama, similar to the ground row units. Usually, the 4-unit top cyclorama luminaires are interconnected using special 9-way cables, used in a similar manner to the ground row cables, again sharing lighting circuits for economy in control, i.e. 4 × 1.25 kW = 5 kW for studios with 5 kW dimmers or 4 × 625 W = 2.5 kW for studios with 2.5 kW dimmers

Plotting cyclorama lights

The basic need to light the cyclorama evenly is satisfied with an even distribution of top cyclorama luminaires. Consequently, it is normal practice to plot the positions of the cyclorama lights as a priority when planning a production. For even coverage, i.e. smooth overlapping horizontally and even illumination top to bottom of the cyclorama, the *minimum* distances and spacings are as shown in Fig. 4.54.

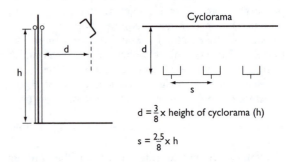

$$d = \frac{3}{8} \times \text{height of cyclorama (h)}$$

$$s = \frac{2.5}{8} \times h$$

Figure 4.54 Plotting of top cyclorama units.

Always plot the cyclorama corners first, then work along the straight sections. The larger the radius of the cyclorama the easier it is to light it uniformly.

Use of ground row and top cyc lighting

Ground row and top cyc lighting are required for tall cycloramas or where a change in saturation or colour is required, e.g. to produce a sky effect. With only ground row or top cyc lighting the saturation and colour would be the same from top to bottom. Fig. 4.55 illustrates the principle of lighting the cyc to produce a sky effect.

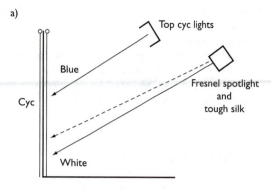

a)

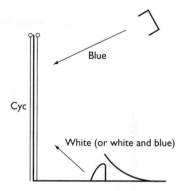

Figure 4.55 Use of ground row and top cyc lighting.

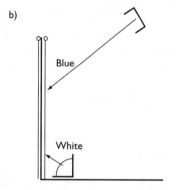

b)

Figure 4.56 (a) Graduated cyc without ground row; (b) use of close ground row for 'low horizon' effects.

The reduction in saturation achieved with this arrangement will be gradual. When a more rapid change is required, say for a distant horizon effect, one could use an extra row of ground row units, all white (clear) very close to the cycloramas, or use Fresnel spotlights (Fig. 4.56). The barndoors on the Fresnel spotlights can be used to 'shape' the horizon effect; using tough silk or brushed silk enables a soft horizontal overlap between adjacent spotlights.

This technique could also be used for a cyc lit only with top cyc units.

Filter material

Two basic types of colour filter are available:

- polyester – in which a clear plastic base is coated with the appropriate pigment; these can be identified by scraping away the pigment with a pen-knife;
- polycarbonate – in which the base and the pigment are mixed together; this is known as a 'dyed in the mass' filter.

The polycarbonate filters are referred to as HT or high temperature filters; these are not affected by heat as much as the polyester filters but are more expensive. If long filter life is needed, or when using dense filters, it is recommended to use the polycarbonate filters.

Choice of filters

Where specific colour filters are used to create sky effects, instead of colour mixing, typical filters used are:

Light Blue	–	for a light blue sky of high luminance
Medium Blue	–	for a strong blue sky
Congo Blue	–	for a deeply saturated, dark blue 'night' sky
Medium Blue	– ⎫	in separate units, when mixed
Steel Blue	– ⎬	together give a choice of
	⎭	summer or winter sky
Apricot	–	good for ground row 'dawn' effect

Note that when lighting cycloramas one should aim to avoid any of the artiste lighting or set lighting spilling onto the cyclorama; similarly, one should not allow any of the cyclorama lighting to hit the artiste.

Any soft sources lighting the cyclorama will desaturate the cyclorama colour; consequently, there is a need to consider using hard fill-lights for variety type performances and use the barndoor to select the area lit, i.e. not the cyclorama.

Clouds

Cloud effects can be realized by:

*   using a transparency projector with a suitable rotating 'cloud wheel' to produce a moving cloud effect. Several projectors will be needed to light a large cyclorama. Care has to be taken to ensure that all the wheels move the same way, at the same speed, and that the projectors are similarly focused;
*   using gobo projectors with a suitable de-focused cloud gobo;
*   using a 'cookie' in an out-rigger frame to give soft clouds (see Section 4.6).

Cyclorama lighting power

The 1.25 kW top cyc lighting units were designed when lighting levels of 1600–2000 lux were required. Consequently, with the increased camera sensitivity it is worth considering reducing the lamp wattage to 625 W, except for studios using very high cycloramas, i.e. >8 m.

If the 1.25 kW lamps are used with, say, a 5.0 metre high cyclorama there will be a need to dim the lamps significantly, resulting in a colour change which may not be desirable – colours will look 'warmer'.

Cyclorama lighting using fluorescent lights

An alternative to using tungsten halogen sources to light the cyclorama is to use fluorescent lights. This system uses a combination of tubes which have red phosphors, green phosphors and blue phosphors, and in some cases white phosphors, to light the cyclorama from behind (Fig. 4.57).

In large studios with a fire-lane this can be used effectively for this lighting. The spacing between the group of red, green and blue tubes, and between the cyclorama and the tubes, is usually the basic light-box dimensions assuming a good diffuser (cyclorama) is used (Fig. 4.58).

The advantages of using fluorescent lighting for the cyclorama are:

*   permanently lit cyc;
*   significant power savings over tungsten halogen sources;

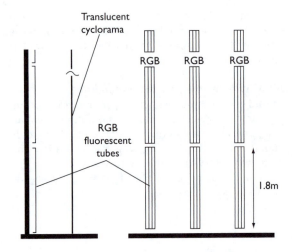

Figure 4.57 Use of RGB fluorescent tubes to light a translucent cyc.

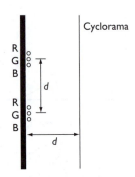

Figure 4.58 Details of RGB tubes/cyclorama spacing (typically $d = 1$ metre).

*   no radiant heat;
*   mixture colours can be set up and memorized for future use on a long-term basis;
*   no shadows of backlights on cyc from cyc lights;
*   excellent for chroma key operations;
*   total freedom to light inside cyc area, i.e. no compromise brought about by cyc light positioning;
*   no filters needed as the lights have appropriate Red, Green and Blue phosphors;
*   shading in luminance and saturation possible without the need for a ground row.

The disadvantage is the high initial costs.

If a peripheral lighting bar is installed adjacent to the studio wall the fluorescent fixtures of groups of three (or four) tubes can be suspended from a luminaire trolley. The lighting units may then be manoeuvred as required.

4.5.6 PAR lights

The parabolic aluminized reflector lights known as PAR lights or PAR cans were first introduced into the world of 'pop' before gaining popularity in television applications. The PAR can, as its name suggests, has a parabolic reflector to collect the light from the lamp into a very narrow beam (Fig. 4.59).

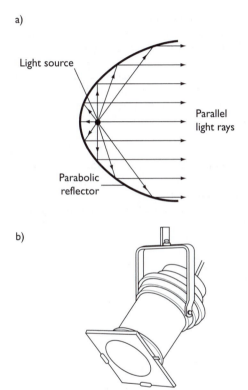

Figure 4.59 (a) Parabolic reflector action; (b) typical PAR can.

The lamp, together with its reflector, are part of a sealed beam unit, the front element of which may be plain, diffused or in the form of a lens, similar to a Fresnel lens, except that it is a diverging lens, i.e. concave.

The merits of these luminaires are:

- a very intense and very narrow beam is available which when used with smoke results in the production of dramatic shafts of light;
- the short thermal capacity of the lamp filament which allows it to be switched on/off very rapidly, e.g. in time with music.

PAR cans are normally expressed as PAR 64, PAR 56, PAR 16, etc. Dividing the number by 8 gives the

Table 4.11 1 kW PAR can data.

		Beam angle	Effective candlepower
CP60	Narrow spot	9° × 12°	320 000 candelas
CP61	Spot	10° × 14°	270 000 candelas
CP62	Flood	11° × 24°	125 000 candelas
CP63	Extra wide	70° × 70°	15 000 candelas

luminaire diameter, e.g. PAR 64 is 8″ in diameter. The performance of the 1000 W PAR cans is shown in Table 4.11.

The long throw CP60 and CP61 sources have a long throw capability which makes them particularly useful for outside broadcast work when lighting at a distance. For example, for the CP61 at 10 m:

$$\text{Illuminance} = \frac{\text{candlepower}}{\text{distance}^2} = \frac{270\,000}{10 \times 10} = 2700 \text{ lux!}$$

The 1 kW PAR can is rapidly being replaced by the 500 W version, following the development of more sensitive cameras (Table 4.12).

Table 4.12 500 W PAR can data.

		Beam angle	Effective candlepower
CP86	0.5 kW	7° × 10°	240 000 candelas
CP87	0.5 kW	9° × 11°	140 000 candelas
CP88	0.5 kW	10° × 21°	65 000 candelas
HX115	0.5 kW	66° × 66°	7000 candelas

The Raylight is similar to the PAR can, except that it uses a separate reflector and lamp, i.e. no-sealed beam unit, with the reflector providing the appropriate beam angle. This has the advantage of only needing the lamp to be changed, rather than a complete sealed beam unit, when the lamp fails.

A further evolution has been the development of a unit which has a fixed reflector, a special axially mounted 575 W lamp and a selection of five interchangeable lenses. The axially mounted lamp is a more efficient system, resulting in almost the same light output as a 1000 W PAR can (Fig. 4.60)!

An option is available to use a dichroic mirror as a reflector. This reflects light but transmits heat; consequently, any filters mounted on the lamp have a significant increase in light, and the stage is cooler!

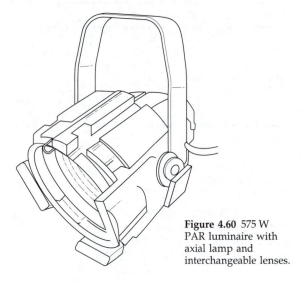

Figure 4.60 575 W PAR luminaire with axial lamp and interchangeable lenses.

Discharge PAR lights

The advantages observed in using an axially mounted lamp have been developed for use in a range of PAR lamps with HMI and MSR light sources (single-ended). These use a fixed parabolic reflector with interchangeable lenses. They have the advantage of being more efficient than a Fresnel spotlight with a similar light source and provide a very 'punchy' light, very useful for 'bouncing'. It should be noted that the interchangeable lenses do not give quite the smooth beam enjoyed with a Fresnel spotlight, i.e. in wide angle condition the beam is not so uniform.

Discharge PAR lights are available from 125 W–6 kW.

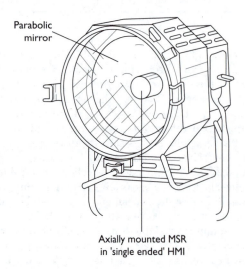

Parabolic mirror

Axially mounted MSR in 'single ended' HMI

Figure 4.61 Open-faced PAR 2.5/4 kW HMI with five different interchangeable lenses.

4.5.7 Moving lights (intelligent lights)

One of the most interesting and exciting developments has been the evolution of moving lights. They fall into two basic categories:

- effects lights;
- colour wash lights.

Effects lights provide a wide range of effects in addition to being able to move the light beam. They break down into two further sub-categories:

- luminaires where the beam is moved by moving the complete luminaire;
- luminaires in which a mirror is used to move the beam.

Luminaires in the first sub-category have the advantage of small size and greater angles of rotation and tilt (360° and 270° respectively), but are slower in moving than the second sub-category.

Luminaires in the second sub-category have the advantage of a lightweight, low inertia mirror which

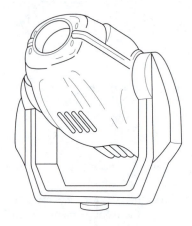

Figure 4.62 (a) Moving effects light.

Figure 4.62 (b) Moving colour washlight.

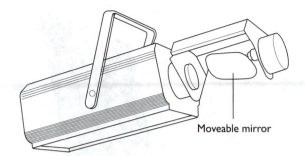

Figure 4.63 Moving mirror light.

can move much faster, but have restricted rotation and tilt angles of 170° and 110° respectively. They are also larger in physical size.

The light source used in these luminaires is usually a compact HMI (HTI) of 1200 W or 575 W rating.

All moving lights offer a variety of effects. For example:

- pan and tilt;
- colour change of light beam (infinite or limited colour wheel);
- beam angle change;
- beam focus change;
- gobo wheel;
- rotating gobo effects;
- diffusion;
- colour correction;
- mechanical dimmer.

Generally, moving lights are used upstage of the artiste, from above, at ground level or side lighting positions.

Note: All moving light systems, including scrollers (see Section 4.13.4), generate some noise either from cooling fans or motors.

Most moving lights use DMX 512 for transmission of the control signals to the luminaire.

It is recommended to use a dedicated control console for moving lights. The Cyberlight, for example, can require over 20 channels! With, say, 20 such fixtures, 400 control channels would be needed on a conventional control console. Using a separate console means that the moving-light operator can programme the lighting changes while working on the studio floor during the rehearsals and move to the lighting control room for the transmission/recording.

Colour wash lights use 575 W HTI or 1000 W tungsten light sources and are based on the first category of moving lights. They provide a variable colour wash and variable beam angle, but no gobo effects. Their pan/tilt range is typically 370°/240°.

Auto pilot

This is a system which enables moving lights to 'follow' the performer. The artist carries a small transmitter which sends signals to six receivers around the edge of the 'stage'. The information received is used to modify the DMX control signals to the moving lights.

Open-faced luminaires

These were developed to provide an efficient, lightweight wide-angle luminaire for location work. They use a special mirror to collect as much light as possible and project it forward. The original open-faced luminaires were the 'redhead' at 800 W and the 'blonde' at 2 kW.

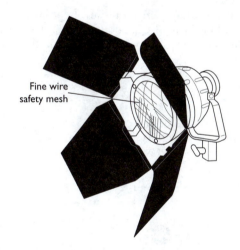

Fine wire safety mesh

Figure 4.64 800 W open-faced luminaire.

They were designed for use with cameras needing 1600–2000 lux; consequently, with modern sensitive cameras they provide an abundance of light over a wide beam angle, 70–80°. The major drawback of this type of light is the lack of good barndooring control – a double shadow of each barndoor is produced. However, this can be minimized by using Hamburg or Hampshire frost on the front of the barndoors.

All open-faced luminaires *must* be used with either a safety glass or a fine wire safety mesh between the lamp and the barndoors. This is to ensure that in the event of a lamp exploding, it is contained within the luminaire housing.

4.6 Control of beam shape and light intensity

4.6.1 Control of beam shape

Basic control of light intensity and beam shape is paramount to effective lighting. Always the light which 'misses' the artiste has to be considered and decisions taken on the best way to shape the light beam.

Generally, Fresnel spotlights are used in the full flood mode to provide uniform coverage over a wide area; the basic beam shape can be modified from a circular beam to a rectangular beam using the barndoors. Barndoors are normally fitted as a pair of short and a pair of long doors; the smaller doors when tucked inside the larger doors give 'tighter' control. So, for example, when lighting a presenter at a desk, keeping the light off the background is best achieved by:

- rotating barndoors to give small doors top and bottom;
- setting the luminaire on the artiste position;
- adjusting the top barndoor until it is just above the **hot-spot** of the luminaire, viewed from the artiste position;
- box side doors to the small doors to avoid unwanted spill.

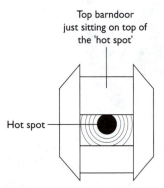

Figure 4.65
Barndoored Fresnel spotlight.

If, however, there is a requirement to have a broad coverage horizontally, the barndoors will have to be used with large doors top and bottom. If the side doors are not needed, one can simply adjust the top door as before, i.e. until it is just 'sitting' on top of the hot-spot. However, if the side doors need to be tucked inside the large doors (to control sideways spill) there could be a problem of keeping the light off the background. Tipping down the luminaire is not recommended because the beam centre is no longer set on the centre of interest. Control can be achieved by using:

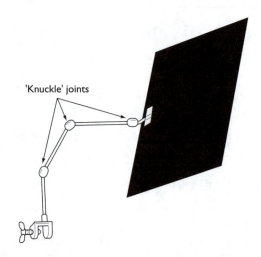

Figure 4.66 French flag (250 mm × 400 mm).

- a French flag – this is effectively an extra barndoor on the end of a 'knuckle-jointed' arm, which can be clamped to the luminaire (Fig. 4.66);
- Black wrap – a matt black tin foil, which can be clipped with crocodile clips to the top barndoor, and shaped to provide the appropriate barndooring action (Fig. 4.67).

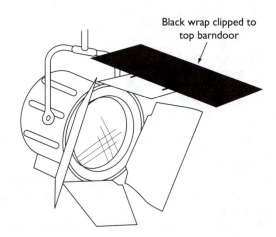

Figure 4.67 Use of black wrap.

Note that barndoors have a limitation on their effectiveness, namely that when they are closed in to the point where they cut across the 'hot-spot', their action becomes one of dimming! Hence the barndoors have little effect on a full-spotted Fresnel spotlight except to control the light scattered by the lens.

The large barndoors should ideally be large enough to cover the complete light beam. If this is not the case, **black wrap** can again be used to prevent 'pigs ears' (Fig. 4.68).

Figure 4.68 'Pigs ears' caused by barndoors which are too small.

Where 'sharper' or 'crisper' control of the beam shape is required this can be achieved with a **black flag**, a four-sided wire frame with a black serge covering. It is rigged in front of the luminaire on flag-arms to give flexible positioning (Fig. 4.69).

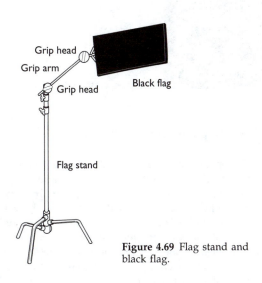

Figure 4.69 Flag stand and black flag.

The further the flag is from the luminaire the 'harder' is the shadow created. Flags are usually rectangular in shape (4:3); when they are long and narrow they are called **cutters**. Cutters are normally used to provide a hard 'cut' of light, e.g. when using a large keylight, say 10 kW, to cover a large dance area it will have a long throw. Consequently, it will be difficult to achieve a 'hard' barndooring action at the join between cyclorama and floor unless a cutter is used, rigged a little way in front of the luminaire.

4.6.2 Control of light intensity

The simplest way to control light intensity from a tungsten halogen source is to use an electronic **dimmer** on every lighting power outlet. This is covered fully in Section 4.18.1.

Discharge sources such as CSI, CID, HMI, MSR and xenon require a mechanical dimmer system if the light source is to be dimmed fully.

Alternatives to using a dimmer are:

- Use of the inverse square law
  – moving the luminaire position to be closer or further away as necessary.
- Use of spot/flood on the luminaire
  – usually luminaires are used in their full flood condition; an increase in illuminance can be made by 'spotting' but, of course, the beam angle is reduced.
- Use of neutral density filters
  – these can be used to reduce light by ½ stop, 1 stop, 2 stops, 3 stops or 4 stops (see Section 4.16.1 on ND filters).
- Use of wire scrims – discussed below.
- Use of veils, nets or yashmaks – discussed below.

A wire **scrim**, fitted between the Fresnel lens and the barndoors, can be used to reduce the light intensity, with no change in colour temperature.

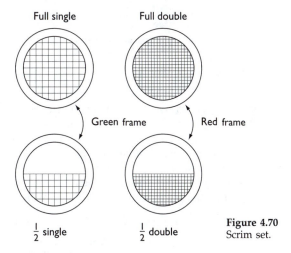

Figure 4.70 Scrim set.

Scrims are available as:

- full single with a transmission of 70% (½ stop loss) (Green);
- full double with a transmission of 50% (1 stop loss) (Red);
- half single with a transmission of 70% (½ stop loss) (Green);
- half double with a transmission of 50% (1 stop loss) (Red).

Full-scrims are useful for simply reducing the overall level, with no change in colour temperature.

Half-scrims are useful for providing a reduction in lighting level for one half of the light beam (see Section 4.9.2), for equalizing illuminance when the artiste walks towards the luminaire (see Section 4.11), or to equalize the illuminance on scenery.

Often it is necessary to have more precise control than that offered by a half-scrim. This can be achieved using a **veil**, **net** or **yashmak**, an open-ended wire frame fitted with black nets to give light loss of ½ stop, 1 stop and 1½ stops. Veils are available in a wide range of sizes to accommodate the beam angles of most Fresnel spotlights.

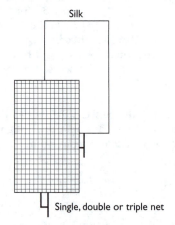

Figure 4.71 Veil, net or yashmak.

Veils are rigged on flag-arms similar to black flags. Like flags, they can be set a little in front of the luminaire to give precise control of the area to be reduced in intensity, e.g. reducing the illuminance on the downstage area of a demonstration area (such as the front of a demonstration desk) when the keylight is used to light the artiste behind the desk as well as the desk front.

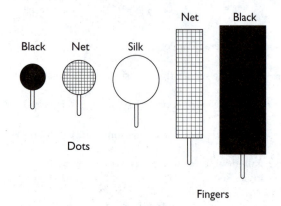

Figure 4.72 Fingers and dots.

Finger and **dot kits** provide the facility to modify a light beam in a localized way. Usually a kit has a range of dots from 3″ diameter to 10″ diameter and 2″ × 12″ fingers to 4″ × 14″ fingers, and fitted with nets, silks or black serge.

Cookie or **cucoloris** is the name given to a dapple plate placed in front of a Fresnel spotlight to provide 'break-up' of the light beam. Again, the further it is placed from the luminaire, the harder is the resulting shadow. Cookies are rigged on flag-arms similar to flags.

Figure 4.73 Cookie or cucoloris.

4.7 Basic portraiture

Good portraiture is an essential part of television lighting, that is, to portray or create a good likeness of the subject. Drama lighting is portraiture in a given environment, where there will be clues to how the person should be lit to 'look right'. Most other applications of news, current affairs, documentary programmes, variety programmes, etc. rely on the observation and technique of the lighting director to ensure that the artistes are 'seen in a good light'!

Ideally, the aim is to light artistes separately from their backgrounds, thus enabling control of the lighting of both areas to be achieved. Three lights are used to light a basic portrait, namely:

- keylight;
- fill-light or filler;
- backlight, hairlight or rimlight.

4.7.1 The keylight

As its name suggests, it is the main light in any lighting set-up:

- It is usually a hard source such as a Fresnel spotlight, providing crisp shadows and good control of the lit area. Note that it could also be a softlight, if the situation so required.
- It establishes the direction of light within a set, e.g. from a window or practical light.

- It creates shadows (modelling) on the subject to reveal its shape and texture.
- The effect seen on camera is determined by the angle between the keylight and the camera.

This point is really a most fundamental statement about lighting. If one experiments with a small Fresnel spotlight on a floor stand together with a television camera and monitor, one can quickly establish some important principles of portraiture, for example: the larger the angle between keylight and camera, the greater the degree of modelling (shadows) and texture revealed. This is true in both the vertical direction and horizontal direction. (See Fig. 4.74.)

Much stress is often made of the effects of horizontal angle in portraiture. In most instances it is the vertical

keying angle which can change the look of a subject from acceptable to unacceptable, e.g. too steep a keying angle. (See Fig. 4.75.)

- The need to keep 'catchlights' in the eyes is also important to give the eyes 'life'. Without 'catchlights' the eyes will look dull. If there is no light in the eyes at all, the subject will tend to look 'shifty', even 'menacing' – fine for the appropriate dramatic moment but totally unsuitable for lighting politicians! (See Fig. 4.76.)
- The subject's shadow should be kept out of shot. In any formal set-up, e.g. news presentation, it is essential to avoid an in-shot shadow of the artiste on the background – it will be a distraction for the viewer. If, however, it is unavoidable, the shadow can be made less of a distraction by

(a)

(b)

Figure 4.74 Modelling and texture: (a) large angle between camera and light source; (b) small angle between camera and light source.

Figure 4.75 Excessive vertical keying angle.

Figure 4.76 Illustration of lack of catchlights.

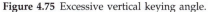

(a)

(b)

Figure 4.77 Use of diffusion.

using diffusion on the keylight to 'soften' the shadow. (See Fig. 4.77.)

- Any light source below the artiste's eyeline will result in underlighting, an unnatural way to light people, especially if taken to extreme angles (Fig. 4.78). This is a technique usually used for 'horror' lighting; or with less extreme angles together with a 'flicker' pole to create a fire-flicker effect (see Section 4.14.4).
- An 'open and honest' look is achieved with minimum shadows on the face. However, it will look very flat if the light is literally just above the camera lens. This will be too blinding for the artiste, who will be unable to read on teleprompter, and the light would be all over the background. A typical newsreader set-up would be to use a keylight with an elevation of about 25° and offset about 15° from the camera axis. (See Fig. 4.79.)

- For dramatic lighting, it can be useful to join the nose shadow to the cheek shadow to produce a triangle of light on the shadow side of the face. This is often referred to as **Rembrandt** lighting, after the famous painter, who incorporated this lighting feature in many of his portraits. (See Fig. 4.80.)

Note that very few faces are truly symmetrical and often actors will talk about their 'better side'. This is perfectly true – they may look better if lit from one side. A simple test with two lamps set up symmetrically to the camera will help to identify the 'better side'. (See Fig. 4.81.)

Switching between lamp A and lamp B will show if one side produces the better portraiture. Often one does not have to analyse the picture – the differences are obvious. The features which affect the portraiture, or portrayal of likeness, include:

Figure 4.78 Under-lit subject.

Figure 4.79 Typical keylight position.

(a)

(b)

Figure 4.80 Rembrandt lighting.

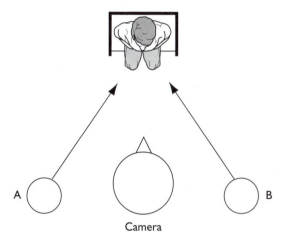

Figure 4.81 Portraiture test.

- shape of the face – round, oval, egg-shaped;
- shape of the jawline – square or rounded;
- asymmetry of the face about the centre-line. The modelling will make the shadowed side of the face appear to be narrower. Clearly one needs to avoid making the naturally narrow side even narrower;
- line of the eyes;
- line of the mouth;
- bent nose – if the subject is keyed the same way as the bend of the nose this will exaggerate the nose bend. If keyed in the opposite direction it will tend to straighten out the bend;
- hair line – this may be higher on one side, so if keyed from that side will tend to make the face look longer than if keyed on the opposite side;
- Sticking out ears – try to avoid lighting the ear which stands out the most;

- scars, bumps, etc. – the principle here is to avoid revealing texture in the area of the blemish, i.e. 'key' into the blemish.

Watch out for deep-set eyes or artistes who use their eyebrows to shade the light from their eyes.

Reading a teleprompter is not the easiest of jobs when you have a Fresnel spotlight close to the camera lens. It used to be said, 'If it doesn't hurt it isn't right!' With the high sensitivity of current cameras this does not have to be so. To make it easier for the artiste:

- Use half white diffusion on the keylight, which will reduce the glare from it. The light will no longer be a dazzling point source but a large area source. The barndoors no longer work, so there may be a need to use a flag to keep the light off the background. Note that a small area of diffusion will not transform the lighting into a softly-lit scene like on an overcast day! The modelling from, say, a 0.25 m × 0.25 m light source will still look crisp, but you will have made the presenter's life more bearable.
- Light the area behind the camera so that the artiste is not looking into a single point source against an area of black.

So much for our discussion on keylights. We have now identified the best place for the keylight for:

- an 'open and honest' look, i.e. not dramatic;
- best portrayal of likeness – avoiding blemishes etc.;
- avoidance of artiste shadow, in shot;
- catchlight in the eyes;
- minimum dazzle of presenter.

Figure 4.82 Background shading.

Use the barndoors, plus flag if required, to keep the light off the background, or at least shade the keylight to the top of the presenter's head to give a shaded background (Fig. 4.82).

In the foregoing discussion, the placing of the keylight has been with reference to a single camera position. The portraiture will have been designed to have been viewed by one camera. Obviously, if a second camera views the same artiste, and same eyeline, it will see a different portrayal of the scene (Fig. 4.83).

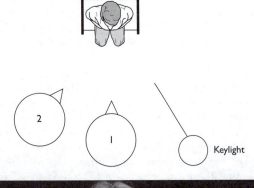

Figure 4.83 Multicamera shooting.
Multicamera shooting using camera 2.

Figure 4.84 Multicamera shot, change of eyeline to camera 2.

Similarly, if the artiste turns to look at camera 2, the portraiture will be different (Fig. 4.84). This illustrates a basic problem when shooting multicamera, namely the possible need to compromise on the lighting to satisfy the portraiture requirements of several cameras.

Having revealed the shape of the subject, however, the shadows will be too dark, too contrasty for a newsreader application. There is a need to **fill in** the shadows with an additional light – the fill-light.

4.7.2 The fill-light or filler

The role of the fill-light or filler is to add light in order to reduce the density of the shadow areas, i.e. make the shadows transparent. Ideally, the fill-light should not introduce modelling or result in a second shadow being created, so it needs to be a soft source. Note that often this light is simply referred to as a **fill**.

Placement of the fill-light
This needs to be placed in a position where it will do the most good in reducing shadow contrast. Normally it is placed on the opposite side of the camera to the keylight, at a low elevation so that all the shadows are filled.

Placed in position A (Fig. 4.85) it will satisfy the needs of the camera. However, it suffers from several drawbacks, namely:

- It lights the key side of the face and the shadow side; consequently it is not possible to 'balance' the key and fill-lights independently.
- If the camera is required to crab left a little to improve a shot, the key and fill are on the same side of the camera.
- It can give rise to a 'muddy' shadow of the presenter on the background.

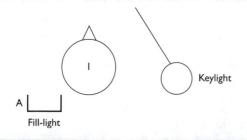

Figure 4.85 Basic fill-light position.

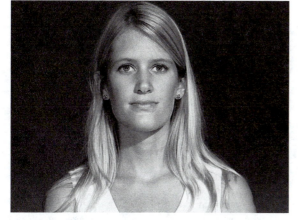

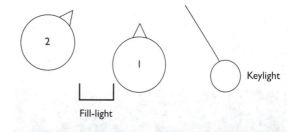

Figure 4.86 Multicamera shooting.

- It does not satisfy the needs of a second camera taking a semi-profile shot (Fig. 4.86).

The latter point can be addressed by adding a second fill-light at 90° to the camera axis. A compromise balance can be set up which satisfies both cameras (Fig. 4.87).

An alternative is to place the fill-light opposite the shadow areas, that is about 90° away from the keylight.

Provided the source used is of a large enough area, i.e. soft enough, it should not create a second nose shadow. It should also satisfy the needs of

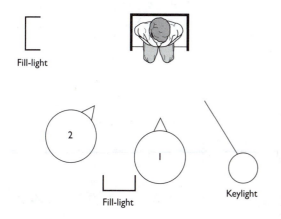

Figure 4.87 Multicamera shooting with additional fill-light.

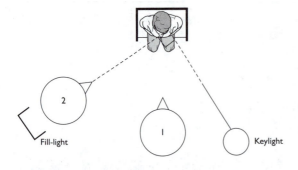

Figure 4.88 Multicamera shooting with compromise fill-light.

multicamera shooting and also allows for individual balance of the fill-light to the keylight.

Note: The addition of the fill-light will reduce the texture revealed as well as reducing the tonal contrast.

The low elevation requirement for fill-lights (when they have to be rigged at a high level) is often met by moving the luminaire away from the acting area. To restore the 'softness' or apparent area of light source several softlights are grouped together.

On occasions, when tight control of the filled area is required, e.g. low key drama scenes or variety shows using coloured cycloramas, a hard fill is usually used (Fresnel spotlights or profile spotlight).

The result of adding the fill-light to the keylight provides the appropriate filling of shadows to give pictures which are not over-dramatic or with washed-out shadows. Typically, for a newscaster one is aiming at a 1:2 or 1:1.5 contrast ratio between key and shadow areas on the face.

There is, however, still a need to separate the artiste from the background and provide some 'life' to the hair. When viewed from the camera position the artiste's hair will look rather dull and lack life; however, when viewed from upstage (behind the

artiste) it will sparkle. Each strand of hair acts like a direct reflector so most of the light hitting the hair is reflected upstage!

4.7.3 The backlight

The backlight, normally a hard source of light, is used to light the artiste from upstage to provide:

* separation of the artiste from the background by providing a rim of light around the artiste;
* depth to the head;
* roundness to the shoulders and arms;
* life to the hair.

A single backlight is normally used so that it is backlight with reference to the camera, not the artiste's back. In the case of a newsreader this will, of course, be one and the same.

* Because of its dramatic effect in providing separation, great care needs to be exercised to ensure that it is not too bright.
* The backlight is excellent as a glamorizing light for female artistes, in the right circumstances. A single backlight aimed at the 'hair parting' can be very effective for females. Beware of excess backlight on male presenters!
* The optimum position for a backlight is usually just above the scenery (Fig. 4.89). Rigged as shown it can light into the set.

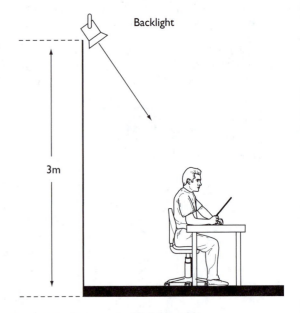

Figure 4.89 Optimum backlight position.

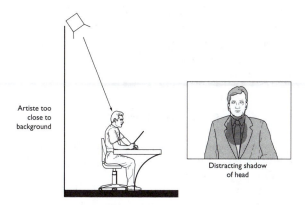

Figure 4.90 Backlight too steep.

* Typical backlight elevation angles are 45–60°. If too shallow it will create problems of camera flare. If too steep it will create a distracting shadow of the artiste's head on the front of the artiste.
* Although the backlight is normally a hard source, there are occasions when a softlight is used – see later discussions on demonstrations (Section 4.10) and chroma key (Section 4.12).
* Two backlights, separated by about 50–60°, can be particularly useful for long-haired artistes, chroma key set-ups and newsreaders. Apart from providing a greater feeling of roundness to the subject the two off-set backlights avoid the newsreader having a single heavy shadow all over the script.

The lighting 'plot' evolved above of keylight, fill-light and backlight is known as **three-point lighting**. It

forms the basis for lighting artistes for most television applications.

4.7.4 The background light

A fourth light is the background or scenery light. This has the basic function of:

* revealing the nature of the background, background shape and texture;
* adding depth to the picture by separating the artiste from the background;
* revealing the shape of the artiste by silhouetting.

The background light is normally a hard source, e.g. Fresnel spotlight, which can be focused and barndoored to light the appropriate area of the background. (Usually the barndoors are used to darken off the top of the set to create the feeling of an out-of-shot ceiling.) A softlight would tend to light the top of the set more than the bottom part. This is the reverse of what is needed.

Plain backgrounds can benefit from the addition of coloured light, shafts of light, or simple gobo patterns using profile projectors.

Backgrounds which include drapes should be side lit to reveal the texture, i.e. the folds of the drapes.

With single presenters it is recommended to position the subject at least 1.5 metres from the backing:

* to ensure no distracting 'in shot' shadow of the artiste on the background;

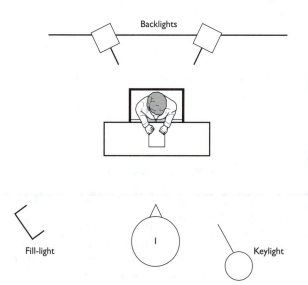

Figure 4.91 Typical newsreader plot.

Figure 4.92 Background lighting.

- to enable the background to be lit separately;
- to ensure that the backlight is not too steep.

4.7.5 The kicker light

No discussion on portraiture would be complete without mention of the **kicker** light or just simply 'kicker'. The kicker is an extra modelling light which is used from upstage of the artiste to 'kick' the side of the artiste's head. It should be rigged at head height and aimed towards the temple of the subject (Fig. 4.93).

It can be a hard or soft source and is positioned to 'kick', i.e. cause a **glare** reflection which models the shape of the face and reveals texture.

When it is motivated, the kicker is an extremely useful light to use:

Figure 4.93 Kicker light.

- reinforcing the direction of sunlight when used on the same side as the keylight;
- reinforcing the multi-light aspect of night-time lighting when used on the opposite side to the keylight.

4.7.6 Lighting the offset presenter

When a presenter is offset in the television frame to allow for the inclusion of, say, a 'window' or logo, the lighting of the presenter tends to look more correct if they are lit from within the picture (Fig. 4.94). Lit this way the lighting looks part of the picture; lit from camera left creates the illusion of a light source 'outside' the picture, plus it creates the possibility of an in-shot shadow of the artiste.

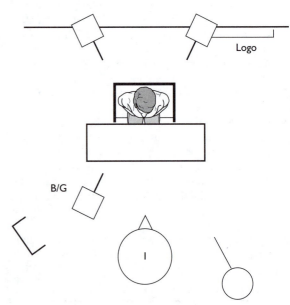

B/G = Background light, angled to create shadows of logo running out of the picture

Figure 4.94 Lighting the off-set presenter.

4.7.7 Single-camera and multicamera operations

The discussions so far have concentrated on lighting for a single-camera position. This has made the lighting straightforward, in that only the portraiture needs for one camera have to be satisfied. This has given an element of freedom in positioning lights, especially if on location and working with lighting stands.

As soon as two cameras are involved there usually is an element of compromise to satisfy the portraiture needs of both cameras. This could, for example, be where the second camera takes a semi-profile shot, ideally shooting the modelled side of the face; the modelling (shadows) may be satisfactory when viewed on camera 1, but on camera 2 they may be too heavy (Fig. 4.86). This point has been discussed earlier when looking at the position of the fill-light.

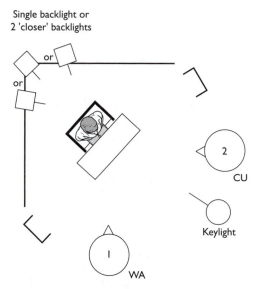

Figure 4.95 Multicamera shooting plus change in eyeline.

A second camera may, in fact, be used to take a second eyeline. If in Fig. 4.95 it is required to cut from camera 1 (wide angle, WA) to camera 2 (Close Up, CU), it would be impractical to make a lighting change at the instant of the cut in order to make the portraiture 'ideal' on both cameras, so a compromise has to be made. On the basis that the 'tighter' one shoots the artiste the more important the portraiture becomes, one tends to 'favour' the close-up shots. On a documentary-type programme there is usually no need to preserve an inferred lighting direction so the change of keying angle, camera right to camera left, should not be a problem.

If, of course, the action is not continuous between camera 1 and camera 2, e.g. a videotape insert between the two shots, then one could have two separate lighting plots to maximize the portraiture for each camera.

To determine the position of the fill-light, identify where the shadows will be for each eyeline. This will indicate the best position for the fill-light.

In this example, it is probably best to use only one backlight on the basis that two separate backlights, one for each camera position, would probably hit the artiste's nose when the artiste turns towards the backlight.

Generally, highlights on noses are to be avoided – they draw attention to the nose, and any object brightly lit looks larger than the same object dimly lit! (See Fig. 4.96.)

Figure 4.96 Optical illusion of brighter objects appearing larger.

The background in the simple set of Fig. 4.97 can be lit with two Fresnel spotlights. Positioned as shown they will reveal texture on the set which will be seen on camera; shadows on the background will be filled with the downstage full-lights. The only problem with this is the uneven lighting of the set due to the difference in lamp throw – to overcome this a **half-wire** or **half-scrim** can be used.

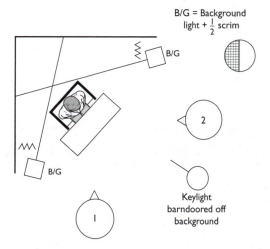

Figure 4.97 Illustrating the lighting of the background.

4.8 Studio lighting

In developing the basic lighting plots we have enjoyed total freedom in luminaire placement, i.e. no restrictions on where luminaires may be rigged. This, of course, is an ideal situation that rarely happens in practice. The planning of any lighting plot requires recognition of the studio 'mechanics', that is the method for suspending the luminaires and the **flexibility** offered by the suspension system. Total flexibility means, to a lighting director, the ability to plot a luminaire anywhere in the studio and to be able to rig it at any height. To a manager, flexibility means the ability to have a fast turn-around time between productions and to achieve a fast turn-around time for any set changes within a production. These two viewpoints of flexibility may sometimes be in conflict, but usually a compromise is adopted which satisfies the particular needs of a studio.

4.8.1 Lighting suspension systems – the lighting grid

Lighting suspension systems, often referred to as the **lighting grid**, have been developed to provide varying degrees of flexibility.

In order of cost, most expensive first, they are:

- *powered tracks with remotely operated telescopes and luminaires (ICARUS);
- *slotted grid with telescopes;
- motorized hoists with lighting bars or barrels;
- self-climbing motorized hoists with lighting tracks or bars;
- trackable self-climbing hoists;
- flying grids;
- *motorized telescopes on pantographs or steel bars;
- track and beam systems;
- *rolling pantographs on steel bars;
- lightweight track and beam systems;
- simple pipe grid.

Those systems marked with an asterisk are known as point-suspension systems, which offer individual height adjustments; the other systems provide a multipoint suspension system which requires additional pantographs or drop arms to achieve any required height differential.

The choice of suspension system will depend on:

- studio area;
- available studio height;
- type of productions;
- turn-around required between productions;
- budget.

Typical uses are indicated in Table 4.13.

The desirable operational features for a lighting grid can be summarized as:

- good turn-around time between productions and any set changes during a production;
- flexibility in positioning lamp, in plan view and in height;
- allowing a permanent arrangement for cyclorama lighting, with ease of lamp change and filter change;
- safe working load (SWL) which does not place unnecessary restrictions in using the grid. This is particularly important with some moving lights, each weighing in excess of 40 kg;
- easy powering of luminaire. Ideally this should be a hard-wired system from the dimmer to the lighting power outlet, easily identified from the studio floor. Patching systems are not user-friendly from an operational viewpoint;
- ease of positioning a luminaire and any repositioning which may be required;
- ease of lighting operations, above a set, e.g.
  - change a lamp
  - change a colour filter

Table 4.13 Lighting suspension by studio area.

System	Small studio <150 m²	Medium studio 150–350 m²	Large studio >350 m²
Barrel system (i) conventional hoist			•
(ii) self-climbing hoist		•	•
(iii) trackable self-climbing hoist		•	•
Slotted grid with telescopes		•	•
Movable beams with telescopes/pantographs		•	•
Powered tracks with telescopes or pantographs	•	•	•
Flying grids	•	•	•
Track and beam system (i) swivelling beams	•	•	
(ii) orthogonal beams	•	•	
Rolling pantographs on steel bars	•		
Fixed pipe grid	•		

– add an extra luminaire
– add a flag or cutter.
- ease of rigging
  – can the suspended lighting plot be rigged over an existing set, or is a completely clear studio required?
  – can rigging work be carried out whilst the scenery is being set below?
- minimum of staff required to operate the lighting system, speedily and safely.

Other factors influencing the choice of system at the time of installation include:

- height loss introduced by the rigging system;
- weight of grid plus luminaires to be imposed on building structure;
- ease of maintenance;
- cost;
- system which best satisfies the studio's needs.

4.8.2 Point suspension systems

Slotted grid with telescopes
This system is based on a structure of slotted grids or tracks, typically 0.6 m apart, which span the studio. The suspension unit, which can be pushed along the slot, is in the form of a **telescope** or **monopole**. Transverse slots or tracks are usually provided to allow the transfer of telescopes between tracks. The telescopes may be manually operated or motorized. This form of lighting grid requires at least 2 m of space above the slotted grids/tracks to enable the electricians to move around. The power lead to the telescope is 'patched' to an appropriate outlet in the 'grid', i.e. no hard-wiring, consequently great care is needed in ensuring that the lighting plot is correctly labelled and kept up to date.

This is generally regarded as the most flexible system for a lighting director but, unfortunately, is the most expensive to install.

Powered tracks with remotely operated telescopes and luminaires (ICARUS)
This uses heavy duty tracks with integral power rails and a system of brushes to make a sliding contact on the rails. Consequently, the telescope and luminaire are always connected to the power supply. The telescope unit is motorized in the vertical direction and in the horizontal direction; similarly, the luminaire has motorized pan/tilt, spot/flood and individual barndoor operation. The complete system is computer-controlled to give rapid turn-around time

(a)

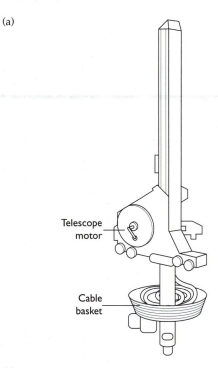

Telescope motor

Cable basket

(b)

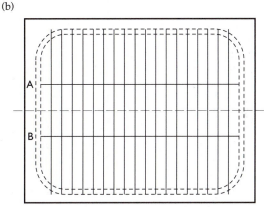

A + B transverse slots

Figure 4.98 (a) Telescope; (b) slotted grid layout (250 m² studio).

and rapid repositioning of luminaires. Ideally, it should be rigged with dual source luminaires. It does not have transverse slots, so luminaire movement is limited to its own particular track. The ICARUS system does not require space above the powered tracks but, of course, the retracted or collapsed telescope will occupy some studio space. When 'specials' are required, e.g. profile projectors, they need to be rigged in the normal way. Usually a

Table 4.14 Comparison of suspension systems.

Feature	Telescopes	Hoists	Flying grid	Lightweight track and beams	Rolling pantos on bars	Pipe grid	Tracks and beams and telescopes/pantos	Motorized telescopes/pantos on tracks
Turn-around time	•••	•••••	•••••	••	••	•	•••	•••
Accurate position of luminaires (without pantographs)	•••••	••••	•••••	•••	•••	•••	•••	••••
Permanent cyc lighting	••••	••••	••••	•••	•••		•••	••••
Ease of changing filters on cyc	••••	••••	••••	•••	•••	•	••••	••••
Weight of total lighting grid	••••	•••	•••	•••	••	•••	•••	••••
Ease of adding extra fixture	••••	•••	•••	•••	•••	•	•••	••••
SWL	•	•••	•••••	•••	•••	••	•••	•••
Hard-wired power?	No	Yes	Yes	Yes	Yes	No	Yes	Yes
Height required for lighting grid	2 m	1.2 m	1.2 m	3 m	.5 m	2 m	1.2 m	1.2 m
Maintenance	••	•••	•••	••	••	•	•••	•••
Speed adjustment of luminaire position	••••	•••	•••	••	•••	••	••	•••
Rigging – clear studio	No	Yes	Yes	Yes	Yes	Yes	Yes	Yes
Expense	$$$$	$$$$	$$$	$$	$$	$	$$$	$$$$

Excellent •••••; Very good ••••; Good •••; Average ••; Poor •

separate system is integrated with the ICARUS system for cyclorama lighting. The major drawback is the cost for this system.

Motorized telescopes or pantographs on steel bars
This is similar to the ICARUS system above, except that the luminaires are not remotely controlled. The raising and lowering of the telescopic units or pantographs is motorized, as are the transverse movements.

Track and beam system (heavy duty)
This uses a system of fixed tracks, typically 3 metres apart, with movable beams sliding along the tracks. Each beam has 2–3 motorized telescopes or motorized pantographs. With the adjustment of height possible for each luminaire, this offers greater flexibility than the self-climbing hoists. However, the number of luminaires/beam is limited by the number of telescopes/pantographs available.

Rolling pantographs on steel bars
Usually used in smaller studios, this system employs pantographs which can be moved manually along steel bars. The pantographs may be wire-wound, manually operated or employing a simple motor for raising and lowering. The pantograph lighting outlet is usually fed via a catenary system to allow the power cable to 'follow' the pantograph (Fig. 4.99).

4.8.3 Multi-point suspension

Motorized hoists
This system uses a motor to raise and lower a **lighting bar** or **barrel** typically 2–3 metres long, on which the luminaires are rigged.

The lighting barrel may be a 48.3 mm diameter steel bar or a simple lighting track. Ideally, the barrel should have braked luminaire trolleys (3–4) as appropriate, to enable easy positioning/repositioning of the luminaires.

The motorized hoist may be one of several types:

- Conventional hoist, original BBC type, where the hoist motor is located above the studio in the lighting 'grid'. This requires a 2 m space above the studio for a 'walk-on' grid.
- Self-climbing hoist, developed to satisfy the needs of studios with low ceilings. The hoist motor is located above the lighting bar, and travels with the lighting bar.
- Trackable self-climbing hoists in which the hoist is suspended from a trackable beam. This typically offers movement of the hoist ±1.5 metres in the lateral direction, i.e. hoists may be repositioned to suit the scenery layout.

Power to the lighting barrel is via folding trays (Fig. 4.100).

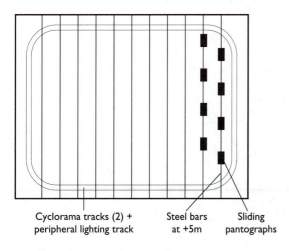

Figure 4.99 Steel bars with sliding pantographs (100 m² studio).

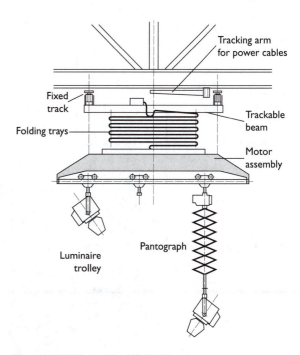

Figure 4.100 Trackable self-climbing hoists.

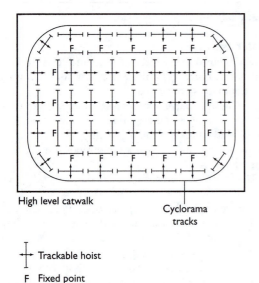

High level catwalk

Cyclorama tracks

┼ Trackable hoist

F Fixed point

Figure 4.101 Typical hoist layout using trackable self-climbing hoists (400 m² studio).

Typical hoist spacing is about 1.4 m between hoists and 0.3–0.5 m between the ends of barrels.

An important aspect of this system, and any other suspension system, is clear labelling of the hoist number and lighting power outlets so that they can be read easily from the studio floor.

Height differences for luminaires on the same hoist may be achieved with mini-pantographs, variable or fixed length drop-arms.

Hoists may also include feeds of DMX, non-dimmed mains supply plus video and audio tie-lines.

Flying grids

This system uses a number of miniature 'grids', typically 3 m × 3 m, to provide a comprehensive suspension facility at a cheaper cost than using self-climbing hoists. Flying grids normally use a self-climbing principle, i.e. motor on the grid. Each flying grid has three movable cross-bars each having 2–3 luminaire trolleys. Height differences for luminaires on the same grid are achieved in the same way as with hoists.

Lightweight track and beam systems

These are common in smaller studios and fall into two basic types:

- tracks with orthogonally sliding beams (at 90°) which fit within the tracks (Fig 4.103(a));
- tracks with swivelling sliding rails which extend beyond the tracks (Fig 4.103(b)).

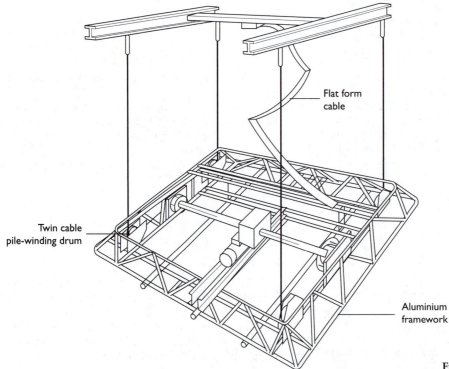

Flat form cable

Twin cable pile-winding drum

Aluminium framework

Figure 4.102 Basic flying grid.

a)

b)

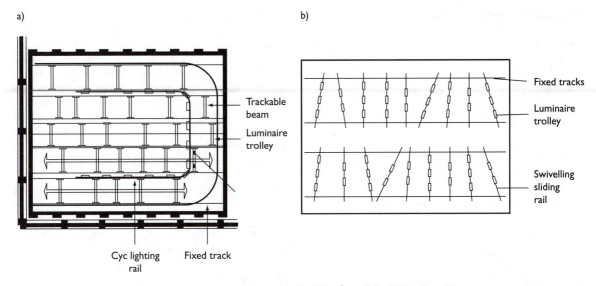

Figure 4.103 (a) Track and beam system using orthogonal rails (200 m² studio); (b) Track and beam system using swivelling rails (100 m² studio).

Each sliding beam or sliding rail will have 2–3 luminaire trolleys. Height differentials can be established using mini-pantographs, adjustable or fixed length drop-arms.

Although the sliding beam system is more robust, both systems have their merits. Both allow the easy addition of extra beams or rails and luminaire trolleys at a later date.

Fixed pipe grid

This is a very common form of lighting grid in smaller studios, consisting of a 'matrix' of 48.3 mm aluminium or steel bars at 1 m spacing. When supplemented with short bars, 1.8 m long, and swivel clamps this becomes a very flexible grid – the luminaires may be placed anywhere! Height differential requires the use of mini-pantographs, adjustable or fixed length drop-arms (Fig 4.104).

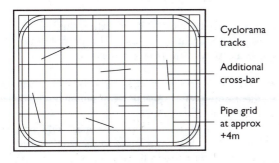

Figure 4.104 Fixed pipe grid (100 m² studio).

All rigging has to be done from step ladders, and consequently this grid does not offer a fast turn-around time.

A variation on this principle would be to use bars installed across the width of the studio at 0.5 m spacing. This usually avoids the need for cross barrels, but does require more grid 'hangers'.

4.8.4 Safety

The safe working load of any suspension system must be clearly displayed on each element, and must be adhered to!

All new lifting equipment in studios should have double suspension cables, i.e. telescopes should have two independent cables and hoists should have four independent cables.

All motorized lifting equipment will have operational safety features:

- top and bottom limit trip;
- overload trip;
- slack wire trip (e.g. when hoist is lowered onto a set!).

All rigged equipment *must* be fitted with a safety bond, correctly used, to ensure that it cannot fall accidentally onto personnel below.

All electrical equipment must be fitted with a correctly connected 3-pin plug, with all metalwork connected to the earth connection.

4.8.5 Lighting plots and symbols

The **lighting plot**, drawn to a 1:50 scale, is an essential part of the lighting process. It is a communication document for everyone in the lighting team, indicating:

- type of luminaire, its position and aiming direction;
- colour filters, usually shown by a colour 'key' plus the colour reference number (swatch number);
- any flags, cutters, half-wires, etc.;
- floor luminaires;
- practical lamps, e.g. wall lights, table stands.

On a large production, the lighting director may produce separate plots for suspended rig, floor rig, colour filters and practicals, to ensure that there is no ambiguity of instruction and make it easier for the electricians to spot the elusive practicals on a complicated plot.

Unfortunately, unlike theatre lighting, there is no international agreed set of symbols for use in television lighting. Many television companies have evolved their own set, the main criteria being that the symbols should be easily recognizable with no ambiguity possible – for example, avoiding three different diameters of circle to represent 1 kW, 2 kW and 5 kW Fresnel spotlights. It is a better scheme to use different shapes where possible, unless there is a significant difference in size of similar shapes. The BBC, for example, has adopted such a scheme (Fig 4.105).

At one time the symbols were to scale – the luminaire symbol occupied the same space on the lighting barrel plot as in the studio. This is a very useful idea, as when the barrel is plotted full of luminaire symbols it means that the lighting barrel is also full. With the compact versions of luminaires available, however, it means that this concept may not always be feasible, unless a different symbol is used for the compact luminaires.

It is paramount that any changes to the lighting rig are immediately indicated on the lighting plot – it must be kept up to date!

4.8.6 Rigging luminaires

Unless the studio has a lighting suspension system which allows the luminaires to be rigged above a set (telescope system), the normal practice would be to rig the luminaires in an empty studio, i.e.:

- drop in lighting hoists to floor level (+1.2 m);
- rig luminaires as required, pointing in the right direction, setting spot/flood to flood condition;
- add colour filters, flags, cutters, half-wires (scrims);
- check that all luminaires work, including both filaments on a dual filament lamp;
- raise all lighting hoists, usually to maximum height.

The scenery is then rigged in the studio as a basic set or sets.

4.8.7 Setting luminaires

The set/light time involves adjusting the lighting rig to satisfy the lighting needs of the programme. The following procedure is recommended:

- Give an overview of the production and the rig, mentioning any special requirements which are needed, to the electrician.
- Lower in all hoists (or telescopes) which have luminaires on them relative to the production.
- Set each luminaire individually, only switching on at fader 7 the luminaire you are setting. Ideally,

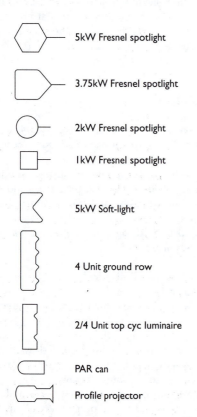

Figure 4.105 Examples of BBC symbols.

5kW Fresnel spotlight

3.75kW Fresnel spotlight

2kW Fresnel spotlight

1kW Fresnel spotlight

5kW Soft-light

4 Unit ground row

2/4 Unit top cyc luminaire

PAR can

Profile projector

stand at the artiste position and view the luminaire through a suitable viewing filter (ND 2.0 viewing filter). A viewing filter is invaluable when setting luminaires. It enables accurate setting without flare in eye and prevents 'after-images' of the light source interfering with your vision, such as your ability to read a lighting plot after looking into a luminaire.

Fig. 4.106(a) shows the appearance of a centred luminaire viewed from the artiste's position. Figs 4.106(b) and (c) illustrate the luminaire incorrectly set.

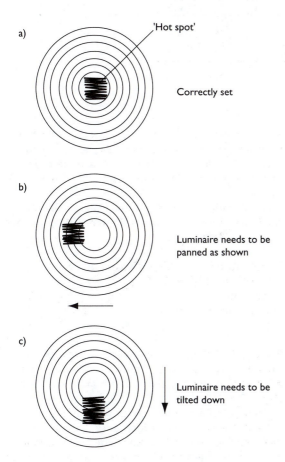

Figure 4.106 Setting a fully flooded Fresnel spotlight.

It is useful to adopt a definite procedure when setting luminaires – say, start upstage and work downstage or the reverse. For each Fresnel spotlight:

• Check that the height is correct.
• Rotate barndoors to the configuration you think you require. This avoids the disturbance of a 'set' luminaire if you leave this to last. Many barndoors

develop a reluctance to rotate smoothly, requiring some additional force which often displaces the luminaire setting!
• Open barndoors so that you can see the hot spot.
• Adjust pan/tilt as necessary to 'set' the luminaire. It is useful to check that the illuminance is satisfactory for keylights.
• Adjust barndoors as necessary.
• Avoid trying to set a luminaire while others are on.
• When all the luminaires are set, have a look at each lighting condition.
• Check illuminance and make up basic memories.
• Finally set the line-up lamp.

Incidentally, it is often difficult to judge the height of a luminaire in 'free space', i.e. not set adjacent to scenery (normal scenery height is 3 m); check the length of the electricians' operating poles or lighting sticks and use them to help judge the luminaire height.

4.8.8 Plotting

Having discussed the principles of portraiture and the hardware, we need to see how a lighting plot may be completed, taking into account the particular studio facilities. The questions to be answered are 'what lamp to use, and where to place it?' It is useful to adopt a strategy when plotting to ensure that nothing gets overlooked:

• If a cyclorama is included, plot the luminaires to light this, plus ground row if required.
• Consider the lighting of each artiste position, plotting keylights first, then fill-lights, then backlights.
• Consider the lighting of each part of the set; plot appropriate luminaires.
• Add a line-up luminaire. Ideally this should be plotted in a downstage area so that cameras can be put on a line-up chart away from any activities within the set.

As a general principle, one should aim to use as long a luminaire throw as is practical. This will obviously give a wide coverage of uniform illumination (luminaire in full flood mode), but will minimize to some extent the effects of the inverse square law if the artiste should move towards the luminaire. For example, if an artiste were lit at a 2 metre luminaire throw and moved towards the luminaire by say 0.5 m, the illuminance would increase by 77%; however, if lit from 5 metres, the change in illuminance would only be 23%.

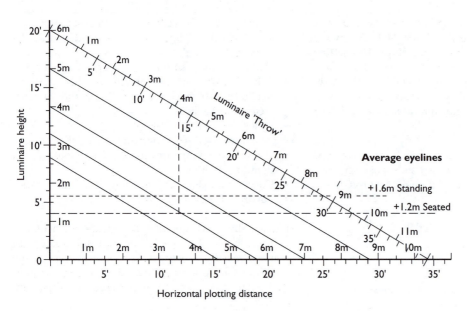

Figure 4.107 Luminaire plotting guide.

The only time we would consider placing the keylight closer than 'normal' would be where 'tight' barndooring is required. Having established a nominal vertical keying angle of about 25–30°, the maximum luminaire throw for any studio will be dictated by the maximum height of the lighting grid. In many small studios this may be as low as 3 m (or even lower!). Consequently, the luminaire throws will be much shorter than, say, in a studio with a 6 m high 'grid'.

Fig. 4.107 illustrates the typical vertical keying angles and plotting distances for a seated and a standing artiste.

The minimum height for luminaires should be well above head height, for obvious reasons. If luminaires are required to be below this level they are normally rigged on lighting stands: we are more aware of objects standing on the floor and growing upwards than objects hanging down from the ceiling – until we bump our head on them! In some very small studios, e.g. presentation studios, special arrangements may be made to operate with low luminaires.

So, from Fig. 4.107, we can establish the luminaire plotting distance and the actual luminaire throw. From this we can estimate the luminaire needed, for example:

Illuminance needed say	500 lux
Luminaire throw say	4.0 m

$$\text{Illuminance} = \frac{\text{candlepower}}{\text{distance}^2}$$

so

Candlepower = illuminance × distance²
= 500 × 4 × 4 = 8000 candelas

If this is required at fader 7 (50% light output) as a nominal setting, then the luminaire needs to provide 8000 × 2 = 16 000 candelas as full output. This is typical of many 1 kW Fresnel spotlights. (ARRI 1 kW = 18 000 candelas.)

Incidentally, it is useful to calculate maximum and minimum throws for each of the luminaires that you use in your studio, e.g.:

If the throw for fader 7 is	500 lux at 4 m
then at fader 10 it will provide	500 lux at 4 × √2 = 5.6 m
and at fader 5 it will provide	500 lux at 4/√2 = 2.8 m

These calculations are all based on the use of the inverse square law. From this can be seen a simple relationship between lamp throw and fader setting (Fig. 4.108).

What is the significance of these fader settings?

Recall the need to consider fader 7 as the nominal fader setting (at 2950 K) and fader 10 and fader 5 representing the upper and lower limits for colour temperature tolerance when dimming a tungsten source.

This may seem very theoretical. However, it is a useful procedure to adopt in any new studio or new application and will give you a ball-park figure. Remember, the only calculations that have to be done are for your particular 'hardware'. It is far better to be in the ball-park for illuminance, rather than struggle with too little illuminance or be embarrassed with excessive lighting levels (and unnecessary heat!).

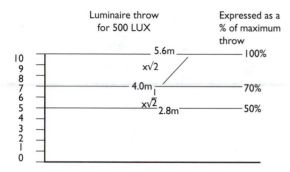

If maximum throw for a given illuminance is known it
is a simple calculation to find the 'throw' at any fader setting,
or vice versa

Figure 4.108 Fader setting and luminaire throw.

Incidentally, the luminaire manufacturers will
quote performance of their luminaires for a new
lamp, clean optics and full mains voltage. It is a good
idea to allow a 15–20% maintenance factor to take
account of the practical situation of ageing lamp, dirty
optics and possible reduced mains voltage!

4.9 Interview lighting

A common situation is that of the two-handed interview, referred to as a 'two-hander' or a '1 + 1'. This
is usually shot as a multicamera shoot in studios, and
single-camera on location. Lighting has to satisfy the
portraiture needs of a 2-shot (2S) on camera 2 and
over-the-shoulder 2-shot (O/S 2S) and single close-up
(CU) shots on cameras one and three.

Cameras one and three will normally try to get
close to the 'eyeline' of A and B to ensure that the
shots are not too profile.

If one assumes that there is no introduction to
camera from A or B, then the normal eyeline of the
participants will be shown, i.e. towards each other.
Clearly a single keylight, say over the top of camera

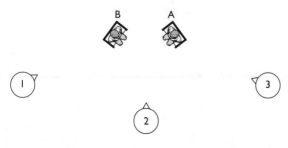

Figure 4.109 Basic staging for a 1 + 1 interview.

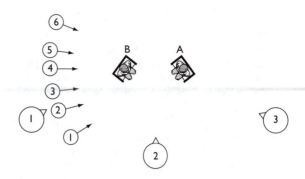

Figure 4.110 Keylight options for a 1 + 1 inteview.

2, will not suffice because its effect on A and B will
not be flattering. A and B require to be lit separately.

The position of the keylight for the artiste A could
be anywhere shown by the arrowed lines (Fig. 4.110).
However, it is worth just examining the consequences
of choosing particular positions:

(1) A keylight placed here provides an angle
between it and the camera, however, the modelling produced by it is mainly upstage and little
of it is seen by the camera. Where the artistes are
close to a background it will be difficult to isolate
the lighting to the subject without also lighting
the background, plus artiste's shadow. The
artiste's shadow would become a distraction as it
falls 'ahead' of the artiste in a mid-shot on
camera 1.
(2) This keylight position, over the top of the camera,
produces little modelling. Again, it is difficult to
keep the light off adjacent backgrounds – the
artiste's shadow will be directly behind them and
should therefore not be visible to camera.
(3) With a small angle between the keylight and
camera, there will be some modelling of the face,
but the nose shadow will still be on the upstage
side of the face. With care it may be possible to
keep the artiste's shadow out of shot. Note that
the artiste's shadow would appear 'behind' them
in any mid-shot on camera 1. It may be difficult
to barndoor this light off artiste B. If A is to make
links to camera this is, however, a good compromise for the keylight, especially if one wants to
use a 'flattering' light, i.e. little texture revealed,
compared with using lamp 5. Problems with
spectacles can also be reduced by using lamp
position 3.
(4) This keylight position establishes good modelling
for documentary interviews, and will also prove
satisfactory for artiste A doing a 'link' to camera
1. The main problem with this is the difficulty of
keeping a shadow of B off artiste A. The vertical

angle may have to be increased with consequent poor vertical keying angle for A, i.e. no light in the eyes. Physically separating the artistes could help, but in small studios this may not be possible – it would certainly alter the perspective and cause the artistes to appear to be far apart in 2-shots.

(5) If the keylight is placed slightly 'upstage' of the artistes, the modelling increases and the mutual shadowing problem is overcome. This is a good position for the keylight if a boom microphone is used for sound pick-up, because the boom shadow will be thrown downstage. Careful barndooring is needed to avoid lens flare on camera 3.

(6) This keylight will provide excessive modelling of the artiste, especially when the artiste turns downstage. However, although generally not suitable for documentary interviews it could be perfectly acceptable in a drama situation.

So, having established preferred keylight positions, we have a lighting plot.

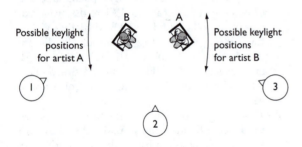

Figure 4.111 Basic key light positions for a 1 + 1 interview.

Note: When lighting a semi-profile shot the terms **narrow** and **broad** lighting are sometimes used. Lighting from upstage is known as narrow lighting when the modelling (shadows) is thrown downstage causing this side of the face to look narrower. Conversely, when lit from downstage the modelling is upstage; the downstage side of the face is seen with very little modelling and as a broad side of the face. Narrow lighting is more dramatic and more three-dimensional. Broad lighting is clearly less dramatic, but may be required to provide a more flattering lighting result, although less three-dimensional.

4.9.1 Filler

Depending on the size of the studio and set-up one could use a single filler light above camera 2. However, unless this is a large area source, it could

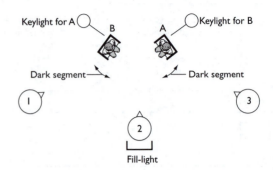

Figure 4.112 Single fill-light position for a 1 + 1 interview.

result in dark segments on the downstage shoulders of the artistes, i.e. A would be satisfactory on camera 1, but in the over-the-shoulder 2-shot on camera 3, would look too dark.

To overcome this problem, two fill-lights are used, each making a contribution to the 'fill' required on each artiste.

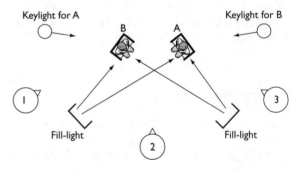

Figure 4.113 1 + 1 interview, keylights plus two fill-lights.

4.9.2 Backlight

The backlight should be with reference to the camera position. The upstage keylights already plotted are therefore ideally placed for backlight purposes.

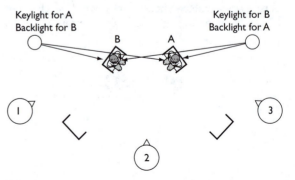

Figure 4.114 1 + 1 interview with combined keylights/backlights.

However, because of the shorter 'throw' to artiste B, the keylight for A will provide far too much backlight illumination on artiste B. This can be reduced by using bottom half-wires (Fig. 4.115). They may be doubled or overlapped as necessary to obtain the correct backlight illumination.

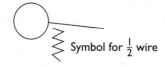

Symbol for $\frac{1}{2}$ wire

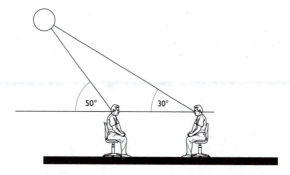

Figure 4.117 Combined keylight and backlight vertical angles.

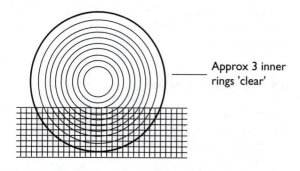

Approx 3 inner rings 'clear'

Figure 4.115 Bottom half-wire technique.

Note the need to keep the inner three rings of the Fresnel lens completely clear to ensure that the light may be accurately 'centred' on artiste A with no loss of illuminance.

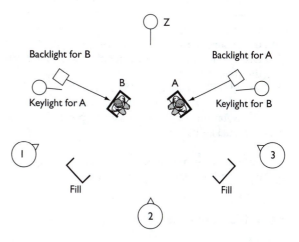

Figure 4.118 1 + 1 interview using separate keylights and fill-lights.

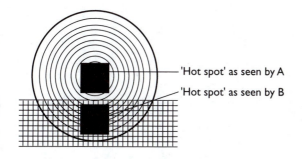

'Hot spot' as seen by A

'Hot spot' as seen by B

Figure 4.116 Correct setting of keylight/backlight.

Note also, for the half-wiring technique to work there must be a significant lighting angle difference between artiste A and artiste B (Fig. 4.117).

A better way, giving greater control of backlight and keylight illuminance, is to use separate keylights and backlights (Fig. 4.118).

Usually, the backlight need only be half the power of the keylight, while the filler light should be of similar power to the keylight.

Barndooring notes
(1) To enable effective barndooring, all spotlights should be fully flooded.
(2) Set keys and backlights onto A and B as appropriate.
(3) Note appearance of backlight on B from A's position (Fig. 4.119).

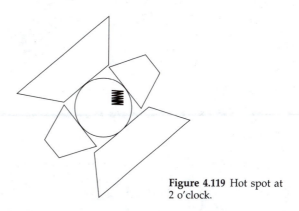

Figure 4.119 Hot spot at 2 o'clock.

(4) Rotate barndoors until the small door is at '2 o'clock'.
(5) Fold small door over hot-spot; box doors to give Fig. 4.120.

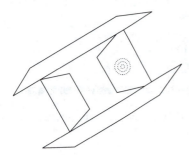

Figure 4.120
Barndooring detail.

(6) Use a similar procedure for the keylights.
(7) Don't forget to use the barndoor to keep light off the floor.
(8) Avoid a light-toned coffee table between the interviewer and interviewee. It may look excessively bright – it is the 'meeting point' for keys and backlights.

It is useful to add a central upstage backlight for opening/closing silhouette shots on camera 2.

4.9.3 1 + 2 interview

The technique developed above can be used to light more involved interviews, such as a 1 + 2 interview.

Two guidelines when plotting are:

• keep it simple;
• control.

In the above example, one keylight is suggested for artistes B and C. Remember the Fresnel spotlight has a wide, useful beam width of typically 45°, so two artistes can be covered easily with one luminaire. Note, however, that each interviewee has a separate backlight; this is to enable individual control of backlight levels. One backlight for both interviewees could create problems, e.g. with a brunette next to a blonde or bald-headed artiste. The filler light, again from downstage, can be lowered in to preserve a low elevation filler.

4.9.4 3-handed interview

Although a common interview, the 'deep' three-handed interview is not necessarily the best staging for coverage of an interviewer plus two interviewees (Fig. 4.122).

Artistes A and C can be lit in a similar way to a 2-handed interview, Artiste B with a frontal keylight X or an offset keylight Y. The compromise on lighting is when artiste B is shot on camera 1 or camera 3. When lit with keylight Y, shots of artiste B on cameras one and two will look satisfactory, but, on camera 3 (artiste looking well away from the keylight) the portraiture will not be so good. When lit with the

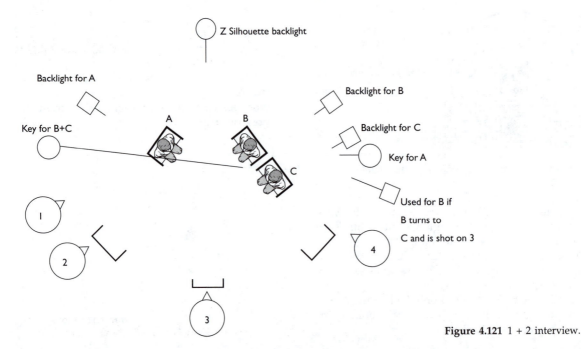

Figure 4.121 1 + 2 interview.

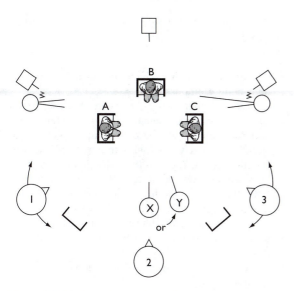

Figure 4.122 3-handed interview (deep arrangement).

frontal keylight X, camera 2 will be satisfactory (although, of course, frontally lit) and the shots on cameras one and three will be acceptable compromises.

The two side-lights on artiste B bring out the texture in artiste B, as well as providing upstage fill-light when looking to artistes A and C.

The major disadvantage of the above shooting arrangement is when artistes A and C look towards the interviewer (B). Cameras one and three can only provide one-eyed shots (profile shots) of artistes A and C.

A better shooting arrangement is that of the shallow three-handed interview (Fig. 4.123). This arrangement works much better for getting two-eyed shots of artistes A and C. The lighting of this set-up provides one of the most interesting problems in television lighting.

Most lighting problems may be analysed as lighting for news/documentary/demonstration/variety with the artiste facing downstage, or drama/interviews with the artistes facing across the 'stage'; in this problem we have a combination of both scenarios (Fig. 4.124).

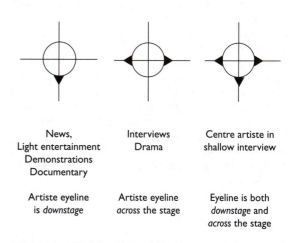

Figure 4.124 Basic eyelines.

As always, there are several possible solutions. However, as a starting philosophy it is worth remembering that for multi-way interviews the artistes need to be keyed from whichever direction they look. Artiste B is the compromise position for lighting. A compromise lighting plot is shown in Fig. 4.125.

This lighting plot works well for artiste B, shot on camera 1 or camera 3. Any close-up on camera 2, however, will not be good portraiture as the artiste is heavily cross-lit. The hard fill-light (Z) on artiste B

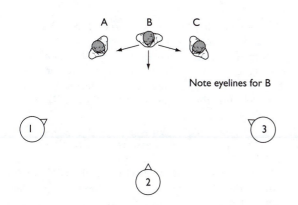

Figure 4.123 Staging of a 'shallow' 3-handed interview.

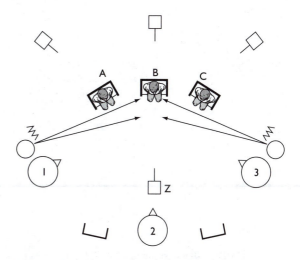

Figure 4.125 3-handed interview (shallow arrangement).

helps to reduce the effect of the cross-lights and provide a catchlight; it is recommended to keep shots of B, on camera 2, to mid-shots.

An alternative to this would be to fade up appropriate keys to follow the head-turns of artiste B. This could only be practical if it could be done 'out-of-vision' and with localized lighting of B, i.e. no spill light on artistes A and C.

The above technique can be extended to include 5 artistes, i.e. 2 + 1 + 2.

Note: The position of the fill-light in interview lighting is downstage of the action. This is especially useful in that the fill-light may be lowered-in to achieve a low elevation to the artistes, without fear of the luminaires being in shot. If the fill-lights are upstage, it will be difficult to achieve a low elevation. This principle is adopted for many similar applications, e.g. panel games, drama, variety shows.

4.10 Lighting demonstrations and pack shots

4.10.1 Demonstrations

The simplest demonstration is a single artiste to a camera, providing mid-shots and medium close-ups of the presenter, with a second camera providing the close-ups of the item(s) being demonstrated (Fig 4.126).

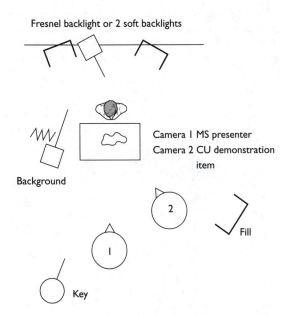

Figure 4.126 Basic demonstration, lighting for a single presenter.

The lighting plot for the demonstration is based on the need:

- to provide modelling (shape) for the artiste and the item being demonstrated;
- to avoid camera shadows from both cameras; camera 1 will probably have a teleprompter system and the camera will be craned up to get on the standing artiste's eyeline. Camera 2 will also be elevated to be able to look down on the items being demonstrated. Both of these situations pose potential camera shadow problems;
- to avoid strong shadows of the artiste from the backlight over the items being demonstrated;
- to avoid over-lighting the front of the demonstration table;
- to avoid flare, i.e. specular reflections off demonstration items.

Note:
(i) The lighting plot indicated above may not always work. Depending on the item being demonstrated, there may be a need to reverse the direction of the lighting, e.g. flat items of low reflectivity may need to be lit more frontally.
(ii) The use of a veil on the keylight is a more precise way of controlling the light on the front of the demonstration desk; it is better than using the bottom barndoor.
(iii) The use of soft backlight is especially useful to avoid hard forward going shadows from the backlight. Ideally, two soft backlights should be used, tipped well down to avoid camera flare. If there is not an effective eggcrate on the softlights, there may be a need to add a flag to these lights to avoid spill light on the upstage wall of the set.

The above basic plot can be extended to include two or more persons (Fig 4.127).

Note that, in the above situation, the need is to place the guest camera right so that he or she is 'favoured' by the lighting for their close-up, i.e. they turn *towards* the keylight when they talk to the presenter.

An alternative technique would be to use cross-lighting, if only two persons are involved (Fig. 4.128).

Note the use of side half-wires on the keylights to reduce the illuminance on the closer artiste. The bottom barndoors would need to be used to ensure that the table-top is not over-lit.

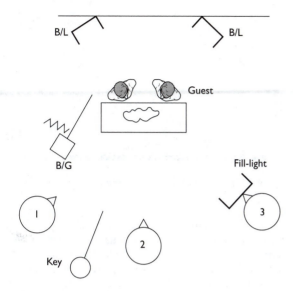

Figure 4.127 2-handed demonstration, basic plot.

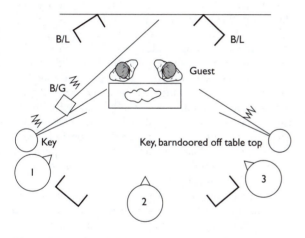

Figure 4.128 2-handed demonstration, cross-lit.

4.10.2 Pack shots

These are shots of 'packages' which exclude a presenter, e.g. a product or a prize, seen in isolation. The general principle, as always, is keep it simple. Try to avoid conflicting shadows. One of the basic 'plots' involves lighting a plate of food – often effective lighting can be achieved by using a soft keylight from upstage, offset to one side, and a complementary soft fill-light from downstage.

Pack shots may give rise to **glare** reflections of the light source. These can be controlled by using a polarizing filter on the camera. If direct reflections of the source cause problems, these can be controlled by

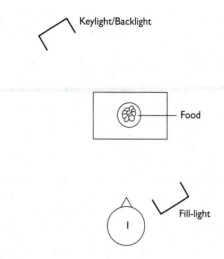

Figure 4.129 Basic lighting of food.

polarizing the light source as well as using a polarizer on the camera.

Glass and metal objects require special mention as subjects requiring careful treatment.

Lighting glass

Glass, being transparent, is difficult to light: most of the light is transmitted by the glass, a small amount is absorbed and a small amount is reflected. The light reflected will give rise to a specular reflection that may be a distraction. Two techniques have evolved for lighting glass:

- bright-field method;
- dark-field method.

The **bright-field method** relies on placing the glassware in front of an illuminated background with black drapes either side of it. The glass is unlit! The luminaire lighting the white background must be 'flagged' to ensure that no specular reflections are seen in the glass.

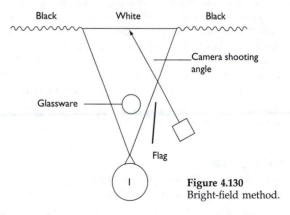

Figure 4.130
Bright-field method.

This reveals the glass as slightly 'smokey', due to less than 100% transmission of the glass, with dark edges to the glassware. The dark edges are the black drapes, refracted by the glass. Coloured filters over the background light can be used to great effect. Note, however, that if translucent liquid is introduced into the glass it will turn the glass/liquid into a lens with consequent reversal of background colour position. If extra shape is required, a reflection of a 'window' can be introduced on the glass by using a white reflector downstage with black tape 'glazing bars' and bouncing a suitable Fresnel spotlight. A similar technique of revealing the shape of, say, a wine bottle can be used; it also provides illuminance for the label.

The **dark-field method**, as its name suggests, is the reverse of the bright-field technique, i.e. the glass object is seen against a black background with out-of-shot white cyclorama either side of it. Fig. 4.131 illustrates this technique.

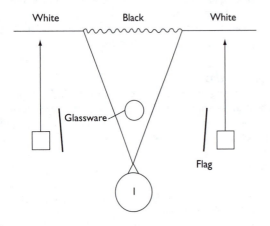

Figure 4.131 Dark-field method.

Again, care should be taken to ensure that no specular reflections of the light sources are visible on camera, unless specifically requested. This technique is especially useful for cut-glassware. The image seen on camera will be that of the glassware against black with the edges showing as highlights – the refracted images of the white drapes. Again, colour can be used to good effect, and downstage soft sources can be used to reveal engravings in the glassware.

If time permits, it is useful to experiment with a piece of glassware using either of the above techniques, or a combination of them.

Lighting metal

Lighting metal, in particular polished metal, usually requires the light source to be revealed (Fig. 4.132).

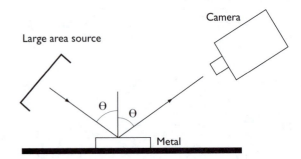

Figure 4.132 Basic technique for lighting metal.

Often, it is useful to add some 'texture' to the reflection by putting small flags or 'charlie bars' over the light source. Silver trophies are usually put in a 'tent' of diffusion which is lit from outside. The camera shoots through a small hole in the 'tent'.

This technique is extended for lighting a car. The usual brief is no 'speculars' – the car must look sleek and elegant! Observe a car, outdoors, on an overcast day, and the technique for lighting a car will be revealed! The convex curves of the car reflect the sky and at the same time produce a minified image. This results in a car with highlights (the reflected sky) on all the curves, which help to accentuate the 'lines' of the car. At the same time, of course, the car is lit with the skylight. In a studio, this can be realized with the car, against a cyclorama, with a large **butterfly** above. The butterfly fitted with silk or diffusion is lit from above, usually hard sources; but if a perfectly diffused light source (from the butterfly) is required, one could use softlights.

The cyclorama can be lit to provide appropriate illuminance of the car sides. If artistes are required to be lit, standing alongside the car, one can use a

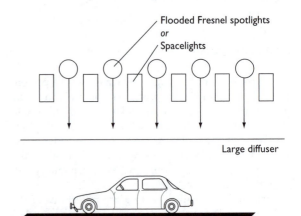

Figure 4.133 Lighting a car – basic technique.

Fresnel spotlight which has been well flagged off the car (to avoid specular reflections).

Lighting captions

This is often achieved with one light. However, to light a caption uniformly with no glare reflections requires two lights at an angle of 45° to the camera axis, and at camera height.

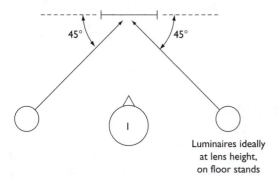

Figure 4.134 Lighting a caption.

Often, because of the need for speed, one light is used some distance from the caption, to reduce the shading in illuminance on the caption. Tilting the caption usually removes any 'glare' reflection.

4.11 Lighting for subject movement

The lighting techniques discussed so far have been for stationary artistes, either seated or standing. However, there is often a need to cover artistes on the move within a set, or walking between a number of sets. There may be occasions where it is quite natural for moving artistes to go in and out of lit areas, for example in drama at night, but many applications require the lighting levels to be maintained during an artiste's move. The main problem is the basic inverse square law, namely as an artiste moves towards a keylight, they will receive more illuminance. There are a number of techniques which may be applied to avoid noticeable illuminance changes:

- stop down the lens as the artiste gets more brightly lit;
- dim the keylight as the artiste walks towards it;
- use a spotted luminaire (see below);
- use a luminaire with a very long throw, so that the effects of the inverse square law are minimized, i.e. follow spot (see Section 4.13);

- avoid the artiste walking directly towards the keylight;
- use half-scrims or veils to even out the illuminance when walking towards a keylight;
- use two identical luminaires to cover the artiste's two acting areas and arrange a suitable 'crossover' or 'take-over' between the two luminaires;
- use the bounce technique to produce a 'graded' walk (see below).

Dimming the keylight is fine if the keylight can be localized to the artiste, i.e. not lighting scenery or other artistes seen in shot, provided it is not a noticeable change in colour temperature. It must not cause problems for the next shot, with the keylight dimmed.

Stopping down the iris is a better option (no change in colour temperature), but the same principles apply – the artiste must be seen in isolation.

A **spotted** luminaire can sometimes solve the problem, where the artiste starts in the beam centre and as he or she walks towards the luminaire they move progressively into the edge of the beam.

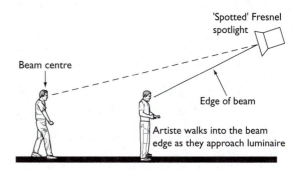

Figure 4.135 Subject movement – use of spotted luminaire.

An alternative to this, often used on location work, would be to start with a spotted lamp and progressively flood it as the artiste walked towards the luminaire. Again, the luminaire must be localized on the artiste.

The use of **half-scrims**, **half-wires**, **veils** or **yashmaks** is the common technique for helping to provide even coverage. These have been introduced during earlier discussions. The essential requirement for these to work is that there must be a significant change in the angle between the keylight and the artiste.

The half-scrim provides a very soft edge to the start of the reduction in illuminance because it is very close to the lens. Veils and yashmaks have to be positioned close to the lens if they also are to give a smooth reduction in illuminance. A small incident light

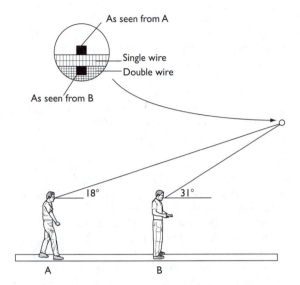

Figure 4.136 Subject movement – use of half-wires/scrims/yashmaks.

meter, e.g. Sekonic, is ideal for checking illuminance at position A and position B before deciding which scrim/veil to use (Fig. 4.136).

Where a large distance separates the two acting areas, and it is not practical to use one keylight, two keylights with a suitable changeover between them is the solution.

Before discussing this technique it is worth examining some salient points about barndooring:

- Barndoors are most effective when the luminaire is fully flooded.
- The barndoor produces the 'sharpest' cut of light when its edge is farthest from the lens.

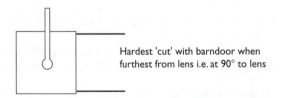

Figure 4.137 Barndooring 'sharpness'.

- The degree of barndooring 'sharpness' increases as you get nearer to the luminaire. This is a particularly important point when setting a crossover, and can be checked by putting a luminaire on a floor stand at head height. Set it to, say, 6 m and put the large barndoor vertical and at 90° to the lens. Observe how much you have to move your head from seeing all the hot spot to seeing none of

the hot spot – at 3 m it will probably be about 0.5 m, and at 6 m it will be about 1 metre. Incidentally, note how the hot spot follows you as you move within the beam.

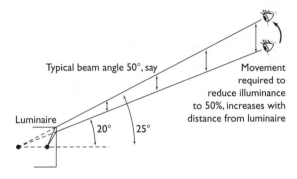

Figure 4.138 Barndooring difficulties at long throws.

- The barndooring sharpness depends on the sharpness of the hot spot image. This is controlled by the particular Fresnel lens and the amount of diffusion introduced on the rear of the lens. A well-defined hot spot will give sharper barndooring than one with a diffused image.

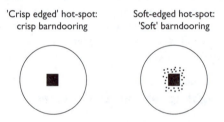

Figure 4.139 Hot-spot 'sharpness' (Fresnel spotlight).

Incidentally, if you see two hot spots, it means that the mirror/lamp base assembly is loose or bent in some way. Normally, the reflected image of the filaments should 'lie' over the actual image of the filaments, to produce one hot spot. Sometimes, 'saggy' filaments can give rise to one image being slightly displaced from the other.

Beware of trying to achieve 'sharp' barndooring from a luminaire which has two hot spots – it will not be possible!

Figure 4.140 Double 'hot-spot' (Fresnel spotlight).

Fig. 4.141 Illustrates the problem of lighting the artiste for position A and position B, with a walk between A and B.

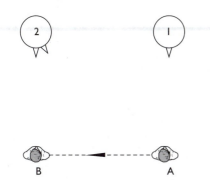

Figure 4.141 Basic artiste movement problem.

To ensure a good crossover, the following points should be observed:

- The artiste should walk towards their keylight, i.e. not turn away from it.
- Both keylights should be identical luminaires and accurately set on position A and position B.
- The keylights need to be at similar heights, similar angle and similar distances to each area.
- The keylights should be fully flooded.
- The illuminance at area A and area B should be adjusted to be the same.

Ideally, the crossover should be disguised by the action so, in the above case, it is suggested to complete the crossover immediately the artiste starts walking, at X. The sequence of operations for setting the crossover would be to adjust the barndoors as indicated in Fig. 4.142.

The above is something of an 'ideal' case. In practice, the barndooring of key A will be sharper than that of key B, and key A will be providing more illuminance than key B (key A is closer to the artiste).

Depending on circumstances, half-scrims or veils can be used to control the change in illuminance as key A is approached. Some practitioners find it easier to simply use scrims/veils or even half white diffusion on key A to produce a gradual reduction in illuminance as key B is moved into.

The above technique is worth practising on a quiet day to perfect your own technique. It is useful to have a small analogue incident light meter to check the evenness of the walk – aim initially at a spread of illuminance within half of one f_{stop} and see if you feel that this is satisfactory. Start with a 30° angle between keylight and camera, then progress

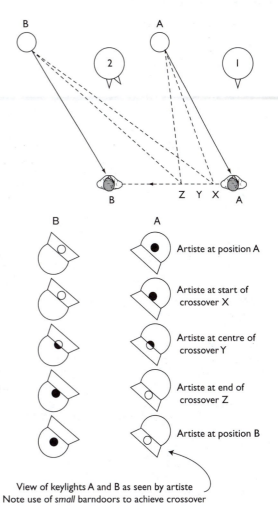

View of keylights A and B as seen by artiste
Note use of *small* barndoors to achieve crossover

Figure 4.142 The setting of a crossover.

to 0°! When confident with two luminaires, try setting the crossovers for three luminaires, i.e. two crossovers.

Obviously, the backlights can be treated in a similar way for barndooring, but are not so critical as the keylights. Fill-lights are used to provide a base light of illuminance.

A variation on the above principle can sometimes be applied for large drama sets where a large keylight is providing major coverage across a set, but artistes walk towards it as they exit.

In Fig. 4.143, the two luminaires are set so that the artiste walks out of the large luminaire into the smaller, lower luminaire on exiting, thus preserving the illuminance and vertical keying angle.

Use of 'bounce' techniques with artiste movements provides a very quick and easy way to cover artiste movement. The principle is illustrated in Fig. 4.144.

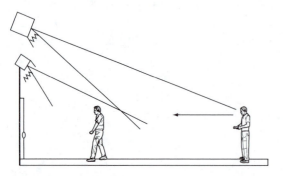

Figure 4.143 Artiste movement coverage in a large drama set.

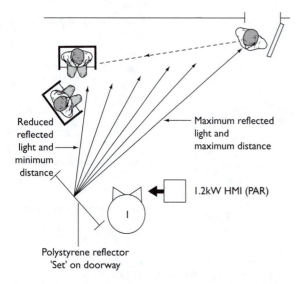

Figure 4.144 Use of 'bounce' to cover artiste movement.

In this technique, use is made of the cosine law nature of the light reflected from a diffuse reflector (Fig. 4.11). The centre of the reflected light is directed at the distant area. The artiste walks out of this central area into the area where the illuminance is reducing as they approach the downstage area.

If there are any 'hot spots' on the walk, these can be reduced by placing an appropriate size of veil between the reflector and the artiste.

4.12 Lighting for chroma key

4.12.1 Introduction

Chroma key is a very common technique in colour television, forming the basis of many news and current affairs programmes. Virtual reality sets are also based on chroma key principles. In establishing the lighting techniques which are useful for chroma key it is worthwhile to take a look at the basic chroma key process to identify the operational and lighting needs.

4.12.2 Chroma key principle

Chroma key is an electronic process whereby part of one picture (foreground) is inserted into another (background). The area to be inserted is determined by placing the foreground subject in front of a suitably coloured **backing**, e.g. blue or green. The RGB signals from the foreground camera are used to devise a suitable **keying** or **switching** signal which is used to operate a fast-acting switch between foreground and background cameras. Whenever the keying signal is of a high amplitude, the background source is selected (Fig. 4.145).

A virtual reality set uses a computer-generated background image, with the pan/tilt/zoom action of the foreground camera being used to control the geometry of the background picture. Often the cameras have completely robotic 'heads'.

4.12.3 Choice of keying colour

The keying colour may be any hue. However, the foreground subject should not contain any of this colour, otherwise spurious switching will occur. Red is avoided for foreground subjects which include face tones; early chroma keying systems concentrated on blue for keying to ensure that face tones did not key. Green is also a useful keying colour allowing foreground subjects to wear blue, i.e. jeans, blue suits, etc. In addition to avoiding keying colour, the foreground subject should not contain 'mirror' type surfaces, e.g. chrome legs on chairs – they will of course reflect the keying colour! Basic chroma key cannot handle transparent foreground material, e.g. glass and smoke, neither will it reproduce shadows (see the note on linear keying systems later in this section). If the camera can 'see' the right luminance of keying colour through the smoke or glass, the background will be inserted with no indication of the smoke or glass. If, on the other hand, the luminance of the keying colour through the glass or smoke is insufficient to operate the switch to the background, the foreground will be reproduced, i.e. glass and smoke against a dark blue background.

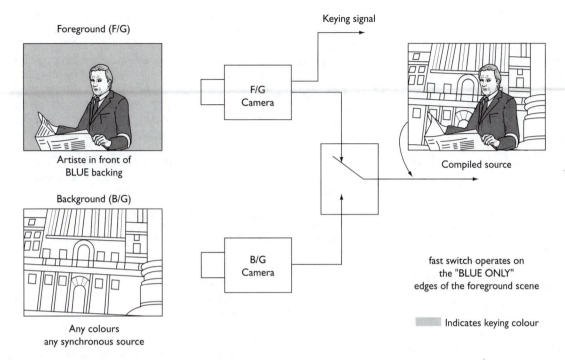

Figure 4.145 Chroma key principle.

4.12.4 The keying signal

It is useful to examine the derivation of the keying signal in establishing the need for a **clipping level** adjustment as well as simply using a coloured backing to the foreground camera. The keying signal may be derived in a number of ways, one of the most basic methods being to use $(B - Y)$ when using blue as the keying colour. This has a maximum value for 'blue only' areas of the foreground; unfortunately, any foreground colours containing blue will produce a positive value for $(B - Y)$, a keying signal. As discussed earlier $Y = 0.3R + 0.59G + 0.11B$.

So, on an area of saturated blue only we could have $R = 0$, $G = 0$ and $B = 0.7$ V, the luminance signal $Y = 0.3 \times 0 + 0.59 \times 0 + 0.11 \times 0.7 = 0.077$ V, and $(B - Y) = 0.7 - 0.077 = 0.623$ V, i.e. a large keying signal.

The requirement for white (or any neutral grey) is that $R = G = B$; for peak white this would be 0.7 V. So, an area of peak white in the foreground picture gives a luminance signal $Y = 0.7$ V, i.e.:

$$Y = 0.3 \times 0.7 + 0.59 \times 0.7 + 0.11 \times 0.7 = 0.7 \text{ V}$$

The keying signal would be:

$$(B - Y) = 0.7 - 0.7 = 0 \text{ V}$$

i.e. zero keying signal for white. The system has therefore discriminated against the blue present in white. Unfortunately, this is a special case – other colours with blue in their make-up produce a keying signal, e.g. magenta.

Magenta, taking fully saturated values, would result in RGB signals of $R = 0.7$ V, $G = 0$ V and $B = 0.7$ V. The luminance signal Y is:

$$Y = 0.3 \times 0.7 + 0.59 \times 0 + 0.11 \times 0.7$$
$$= 0.21 + 0 + 0.077 = 0.287 \text{ V}$$

and

$$(B - Y) = 0.7 - 0.287 = 0.413 \text{ V}$$

Clearly, there is a need to be able to discriminate between the blue only area (the keying colour) and other colours. This is done by introducing a voltage threshold or clipping level, which the keying signal *must rise above*, in order to operate the chroma key switch. All vision mixing desks will have a clipping level adjustment, which has to be adjusted for optimum switching.

Chroma key systems, therefore, use two steps to derive a suitable keying (switching) signal:

(i)   a saturated colour backing – hence **chroma** key;
(ii) an operation threshold or **clipping** level.

4.12.5 The chroma key switch

The basic chroma key switch simply completes a very fast **crossfade** between foreground and background. Early chroma key systems used a very fast-acting switch and this gave rise to lively edges, especially around the hair of the foreground subject.

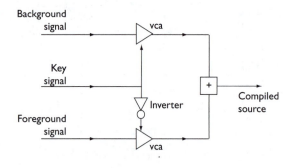

vca = voltage controlled
amplifier (gain controlled by key signal)

Figure 4.146 Basic chroma keyer.

Fig. 4.146 illustrates the basic principle where only one amplifier is conducting at any time. A fast cross-fade between the two sources is made at the transition from foreground to background and vice versa.

This is known as a soft-edged keyer – usually a **softness** control is incorporated on the vision-mixing desk to increase the transition period and hence soften the edge of the transition. Note, however, that the greatest discrimination is achieved with the softness control set to minimum, i.e. 'hardest' transition. Usually a compromise between softness and discrimination has to be established.

This illustrates the three controls, hue, clipping level and softness, which have to be set up with great care to ensure good chroma key. It also illustrates the need for a uniformly lit chroma key backing with no shadows. The darkest part of the coloured backing will determine the clipping level. If this has to be set very low to accommodate unevenness or shadows on the backing, then unwanted colours (with keying colour in their make-up) may well cause spurious switching.

4.12.6 The chroma key backing

This can be obtained in one of two ways:

(i) by lighting an appropriate coloured backing with white light;
(ii) by lighting a white backing with an appropriate coloured light.

The first method is the one normally used. It is unaffected by any spurious white lights used to light the foreground artiste.

The second method has the advantage of being able to change the keying colour with a simple filter change and revert to a non-chroma key coloured backing when chroma key is no longer required for the artiste. The disadvantage of this method is the obvious desaturation of the keying colour by foreground artiste lighting (white light). Ideally, the foreground artiste needs to be lit with hard fill-light to give the required control of beam shape. Appropriate colour filters are shown in Table 4.15.

With chroma key drapes which may have become faded, or painted backcloths which may have become

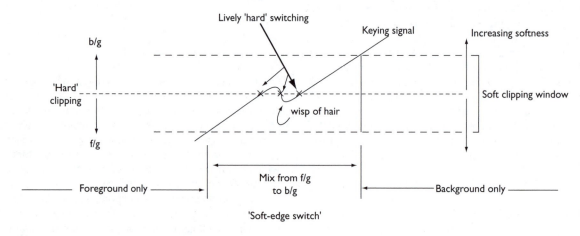

Figure 4.147 Hard clipping and soft-edged switching.

Table 4.15 Colour filters for chroma key.

Keying colour	Typical filter colour
Blue	Medium Blue
	Dark Blue
Yellow	Yellow
	Chrome Yellow
Green	Primary Green
	Dark Green
	Moss Green

wrinkled and cracked, it is useful to use coloured light on them to overcome their deficiencies.

Good chroma key relies on:

- deriving a good keying signal;
- minimizing the colour fringing of the foreground artiste.

4.12.7 Derivation of a good keying signal

- Keying colour – obviously must not be present on the foreground subject. Clearly the foreground artiste *must* be informed of the costume requirements for chroma key operation.

- Uniform lighting – as previously mentioned, the aim is to light the backing as evenly as possible, with no shadows present (unless using a 'shadow' chroma key). See Section 4.12.10.

- Avoidance of wispy hairstyles – the foreground artiste should have a well-defined edge. If using a linear keyer, wispy hairstyles do not usually present a problem.

- Depth-of-field – where deep foreground shots are required it may be necessary to increase the lighting levels, i.e. increase f_{no} and increase depth-of-field so that all of the foreground subject is in focus. An out-of-focus transition between foreground planes and the backing will result in a mix of foreground and key colour which will lead to either keying in this area of keying colour (reducing area of foreground) or leaving the area of foreground with a strong colour fringe!

Note: The use of a decoded $(B - Y)$ signal from a PAL composite signal does not provide a good keying signal.

4.12.8 Minimizing colour fringing of the foreground artiste

A basic problem is that the chroma key backing, when lit, acts as a large area coloured backlight for the foreground artiste. This can sometimes create colour-fringing problems of the foreground artiste. The fringing may be minimized by:

- maintaining the luminance of the backing at as low a level as possible consistent with 'clean' switching being obtained;
- keeping the foreground artiste well clear of the backing;
- using the minimum area of chroma key backing consistent with no 'shoot-off' problems. Any out-of-shot coloured backing is only adding to any colour fringing problems. A rule-of-thumb set-up for minimum fringing is shown in Fig. 4.148;

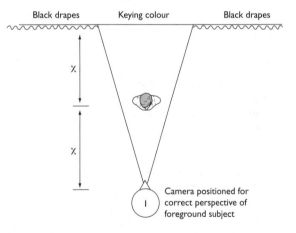

Figure 4.148 Rule-of-thumb for minimum fringing of foreground subject.

- using two backlights on the foreground artiste to provide backlight and to 'wash-out' any keying colour spill on the artiste. Use of an amber filter on the backlights to help to cancel the blue fringe is a matter for personal choice. It is usually more effective to control the size of the area lit and the illuminance on the backing to minimize the amount of blue fringing;
- using a hue suppresser. This is a facility which can be used to reduce the level of a particular hue, say blue, to the level of the greater of red or green. This can help to minimize any colour fringing effect.

4.12.9 Long shots and chroma key

Provided the artistes are not required to move everywhere in the television frame, long shots of the artistes may be obtained by using suitable box wipes on the vision mixing panel (Fig. 4.149). This reduces the area of chroma key backing needed.

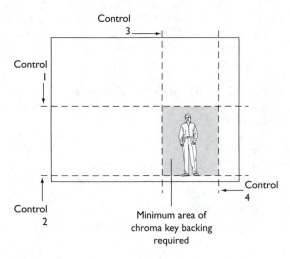

Figure 4.149 Use of a box wipe to produce an electronic vignette.

4.12.10 Lighting for chroma key

The lighting requirements can be summarized as:

- providing an evenly illuminated chroma key backing;
- providing the minimum level of illuminance on the chroma key backing;
- being consistent with clean switching;
- providing an effective backlight.

In addition, there is a need for the lighting of the foreground artiste to match that of the background:

- matching keylight direction and elevation;
- matching keylight source – hard or softlights;
- matching the colour of the background lighting – cool or warm;
- matching the lighting balance – contrast in shadow areas;
- correct exposure of foreground face tones to match with background picture.

Incidentally, for most applications, the illuminance on the foreground artiste and on the foreground backing need to be similar. There is no need for the backing

to be lit to an excessively high value, as this will only cause excessive fringing of the foreground artiste.

4.12.11 Basic set-up for chroma key

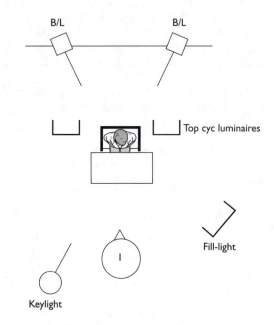

Figure 4.150 Basic lighting plot for chroma key.

Fig. 4.150 illustrates a typical chroma keylighting set-up:

- **Keylight**   Positioned to give good modelling for a news/documentary programme. If appropriate its direction, elevation, colour and softness should match that of the background picture.

- **Filler**   Positioned approximately 90° from the keylight. Usually a soft source. Facial contrast should relate to background picture, if appropriate.

- **Backlight**   Always use two backlights. A single backlight would be too 'toppy' and would not wash out the colour fringing on the artistes. Consequently, the sides of the subject, head and arms may give rise to spurious switching. If long shots are required, one needs to minimize the shadows from the backlights. This can be achieved by using softlights or spacelights as backlights. Spacelights are especially useful for large area chroma key set-ups.

- **Backing** This has to be uniformly lit. Cyclorama units are preferred for this, as they are designed to light a vertical surface uniformly. An alternative to this is to use fluorescent lights. They have the advantage of producing good outputs of blue and green energy (Section 4.4.1) and no radiant heat. Fig. 4.151 illustrates the principle of lighting a chroma key backing using these lights.

A further alternative is to use a rear lit screen with suitable red, green and blue fluorescent lamps.

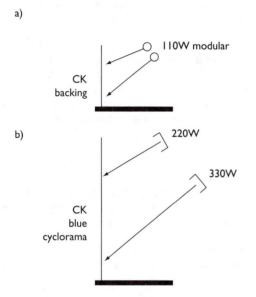

Figure 4.151 Use of fluorescent lighting for chroma key cycloramas: (a) 3 m high backing; (b) 8 m high cyclorama.

4.12.12 Coloured light on a white backing

Cyclorama lights with coloured filters can be used to turn a white backing (cyclorama) into a chroma key backing. The aim is to keep the backing colour as 'pure' as possible by preventing the foreground artiste lighting from reaching the backing, as illustrated in Fig. 4.152.

One of the most common uses for chroma key is the weather presenter set-up, i.e. a weather presenter standing next to a blue 'window' in the set. The chroma key backing enables different weather information to be inserted into the 'window' behind them. The main problem here is the artiste's shadow on the wall; if they are very close to the set it will be difficult to fill the under-arm shadow. Fig. 4.153 illustrates one solution.

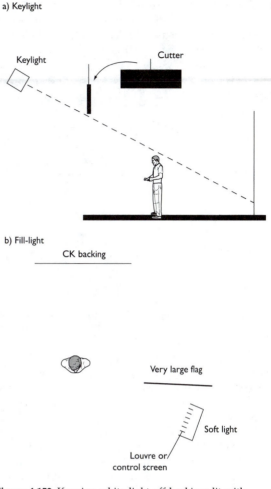

Figure 4.152 Keeping white light off backings lit with coloured light.

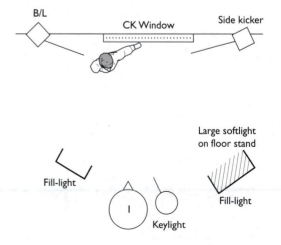

Figure 4.153 Weather presenter plus chroma key (basic version).

An alternative is to 'cheat' the weather presenter so that they are about 0.5 metre downstage, in which case the shadow may be filled using a barndoored Fresnel spotlight (Fig. 4.154).

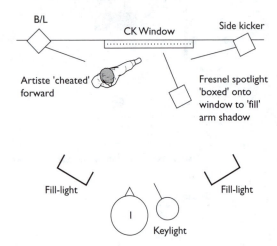

Figure 4.154 Weather presenter plus chroma key (alternative).

4.12.13 Large chroma key set

Chroma key set-ups which include a vertical plane and a horizontal plane, i.e. wall and floor, pose a number of problems:

- Possible difference in wall and floor material, e.g. 'wall' could be a blue drape and the floor of chroma key paint. Ideally, all the keying surfaces should be the same material and the same colour.
- Difficulty in lighting into the join between vertical surface and floor. This is best cured by using **coving**, ideally of at least 0.6 m radius, suitably painted and taped to the floor at the join. An alternative, for sets up to 4 m wide, would be to use linoleum to provide an excellent coving.

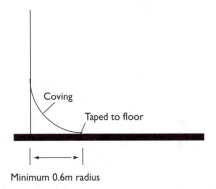

Figure 4.155 Use of coving in chroma key sets.

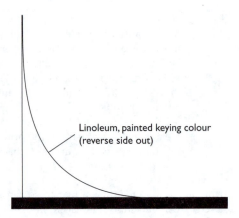

Figure 4.156 Use of linoleum for chroma key backings/coving.

Use of a polarizing filter

A polarizing filter on the camera may be useful to help overcome glare reflection problems caused by backlights on the floor of large chroma key sets (remember, however, loss introduced by polarizing filter, approximately 2 f_{stops}).

Virtual reality sets

These are usually three-sided sets plus the floor, all painted in blue or green. Again it is the joins between two surfaces at right angles which can create problems. Virtual reality sets need to have curved corners of as large a radius as possible, as well as coving between wall and floor.

4.12.14 Linear keying systems

Linear keying systems such as Ultimatte process the foreground and background pictures separately.

The keying signal derived from the foreground camera is used to produce a background signal with a black hole exactly the same size, shape and position as the foreground artiste. The same keying signal is inverted, and operated on the foreground picture to produce an image of the foreground signal against a black background. It then becomes a simple matter to add the two processed signals to produce the composite output.

The significance of the linear keyer is that if the keying background is not *absolutely* uniformly lit, say shaded top to bottom, the keying signal will also be shaded top to bottom, and this will result in the background picture being shaded top to bottom! This is clearly an undesirable condition. However, if the keying signal is reduced by the presence of a shadow,

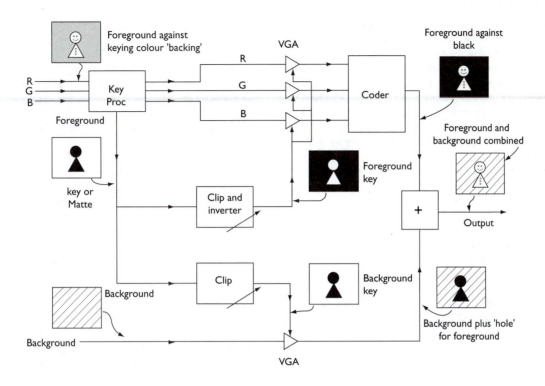

VGA Voltage controlled amplifier

Figure 4.157 Linear keyer, basic Ultimatte.

the background picture will be reduced in amplitude in the area of the shadow, and a shadow will appear on the composite output. Smoke and glass in the foreground are also reproduced by a similar process.

Linear keyers have become very much more sophisticated than the basic principle described above. Together with hue suppression they are capable of excellent results.

4.13 Principles of lighting for variety programmes

4.13.1 Introduction

Lighting plays an important part in realizing the 'look' of variety programmes. As always, good lighting is the result of careful planning, liaison with other disciplines and an effective rehearsal. Typically, a variety programme will be made up of several segments.

The role of lighting is to create a different 'look' to each segment. It is vital that the scenery is such that it allows for colour changes to have an effect. Ideally, the variety set should be created in white, black and greys with avoidance of strong colours. This enables the lighting to be effective in changing the 'look' of the scenery.

4.13.2 Scenic requirements

(1) Set to be in shades of grey, white and black with few inherent colours.
(2) Avoidance of strong set colours.
(3) Use of self-illuminating features, e.g. 'pea'-lamps, neon strips, rear-lit panels, practical lamps, star cloths.
(4) Floor to be grey or even black. Shiny black floors reflect the scenery. Remember, the floor will be the meeting point for all the light – keys, fillers and backlights. Avoid TV white floors.
(5) Translucent panels which can be rear-lit.

4.13.3 Lighting the artiste

Generally, the artiste is lit in isolation using a follow-spot (following-spotlight). Depending on the lamp throw this may be tungsten, CSI, HMI or xenon. Tungsten follow-spots are the most flexible in use, though the maximum wattage is only 2–2½ kW. CSI and HMI spotlights are more powerful but there is a need to correct these lights, usually to be at a colour temperature a little above tungsten, i.e. 3400 K. Remember, there will also be a need to correct CSI or HMI lights to each other if two such lights are used. Xenon lights at approximately 6000 K offer a very stable light source (colour does not change with life) requiring only correction to the required colour temperature.

In plotting follow-spotlights, note the need for the following:

- Maximum vertical angle of approximately 40° to keep the artiste shadow short, and also to keep the shadow and light off the scenery. Remember, the artiste will usually look up towards lights – reducing the vertical keying angle. Circumstances may require a more shallow angle, say 20°, but artiste shadow will be very long.
- Check that follow-spot has a clear 'arc-of-operation', i.e. no luminaires are in the path of the follow-spot.
- If the floor is shiny, the light from the follow spot will reflect onto the set or cyclorama cloth. Often a grey gauze is used in front of the cyclorama to reduce this effect.

Follow-spotlights may be used as backlights and filler lights. The advantage of this is to localize the lighting and to keep the remainder of the set 'clean'.

Although follow-spots are used sharply focused, it is often useful to operate with a soft-focused spotlight. This is easily obtained by using Hamburg Frost or Hampshire Frost on the front of the follow-spot.

Note: When operating a follow-spot use the same 'framing' of spot size as with a camera, i.e. long shot, medium long shot, mid-shot, medium close-up, etc.

Use of kicker

The use of a kicker light is often desirable in variety lighting. Ideally, it should be at eye-height from upstage, and consequently it has to be used with great care if it is not to be in-shot. Often, a compromise is made where the kicker is placed at floor level or elevated to avoid in-shot flare.

Lighting musicians

Lighting musicians will depend on the type of musicians and music being played, and the role of the musicians, i.e. whether they are main feature or supportive. 'Put the light where the money is' sums up one philosophy of lighting variety shows; however, it does indicate the principle of using subdued lighting on the supporting singers and musicians. For best results consider lighting for texture.

When lighting orchestras, the main objectives are:

- clarity of musicians, with no shadows on the musician's face from the instrument being played, e.g. violin bow;
- no keylights on the musician's eyeline to the conductor, otherwise the musician will get after-images of the lights, i.e. extra 'black notes' on their score!
- no backlight shadows of the musicians on the musical score;
- avoidance of distracting shadows of the conductor on the orchestra.

One musical instrument, however, does have a unique lighting solution. Namely, lighting a piano keyboard. The basic technique is to light the keyboard from upstage of the keyboard, which acts as both keylight and backlight to the keyboard and the pianist. Fig. 4.158 illustrates the typical arrangement.

The keyboard light has to be positioned as shown:

- at an elevation of 45–55° to ensure that the 'black-note' shadows are not too long;

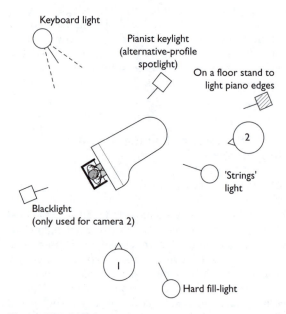

Figure 4.158 Lighting a piano.

- to avoid a shadow of the pianist on the downstage end of the piano (if too far camera left);
- to avoid a shadow of the piano front over the keyboard (if too far camera right).

The keyboard light can be spotted as necessary to provide a disc of light on the floor – this can be useful for an opening and closing silhouette shot.

The remaining lights shown in Fig. 4.158 assume that the piano has its lid up. If the lid is down, or removed, the musician's keylight could usefully be a localized follow-spot. The musician's keylight should be carefully set so that there is no light on the hands; this is a particularly critical setting, so that the hands on the keyboard look clean. After setting the lighting, check lighting levels across the keyboard.

Large groups
When lighting large groups use Fresnel spotlights. Ideally, use a large spotlight to cover the complete area as simply as possible.

Use a cutter or flag to obtain a sharp cut-off of the light at the cyclorama/floor join. Usually hard light plus diffusion is used to provide fill-light.

Dance groups
If possible try to use side lighting from the floor when lighting dancers. This will reveal the limbs to best advantage.

It may, however, not be possible to do this if the stage is shot from extreme left and right (lamps in shot!).

4.13.4 Lighting the set

Generally, hard light is used for lighting the set, using the control offered by the barndoors. Coloured filters should be clipped to the barndoor or fixed on outrigger frames to ensure that the filter life is as long as possible.

Choice of colour
A colour scheme needs to be designed for each programme segment, usually using colours which complement or contrast with the artiste's costume colour, or even similar colours when only lighting small areas of the set. It is useful to remember the colour wheel in choosing colours (Fig. 4.159).

In lighting the set, points to consider are:

- Shorter wavelength colours, the blue hues, 'recede' to enhance depth; while the longer wavelength

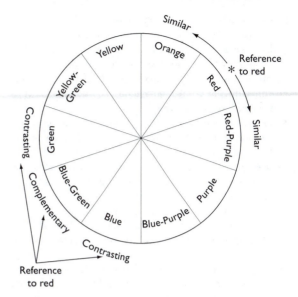

Figure 4.159 Basic colour 'wheel'.

colours, the red hues, 'advance' towards the viewer reducing the apparent depth when on the background, but assisting depth when on the foreground areas.
- Avoid over-lighting the foreground areas.
- Use a limited palette of colours for each segment, i.e. one colour plus black and white, or two colours plus black and white, unless a kaleidoscope of colours is required.
- Change the look of the set by lighting it from different angles, i.e. front/side/rear/floor/silhouette etc.
- For in-shot lighting changes, make sure that you introduce good changes to the luminance values of the set. This is where a monochrome monitor is particularly useful in assessing the changes in luminance values.
- Beware of potential shadows created by camera cranes and sound booms.
- Keep the coloured light 'clean', i.e. avoid overlapping of colours otherwise a mixture colour will result.
- Avoid shadows on the cyclorama.
- Light the floor and any steps/staircases from upstage to reveal texture and to avoid coloured light on the front of the artiste.
- Light translucent screens from behind for the best effect.
- Beware of creating illegal colours when adding coloured light to a set. It is possible to produce colours with luminance values which do not exist in the real world. When using coloured light to

light areas of the scenery, it is possible to achieve luminance levels of the colour which do not exist in nature. For example, a deeply saturated blue surface does not normally have a high luminance, but when using a light of this colour in excess, so-called illegal colours are achieved. It usually does not look right anyway!

- Gobo projectors or profile projectors may be used to project patterns on the set, the cyclorama or the floor. Remember to project on the floor from upstage – the pattern will diverge towards the downstage area thus enhancing the illusion of space. When purchasing gobos, unless using a particular unique gobo, it is useful to buy them in sets of six identical patterns. This will allow the set, cyc and floor to be given a complete treatment.

Always set the focus with all the remaining lighting on. This will allow you to see the subtle effects which exist. If you focus in isolation, the addition of the extra lighting will wash out the more subtle effects.

Usually, gobo projectors are used de-focused to enhance the depth in a scene; however, if pin-sharp effects are required the focus can be improved by using a 'doughnut'. A doughnut is a metal mask (could be black-wrap) with a small circular hole, 3–4 cm diameter, placed in front of the gobo projector lens. Gobos may be used singly or in combination to produce an appropriate effect.

Remember, for a gobo to be seen there must be contrast between the gobo lit area and its background. Consequently, a gobo projected onto a pale yellow cyclorama will not show very strongly. When 'white' gobo effects are required with a projected coloured background, it is useful to use an appropriate complementary colour filter on the gobo projector, for example:

- cyc lit blue + white gobo, may give pale blue gobo effect;
- cyc lit blue + pale yellow gobo, to give 'white' gobo effect.

It can be effective to project gobos onto 'blobs' of colour, or link gobos to blobs of colour, i.e. overlapping. Strips of colour filter (20 mm wide) clipped to the projection lens can be used to produce interesting colour fringes to a de-focused gobo.

Use of the PAR can
The PAR can, originally developed for the pop world, has become well established in television lighting. It may be used with a wide-angle lamp for colour washes, or a narrow angle projector to provide

intense beams of light which can be revealed when used with smoke or haze.

Generally, PAR cans are used upstage or as side-lights for greater impact, i.e. light beams and light sources are seen in-shot. Scrollers can be used to provide changes of colour on PAR cans; however, the lit area will be identical.

Remember that a lighting change involving only a change in colour will not have the same impact as one which involves large changes in luminance (lit areas) and colour.

Note that the PAR can be very effective when aimed at black drapes! The narrow beam PARs have an intense beam, which can produce interesting effects when used in this way.

Use of smoke, fog, haze and dry ice
Smoke, fog or haze are used to reveal light beams to their maximum effect. Smoke and fog machines tend to be difficult to control in ensuring that the right amount of smoke is available when required. Recent advances have seen the use of cracked-oil and haze machines. These produce a very fine suspension of oil vapour or water vapour droplets in the studio – which are made visible when hit by a high intensity beam of light. Usually, the studio is filled with the appropriate vapour by building up the haze during several hours of operation of the haze generator (in rehearsal time). Dry ice, unlike smoke and haze, falls towards the studio floor. It should be remembered that it will spread all over the floor and as such should be contained to the required area using appropriate boards. Dry ice will make the floor wet and slippery, and should therefore be avoided for fast-moving dance routines. Incidentally, it is ideal that the light beams are revealed in isolation, i.e. against a black cyc. If a white cyc is used the light reflected by the haze will reveal the cyc, i.e. light it, thus reducing the impact and clarity of the light beams.

Use of star cloths
There are two types of star cloths:

- tungsten 'pea' lamps stitched to a black serge cloth;
- fibre-optics which feed light from a remote light source to points on a black serge cloth.

The advantage of the latter is that when extinguished the fibre-optic ends tend not to show as strongly as the extinguished 'pea' lamps. The fibre-optic also allows a colour wheel to be used at the light source enabling the 'stars' to be coloured in a random way or just to extinguish in a random way, i.e. 'twinkle'.

Use of scrollers

When there is a limited number of fixtures and a need for colour changing, a scroller can provide a useful solution.

A scroller enables any one of 11 or 16 colours to be selected from a filter roll which 'scrolls' in front of the luminaries. Although originally designed for PAR cans it is now possible to obtain scrollers for most fixtures. Scrollers are normally controlled via DMX 512.

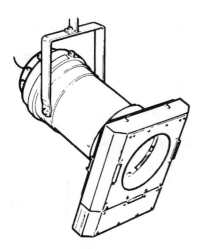

Figure 4.160 PAR can with scroller.

Lighting changes

The decisions needed at the planning stage, for each segment, will be choice of colour treatment and what lighting changes may be needed, i.e. static or dynamic lighting. The latter is clearly influenced by the nature of the segment.

Most lighting consoles will provide a range of **chase** type effects for built-in practical lamps. A minimum of three separate channels are required to give the illusion of moving lights, that is the practical lamps need to be connected as A, B or C, with a 'loop' or chase set up to switch between A, B, C and back to A. If only two circuits are used, the lamps will simply 'flip-flop' between the two conditions. If the lighting change is reversed after a sequence of loops, the lamps will appear to reverse direction, i.e. 'bounce'. Careful thought needs to be given to the connection of practical lamps if more involved effects are required, e.g. single light moving would require individual lamps each to have a lighting channel!

With moving lights, the desire to reveal everything on the first number should be resisted. Instead use the range of effects to provide a different look to each segment, for example:

- stationary beams;
- stationary beams + changing colours;
- moving beams;
- moving beams + gobo;
- moving beams + rotating gobo;
- stationary beams + gobo;
- stationary beams + rotating gobo;
- stabbing beams (change between two pre-set conditions);
- moving beams, moving gobo plus zoom angle changing;
- moving beams, moving gobo, changing colour etc.

Whatever you decide, do make sure that the lighting conditions suit the particular segment, e.g. a slow-moving song would not look right with a rapidly changing lighting condition!

Remember that the luminaire/mirror has to be moved during an 'off' period when a new condition is required to be 'cued', i.e. the change to the new condition is not to be seen.

Lighting cues

One of the hallmarks of good lighting is that of 'slick' execution of lighting cues. These may be during a programme segment or the joins linking segments:

- All lighting changes should be motivated.
- All lighting changes *must* be at the right moment, i.e.
  - linked to 'on-stage' action
  - linked to sound, that is usually the 'beat' of music. Note, however, that with pop and rock music it is more effective to link lighting changes to the OFF-beat, rather than the ON-beat of the music.
- Speed of lighting changes should be related to the nature of the production number – song or dance.
- Moving lights should start on music cue and stop on music cue. This is especially vital to ensure an ending which looks right!

4.13.5 Audience lighting

Unless required for a specific purpose, avoid lighting the audience with full intensity white light. Generally, low-level coloured light is preferred, often two colours used at >180° apart can be effective – aim for texture rather than 'illumination'.

4.13.6 Warm-up lighting

Always provide lighting for any 'warm-up' artiste; also lighting for the audience to find their way to their seats.

Avoid using house lights unless they are on a dimmer.

The transition to 'show' lighting condition should be on a crossfade, not by crashing-out the house lights!

4.13.7 Allocation of time

There is usually never enough time to do everything as you would like. Care should be taken to allocate your time in an even-handed fashion. Guard against spending too much time on one segment to the detriment of the other segments.

4.14 Principles of drama lighting

4.14.1 Introduction

Obviously, lighting plays a very important role in any drama production. Good lighting is again the result of careful planning, liaison with other disciplines and effective rehearsal.

The **illusion of reality** is the aim of lighting for drama rather than absolute reality. One is aiming to satisfy the criterion of 'when it looks right – it is', by using one's observation and judgement to decide how close we need to go to realism.

For example, a night domestic interior scene may in reality be lit with a single overhead lamp. If one were to create this exact lighting in the studio, the portraiture would be unacceptable because of the high elevation of the light sources.

There are many factors to consider when lighting for drama, and often the final lighting plot is one of compromise. One should avoid developing a too rigid technique, but be prepared to meet each situation with an open mind. This way, one should develop a flexible technique which will produce good results most of the time.

The factor of time is all-important with any lighting, and in a rehearse/record situation extremely precious. So make sure you will have enough time to rig, fine set and balance the lighting plot. A good rule is 'keep it simple', but be flexible in your approach, i.e. try to anticipate possible problems and have the odd extra luminaire available to cope with the problem.

4.14.2 Planning

Effective planning relies on getting the right information. For drama one needs to know:

- artistes' positions and movements;
- camera positions and movements – single-camera/multicamera shooting;
- desired mood (**implicit** requirement);
- day/night (**explicit** requirement);
- sound pick-up (generally by means of a microphone boom);
- direction of the inferred light source, i.e. sun or practical light;
- position of the scenery, ceiling pieces etc.;
- position of the lighting hoists/lighting grid;
- luminaires available;
- costume – contrast ratio, large hats, etc.;
- motivated lighting changes required.

4.14.3 Lighting techniques

The lighting technique adopted will be affected by four factors:

Nature of the production
Technology available –   luminaires, grip, etc. } All related to the programme BUDGET!
Time available
Single- or multicamera shooting

For example, on a larger budget period drama, shooting single-camera, one could strive to produce the best possible lighting quality for each shot without the compromise of multicamera shooting.

As soon as a production becomes multicamera, some of the freedom enjoyed by single-camera shoots is lost. For example, luminaires which would have been on floor-stands for single-camera shooting have to be rigged at a higher level in the lighting grid, to avoid the luminaire and the stand being in shot. This can result in a more 'toppy' look to the lighting. Luminaires on stands may of course be a camera obstruction when using several cameras on a set.

Direction of the inferred light source

To decide which direction the inferred light source should come from, consider the script, the set, and any shooting of exterior location scenes.

The script will indicate day/night, sunny/cloudy, interior/exterior and may also give an indication of the light flow within a set.

The set usually contains a lighting feature which will assist in setting a lighting direction:

- windows within the set;
- practical lamps;
- chroma key background or painted backcloths.

In the last of these the direction and colour of the light will be dictated by the direction and colour of the light flow in the added background.

When location shots relate directly to the studio sets, they should be matched by the studio in terms of direction and type of lighting on the location.

Basic techniques

Generally, drama situations consist of two or more persons talking to each other. The usual method of positioning the artistes is across a set and they then 'play' to each other, *not* to the cameras. This is different from stage productions, in which the artistes would tend to face downstage (towards the audience) and also 'play' towards the audience. This placement of the artistes allows for cross-shooting between two cameras (Fig 4.161).

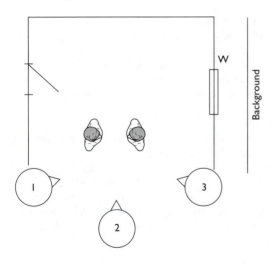

W = Window

Figure 4.161 Basic drama shooting.

A daylight drama set will usually have some lighting features in it to give a sense of direction to the lighting, e.g. windows. Windows, in reality, may have two sources of light from outside:

- sunlight – a hard source of light;
- skylight – a soft source of light.

It is unusual to sit by windows in direct sunlight – in reality it would be too uncomfortable. Consequently, one is normally lit by skylight and/or light which has reflected off the walls/floor/ceiling of the room.

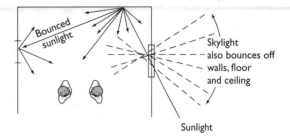

Figure 4.162 Natural light sources in a basic drama set.

A basic technique to light the action shown in Fig. 4.162 would be to use a hard source through the window to suggest sunlight, aimed upstage so that its effect is seen in-shot. The artiste lighting would also be a hard source, not a soft source, to have good control of the beam shape, to create more texture and to create more modelling. Often, the keylights are used as backlights and are fitted with bottom half-wires or a light diffusion in the bottom half of the lens.

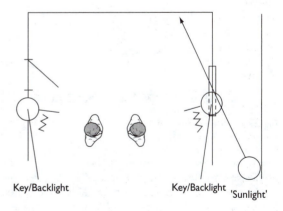

Figure 4.163 Basic drama keylighting.

The degree of modelling on the artistes' faces can be controlled by how far upstage the keys are placed. If their keys are exactly opposite the artistes then there is the risk of mutual shadowing of the artistes. When lit as shown, there should be no difficulty of sound pick-up using a microphone boom (Fig. 4.164).

The **lighting balance** should indicate that one person is standing with their back to the window, that is, key A is brighter than key B. The optimum position for the keys is usually just above the scenery (Fig. 4.165).

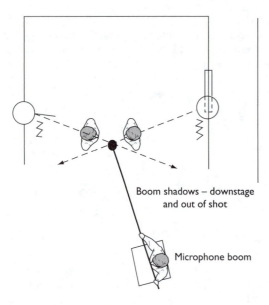

Boom shadows – downstage
and out of shot

Microphone boom

Figure 4.164 Boom shadows.

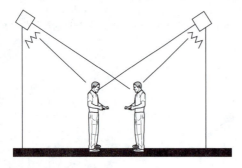

Keylights just above scenery

Figure 4.165 Optimum keylight positions.

If there is movement of the artistes close to the walls of the set, a bottom half-wire should be used in the keys to make the illumination reasonably even. Often the lighting barrels do not coincide with the scenery flats, and one has to decide in the light of artistes' positions whether to use a barrel inside the set or outside. At the planning stage, it is useful to get the position of the sets adjusted so that they do coincide with the lighting bars if at all possible. Cross-barrelling can be used to position a luminaire in a precise location, but this will fix the height of two barrels.

Referring to Figure 4.165 again, careful barndooring of the keys must be done to avoid camera flare. A camera-mounted flag is useful in preventing flare problems (zoom lenses do not have effective lens hoods). The filler light can be added as shown, usually at least 3 metres away from the artistes (Fig. 4.166).

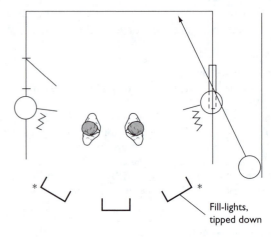

Fill-lights,
tipped down

Figure 4.166 Addition of fill-lights.

The number of filler lights used will depend on the size of the set and the mood to be created. The fillers marked with an asterisk in Fig. 4.166 should be angled away from the side walls to avoid over-lighting them and reduce the risk of 'muddy' boom shadows on the side walls, should the action be close to them. The filler luminaires should be lowered in to provide illumination of as low an elevation as is possible. Always tip the filler down so that the risk of muddy boom shadows on the upstage wall is minimized.

To ensure that the filler is always of a high colour temperature, i.e. within the tolerance of 2960 K ± 150 K, use a heavy frost or half white diffusion filter over them. This:

- diffuses the light source slightly, and reduces the clarity of boom shadow;
- increases the spread of the light, again only slightly, but this is useful when overlapping fillers;
- reduces the light output by about one-third. To overcome this loss of light the fader has to be raised up, and so a higher colour temperature is achieved.

The boom should be placed in the centre of the set if possible. If it is too much to one side it will be difficult for the boom operator to see all the action, and the boom arm will cause muddy boom shadows of the complete arm on the upstage wall.

In the situation where the spill from the filler light causes unnecessary illumination of the scenery, it may be desirable to use either a hard source of light or a camera head-lamp as a filler. The barndoors on a hard light source can be used to restrict the filler light to the desired area. The use of a hard filler may create boom shadows and a double nose shadow so generally the

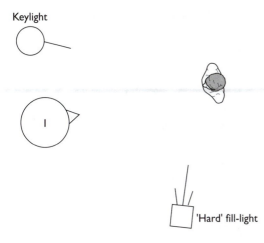

Figure 4.167 Use of hard fill-light.

filler is placed at about an angle of 90° to the camera axis (Fig. 4.167).

A hard filler used in this way should also be of low elevation. It must be remembered that the filler position is always something of a compromise – however, when placed as shown it should be satisfactory for most dramatic situations and will reveal texture on the subject.

Use of 'bounced' softlights

The high sensitivity of CCD cameras has made it possible to use fill-lights derived from bouncing a hard source off a suitable white board. These are particularly useful in drama set-ups, resulting in a very soft fill-light. The drawback is the difficulty in keeping the light off the upstage wall; the size of any flags or cutters has to be comparable to the reflector board to be effective.

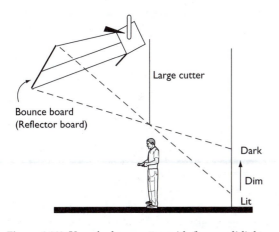

Figure 4.168 Use of a large cutter with 'bounced' light.

Small sets

The standard height of scenery is 3 metres, so with luminaires rigged above the set walls the lighting in a small set would be very 'toppy'. A technique often used to overcome this is to use a dimpled reflective material on a board about 0.5 m × 0.6 m rigged near the set wall and to 'bounce' a suitable Fresnel spotlight. The dimpled reflector gives a softening of the keylights but still maintains a reasonably punchy light beam.

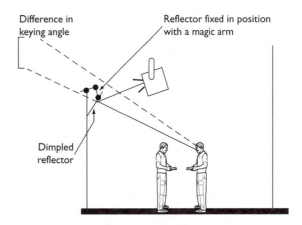

Figure 4.169 Use of directional 'bounce' light.

This technique puts the apparent light source at a much lower elevation to the artistes, thus reducing the 'toppy' look. With the sets being small it is unlikely that the reflector will be seen in shot.

Larger sets

Although the situations discussed above may be considered as general ones, often the drama situations involve several artistes' positions as in Fig. 4.170.

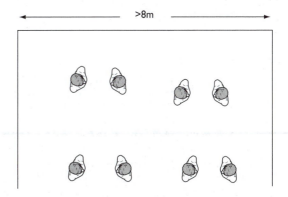

Figure 4.170 Possible coverage required in a large set.

It now becomes necessary to use several pairs of keys and backlights to maintain a reasonable keylight angle (both horizontal and vertical). The barndoors are adjusted on the lamps to ensure a smooth take-over between the keylights.

Normally one would arrange the take-over to be in a place where the doubling of shadows was least visible (Fig. 4.171). For night interiors and in apparent multilight situation, lit and unlit areas may be perfectly acceptable.

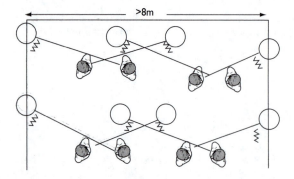

Figure 4.171 Coverage of a large area with multiple keylights.

With a deep set, two rows of filler lights may be necessary to reach the upstage artistes. If the action is angled across the set, then the keys can be angled in a similar manner (Fig. 4.172).

In fact, with a large set it is often an advantage to rig several keys set for different angles and only use the appropriate 'pair' of keys at any one time (Fig. 4.173).

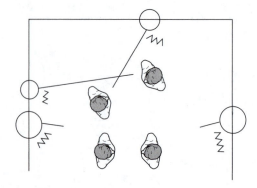

Keylights barndoored off set

Figure 4.173 Use of alternative keylights.

In other words, one should not consider the lighting plot as being static. Be prepared to change keylights according to the action – but of course the change *must not be noticed* by the viewer unless it is a motivated lighting change. It must also be remembered that in drama one is lighting 'portraiture within a given environment' and it is to be expected that the degree of modelling will change when the artistes move around a set. If the modelling always remained the same, irrespective of the artiste's position, then an element of realism would be lost.

Sometimes it is required to consider the lighting of the artiste when their eyeline is downstage (Fig. 4.174). The keylight in Figure 4.174 should be carefully barndoored to avoid the possibility of a boom shadow falling upstage.

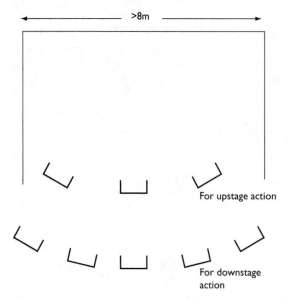

Figure 4.172 Fill-light in a large set.

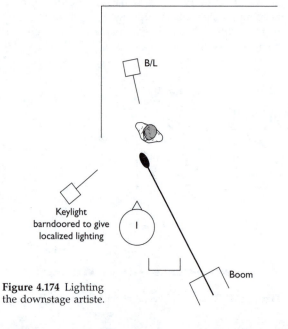

Figure 4.174 Lighting the downstage artiste.

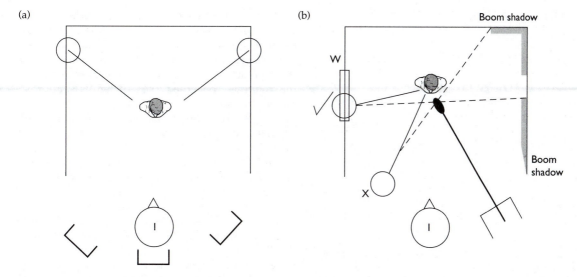

Figure 4.175 (a) 'Contre jour' lighting; (b) dangers of frontal keys for upstage lighting.

In Fig. 4.175 the keys used for the 'across the set' action are producing a 'contre jour' form of lighting of the artist. Depending on the action, and its duration, this may be a perfectly acceptable form of lighting for this shot – if a frontal key were to be used then boom shadows could be difficult to avoid, unless the shot is restricted to close-ups.

If the action is upstage, then again the use of a frontal key could cause boom shadow problems. The lighting of the artist should be dictated by the direction of the inferred light source.

One other solution is to use a hard-edged projector to key the upstage artist, e.g. a boardroom scene (Fig. 4.176).

The hard-edged projector has shutters which can be adjusted to shape the beam to any desired profile and so enable the upstage artist to be lit in complete isolation. There should be some space between the artist and the upstage wall otherwise the localized lighting may show as an isolated patch of bright light. Even with upstage keys, it is still possible to get boom shadow problems, as illustrated in Fig. 4.177.

In this, camera 2 is taking a tight 2-shot of the upstage artistes. This requires the boom to be upstage and close to them to get the right sound prospective.

Profile projector to give localised lighting
of chairman X

Figure 4.176 Use of hard-edged projector to avoid boom shadows.

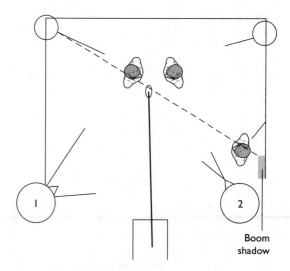

Figure 4.177 Boom shadows and upstage action.

Key localised to upstage action

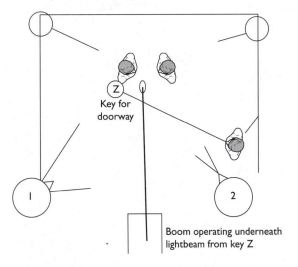

Figure 4.178 Coping with the upstage boom.

The next shot is a shot of the newcomer at the doorway, seen in long shot + the *boom shadow*! One way of avoiding this is to light as shown in Fig. 4.178.

This technique should also reduce the problem of camera flare for camera 2. In general, one should adjust the luminaire position to cover about 8–10 feet within an average size of set. This should allow for fairly sharp barndooring and with the vertical angle not being too shallow, camera flare will be reduced.

4.14.4 Lighting the set

Ideally, the set should be lit separately to the artistes. However, where small sets are involved, or the artistes work close to the walls, this is not always possible.

All lighting features in a set must look correct if they are going to be believable:

- windows and exterior views;
- night-time 'in-shot' practicals;
- interim shot from an exterior position.

Look back at our basic situation of Fig. 4.163. We left the set with a single hard light through the window (sunlight). Unless we are creating early morning or late evening the window glazing bar pattern will only be seen on the window 'return' and 'curtains'; it will not reach the upstage wall.

The upstage wall needs some treatment – in reality it is lit with skylight plus light reflected in the room, i.e. a soft source. Note a very important

observation about softlight, namely, when objects very close to a wall are lit with softlight there is a shadow. Consequently, it is possible to use a hard light to light the upstage wall which almost mimics the skylight (of finite area not infinite area: as far as the room is concerned the 'skylight' is approximately the size of the window!) *and*, more importantly, gives barndoor control in lighting the wall, i.e. using the top barndoor to darken off the top of the set (Fig. 4.179).

The lighting of the backcloth with cyc lights (and ground row if it is very tall) plus softlight into the window completes the lighting of this set.

If the window is upstage, cross-keying can still be used plus a light above the window to reveal texture on the artistes and help to give a sense of direction in the lighting. This is an example of where single-camera shooting would have the advantage of being able to place the 'window-light' on a low stand to create a better window effect.

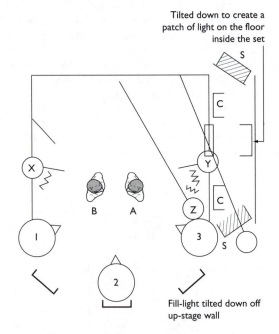

X = Keylight for A, Backlight for B, barndoored to approx halfway up RH wall

Y = Keylight for B, backlight for A, also LH wall

Z = Upstage wall, barndoor used to darken top of the set

S = Fill-light on floor stands to create the illusion of skylight for artistes at the window

C = Cyclorama lights for backdrop

Figure 4.179 The completed drama set.

Try to avoid double shadows when possible, especially cross-lit double shadows. Although one would set luminaires individually with all others off, it is good practice to observe the complete set lit with all lights roughly balanced to check for potential problems:

* double shadows;
* camera flare;
* luminaires in shot;
* cables in shot;
* unwanted spill light from luminaires;
* unwanted spill light from one set into an adjacent set;
* unlit area.

Lighting balance

It is a good plan to obtain a rough balance during the set/light time, using an incident light meter to determine levels. Then at the start of rehearsals, ask the camera operator for a wide-angle shot of the set and, with the camera aperture set to the nominal working aperture, use the lighting console to achieve a lighting balance.

Drama lighting effects (explicit requirements)

So far our discussion has been centred on interior daytime lighting. Any requirement for a departure from daylight requires appropriate planning to ensure that the correct effect can be easily obtained. For example:

* Sunrise/sunset — This requires that the 'sunlight' has a lower colour temperature. Typically a ½CTO filter on a low elevation Fresnel spotlight will help create the illusion, provided the light is seen cleanly, i.e. not contaminated with other light.

* Night-time — Interiors usually require in-shot practicals to be on and curtains to be drawn. It is useful to reverse the direction of the set lighting at night to change the 'look' of the set. More localized lighting can be used.
  — For exteriors, typically a ½CTB or ¾CTB can be used on spotlights to create a moonlight effect. Note that opinions are divided on this (see Section 4.16.5.).

* Exterior daytime — Ideally, try to use one large light to give the feel of a sun, plus bounced softlight to preserve the single-shadow philosophy.

* Fire-flicker effect — Despite technology being available, the original technique of using strips of rag on a broom handle shaken in front of a floor-mounted spotlight is still one of the most effective ways of achieving this effect. Use full CTO or ¾CTO on the light source to give the appropriate colour.

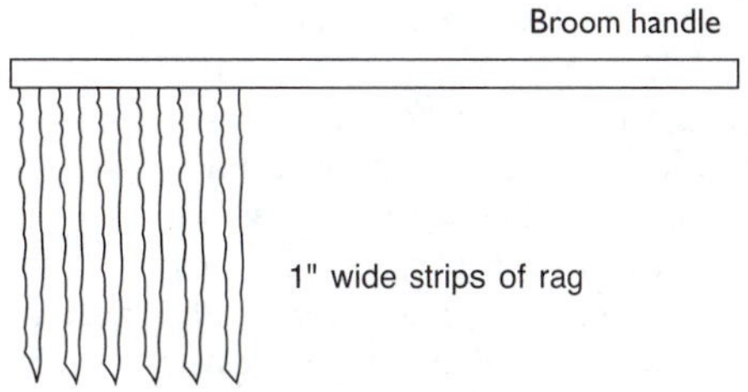

Figure 4.180 Fire-flicker device.

* Water ripple effect — To suggest that the action is near water, use a water tray 0.6 m × 0.6 m × 0.1 m with broken mirror in the bottom, half-filled with water. Bounce a Fresnel spotlight from very close to the tray (it must collect all the light beam) and disturb the water slightly to obtain water ripple effect on the set or artistes.

* Candlelight — This effect is clearly enhanced by having the candle flame in shot, at least for some of the time. To maintain the right warmth, it is important that the candle itself should appear warm. This is best achieved by moving the white point on the camera, i.e. white balance through ½CTB or ¾CTB, to ensure that the complete scene is 'warmed up'.

- Lightning — Use a special lightning discharge source, or a semaphore shutter on an HMI/MSR Fresnel spotlight.

Creating mood or atmosphere (implicit requirements)

The main lighting-related parameters which affect the mood or atmosphere are:

- texture;
- ambiguity;
- clarity;
- colour;
- lighting balance – relative lighting levels;
- exposure.

Texture – subjects look more interesting and appear more realistic when texture is revealed to a maximum, i.e. the nature of the surface of the subject is revealed by using a large angle between the keylight and the camera. This applies equally to buildings and to people. Dark clothing, for example, is best revealed when lit for texture. Maximum texture will help in the creation of dramatic-looking pictures.

Ambiguity is one of the major factors in creating mood, namely the degree of ambiguity created by the lighting, i.e. uncertainty of what we are seeing; the greater the ambiguity, the more mystery created. An example of this would be the lighting of a scene depicting moonlight, by introducing a 'cookie', dapple-plate or tree-branch gobo in front of the light source. The scene is transformed from a 'clear moonlit' scene to one of uncertainty and mystery.

Clarity in terms of image sharpness and contrast is another factor affecting mood. Camera filters can be used to modify these parameters:

- Black nets — reduces image sharpness, excellent in reducing harshness on face tones.
- White nets — as black net, but also 'lifts' the blacks, halation on highlights.
- Fogs — creates the effect of natural fog.
- Double fogs — as fog filter, but with clearer subject detail.
- Promist — removes harshness, adds small amount of flare and slight reduction in contrast.
- Black promist — removes harshness, with less flare than promist, useful for the 'film' look.
- Warm promist — as promist but with additional warming, useful for exterior skin tones.
- Warm soft/fx — retains clarity, but softening details, with warming, useful for skin tones.

Normally, filters are graded in sets of 5, where 1 is the most subtle effect and 5 is the most severe effect. This enables the choice of filter to suit each situation, i.e. zoom angle and severity of effect required. These filters are most effective at wide apertures, i.e. $f2.0–f2.8$.

Some of the filters have more subtle grades, i.e. ¼ and ½.

Before using the filters for a particular requirement, it is recommended to experiment with them to determine the most appropriate filters (again, saving studio time on the recording day), using a large, good quality picture monitor to assess the effects.

The following effects of the above filters should be noted:

- reduction in picture sharpness;
- reduction in picture contrast;
- 'lifting' of black level;
- 'star' filter type effects on extreme highlights;
- effect on highlights – candles, windows, practicals, etc.;
- effect on skin tones.

Record also the camera parameters of f_{no} and focal length.

Colour

The effect of colour has already been discussed in terms of warming a picture or cooling a picture.

Basic principle 'reminder'

A useful concept is that of considering an artiste in plan view and ensuring a lit/dark/lit/dark scenario. Fig. 4.181 illustrates this principle.

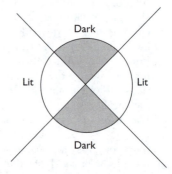

Figure 4.181
Lit/dark/lit/dark scenario.

Provided two of the segments are lit to a lower level than the two 'lit' segments, the artiste will look three-dimensional from any angle. If all four segments are lit to be the same value, the artiste will be illuminated only, and not have a three-dimensional look.

4.14.5 Summary

From all that has been said it can be seen that drama lighting has to be something of a compromise because:

(a) Shooting is multicamera.
(b) Artistes are moving and changing their eyelines.
(c) There cannot be a separate key/backlight/filler for every single position the artist may take up – for example 1 artiste with, say, 10 positions in one set would require 30 luminaires.
(d) Multicamera techniques require that long shots and close-ups are lit for at the same time!
(e) Sound pick-up is usually by means of a boom microphone. Careful positioning of luminaires is essential to avoid boom shadows (see Section 4.15).
(f) Lighting hoists may not be in the ideal position.
(g) The optimum position for two or more luminaires may be in the same physical position; some compromise has to be reached on their final position.
(h) The planned artiste and camera positions may need to be changed during the rehearsals if problems arise.

All these factors point to the need for careful planning of the lighting facilities. Ideally, the lighting director should be very familiar with the script and the action and know the main acting areas. He or she should strive to achieve the illusion of realism within the allotted timescale.

Unless called upon for some spectacular lighting effects, the lighting director can assume to have done a good job if no one notices the lighting!

4.15 Coping with sound

At one time, the microphone boom, with its operator, was regarded as the principal method of sound pick-up in a television studio. Its main advantage is that it allows for very flexible sound pick-up, providing the facility to:

- follow artistes' movements within a set;
- adjust sound perspective as required by adjusting microphone distance to artistes;
- help with sound balance by favouring artistes as necessary.

The disadvantages are:

- it requires an operator;
- it requires space in the studio;
- it creates a shadow, which may be seen in shot!

Often, a **fish pole** is used in a similar way to the microphone boom, both in the studios and on location. This requires less space, is very flexible in its use, obviously still requires an operator, but can still give rise to an in-shot shadow!

The use of compact personal microphones has reduced the need for boom coverage for many situations; nevertheless, the boom is still usually used for audience chat shows as well as being the main method of sound pick-up for drama productions.

As soon as it is clear that a microphone boom or fish pole is to be used on a production, the lighting and shooting techniques *must* take this into account to ensure that in-shot shadows are avoided.

4.15.1 Minimizing boom shadows

Plotting keylight positions without due recognition of the presence of a sound microphone boom is a sure recipe for in-shot shadows! With artistes working downstage towards cameras, typical of many documentary programmes, an angle between keylight and camera of 25–30° is required to minimize the possibility of in-shot shadows. The angle between keylight and camera should relate to the lens angle of view. This is shown in Fig. 4.182.

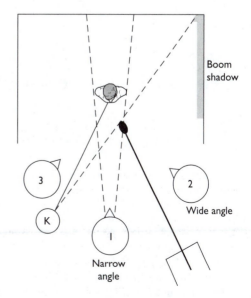

Figure 4.182 The basic principle for avoiding boom shadows.

Clearly, when microphone booms are in use, the position of the boom has to be decided at the planning stage so that the director and lighting director may plan accordingly.

From Fig. 4.182 it can be seen that, provided camera 1 avoids taking a wide-angle shot, its shot will be clear of boom shadows. Camera 2, with a large angle between it and the keylight, will have no boom shadow problems, shooting from close-up to wide-angle. Camera 3, positioned under the keylight, taking a wide-angle shot with no angle difference to the keylight, will have tremendous boom shadow problems unless the keylight is very steep or the set is a long distance behind the artiste (shadow is then on the floor).

Note that if the artiste moves upstage, the boom shadow moves towards the artiste (Fig. 4.183).

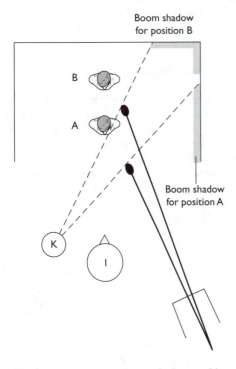

Figure 4.183 Upstage artiste – boom shadow problem.

In drama sets, the basic lighting treatment as discussed earlier should result in the boom shadow appearing downstage and out-of-shot (Fig. 4.184). However, even this can cause problems, as shown in Fig. 4.185(a). Fig. 4.185(b) shows how this problem may be overcome.

Similarly, with a large set, one can avoid boom shadows by using two keylights, as seen earlier in the discussion on drama lighting (see, for example, Figs 4.177 and 4.178).

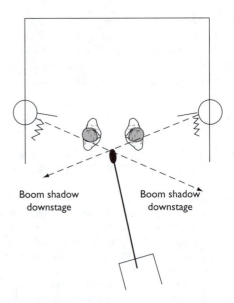

Figure 4.184 Upstage keylights and boom shadows.

4.15.2 Getting rid of boom shadows

When boom shadows appear, despite planning to avoid them, it is good to have a strategy, namely, check that everything is as planned:

- artiste position;
- camera position and shot size;
- boom position and position of microphone.

Based on the premise that artistes, cameras and booms can usually be moved more easily than luminaires, ask:

- Can anything be modified to help?
  - artiste position, move away from set
  - camera position, shot size and framing
  - boom position and microphone position
- Is there an easy alternative method of sound pick-up?

The ball is now in lighting's 'court' if you get this far! So what can be done?

- Check barndooring on keylight.
- Increase horizontal keying angle.
- Increase vertical keying angle.
- Use a cutter to get a harder 'cut' of keylight on the background.
- Localize keylight to artiste only and use a second light for the background.

(a)

(b)

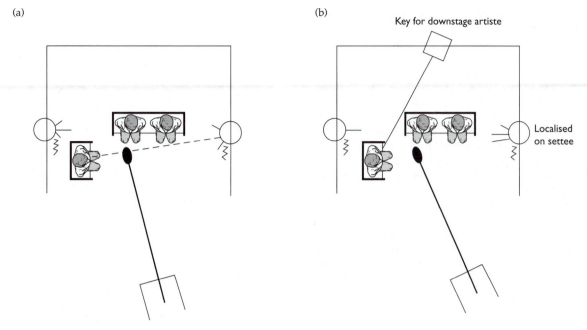

Figure 4.185 (a) Boom shadow problem; (b) use of an extra keylight to solve the boom shadow problem.

- If it is a 'muddy' shadow, i.e. softlight shadow, it may be possible to 'light it out' with an additional light. This is not a preferred method – the set may be over-lit and, having added an additional light, we have an additional set of shadows!
- Sometimes it may be possible to change the keylight position and use a spotlight on a stand, which can 'reach' the artiste underneath the boom arm.

4.16 Lighting on location

Why should we need lighting on location with today's sensitive cameras? The answer is that natural or artificial lighting may provide sufficient illuminance, but it may not result in pictures which look correct.

Lighting may be required to:

- correct picture contrast;
- correct the level of illuminance;
- supplement nature, to provide
  - keylight
  - fill-light
  - backlight
  - kicker light
  - set lighting;
- provide continuity of lighting treatment – natural lighting changes continuously;
- provide corrective lighting, e.g. middle of the day, steep sunlight;

- provide suitable lighting treatment where no natural lighting exists.

4.16.1 Problems of lighting on location

The main production problem is lack of control of the environment – weather, extraneous noises, etc. The main lighting problems are the same as in a studio but are larger:

- **Illuminance** – direct sunlight can be as high as 100 000 lux! On a dreary winter's day it can be as low as a few hundred lux.
- **Colour temperature** – this can vary from 2000 K to over 10 000 K depending on conditions:

dusk/dawn	>6500 K
sunrise/sunset	2000–3000 K
average summer sunlight	5500 K
sun through clouds	6000 K
overcast cloudy day	6500 K
blue sky	8000–20 000 K.

- **Contrast ratio** – average scene contrast ratio is approximately 150:1 with contrast ratios of 1000:1 possible.

In addition, the following logistical problems have to be solved:

- Providing sufficient power:
  - available domestic mains – sufficient?

– special mains feed
– generator (silenced).
• Providing appropriate lighting suspension:
  – stands
  – trussing
  – scaffolding
  – scissor lift
  – hydraulic platform ('cherry picker').
• Providing a wide range of appropriate luminaires on site, including waterproof covers.
• Providing appropriate lighting grip equipment.
• Providing a range of appropriate filters which may be required.
• Providing appropriate transport.

Very few locations in the world can guarantee consistently fine weather over a prolonged period – usually the weather is somewhat unpredictable. Consequently, there is a need for a wide range of suitable luminaires to enable the day-to-day lighting needs to be met. For most exterior lighting applications, luminaires with daylight matching light sources are used, e.g. HMI, MSR, CID. These have the obvious merit of colour matching to average summer sunlight and have a much greater light output than an equivalent tungsten source, i.e. better lumens/watt (efficacy).

On small-scale operations one of the most useful discharge sources is the 1.2 kW HMI, which can be handled by one person and can be fed safely from a domestic 13 A socket.

Mixed lighting

For many location shoots there is a need to cope with the problem of mixed lighting, i.e. daylight and tungsten sources. Typically, this would be when lighting indoors during daylight hours. There is a need to correct the light sources to a common colour temperature by using appropriate filters:

• to correct the tungsten sources to daylight (5500 K);
• to correct the daylight to tungsten (3200 K);
• to correct both sources to an intermediate value, say 4300 K.

There are two basic colour correction filters: colour temperature blue (CTB) and colour temperature orange (CTO).

The colour temperature blue (CTB) filters transmit more blue wavelengths than orange/red wavelengths. The increase in the proportion of blue light and decrease in red light results in an increase in colour temperature (Fig. 4.186).

Often it is necessary to make intermediate or minor adjustments to colour temperature. A range of CTB

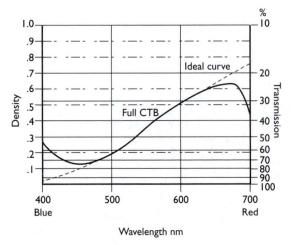

Figure 4.186 Filter characteristics for full colour temperature blue (CTB).

Table 4.16 Colour temperature blue (CTB) filters – basic conversion.

Filter	Conversion	Transmission
Full CTB	3200–5700 K	34%
¾CTB	3200–5000 K	45%
½CTB	3200–4300 K	55%
¼CTB	3200–3600 K	69%
⅛CTB	3200–3400 K	81%

Note: Please see later tables for complete data on conversion.

filters is therefore available for this purpose, as shown in Table 4.16.

Note that the transmission of a full colour temperature blue, often referred to as a 'full blue', is only about 33%! This represents a significant loss of light; for example, a 2 kW tungsten lamp effectively becomes a 660 W lamp. Often a compromise is made on correction and light loss by using a ½CTB, or the recently developed ¾CTB.

The colour temperature orange (CTO) filters behave in the opposite way to the CTB filters. They transmit more orange/red wavelengths than blue, and consequently the colour temperature is decreased (Fig. 4.187).

A similar range of CTO filters is available to make possible intermediate or minor adjustments to colour temperature (Table 4.17).

Note that the transmission of a full CTO (full orange) is 55%, significantly more than a full blue.

When using CTO filters on 'in-shot' windows, the filter must be placed on the outside of the window, otherwise the window glazing bars will be changed

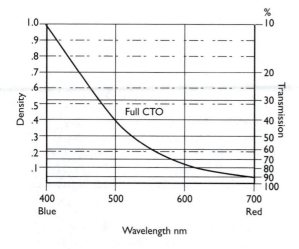

Figure 4.187 Filter characteristics for full colour temperature orange (CTO).

Table 4.17 Colour temperature orange (CTO) filters – basic conversion.

Filter	Conversion	Transmission
Full CTO	6500–3200 K	55%
¾CTO	6500–3600 K	61%
½CTO	6500–3800 K	71%
¼CTO	6500–4600 K	79%
⅛CTO	6500–5500 K	85%

Note: Please see later tables for complete data on conversion.

in colour by the filter. With large plate windows it may be possible to squeegee the filter onto the window.

Ideally, the CTO filters should be stapled to wooden frames and wedged in place. Care should be taken to avoid any wrinkles in the filter as these will cause reflection of lights.

Acrylic filters, 3 mm thick, are available which overcome the problem of maintaining a rigid, wrinkle-free filter. These are more expensive than the normal flexible (polyester) filters.

MIRED

Often it is required to estimate which filter to use for a particular application. Unfortunately, the change in colour temperature produced with a particular filter depends on the starting colour temperature.

A full blue causes a bigger change on a 4000 K source than a 2800 K source:

2800 K + Full Blue = 4600 K (1800 K shift)

3200 K + Full Blue = 5700 K (2500 K shift)
4000 K + Full Blue = 8850 K (4850 K shift)

Fortunately, it is possible to predict the effect of a filter by using the concept of MIREDs.

MIREDs are based on the observation that a given filter causes a **constant** shift in the **reciprocal** value of the colour temperature of a light source. Unfortunately, the reciprocal value of a colour temperature will give a very small number, so to make the numbers easier to handle we use MIREDs where MIRED stands for 'micro-reciprocal degrees'.

The MIRED value of a light source is given by:

$$\frac{1}{K} \times \frac{1}{10^{-6}} = \frac{10^6}{K}$$

For example, the MIRED value for 5000 K is:

$$\frac{10^6}{5000} = 200 \text{ MIREDs}$$

Manufacturers quote the MIRED shift for all colour temperature correction filters. CTB filters reduce the MIRED value of the colour temperature and therefore have a negative sign (Table 4.18).

Table 4.18 MIRED shift of CTB/CTO filters.

Filter	MIRED shift	Filter	MIRED shift
Full CTB	−137	Full CTO	+159
¾CTB	−113	¾CTO	+124
½CTB	−78	½CTO	+109
¼CTB	−35	¼CTO	+64
⅛CTB	−18	⅛CTO	+26

Using this concept we can estimate the filter required to cause a particular change in colour temperature, or predict the new colour temperature when using a particular filter.

For example, what filter is required to simulate moonlight (4100 K) when using a 3200 K tungsten source?

$$\text{MIRED value of 3200 K} = \frac{10^6}{3200} = 312$$

$$\text{MIRED value of 4100 K} = \frac{10^6}{4100} = 243$$

Required MIRED shift = 69, i.e. ½CTB (−78 MIREDs)

Note that the tolerances of 3200 K ± 150 K and 5500 K ± 400 K, discussed earlier, represents a MIRED shift of approximately 14 MIREDs. Consequently, use of the ½CTB filter would be within this tolerance.

As another example, what is the new colour temperature if a ¾CTO is used on a 3200 K source?

$$\text{MIRED value of } 3200\,K = \frac{10^6}{3200} = 312$$

MIRED shift of ¾CTO = +124

New MIRED value = 436

$$\text{New colour temperature} = \frac{10^6}{436} = 2293\,K \simeq 2300\,K$$

Colour temperature correction filters are often used to create appropriate lighting effects, e.g. moonlight, sunset. Tables 4.19–4.21 give the appropriate colour temperature change introduced when using them.

Colour temperate correction filters may be used to change the white balance or white point on the camera. For example, if one wished to have warmer pictures, say in a tungsten lit scene, rather than putting ¼CTO filters on all the light sources one could

Table 4.19 Tungsten light conversion.

Filter	Conversion	MIRED shift	Transmission
Full CTB	3200–5700 K	−137	34%
¾CTB	3200–5000 K	−113	45%
½CTB	3200–4300 K	−78	55%
¼CTB	3200–3600 K	−35	69%
⅛CTB	3200–3400 K	−18	81%
Full CTO	3200–2100 K	+159	55%
¾CTO	3200–2300 K	+124	61%
½CTO	3200–2400 K	+109	71%
¼CTO	3200–2650 K	+64	79%
⅛CTO	3200–2950 K	+26	85%

Table 4.20 Daylight conversion.

Filter	Conversion	MIRED shift	Transmission
Full CTO	6500–3200 K	+159	55%
¾CTO	6500–3600 K	+124	61%
½CTO	6500–3800 K	+109	71%
¼CTO	6500–4600 K	+64	79%
⅛CTO	6500–5550 K	+26	85%
Also			
¾CTO	5300–3200 K	+124	61%
½CTO	4900–3200 K	+109	71%
¼CTO	4000–3200 K	+64	79%
⅛CTO	3700–3200 K	+26	85%

Table 4.21 Average summer sunlight conversion.

Filter	Conversion	MIRED shift	Transmission
Full CTB	5500–22 000 K	−137	34%
¾CTB	5500–14 500 K	−113	45%
½CTB	5500–9600 K	−78	55%
¼CTB	5500–6800 K	−35	69%
⅛CTB	5500–6100 K	−18	81%
Full CTO	5500–2950 K	+159	55%
¾CTO	5500–3270 K	+124	61%
½CTO	5500–3450 K	+109	71%
¼CTO	5500–4100 K	+64	79%
⅛CTO	5500–4800 K	+26	85%

simply move the white points to ¼CTB by holding a ¼CTB filter over the lens at the time of white balancing the camera. The 3200 K lit scene would look warm, with only scene elements lit with 3600 K (3200 K + ¼CTB) looking 'normal' (Fig. 4.188).

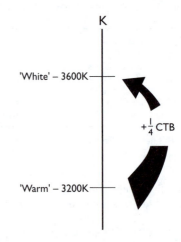

Figure 4.188 Change of 'white' point.

Note that colour temperature correction filters may be used in combination. Simply add the MIRED shift of each filter to determine the effect of a combination, and multiply the transmission factors to determine the overall transmission, for example:

½CTB + ½CTB = Full CTB
(−78) + (−78) = −156 MIREDS

Note that this is about 19 MIREDs greater than a full CTB (−137), i.e. a noticeable departure from average daylight.

Some camera operators only carry ½CTB as a compromise on correction/transmission; this is usually satisfactory, but one needs to be aware of the over-correction when used together to produce full CTB.

Similarly, overall transmission factor = 0.55 × 0.55 = 0.30, i.e. 30% transmission.

Beware of using filters in combination on luminaires – heat absorbed by the filters becomes trapped between them, resulting in a short filter life.

Excessive contrast

A common problem encountered on location is that of the excessive contrast, i.e. greater than 32:1 (5 stops), when shooting against windows (Fig. 4.189).

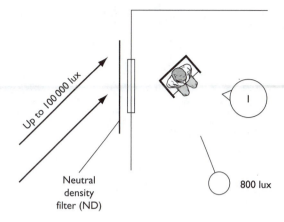

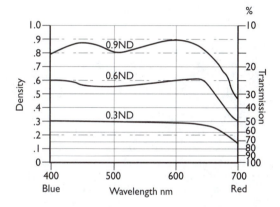

Figure 4.190 Use of ND filters to overcome problem of excessive contrast.

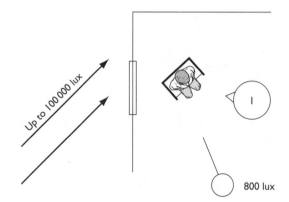

Figure 4.189 Basic problem of excessive contrast.

The outside lighting illuminance may be very high, up to 100 000 lux. Consequently, it will be over-exposed compared with the interior or the interior under-exposed when the exterior is correctly exposed. There is a need either to reduce the exterior illuminance or to increase the interior illuminance. Normally it is impractical to achieve daylight lighting levels indoors; in addition, the excessive heat and light levels would make it very uncomfortable for the artistes. The solution is to introduce neutral density filters between the interior and exterior scenes, i.e. on the window (Fig. 4.190).

Neutral density filters (ND filters) are filters which have very little colour bias and simply reduce the light equally throughout the spectrum (Fig. 4.191).

$$\text{Density} = \log_{10} \frac{1}{\text{transmission factor}} \text{ or } \log_{10} \text{opacity}$$

So a filter with a 50% transmission (0.5 transmission factor) has a density of:

$$\log_{10} \frac{1}{0.5} = \log_{10} 2 = 0.3$$

Figure 4.191 Characteristics of typical ND filters.

Again, it is useful to think of the change in exposure introduced by the ND filter in terms of f_{stops}. The 0.3 ND filter would therefore introduce a one f_{stop} loss.

A range of ND filters is available (Table 4.19). Note that the ND filters may be used together, e.g. 0.3 + 0.6 will result in 0.9 ND.

The density scale is obviously a logarithmic scale so equal changes in density are perceived equally by the eye, i.e. 0.3, 0.6, 0.9, 1.2.

Estimation of the required neutral density

A simple test can be used to determine the required neutral density filter (Fig. 4.192):

(1) Assume that the camera is required to operate at f2.8 to give the appropriate depth of field.
(2) Expose the camera for the exterior scene and note f_{stop}.
(3) The difference between f2.8 and the derived f_{stop} indicates the required ND. For example, if

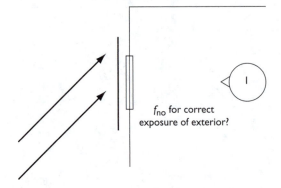

Figure 4.192 Determining the value of an ND filter.

exterior f_{stop} is $f8.0$, the difference between exterior and interior exposure is 3 stops, so the filter required is 0.9 ND.

Notes

- Always err on the side of under-correction, not over-correction. The exterior should always look brighter than the interior, otherwise it will look wrong.
- Normally the ND filter has to be used outside the window to avoid darkening window glazing bars, in a similar way to CTO filters.
- For large plate glass windows it may be possible to squeegee the filter onto the inside of the window.
- Acrylic ND filters, 3 mm thick, are available which also avoid the problems of flexible filters, i.e. they are flat and rigid.
- When 2 f_{stops} of loss are required a perforated filter known as 'scrim' may be used instead of ND filters. This is a reflective material, shiny on one side and black on the other. It is easier to handle than ND but always needs to be used on the outside of windows to avoid internal reflections onto the window. It cannot be used as a double layer because of moiré patterns created when the two perforated filters are placed in contact.
- Care has to be taken with exterior backlit scenes. If the ND filter is chosen to give correct exposure of the sky, the exterior scene will look underexposed. It is better to compromise on the sky to get a correctly exposed exterior scene, allowing the sky detail to 'burn-out' (limit).
- If possible, avoid sunlight shining directly onto the subject; it creates problems of excessive contrast, is of a constantly changing angle, and may be variable (clouds).

When shooting anyone against a window, apart from getting the exterior to look correct, it is *essential* that

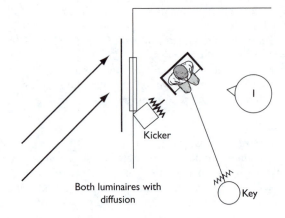

Figure 4.193 Use of a 'kicker'.

the artiste is *apparently* lit with light from outside the window. This is vital if the artiste is going to look like they belong in the scene. This can often be achieved by using a kicker placed inside the room, placed as far upstage as possible (Fig. 4.193).

Note: Polarizing filter may be helpful with backlit scenes.

4.16.2 Strategy on location

A basic strategy when lighting on location is to 'add what is necessary'. Don't automatically reach for your three-lamp kit but set up the shot to see what nature has given you, then add what is necessary to make it look correct. Only use the minimum area of ND filter, consistent with shot size, to ensure that the natural light entering the room is not reduced by too much, i.e. it still has an effect as a backlight. When complete windows are fitted with ND filters it may be necessary to add suitable HMI sources outside the window to maintain the appropriate lighting effect inside the building.

To summarize:

- set up camera
- evaluate natural lighting
- decide what is needed:
    - tungsten/daylight sources?
    - ND filters?
- rig lights/filters
- balance light sources.

Note: 0.15 ND and 0.3 ND filters are useful on light sources to enable a lighting balance to be achieved quickly. Always mark pieces of ND with their value using a white chinagraph pencil – this can save time later in identifying them!

4.16.3 Lighting continuity

On long shoots it may be easier to block the direct sunlight through south-facing windows and introduce your own 'sunlight' through north-facing windows using appropriate daylight sources.

One of the major problems when shooting single-camera is that of lighting continuity. When, say, shooting a two-handed interview it is important that the **reversal** shots are compatible with the initial shots. To ensure that the pictures match one should aim for:

- identical camera angles and camera-to-subject distance;
- identical f_{no};
- similar illuminance on subject and background.

If the luminaires are used at similar 'throws', the requirements for similar illuminance should be met. A useful aid in any lighting set-up is a small incident light meter. This can be used to check lighting levels to achieve a rough balance before the artiste is 'on-set'. An alternative is to use a spot-meter to check face tone values and background values. For good separation of face tones from the background, tonal separation of about 1½ EV is recommended (1½ stops) or approximately 1:3 ratio (remember that this is the *relative* luminance indicated by reflected lighting levels).

Other aids to lighting continuity include devices like Hamlet, which enable the television waveform to be displayed on a picture monitor. A variable **cursor** is included so that a particular signal level can be indicated for continuous reference. This is particularly useful for night shots and location chroma key set-ups.

4.16.4 Exterior lighting on location

The changing state of natural lighting has already been stressed. Lighting may be needed to help in making the pictures 'look right'.

Excessive contrast
Bright sunny days result in very dark shadows on the face:

sunlight illuminance $\simeq$ 100 000 lux
skylight illuminance $\simeq$ 12 000 lux

The resulting contrast is approximately 8:1, i.e. 3 stops (Fig. 4.194). Remembering the 5-stop dynamic range,

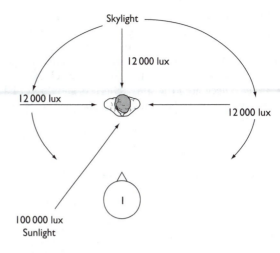

Figure 4.194 Sunlit artiste – basic problem.

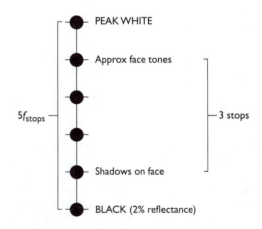

Figure 4.195 Dynamic range of sunlit artiste.

with face tones approximately one stop below peak white exposure, then the shadow areas are 4 stops down on peak white (Fig. 4.195).

Clearly there is a need to add fill-light into the shadow areas otherwise the pictures will look too harsh, with heavy shadows. This can be achieved in one of two ways:

- use of a suitable reflector board to reflect sunlight into the shadow areas;
- use of a daylight source to add light to the shadow areas.

Use of reflectors
This is a simple solution provided the relationship of the sun to the action allows easy positioning of the reflector.

The reflector may be a matt-white surface if used close, while for longer throws a metallic reflector is used. Ideally, the surface used should result in a soft reflection, i.e. a dimpled, perforated or multi-faceted reflector medium, so that the artiste is not blinded by a direct reflection of the sun. Reflectors should not be used directly on the artiste's eyeline, again to avoid blinding the artiste.

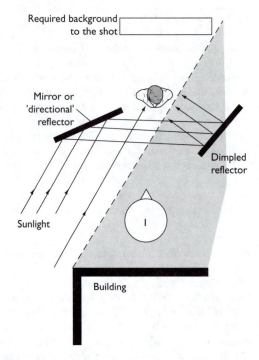

Figure 4.197 Use of two reflectors.

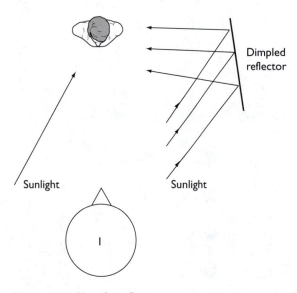

Figure 4.196 Use of a reflector.

Reflectors should always be manned to ensure correct setting and to prevent them from being blown over. After use the reflectors should be turned towards the ground to avoid accidental blinding of motorists!

The advantages in using a reflector are:

- it is simple;
- it does not require a mains supply;
- once the appropriate lighting balance has been achieved it is self-maintaining, i.e. if the sun fades, the 'fill' also fades in direct proportion.

The disadvantages in using a reflector are:

- the sun may not be in an appropriate place;
- it requires an operator;
- it is difficult to follow subject movement.

Sometimes it may be necessary to employ two reflectors to get the fill-light where it is needed, i.e. a mirror is used to reflect the sun onto the reflector (Fig. 4.197).

Use of daylight sources (HMI etc.)

Daylight sources, of course, can be used from any angle, provided the lamp stand shadow is not seen in shot. Usually an HMI is used together with diffusion to reduce the possibility of a second hard shadow.

The advantages of using a daylight source are:

- does not require continuous adjustment as with the reflector;

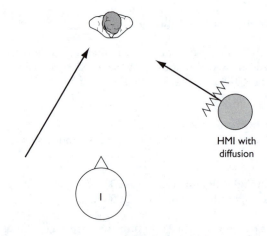

Figure 4.198 Use of a daylight source as fill-light.

- can be used from any lighting angle relative to the sun;
- can cover a wider area than a reflector;
- easy adjustment of illuminance with spot/flood mechanism or movement of luminaire position;
- easy to cover artiste movement with simple pan of the luminaire.

The disadvantages of using a daylight source are:

- requires a suitable mains feed;
- does not adjust automatically if the sun 'fades', unlike a reflector;
- any discharge source of 2.5 kW or larger will usually require two electricians.

Corrective lighting – sunlit scenes

It has already been mentioned that there may be an abundance of natural light but it may not produce pleasing pictures. Take, for example, someone standing under the noon-day sun during summer. This will result in most unflattering lighting and is probably not acceptable. Corrective lighting has to be applied by diffusing the direct sunlight using a **butterfly** (6' × 6') rigged over the artiste and then re-lighting under the butterfly with appropriate daylight sources (Fig. 4.199).

Corrective lighting – overcast

A similar requirement for corrective lighting exists with exterior scenes on a totally overcast day.

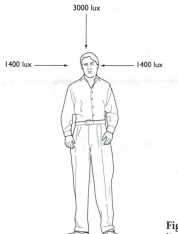

Figure 4.200 Overcast lighting, typical levels.

Typically, the conditions will produce a 'toppy' effect with twice as much light measured vertically as horizontally (Fig. 4.200).

This will result in the artistes having 'dark' eyes and over-lighting of bald-heads! The problem can be corrected by using a diffused daylight source at a low elevation, which will lift the darkness around the eyes and introduce a catchlight in them. An overhead diffuser could also be useful to reduce the 'toppy' lighting effect and the over-lighting of bald heads. However, do beware of over-lighting the foreground subject – they will no longer look as though they belong in the picture!

Negative lighting

When no light sources are available, it may be possible to introduce some modelling, light and shade, to an otherwise flatly lit subject by removing light, i.e. using a black flag to shade one side of the subject. An alternative would be to place the artiste near a dark-sided building (Fig. 4.201).

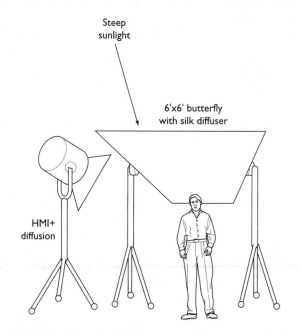

Figure 4.199 Use of a butterfly.

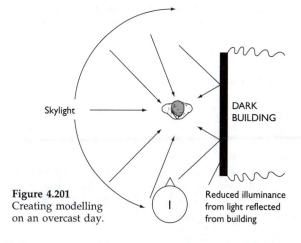

Figure 4.201 Creating modelling on an overcast day.

Overcast day and excess contrast

Avoid shooting artistes' heads against the sky. The sky is a light source and as such can be very much brighter than the daylight lit skin tones (Fig. 4.202).

Figure 4.202 Overcast sky and face tones.

Use of kickers on location

A small daylight source, such as a handlamp, can be used to create a **kicker** on overcast days. This helps to reveal more texture and will make the artiste look more three-dimensional. Alternatively, side-lighting the artiste will help to bring out texture.

Use of camera ND filters

On overcast days it is especially useful to use the camera ND filter to introduce neutral density filter into the optical path. The consequence of this is to create the need to open up the lens iris, with a resultant reduction in depth-of-field, i.e. thus making the artiste better separated from the background.

Use of polarizing filter

Remember, a polarizing filter can be used to control glare reflection. This can be useful to use, on the camera, in circumstances where there is no control of heavily backlit sunlit scenes, i.e. reducing the intensity of a kicker on the artiste, plus any other glare reflections in the scene.

A polarizing filter may also be used to darken blue sky (polarized), making white clouds become more dramatic, and also to improve the colour purity of costumes.

4.16.5 Night lighting on location

The points to be considered for lighting at night on location are similar to those identified for creating mood, i.e. texture, ambiguity, colour, lighting, balance and exposure.

Texture is so important when lighting a shot at night. Typically, one is lighting a location so that it looks like night, i.e. dimly lit; without texture being revealed the result will be uninteresting and flat. Clothing, especially dark clothing, is more readily revealed when lit for texture. The same is true for buildings.

Ambiguity, as discussed earlier, is a major parameter in creating an element of mystery. Night lighting is very much an area for using dapple-plates (cookies) and simple 'dingles' (tree branches) in front of lights to create a shadowed and mysterious look to the location.

The **colour** of light used at night is an area for a major debate, and there are several opinions on what is best. Some lighting directors avoid coloured light completely, while others use colour according to their own observation and what looks right for them. The correct placing of luminaire is important to create the right effect before considering the use of colour.

The potential light sources at night are:

- moonlight at 4100 K;
- domestic tungsten at 2760 K;
- street lamps (sodium) at 2000 K (low pressure) to 2400 K (high pressure).

So, what about the use of coloured light at night?

The stylized film treatment of using a fairly strong blue filter on lights or camera lens originates from the observation that at extremely low levels of illuminance, i.e. moonlight (0.1 lux), human vision becomes monochromatic and we no longer see any colour, only a black/white landscape. One way to remove the colour from a scene, except of course blue, is to use a blue filter. This leaves the scene very blue.

Another argument for using blue is that when the eye/brain changes from photopic vision (full colour) to scotopic vision (night vision – monochromatic), there is a small shift in the peak response towards the blue end of the spectrum; this is sometimes used as an argument for using blue. However, the eye/brain sees this as a black/white image – not a very convincing argument for using blue!

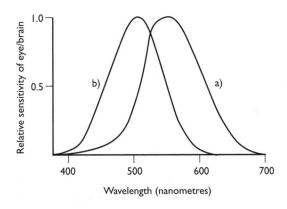

Figure 4.203 Relative spectral sensitivity of the eye/brain: (a) photopic; (b) scotopic.

Probably the best way to tackle the use of colour at night is to look at relative colour differences, say between moonlight and domestic tungsten. Moonlight is reflected sunlight, but without the presence of skylight, so it will be less than average summer sunlight; a colour temperature of 4100 K is usually quoted.

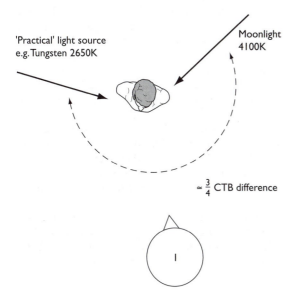

Figure 4.204 Night exterior scene – 'reality'.

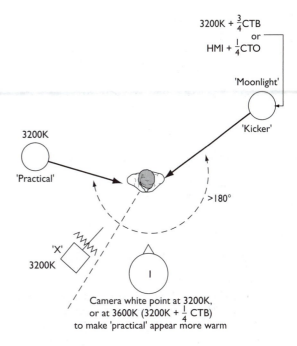

Note: Luminaire 'X' to give catchlights and provide appropriate fill-light

Figure 4.205 Night exterior scene – practical arrangement.

A scene involving absolute reality is shown in Fig. 4.204. This lighting plot could be realized with filtering of light sources, for example:

$$\text{Moonlight} \left\{ \begin{array}{c} \text{Tungsten halogen} \\ 3200\ \text{K} + \frac{1}{2}\text{CTB} \\ \text{or} \\ \text{HMI/MSR } 5600\ \text{K} + \frac{1}{2}\text{CTO} \end{array} \right\} = 4300\ \text{K}$$

$$\begin{array}{c} \text{Domestic} \\ \text{tungsten} \end{array} \quad \begin{array}{c} \text{Tungsten halogen} \\ 3200\ \text{K} + \frac{1}{4}\text{CTO} \end{array} = 2650\ \text{K}$$

A simpler solution would be to minimize the amount of filtering by just ensuring that the *difference* between the sources is the correct colour shift – that is the correct MIRED shift, in this case a ¾CTB difference.

An alternative, practical solution is shown in Fig. 4.205. Or use full CTB + white flame green filters to give a cool moonlight, which is not so harsh on face tones.

Yet another alternative, depending on personal preference, is to reduce the colour temperature difference to ½CTB. There will be slight differences in the

effect achieved from one manufacturer's camera to another. Certainly, the older tube cameras had an enhanced blue response so ½CTB correction was satisfactory. Generally, aim at subtle use of colour – if it is too strong the effect will look too theatrical. Note the use of a kicker as opposed to an off-set elevated backlight – the kicker should be at eye level and aimed at the subject's temple. This reveals more texture on the side of the face and although a 'cheat' on reality, generally produces a better result than the elevated backlight.

It is important to note:

- The two main lights must be greater than 180° apart to avoid contamination of coloured light.
- For best results avoid symmetrical lighting on the face from the keylight and kicker.
- The small filler light, plus diffusion, provides a catch-light in the eye. It *must* be positioned to camera left of the eyeline to avoid contamination of coloured light and to maintain good texture on the face. The lighting balance of this light is crucial to the mood created. If only a hint of light around the eyes is required this can best be achieved with a small plastic mirror (Fig. 4.206).

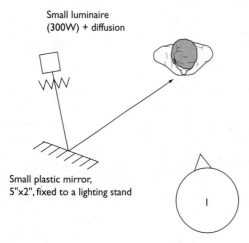

Figure 4.206 Use of a small mirror for 'catchlights'.

If no diffusion is used, the projected image will have a hard edge. The lit area can be reduced by masking off part of the mirror with gaffer tape. This is a much better way of achieving this effect than trying to barndoor a Fresnel spotlight.

- Remember, moonlight should be less intense than the 'practical' lights.
- Avoid over-exposure – generally, exposure will be approximately one stop down on daylight exposure settings.
- Remember that the eye/brain will adapt its 'white' point to the prevailing conditions. Consequently, a building lit with an HMI/MSR may not look as blue as you might expect if the eye/brain has adapted to the HMI 'white'. A yellowish building will of course look white!
- Buildings do not need to be lit to high lighting levels, they only need to be made visible. Typically, floodlit buildings are lit to 50–70 lux!
- Ideally, use a waveform monitor, e.g. Hamlet picoscope, to verify levels or check relative signal levels by flicking to colour bars to re-establish normal levels on the picture monitor.
- It is recommended to experiment with the above ideas to establish your own preference for use of colour, lighting balance and exposure on night shoots.
- Avoid using unfiltered HMI/MSRs to produce moonlight – this tends to produce a very blue coarse look which is not subtle enough.
- Remember that when using minimum lighting levels any ambient light may influence your lighting balance.
- When using a mixture of tungsten and HMI/MSR light sources, remember that HMI/MSRs have 3 to 4 times the efficiency of tungsten sources.

When shooting wide shots, typical techniques are:

- Use a large HMI/MSR + correction as a single major backlight.
- Use smoke upstage, backlit with a suitably corrected HMI/MSR.
- Use the fire brigade to dampen roads, roofs, etc. to help reveal texture.
- If long shots are required, try to 'flag' or barndoor one of the lights off the ground to avoid conflicting floor shadows.

Remember that at night the moving subject will not necessarily be lit constantly, but could be lit from 'practicals', e.g. street lights, lights from windows, car headlamps or lights on buildings. A technique to cover periods of walking through unlit areas is to ensure that the artiste is always seen in silhouette. Used by itself, this is another way of introducing ambiguity; another would be to throw the shadow of the subject onto a building and then shoot the shadow only.

Sodium street lights can be simulated by using ¾CTO on a tungsten source. One could use a similar technique to the moonlight set-up, using a tungsten + ¾CTO as a kicker to suggest the street light.

4.17 Lighting grip equipment

Lighting grip equipment refers to the lighting accessories which may be used to position a luminaire or to control the light beam shape or intensity. Many of the items have already been introduced in this chapter:

Flag stands	Reflector boards	Polecats
Lighting stands	Veils/yashmaks	Super clamps
Scrims/wires	Flag arms plus grip heads	Magic arms
French flags	Butterflies	Barrel clamps
Black flags and cutters	Scissor clamps	Gaffer grips
Finger and dot kits	Sandbags	TV hook clamps

In studios, it is recommended to use stands which have lockable wheels. Always note the load bearing capacity (SWL) for stands.

On location it is recommended to use stands with lockable wheels and also a 'lazy' leg – an adjustable leg which enables the stand to be used on sloping ground or stairs. For maximum stability the lighting stand should be vertical.

Television spigots are 16 mm diameter for lightweight luminaires and 28 mm diameter for standard luminaires. Except for lightweight stands with 16 mm spigots or sockets it is recommended to use a universal head which includes a 28 mm and 16 mm socket plus a pop-up 16 mm spigot. Similarly with barrel clamps, i.e. 28 mm and 16 mm sockets.

Sandbags should be used to add extra weight to flag stands, lighting stands and butterflies to provide extra stability when required.

Scissor clamps, used with lightweight luminaires, provide a 16 mm spigot which can be fastened to the metal supports of a suspended ceiling.

Polecats is the term used to describe lightweight telescopic poles which can be used vertically, horizontally or as a 'goal post' for rigging lights. The polecat is adjusted to fit between, say, floor and ceiling then tensioned to 'jam' in place. Beware of using these on weak ceilings and avoid leaving a black mark on the ceiling by using a piece of card on the top rubber pad (unused beer mats are ideal).

Super clamps were designed for use with polecats. A super clamp is an adjustable clamp with a 16 mm socket, and can be used to clamp onto any suitable fixed shelf, pipe, etc. to provide a rigging position.

Magic arms provide two hinged arms with a 16 mm spigot on the end of each arm. All three movements are locked with one locking arm on the hinge. (Usually they are used with a super clamp on one end.) They are ideal for rigging small lightweight luminaires in awkward places.

The **gaffer grip** is a large adjustable clamp with 16 mm spigots and sockets, again for use with lightweight luminaires.

Collapsible reflectors, with universal brackets, are one of the most useful location items. The universal bracket adjusts to fit the 20″, 38″ or 48″ reflectors which may be white/gold, white/silver diffusion or black.

Also available are large collapsible chrome key backgrounds.

Consumables
These are the items which are generally used once and discarded, or have a limited life:

Gaffer tape
Black wrap
Correction filters
Colour effects filters (gels)
Diffusion media

It is a good practice to have templates for all the different sizes of colour frame used, thus enabling filters to be cut very quickly to size. Use a chinagraph pencil to indicate filter swatch number for easy reference to the filter.

4.18 Lighting control systems

Everything under control! That is really a statement of intent rather than a question. The lighting director ideally wants to have as much as possible under control, and fundamental in this is control of the studio lighting condition, together with a comprehensive monitoring system. The lighting control system should therefore provide:

- a centralized control point – the lighting console;
- control of dimmer levels;
- control of scrollers;
- control of moving lights;
- control of remote machines;
- control of on/off devices;
- comprehensive monitoring facilities;
- remote control from studio floor – riggers panel.

The lighting console provides the necessary control signals to remotely operate dimmers etc. The earlier analogue dimmers used a 0–10 V control signal with 0 ('zero') representing OFF and +10 V representing fully ON. Modern consoles usually convert this to a digital number for sequential transmission over one pair of wires using a digital multiplexing system (DMX 512) (see Section 4.18.2).

An overview of the lighting control system is shown in Fig. 4.207.

Current practice is to include a dimmer for each lighting circuit (outlet) whenever possible. The earlier practice of using a patch-panel to 'patch' (connect) the outputs from a limited number of dimmers to selected outputs is less attractive with the relatively low cost of dimmers and high cost of a patch-panel operation.

From convenience of operation it is very desirable to match a lighting outlet with its associated lighting channel number (dimmer number). With a patching system this is not possible and makes it a less user-friendly system.

Soft patching refers to the facility of patching the control signal from a channel fader to one or more dimmers. This enables a console with 120 control channels to be used to control 512 dimmers.

Proportional soft patching refers to the facility of being able to allocate a proportion of the control signal to a particular dimmer, e.g. 50%, in which case the dimmer would always operate at 50% of the control channel setting.

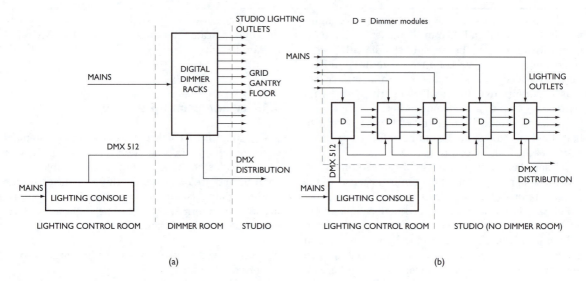

Figure 4.207 Lighting control system using: (a) central dimmer room; (b) distributed dimming.

4.18.1 Dimmers

A dimmer provides an electronic means for controlling the current to a luminaire, and hence its light output. The **thyristor** or **silicon controller rectifier** (SCR) has until recently been used as the most suitable dimmer for television studios. New technology has seen the development of a **transistor** switching element which is gaining popularity.

Thyristor dimmers are sometimes referred to as forward-phase control and transistor dimmers as reverse-phase control.

Thyristor, silicon controlled rectifier dimmer – (forward phase control)

The 0–10 V control signal from the fader is used to control the instant of switch-on for the thyristor

dimmer; once triggered to conduct electricity, the thyristor cannot be switched off until the mains voltage falls to zero or is reversed (Fig. 4.208).

The rapid switch-on of the thyristor causes lamp filament vibration and electrical interference; this interference can be particularly annoying if induced onto microphone circuits as a 100 Hz buzz ('buzz' not 'hum' due to harmonics of the 100 Hz waveform). To increase the switch-on time, a choke (inductor) is included in the circuit. Typical specification for the time-of-rise would be 240 µsec (Fig. 4.209) (BBC specification is 480 µsec).

A special 'star-quad' microphone cable is effective at reducing the electrical interference on audio circuits; it can reduce interference levels by as much as 28 dB (Fig. 4.210).

Thyristor dimmers are heat-sensitive and usually have forced air cooling; they are normally located in

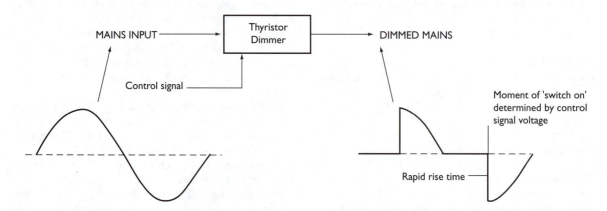

Figure 4.208 Thyristor dimmer principle.

a)

b)

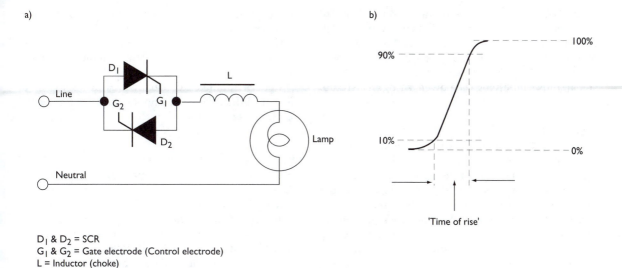

D$_1$ & D$_2$ = SCR
G$_1$ & G$_2$ = Gate electrode (Control electrode)
L = Inductor (choke)

Figure 4.209 (a) Basic thyristor dimmer; (b) 'time-of-rise'.

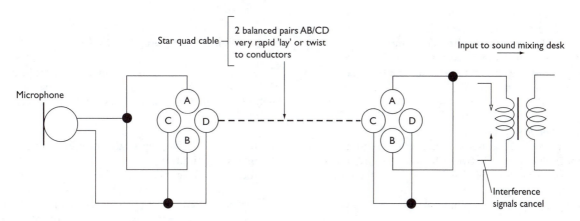

Figure 4.210 Use of star-quad microphone cable.

a dimmer room adjacent to the lighting grid. Cable runs from the dimmer room to the studio outlet should be kept as short as possible to avoid an excessive voltage drop on the cable; this should be less than 4% of the mains voltage.

Transistor dimmers – reverse phase control

The principle of operation for a transistor dimmer is the opposite to the thyristor dimmer in that the device is switched off during each half-cycle (Fig. 4.211). The main advantage of the transistor dimmer is that its switch-off time is longer than the thyristor dimmer switch-on time and it does not involve large current surges on 'switch-on'. It always switches on at the zero point (cross-over point) on the mains

waveform. Consequently, this is a much quieter dimmer and can be located in the studio, adjacent to the studio outlet. Similarly, filament vibration is eliminated, resulting in a quieter studio.

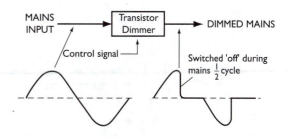

Figure 4.211 Transistor dimmer principle.

Transistor dimmers may be rack-mounted or are available in modules (small dimmer packs), which may be used for distributed dimming. For example, a dimmer strip located on a lighting hoist would only need a single power cable plus a feed of a DMX signal, thus simplifying the power wiring in a studio.

Digital dimmers

As previously mentioned, early control systems used a 0–10 V signal between the console and the dimmers. When DMX 512 was introduced this was used between the consoles and the dimmers, converting the DMX signal back to 0–10 V at the dimmer.

Modern digital dimmers use the DMX data signal directly for processing the control of the dimmer, i.e. the dimmer is operated with a 'number' not an analogue voltage.

Consequently, digital dimmers provide:

- a cheaper dimmer;
- a more reliable and more accurate dimmer;
- faster response to level changes;
- a selection of a number of dimmer laws;
- protection against overloads and short circuits;
- monitoring of dimmer load, control status and temperature.

Dimmer law

An important feature of a dimmer is the dimmer law, the relationship between fader setting and light output. The desirable law is one where the change in lamp brightness appears to be linear. This has to compliment the logarithmic nature of the eye/brain

in the perception of brightness changes – a square law is generally desirable for television (Fig. 4.212).

The law of the dimmer should be constant irrespective of the load placed on the dimmer, i.e. lamp wattage.

Modern dimmers can usually provide a selection of laws including ON/OFF and special laws for control of fluorescent lighting.

Pluggable or hard-wired dimmers

Studio dimmers may be pluggable or hard-wired. Pluggable dimmers are more expensive but provide easy replacement of a faulty dimmer, usually have a better specification than hard-wired dimmers and include a comprehensive back-up and monitoring system. Usually, major studios will use pluggable dimmers; nevertheless, digital hard-wired dimmers are very reliable and offer a cheaper option for small/medium sized studios.

4.18.2 Digital multiplex 512 (DMX 512)

This system was developed initially to meet the needs of distributed dimmer packs and the use of scrollers. Sending an analogue 0–10 V signal long distances meant:

(a) the provision of long lengths of multiway cable, one wire/dimmer;
(b) the received signal could be less than 10 V due to voltage drop on the cable; consequently, a dimmer would never reach 100%, or a colour scroller would never reach the colour dictated by fader 10! This could be particularly problematic if several scrollers, at different distances from the lighting console, were required to display the same colour.

DMX 512 provides a digital multiplex system capable of handling the control information for 512 channels, as a single data channel. The fader setting between 0 and +10 V (analogue signal) is sampled in channel sequence at a regular interval and converted into an 8 bit binary number, providing 255 discrete fader levels plus OFF (Fig. 4.213).

This data is sent as a sequence down a single cable to all devices using DMX 512:

- dimmers;
- scrollers;
- moving lights;
- fog machines.

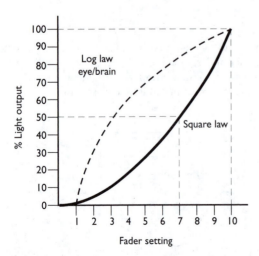

Figure 4.212 Basic dimmer law.

Channels are addressed sequentially as frames of data:

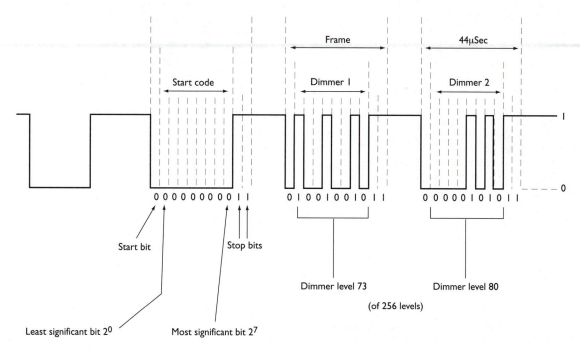

Figure 4.213 DMX 512 signal.

The rate of sampling the fader voltage is approximately 44 times per second; this is generally considered a fast enough 'refresh' rate for most applications.

In situations where finer control than that obtained with 8 bits (255 levels) is needed, a double system is used, the first 8 bits providing the 8 'most significant' digits and the second providing the 8 'least significant' digits.

In designing a DMX system, whether permanent or temporary, one must remember that 1 'bit' has a duration of 4 µsec, i.e. a frequency of 250 MHz. Consequently, the signal should be treated in a similar way to video if disturbing reflections of data are to be avoided:

- no teeing or paralleling of the DMX signal;
- the last DMX device should be terminated with 120 Ω.

Up to 32 DMX devices may be 'daisy-chained'.

A specific data cable (EIA 485/RS 485 rated) should be used for distributing the DMX signal. This is a screened twin twisted pair cable (only one pair used at present). Connections should be made using 5-pin XLR connectors. There is an appropriate version of

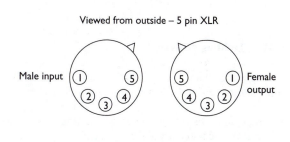

Viewed from outside – 5 pin XLR

Male input

Female output

1 – (Shield) ground/return/0v
2 – Data complement (–, inverted)
3 – Data true (+, inverted)
4 – Spare
5 – Spare

Figure 4.214 DMX 512 cable connections.

the DMX cable which can be run alongside power mains cables.

It is essential that all lighting consoles are opto-isolated from the devices using the DMX signal. This is to avoid the risk of damage when, under fault conditions, mains voltages could be sent along the DMX cable to the console – with dire consequences!

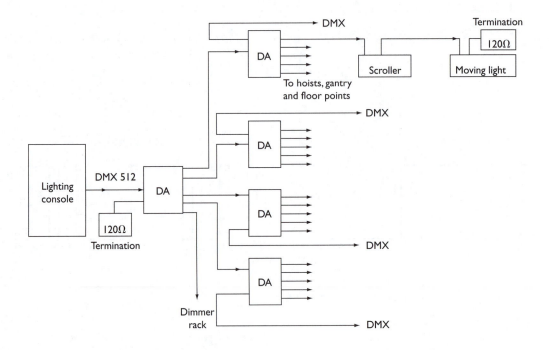

DA = Opto-isolated Distribution Amplifier, 1 input and 5 isolated outputs
DMX Cable = Data cable to EIA 485/RS 485 rated
Connectors = 5 pin XLR

Figure 4.215 DMX 512 distribution system.

4.18.3 Lighting console

The lighting console provides remote control of all the light sources. Its basic functions are to enable:

- quick and easy adjustment of lighting levels to achieve a satisfactory lighting balance;
- changes in lighting conditions (lighting **cues**) as required by the production;
- reduction in heat build-up in the studio by switching off luminaires not required;
- comprehensive monitoring of lighting conditions.

It should be located next to the vision control area, be compact and capable of being operated by one person.

It is essential for good lighting control and vision control that these two functions are carried out in the same area. Fig. 4.216 illustrates the ideal layout for a medium to large studio. In small studios the vision control and lighting function may well be the responsibility of one person.

This arrangement ensures that the team responsible for picture quality are looking at the same monitors!

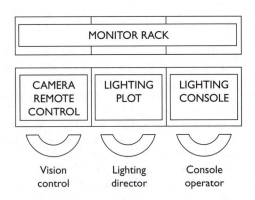

Figure 4.216 Recommended control room layout.

Lighting and vision control should each have a switchable high grade monitor for assessing picture quality in addition to the monitor stack displaying each source, plus a non-switched transmission/on air monitor.

Being in the same area ensures good teamwork, good communication and easy liaison when chasing picture faults.

Current consoles offer a wide range of facilities. The simplest manual console typically provides the facility to crossfade between two sets of pre-sets for each lighting channel. This can be expanded to include simple effects such as 'chases', flicker, etc. (Fig. 4.217).

(a) Manual console plus simple effects

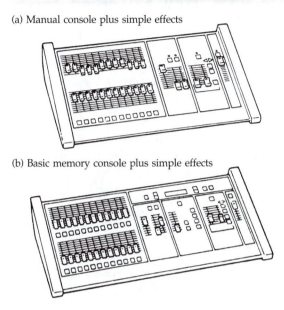

(b) Basic memory console plus simple effects

Figure 4.217 Basic lighting consoles.

Many consoles or computer-type consoles can provide comprehensive facilities, some of them retaining the ability to be operated as a manual console as well as operating automatically between lighting cues (Fig. 4.218).

What should a lighting console provide? This, of course, is reflected by what the lighting operation requires. Typical facilities are:

- easy selection of channels and level adjustment;
- recording of selected channels into memories (cues);
- memory protect key;
- recording of fade-up and fade-down times;
- timed playback of lighting cues as recorded;
- proportional soft-patch;
- large number of memories (greater than 100);
- DMX 512 outputs;
- provision to make-up memories 'blind', i.e. without affecting studio lighting;
- provision of manual sub-masters, which can be loaded with channels or memories either 'live' or 'blind';
- control of chasers from an audio input, allowing bass, middle and treble audio frequencies to determine the pattern of the chasers;
- special effects such as chasers, flicker, lightning, etc.;
- split, dipless, crossfaders used as main playback of lighting cues; to be operated manually, automatically with recorded times, run in sequence or held on hold until released;
- master fader with blackout switch, operating only on the dimmer DMX output;
- selection of appropriate dimmer, on a channel-by-channel basis;
- provision of **macro** keys which can be programmed to initiate many keyboard steps;
- capable of accepting a MIDI input, producing a MIDI output and providing a MIDI through facility;

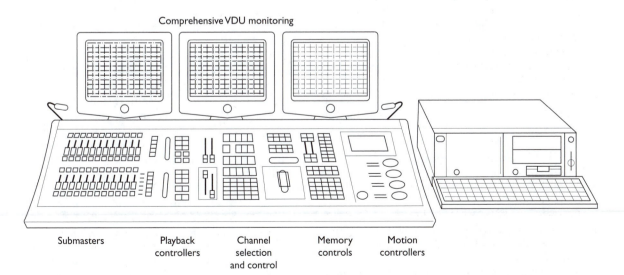

Comprehensive VDU monitoring

Submasters　　Playback controllers　　Channel selection and control　　Memory controls　　Motion controllers

Figure 4.218 Full facility lighting console.

- infrared control of basic console operation, e.g. channel on/off and level adjustment and recording of memories (cues) from the studio floor;
- comprehensive monitoring of studio lighting conditions, blind plotting, sub-masters, crossfade status, using VDUs;
- built-in help programme;
- built-in back-up;
- library storage on 3½" floppy disk;
- control of scrollers;
- control of moving lights.

Note: For major productions using scrollers and moving lights a portable moving light console is recommended, as discussed in Section 4.13.

Load meters

Studio lighting power is usually calculated on a diversity basis, that is, on an assumption that not all the luminaires will be on at full at any time. Consequently, there is a need for load meters to be installed alongside the lighting console so that the load current for each phase can be monitored.

The role of the lighting console operator

Working with the lighting director, the console operator's role is as follows.

Set/light period – usually operating on the studio floor, if possible, using a remote rigger panel or lighting console if it is portable:

- switch on luminaires as required for setting;
- make up basic memories (cues) as identified;
- become familiar with the lighting plot and the geography of the studio sets;
- update lighting plot as necessary;
- identify and set the 'line-up' lamp.

Rehearsal period – during which time the lighting director may spend some time 'trouble-shooting' on the studio floor:

- provide line-up lamp for camera line-up;
- control studio houselights!
- establish and memorize the final lighting balance for each cue;
- establish and memorize the timings for cues;
- assist in identifying any potential lighting problems – camera flare, camera shadows, double shadows, etc.;
- keep an accurate paper record of cues, usually in the form of a 'marked-up' script;

- update the lighting plot with any changes to the plot;
- note any potential power loading problems (when load meters are fitted).

Transmission – during transmission the console operator should be able to:

- control studio house lights!
- reproduce lighting cues as rehearsed;
- respond to any last-minute changes, e.g. delay cues, artistes not on their marks, conditions not as rehearsed.

With the complexity of modern consoles, **user-friendly monitoring** is an absolute requirement. The console operator needs to be able to:

- monitor studio condition;
- preview the next cue, including channel levels and timings;
- preview any cue;
- monitor sub-masters;
- 'blind' plot memories and sub-masters without affecting the studio lighting.

Lighting console practices

Where an initial lighting balance has not been obtained during the set/light period, it is a common practice to switch on luminaires at fader 7 (50% light output) – this should be approximately in the 'ballpark' if the planning has worked! The vision controller, having set all cameras to the 'nominal' lens aperture and adjusted the black level if necessary, should leave the lens apertures fixed while a lighting balance is being established.

If a rough balance had been achieved during the set/light period, this can be recalled and the final balance established, and memorized. At rehearsals, progress there is often a need to update a memory – rather than re-record over an existing memory it is advisable to make a new memory, e.g. keep cue 23 and call the revised cue 23.1. Often, there is a need to return to an original condition!

With the abundance of memories available on modern consoles, it is good practice to duplicate the memory well away from the operating memories, e.g. use cue 23 and also cue 123. This is particularly useful for news/current affairs programmes, using a regular daily plot. On a day-to-day basis this may need modifying in levels to accommodate different presenters, hence the need to keep a master cue well away from the everyday operations.

Crossfades may be achieved manually or automatically – clearly the speed of a crossfade is dictated by the action and the nature of the programme. Consoles usually provide a **dipless crossfade**, where any channels duplicated in both cues at the same level are held at that level during the crossfade. Crossfade operations often look better if the fade-up time is half the fade-down time, e.g. 2½ seconds and 5 seconds.

Where cues are required to change in time with music, it is useful to pre-warm the lamp filaments by recording the cue ON at a low level. This will speed up the rate of build-up of the light intensity when requiring a rapid switch-on.

Taking cues – it is absolutely vital that the cue is at the right instant! It is usually best for the console operator and lighting director to agree, when appropriate, that the cue is taken from the picture, i.e. the console operator is to anticipate the moment of the cue. The console operator is more likely to get it right than if the director or lighting director gives a verbal cue.

Music cues have already been mentioned when discussing variety lighting, including the importance of making the cue on the OFF-beat for modern pop/rock music.

Memory key – the memory function of computer-type consoles requires that a memory key (small, removable Yale-type key) is switched to the ON position. It is good practice always to leave this in the OFF position, except when actually recording cues, and remove the key when on meal breaks, etc.

Important discipline – it should be clearly understood that nobody, absolutely nobody, touches the lighting console except for the lighting console operator! It is so easy for a morning's work to be lost because someone has been 'playing' on the console.

4.19 Vision control

Good vision control is fundamental to the production of good picture quality. The vision controller may be an operator, engineer or technical director, depending on the organization – nevertheless, the role is similar:

- align cameras prior to rehearsal and transmission/recording;
- align control room monitors (this may not always be the practice; however, it is strongly recommended that only one person should be responsible for monitor alignment – the vision controller);
- adjust black level and iris settings, after a lighting balance has been achieved;
- match picture between cameras, i.e. colour matching;

- check vision sources to the vision mixer (engineers/technical director);
- adjust camera 'detail' as appropriate;
- adjust colour balance as necessary;
- in liaison with the lighting director, adjust gamma and knee as appropriate;
- switch appropriate video feeds to camera viewfinders;
- diagnose vision faults;
- indicate any lighting-based problems to the lighting director.

The vision controller should have a switchable Grade 1 colour monitor coupled to a waveform monitor/vectorscope. Ideally, the black level and iris controls should be in the form of joystick controllers, allowing easy control of black level (rotation) and iris (forward/backward movement). Pressure on any camera joystick operates a micro-switch, which replaces the picture being monitored with that particular camera's picture. This is particularly useful for matching pictures; the transmission picture is selected on the monitoring selection buttons and then replaced, when the joystick is depressed, with the camera being set up/adjusted ready for transmission.

The adjustment of black level is very critical. A few percent of picture **lift** or picture **sit** can make a big change to the picture, whereas a few per cent change in iris setting will not have the same impact (remember the logarithmic nature of the eye/brain). Usually, the control of the iris can be either COARSE or FINE. For studio work, the iris control is normally operated in the FINE mode, which allows one f_{stop} either side of the central position (the central position having been set to the nominal lens aperture).

The COARSE iris control is normally used on outside broadcasts where large changes in lighting levels can be expected!

Normally, the vision controller will check each camera prior to it being put on transmission. 'On-air' adjustments are not recommended. However, when required, they need to be done very slowly to reduce the viewer's awareness of the changes, unless motivated, e.g. the sun disappearing behind a cloud at a sports event.

Usually the vision controller will continually check all cameras against the transmission picture to check exposure and black level, and also to check that face tones and backgrounds match.

The vision controller will use the picture monitor for the majority of his or her work, only using the waveform monitor as an occasional check of signal levels. This illustrates the importance of correct monitor alignment and the need for regular checking of monitor alignment. Picture monitor alignment should be regarded as one of the most important adjustments made in any studio complex, especially:

brightness – monitor black level
contrast – monitor gain
chroma – saturation of monitor colour.

Many modern monitors use an internal system plus a sensor held against the monitor face to carry out an automatic alignment. It is, however, common practice to have the second input of a monitor fed with a switchable test signal. This enables the monitor to display a special test signal called PLUGE (Picture Line-Up Generating Equipment) (Fig. 4.219).

a)

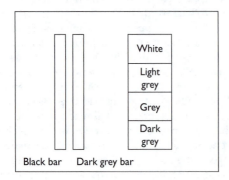

b)

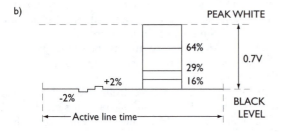

Figure 4.219 PLUGE signal: (a) picture display; (b) waveform.

This is used to set brightness and contrast. **Brightness** is adjusted so that the lighter bar is just visible, but the darker bar is not visible. Using a spotmeter, the **contrast** is adjusted to give 25 foot lamberts off the peak white signal. The other 'steps' may be used to check the gamma of the monitor.

The chroma adjustments can be checked by feeding colour bars to the monitors and switching the monitor to **Blue only**. Under this condition, the three right-hand colour bars should look the same brightness. The eye can be made more critical for this test by

viewing the screen through a suitable ND filter or by turning down the brightness control (to be reset later). All adjustments of monitors should be done under normal viewing conditions, i.e. 'script' lights only on.

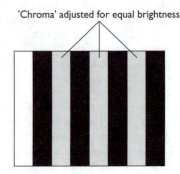

Figure 4.220 Colour monitor display with EBU bars, switched to 'Blue only'.

Ideally, brightness and contrast should be remotely controlled from the vision controller's desk.

4.19.1 Make-up and lighting

Good make-up is a vital part of the televised scene. It falls into two basic categories:

- corrective make-up;
- character make-up.

The make-up department can often help with particular lighting problems:

- shiny bald heads;
- shiny spectacle frames;
- problems with spectacle lenses;
- fair-skinned artistes in company with dark-skinned artistes.

The reflection of backlights on bald heads can sometimes result in distracting highlights. Use of corrective make-up can usually be a quick remedy – however, if it is known beforehand that the problem may exist, then using diffusion on the backlight will help to reduce the effect. The offending highlight, a reflection of light source, becomes a larger area source, i.e. spread out and therefore of a lower intensity. With static presenters, e.g. newsreaders, it may be possible to 'spot' the backlight onto the presenter's shoulders, leaving a small amount of backlight on the head. An alternative would be to use a veil to reduce the intensity of the backlight on the head.

Note: Rather than have a distracting backlight it is preferable to dim the backlight, provided there is separation with the background (background is lit).

If the reflection of lights in metal spectacle frames causes distracting highlights, a thin layer of make-up on the frames can be used to overcome this problem.

Reflections of lights in spectacles can be reduced by encouraging or advising the presenters to use multi-coated lenses. As a temporary measure, reflections can be avoided by a small tilt-down of the spectacles – with help from make-up to discreetly tape them in place.

An exposure problem can sometimes exist with very fair-skinned artistes sitting next to a dark-skinned artiste, e.g. during a panel game. When lit with a common keylight the difference in skin tones may be reduced by:

- using make-up to darken the very fair skin;
- using a net 'finger' in front of the keylight for the fair-skinned artiste.

Note: It is not usual to try to lighten dark skin because the dark skin shows through the make-up.

Another call for make-up assistance is when personal microphones need to be concealed in the hair of the artiste. This is a particularly useful technique and avoids the use of a microphone boom (and problems of boom shadows).

Make-up is similar to lighting in that if no-one notices the make-up it has been well done! Modern make-up techniques rely on subtle application of make-up, skilfully applied – again, the criterion is 'does it look right?'

4.19.2 Costume and lighting

Costume problems which affect the vision control operation are:

- clothing which is too dark or too reflective, i.e. outside the camera dynamic range;
- clothing which has a fine check pattern or any regular fine detail.

Detail in dark clothing could be made more visible by opening up the lens iris. However, this would affect the face tone, making the face tone over-exposed. Increasing the lighting level would have the same effect, unless one could add light selectively to the area of dark clothing. This would be most impractical for moving artistes. The solution is to introduce some additional black stretch or change the gamma correction. Unfortunately, both of these introduce extra noise, the price one has to pay for providing extra gain in the dark areas of the picture.

Detail in light-coloured costume which reflects more than 60% of the light will be lost. To make it visible one could stop down the lens iris; however, this would make the face under-exposed. If practical, one could selectively reduce the light on the costume. With a fixed presenter such as a newsreader this is possible, using a veil on the keylight to reduce the illuminance on the front of the artiste – but not the face (Fig. 4.221)!

An alternative to this would be to introduce a knee in the camera transfer characteristic (Fig. 4.222).

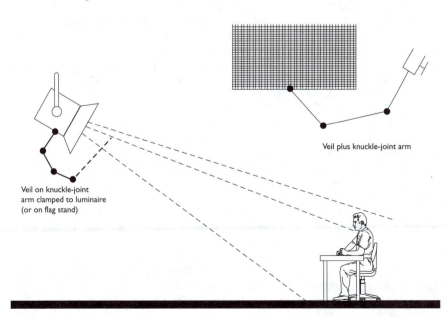

Veil plus knuckle-joint arm

Veil on knuckle-joint arm clamped to luminaire (or on flag stand)

Figure 4.221
Use of veil on a keylight.

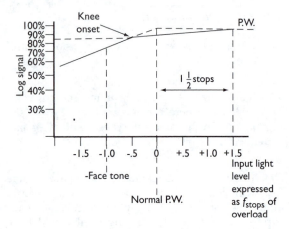

The knee facility therefore gives 1.5 stops extra latitude on highlights

Figure 4.222 Camera 'knee' characteristic.

This provides a compression of the tonal values above the knee and provides more 'headroom' for the range of input light. It should, however, be noted that:

- the face tone must always be below the knee value, otherwise tonal detail will be lost in the face;
- above the knee the tonal gradation is compressed, i.e. no longer a true tonal representation of the original scene.

Another easy option is to 'dip' the offending costume in a light grey dye or cold tea for a few seconds; after drying, the costume can be put against a grey scale and checked to see that its tonal value is below 100% video signal, i.e. less than 60% reflection.

This technique is used in drama, especially period drama, when a costume is too reflective or too vibrant a colour and is too distracting.

Costumes with regular fine detail create a problem of 'cross-colour'. When fine detail in the luminance signal represents a high frequency, comparable to the colour sub-carrier frequency, the decoding systems decode it as colour information (switching on alternate lines for the PAL system). This results in an annoying 'twitching' colour pattern being displayed. Usually, a small change in shot size is sufficient to reduce this effect, i.e. change the size of the detail.

4.20 Lighting standards

Whilst accepting that many aspects of programme-making rely on compromises to be made, nevertheless,

there is a need to maintain good standards of lighting. Good lighting has already been defined as 'when it looks right!', in other words when the lighting director sees the mental image which 'evolved' at the planning stage.

One of the difficult decisions is knowing when to stop making further lighting adjustments (lighting 'tweaks'), since often these are made to the detriment of the lighting look. Nevertheless, there are some things which need to be recognized and attended to. Any adjustments made on the studio floor in rehearsal time need the agreement of the director; consequently, it is a good practice to use the set/light time to best advantage.

Typically, 'when it doesn't look right' may be due to:

- incorrect lighting balance;
- over-exposure of part of the picture;
- colour temperature problems – mixed lighting;
- camera shadows;
- boom shadows;
- distracting shadow of the artiste on the background;
- double keying of the artiste;
- over-lighting of the foreground;
- keylight too steep or too shallow;
- keylight too frontal or too large horizontal angle;
- 'loose' barndooring – light spill onto the set;
- spill from lights onto the cyclorama;
- shadows from lights onto the cyclorama;
- lighting changes unmotivated;
- lighting changes out of step with the motivation – action/sound;
- light direction not as motivated;
- lack of continuity of lighting condition;
- face tone not 'placed' as appropriate within the dynamic range of the camera;
- background tone much brighter than the face tone;
- quality of light not correct – softness/colour;
- lack of texture;
- lack of tonal contrast;
- objectionable 'flare' from light sources;
- reflections of hard sources from shiny objects – direct or glare reflection;
- colour fringing on chroma key set-ups;
- wrong choice of gobo;
- wrong focus of gobo;
- gobo effect too dramatic or too weak;
- wrong choice of colour to match artiste/dance item;
- incorrect sequencing of moving lights;
- too large a depth of field – no optical separation of artistes from the background;
- too small a depth of field;

- generation of 'illegal' colours when lighting with coloured light;
- excessive use of colour in creating a particular mood;
- excessive use of smoke;
- lighting 'statement' too strong – easily done if you like a particular effect which you have created!
- 'flat' illumination – the ultimate 'brickbat' from your lighting critics!

Good vision control is an integral part of the picture-making process.

Things to be avoided are:

- 'tweaking' on air, unless done very slowly;
- over-exposure;
- colour cast to pictures;
- pictures not matching between cameras;
- too much 'detail', especially on faces;
- black level set too low or too high;
- gamma setting incorrect;
- excessive noise.

So, at the end of all this, if no one notices the lighting, you can relax and take a bow!

5 Sound

Introduction – some background about sound

Before learning how to record sound it is important to consider how it relates to the picture and the dialogue, and to understand the way that sound affects the viewer's senses. A clear understanding of this will make the difference between an operator who can make the equipment work and someone who is a valued part of the production team, producing sound that really enhances the pictures. Hopefully this section of the book will lead the reader on, via the theoretical background, through the knobs and buttons to a real understanding of the sound–picture relationship.

There are a large number of areas to be understood, from the recording process through to the point when the material is being transmitted to the viewing public. All of the technological understanding relies on a more important understanding of how the sound and pictures combine to give the viewer the experience that was intended by the programme producer. The audio section of this book will take the reader through the following topics:

- Hearing
- The physics of sound
- Sound levels
- Acoustics
- Ambient effects
- Analogue recording
- Digital recording
- Levels
- Metering
- Connections
- Monitoring
- Microphone techniques
- Sound requirements in a television studio
- Sound on location
- Stereo and ambisonics.

The requirements of post-production and the appropriate audio techniques are discussed in Chapter 12.

Also included is the role of the transmission suite, with a description of the presentation process, the final stage before the viewer finally sees and hears the programme.

5.1 What is sound?

Sound is made up of vibrations; these vibrations are created many ways, from a guitar string to the vocal cords. The vibrations move the air and create compression waves, which radiate out from the original source. This is rather like dropping a stone into a pond – the ripples move away from the centre where the splash occurred. It is similar with sound. The vibrations of the vocal cords, or any other device, make waves of compressed air which move outward like the ripples in the pond. The differences are that the sound waves travel at about 340 metres every second, and move out in three dimensions, up and down as well as horizontally!

5.1.1 What makes sounds different from each other?

One obvious difference between sounds is how loud they are. There is quite a difference between a quietly spoken person and a jumbo jet taking off! When the sounds are recorded these variations in level will need to be considered very carefully. The considerations are not only the technical limitations of the equipment in use, but also what the listener will reasonably want to hear.

The other fact that makes the sound of a human voice appear different from an aircraft, or even a guitar string, is its pitch, or more realistically a whole range of pitches. Whistling a single note can be matched to the pitch of an instrument like a guitar. Such a note is almost a pure tone and is made up of a particular number of vibrations per second. For a high-pitched sound there are more vibrations per second. For a lower-pitched sound there are fewer. The pitch or **frequency** of the sound is measured in Hertz (or cycles per second) and this helps define the different sounds heard by the human ear.

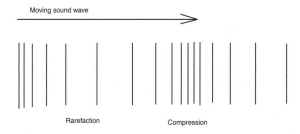

Figure 5.1 Sound pressure wave.

Sound transmitted through the air as vibrations cause the molecules of the air to vibrate against each other, producing pressure waves, which travel outwards. Whilst the speed of sound is independent of air pressure, it changes with temperature because the molecules move faster when they are hotter. The actual speed of sound is important, as it is the time sounds arrive at the ears that influences the brain, giving important clues about the location. At normal temperatures the speed of sound is approximately 1100 feet per second or 340 metres per second.

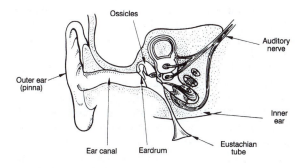

Figure 5.2 The ear mechanism.

The pressure waves travel through the air, eventually reaching the ear, causing vibrations of the eardrum. This in turn vibrates the bones of the ear and the 'sound' is passed to the inner ear and eventually the basilar membrane. This membrane is made up of hairs sensitive to different frequencies. It is these hairs that produce electrical impulses, transmitted via the auditory nerve, which the brain can then interpret as sound.

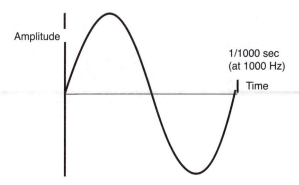

Figure 5.3 Audio sine wave.

Sound can be represented graphically illustrating the changes in air pressure over a period of time. The number of changes or cycles per second will give the frequency. The height of the graph will show the level or loudness of the sound. For a pure tone this is represented by a smooth curve, known as a **sine wave**. The importance of this graphical representation will become clear in the discussion of frequencies as it will illustrate how these curves can become damaged by careless handling of the signals.

5.1.2 Frequencies

The lowest frequency humans can hear is approximately 20 Hertz (Hz) and the highest around 20 000 Hz. That is, 20 000 vibrations every second.

Male vocal cords start producing sounds at about 75 Hz and go up to about 800 Hz – these are the **fundamental frequencies**. These fundamental frequencies become more complex because of the shape of the mouth and nasal passages, which modify these sounds producing other frequencies, called 'harmonics'. These can include frequencies up to 8000 Hz even though the vocal cords do not produce them as fundamental frequencies.

Harmonics make musical instruments all sound different. The piano and the trumpet might produce the same note, but they sound different because of their harmonics, created by their individual construction.

5.1.3 The human ear

The human ear is not a linear device, as it is more sensitive to low-level changes of sound than those that occur at high levels. The ear recognizes a doubling of sound level as a similar increase whether

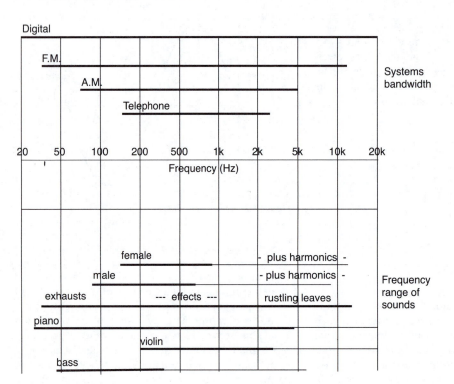

Figure 5.4 Examples of the frequency range of various sounds.

the sounds are quiet or very loud. This allows changes in loudness of both small and very large sounds to be heard.

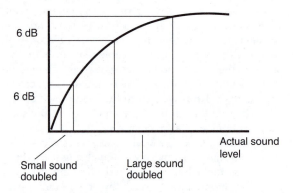

Figure 5.5 Human perception of sound levels.

The way the ear and brain perceive sound level changes must also affect the way in which the different sound levels are to be controlled. There is therefore a need to have a way of measuring changes in audio level that relates to the way the ears perceive the changes.

The decibel

The measurement used is the **decibel**. It follows a logarithmic law and provides numerical values that can be used to quantify changes in sound level. This decibel law is used to calibrate audio meters, i.e. is used to control levels. This will result in level changes that have a close relationship with human hearing.

Some illustrations of decibel values can be found at the end of this chapter.

The decibel is a unit of comparison rather than an absolute value. It is important always to remember that the units are meaningless without the reference level to which they refer. In broadcasting, sound is commonly referred to a level known as **zero level**. In actual voltage terms this value is 0.775 volts and is used throughout Europe and much of the rest of the world to align equipment. It is correctly shown as $0 \, dB_u$ and if written in this way no further reference is required. If this voltage of 0.775 volts is being fed into a standard resistance of 600 ohms it will produce a power output of 1 milliwatt. This reference is known as $0 \, dB_m$.

Some voltage decibel ratios are:

dB	Multiplication factor
+3	1.414
+6	2
+20	10
+60	1000

5.1.4 How loud are sounds?

All sounds are not just a range of different frequencies – they vary in loudness. This range of levels, from the quietest sound we can hear to the loudest we can tolerate, is known as the **dynamic range** of human hearing. Such a range exists not only for hearing but also for all the technical equipment in use and the transmission systems that are employed.

Dynamic range

Every programme type will have a bearing on dynamic range, as will the recording equipment or system used for transmission. This may be less than the range we can hear, so a method must be employed to restrict these levels or balance the overall sound. This is described more fully later in Section 5.6.8 in the discussion on mixing and compression, explaining the techniques and equipment that can help overcome this problem.

Examples of the levels of real sounds in relation to the threshold of human hearing (the smallest sounds we can hear) are:

Explosions and close aircraft	120 dB
Loud alarms or chainsaw	110 dB
Full orchestra or loud pop band	100 dB
Tractor or digger	90 dB
Electric saw	80 dB
Rough sea or loud radio	70 dB
Office interior	60 dB
Normal home TV	50 dB
Quiet conversation	40 dB
Whisper	30 dB
Quiet countryside	20 dB
Studio background	10 dB

Real life produces a very large range of sound levels, requiring very careful and considered control if satisfactory recording and transmission of these sounds is to be achieved.

Artistically it is not right to simply balance all the sounds to the same level. Whilst this might solve the problems of trying to record levels that are either too great or too small, the range and reality of sounds in a real world will be lost. First it is necessary to decide on a dynamic range that the viewer at home can accept and would be suitable for the programme material in question. When this has been decided there might then be an additional need for control in order to ensure the dynamic range is technically suitable for the equipment and systems in use.

5.1.5 Home viewing environments

It is very important to consider the conditions in which the viewer is listening. From the list of sound levels given in Section 5.1.4 it can be seen that the level transmitted to the viewer must not drop below the level of a quiet conversation, or the sound might be lost in their background sounds. Fans, air-conditioning, traffic outside or playing children may well decide the quietest sounds that will be acceptable. At the other end of the scale, the loudest sound must be held to a reasonable point that the TV can reproduce without distortion and will not be so loud as to be uncomfortable.

In an average listening home this might well be a range as small as 25 dB from the loudest to the quietest sounds. All of the range of real life will need to be squashed into this much reduced **transmitted dynamic range**.

The artistic requirement is to define a suitable range and then place the sounds within this range, still maintaining a realistic relationship between the different sounds. It would be expected that a loud aircraft will sound louder than a lorry and that this would be expected to be louder than speech. In fact some cheating needs to take place, and sounds allowed to compete, one with another, to give the illusion of loud planes or traffic. In fact the speech will actually be peaking at a higher level than the noisy effects. This ensures that the voice can actually be heard where in reality the voice would be inaudible if the sound levels were left at the real level. Progressive and almost imperceptible changes may also help, allowing the speech to gradually decrease so that further sounds can be added without exceeding the maximum peaks for the system in use. From an artistic point of view there is some further discussion on balancing various types of sound in Section 5.6.8 and Chapter 12.

5.1.6 The correct level

One of the most important technical issues for all sound operators is the maintenance of correct audio levels. This factor must be considered all the way through the audio chain. Consideration of the correct microphone for the type and loudness of the sound, adjustment of the mixer input and properly metered and controlled levels must be achieved.

All good audio equipment is fitted with some metering device to ensure the correct operating audio level. This will ensure that the equipment in use will be operating in the way in which the manufacturer designed it. The object is to record the sound as accurately as possible and do nothing, throughout the audio chain, that might change its characteristics. This is an important topic and will be discussed fully in Section 5.3.

5.1.7 Sound level and distance

One very important fact relating to the transmission of sound is that as the pressure wave moves through the atmosphere it reduces in level. This is partly due to losing some of its energy to the air, occurring as the sound, vibrating air molecules, cause them to heat up. However, the main reason for a reduction in the level of sound is that, as the sound travels further and further from its point of creation, the energy is spread over an ever-increasing area. The energy level at any particular point on the outside of this imaginary sphere will become considerably lower as the sphere expands.

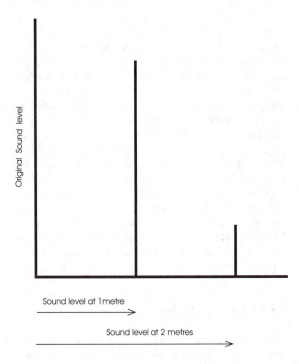

Figure 5.6 Reduction of sound level with distance.

With sound, the reduction in energy level happens in three directions. A good analogy is in blowing up a balloon, where the energy is spread over an ever-increasing sphere. For sound, a reduction of level may be obvious – it is expected that the further away from a sound source the listener is, the quieter the sound will become.

Just how dramatic the effect is may not be so clear unless this is considered carefully. If a microphone is 1 metre away from a speaker a reasonable sound level may be picked up, but if it moves to 2 metres, the doubling of the speaker-to-microphone distance will divide this sound level by four. The surface area of a sphere is πr^2. In this example the reduction of sound level will force the sound operator to increase the microphone gain by a factor of four, to compensate for the loss of level, resulting in four times as much background sound being recorded.

This reduction in level is known as the 'inverse square law' ...

The inverse square law must be clearly understood, as this relationship between distance and audio level determines the characteristics of all the sounds that are recorded in any location. It has a major effect on the placement microphones and the methods used to achieve an accurate match between sound and pictures.

... and that's all there is to know about sound!

In theory these parameters define everything about sound: it travels in waves, it varies in pitch (frequency) and it varies in loudness (amplitude). All the sounds that the ear can hear are made up of lots of different frequencies, at differing amplitudes all added together to make the complicated sounds that are encountered every day.

Unfortunately, that's not the whole story. In reality any recorded sound will be modified by the location in which it is recorded. Of course there will be unwanted noises and sometimes there may be ways of reducing these. The most difficult part of recording sound has many implications; this is the effect of **acoustics**.

5.1.8 Acoustics

It is important to consider what happens to the various different sounds when they are recorded in a real location. The sound will be quite different when the recording is made inside a room, or a church, or just near a building. The design of a studio set will have a considerable impact on the characteristics of sound recorded within it. The sound waves travel from the person speaking and the microphone hears their voice, then the sound waves carry on and hit the walls around the room. Some of the sound is absorbed by the wall and the rest bounces off and travels back to the microphone. The words are heard once and then a second version is heard, slightly later, with a few changes to the quality. This repeats itself many times until the air or the walls have absorbed all of the original energy.

These reflected sounds all appear to be quite normal when the listener is actually in the room along

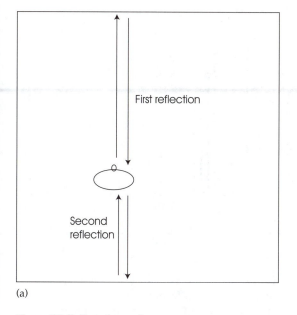

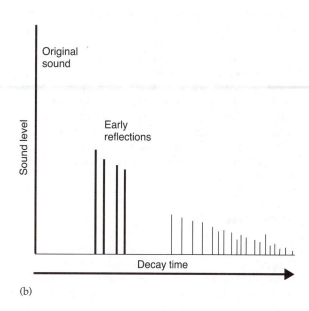

(a)   (b)

Figure 5.7 Reflected sound waves.

with the person or sound they are listening to. The human brain is very clever – the message from the eye identifies a small room and with no soft furnishings or curtains, the brain must expect to receive a certain kind of sound. What is heard agrees with what can be seen.

What does the viewer hear?

The problems start to occur when sound is recorded and played back later. The eyes are separated from the ears by the process of television. If the recording is being made in a room, the eyes are telling the brain about the part of the room that is visible in the camera shot. At the same time the ears are listening to the effect that the whole room had on the sound. If the acoustics of the listening room are poor, a further effect is added to the recorded sound and the situation becomes worse! What is seen and experienced in any location affects the total human perception of the environment, and the brain gets a preconceived idea of the sound that is expected to accompany it.

The way in which any space modifies sound is extremely elaborate. The actual effect depends on the structure of the environment. The construction of the walls and all of the furnishings in any room or hall absorb the sound in varying amounts. Certain frequencies will be absorbed first, the effect varying with different wall materials. Each material has its own particular coefficient of absorption, and the coefficient varies with frequency. If the wall surfaces are hard and smooth, sound waves, especially the middle and

higher frequencies, are reflected off them with very little attenuation, that is loss of energy. Soft furnishing, carpets, curtains and crowds of people tend to absorb the high and mid-frequencies so that the reflected sounds will be muffled, containing relatively more bass sounds. Large rooms produce reflections that have correspondingly large delays, whereas in a small room the reflections will return more quickly. Added to this effect is the total time it takes all of the sound to be effectively absorbed, the point at which the reflections have reduced to a level where they are inaudible. This is the **reverberation time**, or the time for nearly all (a reduction of 60 dB) of the sound energy to be absorbed by the structure of the room.

At an exterior location, away from any hard surfaces, the sound disappears off into the distance and only the initial sound is heard. In this situation the brain does not expect any secondary sound images. If near to a single large building or rock face, a single clear echo might be heard. These echoes are sometimes a surprise in real life – the listener may even look around to see where the echo is coming from.

Echo effects can be very obvious in a large sports hall. These spaces produce high amplitude reflections at long, regular reflection times, which take an equally long time to decay. These echoes are so dramatic that sound recorded in this type of location will be difficult to edit to sound recorded in quieter locations, even when both sounds are perfectly correct. This may be a situation when the sound quality will dictate how often to cut from one location to another in order not to disturb the viewer.

From the examples given it can be seen that reflected sounds are very complex, with the walls and furniture of a room returning the sound to our ears at varying times, in varying amounts, and with varying effects on different frequencies. Every room has its own distinct characteristics. The human brain is used to interpreting these signals quite automatically and will simply accept the reality of the sounds when moving from one area to another. These expectations need to be maintained within the sound and picture relationship in television material, or the brain will be distracted by the discontinuity.

5.1.9 Ambient effects

As well as the acoustics, the sound effects must be properly considered. Just as the viewer will have an expectation of the acoustic effect for any particular shot, they will also expect to hear certain ambient sounds. These sound effects may be very obvious from the shot, as the sound sources are visible. Further, there will be an expectation from the context of the item. If the action takes place in a school, it would be perfectly reasonable to hear children playing, even if they cannot be seen. In fact it might be desirable to hear them, as they will help create the overall image.

Whilst general effects and backgrounds will be an important part of the overall sound, helping to produce an appearance of reality, spot effects are also needed. This is important where anything that makes a short duration sound appears in the picture, or the effect may be implied from the dialogue. Care is needed here as the effects may make the edit very difficult. It is often best to 'cheat', pretending that the door bell rang during the shoot, recording a wild track version to add at the dubbing stage.

Sound effects are a big subject and are further discussed in Section 12.2.

Re-creating the effect

The velocity of sound in air varies with temperature but is roughly 340 m/s. Using this fact, the length of time taken for a reflection to return to the ear can be easily calculated for any specific environment. Adding equalization to the delayed sounds will make the appropriate allowance for the construction. Consequently it is possible to use echo processors to re-create a good approximation of any given acoustic by defining the time taken for each reflection to return and the amount by which it will have decayed. When interpreting acoustics, the brain can interpret very small time differences, as small as a few milliseconds.

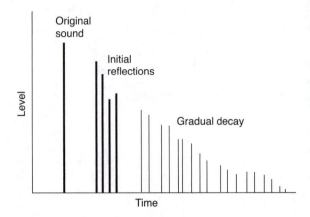

Figure 5.8 Echo – early reflections and decay time.

Time delays between each ear also give clues in interpreting the direction from which sound is heard.

To summarize; as well as ensuring that the frequencies and levels of sounds are properly considered, the acoustic and ambient effects need to be recognized when recording and handling audio. The most important consideration is that the sound should match the pictures and be as consistent as possible. To achieve this requires careful planning. There may be occasions when less than perfect recording locations can be quite acceptable provided that, in the final edited item, there are no dramatic changes between adjacent recordings.

Matching the sound to the pictures

In radio programmes, high quality sound is recorded in good, acoustically absorbent rooms, using close microphone techniques. The only acoustic effect the listener gets is their own listening room. Any acoustic changes to the recorded sound can be used deliberately, to help tell the listener where the action is, provided the changes agree with the script.

In television the situation may be much more difficult because the viewer can see a picture and this carries an expectation of a particular quality of sound. On location, or sometimes even in a studio, the solution is quite involved, and takes not just skill on behalf of the sound operator but a close teamwork between the whole crew. It means that the camera operators and producers need a clear understanding of the relationship between the sound and pictures if the viewer is going to enjoy a complete and harmonized experience.

Each location needs to be checked, and the producer must know how he or she will shoot and edit the material. If the sound does not match the pictures, it may be necessary to use a different micro-phone technique, or perhaps change the shot. The sound operator must know what sort of shot it is and how it is going to be used in the final edit, in order to record something with the correct characteristics. It may be too late to put it right when it gets to the post-production stage.

What can be fixed later?

There is a lot that can be done in editing and dubbing and this is discussed more fully in Chapter 12.2. The trick is to know what must be done at the recording stage so that the editor and dubbing mixer have good clean sound to work with.

If the recorded effects and acoustics from the location match the shots then they can be included in the location mix. Care must be taken to ensure that any changes in the background sounds do not make the edit difficult. If the end result is very complex with many different sound effects, it may be much better to record the location sound with as little background and acoustic effects as possible. Wild tracks (sounds recorded separately from the picture) can be easily added at the dubbing stage, so plenty should be recorded on location. With the correct equipment it is possible to add any acoustic effects that may be required; however, unwanted effects or acoustics cannot be easily removed.

Communication between operators

It helps considerably if the location sound operators know what will be available in post-production. This will enable them to leave out things which are better done at the later stages. They must further ensure that the audio tracks are presented in a way that will be acceptable to those who will be using the sound in the post-production processes. This includes microphone techniques like M/S or A/B stereo and acceptable formats for wild effects – must they be analogue tape, or can they be digital tape or disc-based systems like MiniDisc? It is important to know what technology is available in dubbing.

5.2 Recording the sound

5.2.1 Analogue

Both the sound and the picture are recorded onto tape using a sophisticated application of some simple theories. When an electrical conductor is passed through a magnetic field, this field will induce a small electrical current in the conductor. Microphones will be discussed later, but some use this principle, connecting a diaphragm to a coil that is held in the centre of a permanent magnetic field. The sound waves vibrate the diaphragm, and thus the coil, moving it through the magnetic field. This produces an electrical current proportional to the sound in both amplitude and frequency.

The way a recording is made onto tape is a reverse of the principle of the moving coil microphone. Passing an electrical current through a wire conduc-tor will produce a magnetic field around the conduc-tor, proportional to the original current. Taking this principle one stage further, many turns of wire wrapped around a magnetizable material can be designed so that it will increase and concentrate the magnetic field, producing an electromagnet. If the electromagnet is driven by an audio-derived alternat-ing current, the magnetic field produced will vary in proportion to the audio. If a magnetizable material, like a tape, is passed at constant speed over this magnet, a magnetic imprint relating to the original audio will be recorded onto the tape.

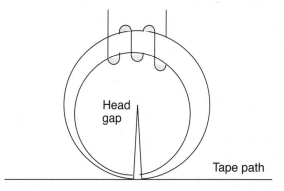

Head gap

Tape path

Figure 5.9 Analogue tape and tape head.

Whist in principle that is all there is to the produc-tion of magnetic recordings, this rather over-simpli-fies the actual process. Tape has a poor magnetic retention and further its characteristics are not linear, so methods need to be employed to overcome these problems. To help overcome these shortcomings, a bias frequency (100–200 kHz) at a fixed level is added to the audio, which means the recording is made where the recording characteristic is more linear. The bias frequency is too high for the replayed tape to reproduce it. A high frequency filter is included in the circuit to ensure that it is not present in the replayed signal. There is no perfect level for the bias setting, rather a compromise needs to be found between distortion and frequency response. For the best results the bias may have to be set for each tape type in use. Some recorders have the ability to store bias settings for more than one type of tape.

The recorded signal is replayed by running the tape back over an electromagnet (replay head) and a current, corresponding to the magnetic recording, will be induced in the head's coil. This signal can be amplified and equalized, or frequency adjusted to allow for the system's inherent response, and the result is an audio signal virtually identical to the original sound.

Signal levels

One problem with magnetic theory is that very careful mechanical manufacturing and system alignments need to be made to ensure the good frequency response of the system. Magnetic systems have the problem that they become **saturated**, that is can only take a certain amount of magnetizing force. This requires careful regulation of the electrical input, so that it does not try to produce a magnetic field that the system cannot achieve. The recording must be made in the linear part of the magnetic **hysteresis curve**.

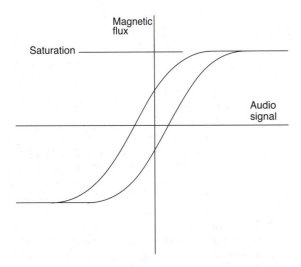

Figure 5.10 The relationship between the audio signal and the recorded magnetic flux.

Magnetic distortion

Distortion is in the direct control of the operator and once the equipment has been properly manufactured and aligned, distortion can be minimized by using correct recording levels. This level is set up by the correct line-up of the equipment and the controlling of levels during the recording process. If too great a signal is applied to the recording head any increase

which cannot be accommodated by the electromagnetic properties of the material will not be properly translated. A sine wave at too high a level will have its peaks squared off resulting in over-modulation distortion. Magnetic theory needs to be remembered and correct line-up procedures need to be employed to avoid any problems.

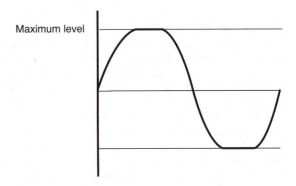

Figure 5.11 Signal clipping – if the audio signal exceeds the level that the magnetic system can accommodate, clipping of the signal will occur.

Electronic distortion

Distortion is not just a problem of magnetic theory, as it is possible to drive too high a level into an electronic circuit such that it distorts the signal. The resultant effect will depend on the circuit design but simply reducing the recording gain may not stop the distortion if it is occurring in circuitry in front of the control being adjusted.

It is important to match the input of any equipment to which an audio signal is being applied. An extreme example of an error in matching is to connect the line output of a portable mixer to the microphone input of a camera. Even if the input of the camera were correctly adjusted for the tone output from the mixer the result would be a considerably distorted recording. In this case the level recorded on the tape would be correct but the circuit at the front of the camera would have been badly overloaded by the equipment mismatch.

Recorded noise

As has been shown, the result of trying to record at levels that are too great is distortion. A further consideration when adjusting the signal levels is noise. All electronic devices produce noise and the process of recording an analogue signal onto magnetic tape will produce a level of background noise (measured as the signal-to-noise ratio). In fact noise is recorded onto the tape even when no signal is being recorded. It is therefore very important to reduce the effect of this residual noise as much as is possible. Transferring this signal from one tape to another, as happens in editing, multiplies the problem on each pass. Whilst not wanting to cause the distortion problems described above, a good level should be recorded onto the tape at all times. Dolby (and other) noise reduction systems help considerably here. These systems encode the signal prior to recording it and decode the audio during replay. The end result is to considerably reduce the background noise and enhance the effective **dynamic range** (the difference between the quietest and loudest sound that can be reproduced).

Noise reduction

With noise reduction it is important to ensure the correct levels in recording and replay. This is because the effect of the noise reduction systems changes with level. The signal must be correctly encoded and decoded. It is important that they are enabled during both recording and replay or the result will be unacceptable!

There are a range of noise reduction systems in use.

- **Pre-emphasis**
  Pre-emphasis is a simple technique which applies an equalization to the signal prior to the recording process. This is then decoded by applying an exact opposite process to the audio when it is replayed. Increasing the high frequencies in the signal before recording will allow an opposite reduction in these frequencies after the signal is replayed. This reduction, applied during the replay, will also produce a decrease in any high frequency noise, whilst leaving the original audio unaffected.
- **Dolby A**
  Introduced in the mid-1960s and used extensively in professional broadcasting, especially in the film industry, Dolby A divides the signal into four frequency bands having its maximum effect when the level is 40 dB below reference. The system provides between 10 and 15 dB of noise reduction.
- **Dolby B**
  This system was employed in domestic equipment in the early 1970s mainly to overcome the noise produced in smaller tape formats like cassette. It is primarily a system of equalization with some compression applied to the signal. This can increase the signal-to-noise ratio of domestic cassettes to about 60 dB.
- **Dolby C**
  Designed in the late 1970s, this system uses a larger compression and expansion ratio as well as

frequency adjustments and can produce an improvement of around 10 dB over Dolby B.
- **Dolby SR**
  This Spectral Recording system was developed in the mid-1980s in an attempt to extend the operating life of analogue equipment against the growth of digital technology. The system uses ten separate bands of frequency processing operating signal compression that varies with its level. The result can be a reduction in noise of approximately 25 dB.
- **DBX**
  This system, developed in the late 1970s, uses compression across the whole frequency range. There is frequency pre-emphasis and corresponding de-emphasis on replay, the whole system providing up to 30 dB of improvement in the system signal-to-noise. There are two versions of the system: type 1 installed in professional equipment and type 2 used in the domestic market.

All systems employing noise reduction must be carefully aligned for the record and replay levels, plus adjustments of the noise reduction thresholds. The systems may use standard tone, Dolby tone or even pink noise (a wide band signal) to achieve the line-up.

Noise gates

A further method of reducing noise present in a signal is to use a gating technique. The equipment may be a purpose designed gate, or some compressors have gating available as a function. The principle is to define a set level below which the signal gain is reduced or even cut altogether. This process can be very unpleasant if not used with care. One good example might be the feed to an audience PA system. Here, setting the gate threshold to around 20 dB (ref. 0.775 V) would ensure the speakers had no output unless the signal exceeded this level, thus reducing unwanted hum from the speakers.

5.2.2 Digital

When audio is recorded using analogue techniques the sound pressure waves are converted into electrical signals by the microphone which, in turn, are converted into a magnetic field to be recorded on the tape. This recorded information still retains the same frequencies and an amplitude, or level, proportional to the original sound. The process, whilst fairly simple in principle, is unable to differentiate between the desirable original signal and noise or distortion created during the recording or processing operations. Even with the best techniques, high quality tapes and the use of noise reduction methods, some damage or distortion will have been recorded. The replayed sound will not be quite the same as the original; even worse, the more times the sound is recorded via editing, programme compilation and signal routing, the more noticeable the problems will become.

Digital recordings use techniques that convert the electrical signals into a series of binary codes or numbers. Each of these numbers represents the signal level at a given point in time. This process enables the decoding to recognize only the desirable information, and thus the system is not subject to the same problems as the analogue ones.

Sampling

The analogue waveform is sampled at a fixed rate, thus producing a stream of pulses of varying amplitude.

Enough samples have to be taken to ensure that the decoding process will exactly mimic the encoding. To achieve this at least two samples must be taken during each complete analogue cycle or false alias frequencies will be created. Thus the sampling frequency needs to be at least twice the maximum audio frequency that it is required to reproduce. Filtering the audio signal is required to ensure that no audio exists at more than half the sample frequency.

It has been shown that to achieve a frequency response of up to 20 kHz, the sample rate needs to be 40 kHz or greater. It is important to be aware that producing pulses that are effectively amplitude modulated will produce harmonics. These harmonics will be the sum and difference of the audio and the sampling frequencies.

For example, had it been decided to sample at a rate of 20 kHz, an 8 kHz sine wave would produce harmonics at 20 − 8 = 12 kHz and 20 + 8 = 28 kHz. 12 kHz would be an audible problem and requires an audio filter to be introduced to remove any harmonics occurring above half the sampling frequency. In

this system the maximum audio frequency will be restricted to 10 kHz.

In practice, sampling rates have been chosen to be higher than the basic minimum that would be required to achieve the required system bandwidth:

- For compact discs the rate has been set at 44.1 kHz. This allows the anti-aliasing filters to have less steep responses.
- The professional rate in many broadcasting stations is 48 kHz.
- For the transmission systems like that of NICAM 728 the system design uses 32 kHz giving a practical limit to the audio of 15 kHz.

Quantization

Having set the rate at which the audio is to be sampled, the pulses need to be converted into numbers that represent the amplitude of each pulse. The accuracy of the conversion will depend on how many levels are chosen to make the representation. If there are a greater number of levels used in the encoding process the decoded signal will be nearer to the original sound.

As a binary code is to be used, the result will be 2 to the power of the chosen number of bits.

For example: 4 bit sampling would give 16 different values (2 to the power of 4).

Levels in between these samples will be rounded up or down to the nearest value, resulting in a change or distortion to the signal. This is known as the **quantization error**.

The result of these errors appears mainly as low-level noise in the signal. It has been found that the addition of intentional noise, prior to conversion, makes the effect of this error more random and less noticeable. This addition of noise is called **dither**.

Thus the dynamic range of the system will be limited by the way in which this conversion is defined. A large number of quantizing steps can therefore decrease the quantizing error and allow for

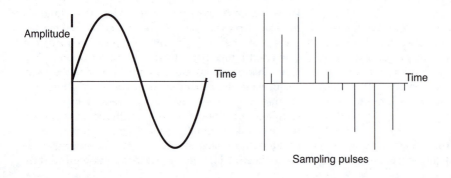

Amplitude

Time

Sampling pulses

Time

Figure 5.12 The audio is sampled, producing a series of pulses representing the level at each moment in time.

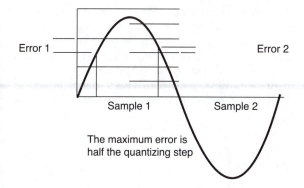

Figure 5.13 Quantization – signal errors will occur if insufficient levels are used.

a correspondingly greater dynamic range. In the compact disc the system uses 16 bit sampling which allows for 65 536 intervals (2 to the power of 16), ensuring very low quantization errors, and as the dynamic range is approximately 6 dB per bit, 96 dB is theoretically possible with this system.

Channel coding

The binary data produced by the quantization is not suitable to be directly recorded onto magnetic tape as the samples must be accurately timed. This timing is vital to the correct decoding of the signal. Coding converts the data into a regular pattern of signals that can be recorded and later recovered correctly. It involves the newly coded material being recorded along with a clock signal. When the signal is replayed, the recorded clock information can be compared with a stable reference clock in the replay equipment. This ensures the correct timing of the digital information. This timing and reference information not only ensures an accurate decoding of the signal, but also allows error correction techniques to be applied to the samples.

Error correction

There are two main types of error that have to be corrected in digital audio systems. These are **burst error**, the errors that are due to the loss of a number of consecutive samples, possibly caused by tape drop-out, and **random error**, the loss of single samples in the material, often due to noise or poor signal quality.

Burst error correction is made possible by interleaving the audio data prior to its being recorded. This process, a kind of shuffling, is carried out in a controlled way so that unshuffling can occur during the decoding; this effectively separates the missing

data, ensuring that consecutive values are less likely to be lost. More accurate error correction is thus possible.

Error correction methods incorporated into the systems include:

- **true correction**, where an exact replacement value can be inserted;
- **interpolation**, where a mathematically derived replacement is calculated from the average of the data immediately before and after the missing piece;
- **hold**, where the missing data is simply replaced by a copy of the data immediately in front. This is the simplest correction and can only be sustained for a few samples.

Eventually when the error cannot be resolved the system will mute until sufficient samples can be recovered for the conversion to continue.

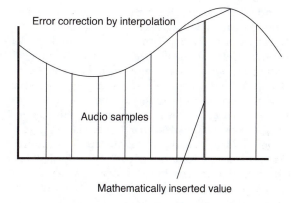

Figure 5.14 Error correction – replacement data can be calculated from the adjacent data.

Recording

The recording process is limited by the need to record very high data rates and thus conventional analogue tape speeds are unsuitable. There are two basic methods used to satisfy the requirement for a high write speed.

(1) The first method follows video technology and uses a relatively low linear tape speed, but employing a helical tape wrap of the tape around a rotating head drum. This produces a series of diagonal tracks producing a write speed that is suitable for the required bandwidth. This tape cannot be physically edited but requires two machines to achieve the electronic splicing of material. The tapes are compact but fragile and for

this reason are held in totally enclosed cases like those used in video cassette machines.

(2) The second approach is to use stationary heads having multiple tracks and to use several tracks for each channel of digital audio, so allowing the large amount of information to be recorded. The tape speed needs to be quite high but can be reduced if the number of tracks is increased.

The use of digital techniques allows the recording of audio to be made on any of the standard digital storage systems used in computers. Winchester disks, worm drives and optical disks and solid state devices can all be used. These systems all have their applications and although not all transportable for field use, are very useful in studios for mastering or editing due to their reliability and high storage capacity. Most are easily obtained due to the large numbers in use for other applications.

Data compression

In order to record or route very large amounts of data most systems allow extra signals or longer recording time by the use of data compression. The AES/EBU interface that is commonly used to interconnect digital equipment uses a time compression of 2:1 and it is thus possible to carry twice as much audio data. For example, stereo can be routed onto a single cable. In picture formats various data compression techniques rely on only small parts of the picture changing from frame to frame. The compression technique utilizes this fact and only records that part of the signal which changes. Similar techniques can be applied to the audio, designing circuits that copy the characteristics of the human ear, and leaving out information that will not be identified by the listener. This system is known as Precision Adaptive Subband Coding, and can allow effective compression of 2:1 and greater.

The difficulty with data compression is that there can be undesirable effects where the individual pieces of audio equipment in a system chain use differing compression techniques. In this case no one piece of equipment will significantly damage the audio signal but the combined effect of all will be unacceptable. Most studio and location recordings are made using the minimum compression that cost, time and the volume of recording medium will allow.

5.3 Audio engineering

The routing and recording of audio signals requires the signal levels to be correctly maintained within the specification of the equipment in use. Care must be taken not to exceed the maxima of both electronic and magnetic levels, or to exceed the available quantity of samples where digital systems are employed. It is equally important not to allow levels to drop too low, particularly with analogue equipment, if the system noise levels are not to become a problem.

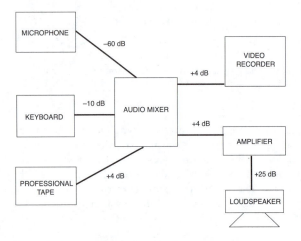

Figure 5.15 Signal levels in an audio system.

5.3.1 Maintaining the levels

Correct levels within a system can be achieved using many metering methods, ensuring the engineering specifications are maintained throughout the audio chain. Whenever a number of devices are connected a line-up should be carried out. Tone (usually at 1 kHz) is routed through the chain, the level is read, and if required, adjusted to set up the gain of each piece of equipment in use. Whilst most meters will achieve this engineering line up, they may not clearly show how loud the sound will appear to our hearing. Equally important, some may not indicate the maximum peaks, vital if over-modulation is to be avoided.

5.3.2 Meters

In order to interpret any meter it is first necessary to have a basic understanding of the difference between the peak level, signal power and perceived loudness. This book has already described the use of the decibel as a reference. This ratio of levels is useful as it has a close relationship with the way sound is actually perceived by our hearing.

Peak level is a simple concept in that is simply the maximum voltage that the signal reaches. For any given piece of equipment the **maximum acceptable level** is important – it is at this point that damage will begin to occur as the signal begins to clip.

Signal power can be determined mathematically and is represented by the root mean square (RMS) of the signal. The signal power is a useful figure as it has a close correlation to the way in which sound levels are heard.

To the viewer at home peak levels are not important unless they cause distortion. The way the sound affects the viewer is the **perceived loudness**. This is difficult to measure in a definitive way, which is why loudspeaker monitoring is so important. Meters can help with this process if the indicated values are fully understood.

VU (volume units)

The VU meter is designed to give a reading of the average signal level over a period of time. For this reason the meter is constructed with a time constant of 300 milliseconds (ms), that is, it takes 300 ms to reach 99% of its final value, and the same time to decay. This means that the meter will not show the maximum level of a peak that occurs in a time of less than 300 ms. To give this some perspective the human ear can identify distortion in signals as short as 5 ms duration.

Unfortunately many manufacturers produce meters that are calibrated to appear as a VU meter but for cost reasons do not comply strictly with this time constant. This means that interpreting the readings on anything other than a pure tone is difficult.

- VU meters give an average reading of signal volume.
- They are calibrated from –20 to +3 dB (some may have extended scales).
- They are good for reading continuous signals such as tone but care is needed to interpret

programme material. It is difficult to read low-level signals.

- To achieve the approximation of volume they have a time constant of 300 ms and hence will not show short transient signals. With these short peaks they may indicate as much as 10 dB below the actual level, resulting in possible over-modulation if care is not taken.
- The decay time, identical to the rise time, may be too fast to read the signal.
- They are cheap to manufacture (cheap ones may be not very accurate) and therefore many meters can be installed rather than having to switch signals to a single meter.

With VU meters it is difficult to give an operational guide. To some extent the VU will help to indicate the signal loudness but many transient sounds will barely move the meter. The absolute maximum is 0 dB or 100%, and this value is sometimes used for tone alignments. Reading programme material can be very difficult – some high peak, low energy material may cause distortion before any real level is shown on the meter. Peak indicators are sometimes fitted to help with this.

The following may be used as a guide to help prevent over-modulation:

- Pure speech may have to be held back to –6 dB or lower (50% mod.).
- Musical instruments that produce short duration peaks may have to be limited to –10 dB.
- Loud crowds or compressed material can reach 0 dB without causing problems.
- Readings over 0 dB (100%) must be avoided to ensure quality undistorted recordings.

PPM (Peak Programme Meter)

There are a number of scales used on PPMs but all have the same mechanical characteristics. The PPM has a very fast rise time (the actual integration time is 10 ms) with a decay time of 2.8 s, allowing short duration peaks to be clearly seen. This means that the meter is very good for identifying signals that would cause over-modulation of recordings or on-air transmitters. The PPM is less good as a method of illustrating the loudness of the signal being monitored. The scale covers a range of 24 dB with 4 dB steps.

- These meters indicate the signal peaks.
- The BBC versions are calibrated from 1 to 7 with 4 dB between graduation.
- PPM 4 is used as a reference line-up, representing a signal of 1 mW (0.775 V into 600 ohms).

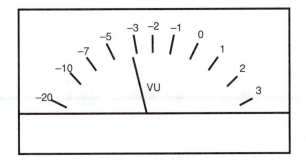

Figure 5.16 VU meter.

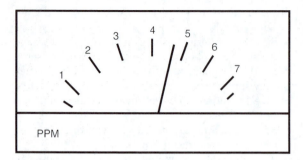

Figure 5.17 PPM meter.

- PPM 6 represents the maximum allowable signal.
- The meters have a very fast rise time (peak levels likely to cause overloads are therefore clearly visible), a parameter set by their associated electronics.
- The slow decay time makes the meter easy to read, even with short transients.
- PPMs are very expensive as the mechanical construction has to be very accurate and requires associated electronics to enable the parameters to be adjusted.

Operational guide to assist with balance:

- PPMs give little indication of the perceived loudness of the material. The audio may be allowed to peak up to 6 but needs to be controlled according to the programme material and its loudness, monitored on loudspeakers.
- Pure speech should be normally peaking 5 with only occasional peaks to 6.
- Some acoustic instruments might be allowed to peak 5 as well but more complex music mixes will need to be lower.
- Compressed music (rock bands for example) will need to be held to a maximum of 4. The use of heavy compression on TV commercials may mean these also need to be held at this level. Compression can be seen on the meter as the range of levels becomes

reduced. This will at least warn that close attention needs to be paid to the loudspeaker monitoring.
- Small crowds may peak 5 but very energetic ones only 4.
- Background effects behind a voice should be no greater than PPM 2 to 3.

Bargraph meters
Bargraph meters are constructed using LEDs, plasma or liquid crystal displays. They have no mechanical inertia to overcome and so can have associated electronics to provide them with any characteristic.

Both VU and PPM calibrations are used and some manufacturers build in the facility to view either. Peak hold indication is included in some versions but the precise ballistics may vary.

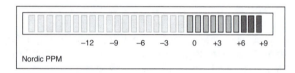

Figure 5.18 Bargraph meter – can be manufactured to any characteristic.

Dorrough loudness monitors
The development of the Dorrough meter was based on identifying the strengths and weaknesses of both VU and peak metering methods. It was realized that a more satisfactory solution would be to provide actual peak and quasi-average readings simultaneously.

The unit is based on forty LEDs calibrated from –25 dB to +14 dB in 1 dB steps. The display shows peaks as a single dot with a rise time of 10 µs and a bar with a time constant of 600 ms to indicate the quasi-average or persistence. These qualities enable the meters to be used to judge signal loudness whilst ensuring the engineering parameters are simultaneously maintained.

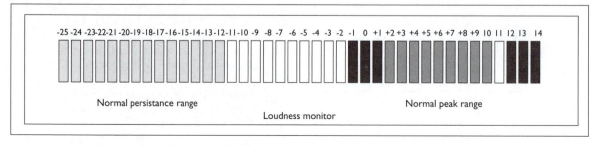

Figure 5.19 Dorrough meter (courtesy of Dorrough Electronics).

- Forty segment LEDs representing 1 dB per division.
- Peak rise time of 10 µs. Fast enough to show transients even at 15 kHz.
- Peak decay time 18 ms/dB. Equivalent to 720 ms for FSD.
- Persistence rise time approx. 600 ms.
- Selectable 3 sec, or indefinite peak hold facility.

Digital meters

Unlike analogue systems where there is some headroom, above which the signal becomes progressively more distorted, digital signals do not exist above the maximum quantized level.

The meters used for digital systems are calibrated from infinity (∞) to 0 (maximum level). Many have a calibration mark at −18 dB which is intended to be aligned with tone at zero VU. In fact some signals may produce digital clipping when aligned in this way and in the UK many users align 0 VU to −20 dB which places the zero level of 0.775 volts at −24 dB.

Figure 5.20 A typical digital meter.

In-picture display

One very effective way of placing the audio metering in the operator's eyeline is to insert the information into a picture monitor. This will help to ensure that incorrect levels do not go unnoticed, especially a problem in editing areas where the picture often takes precedence and metering may be on a sound console away from the eyeline. A small control unit is normally mounted in the equipment bay and the video feed to the monitor passes through the unit so that the audio information can be added to the picture. In-picture audio metering can display the signal in a bar-graph form from mono through to multi-track and the display position, within the picture, can be user selected to be horizontal, top or bottom or vertical, left or right of the picture.

Figure 5.21 Audio levels can be displayed in a picture monitor (courtesy of Chromatec).

The display can be switched to use VU or PPM type ballistics with the ability to hold peak levels to ensure over-modulation cannot be missed.

Graphical display

An alternative approach to complex audio monitoring is a purpose-designed vectorscope. This device displays the audio signals in a bar graph form on one side with the main part of the display showing a plan view of the audio image.

These units can handle any signal from stereo to full surround sound clearly indicating not only the level but also the average position of the sound. The great advantage of these displays is that they show

Figure 5.22 Complex audio levels are clearer displayed graphically (courtesy of RTW).

mono compatibility of stereo signals and stereo compatibility of surround signals. The bar graphs can be calibrated to comply with the required standard, VU, PPM (in its various international forms) and digital scales.

Metering summary

Whatever metering is to be used, the relative levels between each sound source must be balanced by careful monitoring. The mix heard on loudspeakers, or even on headphones, should be used to illustrate real energy levels. This is the correct place to balance the various sound sources, using meters as a guide. The meters will also ensure that the engineering parameters are correctly fulfilled.

5.3.3 Engineering connections

Unbalanced systems

Most domestic audio equipment is based on unbalanced circuits. In these systems the signal return acts as a screen or earth connection as well as being a part of the signal circuit. This can produce problems in the possibility of interference being induced into the circuit, especially as the signal levels of unbalanced systems are lower than professional ones. Further to this, loops between systems with separate earths can produce hum due to small differences in the earth potentials.

Balanced systems

In a balanced system the signal paths and the system earth are separated. This ensures that the screening of the system is more effective and any current flowing in the earth circuit will have little effect on the signal itself.

In order to interconnect balanced and unbalanced systems it is important to ensure that the balanced audio signal path remains separated from the earth. This can only be achieved with a purpose-designed transformer.

Cable types

The correct use of cable is vital to the integrity of audio signals, especially where long cable paths are required. Cables must have as little effect as possible on the signal they will be carrying. Balanced audio cables are specifically designed to match with the impedance of the system and resist unwanted pick-up from interference. The impedance of the system is particularly important with high impedance microphones (1000 ohms or more), where the wrong cable will produce a loss of signal level, as well as affecting the frequency response. Most broadcast microphones are only 200 ohms and therefore this problem is less significant. It becomes very important with high frequency signals. The correct, low loss cable must always be used on radio frequency (RF) systems like radio microphone aerials.

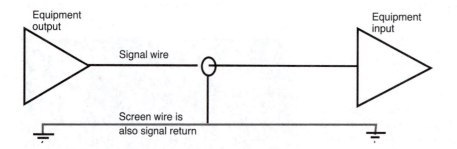

Figure 5.23 Unbalanced system.

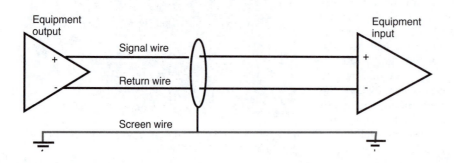

Figure 5.24 Balanced system.

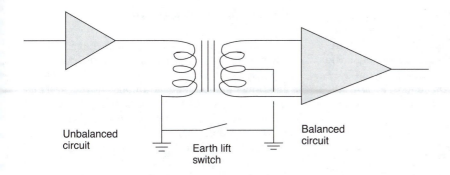

Figure 5.25 A balance transformer is required to connect an unbalanced system to a balanced one.

Unbalanced circuit

Earth lift switch

Balanced circuit

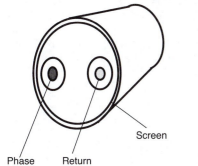

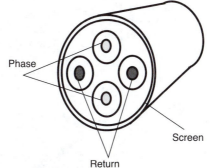

Figure 5.26 Cross-section of audio screened and star-quad cables.

Phase

Screen

Phase   Return

Phase

Screen

Return

The balanced microphone cables come in two forms:

- screened balanced cable which will help reduce unwanted pick-up of interference;
- star-quad cable where there are two pairs of conductors, laid in opposing directions. This lay produces an anti-phase component of the interference which tends to cancel as the pairs are connected together at each end of the cable.

Cables are further designed to have mechanical characteristics to suit the purpose to which they are to be used. In a microphone cable this includes an ability to resist abrasion, and be flexible, to help with handling and prevent the work-hardening and eventual fracture of the internal cores. On permanent installations thinner cables with foil screens can be used. These will be routed in special conduits and laced together to support their weight.

Multicore cables are designed for permanent installations and different types can be used for microphones allowing the use of break-out boxes to simplify large rigs.

Figure 5.27 Special cable is used where it will be laced into a permanent installation.

Figure 5.28 Purpose-designed cable must be used for multicore cables on drums.

Connectors for balanced systems

There are many audio connectors in use, some special types being used because of special requirements of the systems to which they are designed to connect. This might be a size requirement like the miniature connectors used on microphone radio transmitters or multiconnectors used to carry several audio circuits.

- **XLR (Xternal, Live and Return)**
  The common connector used for all balanced microphone connections and balanced high-level signals is the XLR. This has three pins to make the earth, live and return connections. These are manufactured in cable-ended plugs and sockets as well as in chassis-mounted versions.

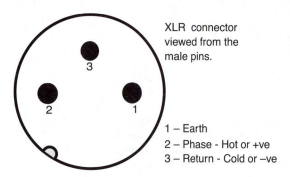

XLR connector viewed from the male pins.

1 – Earth
2 – Phase - Hot or +ve
3 – Return - Cold or –ve

Figure 5.29 XLR connector.

- **Jack**
  Connections on studio jack fields are always made with either 3 pin ¼″ PO type jacks or bantam jacks. These are connected: sleeve–earth, ring–return and tip–live. They are not the same shape as the domestic stereo ¼″ jacks which are not normally used to carry balanced signals and may damage the PO type sockets due to the larger tip size.

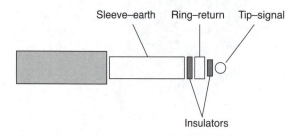

Sleeve–earth   Ring–return   Tip–signal

Insulators

Figure 5.30 PO type ¼″ jack.

Connectors for unbalanced systems

- **¼″ Jack**
  This is used for microphone connections and also for musical instruments like electric guitars or keyboards. It is therefore fitted to the input of instrument amplifiers and public address systems. Stereo versions of the ¼″ jack plug are used for most headphone connections on equipment like field recorders and mixers and studio tape machines. These headphones will have an impedance of between 8 and 50 ohms. Note that high impedance headphones, normally 2000 ohms, are fitted with PO type jacks and are designed for use with jack-fields and studio wall boxes. These do not appreciably affect the line to which they are connected due to their high impedance and further allow many pairs to be connected in the studio for talk-back and monitoring.

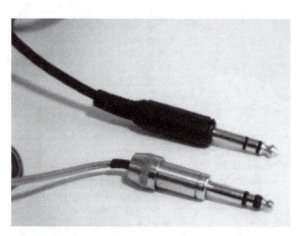

Figure 5.31 Unbalanced stereo jack at rear – note the smaller tip size on the P.O. version in the foreground.

- **RCA phono plugs**
  This is the input connector found on most domestic hi-fi systems and is used for the high level inputs on some lower priced sound mixers. It is considerably cheaper than the XLR and may be considered adequate where the susceptibility to induced interference is lower at the higher signal level.

5.4 Monitoring the sound

In establishing the requirements for good metering it has been stated that this is only an aid to proper audio monitoring. In order to record or broadcast television programmes it is vital to ensure that the viewer can clearly hear the audio that makes up the total programme image. This means that care must be taken to properly monitor the audio at all stages and ensure that the audio is appropriate for the image it is complementing.

To monitor sound effectively the listener must have suitable equipment and an environment to hear the audio clearly. The listener must be suitably trained to be able to recognize any errors that have occurred and then have the knowledge as to how these errors should be rectified. The listener must also have an understanding of the effect of the viewer's listening conditions, in order that they know how the end result will be perceived at home.

There is little point in transmitting any signal that makes it difficult to hear dialogue clearly. Such a problem may be due to poor recording or to a poor mix between the dialogue and any other sounds. Further, it is vital that the audio complements the pictures, particularly in drama where any discrepancies will significantly disturb the viewer's enjoyment.

To appreciate good audio the main requirement is for a quality monitoring environment. In a studio, outside broadcast vehicle or post-production area, it is reasonably straightforward to define an appropriate set-up. On location the problem is very different. A suitable pair of headphones is obvious but it is difficult to quantify the ability to interpret what is heard.

5.4.1 A professional monitoring environment

Monitoring audio requires care to ensure three main factors:

- Quality loudspeakers that produce a flat frequency response and can reproduce fast transients or changes in level.
- A listening environment that is quiet and has suitable acoustics, such that the room itself should not have any significant effect on the sound.
- A method of ascertaining the actual signal level; this assumes a clear understanding of how to interpret the various metering methods.

The mechanical factors in the room being used that must be considered to achieve good monitoring and thus minimize the errors include:

- **Loudspeaker power** – must be adequate to allow reasonable levels operating well within the system rating. Low frequencies require much greater output, in terms of energy, than the higher

frequencies. The speakers need to be capable of producing a power output up to four times greater than the average output, in order to ensure a flat response and an undistorted bass.
- **Loudspeaker frequency response** – needs to be as flat as possible, ensuring a true rendition of the whole frequency range. An operator balancing audio on an overly bright loudspeaker will automatically produce a dull recording.
- **Loudspeaker axis and position** – the speaker should be located in free space and pointing at the operator. The high frequency output from many loudspeakers will begin to reduce from as little as 15 degrees off axis. The speaker should not be placed close to flat surfaces or bass tip-up may occur, where sound reflections from nearby surfaces enhance the low frequency response.

For television production, the relationship between sound and picture is the primary consideration; the speaker must be close to the picture monitor to achieve this relationship. Loudspeaker position becomes even more important if stereo is a consideration as the system must be symmetrical.

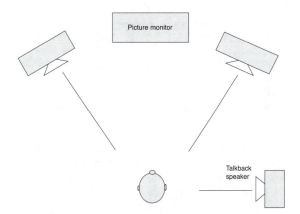

Figure 5.32 Loudspeakers should be symmetrically placed around the picture monitor with talkback well away from the programme sound image.

Talkback speakers must be placed so that they are well away from the programme speakers, avoiding any risk that sound coloration from these sources could influence the monitored sound. Coloration is caused by the partial cancellation of some frequencies; it occurs when sounds are repeated from a second loudspeaker, delayed in time from the original version.

- **Listening level** – many operators monitor broadcast audio at quite a high level in order to hear inaccuracies. The level should be reasonable, but not too loud, and must remain constant if consistent sound balances are to be achieved. It must be remembered that, as the monitoring level changes, the way in which one sound will mask out another will result in an overall change in the perceived balance.

5.4.2 The effect of incorrect monitoring levels

It is important to remember that the ear works in a non-linear way in order to cope with both low and high levels of sound.

Ear's perception

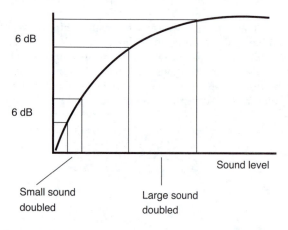

Figure 5.33 Human hearing sensitivity changes with level.

The effect of too high a monitoring level on an audio mix is that the brain will perceive sound levels as quite near each other.

Take an example of voice with music mixed under:

- With a high level of monitoring affecting the mix, the balancer will tend to keep the music at a lower level relative to the voice. The resultant effect will be that the viewers may barely hear the music because they are listening at a much lower level.

- If the monitoring level is too low the balancer will not hear the music clearly – the resulting balance contains music that is too high and may drown out the voice when listened to at normal levels.

The figures in the graphs (Fig. 5.34) are only an illustration. The real difference in level between voice and background music will depend on the voice, the music and the type of programme. Sound should be monitored at a level that is only slightly louder than the home viewing level. This will ensure a good mix whilst still enabling faults or distortions to be heard before they get transmitted.

There will be occasions when it is necessary to change the level of the control room monitors when communicating with other areas: to answer the phone, to have a conversation, or when using talkback (in which case the monitoring may be reduced automatically by the talkback system). To achieve these temporary changes in monitoring level, speaker 'dim, cut and lift' controls should be used, ensuring the level returns to exactly the same point when ready. This is impossible using a continuously variable control.

5.4.3 Room acoustics

When planning the acoustics of a monitoring area there are two primary considerations:

(1) **Reverberation.** This relates to the time delay before sounds reflected from the wall and other surfaces reach the operator's ears. These reflected sounds will have their own frequency characteristics, as some frequencies will be partially absorbed by the walls. Sound absorbers are needed to reduce the reflections evenly across the whole audio spectrum. The overall reverberation time should be low enough to ensure that the monitored sound is clear and not coloured by the room acoustics.

(2) **Standing waves.** This effect is due to the room having resonances where the parallel walls act like an organ pipe, enhancing certain frequencies.

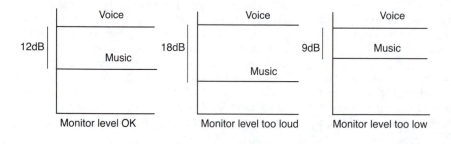

Figure 5.34 Sound balancers will achieve varying results at different monitoring levels.

In the same way that a non-linear frequency response in the loudspeakers affects the mix, poor room acoustics will force operators to accommodate for errors in the listening environment, producing a less than perfect overall balance.

Glass, hard surfaces and parallel walls are all to be avoided. Windows need to be kept to minimum, with the glass surfaces angled to make the reflected paths as long as possible and to confuse the reflections.

Any audio mix is a subjective matter but most operators will agree on technical quality and voice clarity. It is important to realize that personal factors like tiredness can affect judgement of audio mixes. Television sound quality will be difficult to judge if the loudspeakers are not reasonably close to the main picture monitor. Metering must be close to the eyeline, as should gain reduction meters fitted to compressors, or they might be ignored.

It is vital that persons making judgements of audio quality are able to recognize the effect these devices have and can judge where they are incorrectly employed or adjusted.

Operators must be sure that they correctly interpret the metering and combine their readings with loudspeaker monitoring if the viewer is to enjoy the programme material.

5.4.4 Domestic viewing environments

Sound levels
Viewing conditions vary significantly, from the family home with open windows and much noise (children playing, traffic and so on) to quiet well-designed rooms with soft furnishings, preventing reflected sounds from colouring the audio.

There will be a range of receivers in use, from small televisions with even smaller loudspeakers, not always pointing at the viewer (the high frequency dispersion of some loudspeakers may be as little as 20 degrees) to high quality systems with stereo or even surround sound systems capable of reproducing high sound output levels with a flat frequency response.

Sound operators normally operate in high quality environments, using the best equipment. This means that background sounds will be low, monitoring a wide dynamic range on equipment capable of producing high audio levels, with very linear frequency responses. Most viewers at home are in a very different position. The quality of their television audio may be quite poor by comparison, producing only fairly low levels of sound, which often lack a good bass response. This, combined with the noise from the viewing environment, reduces the ability to hear wide dynamic ranges as the low-level sounds are lost into the local ambience.

The viewing conditions may vary from country to country and different programmes will have an effect on the range of sounds that are acceptable. It is generally agreed that: the transmitted dynamic range should not exceed 26 dB. This will ensure that in all but the noisiest of homes the whole range of sounds can be heard satisfactorily.

Check monitors
An aid to keeping the operator aware of this concern is the parallel use of small check loudspeakers that more nearly match the home monitoring quality. They will enable the operator to adjust the balance in order that all the information can be heard clearly. The example of monitoring only on high quality speakers, operating at fairly high levels, and producing mixes with music or effects that are too low has already been given. In these mixes the music becomes a background annoyance rather than an effective part of the audio.

Very high monitoring levels will also increase the relative clarity of both bass and treble frequencies. Adjustments made may result in a corresponding reduction of these frequencies for the viewer. This will always be a compromise as some viewers will have high quality equipment that more nearly matches that used by the professional, so the allowance for domestic conditions must not be taken too far.

Stereo images
For stereo, home considerations become more complex and discussion needs to take place regarding image width as well as the frequency response and dynamic range considerations.

In order to decide on the operational practices, information on the way in which the viewers are listening and the equipment that they are using is essential. This information can be used to provide a compromise as to the width and other qualities of the sound, allowing for the local viewing conditions.

5.4.5 What qualities should be judged?

In practice, to understand audio quality there are two areas to consider: the technical matters and the artistic criteria.

Technical
- **Frequency range.** Is the sound even across the whole range from treble to bass? Is the correct microphone being employed and is the equalization correct?

- **Level.** Is the signal properly controlled to ensure a technically correct recording? This will depend on the equipment in use; the range of acceptable levels will be lower for analogue equipment than it is for digital. See also dynamic range, noise and distortion.
- **Distortion.** Are the microphones suitable for the instrument or voice, and are all levels set accordingly to ensure the equipment is functioning within its specification? Distortion includes poor equalization and problems such as sibilance, not purely engineering parameters like over-modulation.
- **Noise.** Are the levels high enough to ensure that the signal-to-noise ratio for the system in use is properly maintained? This will be most important for analogue methods.
- **Dynamic range.** Are the maximum and minimum levels appropriate to the material being recorded (and within the capability of the recording device) and controlled according to the viewer at home? See Section 5.4.4.
- **Wow and flutter.** Are there any unwanted variations in equipment speed or pitch variations?
- **Sync.** Are there any time delays between the pictures and sound?
- **Phase.** Are there any time delays between the left and right legs of a stereo signal? Time delay is recognized by a hollow sound, lacking clear imagery. Phase or correlation meters will show the errors. In M/S (mid and side) stereo recordings, S must be less than M.

Artistic

- **Balance.** Is the relationship between each sound source correct? This may mean the balance between each microphone, or may be achieved by the position of one microphone to ensure correct coverage of the sound sources, or a combination of both.
- **Perspective.** Do the sounds appear at the correct distance from the camera? If a speaker is close to the camera lens their voice should sound close, it will contain much less background sound and the effect of the acoustics will be low.
- **Ambience.** Is the relationship between the primary sound sources and the background effects satisfactory, and is the effect of the acoustic suitable?
- **Stereo.** Are the left–right position images correct relative to the picture? Decisions will have to be made in the planning stage as to how to match the sound and picture images. Care must be taken to allow for the editing of the material.

The first group of criteria are technical and can be clearly defined. The second group are judgements on the artistic content of the programme and must be considered in relation to the picture. It might be thought that the artistic criteria cannot be judged objectively, varying from person to person. Surprisingly, it has been found that most will have a very close agreement as to what is right or wrong for a given picture. When audio is graded, both the technical and artistic criteria must be taken into account.

5.4.6 Location monitoring

All the factors already outlined have to be considered during the recording or transmission of items when on location. On an outside broadcast, a control environment is created so that near conventional monitoring can be achieved. This becomes more difficult with single-camera operation where headphones will have to be used.

The perception of sound balances on headphones is very different from that monitored by loudspeaker. Like the effect of monitoring at too high a level on loudspeakers, sounds monitored on headphones will appear to be at a very similar level to each other. This is enhanced by the fact that the listener is removed from any effect of room acoustics, making the balance appear even more artificial.

In order to make a judgement on the balance between speech and background sounds, the headphones must be of a closed back type. The headphones will therefore reasonably isolate the operator from the sounds in the working environment, ensuring that the operator is monitoring only the sound being picked up by the microphones in use.

Quality

The main quality criteria of frequency range, dynamic range and distortion can be satisfied quite well. The headphones should be of good enough quality in order to judge these parameters as effectively as can be achieved with loudspeakers.

Balance and ambience

Balance between the various featured sounds can be achieved on headphones, with experience.

The relation between these featured sounds and the ambience is much more difficult. To achieve this it is important to ensure the headphones provide a good isolation from the outside world. Open back headphones on location are therefore quite unacceptable. The difficulty increases as ambient levels get higher, and the headphones do not adequately separate the recorded and direct sounds. Operating at a reasonable level will help, but it must not be forgotten that level changes will affect the perception of balance.

In order to get an understanding of how balances appear different on headphones from those on loudspeakers, some time should be spent listening to good recordings alternately, firstly on loudspeakers and then on the headphones. Try to identify just how loud the backgrounds appear on the headphones, as this needs to be remembered when on the location. It is difficult and takes quite a lot of experience to make good judgements under the pressure of a location shoot.

Perspective

Perspective is much more difficult as, on headphones, it is difficult to recognize the difference between varying acoustic effects at different recording levels. Just like judging ambient effects, some guidance can be achieved by listening to recordings alternately on loudspeakers and headphones.

Stereo

Stereo on location is difficult as the image is placed through the head rather than displayed in front of it. Absolute position is quite hard to determine and the use of a number of microphones being panned into position may be outside the scope of headphone monitoring. Experience of what worked in the past may be the only solution.

One method of achieving good stereo is to use the tried and tested stereo combinations, like an M/S pair, or known stereo coincident pairs, thus relying on the microphones to achieve the image. To match the sound to the picture the microphone must be placed in the same axis as the camera lens (more of this in Section 5.8).

It is worth noting that some manufacturers recognize this problem and produce a solution in the form of monitoring 'black boxes'. These take the left and right signals and process them, using time delay, and feed an amount of each signal into the opposite channel, prior to the headphones. The effect is to provide the sound the brain would normally experience when listening to loudspeakers. If it is important to adjust the positional balance during the recording, this may provide a solution.

5.4.7 Grading

Grading is the process of scoring both sound and pictures to enable a report to be made about the quality of the transmitted material.

In most countries a five-point grading structure is used to quantify the various criteria, with 5 being the best and 1 the worst:

5	EXCELLENT	The best that can be technically achieved
4	GOOD	Very little technical impairment
3	FAIR	An acceptable normal standard
2	POOR	Below the normal with noticeable errors
1	BAD	Seriously degraded, not for transmission

This is a useful process as it can be used to feed back to programme makers information regarding both technical and artistic criteria. The process is helpful in maintaining consistent overall standards.

5.5 Microphones

The job of the microphone is to convert the sound pressure waves into the electrical signals required for recording or transmitting sound information. These electrical signals must be the same frequencies as and be proportional in amplitude to the original sound. There are many techniques for achieving this and each microphone type will have different characteristics, both in how faithfully it reproduces the original sound and in whether it has directional properties, as the microphone tries to reject any unwanted sounds.

5.5.1 Microphone types

There are many principles by which sound pressure waves can be translated into electrical signals. In order to keep this volume reasonably simple this section will describe the three methods most commonly used: dynamic moving coil, dynamic ribbon and condenser.

Microphones can be grouped into two categories:

- **Pressure operated.** These produce a varying output proportional to changes in air pressure. They are built with only one face of their diaphragms open to the atmosphere.
- **Pressure gradient.** These measure pressure difference as both sides of the diaphragms are open and the pressure on each side must be different for them to operate.

The shape of the area of sensitivity of a microphone is known as its **polar pattern**. Most types can be

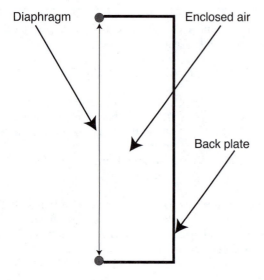

Figure 5.35 Pressure operation – the capsule produces an output with changes of air pressure.

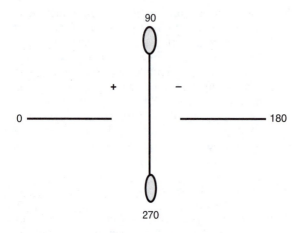

Figure 5.36 Pressure gradient – produces an output only if there is a pressure difference on opposite sides of the diaphragm.

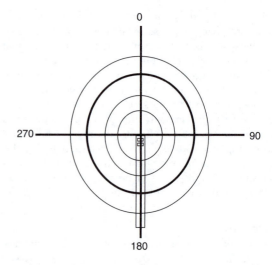

Figure 5.37 Omni-directional response – picks up sound from all around.

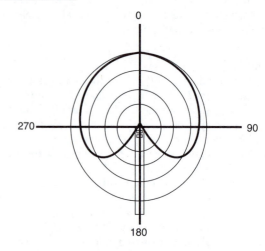

Figure 5.38 Cardioid response – heart-shaped pick-up.

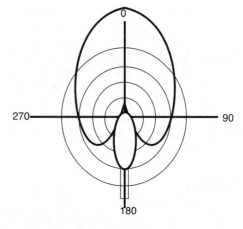

Figure 5.39 Hyper-cardioid response – slightly narrower response with small rear lobe.

manufactured to have different polar responses, regardless of the operating method, as mostly the directional characteristics are produced by the way in which the heart of the microphone is mounted within its body.

The polar responses should always be shown for a particular frequency range, as the directional characteristics will vary with frequency. Microphones may be quite directional at high frequencies, 1000 Hz or more, and progressively less so as the frequency decreases. This is due to lower frequencies, below 250 Hz, being of such long wavelengths that making directional microphones is practically impossible.

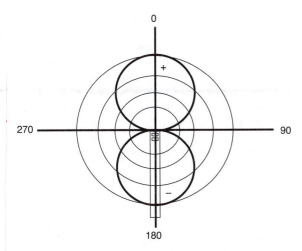

Figure 5.40 Figure-of-eight response – picks up sound from either side.

Figure 5.42 Cardioid and omni-directional moving coil microphones.

Dynamic moving coil

Moving coil microphones depend on the principle that when an electrical conductor moves through a magnetic field there will be a small electrical current induced in the conductor. A coil of very fine wire is attached to the rear of a diaphragm. It is arranged so that the coil is in the centre of a fixed magnet.

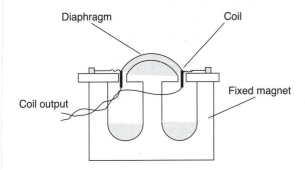

Figure 5.41 Moving coil operation.

Sound pressure waves cause the diaphragm to move in time with the sound and correspondingly move the coil within the magnetic field. If the output of the coil is connected to an electrical circuit a small current will flow, and this will be proportional to the original sound. This type of microphone is effectively a small electrical generator.

This principle is most commonly employed in the manufacture of stick microphones. These can be designed for many applications from news broadcasting, used for interviews, to hand-held vocal microphones for singers.

Advantages of moving coil microphones are:

• They are robust and reliable.
• They are relatively inexpensive.
• They can be made to have a range of uses and pick-up patterns.
• They are less sensitive to wind noise, handling noise or atmospheric moisture and temperature changes.
• They need no external power for operation.

Disadvantages of moving coil microphones are:

• Frequency response is generally limited, particularly at high frequencies. Because of their mechanical nature, the highest response would normally be around 10 kHz.
• They have a rather poor transient response due to the relatively large mass of their moving components. The transient response is the rate at which the device will respond to changes in sound level.
• Fairly low output will require gains of 60 or 70 dB at the input stage and may be unsuitable for very low level sounds.

Dynamic ribbon

The ribbon microphone, as its name implies, has a thin metal ribbon suspended in a concentrated magnetic field. The principle is the same as the moving coil where the ribbon is both the diaphragm and the conductor. As a result of the very low impedance of this conductor a transformer must also be included in the design.

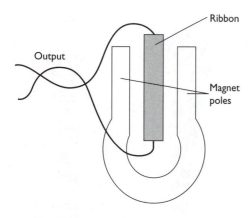

Figure 5.43 Ribbon operation.

This is a true pressure difference device and will therefore have a figure of eight response. This response is independent of frequency. This microphone is very popular in radio as a two-person interview could sit across a table with the producer off-response at the side. Virtually no pick-up exists at the side at all frequencies. The most common version of the ribbon microphone is the commentator's lip-ribbon. This is a very close talking version and is able to considerably reduce the level of unwanted background sounds.

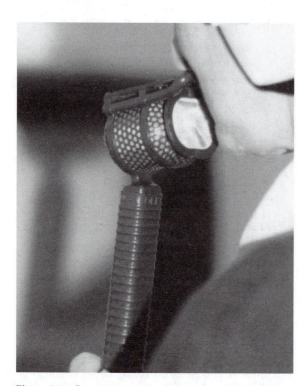

Figure 5.44 Commentator's lip-ribbon.

Advantages of ribbon microphones are:

- They have a good frequency response.
- They have good transient response due to the low mass of the diaphragm.
- They have figure of eight response, making them ideal for noise cancellation and use as a commentator's microphone.

Disadvantages of ribbon microphones are:

- They are more expensive than moving coil microphones.
- They are very fragile.
- They are sensitive to air movement – they will need protection from wind noise and breathing if used as a close-talking microphone.
- They have very low output, needing 70 to 80 dB of gain.

Condenser

The most commonly used microphones today are condenser microphones as they can be manufactured almost any size and, by using a combination of mechanical construction using one or more capsules, can be designed to produce virtually any polar pattern. They use the principle of a condenser or capacitor that has the capability of storing electrical charges. The density of this charge is proportional to the size of the plates, the medium separating the plates and the distance between the plates.

A polarizing voltage is applied between the plates, one of which is made of thin foil in the form of a diaphragm. The only variable is the distance between

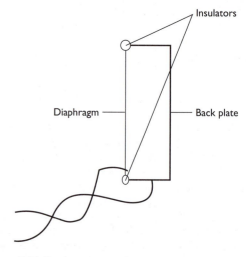

Figure 5.45 Condenser operation.

the plates, and this distance will vary in proportion to sound pressure. The result will be an electrical charge which varies with the changes of sound pressure.

The output is very low and must be amplified within the body of the microphone, requiring the microphone to have a power supply connected or a battery within. This supply is commonly provided via the connecting cable and is known as **phantom powering**.

These microphones can be designed to have virtually any response including being attached to an acoustic labyrinth to produce more directional responses, as in shotgun and rifle microphones.

They can also have accessories which allow cables or tubes to separate the condenser capsule from the body of the microphone. This allows a large range of operations and is especially useful in producing very neat alternatives to having unattractive microphone stands in shot.

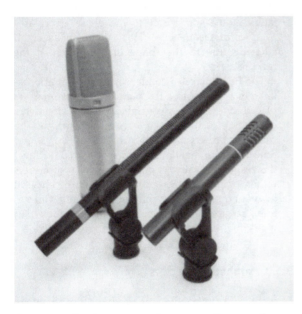

Figure 5.46 Condenser microphones can take many forms.

Advantages of condenser microphones are:

- They have a full range of frequencies.
- They have good transient response.
- The system is very flexible and can be manufactured to have virtually all polar responses.
- Their flexibility means they can be manufactured in varying forms: stick, shotgun or rifle, lapel and large capsule or multicapsule switchable versions.

Disadvantages of condenser microphones are:

- They are quite fragile, especially as they contain electronics within the body of the microphone.
- They range from fairly expensive to very expensive.
- They are sensitive to air movement and wind noise.
- They are sensitive to handling noise.
- They can be sensitive to temperature changes and moisture caused by condensation.
- They require powering.

Apart from fitting internal batteries to those microphones so designed, there are two types of powering methods in use for condenser microphones, with Phantom 12–48 volt systems the most commonly used:

- Phantom 12–48 volts – connected between both signal paths and earth.
- AB (or T) 12 volts – an older system, most commonly found on film equipment. The voltage is connected between the two signal paths. Applying this to some non-condenser microphones may damage them.

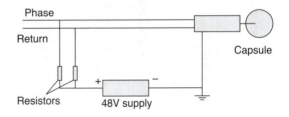

Figure 5.47 Phantom wiring – used for studio and most location microphones.

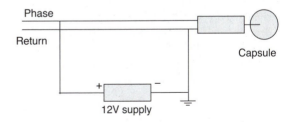

Figure 5.48 T-power wiring – may be found on older film equipment.

Other microphone types
- **Electret microphone**

    The true condenser microphone requires a polarizing voltage to produce the varying charge and the subsequent electrical output. It is possible to produce a capsule where the diaphragm has a permanent charge and no polarizing voltage has to be generated in the microphone. These have a similarly low output and still require amplification very close to the capsule, so a power supply will still be needed.

One advantage of this type is that they can be made at a lower price although care is needed in selection as some have rather uneven mid and high frequency responses.

Figure 5.49 Dual condenser microphone capsule.

- **Dual condenser microphones**
  Two of the condenser type capsules can be placed back-to-back and their combined responses switched by varying the polarizing voltages. By this method microphones can be manufactured that have switchable responses covering omni-, cardioid- and hyper-cardioid patterns.

- **Shotgun or rifle capsules**
  Condenser capsules can be given much narrower angles of acceptance by the use of cancellation of 'off-axis' signals. These microphones have a hyper-cardioid capsule mounted at the end of an acoustic tube. The tube has slots along its side which allow sound pressure waves to enter and these produce phase shifts, and hence cancellation of the off-centre sounds. These effects are very frequency dependent and the directional characteristics are considerably reduced at lower frequencies.

- **Pressure zone microphones (PZM)**
  Pressure zone or boundary microphones are a specialized use of a condenser or electret capsule. The problem of positioning any microphone near a table or floor is that sound sources that are well away from the microphone will not only be heard directly by the capsule but a second version of the same sound will be reflected off the surface of the floor. This second version will be delayed in time from the original sound, producing partial cancellation of the sound due to the phase errors at a number of frequencies. This is known as **comb filtering** due to the shape of the graph of the response.

  The PZM places a condenser capsule at approximately 1 mm from a flat plate. The microphone is placed on the floor or table, which effectively becomes part of the same reflecting surface. The construction ensures that the delay to sound reflected from the 'flat surface' is too small to affect the response. Many users define the response as rather 'open', but these microphones can be useful to avoid the frequency combing effect and, further, they reduce the number of microphones that would be required to cover large areas of action.

5.5.2 Parabolic reflectors

It is virtually impossible to produce a microphone that has a very narrow angle of response at a good

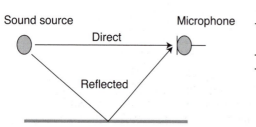

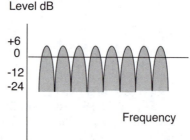

Figure 5.50 Reflected sound produces a comb filter effect.

range of frequencies. One useful solution to this is the use of the parabolic reflector. It is a very specialized piece of equipment and may cost as much as the microphone with which it is to be used. The units, which vary from 0.5 to 1 metres across, are designed as a parabola with the microphone mounted facing inwards. Incoming pressure waves are reflected off the inner surface and concentrated at the microphone, considerably enhancing its sensitivity. The microphone used needs to have a wide enough polar response so that the whole surface of the reflector is 'heard'. In fact omni-directional microphones can be used, as unwanted off-axis sounds are scattered by the reflector and add little to the overall pick-up.

Care is needed in their use as they are very narrow at high frequencies. These units may be used for sport but are particularly useful in recording wildlife as good sound can be achieved from quite large distances.

5.5.3 Microphone mounts

There are a large range of devices designed to position microphones where they are needed. Floor stands must be well designed and heavy to ensure that the expensive microphones that they will be supporting cannot easily be damaged. Weight is also helpful, as it will reduce any unwanted noises being transmitted to the microphone.

Boom arms can be fitted to the stands to reach over instruments or help with obtaining good camera shots. Microphone clips are important both for security and the reduction of mechanical pick-up.

Table stands can be used, but here it is even more important to consider sounds transmitted through the stand as the table may act as a sounding board making mechanical pick-up more likely. Heavy bases with soft rubber bottoms will help with this. Special clips can be used to connect small microphones directly to musical instruments and clamps of various designs are useful to clamp spot microphones to sets or scaffolds. Lighting clamps are very useful here so it is worth looking at lighting catalogues as well as purpose-sold sound accessories.

Booms

Microphone booms are very valuable in the television studio and may be available on some location sets for drama use. The boom is a specialist wheel-based unit that allows the operator very flexible positioning of the microphone. A second operator can track the platform base and one wheel can be steered or all three locked to steer them altogether, in order that the base can be 'crabbed' sideways. The operator stands on the platform, which can be raised to give an arm position of approximately two to three metres high. With one hand the operator can 'rack' the boom arm in and out, which allows the position of the microphone to telescope from two to nearly five metres from the centre of the boom. The other hand controls the rotation and tilt of the microphone mount. The microphone needs to be mounted very carefully to reduce mechanically transmitted noise and the whole boom arm is then balanced in order that the operator does not have difficulty in operating the boom for long periods.

The boom is extremely versatile, allowing very quick and accurate positioning of the microphone. The operator must have a good knowledge of camera angles and lighting techniques as the microphone needs to be carefully positioned in order to achieve the required sound quality, whilst keeping out of shot and not casting visible shadows.

The prevention of shadows and keeping the microphone out of shot are a team effort. Careful planning of the required action should indicate an appropriate lighting technique and rehearsal of the moves will produce the required compromise. It is vital that both sound and camera operators mark their positions and maybe even take notes, so that the positions can be accurately repeated during recording. For a boom operator, one useful way of identifying the microphone position accurately is to note the out-of-vision shadows, which should help in returning the microphone to the exact same position during the recording.

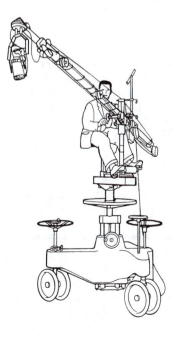

Figure 5.51
Microphone boom mounted on a wheeled base.

Fish poles

Where a large boom platform is not practical, especially on location shoots, short hand-held 'fish poles' or lightweight booms are used. These allow an operator to get the microphone in over the action and with the close cooperation of the camera operator can be held very close to the edge of frame and produce very good results.

Experience is needed here with regard to shots and lighting, and on location the operator may also have to adjust the mixer levels as well!

5.5.4 Problems

All microphones have to be used with care. They are precision pieces of engineering and thus they all can be damaged, or their characteristics be changed, by misuse. Severe shock loads, caused by dropping them, will obviously cause problems. They should all be protected from moisture or very large changes in temperature. They will all pick up handling noise to some degree and air movement like wind noise, or even breathing on them, which will cause severe overloads or distortions.

Wind noise

Condenser microphones are extremely sensitive to air movement and will even need some protection for interior shoots if the microphone is to be moved. Most stick versions have built-in windshields which will be enough to allow hand-held interviews, but if a rifle type is to be used on a fish pole or boom it will need a foam shield to protect it from air movement. In some cases the movement due to air-conditioners will be enough to produce background rumbles.

The microphones need to be properly protected from wind noise with a basket-type windshield that will keep the air movement away from the microphone. In very windy conditions even these will howl. To reduce this effect a hairy cover can be fitted over the basket; this is very effective, making it possible to obtain good sound in almost any conditions.

Whilst **lapel microphones** are also condenser types, they require a rather different approach when dealing with wind noise. Air movement will be a problem on exterior locations even on an apparently still day and the use of foam windshields is only part of the solution. The principle is to try to move the air movement away from the microphone, but clearly large baskets are not a practical solution here. Rigging under clothing is a more satisfactory way of reducing wind noise, and it is worth experimenting with different fabrics to ascertain which help reduce the wind

(a)

(b)

(c)

Figure 5.52 Microphone correctly mounted to avoid handling noise; (b) basket shield used to reduce wind noise; (c) a long-haired cover may be required for extreme wind conditions (courtesy of Rycote Microphone Windshields Ltd).

noise without a noticeable loss of high frequency response or the production of unpleasant fabric sounds. Open-weave fabrics are best but they should be soft in order to reduce rubbing noises. Wind noise is further discussed in Section 5.5.5.

In general, **dynamic microphones** are much less sensitive to wind noise and most are fitted with some sort of wind protection within the body of the unit. They may need extra protection in extreme conditions, where foam windshields should be sufficient. One other advantage of an extra windshield is that if the microphone is being used in the rain it will help provide some short-term protection. Spare windshields should be available to replace wet ones, keeping most of the water away from the microphone.

Phasing (acoustic)

Where the artistes are individually miked and are close to each other, coloration or phase cancellation can be very serious, especially where one person's voice is very quiet. This requires the microphones to be set at very different levels. The louder person is picked up on the wrong microphone as well as their own, with a time delay that is proportional to the distance between the speakers. This delay will cause cancellation of some frequencies – **phasing**. The solution is to balance the two channels so that only one at a time is at the working level. This is impossible for a one-person operation, where the best solution is to record the microphones separately onto two tracks, leaving the editor or dubbing mixer to get the mix right. Make sure that a detail of how the tracks have been used is written on the tape or log sheet.

Electronic phase checks

Whenever a number of microphones are to be used in close proximity they should be checked for electronic phase. Electronic phase is caused by the reversal of the balanced circuit – either incorrect microphone manufacture or cable errors can cause this. The check is to hold all the microphones together and, using one as a reference, mix in the others one by one whilst taking a level. If errors are present a very noticeable loss of the bass response will be heard and should be temporarily corrected with a phase lead (coded yellow). This fault should be noted and permanently corrected later.

Proximity effect or bass tip-up

The effect of getting very close (this might be tried to reduce background noise), perhaps 200 mm or closer, to many microphones is to increase its output at low frequencies with respect to the middle and high frequencies, known as **proximity effect**. This effect, of enhancing the lower frequencies, is most noticeable with male voices where there is a larger amount of bass in the voice. In general this is an unpleasant effect, and may reduce the continuity between takes or shots.

Some stick microphones, particularly the music vocalist types, are designed to reduce this effect, allowing them to be operated at very small distances. This will make these microphones unsuitable for operation at larger distances where they will sound very 'thin' and lacking in bass response. It is normally bad practice to use a microphone designed for singing as a hand-held stick microphone for interviews.

5.5.5 Microphone technique

This sub-section is intended to provide a basic guide to using microphones. There are many solutions to every sound problem, so the methods described should be regarded as starting points. Experience will produce more techniques and all sound operators are constantly exchanging ideas, especially in more complex topics like stereo and surround.

The sub-section is divided into five areas:

(1) Effects
(2) Voice-over recording
(3) Pieces to camera and interviews
(4) Music
(5) Radio microphones

1 Effects

In general, effects are fairly straightforward to record. If the level is fairly constant any good quality microphone will achieve acceptable results. It is important to be consistent in both quality and level in order that the material can be easily edited.

Short rifle or shotgun types are the most popular, as the sound required to match the picture can be selected. These microphones are sensitive so will always need to be protected from wind noise. They should be properly mounted in a lightweight suspension to decouple the microphone from the pole on which it is mounted in order to remove any handling noise.

On location it may be desirable to mount the microphone on the camera, but it must be positioned so as not to pick up servo zooms or handling noise. The microphone provided by the camera manufacturer may not be of good enough quality as these often lack adequate low-frequency response, possibly deliberately to reduce the effect of wind. A lightweight condenser can be mounted in a soft windshield, which provides both the microphone suspension and the wind protection, all mounted simply on the camera.

Omni-directional microphones are useful, particularly if there is to be a lot of movement in the shots; here using a rifle on the camera will not give consistent effects, making the edit difficult.

Care must be taken with effects to ensure that the results can be easily edited. Often it is preferable to have consistent sound effects rather than a different sound on each shot. Unless the noises are specific, and in vision, one long sound take will speed up the edit, reducing the need to crossfade the sound between every shot. It is vital to make sure there are enough effects tracks, even if some of the shots are much longer than needed for the pictures alone – the editing can be speeded up considerably if one take of effects can be laid over a whole sequence of shots.

If separate sound equipment like a portable MiniDisc or DAT (Digital Audio Tape) machine is available, the extra sound effects takes can be recorded onto this medium.

For news-type shoots, the effects levels should be recorded so that they are approximately consistent with the background effects recorded during the pieces to camera or interviews. This makes the edits much quicker as the backgrounds will be consistent throughout the whole shoot.

Auto gain, on the input of the camera, should generally be avoided as it will cause level variations, making the results unpleasant to listen to and difficult to edit. In very bad cases the background effects will be quickly lifted in level between each spoken sentence, producing a sound that will be very distracting.

Featured spot effects (bombs, door slams, etc.) may be adjusted so as to peak up to 6 PPM or 0 VU (100% modulation). This is the only occasion where an unrehearsed, one-off, event might justify the use of auto gain on the input, although setting a second channel 12 dB below the first should produce one that is close enough. A hand-clap near the microphone, used to adjust the gain, can give a good guide. It is good practice to use a moving coil microphone for very loud, transient sounds. These short-duration, very large pressure changes can produce rather flat results on condenser microphones. If there is any uncertainty one solution is to use both types, recording on two tracks, allowing a choice of the most effective track in the edit.

2 Voice-over recording

A whole range of microphones can be used for voice-over recording, from the very best variable pattern condensers to moving coils, lip ribbons, or even lapels. The object is to make a recording that is clear, without echoes or background noise and at a consistent level. It must match any recordings that have already been made by the same artiste in the studio or on location.

The most usual is to use a good quality cardioid microphone at about 300 mm from the mouth in a dry voice-over booth. A pop shield will be needed, either a foam windshield or, better, a purpose-made gauze shield mounted in a clamp in front of the microphone.

Figure 5.53 Separate shields are needed on voice-over microphones to prevent popping.

If the voice-over artiste also speaks in vision it is important to make the two recordings sound as similar as possible. It can be very confusing when the voice-over material sounds like a different person to the one already recorded in vision. It may help to position the artist away from the microphone and get them to speak up or even shout (particularly with sports commentating) so that the voice cuts through the backgrounds that it will be laid against. The use of headphones will be needed in the voice-recording booth for communication. Background music or effects are played to the artiste, mixed with their voice-over. The artist will tend to speak up in competition with the effects, and this will help the voice presentation. Compression may be needed to give the voice enough punch to be clearly heard through the effects. One way to match voice recordings is use the same microphone as was employed on location.

Occasionally it is necessary to record the voice-over on location. Beware of recording in vehicles as they can sound very boxy and this acoustic will be unsuitable to cover an exterior shot. It is better to find a quiet exterior location to do the voice recording.

Lip ribbons should be used with great care, as many people sound very nasal when recorded in this way. Lip ribbons are really only acceptable for sport where the viewer is used to their effect.

3 Pieces to camera and interviews

Rifle microphones
The most common way to cover this situation is to use a short rifle microphone. This gives a good frequency response, can be protected from wind noise and with careful positioning will give a good balance between the voice and the surrounding effects. This method also has the advantage of being immediately available, whereas rigging personal microphones will take time and might result in the material being lost. Compromise between the sound and the picture may be required to keep this microphone out of shot.

Indoors, where wind noise is not a problem, the basket windshield should always be removed; a simple foam windshield will protect the microphone from air movement. This smaller unit is lighter to hold and is less likely to get in shot and, if it does, it might be acceptable just on the edge of frame.

Stick microphones
Single-person operation may make the use of rifle microphones difficult and so hand-held stick microphones are good if they are acceptable in shot. These must be handled firmly, ensuring that the cable connector does not rattle and that the microphone is 'worked' between the persons speaking if it is a cardioid response. Moving the microphone correctly takes skill on behalf of the interviewer – learning to favour the more quietly spoken whilst ensuring the correct distance from the mouth to overcome backgrounds and still keeping in sync with the questions and answers all takes practice.

Omni-directional microphones are often better as they are easier to use. Provided they are kept reasonably close, about 300 mm, from the mouth they will give a good rejection of background sounds. These will still need to be kept in the correct place to ensure a good balance between the speakers.

Lapel or personal microphones
Another alternative to the rifle microphone is the use of lapel or personal microphones, which can be unobtrusive or even hidden. These can be connected to radio transmitters, which allow greater freedom to the presenter, particularly on location shoots. Getting the correct balance between the microphones can be quite difficult, but the rejection of background sounds should be good, as they will be close to the speaker's mouth. These microphones are normally omni-directional and, as their sensitivity falls off rapidly with distance, the voice will sound close with the background effects levels suitable in all but extreme situations. The disadvantage is that they do not provide any perspective to the sound, being constant in their output regardless of shot. This effect will be acceptable for documentary shoots but drama material will require the addition of acoustic effects and extra background sounds. These can be added at the dubbing stage.

It is possible to purchase directional versions of personal microphones. Directional types can be identified by the slots around the side of the casing. These versions help with feedback where PA systems are to be used. This type will be a little larger and must be rigged pointing upwards.

Rigging of personal microphones
Personal microphones are of the condenser type, but vary considerably in their methods of construction, and therefore in operation. Care is needed to use those that are the most suitable for the type of recording that is going to take place. Some types sound very good when used in a studio, especially where they can be rigged in shot on the clothing. Whilst they sound fine in the studio, they can be so prone to disturbance from wind noise and clothes rustling that they are quite unsuitable for exterior use, due to the difficulty in rigging. The microphone needs to be placed at about 200 mm from the mouth, either mid-chest or in the hairline above the forehead. This latter position is useful for interior drama and stage shows, but will probably be unsuitable on an exterior location as protection from wind noise is virtually impossible. The microphones can be purchased skin-coloured, to help disguise them, but a head of hair is required if the capsule is to be fully covered!

On the chest the omni-direction types can be rigged pointing up or down. Downward pointing may be required if the speaker is likely to look down and may breathe across the capsule.

All manufacturers produce a range of clips to attach personal microphones. The clips are designed to fix to lapels or ties or to tape to the wearer. They are fine when the unit is in shot but the use of adhesive tape is often a better way to secure the microphone, when hidden under clothing, as this should ensure that it cannot move and rub against the fabric. If microphones are to be fixed directly to the skin, non-allergenic plaster or sterilized strips should be used.

Wind noise

The manufacturers of personal microphones all produce windshields to help reduce the disturbance of air movement across the capsule. The mechanical construction will have an effect, the side-facing capsules being less prone to problems than those facing upwards. The types of windshield vary, with miniature metal ones being quite effective, and the foam ones varying considerably. The harder foams may cause fabric rustling, the best of all being made with very soft foam of about 20 mm diameter. Careful rigging under clothing will probably be the most effective way of reducing wind noise.

Fabrics

Rigging lapel microphones requires great care if rustling sounds are to be avoided. Certain man-made fibres can cause considerable noise and static electricity. Some fabrics are so dense in their construction that they do not satisfactorily allow the sound through. The use of windshields or small cages will lift the fabric away from the microphone, which will reduce unwanted noise. The shape of the person may help in hiding the personal microphone, for example the female shape helps hide the microphone, as it can be supported on the brassiere where the fabric of the outer clothing will be held away from the microphone.

Other problems

Be cautious of necklaces or brooches, which can make jangling noises and sound terrible if they actually hit the microphone. Jewellery might be better removed, or in drama shoots where the jewellery is part of the character, it might be best to use a stitch to prevent it from moving around and thus from hitting the microphone.

4 Music

Whilst the recording of music is beyond the scope of this book, it is important to realize some basic facts about handling music recordings. Firstly the overall dynamic range may be quite large. Microphones that can handle these large ranges must be employed. When initially adjusting input levels, ensure that this is done for the maximum level for each mike. The balance of each channel will then be achieved with the fader in its optimum position, reducing the possibility of overloading the input stage of the mixer in use.

In good acoustics it may be possible to group several instruments onto one microphone. Cardioid, condenser microphones, for their wide frequency response, will normally give good results. If stereo is required this could be a coincident stereo pair. To find a suitable microphone position, stand in front of the group of musicians or soloist and find a point where everything can be heard. Slinging the microphone over that point or mounting on a stand, if it does not compromise the shots too much, should produce a usable result. Small choirs and other vocal groups can certainly be single-mike balanced even where there is some room echo as this can enhance the voices naturally.

On a location shoot, drawing curtains may help reduce the unwanted sound reflections (even if it means a bit more lighting) – no-one will be pleased with a muddled 'echoey' sound. Don't be fooled by the brain's ability to become used to the echo of the room – do listen carefully on headphones or on the control room monitors, and adjust the position until the balance is good.

If there are vocals as well as instruments, or the instruments are at very different levels, they will be best miked individually.

Single instruments are reasonably easy – moving around during a performance should find a position where a microphone can be placed to give good sound without being too obtrusive. Sometimes lapel microphones can be fitted to the instrument with specialized clips or carefully taped for acceptable results and clear camera shots. Always discuss this with the musician and beware of damage to valuable instruments.

In general, rifle patterns are not the best solution as they have a too narrow acceptance for all but spot recordings. Remember to remove windshields, as they may reduce the high frequencies, and switch out bass cuts for a full range recording.

5 Radio microphones

Any microphone can be connected to a radio transmitter so that no cable is required to connect it to the mixer or camera on a location shoot. The most common application of this is where a lapel microphone is connected to the transmitter, allowing the artist free movement anywhere within the range of the receiver. The range should be at least fifty metres and more is possible with special techniques. Provided that the system is used with care there will be no difference in quality from that of a cabled microphone.

There are a number of systems in use, with different legislation applying in different countries regarding the power and frequencies that can be used. In most countries, VHF (138–250 MHz) systems are licensed for broadcasters to use on locations within their normal operating region and UHF

(574–960 MHz) systems are more commonly used for fixed studio applications. In order to give good signal-to-noise and an acceptable bandwidth, most wireless systems are fitted with **companders**. This means that the signal is compressed prior to transmission and expanded in the receiver. Where these companders are switchable, both transmitter and receiver must be similarly enabled or the audio will be unacceptable.

To increase the range and reliability of the systems they can have **diversity receivers**. This means that for each transmitter there will be two receivers and a switching device, built into one case. They will need two receiving aerials and the result is very reliable as the better of the two received signals is chosen automatically.

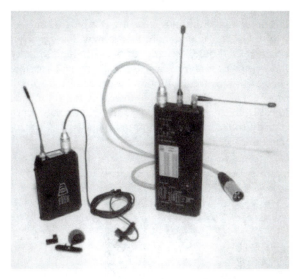

Figure 5.54 A diversity radio system (courtesy Audio Limited).

Operating a radio microphone

The transmitter is first adjusted for input level. The purpose is to match the output of the microphone, and the voice level of the artiste, to the input stage of the transmitter. This prevents any input overload and unnecessary limiting of the signal. The level is usually checked with a simple LED on the transmitter, which flashes to indicate the onset of limiting. The ideal method is to set a gain that just begins to operate the limiter and then turn the gain down a very small amount so limiting will only occur on unexpected peaks.

Where a lapel microphone is to be used it should be rigged with the precautions outlined above. The transmitter should be placed in a pocket, or if required in a purpose-made pouch on a belt, away

from any metal objects, keys, coins, etc. The aerial should be a straight line, hanging down or taped vertically upwards. This is especially important if the person is going to sit down, as bending the aerial or pressing it against a metal chair frame may reduce its range or cause interference.

The receiver is connected to the input of the sound mixer or camera and may be either high level or microphone level, depending upon the system design. This input needs to be adjusted for correct modulation. A level can be achieved accurately if the radio system has a tone oscillator. The level will need to be carried out with voice if there is no oscillator.

The receiving aerial (aerials for diversity systems) should also be upright. Most commonly helical coil aerials are used here, with more complex high gain and directional aerial types available if it is required to increase the range or help the system reduce unwanted interference.

Batteries

It is best to use good quality alkaline batteries in radio systems for reliability. Beware of very cheap batteries that depend on pressure from their plastic cases for the electrical connections within. These can fail if the plastic softens when in a warm pocket. Nickel cadmium rechargeable cells can be used but die with very little notice, which can be embarrassing half-way through an important interview. If wireless systems are regularly used it is an advantage to power the receivers from the mixer as this will mean only one set of batteries to monitor and will reduce the number of stops for battery changes. If weight is not a problem then the use of NP1-type camera batteries will keep the whole operation going all day without any changes at all.

Radio microphone problems

A number of external forces may affect radio transmissions. Steel framed buildings, solid walls or rock faces may all cause reflected signals and interference can be produced by many types of electrical machinery, car ignition systems and other transmitting equipment.

It is a good idea to switch on the receiver first and monitor its output for a while to see if it picks anything up. The muting or squelch circuit is set so that no output is heard unless there is a reasonable level of radio frequency signal being received. This should mean that with the transmitter switched off, there will be no output; sounds heard in this state may indicate that there are problems. The solution is to find the source of interference or try an alternative frequency.

Before recording it is good practice to get someone to wear the transmitter and walk around the location to try to find any source of interference. Check aerials carefully and if necessary move the receiver nearer to the transmitter to help overcome the problems. Time spent checking the systems, before the artistes arrive, will result in the actual recording being less pressured and give a better end result. Everyone is more relaxed if technical problems can be avoided.

5.5.6 Microphones, summary

- Plan the work and choose the microphone that will not only produce a suitable frequency characteristic but can handle the loudest sound it is likely to encounter.
- The polar pattern should be chosen to help isolate the required sounds and also help to match the sound perspective with the shot.
- Be consistent throughout – try not to produce changes in voice quality.
- In a poor acoustic, close microphone techniques are the solution – extra wild-tracks may be needed for audio post-production.
- When away from a studio, background sounds, air-conditioners, refrigerators, telephones and other interference may need to be switched off. These can not only be a distraction but if they are inconsistent will make the edit very difficult.
- Record an effects track for each shot – this will help to cover variable backgrounds and make the edit much easier.
- Highly directional microphones are not always good for operating very close. They may still pick up a lot of background and will give bass lift if too close. The directional characteristics work for voices and higher frequencies. It is not possible to make a microphone directional at very low frequencies. That means that aircraft, generators and large vehicles (particularly exhaust noises) may be picked up wherever the microphone is pointing.

Remember!

Microphones are not clever like the brain and cannot reject the echoes and backgrounds that should not be featured. Careful recording techniques are required to produce a sound quality that matches the picture.

The visual image is most important in television. The appearance of the microphones must be carefully considered in order that they are not unnecessarily conspicuous. A microphone in shot on a news programme may be acceptable but in discussion or light entertainment it should be as inconspicuous as possible whilst still providing good sound quality.

The use of microphones with long thin stems or lapel types will help with this. In drama the microphones will need to be hidden completely.

5.6 Studio sound

Studio Sound Control is the room where sound operators provide appropriate sound to complement the television pictures. Sound can be a very complex area, allowing for a large range of programme types, or designed to produce one specific programme type, where the control room contains less equipment. As well as mixing the various sound sources, Sound Control may be responsible for the studio talkback. This is the communication system that allows all areas involved in the production, in their different locations, to communicate during the programme.

A television sound control room will be centred around the sound mixing desk with high quality loudspeaker monitoring, used to make accurate checks of both the quality and balance of the sound. Traditionally all of the equipment in the room, the lines from the studio floor and many lines from outside the studio are connected via a bay of equipment and connection points.

Figure 5.55 Studio jack-fields can get very complex when all the connections are made.

These connectors are commonly ¼″ jack plugs or a miniature version called bantam jacks. This panel is known as the **jack field**. An alternative to the jack field is to connect all of the equipment lines to a switching device, known as a **matrix** or **routing switcher**.

Figure 5.56 Assignment switchers make the connections electronically.

This complex device allows any chosen connections to be made, and controlled with a computer terminal or a dedicated control panel. Put simply, either system allows the operators to make all the necessary connections, for example connecting the newsreader's microphone to an appropriate channel on the mixing console.

5.6.1 Mixing console

The main function of the mixing console is to control the levels of each individual sound source, producing one composite mix. The sound may come from microphones on the studio floor, tape recorders, compact disc players or computer-controlled sources within the control room. It may also come from outside the studio area: video tape machines, other studios, outside broadcasts, satellite feeds or telephone lines, both analogue and digital.

The console contains a number of inputs, often in multiples of twelve, so a news studio might have a twenty-four channel desk. On an analogue desk each of the channel inputs will have similar controls.

Input select and gain
Line level is selected for tape machines or incoming lines, or the microphone input is chosen and the gain adjusted as required for the type of microphone in use. The channels may be mono or stereo, where both the left and right signals will be adjusted by each of the channel controls.

Auxiliaries
Auxiliary outputs allow the operator to produce separate mixes of the input channels. There may be as many as six or more auxiliary outputs.

Auxiliaries can be used to provide **foldback**. Foldback is sound fed to a loudspeaker in order that the programme participants on the studio floor can hear remote studios or pre-recorded items to be added to the mix.

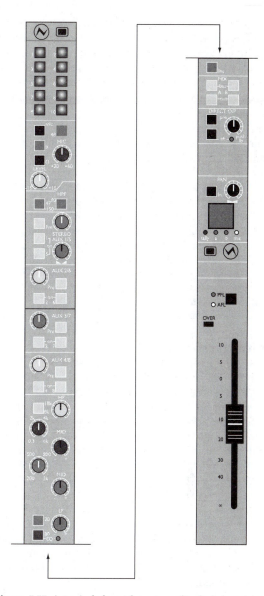

Figure 5.57 A typical channel on an audio desk (courtesy of AMS Neve plc).

The auxiliaries can also be used to provide outputs to other studios or simply to feed the input of audio recorders or echo processors.

Equalization
Adjustments to the frequency response can be made here. There are commonly three bands of adjustment: one for the high frequencies, a second selectable frequency in the middle range and the third for low frequencies. There may also be switched filters operating between 75 and 150 Hz to remove any

unwanted low frequency rumble. These frequencies are chosen as they can reduce the problem whilst having very little effect on male (down to 75 Hz) and female (down to 150 Hz) voice sounds.

Channel fader

This is the main control for each source of sound connected to the console. The fader is a sliding control and will be made of high mechanical quality. This ensures that all the faders feel the same, that is they give an even resistance to movement, and that they will last for many thousands of operations.

The fader is calibrated so the operator can see how much extra gain or attenuation is being applied. Like the location mixers this fader will normally operate 10 dB below its maximum position. This will allow for some adjustment to the channel level whilst ensuring that the signal is being processed at the correct level within the sound console.

Stereo channels

Each input to the desk can be mono or stereo. A mono channel will be fitted with a pan control to allow the signal to be routed to the required image position. A stereo channel routes the signal through two parallel paths with each control on the channel strip adjusting both left and right identically. The output, already split into left and right, will have a balance control to adjust the relative levels of the left and right signals.

Routing

The routing switching allows each, level-controlled, channel to be connected to the output section of the desk. This may be directly to the main output fader or more commonly through another fader known as the group fader.

Group faders

This facility allows a number of microphones or other sources to be controlled or processed together. One example might be a small musical band in the studio that requires six microphones. These could be routed to one group allowing all six channels to be faded up with a single control. Grouping of channels is also useful to process a number of sources together so that they can be routed to a single compressor.

Master fader

The master fader controls the total output of the console. It will normally be left in a calibrated

position. This may be at maximum or at a calibrated 'zero' position, 10 dB below the maximum, like the group and channel faders. This will depend on the design of the console. It can be used to take the level of the whole mix down, for example at the end of a programme.

Monitoring

The monitoring section of the desk is a switching unit that allows the operator to meter and monitor, via the loudspeakers. The sound monitored will normally be the final mix, but the switcher also enables this at various points throughout the console. External connections can be made to this section to enable items not patched to the desk to be monitored. An example of this is on a desk used to mix live programmes will be an external feed of 'Off Air'. This allows the operator to hear the sound as it is transmitted, including the programmes or announcements either side of the studio-originated material.

Metering

In order to ensure that the operator keeps sound levels within the correct engineering parameters, and to assist with the artistic mix, sound desks are fitted with meters. These may be simply connected to the output, but more commonly also are fitted to show the group levels. Meters may be fitted to a monitor switcher allowing the operator to choose which part of the desk is to be metered, as well as that being monitored.

On a music console, auxiliary outputs and even the individual inputs may be fitted with separate small meters.

Metering methods are further explained in Section 5.3.

Other controls

Most consoles will allow the operator to listen to the individual channels without sending the source to the final mix. This is achieved by pulling the fader backwards 'fader over-press', or with a button on the channel called Pre-Fade Listen (PFL). As its name suggests, this allows the sound to be sent to an extra loudspeaker (on some mixers the main loudspeakers) before fading the channel up. If the operator wishes to listen to one channel alone during a mix, this can be done using the control marked After-Fade Listen (AFL or Solo). When pressed, the main loudspeakers will have the output of the chosen channel only. The total mix is not affected even though the operator can no longer hear it.

Clean feeds

Clean feeds are required for telephone links or where one studio is connected to another studio to achieve two-way conversations. All broadcast sound desks need a method of deriving one or more clean feed outputs.

For example, two studios are to be interconnected for an interview. The output from studio one must not send any of the studio two sound mixed into the sound feed returned to studio two. If there are ten channels on the desk in studio one, studio two will need to hear nine of them (the tenth being the studio two sound).

The feed can be derived by producing a separate mix on the auxiliary outputs but is much more quickly done with a purpose-designed clean feed output. This may be derived from the desk group outputs, or it may be provided for each desk channel. In this latter case the clean feed from channel four will be a mix of all of the other channels on the desk, excluding channel four.

The set-up may become more complex where there are many remote studios, requiring a number of clean feeds, set up so that each can hear all of the other studios.

5.6.2 Other types of sound desk

Whilst all of the features above have to be carried out whatever type of sound console is installed in the sound control room, many are fitted with more sophisticated equipment that achieves the same results.

Assignable consoles

Analogue assignable desks are not common as they have been largely replaced by digital technology, but they do still exist in some studios. They use the principle that all audio circuits can be controlled by voltage-controlled amplifiers (VCAs). These allow the audio routing, switching, level control and other processing to remain within a bay of equipment. This bay does not need to be in the sound control area itself. This allows for much simplified installations and smaller control rooms, keeping the cable lengths to a minimum and helping with interference problems. The sound desk, with the exception of its monitoring facilities, is simply controlling the VCA voltages. When a fader is moved or any other surface adjustment is carried out, the voltage information is passed to the bay and makes the appropriate change in the circuits here. This can considerably simplify the overall control surface by centralizing the controls. There will still be a fader on each channel, but many

other parts of the desk will appear quite different, as controls like the equalization and dynamics will be assigned as required. This will usually mean that there will only be one or two sets of controls for these facilities with a button on each channel to enable the facility required. This further means that settings can quickly be copied from one channel to another. This type of desk is quick to use once the operator is familiar with the concept of centralized control operating on the chosen channels or groups.

For even greater speed and flexibility the consoles can be interfaced with a computer. This control will perform the routing and allow regular records to be made to memory 'snapshots' as to the status of each part of the console. Because this type of console includes assignment switching, rather than jack-field routing, all the plugging is made on the studio floor. This is very valuable where a studio is reset to produce another series of the same programmes at a later date. Provided the microphones are connected to the same inputs on the studio floor, the whole sound desk can be reconfigured from a floppy disk that has the settings memorized from previous sessions.

Digital consoles

In a digital console all of the analogue inputs are converted to digital, and digital devices can be connected directly, reducing the chance of noise and other problems associated with the conventional routing and handling of audio signals. The layout of these consoles takes the assignable operation much further, with the desk routing and status shown on liquid crystal displays (LCDs) or computer screens. These software-driven devices allow considerable flexibility and the simpler versions are little more expensive than good quality analogue desks.

Figure 5.58 Digital sound console (courtesy of AMS Neve plc).

Care is needed to ensure that the console is designed in a way that allows an operation that is relevant to the programmes that will be encountered. The computer displays often mean that the operator has to scroll through a number of pages to access the particular channel and facility that is required. An example of this might be on a live programme where access to equalization, especially on an unrehearsed item, is required very quickly. On a conventional analogue desk this is achieved by reaching out and adjusting the parameter immediately. Some of the lower cost digital consoles require the operator to access the correct page and then assign the facility to the channel before the adjustment can be made – a time-consuming operation that might be too slow for, say, a news programme. On other programmes, where the material is well rehearsed, the ability to recall complex settings is a considerable advantage.

5.6.3 Other equipment

Equalization

The equalization provided on a sound desk is not always suitable for specialist applications. There are two types of unit that can be added to the facilities. The **parametric equalizer** is an extended version of that fitted to most mixing desks. It has three or four bands of frequency adjustments with the mid-bands having not only selection of frequency and gain but also a bandwidth control allowing a narrow or wide range, around the chosen frequency, to be adjusted.

The alternative type is the **graphic equalizer**. With these units the whole frequency spectrum is divided into separate bands, each with its own control. These are usually vertically sliding controls, hence the name, as the controls produce a graphical form of the frequencies adjusted. The controls on the professional versions of these units are spaced at musical octaves, each centre frequency being double the one below it, so a smooth control of the whole range can be achieved. The controls may have a fixed bandwidth or this may increase with the increase of cut or boost.

Compression

In Section 5.1.4 it was shown that the dynamic range of sounds that occur naturally is far greater than is desirable for transmission. It is important that levels do not exceed certain values in order to prevent the signals from being damaged. Control of levels can be achieved manually with the fader, but when changes occur too quickly for this then dynamic controllers or **compressors** are used. These may be built into the desk or may be separate pieces of equipment, patched as required via the jack field.

The difficult part of this job is not simply to keep the levels under control but to maintain the illusion of reality.

The basic concept of the compressor is that it monitors audio level and automatically adjusts the level to maintain a reasonable range. The device has a number of parameters it controls. These are: 'Threshold', the level at which it starts to act; 'Slope' or 'Ratio', the amount of adjustment; 'Attack' and 'Release', the speed at which the equipment will react to the changes. These can all be adjusted by the operator, depending on the signal concerned.

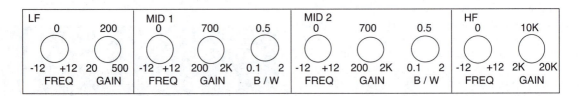

Figure 5.59 Parametric equalizer controls.

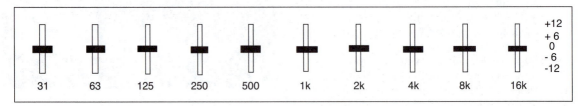

Figure 5.60 Graphic equalizer controls.

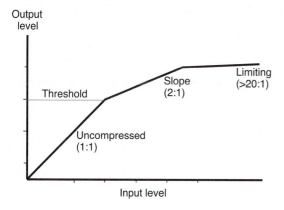

Figure 5.61 Compression and limiting.

As well as complex compression, simple limiting devices are fitted to many pieces of equipment to ensure that signals do not become distorted or damaged because their level is too great. **Limiters** are just that – they simply prevent the signal from exceeding a predetermined level. Limiters need to be used with care and should be considered a safety device operated only occasionally by large signal peaks. If the limiter acts too much, the sound will be dramatically compressed and backgrounds will appear to pump up and down in level.

Echo

Echo and reverberation controls can include everything from special effects to adjustments of parameters for the simulation of room acoustics. The older versions of these pieces of equipment were analogue devices. A number of techniques have been employed; for example long corridors with a speaker and microphone where the distance between them is adjusted to change the effect, or echo plates and springs where a transducer connects the audio signal to the device and the sound is delayed as it travels along it. Digital techniques have meant that complex delays and associated equalization can produce virtually any required effect.

Delay

Simple delay is required not only as part of a special effect, but also to maintain the correct relationship between sound and pictures. One of the common uses of audio delay in television is where the picture has been delayed by frame stores. These devices, designed to overcome the problems of non-synchronous pictures, may delay the picture by several frames causing a visible loss of audio sync. One solution is to delay the sound to match the picture.

Figure 5.62 Compressor controls (courtesy of AMS Neve plc).

Figure 5.63 A typical echo unit that displays the parameters graphically.

Telephone hybrid

In order to connect a separate send and receive circuit to a two-wire telephone system some device is needed to balance the send and receive levels. The telephone hybrid performs this task, compensating for the line resistance and reactance. The connection to the two-wire line is isolated with an internal transformer. There is an output to feed to a channel on the mixing desk and an input, fed from a desk output (which must not include the telephone output). Most units will enable the line to be established in a bypass mode and switch to the desk for transmission. Some may even include the dial pad and handset.

Note that all national telecom companies require approved devices of this type to be used when connecting broadcast audio to their circuits.

Integrated Services Digital Network (ISDN)

Up until the early 1990s there were two ways to link audio to the studio. The conventional telephone line, using a telephone hybrid, was cheap, but with its limited bandwidth really sounded like a telephone call. The alternative was a pre-booked wide-band circuit which was limited to those who could afford to install the required permanent lines to the local exchange. Many places in the world could not provide this and most viewers have experienced long-distance pictures of broadcast quality that were accompanied by sound quality associated with the 1930s. Digital sound technology changed all this with the Integrated Services Digital Network (ISDN). ISDN lines are marketed widely around the world providing not just audio but digital connections that can be used for a range of digitally encoded material. There are two versions of these lines: Basic Rate, connected on a pair of copper wires; and Primary Rate that requires a coaxial cable, fibre optic or microwave link. Various coding methods are used and the connection is made to the Basic Rate lines using a **codec** designed to work with the system. These codecs provide not only wide bandwidth audio but also other outputs for talkback and information circuits like the Internet. The Primary Rate systems are designed for studios where an ISDN exchange can provide access for up to 30 Basic Rate codecs. Britain and most of the world are using compatible systems – the only exceptions are parts of America, Australia and Japan where Euro-ISDN would have to be specified for the systems to be compatible.

Grams

Traditionally all studio control areas were fitted with record playing equipment but with the ease of access

to music using compact discs these are normally only available in transfer areas. This historic use of vinyl records has meant that many directors still use the term 'grams' as a generic term to mean any source of music.

¼" tape

Conventional analogue tape machines are used to provide recording facilities in many studios. They can be particularly useful for cued tracks as leadered cues are very clearly visible and many find this reason alone valuable as miscuing is less likely. Many operators are very skilled at using this medium for editing both speech and music. Tape machines can be supplied with centre track time code, making them suitable for locking to picture machines to produce extra audio tracks for stereo or dubbing operations.

Digital tape

Digital tape is used in many forms. Up to 48 tracks can be provided on reel-to-reel machines, but these machines are expensive to purchase.

Rotary DAT machines have become very popular as they are flexible, can be provided with time code, are also manufactured as portable machines for location work and have the great advantage of using very compact tapes so that libraries of material from this format require very little space. This is a popular format for master tapes in the music industry.

MiniDisc (MD)

MiniDisc is now a very popular format for both music and effects. The machines can have comprehensive editing facilities and so are used to create loops and edit cues.

Figure 5.64 A studio MiniDisc player.

The machines are available as portable recorders with professional facilities. Digital devices like this can be fitted with input buffers that are effectively permanently recording. When the record button is pressed the input is recorded to disc via this buffer and so the material starts to record a few seconds before the operator presses the start button.

Audio cartridge machines

Cartridge machines have been very popular over many years as they can provide endless loops of sound effects for dubbing purposes. They also have tertiary cue tracks which can be used to mark the start of a cue, force the machine into rewind, or start another machine. This facility has made them popular for spot cues and music jingles. They are mechanically rather unsound as they depend upon the use of graphite lubricated tape to allow the tape to slip over itself. They are very prone to mechanical failure and the speed can vary, causing unpleasant wow to the sound.

Computer-based systems

Many manufacturers have recognized the popularity of the cartridge format and so have developed machines that operate in a similar way but are based on digital formats. These machines can be based on any recording format. One popular version uses standard floppy disks as the record medium. They allow the operator to programme the way in which the material shall be formatted in order to best use the storage. If stereo and full bandwidth is required, the storage time will be reduced. If limited bandwidth and mono is suitable for the purpose the recording time will be increased. The equipment allows for editing and the marking of cue points; also loops can be produced, making the system ideal for radio stings or sound effects alike.

Software-based systems are further used to produce workstations that perform a variety of audio tasks. These may be straightforward juke-box devices, particularly suited to radio stations, or can be very versatile, and equally complex, workstations that operate like a multitrack recorder with full editing facilities. These hard-disk-based devices form the basis of the dubbing systems that are further discussed in Chapter 12.

Compact disc

The compact disc is a very inexpensive medium and has made access to music very simple with the cueing of tracks being accessed quickly and cued very

accurately. Recordable Compact discs (CDR) have further helped and these can be useful for making effects discs or recording music tracks that need to be carried from one studio to another. Domestic compact discs use 44.1 kHz sampling so if the music is to be transferred to professional digital systems the material will have to be converted to 48 kHz in order to be processed with other signals.

Balance transformer

The principle of connecting unbalanced equipment to balanced equipment was described in Section 5.3.3. The equipment required is a Direct Injection (DI) box, which may be active (contains electronics and will require powering) or passive (contains purely transformers). The input is usually connected by a ¼" jack plug and the balanced output on an XLR socket. Some of these boxes may have a range of inputs for varying levels: instruments, line level or speaker level. They may have loop output sockets so they can be inserted between a musical instrument and its amplifier, providing a separate output for the balanced connection.

Microphone splitters

Microphone splitters are used when one microphone will be used to feed two audio inputs. This operation is often required when a separate mix is carried out on the studio floor for musicians' foldback. These boxes may be single channels, or multichannel versions can be used where many splits are required. The splitter allows one sound desk to provide the microphone powering and gives a separate feed for the second desk. Any possibility of hum caused by earth loops can be removed as each channel is provided with a switch to disconnect the earth connection to the second desk.

5.6.4 The studio floor

The television studio is a carefully designed area that provides the facilities for many different technical operations. From a sound point of view the isolation from outside audible interference is important. Sound absorption is equally important to prevent unwanted reverberations or standing waves.

Isolation is provided by great care in the construction of the studio. It is necessary to effectively disconnect the walls and floors from other parts of the building structure. Pipes, conduits and air ducting all require special flexible breaks or silencers to prevent sounds being carried in from other areas.

Sound absorption is a very specialist subject. The principal idea is to use special sound absorbers to reduce the reflected sounds evenly across the whole frequency spectrum. This does not mean the area will be totally dead, which would make the area very unpleasant and unreal, but it will have a short reverberation time. Standing waves are a problem and can be created by having reflective surfaces spaced at exactly the wavelength of a particular frequency. This will enhance this frequency, making it boom. The effect is the same as creating sound inside an organ pipe, so ventilation ducts as well as parallel walls or sets can create these.

Wall boxes

Studio wall boxes are provided at convenient locations around the studio to connect the technical equipment to the control rooms. Microphones, foldback speakers, musical instruments, talkback, video and mains supplies will all be present on these boxes. The microphone lines will be specific to a wall box. For example, thirty microphone lines might be fitted, ten to a box on three wall boxes. Talkback and foldback lines will be duplicated to all the boxes. These lines are carried through to the studio jack field, or assignment switcher, and they can there be cross-connected as required.

Figure 5.65 Studio wall box.

The connections between the wall boxes and the control room jack field are very carefully designed and installed taking into consideration the different signals each cable will be required to carry. The cables are grouped into the different signal types and levels to reduce any opportunity for cross-talk and so it is important to use the outlets the way in which they were designed. Microphone lines are the most vulnerable to cross-talk, as they carry signals at very low level, possibly 70 dB or more below the level of other

signals such as feeds to speakers or talkback. These cables will be specially designed to reduce unwanted pick-up and may be routed down individually screened trunking.

Floor cabling

Cabling must be done with care. The planning stages of the programme should mean that cable runs for complex shows are clearly shown on the floor plan.

The correct cable type should be made for each system in use. Microphone cables are particularly designed for low signal levels, with star-quad cables (see Section 5.3.3) available to further reduce the possibility of interference. Good quality cables are designed to have appropriate mechanical characteristics and the colour may be important if the cables are in vision.

In the studio, cables need to be constructed for ease of handling and coiling, and must have a strong outer covering to resist damage. When rigging, it is usual to start at the microphone end and run the cable out, keeping the excess in one place, out of the way of action on the studio floor, near the wall box. Some wall boxes provide a tie rail where the cables can be fastened so the ends do not become damaged if accidentally pulled. Where many microphones are needed in one area the use of a multicore cable to a floor 'Break-Out' or 'Stage Box' considerably reduces the spaghetti on the studio floor.

Figure 5.66 Studio floor multi-box.

Most studios have their own in-house way of coiling cables for storage. The most common is, starting at the wall box end, to coil the cable twisting each loop in alternately opposite directions. This is effectively producing a figure of eight lay within a single coil and thus reducing any possibility of tangles when the cables are run out.

Cable runs need to be made with care, as some equipment in the studio causes interference and microphone cable runs must avoid these. The most common are lighting cables that are connected to dimmer circuits, requiring lighting and sound cables to be kept separate.

Long-term sets

Sets that are to be used over a long period of time may need permanent boxes attached to provide the audio facilities. One example of this will be the presenter positions on a news set. Boxes fitted under or beside the desk could contain connections for the lapel microphone and spare, talkback and level control and outlets for telephones or computer terminals. Video and power feeds for monitors can also be included in separate boxes.

Figure 5.67 Presenter microphone and earpiece connects to permanent outlets under the desk.

Foldback

Studio foldback is provided for the artistes on the studio floor to hear the sounds that are not originating in the studio. This will include music tracks, sound effects, pre-recorded material and feeds from other studios. The speakers should be rigged pointing towards and reasonably near to those who need to hear them. They should also be placed 'off axis' to the microphones on the floor in order to reduce coloration as the sound from the speaker is picked up by the microphones.

Musicians' foldback

Where foldback of a band, particularly one with amplified instruments, is very involved with many musicians and the requirement of individual mixes, it is far simpler to carry out a separate balance of the foldback and PA mixes on the studio floor. A second desk is needed for this and the microphones are split to feed the two desks. This split should be carried out with proper transformer splitters, which prevent one desk affecting the other and ensure that any microphone powering is provided from only one desk. Good communication between the floor balancer and the programme balancer should ensure that nothing is done in the floor mixes that would affect the transmitted end result. Very high levels in floor loudspeakers may help the studio atmosphere but will cause significant coloration of the sound – this needs to be carefully considered.

The floor balancer is in a much better position to achieve the required sound on the floor and will have a good relationship with the artistes in achieving their requirements for the performance. It is especially valuable in television to use 'in-ear monitoring' rather than floor speakers for the musicians. This system puts the sound into the performers' ears using full frequency radio transmitters and body-worn receivers with specialist earpieces. It has many advantages, providing high quality of sound where it is needed without the risk of feedback, and no unsightly speakers in shot – especially popular with camera operators and producers in small television studios. These units are very expensive, and in a small studio that does not produce music programmes very regularly they may need to be hired on a per occasion basis.

Public address (PA)

PA is provided for audiences to hear all of the content of a programme. This may contain a mix of the material on the foldback speakers, but will be primarily the output of some of the microphones on the studio floor. These speakers will be helping the audience to hear the performance action that is taking place. Care is needed to ensure that coloration of the studio microphones is kept to a minimum. In extreme cases 'feedback' or 'howl' may occur as the microphone picks up its own sound, relayed onto the loudspeakers.

There are differing considerations as to how PA speakers are set up. For a discussion programme it is likely that the speakers will be at quite low level, providing some reinforcement of the live studio sound. In music or light entertainment it may be desirable to have the speakers running at a much greater level to create the studio atmosphere. This will considerably alter the way the artistes perform and also the way the sound is perceived by the audience. Be aware that if a stick microphone, fed to the audience PA, is used to interview a nervous guest, hearing themselves on the PA may make them even more nervous. The mix and quality of this sound can have an effect on the performance of its participants.

5.6.5 Studio layout

The layout of the studio will depend on the type of programme to be made. This will normally be planned by the design department who will take into account all the necessary requirements including the set itself and the camera positions to achieve the desired shots. Areas for audiences need to be laid out with care, such that equipment on the floor cannot endanger the safety of the audience. From a sound point of view the most important layout will be the placement and cabling of microphones, allowing for camera moves and the safety of all. Cables need to be laid out with regard to interference as described above. Speakers for the audience need to be planned as they must be safe and not cause problems on shot or shadows from the lighting.

5.6.6 Safety

Some of these problems have already been discussed. All access and fire escape routes must be clear of cables and other equipment. Microphone stands and other equipment on stands must be safe with cables tied off at the base to reduce the chance of them being pulled over. Cables should be made fast to wall box tie rails and routing of cables achieved as tidily as possible. Tidy rigging will have the further advantage of making fault finding easier.

Equipment, especially microphone booms, must be rigged at a safe height, to clear people's heads. Boom operators must be competent and aware of the dangers of the boom, both to themselves and other technicians and in particular to guests who may be unfamiliar with a television studio. The arm should be locked off as appropriate and care taken when mounting and dismounting. The operation of the boom was discussed in Section 5.5.3.

One particular area regarding safety is the rigging of equipment above the studio in the lighting grid. All studios have rules about working above the studio floor – these must be read and observed at all times. Persons walking in the grid should ensure that nothing they are carrying can be dropped – especially cable ends, as one end of a cable can drop and swing causing great damage to anything or anyone it hits. No members of the public should be present when anyone is working on the grid. It is usual to have a safety person below to ensure that those on the floor are aware of what is going on above. Some sound

equipment that is required to be slung is quite heavy – all such equipment must have safety wires to arrest its fall should the main fixing fail.

Electrical safety

There are a whole range of regulations regarding all electrical equipment and any new systems must be approved by the appropriate electrical department before use. Non-standard equipment on the studio floor may need to be connected through an isolation transformer to reduce the danger of faults causing injuries. Remember that television studios use all three phases of the electrical supply. This means that although pieces of equipment are individually using only 240 volts there will be a difference of over 400 volts between them.

5.6.7 Talkback

The talkback system allows all the participants of the programme to communicate – particularly important where remote studios are involved. The director of the programme needs to be heard by the floor manager, camera operators, the sound and vision engineers, etc. The output of a microphone in front of the director is fed to each area; this provides the talkback communication. These operators will be fed all the time – this is known as **open talkback**. Remote studios and operators of video tape recorders in centralized areas may also need to hear the director, but their feeds are only provided when the director chooses. This is called **switched talkback**. In order that an operator on talkback can speak to the director, **reverse talkback** is fed to a loudspeaker in the production area. These sources will be keyed from microphones in each relevant area.

Feeds may be provided to the presenters via earpieces, in order that they, too, can be given information during a programme. These can be 'switched' or 'open' – the choice will usually be made by the presenter, as working with open talkback whilst simultaneously talking on live television takes a particular ability. Talkback to certain people will be provided using radio systems. Floor managers need to be able to move freely without the restriction of cables and presenters on the move may also need radio talkback feeds.

5.6.8 Sound balancing

Exactly how the sound balance is performed depends on the type of programme being produced and the personal methods of the individual sound balancers, who all have slightly different ways of achieving the same result. It is important to realize exactly what sort of mixing process the programme requires as this will dictate the type of information the balancer needs to achieve the required results.

The balancing process requires the operator to perform a number of tasks:

- line-up and input level adjustments;
- equalization;
- foldback and PA;
- fades from one source to another;
- mixes between different types of material;
- musical mixes;
- compression.

This list may not cover all aspects but is a starting point towards an understanding of the role.

Line-up

The line-up is not just a technical operation to ensure that each piece of equipment is correctly connected together but actually requires careful setting of every source of sound that will be encountered in any given programme. It is important that the faders on the sound console are operated in a correct position (they usually have a calibrated 0 dB mark). This helps artistically as it gives the operator a guide as to where to put the fader to start with. More importantly, it ensures that the signal within the console is routed at the correct level. Failure to get this correct will result in the possibility of distorted signals. This means that taking proper voice levels is an important part of getting the correct sound. During this process, input gains will need adjustment and equalization changes are made to ensure that the contributor sounds natural.

Equalization

Equalization has already been mentioned as part of the line-up process. The controls, which can be quite complex, allow frequency adjustments to be made to each sound source, the object being to obtain a clear natural sound. This is achieved by increasing or decreasing each chosen frequency band and so errors from the microphones or their placement – or in some cases the voice quality itself – can be minimized.

Foldback and PA

In its simplest form the balance required on the foldback is an equal amount of each source needed.

For example, in a news or documentary show all that is needed is that the studio floor can hear the pre-recorded material. On a music show it is much more complex, requiring an accurate balance for the musicians to hear themselves clearly. In many situations there may be different balances required for each musician. Where this is very complex, the mix is better achieved by a different operator on the studio floor. (See the discussion on 'Foldback and PA' in Section 5.6.4.)

The actual balance is achieved using the auxiliary outputs. This is a section of the desk which has several extra faders on each channel, allowing many different mixes to be carried out.

Fades and mixes

Fades take many different forms. They may be long, carefully carried out dissolves from one source to another, or in news-type programmes they may be more like a fast switching operation. Fades are usually not linear, but require quite complex thought that depends upon the pace of the material being mixed. Here the hand on the fader acts with the hearing to produce a feedback loop that uses the skill and artistic ability of the balancer to create the mood change required for this sequence.

It is important to think what information the balancer requires in order to decide how and when to perform these crossfades. There are many factors being simultaneously considered at the point of a fade. In the studio, the production assistant will be counting out to the end of the current segment. The balancer will know the scripted out-words or the end phrasing of the music on the segment, and both pieces of information will be used to decide exactly when to perform the fade. The next consideration is the incoming sound. Is it words, music or effects? This transition may be a complete change of mood and pace or it may flow on from the previous segment. Known out-words on the outgoing segment will take precedence and the outgoing fader will need to come down very quickly after the words are heard. If there is music or effects to consider, they may be best mixed into the incoming sound and the transition achieved more gradually.

Music or loud effects on an incoming sequence are often best brought in smoothly, underneath the end of the previous shot, to reduce the shock of the change. Even where the vision is a cut, a very fast fade will soften the transition and appear more natural. These decisions can be made very quickly and effectively so long as the correct information is provided. This illustrates the importance of accurate information, as so many different factors must be considered to produce the correct crossfade.

Compression

Compression is a complex subject and has been described earlier in this section. Its main role is to use the variable parameters to assist with the mix of different signals and to control the overall range of levels that are acceptable for the type of programme being made. Compressors can take some experimentation to get the most suitable settings and adequate rehearsal time is needed to achieve this. Compression cannot be set in advance as it requires the actual sound to be able to set the effect that is required.

5.6.9 Balances and programme types

News and current affairs

In a news or current affairs programme time will be the major consideration, particularly when it is transmitted live. The requirement for making fast decisions is helped by the fact that this type of programme is often a formula operation, carried out on a regular basis. The operators become very familiar with the basic running order, the presenter's methods, and the producer's requirements. This considerably reduces the need for all but the voice checks and simplified rehearsals. The job of the sound balancer on this type of programme is very like that of the vision mixer, fading up the appropriate microphone or video machine in a smooth switching operation. Mixing will usually be the addition of music or extra effects of a reasonably simple nature.

News programmes require a check of each microphone before rehearsal starts and a level from all the other sources and lines from external contributors. These checks will minimize the chance of equipment and lines failure during the programme. The actual programme will be mixed using a running order, on paper or via a computer screen, to give details of the next item and where it originates. Some sound operators prefer paper running orders as they like to write in missing details and equalization or problem notes alongside each item. The most important information is the length of each section and the final words or 'out-words' as it is these that will tell the balancer when to take out the fader. At three words per second, timing is really not accurate enough to get clean in and out points on pre-recorded material.

Light entertainment

Light entertainment has very different and varied requirements, that depend on the exact type of programme to be produced.

In discussion-type programmes, apart from opening and closing sequences, the main task will be to balance the microphones of each contributor to enable their comments to be clearly heard. Good voice checks are vital and rehearsal should point out any problems like jewellery knocking the lapel microphones or, worse, contributors who fiddle with them.

Fades in this type of show are less common, but the balance between sources becomes the main task. The actual balance will depend on careful concentration – not of the content of the programme (listening to the discussion usually results in missed cues!), but trying to guess who is going to speak next. This is important, as to achieve a good sound balance only one microphone at a time will be at full level, the others being at a lower gain to help reduce noises from those who are not currently contributing. This method helps reduce unpleasant coloration, where the sound of one voice is actually picked up by two or more microphones. The balance is considerably aided if the operator can see all of the contributors on a monitor. Sometimes, a permanent wide shot may be required to help with the sound balance. It is certainly not acceptable to have only a transmission monitor in sound as the balancer will be unable to use body language or facial expressions to help with the guessing as to who will talk next.

Where there are many contributors, and especially if there are contributions from an audience, it is wise to group the contributors' channels together, with compression to assist with the balance, leaving the anchor person separately controlled. This will ensure that if the discussion gets really heated, the anchor will cut through to control the situation. Capturing voices from an audience will probably require the use of a studio boom. This makes the job for the balancer quite easy as it is the boom operator who does the work in deciding who will be heard next. The boom operator has a great advantage, as being present on the floor they can see who wants to contribute and will usually beat the camera to the contributor every time. It is perfectly reasonable to hear the speaker before seeing them – the reverse would not make sense.

There may be a need to discuss with producers the priorities in handling a heated discussion, as sound have the ultimate ability to allow the viewer to hear one person over the others in a shouting match. This may have editorial overtones!

Music

In balancing music it is difficult to give rules – the end result will be one person's artistic interpretation of the music. This varies with the type of music; for example, many types of pop music can be very difficult to balance.

No one sound operator can be expected to know what is needed for every type of music. It may be useful to engage the help of the manager, arranger or even the band themselves. It can sometimes be difficult to know exactly what was intended when a band decided on a particular mix. It is certainly not a sign of weakness to ask, and a good professional band will be only too willing to help. They will need to know what time is available and understand that it is virtually impossible to recreate the CD mix in 30 minutes. Generally the most difficult people to please will be the least experienced, for whom an appearance on television is a very great event. In this latter case the balancer will have to make a judgement on whether asking the performer will be a help or a hindrance. It is often advisable to listen to their own studio recording or published record of the band before they arrive.

Classical music may be less difficult to record – there will be less opportunity for personal interpretation as there are conventional methods to record and mix this type of music. Jazz music can also be fairly straightforward – in some cases hearing all the instruments is almost all that is required.

In recording music where there will be many separate microphones on individual instruments it is vital to rig and test all well in advance. No studio time should be wasted on making the equipment work. Labelling the floor cables will assist in ensuring that the microphones are all correctly connected and faults can be quickly traced if they occur. Be absolutely sure that the positions of the musicians have been properly planned – the designer should have produced a floor plan to achieve this. It helps no-one to move things around after the sound balance has been achieved. When all the musicians are in place, check each channel separately and obtain a reasonably even level of all the instruments. This is the time to check the microphone positions as well as adjusting the level and equalization.

The real mixing process now begins and how long this takes will depend on the size of the band, the experience of the balancer and how complex the music is. This whole process is usually best achieved as a sound band balance rather than as part of a camera rehearsal. Band balances allow the check to be stopped by the sound department if required. The process prevents frustration on behalf of the producer or director when they find they can only hear part of the mix as the layers are being built up. In reality band balances save time and tempers and need to be on the schedule so everyone in the studio knows what is happening.

The greatest difficulty in performing a music mix may lie in deciding exactly what the viewer should hear. Should this sound like a concert hall, in which case reverberation will have to be added as studios have intentionally low reverberation times? Or perhaps with small bands or a solo instrument, the performance could sound as if it is in the viewer's home where the acoustic effects will be very small.

There are many considerations, some of which are outside the scope of this basic book. The important thing is that the mix should sound realistic. One of the best pieces of advice is that the balancer should really listen to the piece, on the studio floor, so that some idea of how it sounds is already in the mind before attempting to re-create the sound in the control room.

Drama
Traditionally the real work of a drama mix in the studio is achieved by the careful use of microphone booms. Provided the set does not cause significant problems with sound reflections, the boom allows the microphone to be placed in such a way that the sound perspective matches the shot. There may be more than one boom and, for very difficult positions, spot microphones may be used. It is unlikely that there will be a very large number of microphones, so the skill of the boom operators will have the greatest effect on the sound quality. Good communication is required between the balancer and the boom operators so that they can work as a team placing the microphone and adjusting the levels as required. Swapping the action from one boom to another without audible changes in quality is an example of this teamwork.

If stereo is a consideration in the studio then the boom operators will have the main control with the balancer keeping them well informed on the effect required as headphone monitoring of stereo is quite difficult.

Drama recordings can be made using radio microphones. There are many opinions on this technique. The resultant sound will not include the perspective, with each actor sounding the same regardless of the shot. Some feel that it is acceptable to have sound with less acoustic affect than the shot implies; others may point out that this breaks the dramatic spell by causing discontinuities between sound and picture. If radio microphones are to be used, it is possible, although rather time-consuming, to add the artificial acoustics later. This might be cheaper than extending the studio time and would allow more flexibility in other ways. Certainly the camera shots would not need to consider the boom and there would be no risk of shadows. If radio systems are to be used they must be of the highest quality to achieve reliability and the costume department will need to be well involved to ensure that the clothes and the fabrics used are suitable.

The drama considerations are endless using stereo and ambisonics to enrich the effect, bringing greater reality to the viewer. The recording must be carefully planned and the sound images considered with respect to the overall effect so that there are no unwanted discontinuities between picture, sound and script. If compromises are to be made, they should result in a reduction of complexity and not overall quality, or the end result will not please the viewer and the efforts of artistes and crew are wasted.

5.6.10 Summary

Technicalities

Studio sound is an area containing a very large range of technical equipment which must be clearly understood or its operation will obstruct the process of making the programme. The making of television programmes should be an artistic task not driven purely by the technicalities.

Planning

Because sound is such a technical operation the planning has to be the key. Well defined intelligent rigging and testing of equipment can ensure that no unnecessary time is lost in the valuable rehearsal and recording time.

The mix

Balancing the sound is to some extent a personal interpretation process. If the programme producers have strong views, these must be clearly understood by those in Sound before the programme reaches the studio. Most sound operators will encourage such production input – there are too many occasions when the whole thing is 'left to Sound' with the result that the close harmony between sound and pictures is lost.

5.7 Location sound

The location sound operation requires a good understanding of the sound–picture relationship and a considerable amount of flexibility. Many problems present themselves on location and resourcefulness with limited equipment is often the key. There are great variations in the types of equipment carried by location crews, the following being a minimum that might be expected, for most types of job.

5.7.1 Microphones

The first decision to make is what microphones should be carried on a location shoot. This is perhaps the biggest variable, but basic location units working on a straightforward documentary shoot, would need:

- A dynamic stick microphone, always a useful and reliable workhorse.
- A short condenser rifle microphone. This requires a proper shock mount, a foam windshield for interior use, a basket windshield for exteriors and a hairy cover for extreme wind conditions. If stereo is required this unit could be replaced with an M/S combination. (See Section 5.8.3 for details.)
- A pair of condenser lapel microphones with clips and other mounts, depending on the make, plus a supply of good fabric-backed gaffer tape. Taping these microphones in place is usually better than using the clips provided. Windshields may help a little but careful rigging under the clothing is often better.
- Wireless or radio transmitters are a must – most producers expect to be able to record artistes walking out of the range of cabled microphones. Wireless microphones may be equipped with their own lapel microphones or the pair specified above can be adapted. If these are to be separate it is a good idea for all four microphones to be of the same type. This gives flexibility, four-handed interviews all matching in quality, and the clips and fittings are all the same which will look better when they are in shot. There is an added advantage that familiarity of equipment will speed up rigging. Also, only one set of spares is required.

There may be many other microphones that would be useful, depending on the jobs that will be encountered. Do not forget that every microphone to be used outside will need proper protection from the wind. The simple foam windshield supplied with each microphone is not adequate for wind protection on location.

5.7.2 Mixer

The next part of the chain is the mixer. Most of the units suitable for location operations are designed for four inputs; these can be routed to two outputs to allow for split track or stereo working. This type of mixer covers most applications, the exception being location drama where a portable four-channel mixer is unlikely to have enough facilities.

The mixer facilities required for documentary type work are:

- **Inputs**

  Four microphone inputs, each requiring:
  - T and Phantom powering for condenser microphones (see Section 5.5.1).
  - Bass cuts at 75 Hz and 150 Hz to reduce unwanted low frequency sounds.
  - Input gain adjustments from –30 to –70 dB. Here 10 dB steps are best to ensure that input faders are set properly. It is useful if the mixer can also accept a line level input.

  Stereo units have a phase switch on two of the four channels for switching the S signal. This allows a stereo M/S microphone to be inverted and still maintain the left output on the left after decoding!

- **Routing**

  Each input has a routing switch. With a mono mixer this switch enables the signal to output 1 or 1 + 2 or 2. Stereo units have a pan control. This is a continuously variable control routing the signal anywhere from fully left through centre to right. When a pair of channels on the mixer are ganged together for stereo operation, the pan control becomes a balance control; in this mode the one control adjusts the relative level of left and right signals, leaving just one fader to control the stereo pair.

- **Main out**

  The outputs of the pan or routing switches are fed to the master gain, which adjusts the final output of the mixer. In order that the signal is routed inside the mixer at the designed level, it is important that the master gain and channel faders are operated near their zero positions. This is commonly set to be 10 dB below their maximum positions and so gives some extra gain (20 dB altogether) if required. Should either of these two controls be operating much lower than this, the input gain of the mixer is set too high and distortion is possible on any high-level sounds.

- **Limiters**

  Most location mixers have some form of limiting that can be switched in if unexpected high level signals might be encountered. Limiting should only be an occasional event – if it happens often the system gain may be set too high. With stereo signals the limiters must be set to 'link', to ensure that both sides of the image are limited together. This ensures that the stereo images remain stable.

- **Monitoring**

  Other important controls on the front of mixer are the monitor switching and headphone level. The switch allows for monitoring of all or some of the following facilities:
  - Pre-Fader Listen for each channel, that is, the channel can be monitored without opening the channel fader. This can allow one channel of a mix to be heard solo.
  - The stereo output of the mixer.
  - Left or right outputs individually.
  - A mono mix of the two outputs.
  - An M/S decoded to stereo (for use with M/S microphones).
  - A return feed from the recorder or camera. This is a very important function as it is a confidence check that the camera is receiving the signal at the correct level and no faults have occurred.

  Mixer designs vary, with some the metering also following the monitor switching. This enables levels to be checked even before the channel is opened.

- **Metering**

  Mixers are supplied with either VU or PPM type meters; these are fully described in Section 5.3.2.

  As well as providing a guide during recording, the meter is important when aligning the mixer to the camera. The mixer is provided with a tone generator to allow the alignment. The tone may be at a fixed level or may be adjusted with the mixer master gain. Some mixers ensure that no other signal will reach the output when the tone is activated. To be safe it is best to ensure that the faders are all closed during the line-up.

Reminder on line-up

If the mixer has VU meters, the tone may be set at 0 VU (100% modulation) and as most cameras have VU calibrated meters this should be set to 0 VU on the camera. Digital cameras will normally be set with this tone at –20 dB on the camera meter.

To align a mixer with PPMs, the tone is set to 4 on a BBC type meter (0 on an EBU PPM); this should be set to –4 VU on the camera. This will ensure good modulation on the tape whilst not allowing any high energy peaks to cause distortion. Tone at PPM 4 should be set to –24 dB on a digital camera.

Digital line-up levels may vary slightly – it is important to check that the above is correct for the company for whom the recordings are intended.

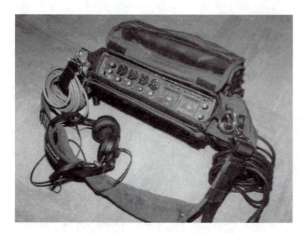

Figure 5.68 Location mixer with good protection and cables neatly coiled (courtesy of Audio Developments Ltd).

Finally the mixer must be fitted into a really good portable case with a comfortable strap. The padded cases are good as they protect the unit from occasional knocks. They also come with a transparent window to help keep rain off the front of the mixer – the best designs allow access to the front controls with this transparent cover closed. The case can be designed to carry wireless receivers, spare batteries, etc.

5.7.3 Other equipment

Cables

Microphone cables are required to connect to the mixer and various lengths are important; 2, 4 and 6 metres is a good start. The cables should be of good quality, star-quad to avoid unwanted pick-up (see Section 5.3.3) and flexible so that they do not easily get tangled.

A location sound operator needs the minimum of things to get caught up in and must be able to move swiftly with the camera operator. If the mixer is connected directly to the camera (rather than with radio links) the connection must be carefully rigged, allowing enough spare cable for the camera operator to move freely. Some mixers have a multipin connector that enables the two send and one return feeds to be connected into a single multiway cable. If individual cables are to be used they can be strapped together or even plaited into a single group. It is a good idea to connect a straining wire to the cables, with a clip at each end. The clips can be fixed to both camera and sound mixer and will avoid straining the audio connectors. This is particularly important on older cameras that use 3.5 mm headphone jacks for the return feed.

Straps of hook and eye fabric (Velcro) or wire hooks on each side of the mixer are useful to keep all excess cable off the ground. Being tidy and having nothing on the ground to get tangled or trip over may be the difference between getting the shot and missing the action altogether.

Fish pole

A good quality lightweight fish pole allows rifle or other cardioid microphones to be positioned over the artistes, near the camera lens, whilst keeping the operator clear of camera moves and out of shot. The best of these poles are made from carbon fibre reinforced plastic making them very light and allowing quite long working times at a reasonable distance. Care is needed with mounting the microphone, ensuring that the mount is suitably flexible to reduce the pick-up of handling noise as well as being lightweight, or the advantage of a light pole would be lost. Like studio boom operation, use of the pole requires good understanding of camera angles and lighting techniques as well as the requirement to match the sound quality to the pictures. A standard pole should extend from about 0.5 to 2.5 metres. The pole must be kept clean to ensure smooth operation and care should be taken not to over-tighten their clamping threads, which can damage the threads and crush the pole itself.

Fish pole for drama

On drama shoots it is necessary to have very long poles as well as the short ones. These might well extend to six metres, allowing the microphone to achieve close-up sound to match a shot at the end of a zoom lens. On a drama operation some operators use a portable meter that can be fixed to the pole and will be in the eyeline of the operator. These are usually provided with a microphone pre-amplifier, and headphone output for monitoring.

Stands

Floor stands are useful, particularly on long interviews when the microphones can be rigged permanently, saving great arm strain. These stands are also useful for the rigging of effects microphones at sport and other events. Table stands may also be needed in conference situations. Clamps are valuable, particularly on sport shoots, where it will often be best to rig the microphones on scaffolds, out of the reach of members of the public.

Microphone clips

Each microphone will need a special clip to fix it to a stand or scaffold clamp. These are only suitable for

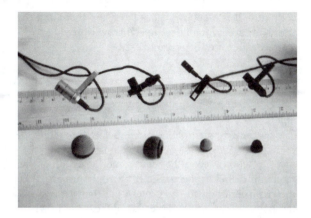

Figure 5.69 Lapel microphones come with various clips and windshields.

static mounting. If a microphone is to be attached to a fish pole it needs a purpose-designed mount to reduce the effect of handling noise.

Lapel microphones have their own special clips. The rigging of these was fully discussed in Section 5.5.

Extras

Cables to connect to domestic systems are often useful although if this is to an unbalanced system the connection should be done with a balance transformer (see below) An alternative method is to have an unbalanced cable, with appropriate attenuation to connect to the input of a radio transmitter. This will provide the required system isolation and the freedom of being able to move around whilst recording the sound source. This can be very useful in theatres or music studios where the camera operator will want to be on the move whilst sound will want to hear the stage or studio mix.

Balance transformer

The requirement to connect professional balanced systems to domestic unbalanced systems is more fully discussed in Section 5.3. The devices used to achieve this are called Direct Injection (DI) boxes. These can be passive versions, those that contain purely a transformer, or active versions, those that have electronic circuits and require internal batteries. In both cases they have unbalanced inputs, usually on ¼" jack plugs and balanced outputs on an XLR socket. Some boxes are designed to have a range of inputs of varying levels, instruments, line level or speaker level, allowing any of these to be connected and provide a balanced line level matching output.

On location the most common use for the DI box is to connect to a PA system or a domestic piece of equipment. It will be necessary to carry some adapter leads to convert the commonly found domestic connectors to the ¼" jack on the box.

Figure 5.70 A simple direct injection box.

Simple tools

A range of simple tools is essential on location shoots. A range of screwdrivers and pliers to correct simple mechanical problems is a minimum. A small soldering iron and associated equipment will allow the repair of cables and connectors which are the most vulnerable part of location operations.

Talkback

Talkback may be required on location if the unit is to carry out live or recorded links to a studio. The simplest form will be to have a return feed, provided as a telecom line or from an ISDN codec (see Section 5.6.3 for details) or even using a mobile phone as the link. This return feed may be fed to the local operators, camera, sound and floor manager. The presenter can be cued by one of these operators. It is common to have a second feed for the presenter which will be fed directly to them on an earpiece.

Where the location presenter needs to hear remote studio presenters, the studio sound can be added to the earpiece feed. This is the safest way as there is no possibility of feedback, which could occur if a speaker is used. The picture monitor for live two-ways on location may be a domestic off-air receiver. Whilst this will provide a visual cue, the sound on the monitor must not be turned up as it will always cause feedback and coloration problems. It is not a good idea to use this sound for the earpiece as, unlike a clean feed, it will include the location presenter in the mix. Very few presenters can perform well with their own voice in their ear, especially if this sound contains audio delays.

Headphones

Headphones are discussed in Section 5.4.6. They must be of the closed back type to ensure that only the mixer output is heard. This is especially important when making judgements of the level of background sounds against a voice.

The headphones need to have a flat, full range frequency response and must be robust. They do need to be strong enough to accept being dropped on the floor without damage. One useful extra is that some are fitted with a ¼″ stereo jack which can be removed to reveal the mini-jack as fitted to many cameras. It allows a direct check on the camera with the same phones, without the use of adapter cables.

5.7.4 Camera controls

When connecting to and setting up the camera, the same rules apply as for setting up the mixer. There are at least two, and on some formats four, audio tracks to

configure. It is a good practice to ensure that all of the tracks are individually set up. This will provide back-up recordings on the spare tracks.

Direct-to-camera recordings

Inputs

The on-camera microphone can be selected to either, or both, of the two tracks and the gain set as required to give a good recording level, not exceeding the maximum level in the peaks. If microphones are to be directly connected to the camera via the rear sockets, these must be selected on the side of the camera. Where VU meters are installed, and they are to be used to balance varying audio levels, it is important to remember that these meters do not respond to very short duration sounds. Care is needed to ensure that the levels do not cause peak distortion – it may be necessary to hold the peaks back by up to 10 dB (see Section 5.3.2).

This set-up is similar if separate microphones are to be connected to the camera. The rear sockets must be switched as appropriate with microphone power switched on if needed. The gain of each input is then set as before.

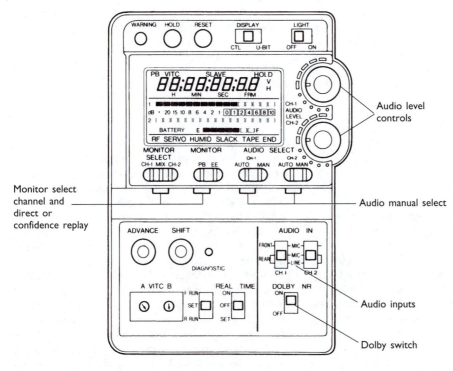

Figure 5.71 Camera controls allow the tracks to be used as required. Note that some cameras will allow up to four tracks to be used.

Setting time code
- if you are using time code and user bits, set user bits first
- maximum value of time code is 23 : 59 : 59 : 24

Auto gain

Most cameras are fitted with auto gain devices which need great care in use. These might help in an unrehearsed situation, but will only be acceptable if there is very little background noise. Where auto gain settings are used, any background sounds will vary as the gain adjusts itself to the dialogue. These background variations cause problems in the editing as they show up the edit points.

Dolby Noise Reduction (Nr)

On SP Beta, Dolby C noise reduction is part of the manufacturer's specification. This means that provided SP tapes are used in the recorder, the Dolby encoding will be automatically enabled, regardless of the switch position. If older oxide tapes are used the Dolby will only be encoded if the switch is on. To get good signal-to-noise figures this should always be used, but it is vital that the use of Dolby is marked on the tape to ensure that it is properly decoded by the player in the edit suite.

With the digital formats many of the audio parameters are adjusted via screen menus on a display on the side of the camera. The settings are recorded by the camera memory. It is vital that the operators understand fully the parameters they are changing and if something unusual is done the settings must be returned to normal afterwards.

As well as the video adjustments, these settings may include:

- noise reduction;
- bass filters;
- equalization;
- signal limiting;
- routing to tracks 3 and 4;
- routing to cue track;
- monitor signal and level;
- time code adjustment.

These settings can be recorded on a removable memory card which would be particularly valuable if the operator regularly works with different cameras.

5.7.5 Working with a mixer

If the sound is all being recorded from a location mixer the line output of the mixer should be connected to the two camera inputs, longitudinal tracks 1 and 2 (LNG), with both switched to line and the audio select switched to manual. Tone is then routed from the mixer and the levels adjusted to ensure the camera is aligned to the mixer as illustrated in Section 5.7.2. Note that track 1 has a separate

gain control on the camera viewfinder – this should be turned to maximum before adjusting the gain on the side of the camera. The return feed from the camera to the mixer should also be adjusted at the mixer to ensure that the mixer still reads the correct level. If this feed comes from the camera headphone output, ensure that this too is set to maximum.

On cameras where there is access to all four tracks, unless they are all required for separate sound recordings, they should be switched to copy the sound from tracks 1 and 2. On Beta SP tracks 3 and 4 are the AFM tracks. On the digital formats only some have access to four tracks. Where all four are available these can be linked to be fed from tracks 1 and 2 as a safety version. The extra tracks can be useful to record stereo effects as well as the separate dialogue tracks. Care must be taken to ensure that the effects tracks do not 'hear' the dialogue or an unpleasant echo may be recorded. An alternative use is where loud sounds are expected but levels cannot be taken. The extra tracks can be set at a lower level, perhaps –12 dB, to act as a safety against over-modulation of the first two tracks.

5.7.6 The location crew

Relationship with camera operator

The key to effective location operations is in the way the crew work together. This is most important with camera and sound. There are many ways in which both can help each other, but this can only be achieved if they both understand each other's job function.

There are many examples of good cooperation. When a camera operator places the camera on the tripod, one of the first things they will do will be to free-off the tilt clutch and slide the base plate back or forwards to balance the camera. They then will readjust the tilt clutch in order to achieve smooth camera movements. Now, along comes the sound operator, who has just finished checking the sound equipment and plugs the umbilical lead into the rear of the camera. A good team player will then carefully tuck the cable around the front of the panning handle so that the cable falls from near the head pivot and barely affects the camera balance. Accidental pressure on the cable will not pan the camera around and ruin the next shot. If this cable is simply left dangling from the rear of the camera, it will unbalance the camera and make smooth movements more difficult.

An effective crew also includes the journalist. It is possible that asking a very nervous interviewee to give a voice level (which is absolutely vital to get a good recording) will make them even more nervous.

It can be pre-arranged, before the interviewee arrives, that a small nod from sound to camera and then from camera to the journalist will allow the journalist to ask a throw-away question, targeted at relaxing the subject. Sound gets a level, from a sensible question that is answered easily, the camera starts rolling and (provided there are no problems) the interview starts on the second question without the interviewee being upset by the process. The interviewee has had no chance to get more nervous, as they haven't been involved in any unnecessary technology. Even an experienced interviewee may give a more honest answer if they do not know the camera is recording.

During an interview or sequence where the sound is being picked up with a microphone mounted on a fish pole or boom, the sound operator needs eyes in several places at once:

- Keep out of shot.
- Do not cast any shadows.
- Get sound that matches the picture.
- Know who is going to talk next.

So many places to look!

Eye contact with the camera operator will help a great deal, especially where camera moves are taking place. A helpful camera operator will give up and down signs, to show how the shots are about to change and avoid getting the microphone into shot. It is important in an unrehearsed interview for sound to look at those who are not speaking, watch for the breath or the body language, which gives clues as to who will speak next, so the microphone is in place before the new contributor joins in. On larger shoots or in drama a monitor may help, but usually a walk through of the action with the attention split between the camera and the artistes should do the trick.

An experienced operator soon 'hears' the microphone position on the headphones, and the lens angles can be guessed pretty accurately from the position of the camera. Headroom, the space between the top of the contributor and the top edge of the frame, is usually fairly constant. This means that on a close-up the camera will be fairly level but on a wide shot the camera will be pointing down. This gives a good clue as to where the microphone can be positioned and how wide the sound image should appear to be.

Safety

Safety should always be considered. When camera operators are concentrating on the viewfinder they will often not be aware of other things that are happening around them because they have a small field of view through the camera. The sound person may be in a much better position to make sure that there are no other threats. Being run over when near road traffic is a good example of this. The camera operator will be focused on the viewfinder and may be quite unaware of traffic dangers. It is important that another person performs the safety role. Where there is no camera assistant the sound operator may be in the best place to do this.

Camera's eyes

For the same reason that camera operators may be unaware of safety concerns, they will often miss actions around them that may have importance to the story. Sound crew are usually working very close to the camera and are well placed to point out important bits of action that are outside the camera's field of view. Care is needed when distracting the camera operator. This close teamwork is vital in achieving the best results.

5.7.7 Recording onto a separate sound medium

One of the biggest problems about location shooting with a camera operator and separate recordist is that they have to be physically connected by a cable. This not only causes frustrations – at best the cable can restrict camera movement at an inopportune moment; at worst the cable can be a real nuisance when the operators have to move locations and maybe can even cause safety problems. One possible solution is to send the audio to the camera via radio signals but at least two channels would be needed and there may already be a radio requirement for microphones. This gets rather complex and in an ideal world a return radio link to the recordist would be needed to provide some confidence that the camera was receiving the signals. Even this has its problems as if break-up was monitored it might have only been in the return feed so the recording would have to be checked for any possible faults.

Time code as a reference

Most crews agree that it would be best to have no direct cable link and, with the use of time code as a reference, a separate medium can be used to record the sound. There are still some problems to solve and these will depend on the type of programme material being recorded.

Continuous time code

Most documentary shoots are recorded with the camera time code in 'Record Run' which means that each time the camera runs it resets the internal generator to the time already on the tape on the previous shot. This ensures one continuous time code track from the start to the end of the tape. This helps with editing as the edit controller can lock anywhere on the tape, reducing the technical need for at least five seconds of code from camera 'run' to the artiste cue. To operate a separate sound recorder and maintain identical time code on both machines would mean transmitting at least a burst of this code to the recorder to reset its generator as well.

Time of day or free run time code

The alternative is to lock the camera code generator and sound recorder generator together and leave them free running. The generators would be quite able to maintain frame-accurate code for several hours and they would always have the same codes. This further allows the sound machine to be used to record some wild tracks without any risk of repeated codes on the same tape. The disadvantage of the system is that at least five seconds must be put onto the front and end of each shot to ensure the edit lock-up. This will certainly be acceptable on feature films and drama where there is a standard practice of running up and having an appropriate acknowledgement from both sound and camera before the artists are cued. However, this disciplined approach might be more difficult on a news-type shoot.

Clapper board for separate sound recording

It is a common practice to continue with the film technique of using a clapper board at the start of each shot. Whilst this is theoretically not required to ensure a lock between sound and picture, as both should have the same frame-accurate time code, it does provide a very helpful visual reference on the picture as to the shot and take number as well. The board is normally used at the start of each take; if missed, it is used inverted at the end of the take.

The clapper board technique is very helpful where code problems have occurred as the visual, and corresponding audio, identification can be used to realign the material. Some crews are so concerned about possible loss of lock that even where a clapper board is not used, the sound operator will 'tap' the microphone in shot at the start of each sequence to give the editor a chance to re-lock the material quickly. Modern electronic clapper boards are made, and have

a built-in time-code generator with the code displayed on large visual displays, clearly visible on the camera. At the point of the identifying clap the code is frozen for a few seconds on the display, allowing the editor to read the time clearly.

The type of programme will most certainly dictate which methods are to be used.

5.7.8 Separate sound systems

Separate sound recordings can be achieved using many techniques, both analogue and digital. The system to be employed will need to take into account many factors, including:

- Programme budget.
- Material to be recorded and location operation. Will complex mixing be required on location? Should the equipment be very light and portable?
- Sound technique. For example, stereo or surround will dictate the number of location tracks required.
- Facilities in post-production. With digital systems the sampling and bit rate must be compatible. Care is also needed where the recording medium uses digital compression. In some cases there may be problems where different equipment uses differing compression rates.

¼" Tape

Analogue time code tape equipment has been around for a long time, and because of the quality of the most popular equipment it is still in use. It has many advantages – it is fairly straightforward to operate, gives off-tape confidence monitoring and is robust and not too prone to failure due to dirt, moisture or temperature changes. The disadvantages are signal-to-noise figures that are lower than modern expectations and the equipment is very heavy, making it difficult to be carried.

Digital ¼" tape

Digital ¼" tape is available to overcome the technical limitations and this equipment too is robust in operation. The advantages are in both quality and flexibility, being able to record up to four tracks as well as the time code, and of using an inexpensive medium of ¼" tape to record the sound. The equipment is rather heavy and slightly more prone to dust and moisture problems than conventional tape equipment but the big disadvantage is its considerable cost. This technology is most commonly found on feature film sets.

DAT

More correctly these cassette systems should be called RDAT as they use a rotary head.

Digital cassette tape has become a popular medium and certainly is capable of recording in high quality. The machines are a similar price to standard ¼″ tape but can be much lighter and the large number of machines in studios and dubbing suites makes this a popular choice. The system is rather more fragile, but much of this is overcome by the fact that the machines are totally enclosed and therefore less likely to be affected by dust. Moisture, particularly condensation, can be a problem and care is needed to ensure that the machines are not subjected to large temperature changes in a very short time. As the video camera is subject to the same problem at least it is something that operators are familiar with.

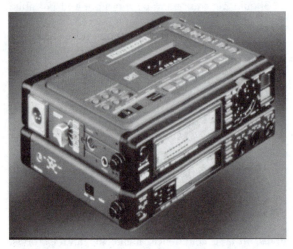

Figure 5.72 Portable time code digital audio recorder (courtesy of HHB Communications Ltd).

Hard disk

Removable hard disk recorders have many advantages, the biggest being that the sound can be transferred to the dubbing theatre without transfer time. The disks are quite expensive and so need to be recycled, a possible problem if the material needs to be stored for future use. A further advantages of this medium is the ability to configure the recording method, making this system very flexible and capable of: mono, stereo, 3 channel encoded surround, or 4 channel recordings – allowing full 24 bit uncompressed audio from 150 minutes of mono to 37 minutes of four track. These devices can also have mixers built in, making this the only piece of location sound equipment required.

Flash disk

Removable solid state cards can be used and very high quality devices are made to record location audio onto this medium. The systems allow multitrack configuration. Because these disks are very specialist and quite new technology they are very expensive and unless a small number of the cards can be recycled, cost may be a deciding factor with this technology.

Optical disk

Optical disk recorders are similarly flexible and have the advantage of easily removable disks. As these disks are used in many industries for data recording they are lower in cost for a given time in recording. The disks allow up to 50 minutes of 16 bit stereo at 48 kHz and have the advantage that the disk can be used directly in editing or dubbing without the need to download the audio data.

Sound effects and non-sync recordings

There are some other formats that can be valuable on location for recording extra effects or separate voice recordings or making transcript copies of the material for production.

These can include any of the above formats plus non-time code DAT machines, MiniDisc recorders or cassette recorders for the transcript recordings. It is important to ensure that the post-production area can use the format chosen.

5.7.9 Drama outline

When moving from documentary-type shots to full drama productions for television or feature films many of the systems outlined above are employed. The system used depends on the budget available.

The big difference in technique relates to the requirements of the location mixer. The mixer needs much more flexibility and the use of rotary faders, as are fitted to a location mixer, will not be adequate for accurate mixes. Slider faders and more comprehensive equalization will mean the mixer will resemble a small version of the types found in the studio.

This desk will have to perform a more complex task providing separate feeds to a video recorder for location playback as well as the main feed to the audio recorder. Even when working on film, a drama shoot will often use video assist. Video assist places a small video camera into the film camera viewfinder to allow the director and others to see the picture on a monitor. If this is to be recorded, a feed of the audio will be needed for the record machine.

Figure 5.73 Location drama mixers require many facilities (courtesy of Audio Developments Ltd).

There may also be a need to feed sound to other members of the crew. Certainly the director will want a headphone feed and lighting or special effects crews may need this for cueing effects, especially if radio microphones are being used and the action is well away from the crew.

Talkback

Talkback, or at least some form of radio communication, is often required on drama shoots and this will frequently be the responsibility of the sound crew. It may be as simple as providing two-way walkie-talkies. On a complex shoot there might be a need for a base station and several remotes with reverse radio talkback for those who need to communicate directly with the director. These units are expensive and there is a requirement to ensure that the frequencies in use are licensed for the region. It is often best to hire these facilities in order to ensure that local regulations are complied with.

Logging the job

One of the most important tasks of the sound recordist on a drama shoot or full documentary is the accurate logging of the material recorded. These logs will show the roll, shot, take number and the reference time code. There will be a short description of the sequence and any notes about the quality of the take. These are quite different from any records that may be made by the production assistant. Logs made by the recordist are sound-specific and are a useful cross-reference with the other records. The log will be used by the production crew, the editor, and most importantly the sound dubbing mixer as they will show the best takes and identify extra sound effects and wild tracks.

How these logs are written will depend on the shoot and the time available. Some may be written at the time of recording; others will need rewriting from rough notes. Some recordists use small memo recorders on location and replay the notes in order to write them up later.

5.7.10 Summary of location recording

Location work varies from the simplest news story, where the camera operator can manage the audio alone, to drama shooting where there may be a sound crew of at least two and often many more. The range of equipment required to carry out these disparate

Location Sound Log.

Programme Working Title	The Seaside calls		Director: V.Able		
Sound Recordist	B.Ears		Sound Assistant	s.Man	
Date	10/01/99		Recording equipment details		
			Portadat - Sample at 48kHz		
Roll No	12		Tone at zero PPM aligned -20dB		

Scene	Shot	Take	Shot details	Sound report	Time Code
23	15	1	Walk to the riverside	NG take serious rustling on mic	12,03:15
23	15	2	Walk to the riverside	Good take - slight wind noise	12,07:15

Figure 5.74 Location sound log.

tasks is therefore very varied, depending on not only the complexity of the task but also the budgets available.

The important discussions follow a logical progression:

- the details of the sequence to be recorded;
- the location and its limitations;
- the number of artistes involved;
- the type of programme;
- the recording format;
- what resources are available in post production.

From this it will be possible to decide on:

- the microphones required;
- the type of mixer;
- the use of tracks on the camera;
- the possible use of separate sound recorders for the primary sound;
- the acceptable formats for voice over or effects recording.

5.8 Stereo and ambisonics

Strictly speaking, stereophony actually means 'solid sound' so this should really include ambisonic or surround sound as well. To most people stereo is understood as two channels and so this section will refer to stereo in this way. Stereo traditionally uses two channels of audio signals, replayed through two spaced loudspeakers to give the image some width. Discrete sounds appear at specific positions within this total image. These 'phantom' centre images are very dependent on both the recording technique and the home environment.

Ambisonics or surround sound takes the stereo image further and allows signals to appear all around the listener. For television, ambisonic is commonly reproduced using five loudspeakers, one either side of the screen with a third placed under or over the screen and two further speakers placed behind the viewer. The ambisonic signals can be processed to feed a larger number of speakers.

In some ways stereo presents more artistic difficulties than ambisonics. In order to achieve an image that works with the picture, just like any other audio considerations, it is first necessary to consider how the material will be replayed by the viewer. It is the home set-up that will dictate the way the sound should be presented.

Stereo image width is a most important consideration. The actual position should ensure that any sound source visible on the screen appears 'in place' in the sound image. In order to achieve this, some clear definition is needed for the distance between the loudspeakers and the size of the television screen. There is a clear problem here. Some viewers may have large screens and separate speakers, whilst others will have smaller sets with the speakers fitted to the sides of the television.

Sound images balanced to stay 'on screen' in the first example may be so narrow that virtually no stereo will appear on the sets with integral speakers. This may be further complicated by the variation in television formats. Sound that works for a standard 4×3 format may be too narrow for 16×9 or other widescreen formats.

Programme producers may have to make their own decisions as to where to place the on-screen images.

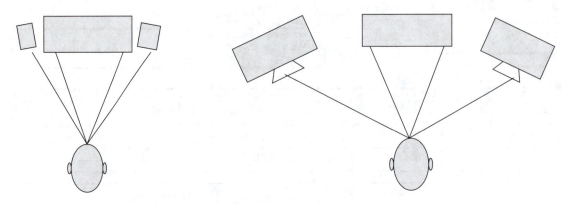

Speakers attached to television   Speakers separate from television

Figure 5.75 Domestic stereo televisions may have different sound image widths.

The result will always be personal and like any artistic interpretation will be open to question. Perhaps there is a bonus here – to get good results audio cannot be 'left to the sound department' to sort out as an afterthought, as is so often the case with other sound considerations. Good stereo programmes must be driven by the overall artistic considerations – the pictures and the impressions the producer wishes to portray must define the stereo spread. Stereo should not be an engineering bolt-on applied to the programme as an afterthought.

Ambisonics need careful planning as well, but the clear definition of the systems means that the variations in home viewing conditions are less variable. Sounds should originate from all around the viewer. Because of the use of a centre loudspeaker, images near the centre, particularly dialogue, should appear clearly on the screen, even if the left and right front speakers are quite a distance from it. A further advantage is that the stereo listening area is quite small. With well produced ambisonics a reasonable effect can be achieved in the home more easily.

5.8.1 Human perception

It is worth considering just how the human ear and brain interprets the direction of sound. Many may think that sound on the left side will simply appear louder in the left ear than the right. In fact, sound on the left will be heard by the right ear at virtually the same level as that on the left. The real difference is that sound from the left will arrive at the left ear slightly earlier than it arrives at the right ear. This 'time of arrival' difference is what must be considered when recording and handling audio signals.

One other consideration is that of frequency. Very low frequencies, certainly those below 150 Hz, have no directional characteristics. This means that the surround systems can be designed with quite small orbital units, with the bass frequencies to come from a separate unit.

5.8.2 Engineering

As accurate stereo positioning depends upon small time differences between the left and right signals, it is important to ensure that timing errors do not occur when engineering these signals. The channels must be routed in such a way that ensures both are processed identically and the careful maintenance of equipment used to record the signals is essential. This is a particular problem with linear analogue tracks that are recorded onto tape with slow write speeds. Betacam

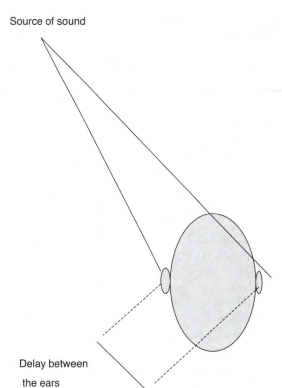

Source of sound

Delay between
the ears

Figure 5.76 Time of arrival differences between the ears.

is one such system. Very small changes in the physical head alignment or the magnetic bias settings (this is described in Section 5.2.1) will produce time delays between the left and right channels. These delays will have an effect that varies with frequency causing cancellations known as 'phasing'. As well as producing an undesirable sound in the mono mix, the effect will seriously damage the stability of the stereo images.

5.8.3 Producing stereo signals – microphone technique

The methods include coincident pairs of directional microphones, microphones in mid–side configurations and microphones dedicated to each sound source, which are positioned electronically on the sound desk.

Multimicrophone

The multimicrophone technique is very common in music recordings where many microphones will be needed to create the balance. Here each source is fed individually to the sound desk and the pan control used to position the sound as required in the image. Care is needed that spill from one microphone to another does not complicate the stereo image. This spill can also cause phase errors which would be a problem for mono compatibility.

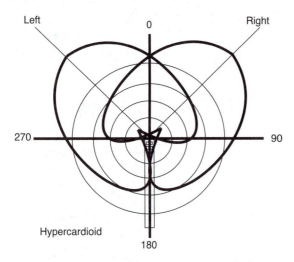

Figure 5.77 Coincident pairs of cardioid microphones.

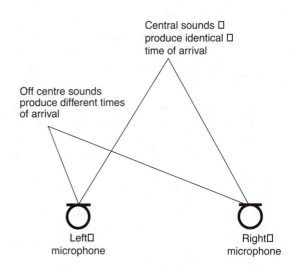

Figure 5.78 Spaced omni-directional microphones.

produce phase errors when they are summed to produce a mono image. Mono compatibility remains a very important issue in television and so this technique is generally not suitable as a recording technique.

Coincident pairs

Coincident pairs produce level differences between the left and right information. When this material is replayed, it is the position of the loudspeakers that creates the time of arrival differences for the listener, and thus the actual sound image. Varying sound images can be produced by using the different directional microphones to produce the stereo image. Cardioid, hyper-cardioid and figure of eight microphones can all be combined to produce stereo signals. They will produce images of different widths and with differing linearity of left–right response.

Spaced omni-directional

Spaced omni-directional microphones actually record time-of-arrival differences. The resultant stereo can produce a very realistic sound with discrete sounds having very clear positions within the image. In classical music a third microphone is sometimes added in the centre and slightly forward of the pair, with its output fed to both sides of the image. This can reduce the hole in the middle of the image sometimes produced with this technique.

The main problem with spaced omni-directional microphones is that the time differences in the signals

Mid–side combination

Coincident microphones will produce a mono-compatible signal and are therefore more suitable for television sound. In the studio and on location where a stereo technique is required to replace the boom microphone, one solution is to use a mid and side combination rather than a conventional stereo pair.

This method has the important advantage of producing mono compatibility, a vital consideration for television sound. Mid–side systems are particularly good for location work or in the studio on the boom, as the microphones can be relied upon to produce the image, provided the operator remembers the rules regarding the relationship between the microphone and the camera lens. Monitoring stereo on headphones can be particularly difficult; relying on the microphone to produce the image is a valuable solution.

The concept of the mid–side coincident pair is to place a forward-facing cardioid microphone together with a side-facing figure of eight. It can be seen from Fig. 5.79 that if the output of the two units is added the negative lobe of the figure of eight will cancel the right pick-up of the cardioid, producing a left-facing image. Conversely if the figure of eight is subtracted (the signals are summed after a 180°

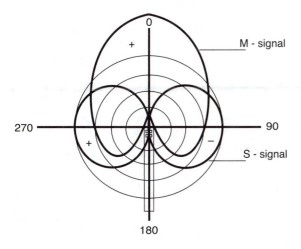

Figure 5.79 Mid–side microphone pair.

phase reversal of the figure of eight output) from the forward signal a right-facing image will be produced:

$$M + S = \text{Left} \quad M - S = \text{Right}$$

The resultant image is roughly equivalent to a hyper-cardioid pair of microphones at 90°.

The stereo microphone channels and most location mixers are fitted with M/S decoders to enable this process. If the signal is to be routed as M/S then a phase reversal switch in the S channel will allow the microphone to be inverted and still retain the correct left–right image.

Figure 5.80 A mid–side combination in a modular suspension (courtesy of Rycote Windshields Ltd).

One great advantage of recordings that are made using this technique is that the mid-signal of material can be used during the edit, saving the image processing for the dubbing stage. It is possible to use the decoding process to control the image width. Increasing the S signal will make the image wider; correspondingly, decreasing it will narrow the image down to the point where S is zero and the signal is mono. Indeed it may be that the side information can be ignored and a simpler dubbing process take place, if time does not allow for the full stereo operation.

5.8.4 Stereo images

Stereo can enhance most programme types. Just to start the programme with a well spaced piece of stereo music will provide the expectation of an interesting experience to follow.

5.8.5 Drama

Drama is a large topic covering the simplest television drama to major film production and so the style that is used will depend on the artistic effect that is required. The basic principle is that the stereo images should complement the viewing angle as well as having the appropriate perspective:

- Close-ups will require a narrower sound image, with the wide shots having correspondingly wide sound. It is necessary to decide how wide is 'wide'. The variations at home are the problem here, but a good starting point might be 50% of the total image width for sounds coming from 'in-vision'.
- Sounds from actors who are out of vision might be wider than this, but care is needed with level, as sounds that are fully left or right will appear lower in level in the mono version.
- Crowds can be full width as can added sound effects or music, unless they are spot effects derived from something that is in vision.
- Panning and moving shots are more difficult. The usual solution is, if the move develops a new overall viewing angle then the sound image should move with the shot.
- Fast cutting between shots presents a problem too. Fast-changing sound images are confusing and unpleasant, so unless this is the intention, it is best to leave the sound alone to match the wide shot or collapse the sound to a narrow image for this sequence. Time is often the deciding factor as to any change of sound image. If the new angle only lasts a few seconds, the action will probably

disguise the temporary error. Such a solution is usually less disconcerting than a fast sound change.

In general it is worth keeping the image reasonably wide, as there is little point in going to all the trouble if no one hears the end result.

5.8.6 Music

With music the solution to the stereo image may be fairly clear. The wide camera shot of the instruments will give the geography and the normal answer is to produce a sound image that matches this. Absolute position is not too critical and if the balance sounds best with slightly different spacing then that is fine.

One problem may be in matching the sound image to the close-ups. If the instrument is close to the centre on the wide shot all is fine; if not then it may be best to move the instrument. This may well be better for cameras as well. If absolutely necessary the sound image can be narrowed for the feature; panning is probably not so good.

All rules are there to be broken and the one good thing about stereo is that if the programme type allows it, anything is worth trying.

5.8.7 Light entertainment

This covers a whole range of programme types and the component parts of the show may well be covered by the suggestions for drama and music in Section 5.6.9.

For quiz shows:

- The sound layout will normally be the same as for the wide shot, but not so wide as to sound strange during the close-ups. It is useful here if the compere of the show is centrally placed as they do talk directly to the camera.
- Bells and buzzers can be put in place or anywhere that works.
- Music should be used to give the image good width.
- The audience can be used to add atmosphere and so can be spread across the whole width of the image. Care is needed to ensure that the audience microphones are correctly placed left and right. If the compere in an audience show looks camera left to react to an audience comment, it is important that the comment does come from the left side of the sound image. The left side of the audience is left with respect to the studio wide shot from behind the audience!

Any microphone method can work for audiences; not only coincident pairs but also spaced microphones are good. They will not suffer noticeably from the problems of mono compatibility, as very few individual parts of the audience sound will reach more than one microphone. In fact any small time errors that are present may well spread the image into the rear speakers of those who are listening to the material in surround.

The presence of the audience in a show adds one extra concern for stereo. There will probably be a need for foldback or public address speakers. Spill between the PA system and the audience microphones is a problem, as it can affect the stereo imagery. Keeping spill to a minimum is important and the use of figure of eight microphones might help with this. The alternative is to keep the speakers in the centre so that the spill does not cause image confusion.

5.8.8 Sport

Sport programmes will follow the general rule for audiences, where a full width image will put the viewer in amongst those at the real venue. Levels of excited crowds always give problems, so proper stereo compression will be required. If the audience is kept very wide, using spaced microphones rather than coincident ones, this should automatically produce a mono mix with the crowd at a slightly lower level. This is helpful as stereo mixes can often stand effects at a higher level with the individual sounds still audible by virtue of their discrete positions. Spot effects, like the bat on ball, or the kick at a football match, need to be placed centrally to produce a clear image and allow for cutting from wide to close-up.

Commentary needs to be considered carefully. The decision may well be fixed if the commentator appears in vision, they will need to be placed centrally. Otherwise the commentary can be slightly off-centre, or if there are two commentators they could be placed left and right. The effect needs to be thought about. Centre images will appear to talk to the viewers, whilst images well off-centre will appear as part of the crowd, along with the viewer.

Outside broadcasts linking with the studio can have a position that is off-centre. This may well complement the practice of using large, in-vision monitors in the studio to make the participants appear to be talking to each other.

5.8.9 Documentary

Stereo sound effects can provide a great sense of reality in documentary programmes. Use of the full width of the stereo image will considerably enhance the show and help bring the material to life. Discussions and interviews should generally be close to centre, although a small amount of width is helpful in giving reality to the sound. This is also true of studio discussions; keeping it fairly narrow will also remove the concerns about matching with wide shots and close-ups alike.

5.8.10 Surround images

It is possible to record surround material using multiple microphones but this is complicated and in reality producers are unlikely to be happy with the time this might take.

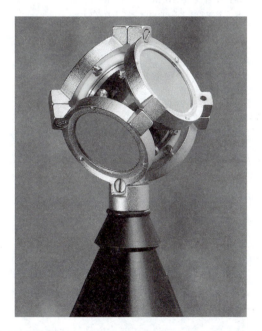

Figure 5.81 Surround sound microphone capsules – the signals can be processed to produce three-dimensional surround images (courtesy of Soundfield Ltd).

Purpose-produced microphones are manufactured and their output is processed using computer software to produce sound in any format from mono through stereo to three-dimensional surround. The signals are actually encoded for transmission and surround has become important to television broadcasters since the development of the Dolby Pro Logic system, which allows surround information to be transmitted via the existing stereo format. Further development with digital broadcasting systems will ensure that surround will be increasingly more common in the viewer's home.

It is true that one of the most important areas of location recording is the sound effects that surround the pictures and the location techniques employed to record these are reasonably straightforward. This is considerably helped by the fact the recorded four-channel surround signals can be processed later in dubbing, to steer the image. This means that even if the microphone was pointing the wrong way on location, it can be redirected later. In a real world, dialogue is normally recorded in mono, in as high a quality as possible, so that a clean version of the sound can be positioned in the image during the dubbing process.

5.8.11 Programme types

The suggestions already discussed for the imagery of stereo can be expanded to cover surround sound – if it will enhance the image by producing a stereo image it will almost certainly be of value to move to the next stage of full ambisonics. A very detailed discussion of surround images is beyond the scope of this book.

The artistic considerations are similar to those already illustrated for stereo; expansion to surround is as varied as the imagination can allow.

Very complex steering of the image will clearly be a job for the dubbing mixer, rather than the location or studio, where the time needed to experiment would be unacceptable. Effects and audience sounds are well worth spreading and the use of purpose-made surround microphones will be of great help as these produce good images which can be always be processed at a later date.

5.8.12 Summary

Stereo is certainly an important addition to television sound. It can bring rather flat audio images to life and is well worth the time and trouble it takes to achieve. Surround is a further extension towards audio reality and many programme types will benefit from its effects. The big caveat is that any form of sound presentation should be an integral part of the production, carefully applied to enhance the viewing experience.

5.9 The decibel

The decibel unit is logarithmic. If it is used to compare two signal powers, the value in dB would be

10 log (P_1/P_2). The log is to the base of 10 and here the ratio is between P_1 and P_2.

Thus, for example, the difference in power between 20 watts and 10 watts is:

$$10 \log \frac{20}{10} = 3 \text{ dB}$$

If it is required to compare voltage, then Ohm's law must be considered. Ohm's law states that there is a constant relationship between current (I), voltage (V) and resistance (R). This can be represented by:

$$I = \frac{V}{R}$$

As power in watts is voltage multiplied by current:

$$P = VI \text{ or } P = \frac{I^2}{R}$$

To compare two voltages, the difference in dB would therefore be:

$$10 \log \frac{V_1^2}{V_2^2}$$

Example

The ratio between 1.55 volts and 0.775 volts is:

$$10 \log \frac{1.55^2}{0.775^2} = 20 \log \frac{1.55}{0.775} = 6 \text{ dB}$$

Note:
A doubling of the power is an increase of 3 dB
A doubling of the voltage is an increase of 6 dB

In some cases the reference is specified by a suffix letter:

dB_u is used in Europe to denote a reference of 0.775 volts
dB_v denotes a reference of 1 volt
dB_m is a power reference of 1 mW.

6 Multicamera camerawork

6.1 Perennial technique

Across the wide range of camera techniques employed by film and video camera operators there are certain shared skills which are common to all forms of camerawork. Standard conventions in composition, camera movement and editing requirements (with small variations) are to be seen in the highest budgeted Hollywood blockbuster through to the modest two-minute regional magazine insert. Multicamera camerawork shares these common characteristics with the addition of a few specialist requirements.

6.1.1 Basic skills

This chapter identifies the following skills needed by a camera operator working on a multicamera production:

- **Technology** – an understanding of camera technology, lens characteristics and studio/OB arrangements.
- **Production methods** – an understanding of television production technique and working practices
- **Basic skills** – anticipation, preparation and concentration.
- **Operational skills** – basic camera and pedestal operational skills.
- **Picture-making skills** – positioning the camera and lens.
- **Intercutting** – matching shots and edit points.
- **Working in a camera crew** – an understanding of the camera operator's role in programme production and within a camera crew.
- **Recording and transmission** – types of multicamera production and transmission procedure.
- **Composition** – an understanding of shot composition.

6.1.2 Teamwork

In addition to the above skills is the crucial fact that television programme making is a group activity and good teamwork is an essential ingredient for its success. The ability to work in a team is often overlooked when discussing camerawork as if this is not part of the necessary operational skills required. It is in fact central to the job of a multicamera television camera operator.

The importance of working as a team and in a team cannot be overestimated. If you have difficulty working with people you will not enjoy multicamera camerawork. A television programme is created by a number of technicians exchanging information, modifying and fine-tuning the original concept.

As we have discussed, the script or brief is brought to the screen via a number of specialist crafts. There is discussion and consensus between all crafts channelled through the director. The ability to discuss, inform and quite often reach a compromise on what one might consider ideal practice is part of working in a camera crew and being part of a production crew.

Not least of the skills required when working in such a group activity is the ability to communicate. If a large part of TV production involves problem-solving then providing and seeking information about the specific project in hand is a key element in multicamera camerawork.

6.2 The basic principles of camerawork

There are a number of basic visual conventions used by the majority of camera operators operating broadcast cameras. Many of these standard camera techniques were developed in the early part of the twentieth century when the first film-makers had to xperiment and invent the grammar of editing, shot-size and the variety of camera movements that are now standard. As we discussed in Chapter 2, the ability to find ways of shooting subjects and then editing the shots together without distracting the audience was learnt by the commercial cinema over a number of years. The guiding concept was the need to persuade the audience that they were watching continuous action in 'real' time. This required the mechanics of film-making to be hidden from the audience; that is, to be invisible. Invisible technique places the emphasis on the content of the shot rather than production technique in order to achieve a seamless flow of images directing the viewer's attention to the narrative. It allows shot change to be unobtrusive and directs attention to what is contained within the frame and to smoothly move the camera to a new viewpoint without distracting the audience.

Figure 6.1

6.2.1 Alternative technique

There are alternative conventions of presentation which intentionally draw attention to the means of production. The production methods and camera movements are emphasized in order to simulate the realism of the unrehearsed shot or to remind the audience that they are watching a piece of fiction. Similar to news coverage, it appears as if the camerawork is surprised by the action. Camera movement in this alternative technique is often restlessly on the move, panning abruptly from subject to subject, making no effort to disguise the transitions and deliberately drawing attention to the means by which the images are brought to the viewer. This breaking down or subverting of the standard convention of an 'invisible' seamless flow of images has a number of different forms or styles. In general, television production has adopted the 'Hollywood' model of invisible technique.

6.2.2 A coherent technique

The point of this brief history of camerawork is rather than simply committing to memory a list of do's and don'ts about TV camerawork it is better to understand *why* these visual conventions exist. There is a coherent technique behind most TV camerawork. The way a shot is framed up, the way a zoom is carried out, the amount of headroom given to a certain size of shot is not simply a matter of personal taste, although that often affects shot composition – it is also a product of ninety-odd years of telling a story in pictures. The development of invisible technique

created the majority of these visual conventions. Knowing why a camerawork convention exists is preferable to simply committing to memory a string of instructions. You can then apply the principles of invisible technique whenever you meet up with a new production requirement.

6.3 Technology and technique

In 1888 the Kodak camera was launched as an easy, simple method of taking photographs. 'You press the button, we do the rest', was a sales slogan to demystify the arcane process of photography. In the early days of the craft, would-be photographers had to prepare their own glass plates, and then develop them in a combined camera/darkroom. After 1888, anybody could press a button and the camera and the chemist would do the rest. Training in photographic competence was condensed to the few minutes required to be instructed on which button to press.

Over one hundred years later, the sales promotion of video broadcast cameras has attempted to follow Kodak's example. In response to the needs of the TV industry, the craft of camerawork is promoted as a simple matter of knowing the position of a couple of buttons on the camera. After a very short training period, anybody can become a competent television camera operator.

If this was true about photography and broadcast camerawork, there should be no visual difference between a holiday snapshot and an advertising brochure of a resort, or a holiday video and a feature film shot at that resort. Of course there are differences, huge differences both in technology and technique. No one can simply press a button and become a photographer without considering the requirements of the technology they are using and an understanding of photographic technique.

Technology and technique intertwine. How you do something in broadcasting is dependent on what equipment you are using. It is not simply a question of being told which button to press in order to get a professional result. In television camerawork, an understanding of camera technology plus the ability to exploit and take into consideration the attributes of the camera and the lens characteristics is the basis of practical programme production. Although television and film production can only be created with technology, there seems to be a growing trend to ignore the mechanics and just press the button. Most camera equipment is now wrapped up with auto features in the hope of being user-friendly to technophobic customers, but technical operators should aim to understand what is happening when they are operating a camera rather than trust the old slogan of 'you press the button, the equipment will do the rest'. The following topics explain how camera equipment functions so that the operator can fully exploit technology to achieve programme requirements.

6.4 Operational aspects of the camera

6.4.1 The tools of the trade

The professional broadcast video camera used in multicamera production consists of a zoom lens (usually servo controlled from behind the camera) attached to a camera body containing three or four light sensors (CCDs – charge-coupled devices), electronic circuits to process the signal, an electronic viewfinder mounted on top of the camera (or a side-mounted monocular viewfinder), and various production facilities such as talkback, filter controls, mixed viewfinder switches, etc.

The three vital facilities that keep the camera operator in touch with programme production are viewfinder, talkback and cue lights. Without a good quality viewfinder the operator is unable to frame-up and focus the shot. Without talkback and cue lights they are unaware when the shot will be taken.

Operational controls which have a significant influence on the operation of the camera and transform it from an electronic device into a programme production tool are:

- servo controls of the zoom lens which allow a smooth take-off, precise control of speed of zoom and positive focus;

- a pan/tilt head to enable the fluid control of camera movement. The pan/tilt head should be adjustable to achieve precise balance in order to cater for a wide range of camera/lens combinations and additional attachments such as prompters. It should also have the facility to accommodate the varying centres of gravity (C of G) of different lens/camera/viewfinder combinations;

- a camera mounting which allows the camera operator to position the camera and lens quickly, smoothly and with precision for the desired shot and for the camera to remain at that setting until it is repositioned.

In addition to the operational controls there is obviously a requirement that cameras produce a high quality electronic picture. This will depend on the design characteristics of the camera's performance such as its sensitivity, resolution, contrast range, colour matrix, etc.

The technical quality of the image produced by the camera has an important influence on how the viewer responds to the production. However, the priorities for a camera operator are often centred on the handling ability of the camera, lens and mounting plus the need to work with a reasonable depth-of-field in an ad-lib situation coupled with the necessity of seeing the focus zone in the viewfinder. In addition, good communications are vital whether in a crowded studio or operating in a remote location. If the operators cannot hear or talk to the control room, then their contribution is severely impaired.

6.4.2 Lightweight v main line cameras

Development in technology has allowed cameras used in multicamera productions to become smaller and smaller. Miniaturization has bought gains and losses for camera operators. The gains have included easier rigs and de-rigs, remote control of cameras on cranes and access to areas previously restricted by the size and weight of larger cameras and mountings. The disadvantages have included tiny switches which are difficult to use at speed, especially when gloves are worn on location, the lack of a full range of production facilities such as controllable cursors in the viewfinder, a range of mixed viewfinder sources, easy access to filter controls, shot box facility and a smaller, limited movement range of the viewfinder.

Lightweight lens servo controls are sometimes not as positive or operationally as sensitive as those found on larger lens packages. A compromise solution is to mount a lightweight camera with large viewfinder and box lens (a large diameter lens encased in a protective cover) in a purpose-built harness which has the same approximate 'feel' and zoom range as a standard, full facility camera.

6.4.3 Facilities found on a multicamera production camera

The operational use of each of the following camera facilities is described in greater detail in a later chapter:

- **An electronic viewfinder** which is usually monochrome although some cameras have the choice of colour or mono. Focusing of a broadcast video camera is through the viewfinder. The definition of the electronic picture therefore must allow the camera operator to be the *first* person in the production chain to see loss of optical focus.
- **Viewfinder controls** – brightness, contrast, peaking (to accentuate edge definition as an aid to focusing); may also have controls for viewfinder image size.
- **Mixed viewfinder** controls to enable the viewfinder picture to be switched to other video combinations.
- **Cue lights** in the viewfinder, on the front of camera and on the front of lens are lit when the camera output is selected at the vision mixing panel. Cue lights outside the viewfinder (on the camera body and lens) can be switched out of circuit if required.
- **Zoom lens** – available in a range of zoom ratios.
- **Lens hood** – to help control flare and degradation and as partial protection against rain.
- **Zoom thumb control** on adjustable pan bar.

- **Zoom focus capstan** wheel on pan bar.
- **Range extender** for zoom lens.
- **Shot box** – to pre-set a range of zoom angles of views.
- **Headset** and headset jack points for talkback from and to the control room staff.
- **Talkback volume** – controlling production and engineering talkback and programme sound level to the headset.
- **Filter wheel** – fitted with a range of colour correction filters, neutral density and effects filters.
- **Crib card holder** and sometimes crib card illumination.

6.4.4 Exposure and vision control

A basic requirement in multicamera productions is that there are no mismatches of exposure or colour rendition when cameras are intercut. This is achieved by remotely controlling the aperture (affecting exposure) and colour adjustment of each camera by Vision Control where the output of each camera is compared, adjusted and matched. Built in ND (neutral density) filters and colour correction filters between lens and CCDs can also be switched in when required (see Section 4.19).

6.5 The zoom lens

6.5.1 Image size

The image formed by the lens on the face of the CCDs is called the image size of the lens. This must match

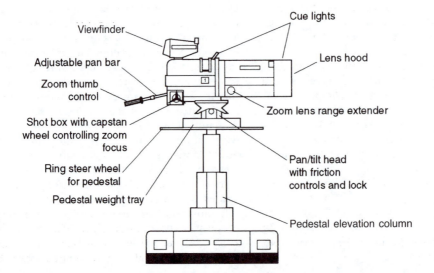

Viewfinder

Cue lights

Adjustable pan bar

Lens hood

Zoom thumb control

Zoom lens range extender

Shot box with capstan wheel controlling zoom focus

Ring steer wheel for pedestal

Pan/tilt head with friction controls and lock

Pedestal weight tray

Pedestal elevation column

Figure 6.2

the size of the camera sensor. Lenses designed for different sized formats (pick-up sensor dimension) may not be interchangeable. The image size produced by the lens may be much smaller than the pick-up sensor and probably the back focus (flange back) will not have sufficient adjustment.

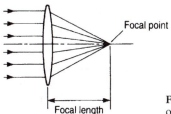

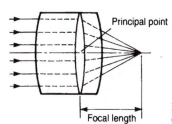

Figure 6.3 Focal length of a single lens.

Figure 6.4 Focal length of a compound lens.

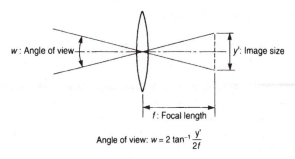

Angle of view: $w = 2 \tan^{-1} \dfrac{y'}{2f}$

Figure 6.5 Calculating angle of view

6.5.2 Focal length

When parallel rays of light pass through a convex lens, they will converge to one point on the optical axis. This point is called the focal point of the lens. The focal length of the lens is indicated by the distance from the centre of the lens or the principal point of a compound lens (e.g. a zoom lens) to the focal point. The longer the focal length of a lens, the smaller its angle of view will be; and the shorter the focal length of a lens, the wider its angle of view.

6.5.3 Angle of view

The approximate horizontal angle of view of a fixed focal length lens can be calculated by using its focal length and the size of the pick-up sensors of the camera.

For a camera fitted with ⅔″ CCDs the formula would be:

$$\text{Angle of view} = \frac{2 \tan^{-1} 8.8 \text{ mm (width of CCD)}}{2 \times \text{focal length (mm)}}$$

Although there are prime lenses (fixed focal length) available for ⅔″ camera/recorders, the majority of broadcast cameras are fitted with a zoom lens which can alter its focal length and therefore the angle of

view over a certain range. This is achieved by moving one part of the lens system (the variator) to change the size of the image and by automatically gearing another part of the lens system (the compensator) to simultaneously move and maintain focus. This alters the image size and therefore the effective focal length of the lens. To zoom into a subject, the lens must first be fully zoomed in on the subject and focused. Then zoom out to the wider angle. The zoom will now stay in focus for the whole range of its travel. If possible, always pre-focus before zooming in.

6.5.4 Zoom ratio

A zoom lens can vary its focal length. The ratio of the longest focal length it can achieve (the telephoto end) with the shortest focal length obtainable (its wide-angle end) is its zoom ratio.

A broadcast zoom lens will state zoom ratio and the wide angle focal length in one figure. A zoom quoted as 14 × 8.5 can therefore be decoded as a zoom with a 14:1 ratio starting at 8.5 mm focal length (angle of view = 54° 44') with the longest focal length of 14 × 8.5 mm = 119 mm (angle of view = 4° 14').

Lenses with ratios in excess of 50:1 can be obtained but the exact choice of ratio and the focal length at the wide end of the zoom will depend very much on what you want to do with the lens. Large zoom ratios are heavy, often require a great deal of power to operate the servo controls and have a reduced *f*-number (see below).

6.5.5 Extender

A zoom lens can be fitted with an internal extender lens system which allows the zoom to be used on a different set of focal lengths. A 2× extender on the 14 × 8.5 zoom mentioned above would transform the range from 8.5–119 mm to 17–238 mm, but it may also lose more than a stop at maximum aperture.

6.5.6 *f*-Number

The *f*-number of a lens is a method of indicating how much light can pass through the lens. It is inversely proportional to the focal length of the lens and directly proportional to the diameter of the effective aperture of the lens. For a given focal length, the larger the aperture of the lens the smaller its *f*-number and the brighter the image it produces. *f*-Numbers are arranged in a scale where each increment is multiplied by √2 (1.414). Each time the *f*-number is increased by one stop, the exposure is decreased by half:

1.4   2   2.8   4   5.6   8   11   16   22

The effective aperture of a zoom is not its actual diameter, but the diameter of the image of the diaphragm seen from in front of the lens. This is called the **entrance pupil** of the lens. When the lens is zoomed (i.e. the focal length is altered) the diameter of the lens which is proportional to focal length alters and also its entrance pupil. The *f*-number is small at the wide angle end of the zoom and larger at the narrowest angle. This may cause *f*-number drop or ramping at the telephoto end on an OB when the entrance pupil diameter equals the diameter of the focusing lens group and cannot become any larger.

6.5.7 Depth of field

Changing the *f*-number alters the depth of field – the portion of the field of view which appears sharply in focus. This zone extends in front and behind the subject on which the lens is focused and will increase as the *f*-number increases. The greater the distance of the subject from the camera, the greater the depth of field. The depth of field is greater behind the subject than in front and is dependent on the focal length of the lens.

f-Number and therefore depth of field can be adjusted by altering light level or by the use of neutral density filters.

6.5.8 Minimum object distance

The distance from the front of the lens to the nearest subject that can be kept in focus is called the minimum object distance (MOD). A 14 × 8.5 zoom would have an MOD of between 0.8 m and 0.65 m, whereas a larger zoom ratio lens (33:1) may have an MOD of over 2 m.

Many zooms are fitted with a macro mechanism which allows objects closer than the lens MOD to be held in focus. The macro shifts several lens groups inside the lens to allow close focus, but this prevents the lens being used as a constant focus zoom. Close focusing (inside the MOD) can sometimes be achieved by using the flange-back adjustment.

6.5.9 Flange-back

Flange-back (commonly called back focus) is the distance from the flange surface of the lens mount to the image plane of the pick-up sensor. Each camera type has a specific flange-back distance (e.g. 48 mm in air) and any lens fitted to that camera must be designed with the equivalent flange-back. There is usually a flange-back adjustment mechanism of the lens with which the flange-back can be adjusted by about ±0.5 mm. It is important when changing lenses on a camera to check that the flange-back position is correctly adjusted and to white balance the new lens.

6.5.10 Adjusting the back focus

Adjusting flange-back (back focus)

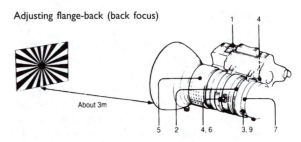

About 3m

Figure 6.6 (1) Open the lens to its widest aperture and adjust exposure by adding ND filters or adjusting shutter speed. (2) Select the widest lens angle. (3) Adjust for optimum focus with the flange-back control on the lens. (4) Zoom the lens in to its narrowest angle on an object at a distance from the camera and adjust the zoom focus for optimum sharpness. (5) Zoom out and repeat steps 2–4 until maximum sharpness is achieved at both ends of the zoom range. (6) Lock off the flange-back control, taking care that its sharpest focus position has not been altered.

6.5.11 Dual format cameras

The transition between 4:3 aspect ratio television and the conversion to 16:9 has produced an interim generation of dual format cameras. Different techniques are employed to use the same CCD for both formats.

If a CCD block design is optimized for the 4:3 shape and is then switched to the 16:9 format, lines are discarded at the top and bottom of the frame in order to convert the image area to a 16:9 shape (see Fig. 6.7(a)). As 4:3 working occupies the same area of the CCD as a standard 4:3 camera there is no change in angle of view or resolution. When switched to 16:9, however, there is a reduction in resolution and a decrease in vertical angle of view.

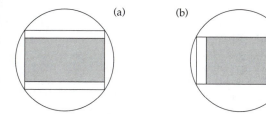

Figure 6.7

If the CCD block is optimized for 16:9 format working (see Fig. 6.7(b)), and is then switched to a 4:3 aspect ratio, the image area now occupies a smaller area than a standard 4:3 CCD image (see Fig. 6.7(a)), and therefore has a reduced resolution and a reduction in horizontal lens angle.

Some camera manufacturers claim that it is not possible to satisfy the competing demands of both formats; one of the formats will be compromised in resolution or change in lens angle. Other camera manufacturers claim that they can offer a switchable camera that retains the same number of pixels in both formats.

The horizontal angle of view is related to the focal length of the lens and the width of the CCD image. In a dual format camera, if the CCD is optimized for 16:9 format, the angle of view will be smaller working in the 4:3 format compared with working in 16:9 using the same focal length of the lens. At the shortest focal length the loss is about 20%. When switched to 4:3 working, there will be a 9 mm diameter image (see Fig. 6.8(c)) compared with the 11 mm diagonal image when working in 16:9 or the 11 mm diameter image of the conventional 4:3 format camera (see Fig. 6.08(a)).

This change in horizontal lens angle when switching formats can be remedied by employing an optical unit in the zoom (similar to an extender but producing negative magnification) which shortens the focal length when working in the 4:3 mode (see Fig. 6.8(d)). This 0.8 reduction of focal length produces the same range of angles of view as a conventional 4:3 camera using the equivalent zoom lens.

It is not essential when working in 16:9/4:3 dual aspect ratio camera to fit a lens with a 0.8 converter, only to have an awareness that the lens angle will be narrower than its equivalent use with a standard 4:3 camera.

6.6 Working as a camera assistant

6.6.1 Keep in touch

Never leave the studio or location unless you know what time working will recommence, especially if you are not on talkback. If you are new to multicamera working, try to keep in touch with the camera crew during production breaks – in television there are frequently last-minute changes to the daily schedule.

6.6.2 Monitors and eyeline

Monitors play an important part on the studio floor and are used by different members of the production crew. Their position is often very carefully sited to provide an unobstructed eyeline for the presenters, floor manager or boom operators (if the booms are not fitted with mini-monitors) and camera crew. Never stand in front of a monitor when watching the show. Stand to one side of the monitor and check that you are not obstructing anyone who is using the monitor. The same discipline applies to standing in front of an audience and obstructing their view of the show.

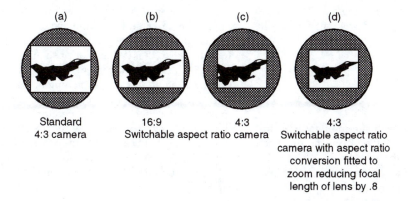

(a) Standard 4:3 camera

(b) 16:9 Switchable aspect ratio camera

(c) 4:3 Switchable aspect ratio camera

(d) 4:3 Switchable aspect ratio camera with aspect ratio conversion fitted to zoom reducing focal length of lens by .8

Figure 6.8

On location, monitors are crucial for keeping reporters, commentators, etc. in touch with the transmitted or recorded output.

In-vision monitors are used to conduct interviews with participants who are not in the studio or to display visual material. Large screen displays and video walls (numerous monitors stacked close to each other displaying a segment of a video image) are also used for a variety of purposes in-vision.

6.6.3 Switched feeds

A monitor can be fed with a single video source such as the output of the studio or location or it can be fed with two or more sources which are switchable on the monitor and therefore serve a dual purpose during a production.

It can also be remotely switched and fed a number of video sources from a technical area or vision mixing panel. It is therefore important when rigging a monitor that the video cable is plugged to the correct monitor video point on the wall box. These monitor points can be cross-plugged in the studio technical area to provide whatever video feed is required.

Studio monitors require a mains cable which is usually bound with the video cable or may be an integral dual video/mains cable. Location monitors may be battery fed if a mains power supply is inaccessible. Check the condition of the power cable before plugging into the technical mains socket. This is a separate power supply to isolate broadcast equipment from any induced interference on the standard mains supply of the studio complex.

Secure the combined power/video cable to the wall box by passing it under the safety bar (if installed) and then tie off the cable using a clove hitch. All monitor cables crossing fire lanes should be ramped or covered with appropriate rubber mats, flown (above head height), or stuck down with special gaffer tape that has been printed with hazard stripes. If the cables are flown, remember to use quick-release knots to avoid wasting time at the de-rig untying tight and complicated 'granny' knots.

6.6.4 Prompters

Prompters attached to cameras are in effect specialist monitors and may require a feed from the prompter controller and a power supply.

Note: Electrical equipment should be periodically tested by a competent person and date-stamped.

6.6.5 Cable bashing

One of the first jobs that may be given to a trainee in a studio production is cabling. This basic job is often essential on a complex, fast-moving show, and it teaches the six basic principles of multicamera camerawork:

- preparation;
- anticipation;
- concentration;
- invisible technique;
- silent operation;
- teamwork.

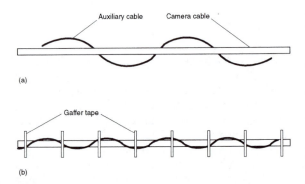

Figure 6.9 Wrapping a cable to a camera cable.

Preparation
Look at the script to find out how the show is broken down into sections, recording periods, etc. Try to get an overall picture of the working day. Check that all camera cables are eighted with no obstruction (e.g. a ladder has not been parked on top of a cable since it was rigged). Check to see where each camera is working and if there are repositions during recording or transmission.

Anticipation
During rehearsal, watch for cameras that work into other camera cable loops and make certain there is sufficient cable laid out in front of a camera tracking into the set so that it does not push another camera's cable. Make certain a camera moving on shot is not pulling a length of cable stretching across the studio. Give sufficient slack cable close to the camera on the move so that the camera operator is pulling the minimum length of cable. Be aware at all times of how much cable is available to each camera and that the cable is free of obstruction (e.g. not snagged around a boom wheel, caught on a stage weight, etc.).

Concentration

Do not let your attention drift towards the content of the show unless it is linked with cues for camera movement you are involved with. You have probably done a good job if, on leaving the studio at the end of the day, you can only supply details of the production which were linked with camera moves and cables.

Invisible technique

Being invisible when cable clearing is an asset to the production. Your activity will not disturb the front-of-camera people or audience and it is good preparation for practising 'invisible' technique when you progress to camerawork. Be aware at all time which camera is 'on-shot' and keep out of shot. Constantly check left, right and behind you to avoid appearing in vision.

Silent operation

One of the reasons that someone is needed on cables, especially in quiet shows such as discussion or orchestral music, is that cables being dragged across the floor can be noisy. Your job in cable clearing is to lift the cable off the floor if it is generating noise. Also remember that you may be ultra-efficient dashing here there and everywhere throwing cables

out of the way as you go, but if you create noise in the process you will have failed. Wear soft-soled shoes.

Frequently, a monitor may need to be repositioned during a recording or transmission. If it is your job to move it, mark up the positions and make a note of when it is to be moved. A basic rule in any simple activity such as repositioning a monitor is applicable all the way through multicamera production practice – if possible, never do something on recording or transmission that was not done on rehearsal. There are many exceptions to this injunction, but until you have sufficient production experience – stick to the rule.

6.6.6 Preparation and anticipation

Each member of the crew has to work in the real time of the programme and all decisions are governed by the timescale of the event. As we discussed in Section 2.6, whilst the planning may have taken months or weeks and the rehearsal days or hours, transmission is governed by the timescale of the event covered. Shot decisions have to be made in seconds with no time-out to consider the best way of tackling a particular situation. Preparation and anticipation are essential in order to create the time for fast camerawork.

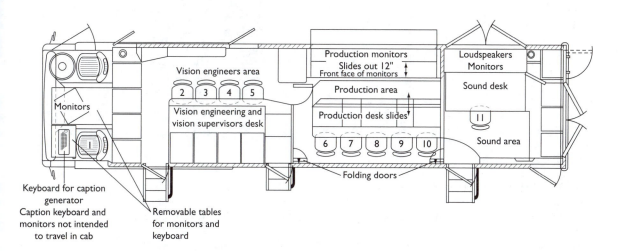

Monitors

Keyboard for caption generator
Caption keyboard and monitors not intended to travel in cab

Removable tables for monitors and keyboard

1	Caption generator operator	6	Engineering manager
2	Vision engineer	7	Editor/producer
3	Vision supervisor	8	Vision mixer
4	Vision engineer	9	Director
5	Vision engineer	10	Production assistant
		11	Sound supervisor

Figure 6.10

6.6.7 Assisting with pedestal work

As we will see in Section 6.8, a camera mounted on a pedestal is a very flexible method of repositioning the camera on and off shot. Most camera operators operating on such a mounting usually like to control all camera movement themselves. The pedestal can be controlled in a very precise manner by the camera operator, but sometimes a shot requires the assistance of a tracker.

Assisting with a pedestal development shot may be the first involvement a trainee will experience with camera movement on shot. There are a number of reasons why a camera operator operating a pedestal may need assistance, but crabbing the camera at speed parallel to the action is one reason for a request for a tracker.

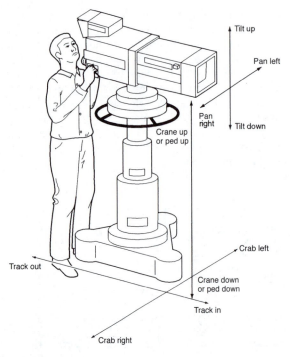

Figure 6.11 The language of camera movement

It is easier to push the pedestal at speed than to attempt to pull it running backwards. Make certain during rehearsal that the start and end positions of the camera are marked and that the end position mark can be seen during the move to avoid an overshoot. Decide on the best method of dealing with the camera cable, keeping it clear of the feet of the camera operator and of the pedestal. Mark up a running order or make a rough camera card for all movements that need your assistance with a description of the action rather than shot number if you are not wearing a radio headset.

Agree with the camera operator how they will signal when the movement is to begin. They may ask you to take your own cue from the artiste movement or they may want to cue you. Always be ready to adapt and adjust to the artiste movement rather than simply going to a pre-rehearsed mark. In general, camera movement will start with artiste movement and end with artiste movement (see Section 6.14.3).

Help with pedestal work may also occur because of the precision needed in focusing whilst moving. The camera operator may need an extra hand to ring-steer the pedestal whilst they reframe and shift focus. Very fast moves on shot and fast reposition between shots are additional reasons why pedestal work requires assistance.

Essential points

- Before rehearsal, equip yourself with marker/pen and marking up material – tape/timber crayon, etc.
- Check cable guard clearance and ensure there are no loops of ancillary cables attached to the camera cable (e.g. lighting cables, prompt, etc.) which could catch under the cable guards.
- Mark the floor according to position and movement.
- Note all positions and movements by marking the card for quick reference.
- Pace the movement to the action.
- Watch your cable and get assistance with cable clearing if necessary.
- All movement must be silent and safe.
- Never endanger yourself, other members of staff, the public or equipment.
- Check that all your marks are still legible before transmission/recording.
- On transmission/recording watch for the camera operator's hand signals.
- Anticipate fast repositions before they occur.
- Work to the cue light and the shot number.

Figure 6.12

6.6.8 Tracking a dolly

The technique required to track a dolly is one step up from assisting on a pedestal because of the important additional responsibility that the camera operator, seated on the front of the dolly, places on the tracker to get him or her and the camera to the rehearsed position. If the rehearsed tracking line is missed or the speed of the track is mismatched with the action, there is nothing the camera operator can do to salvage the shot. The same criterion applies for accurate marking up the floor and camera card plus the need to watch the camera operator for signals to adjust the dolly if required.

The tracker will now be wearing a headset and this will be his or her first opportunity of experiencing the flow of shot numbers, the director's instructions synchronized with programme sound which underpins all continuous multicamera camerawork.

If there are a number of positions on the same tracking line, mark a ladder (i.e. a large 'ruler' on the floor with equal spaced units) and number it alphabetically so that each shot or movement can have a start and a finish letter assigned. Make certain that all shots have an assigned position marked on the camera card and any additional information, such as a fast move, is easily read quickly from the page. There is frequently no time to read long elaborate instructions.

Any movement with a dolly must not endanger yourself or the camera operator, other members of the production crew and cast or any audience or members of the public present. Finally, movement must not endanger the equipment you are using.

6.7 Camera mountings

6.7.1 Choosing a camera mounting

There are a wide range of camera mountings available to cover the diverse requirements of multicamera programme-making in the studio and on location. No one camera mounting will necessarily embrace all styles of camerawork and all weights of equipment.

The first selection criterion is to know if the mounting is to be transported to its operating position (i.e. at a location rather than operated daily in a studio). Equipment that may have to be carried up stairs or rigged in difficult locations will need to be lighter and more easily rigged and de-rigged compared with equipment used permanently in a studio.

The second requirement to be considered is if the mounting is to be used to reposition the camera 'on-shot' or if it is simply to have the ability to reposition 'off-shot'. A tripod on wheels (if the ground surface is suitable) can be repositioned to a new camera position, but is unsuitable for development shots. A pedestal mounting with steerable wheels and smooth adjustment of height will allow a development on shot if operated on a level floor.

The third consideration is the all-up weight of camera, lens and, possibly, camera operator the mounting will need to support. The simplest way of moving a lightweight camera is to carry it on the

shoulder (on or off-shot) although this will not give such a smooth movement as using a harness around the torso to steady the camera. There are a range of lightweight tripods, portable pedestals and jib-arms that can be used with a lightweight camera. There is also the facility to rig a lightweight camera on the end of a boom arm and to remotely control its movement on a servo-driven pan/tilt head and to remotely control the lens. At the other end of the scale there are cranes capable of elevating a full facility camera and camera operator to a lens height of over twenty feet.

6.7.2 Pan/tilt heads

A good pan and tilt head will have adjustment for the centre of gravity (C of G) of the combination of camera/recorder, lens and viewfinder in use. If the C of G is not adjusted the camera will either be difficult to move from the horizontal or it will tilt forwards or backwards. Adjustment of the C of G balance should not be confused with mid-point balance which involves positioning the camera and lens to find the point of balance on the head.

The setting of the friction or drag control of the head depends on the shot and personal preference. Using a very narrow lens for an extreme close shot (e.g. a bird nesting) may require much more friction than that needed to pan the camera smoothly when following rapid impromptu movement (e.g. skating). Some camera operators prefer a heavy drag or 'feel' on the head so that there is weight to push against, while others remove all friction allowing the head to be panned at the slightest touch.

6.7.3 Continuous adjustment

Live or 'recorded as live' television production requires a camera mounting that can be quickly and silently repositioned 'off' shot and which has the flexibility to be smoothly positioned 'on' shot to accomplish pre-rehearsed camera movements. It must also be capable of instant small adjustments in track or crab mode to compensate for masking by artistes or wrong positioning. A usable shot must always be provided in a continuous programme even though the position of the artistes is not as rehearsed.

In a studio these requirements are best served by a pedestal camera mounting controlled by the camera operator who can instantly compensate without misunderstanding or delay between tracker and camera operator.

The camera operator, whilst operating the camera, can also move the camera forwards, backwards or

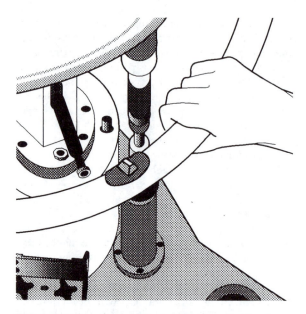

Figure 6.13 The raised pointer indicates the direction in which the pedestal will move and is a constant reminder of the position of the pedestal wheels. Mark up any critical camera position and number or letter the position and make a note on the camera card. The position marked 'STEER' on the base of the pedestal allows one set of wheels to be unlocked and the pedestal base swivelled to the optimum operating position. Return the wheel to 'CRAB' for normal movement.

sideways by means of the ring steering wheel which alters the direction of the double wheel positioned at each corner of the base; the operator can also alter the camera height. This must be accomplished silently, smoothly and with minimum effort. Continuous adjustment of the pedestal requires a smooth floor and complete mastery in the use of a pedestal.

6.7.4 The pedestal design

The most common camera mounting in a multicamera production studio is the pedestal. The majority of studios are equipped with Vinten pedestals which are designed for a range of different weights and models of camera. These mountings have a triangular base with a pair of wheels at each corner controlled from a large ring steering wheel attached to the top of a hydraulically balanced column which can be smoothly raised or lowered.

The larger pedestals (e.g. the Fulmar) with pan/tilt head, full facility camera, lens and lens controls can have an all-up weight of over 300 kg whilst a smaller lightweight pedestal and camera can be less than 140 kg. Moving 300 kg (5.9 cwt) from a standing start, paced to the speed of the action covered whilst

maintaining good composition and focus, requires a specialist technique that is developed with experience. If you are new to multicamera camerawork, do not underestimate the skills needed to move and stop the pedestal fluently, on cue and with precision.

Smoothly positioning the camera 'on' and 'off' shot requires learning skills in the use of the mounting. Practise as much as possible when not engaged in rehearsal, but remember to defocus or cap up the camera to avoid distracting control room staff (who may be involved in rehearsing another sequence) by the moving images on your camera's preview monitor.

6.8 Operational skills

6.8.1 Eye, hand and body coordination

Invisible camera technique requires camera movement to be unobtrusive and matched to content. Panning and tilting the camera is a basic skill that requires considerable practice until there is complete coordination between the eye and the hand on the pan bar. A requirement of good camerawork is the ability to move the camera smoothly and to be able to accelerate movement and decelerate movement. Moving the pedestal 'on' shot should become as familiar and easy as driving a car. Practice and experience, anticipation of the unexpected and the avoidance of impossible moves are all part of good pedestal control.

The control of the camera during panning and tilting requires a combination of:

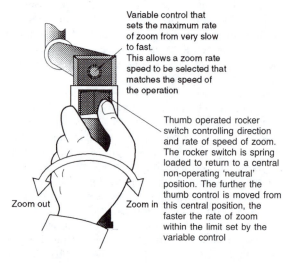

Variable control that sets the maximum rate of zoom from very slow to fast. This allows a zoom rate speed to be selected that matches the speed of the operation

Thumb operated rocker switch controlling direction and rate of speed of zoom. The rocker switch is spring loaded to return to a central non-operating 'neutral' position. The further the thumb control is moved from this central position, the faster the rate of zoom within the limit set by the variable control

Zoom out   Zoom in

Figure 6.14

- correct friction (and cams);
- anticipation;
- correct body posture;
- correct choice of lens angle.

6.8.2 Condition of the pan/tilt head

Controlled smooth camera movement cannot be achieved unless the correct friction has been selected for the programme format. The amount of friction constraining vertical and horizontal movement is often a personal choice. Each camera operator needs to balance out the need for easy flexible movement against the operational difficulties of holding the camera steady when tracking, crabbing and panning the camera without friction.

A compromise amount of friction is therefore selected which suits the programme requirements and weather conditions. Using a long lens continuously at its narrow end in a high wind may require more friction than the same operation in a flat calm. It has been observed that when using the extreme narrow end of a 70-1 zoom lens ($2\times$ range extender lens angle approximately $0.28°$) the pulse in the operator's hand on the pan bar can be detected by a rhythmic movement in the frame.

6.8.3 The pan

The simplest camera movement is the pan. It is often used to give visual variety amongst a number of static shots, but usually the main use of a pan, apart from keeping a moving subject in frame, is to show relationships.

There is obviously the need to begin a pan with a well balanced shot that has intrinsic interest in its own right. The second requirement is to find visual elements that allow the pan to flow smoothly and inevitably to the end framing.

Essential operational points when panning
- Motivate the pan by action, to show relationships or to reveal new information.
- Ensure that the end frame has significance.
- Match speed of movement to mood and content.
- Synchronize all reframing with the action.
- Use dominant lines or movement to bridge first and end frame.
- Use the appropriate lens angle.
- Accelerate and decelerate the pan in the correct ratio.

Figure 6.15

The end frame must be well balanced and again of intrinsic interest. The pan alerts the viewer that the camera is moving to reveal some image of importance or interest. If this anticipation is denied and the end framing is quickly cut away from because it contains no visual interest, then the movement is an anti-climax.

6.8.4 Choice of lens angle

Even the most experienced camera operators will experience difficulties in accomplishing very small detailed pans and tilts when using a very narrow lens angle. The difficulty of controlled movement will be exacerbated if camera and lens are fitted with ancillary equipment such as prompters, lamps or microphones. Panning with a lens angle of less than 1° requires a very small movement on the pan bar for a very big movement in the frame.

6.8.5 Anticipation

Panning along a line of objects of unequal height will quickly demonstrate the need to anticipate change in framing. Good camerawork requires fast reflexes in reframing during a continuous move combined with smooth and unobtrusive transitions. Anticipating the direction of a compensating diagonal move at an early stage will avoid jerky and erratic camerawork. Practise smooth controlled camera movement by panning, in a tight shot, across a camera cable which is snaking across the floor. This also provides focus practice.

6.8.6 Body position

Anticipating the end of a pan or tilt allows the camera operator be in a position so that a comfortable operating stance can be adopted. The more body stress there is in following action the more likely that changes in camera movement will be erratic and noticeable.

6.8.7 Speed of movement matched to mood and content

The speed of a panning shot must be matched to content. Panning fast over complex detail produces irritation – it is impossible to take in the information. Panning slowly over large, unbroken, plain areas may provoke boredom.

The speed of a pan across a symphony orchestra playing a slow majestic piece will be at a different speed to a pan across the orchestra when it is playing at full gallop. Speed of movement must match mood and content. If it is required to be discreet and invisible then movement must begin when the action begins and end when the action ends. A crane or tilt-up with a person rising must not anticipate the move, neither must it be late in catching up with the move. Any movement that is bursting to get out of the frame must either be allowed camera movement to accommodate it or there is a need for a cut to a wider shot.

6.8.8 Using dominant lines and movement

It is almost always necessary to help with the visual change caused by a pan by finding some visual connection between the first and the last composition. One of the ways of achieving 'invisible' movement is to use dominant horizontal, vertical or angled lines to pan along in order to move to a new viewpoint. Panning on lines in the frame allows for visual continuity between two images and appears to provide a satisfactory visual link.

6.8.9 Using movement to motivate a pan

The same visual link can be achieved by using movement within the frame to allow a pan or a camera movement from one composition to another. The most common convention in an establishing shot is to follow a person across the set or location, to allow new information about the geography of the setting as the shot develops. The person the camera follows may be unimportant, but is used visually to take the camera from a starting composition to possibly the main subject.

6.8.10 Control of pedestal

At each corner of the base of the pedestal is a pair of wheels. Their direction is controlled by the large steering ring positioned under the trim weight storage tray. The direction of the alignment of the wheels is communicated to the hand by a raised red indicator attached to the steering ring so that without looking away from the viewfinder, information is always available as to the direction the pedestal will move when pushed.

This centre ring control allows the camera operator to crab, steer and adjust height on shot with one hand (usually the right hand) while controlling framing via the pan bar with the other hand.

The alignment of the base of the pedestal can be adjusted to avoid constantly working with a corner of the base directly behind the camera.

6.8.11 Moving between shots

Practice is required to move the pedestal efficiently and quickly via the ring steering wheel. Multicamera camerawork often involves a number of repositions of the camera during a sequence or scene and so movement 'off shot' has to be fast and precise. Move the pedestal to the new position first before adjusting height.

If the framing of the shot relies on an exact position of the lens (e.g. a reflection in a mirror, an over-the-shoulder two-shot) then the base of the pedestal requires a precise mark on the studio floor. Mark an arc following the base of the pedestal and add a number or letter which corresponds to the shot number and note this on the camera card.

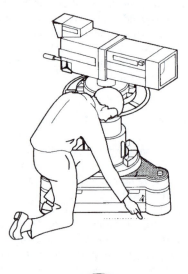

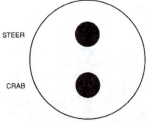

Figure 6.16 Mark up any critical camera position and number or letter the position and make a note on the camera card. The position marked 'STEER' on the base of the pedestal allows one set of wheels to be unlocked and the pedestal base swivelled to the optimum operating position. Return the wheel to 'CRAB' for normal movement.

The marks made with a floor crayon are quickly erased by pedestal and cable movement across them. They will need remarking as there is a great deal of activity across the floor between rehearsal and transmission/recording. 'Lo-tack' tape (designed to be easily removed on de-rig) is more permanent, but there is a risk, if there are too many marks on the studio floor, of bumping over the tape when moving on shot and causing a jump in the framing.

6.8.12 Repositioning the camera at speed

When repositioning the camera at speed across the studio floor, turn the camera in the direction of travel as it is easier to push a camera than to run backwards. Make certain that you walk around the pedestal in a direction that provides sufficient slack cable between camera and cable clamp on the pedestal base rather than winding the cable loop around the column. Pushing the camera onto a new set also allows you to start composing the shot before you come to rest and speeds up the move.

6.9 Focus and depth of field

6.9.1 Introduction to focus

Focusing is the act of adjusting the lens elements to achieve a sharp image at the focal plane. Objects either side of this focus zone may still look reasonably sharp depending on their distance from the lens, the lens aperture and lens angle. The area covering the objects that are in acceptable focus is called the **depth of field**.

The depth of field can be considerable if the widest angle of the zoom is selected and, whilst working with a small aperture, a subject is selected for focus at some distance from the lens. When zooming into this subject, the depth of field or zone of acceptable sharpness will decrease.

6.9.2 Capstan servo control

If the television camera is being operated from behind the camera using a large viewfinder, focusing is usually achieved by a capstan servo control mounted on the right of the camera. The position of the focus control and its operation will vary depending on country, but the standard convention in the UK is to turn the capstan clockwise to focus forward (i.e. objects closer to the lens) and to turn the capstan anti-clockwise for objects further from the lens. If a portable camera is being used with a monocular viewfinder then focus is usually controlled by the focus ring on the lens.

6.9.3 Follow focus

Television is often a 'talking head' medium and the eyes need to be in sharp focus. Sharpest focus can be checked 'off-shot' by rocking the focus zone behind and then in front of the eyes. Detecting 'on-shot' which plane of the picture is in focus is more difficult.

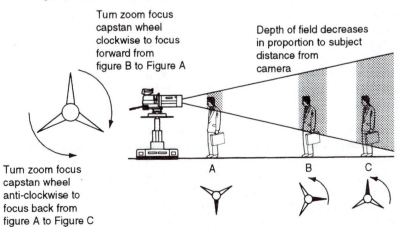

Focus capstan wheel
The three variables that affect depth of field are :
■ distance from camera of principal subject in focus
■ aperture of the lens
■ lens angle selected

Turn zoom focus capstan wheel clockwise to focus forward from figure B to Figure A

Depth of field decreases in proportion to subject distance from camera

Turn zoom focus capstan wheel anti-clockwise to focus back from figure A to Figure C

A   B   C

Figure 6.17

You, as the camera operator, must be the first to detect loss of focus, but this can only be achieved if the viewfinder definition is better than the viewer's image and the plane of sharpest focus can be seen without rocking focus.

As camera or subject moves there will be a loss of focus which needs to be corrected. The art of focusing is to know which way to focus and not to overshoot. Practise following focus as someone walks towards the lens (UK convention – turn the capstan clockwise). Turn the capstan anti-clockwise as the subject moves away from camera. Practise throwing focus from one subject to another.

6.9.4 Pre-focusing

Sometimes it is not possible to focus on a subject before the shot is required. Typically, as a presenter appears in the frame, the camera is cut to. Without some method of pre-focusing, the chances are that the shot will be soft and focus will have to be tweaked 'on-shot'. The solution is to focus up on the subject during rehearsal and then swing the camera (without altering focus) to find another part of the set which is sharp. On transmission/recording pre-focus on that object and then reposition for the subject to enter frame. Make certain that both camera position and subject position are marked.

6.9.5 Zoom lens and focus

A zoom lens is designed to keep the same focal plane throughout the whole of its range (provided the back focus has been correctly adjusted). Even if a zoom has not been rehearsed, always pre-focus whenever possible on the tightest shot of the subject. This is the best way of checking focus and it also prepares for a zoom-in if required.

Some focus demand units have small indentations which can be adjusted (off-shot or during rehearsal) to indicate a specific focus point on the zoom. This allows a pre-rehearsed second focus point to be arrived at by turning the capstan focus and feeling with the hand when the pre-set indentations are aligned.

6.9.6 Blind zooming

When zooming into a subject on which the focus has not been predetermined (blind zooming) it is best to be focused slightly back behind the subject so that you know where your zone of focus is. As focusing becomes more critical at the end of the zoom range, focus can be pulled forward. This helps to correct focus the right way. Correcting the wrong way, for example focusing back when you should have focused forward because you did not know where the zone of focus was positioned, is more obvious than a slight out-of-focus shot for part of the zoom. Practise focusing by fast-zooming into a subject and then hitting the correct focus in one movement. Keep varying the distance of the objects zoomed into so that fast accurate focusing becomes instinctive.

6.9.7 Pulling focus

Within a composition, visual attention is directed to the subject in sharpest focus. Attention can be transferred to another part of the frame by throwing focus onto that subject. Use the principle of invisible technique and match the speed of the focus pull to the motivating action.

If the focus is on a foreground person facing camera with a defocused background figure and the foreground subject turns away from camera, focus can be instantly thrown back to the background. A slower focus pull would be more appropriate in music coverage, for example moving off the hands of a foreground musician to a background instrumentalist. Avoid long focus pulls that provide nothing but a extended defocused picture before another subject comes into sharp focus unless this is motivated by the action (e.g. the subjective visual experience of someone recovering consciousness).

6.9.8 Differential focus

Differential focus is deliberately using a narrow depth of field to emphasize the principal subject in the frame in sharp focus which is contrasted with a heavily out-of-focus background.

A narrow depth of field can be achieved by reducing lighting levels and opening up the lens aperture to achieve correct exposure, or by using a neutral density filter to reduce light entering the lens requiring the aperture to be opened and reducing depth of field, or by increasing the shutter speed.

6.9.9 Split focus

Because of aperture or lens angle it is sometimes not possible, in an unrehearsed situation, to hold two subjects at different distances from the lens in sharp focus. The focus therefore has to be split between them with either one or the other slightly soft.

6.10 Pedestal technique

6.10.1 Checklist of technique

The main elements affecting smooth pedestal movement on shot are:

- the condition of the floor;
- lens angle;
- movement and composition;
- mechanical condition of the pedestal;
- camera cable;
- viewfinder;
- space for the development;
- focus;
- eye, hand and body coordination.

6.10.2 The condition of the floor

Check over the floor for dropped nails or other small debris left from the scenery set and light. Check over painted or 'Martacked' floor areas for over-painted marking tapes, bubbles or general wear and tear of the floor surface. Have the floor swept and if possible plan the camera movement to avoid the worst conditions. The effects of an uneven floor will be exacerbated by working at the top of the pedestal column or by tracking on a narrow lens angle.

> **Essential operational points**
> - The camera and the mounting must be balanced and the head fitted with correct cams to ensure smooth operation.
> - The wheels must be free from any debris picked up from the studio.
> - Always try to operate with the flat side of the pedestal base behind the camera.
> - Whenever possible, position wheels 90 degrees to action so that instant adjustment to avoid masking can be achieved.

Figure 6.18

6.10.3 Lens angle

Select the correct lens angle from the zoom range for the camera development required. A long track on a narrow angle will not only be difficult to hold steady and in focus, but will provide little or no change in the perspective of mass in the shot (see Section 6.16.3). There is no motivation for a camera move if there is no significant change in the composition of the shot.

In general, the wider the lens angle in use (e.g. >30°) the steadier the movement and the greater

control of framing and focus. Often a small amount of camera movement on a wide angle provides a substantial change in the shot.

6.10.4 Movement and composition

Good composition must be maintained throughout the pedestal movement. This can be achieved by starting and ending with good compositions and ensuring a smooth transition between these frames by the use of pivot points, by motivating the movement with action within the frame and at a speed that matches the content of the shot. A good pedestal development shot should provide a smooth, unobtrusive, continuous change in visual interest with no 'dead' area between the initial and final image.

6.10.5 Mechanical condition of the pedestal

Check for pieces of gaffer tape, nails or small debris embedded or stuck to the pedestal wheels. Check that the column of the pedestal is balanced. Changes in temperature affect the hydraulic system of the pedestal. If necessary transfer the trim weights stored at the base of the pedestal to the weight tray above the ring steering wheel. The balance of the camera should have been adjusted in the 'start of day checks' and a check made at the same time that the correct cams are fitted in the pan and tilt head for the camera/lens and prompter (if fitted) in use. Other mechanical checks such as cable guard clearance and slackness in the ring-steer assembly will also identify problems with the smoothness of the pedestal movement.

> **Operational points when tracking**
> - Select a lens angle wider than 25 degrees.
> - Adjust the pedestal to allow you to work within an arc of the base.
> - Adjust the viewfinder to fit the movement.
> - Have sufficient slack cable.
> - Check the floor space is clear for the move.
> - Position ring steer in the direction of track.
> - Use hand on ring steer and foot to kick off movement.
> - Concentrate on steering and shot development before adjusting focus (if needed) when approaching the principal subject in frame.
> - Glide to a halt following a non-linear speed of movement.
> - When tracking out, focus change is critical at the start of the move and movement has to be maintained without the use of the ring steer.
> - Avoid sweeping cable under your feet with the base of the camera when tracking out.

Figure 6.19

6.10.6 Space for the development

It seems self-evident that a camera move can only be attempted if there is sufficient floor space unimpeded by other equipment, set or artistes, that there is sufficient set to cover the whole of the move (including 'shooting off' the top of the set) and that the camera will not end up 'in vision' in the following shot. Although the above criteria may be obvious, it is not unknown for camera operators to set out on a complex development shot to find that they have fallen foul of one of these pitfalls.

6.10.7 Focus

Needless to say, however fluent the camera development may be, the significant subject in the frame must stay in focus during the whole of the move. There is no short-cut technique to focus pulling on the move. You need one hand on the pan bar to continuously reframe the shot, one hand on the ring steer to control the direction and to provide the impetus for the movement and one hand on the focus wheel to adjust focus. Three-handed camera operators are in great demand on multicamera pedestal work!

Some development shots involve staying the same distance from the principal subject and therefore focus is not a problem. A wide angle lens development with a large depth of field may also allow the control of the pedestal with both hands but with most tracks and crabs some stage is reached when the right hand must be freed to give a quick tweak to the focus. The right direction of wheel travel and a 'kick off' with the foot often allows the left hand on the pan bar to keep the camera moving while the right hand can be positioned on the focus wheel. Try to arrange the direction of the pedestal so that this type of movement control is achieved if a large focus pull is required.

6.11 Tracking on a pedestal

6.11.1 Tracking

Tracking is moving the camera towards or away from the principal subject in the frame. The three operational adjustments required in tracking are control of camera mounting and camera, framing and focusing. In addition, there is the need for the track to have a reason or some type of motivation.

6.11.2 Before tracking

If possible, arrange the pedestal base so that you are working within an arc of the base. Position the angle of the viewfinder so that you can see the whole of the image from the start to the end of the track. Have sufficient slack cable for the whole of the track to avoid pulling a large length of cable across the studio floor. Check that nothing will impede your movement throughout the range of the track such as floor coverings, furniture, other cameras, cables or people! Check that your end position will not finish in the succeeding shot. Check that the lens angle selected is suitable for tracking (see Section 6.10.3).

6.11.3 To track in

Position the ring steering wheel to point the wheels in the direction of the track (preferably off-shot) and holding the ring steer with the right hand at the position of the indicator and holding (not gripping) the pan bar with the left hand, push with the right foot to get the pedestal moving and continue the movement with the hand on the ring steer.

Adjust the framing of the shot as you track in (see Section 6.13), and whilst keeping the momentum of the movement with the left hand on the pan bar, the right hand can be released from the ring steer to the focus capstan in order to adjust focus if necessary as you approach the principal subject in the frame. If the design of the focus capstan is sufficiently robust, the right hand can also be used to push the pedestal.

Reduce the push on the pedestal towards the end of the track to allow the track to glide imperceptibly to a halt. Avoid abrupt changes of movement unless this is required by the motivation for the move. Most camera movement follows a non-linear rate of change. The move or zoom is started imperceptibly before accelerating to the maximum speed required and then falling off as the move reaches its end point. Audio fades often use the same technique with the sound gradually receding until it unobtrusively disappears so that the listener is unaware of the exact point of the completed fade. This is another aspect of invisible technique – visual or audio changes are softened to ease transitions.

6.11.4 To track out

Tracking out is operationally more demanding than tracking in as moving backwards is more awkward than moving forwards. Overcoming the inertia required to get the 5.5 cwt pedestal/camera moving has to be provided by the right hand on the ring steer without the benefit of a push-off with the foot. Also, the biggest correction of focus will occur in the first part of the movement, which requires the right hand to be controlling the capstan focus.

The technique is to pull on the ring steer with the right hand to get the pedestal moving and then quickly transfer this hand to the capstan and refocus whilst keeping the pedestal on the move with the left hand on the pan bar. A fast move will cover an unsynchronized focus pull provided the shot is sharp when the movement ends. Focusing is much more critical during a slow move and the camera movement must be activated through the pan bar and focus capstan as the right hand cannot be released to the ring steer or loss of focus will not be corrected in time.

All the conditions connected to a track-in apply to tracking out with the additional requirement to make certain that as you track out, the base of the pedestal does not pile up the camera cable around your feet creating the risk of losing your footing. Avoid kicking the cable guard as you track back.

6.11.5 Craning

An average pedestal has an elevation range of approximately 95 cm (37.5″). Visually, the effect of a three-foot change in lens height can be significantly enhanced if the wider angle of the zoom lens is selected and there is suitable content in the frame. It is usually a shot using the wider lens angle where camera height becomes the most critical. Frequently the camera height is adjusted 'off shot' to improve the composition of the shot by altering perspective of line.

The pedestal counterbalances the combined weight of camera and lens by pressurized gas and small trim weights. These trim weights can be added to the column to compensate for changes in gas pressure due to ambient temperature change. Even though the counterbalance system provides for very little effort to effect a change in height once the column is moving, there is an initial inertia to overcome and care should be taken in craning the camera up or down.

To avoid back strain or injury when lifting a heavy weight it is recommended to keep the back straight and bend the knees. Unfortunately it is often not possible to follow this advice when operating a television camera. Viewfinder height is controlled by lens height, which is frequently below normal standing eye height. Even with tilting viewfinders, the camera operator spends a great deal of operating time crouching in

order to look into the viewfinder. With a bent back in this position they then have to crane the camera, for example to follow an artiste standing up.

The safest body posture and the technique with the greatest control of movement is to position the shoulder over the ring steer and use the torso to force the pedestal down. To crane the camera up, use the reverse of this technique and with the shoulder over the pedestal pull the ring steering wheel up.

The most difficult manoeuvre, and potentially the most dangerous physically, is to attempt to crane up and down gripping the ring steer with the arm outstretched. A small adjustment of the pedestal height in this way can be made 'off shot' but if the crane-up is matched to artiste movement then it is probably prudent to position the shoulder as close to the ring steer as possible before 'lifting' the ring steer.

6.11.6 Viewfinder

Craning the pedestal 'on shot' through its full elevation range will cause problems with viewfinder position. At the lowest operating position of the pedestal, the viewfinder will need to be titled up. As the camera is craned up (if not adjusted) the titled viewfinder will eventually be pointing up at the studio lights and be inaccessible. It is sometimes possible to correct the angle of the viewfinder during the movement with the forehead or to give it a quick 'knock' at the end of the movement.

6.11.7 Crabbing – a combined move

A pure crabbing movement is a camera move where the distance between the principal subject and the lens remains unchanged during the move. Frequently, however, a crab is combined with a track to provide a more visually interesting and dynamic camera development.

The name was probably coined from the ability of the crab to move sideways but it is almost impossible for a camera operator working with a full facility camera on a heavy duty pedestal, unaided, to move a pedestal sideways (parallel to the principal subject) from a standing start. This is because it is not practical to look into the viewfinder and reach around the camera to a point on the ring steer close to 90° from the lens in order to pull the pedestal parallel to the action. Most camera operators are unable to crab the pedestal by gripping the ring steer below the viewfinder. The same move, however, is relatively simple when operating with a lightweight camera and pedestal.

6.11.8 Pan bar conventions

Many countries have adopted the convention of pan bar on the left of camera and focus control on the right-hand side of the camera. The pan bar prevents the ring steer to the left of the camera being used by the camera operator to crab the pedestal.

The usual crabbing technique with a full facility camera and heavy duty pedestal is therefore to turn the wheels slightly into the subject so that the crabbing movement starts as a mixture of crab and track. The movement can be kicked off with the foot and then the shot development controlled with the steering ring. The position of the hand on the steering ring will depend on the degree of rotation of the wheel required by the shot development. The further the hand is positioned away from the wheel below the viewfinder, the less power there is in the arm to keep the pedestal moving. Once the pedestal is on the move, it is usually possible to steer into a crabbing line that is parallel to the principal subject's movement.

A common technique to provide more physical power to move the pedestal is to offset the body on the right side (or opposite side to the pan bar) of the viewfinder in order to reach further around the ring steer and either pull (for a crab right) or push (for a crab left).

6.11.9 From bad to better .

A good rule of thumb for any camera movement which involves at some point a bad body posture for operating or a bad sight-line to the viewfinder, is to start from the worst operating condition and, during the camera development, unwind to a good operating position. This allows framing and focus at the end of the shot to be adjusted when working in the best operating position.

Keeping the whole of the viewfinder image in view is frequently difficult with a crabbing move. A side-opening viewfinder hood or a viewfinder that swivels helps if the final operating position is not jeopardized. A common problem during such a move is that the cue light becomes obscured.

6.11.10 Camera cable

More pedestal movements 'on shot' have suffered from cables being fouled, snagged or stood on than possibly for any other reason. If there is no-one on the crew cable clearing, make certain that there is a sufficient length of unimpeded cable available for the intended movement. If possible, reduce the amount and distance the cable has to be pulled during the move. A long length of cable dragged across the studio floor adds to the weight of the pedestal/camera and the amount of effort required to move the pedestal.

Check that the camera cable is clamped to the base of the pedestal and that the loop of cable between clamp and camera will not become snagged on any part of the pedestal as the camera is panned and moved. Check that no ancillary cable wrapped around the camera cable has loose or exposed loops that could be trapped under the cable guards and stop the pedestal movement.

6.11.11 Viewfinder

If there is a change of height of the camera or, during a crabbing movement, it is necessary to position the

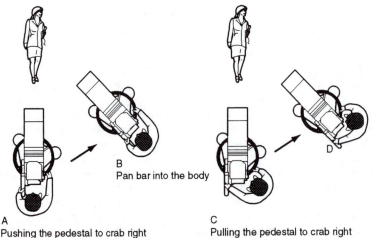

A
Pushing the pedestal to crab right

B
Pan bar into the body

C
Pulling the pedestal to crab right

Figure 6.20

body away from the centre of the viewfinder, provision must be made to alter the viewfinder hood in order to see the whole of the viewfinder image. If this cannot be achieved with a quick adjustment by the right hand released from the ring steer while the camera is moving, then the best compromise is to start in a difficult viewfinder viewing and body position and as the shot develops, to arrive at a comfortable operating position by the end of the move.

(a)

Static frame

(b)

123

Accelerate the pan as the subject moves to provide space in the frame 'to walk into' and begin to zoom out to anticipate the final frame

(c)

125   123

Pace the zoom out to match walk and hold the pan when the end frame is reached and allow subject to move into final position

(d)

123   125   123

Correct final framing anticipated and made invisible by the walk

6.12 Tracking

6.12.1 Frame adjustment whilst tracking

One of the compositional conventions of camerawork with profile shots, where people are looking out of frame, is to give additional space in the direction of their gaze for 'looking room'. Similarly, when someone is walking across frame, give more space in front of them than behind.

This space in the frame to 'walk into' needs to be maintained throughout a development. This can be difficult, for example, if the subject is standing to the left of frame and moves to camera left (i.e. towards the left-hand side of the frame). This requires an accelerated rapid pan left in order to provide space on the left (the direction of movement) before settling down to match the speed of the pan with the walk. The appropriate framing for the end composition must be achieved before the subject stops to avoid the camera reframing after the action has ended. If the subject is walking to take up a similar left-of-frame position, then the camera operator must stop the pan when the required end frame is reached making certain there is sufficient space on left of frame for the subject to walk into. In general, anticipate any change in frame size whilst on the move, and do not leave the reframing until the subject has settled. Come to rest with the subject.

6.12.2 The development shot

Panning, tracking or crabbing the camera to emphasize another visual element in the frame is a standard convention that has been used for many years. A development shot, as the name implies, is a shot which smoothly and unobtrusively moves towards a new viewpoint and is an alternative to a cut. It can start with a composition that emphasizes one set of visual elements and then moves, motivated by action or driven by the audience's curiosity, to an image that emphasizes another set of visual elements. In

Figure 6.21 Frame adjustment during panning. Accelerate and decelerate in the correct ratio: the rate of movement may alter during a camera move. If the composition is such that the subject is close to the edge of the frame when they begin their move, it will be necessary to make a swift adjustment of the frame to give them 'walking' room before settling down to the movement framing. Likewise, at the end of the move, the final frame may have to be arrived at by a similar speedier reframing of the subject to achieve a balanced final frame. If possible, the action should be staged to avoid sudden changes of pace and to provide a fluid, smooth movement.

dramatic terms, it has no real equivalent in theatre or literature and when staging, pace and execution is fully integrated it can provide the most visually exciting images.

To achieve its greatest impact, a development often requires either foreground elements to wipe across the frame to emphasize movement or a significant change in the background of the shot. It requires a progressive change of viewpoint from its starting position and it needs a main subject of interest that can be followed through various dynamic compositions. The movement must be fluid and changing through a series of compelling images. A crab around a performer, for example, will have little visual impact if they are staged against a plain cyclorama. There will be no background markers to indicate movement other than moving from a frontal viewpoint to profile.

6.12.3 Combining tracking and zooming

Many development shots require either a wide opening to the move or they end wide. As we have discussed, camera movement is accentuated when using the wide angle end of the zoom (plus appropriate set design) but if part of the development involves a medium close-up or close-up of a face, then at some stage on a wide angle (>40°) there will be unacceptable distortion and probably camera shadow.

This can be avoided by starting the move on the wide angle and then, at some point in the development, continue the move on the zoom. The transition between track and zoom needs careful selection but usually the movement can be carried over by continuing with a slight crab whilst ending in a tight shot on the zoom. This obviously involves 'blind zooming' with no opportunity to pre-check focus. Critical focus will occur in close-up just at the point when subtle control of framing is required. On a crane or a dolly, the camera lens can be tracked to a predetermined position whilst the camera operator controls framing, pivot and focus. The same type of development shot on a pedestal may require the assistance of a tracker to 'sweeten' the move. The reverse development shot of 'zoom first – track later' requires even more precise focus and attentive camera control.

6.12.4 The distinction between tracking and zooming

Moving the camera towards or away from the subject alters the size relationships between foreground and background objects. The perspective of mass changes in a similar way to our own perceptual experience when we move towards or away from an object. Tracking the camera therefore not only conforms to our normal visual expectations but sets up interesting rearrangements of all the visual elements in the camera's field of view.

Figure 6.22

Changing the camera distance alters all the image size relationships apart from very distant objects near or on the horizon. The size of a range of hills remains unaffected no matter how far we travel towards them until we reach a critical distance where we have a part of the hills as foreground with which to compare a background.

6.12.5 The compositional distinction between zoom and track

Tracking into a scene extends the involvement of the viewer in that they are being allowed visually to move into the two-dimensional screen space. In normal perception, depth indicators can be appraised or checked by moving the head or the body to seek a new viewpoint of the field of view. Viewing a series of static images on a two-dimensional screen does not allow this visual 'interrogation'. If depth is to be indicated it must be self-evident and contained in the composition of the image. A tracking shot provides a change in viewpoint and allows the viewer greater opportunity to experience the depth of the space pictured compared with either a zoom or a static shot.

A zoom in or out contains no change in size relationships – it simply allows either a greater magnification of a portion of the shot or wider view of the same size relationships. The argument for zooming (apart from convenience and budget) is that as a television production is a highly artificial process, the viewer is already experiencing a radically different visual sensation watching a two-dimensional image of an object (which is either magnified or extremely diminished) compared with their visual experience when observing the actual event. If so much is changed in the translation by the film and television medium using techniques of shot size, perspective, two dimensions, small image, etc., why quibble about zooming which fails to reproduce some small physical aspect of human perception?

A television production is an approximation of an event, which often includes attempts to induce an experience of the event in the viewer. Zooming creates a visual experience and therefore, it is argued, is as valid a technique as any other artifice employed.

6.12.6 Accentuating the effect of camera movement

The greatest impression of movement can be observed by using a wide angle lens and tracking between similar size objects such as a row of trees each side of a road. The apparent size of each tree relative to its neighbour changes dramatically as it approaches the lens. There is a constant visual flow of size ratio expansion as we track down the road.

Zooming along the road between rows of trees does not have anything like the same visual dynamics. The camera does not move and therefore there is no change in size relationships. The zoom simply magnifies the central portion of the field of view, preserving the existing size relationships. These remain unaltered as in a still photograph when a portion of it is enlarged. The perspective of mass is decided by the camera distance and zooming simply expands or contracts a portion of the field of view.

The feeling of flatness or deadness of a zoom is because there is no anticipated change to the perspective of mass which in normal perception accompanies changes in magnification or diminution of subject. This compositional inertia can be disguised by building in a camera move such as a pan with action or even a crabbing movement to accompany a zoom. The camera movement provides some relational changes to the visual elements that the zoom is magnifying.

6.12.7 Maintaining good composition when moving

When tracking, it is often necessary to adjust the height of the camera, particularly when moving into the human figure. In shots closer than full figure, lens height is often eye-height; but when the camera is further away, depending on the shot, the lens height is usually lower to reduce the amount of floor/ground in shot. A low lens height places emphasis on the subject by avoiding distracting foreground level surfaces such as roads, grass or floor. Like all 'rules of thumb', this convention is probably ignored more than it is employed, but change in lens height often accompanies tracking movements in order to bring emphasis onto the main subject.

Another reason for altering the lens height when tracking into the subject is to enhance the appearance of actors/actresses by shooting slightly down on faces, rather than shooting up and emphasizing jawlines, double chins, etc.

6.12.8 Finding the right tracking line

We will see in the description of zooming (see Section 6.13.3) that keeping two sides or even one side at a constant distance from the principal subject throughout a zoom or track creates a more pleasing visual result than simply allowing all four sides of the frame to implode in on the subject.

In zooming, the control of the pivot point is achieved by panning and/or tilting to adjust the frame during the zoom. Control of the framing during tracking (to keep a constant distance between one side of the frame and the subject) can also be achieved by panning/tilting but it is more effective if it can be controlled by the line of the track.

Fig. 6.23 illustrates a tracking line to produce an end frame of presenter plus scoreboard. The tracking line chosen requires no constant reframing during the move and no change in the direction of the pedestal wheels to maintain the pre-selected pivot point. It is the tracking line angle that maintains the pivot point. Operationally it is simpler and smoother and visually

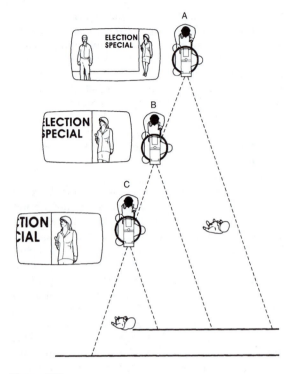

Figure 6.23

unobtrusive – the motivation for selecting a pivot point.

6.12.9 Finding the right camera height when tracking

The same technique can be used to maintain a pivot point at the top of the frame when tracking in or out, for example on a singer. When tracking in, the camera is craned up at a rate which holds the pivot point at the top of the frame without the need to reframe the camera. The lens height automatically arrives at the more flattering position, slightly above eye height, for the closer shot whilst avoiding crossing the keylight and shadowing the artist! When tracking out, the camera is craned down at a rate which maintains the top-of-the-frame pivot point arriving at a lower angle wide-shot which compresses the amount of floor area in shot.

6.12.10 Planned camera positions

Most multicamera productions require pre-planning. The planning includes decisions on design and set, presenter positions, a lighting rig and camera positions. There may not be a camera plan as such,

but frequently the lighting director will have made assumptions on where the cameras will be and what shots they will be taking based on a director's brief. The lighting director requires this essential information in order to produce a lighting plot. Lamps have to be rigged in specific places before rehearsal commences. There is the additional problem of lighting each set for several camera positions. The lighting effect on any subject is determined by the angle between the camera and the light source.

A camera operator has to be aware of the lighting rig and the placing of key, fill and backlight when positioning the camera. Lamps can be re-rigged to accommodate a 'new' camera position during rehearsal but there is a limit to the amount of relighting that can be carried out before the time taken up to relight uses up all the available camera rehearsal to the detriment of the whole production.

6.12.11 Camera position and keylights

Keylights are positioned to produce the desired modelling on the presenter and are typically set to between 10° and 40° either side of the eyeline position to the planned lens position. If the camera is crabbed beyond this point and the presenter turns to face the lens then the modelling on the face becomes either non-existent (camera under keylight) or 'over-modelled', which results in an ugly nose shadow that spreads across the face.

If the camera continues to crab away from the keylight then possibly the backlight will start to illuminate the face with a keylight acting as backlight and there is no fill.

Camera height
Camera height has an influence on the lighting treatment. A high camera position with the presenter looking to lens may tilt their head so far back that the backlight may hit the front of the forehead. A low camera angle always risks shooting into lights.

Flares
Although not always seen in a monochrome viewfinder, coloured flares can have a disturbing and unwanted effect on the composition. Sometimes they can be lost by a slight change in height or position. If this is not possible due to shot content, then either an additional 'impromptu' ray shade is added (a piece of black gaffer tape fastened across the top of the lens hood) or it may be possible to raise the offending lamp to lose the flare, or use a flag on the light source.

Another quick and easy way to overcome 'flare' problems is to have a small flag attached to the camera via a flexible arm.

Shadows on backgrounds

These can occur accidentally when a camera is repositioning or if a camera is forced to take up an unrehearsed position due to the artiste being off their marks or when following impromptu action. Shooting off the lit area can also result from following a spontaneous event. There is a trade-off between achieving good camerawork, good lighting and good sound matched against a production style that attempts to capture the vitality and energy generated by some forms of ad-lib programme content.

6.13 Zooming

6.13.1 Variable lens angle

A zoom lens has a continuously variable lens angle and is therefore useful in multicamera TV production for adjusting the image size without moving the

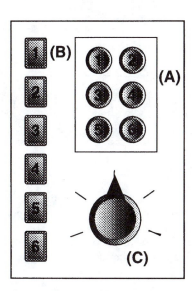

Figure 6.24 Shot box. Each button on the shot box can be pre-set to a specific lens angle by variable controls (A). When a button is bushed (B), the lens will be set to the pre-set lens angle at a speed controlled by (C). The speed of the zoom between the two pre-set positions can therefore be precisely controlled. The speed between the pre-sets is normally set at the maximum setting for rapid change between pre-selected lens angles. The shot box lens angle setting is instantly overridden when the thumb zoom demand is moved away from the neutral central position.

camera position. When operating from behind the camera, the adjustment is controlled on most television cameras via the thumb on a two-way rocker switch which alters the direction and speed of the zoom. A good servo zoom should allow a smooth imperceptible take-up of the movement of the zoom which can then be accelerated by the thumb control to match the requirements of the shot. There is usually provision to alter the response of the thumb control so that a very slow or a very fast zoom rate can be selected for the same movement of the thumb control.

When operating with a monocular viewfinder on a portable camera, the zoom lens can be controlled from a rocker switch mounted on the lens as well as a thumb control remoted to the pan bar or on a pistol grip.

6.13.2 Shot box

As the zoom lens has a continuous range of lens angles, individual settings can be pre-selected on a shot box. This is clamped to the pan bar, sometimes as an integral part of the focus capstan, and has a number of buttons which can be individually set to a required lens angle. When a shot box button is pushed the zoom automatically moves to the pre-selected lens angle associated with that button.

Most shot boxes also have the provision to vary the rate at which the zoom lens moves to a selected lens angle. This allows the lens angle at the start of a shot to be programmed on one button and the lens angle at the end of the shot to be assigned to another button. The speed at which the lens angle alters between the two buttons can then be adjusted to provide a precisely timed zoom-in or out.

6.13.3 Use of the zoom

In general, the zoom is used in three ways in multicamera TV production:

* to compose the shot;
* to readjust the composition on shot;
* to change the shot size in vision.

Composition of shot

The zoom lens allows the desired framing of a shot to be quickly achieved. Shot size can be quickly altered out of vision to provide a range of shots. Each shot can have the required size and framing to match other cameras (see Section 6.20). Extended zoom ranges (30:1–40:1–70:1) allow a wide range of shots to be obtained from a fixed position (e.g. on an OB scaffold tower/hoist) and provide visual movement across terrain where tracking would not be possible.

The speed of response of the thumb control can be adjusted to allow a compromise between the need for a fast reposition out of vision balanced against a slower speed of movement on shot. If the very fastest speed is selected there is a tendency to overshoot on the framing, making small changes in lens angle difficult. At the other extreme, a slow rate of zoom to allow good control of an 'in vision' zoom may be too slow for fast repositioning out of vision.

Readjustment on shot

The zoom is often used to trim or adjust the shot to improve the composition when the content of the shot changes. Someone joining a person 'in shot' is provided with space in the frame by zooming out. The reverse may happen when they leave shot – the camera zooms in to recompose the original shot. Trimming the shot 'in vision' may be unavoidable in the coverage of spontaneous or unknown content but it quickly becomes an irritant if repeatedly used. Fidgeting with the framing by altering the zoom angle should be avoided.

Change of shot size

Zooming into a subject or away from the subject occurs in many programmes. There is a significant distinction between the perspective changes provided by tracking and zooming but zooming is often the only choice to alter the image size because of the inability to move the camera. Zooming can be smoother, quicker and provide a greater change in image size than would be practical in tracking. It allows multicamera coverage at a distance from the principal subjects and avoids cameras moving close to the subject and appearing in adjacent shots. Working at a distance also helps to keep clear the audience's view of the performers and to reduce the distraction of camera movement.

Like all changes in shot, the application of invisible technique requires this type of visual transition to be unobtrusive (except that type of programme content which draws attention to its method of presentation). Because a zoom involves no change of perspective, its harsh abrupt magnification or diminution of an image often requires some means of softening or disguising the transition. This can be achieved by combining the zoom with a camera movement and by the use of a pivot point.

Pivot points

A common mistake with users of domestic camcorders is to centre the subject of interest in the frame and then to zoom towards them keeping the subject the same distance from all four sides of the frame. The visual effect is as if the frame implodes in on them from all sides.

A more pleasing visual movement is to keep two sides of the frame at the same distance from the subject for the whole of the movement. This is achieved in a track or a zoom by pre-selecting a pivot point in the composition, which is usually the main subject of interest, and whilst maintaining their position at a set distance from two adjacent sides of the frame, allow the other two sides of the frame to change their relative position to the subject. This allows the subject image to grow progressively larger (or smaller) within the frame whilst avoiding the impression of the frame contracting in towards them.

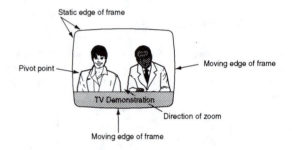

Figure 6.25

It may be necessary on a combined track and crabbing movement to change this pivot point during the move but again, as in all camera technique, the changeover to a different pivot point must be subtle, unobtrusive and controlled by the main subject of interest.

6.14 Camera movement and invisible technique

6.14.1 Invisible movement

There is the paradox of creating camera movement to provide visual excitement or visual change whilst attempting to make the movement 'invisible' – that is, invisible in the sense that the aim of the technique is to avoid the audience's attention switching from the programme content to the camerawork. Invisible movement is achieved when camera movement matches the movement of the action and good composition is maintained throughout the move. The intention is to emphasize subject/picture content, rather than technique.

Intrusive and conspicuous camera movements are often used for specific dramatic or stylistic reasons (e.g. pop promotions), but the majority of programme formats work on the premise that the methods of programme production should remain hidden or invisible.

6.14.2 Motivation

A camera move is usually prompted:

- to add visual interest;
- to express excitement, or increase tension or curiosity;
- to provide a new main subject of interest;
- to provide a change of viewpoint.

A camera move is therefore a visual development that provides new information or creates atmosphere or mood. If the opening and closing frames of a move, such as a zoom-in, are the only images that are considered important, then it is probably better to use a cut to change shot rather than a camera move.

6.14.3 Match the movement to the mood or action

Two basic conventions controlling camera movement are: firstly, to match the movement to the action so that the camera move is motivated by the action and is controlled in speed, timing and degree by action; and, secondly, to maintain good composition throughout the move. A camera move should provide new visual interest and there should be no 'dead' area between the first and end image of the movement.

Movement that is not motivated by action will be obtrusive and focus attention on the method of recording the image – it will make the camera technique visible. It is sometimes the objective of obtrusive camera movement to invigorate content that is considered stale and lacking interest. However, if there is a lack of confidence in the content of a shot, then possibly it is better to rethink the subject rather than attempt to disguise this weakness by moving attention on to the camera technique employed.

6.14.4 Two types of camera movement

There are broadly two types of camera movement: functional – the camera is moved to keep the subject in frame; and decorative – the camera is moved to provide variety and interest or to explain an idea.

6.14.5 When to reframe

A common dilemma is when to reframe a subject who is swaying in and out of reasonable framing. The shot may be too tight for someone who can only talk when they move or who makes big hand movements to emphasize a point.

The solution is to loosen off the shot. It is seldom a good idea to constantly pan to keep someone in frame as inevitably you will be 'wrong-footed' and compensate for an anticipated movement that does not happen. If the shot cannot be contained without continuous reframing then the incessant moving background will eventually become a distraction from the main subject of the shot.

6.14.6 Basic advice for movement

- Try to disguise camera movement by synchronizing with subject movement. Start and stop the movement at the same time as the subject.
- When zooming, hold one side of the frame static as a 'pivot point' rather than zooming in to the centre of the frame.
- Try to find a reason to motivate the zoom and to disguise the zoom. Use a combination of pan and zoom.
- Panning and zooming are done to show relationships. If the beginning of the shot and the end of the shot are interesting but the middle section is not, it is better to cut between the start of the shot and the end frame rather than to pan or to zoom. Begin and end on a point of interest when panning. If the end of the shot is uninteresting why pan to it? Have a reason for drawing attention to the final image of a pan.
- Pace the pan so that the viewer can see what the camera is panning over. Hold the frame at the beginning and end of the pan.
- Use dominant lines or contours to pan across or along. Find some subject movement to motivate the pan.

- When panning movement, leave space in the frame in the direction the subject is moving.
- A zoom-in has the same effect as enlarging a section of a photograph. The perspective of the photograph is fixed and there is no change in the size relationships depicted between the whole photograph or a portion of it. The image is frozen – an unchanging perspective whatever part we look at. This is contrary to our normal experience of a changing perspective when we move closer to a subject. Use the zoom with discretion to avoid increasing the two-dimensional quality of the TV image.

6.15 Camera movement and subject movement

6.15.1 Static camera – moving subject

Lens angle, camera distance and camera height will dictate the characteristics of a moving subject composition. On a long lens with the subject at a distance from the camera, space will be compressed and movement will appear to be disproportionate to the change in image size. For example, a subject can walk ten paces towards the camera on a long lens in midshot and hardly register a change in size. This contradicts our normal perception of perspective change and sets up a surreal 'running on the spot' feel to the image.

A close position with a wide-angle lens will accentuate movement and any movement towards camera will make the subject size change disproportionately to the actual movement taken. Action that crosses from corner to corner of the frame will be more dynamic than action which sweeps horizontally across the frame.

6.15.2 Moving camera – moving subject

One of the most common forms of moving camera/moving subject shot, is to follow, in the same size shot, someone walking or driving. This provides a static principal subject against a continuously changing background. A popular version of this effect is the parallel tracking shot where two people in conversation walk with the camera crabbing with them, often slightly ahead so that both faces are seen. For this technique to be 'invisible' the frame must be steady, horizontally level and the same size shot maintained over most of the move. The effect is as if the audience is a third person walking with them and listening in to their conversation. Other variations of this visual convention are people in cars, trains and even the

interiors of glass-walled lifts which are used to frame a static principal subject against a moving background.

Moving the camera whilst the subject moves towards or away from the lens can be more difficult to handle. Unless there are other visual elements

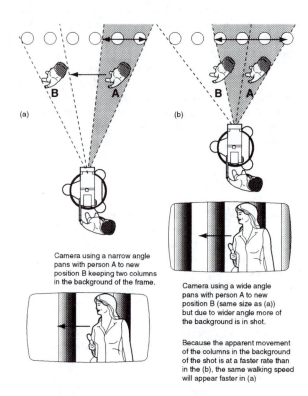

Camera using a narrow angle pans with person A to new position B keeping two columns in the background of the frame.

Camera using a wide angle pans with person A to new position B (same size as (a)) but due to wider angle more of the background is in shot.

Because the apparent movement of the columns in the background of the shot is at a faster rate than in the (b), the same walking speed will appear faster in (a)

Figure 6.26

moving in and out of the frame, the change in size of the subject can appear as if the camera is unable to keep up or is gaining on the subject. When the movement is across the frame, as in a crabbing shot, then change of size may not be so apparent and is visually acceptable.

6.15.3 Understanding the image

It is important to understand the content of a moving shot. If the camera movement, pan or zoom is too fast then the information will be unreadable. If the shot development is too fast for content then there will be a mismatch of a mood.

6.15.4 Movement within the static frame

In setting up a shot where, for example, a background figure walks to join a foreground figure, try to find a camera position that avoids constant reframing. Try to contain the action by appropriate lens position and lens angle without the need to reframe for small movements.

One of the weaknesses of television camerawork is that there is a tendency to cover action by small zoom movements or camera movement. Single-camera film or video usually settle on either staging the action so that it can be contained in a static frame or have tracks laid down and devise a positive camera movement to contain the action. In television productions, continuous small minor adjustments of framing detract from content and become an irritant – although with unrehearsed action there is no way of avoiding constant frame adjustment.

6.16 The depiction of depth

6.16.1 Three dimensions

One of the perceptual methods we use to determine depth is to assess the rate by which objects appear to diminish/increase in size as they recede/approach us and the appearance of parallel lines that converge and vanish at the horizon.

Other depth indicators are atmospheric or aerial perspective. This is the optical effect of light being absorbed by mist, dust or moisture causing colours to become desaturated and bluer, and a reduction of contrast between tones with increasing distance from the observer. Binocular vision allows depth to be assessed by contrasting the two viewpoints of our eyes. This form of depth calculation is obviously not available in a two-dimensional image but overlapping of objects is and gives clues to relative distance.

6.16.2 Two dimensions

When a camera converts a three-dimensional scene into a two-dimensional TV picture, it leaves an imprint of lens height, camera tilt, distance from subject and lens angle.

We can detect these decisions in any image by examining the position of the horizon line (or determine where it would be) and where it cuts similar sized figures. This will reveal camera height and tilt. Lens height and tilt will be revealed by any parallel converging lines in the image such as the edges of buildings or roads. The size relationship between foreground and background objects, particularly the human figure, will give clues to camera distance from objects and lens angle. Camera distance from subject

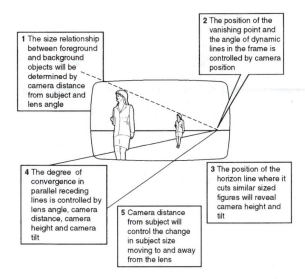

1 The size relationship between foreground and background objects will be determined by camera distance from subject and lens angle

2 The position of the vanishing point and the angle of dynamic lines in the frame is controlled by camera position

4 The degree of convergence in parallel receding lines is controlled by lens angle, camera distance, camera height and camera tilt

5 Camera distance from subject will control the change in subject size moving to and away from the lens

3 The position of the horizon line where it cuts similar sized figures will reveal camera height and tilt

Figure 6.27 Basic influences on a shot

will be revealed by the change in object size when moving towards or away from the lens.

For any specific lens angle and camera position there will be a unique set of the above parameters. Each one can be adjusted when setting up the shot.

6.16.3 Perspective of mass

The composition of a shot is affected by the distance of the camera from the subject and the lens angle that is used. This will make a difference to the size relationships within the frame.

The size relationship of objects in a field of view is known as the perspective of mass. Put simply, the closer an object is to us the larger it will appear, and vice versa. The image of an object doubles in size whenever its distance is halved. This is a simple fact of geometric optics and it applies to a camera as it does to the eye. Adjusting the camera distance and the lens angle can provide the size relationships required for a composition.

6.16.4 Camera position/lens angle

Lens height and tilt will control the perspective of line. Shooting low with a level camera will produce one type of line perspective; shooting from a high vantage point tilted down will produce another set of line relationships in the frame. The camera doesn't lie – much. It simply reproduces an image conditioned by one of the four parameters mentioned above – lens angle, distance from subject, lens height and camera tilt.

Camera distance

Figure 6.28

Mid-range	Wide angle	Narrow angle

The distance between the two figures remains unchanged in all three illustrations.
 The distance between foreground figures and camera has altered.
 With each re-position, lens angle of zoom is adjusted to keep foreground figure the same size in frame.
 The 'wide-angle' effect and 'narrow-angle' effect is a product of *camera distance* from subjects.

6.16.5 Horizon line and camera height as a compositional device

American silent film production at the turn of the twentieth century used a convention of a 50 mm lens at eye level and actor movement was restricted to being no closer to the lens than 12 ft. With an actor standing twelve feet from the lens, the bottom of the frame cuts them at knee height. By 1910, the Vitagraph company allowed the actors to play up to 9 ft from the lens and the camera was lowered to chest height.

From these static camera positions developed a Hollywood convention of frequently placing the camera at eye level, which in turn allowed the horizon line to cut the foreground actors at eye level. Whether the artistes are standing or sitting, the camera is often positioned at eye height, which places the horizon behind the eyes. This emphasizes the main subject of the frame – the face; and the main area of interest of the face – the eyes.

A more prosaic factor controlling lens height is the need to avoid shooting off the top of studio sets. Keeping the camera at eye level speeds up production as actor movement to camera can be accommodated without panning up and shooting off the top of the set or the need to relight.

A lens height of slightly above presenter eye height (whether standing or sitting) is usually kinder to the face, provides a more alert and positive body posture

and often improves the lighting on artistes with, for example, deep-set eyes.

6.16.6 The subjective influence of camera height

Lens height will also control the way the audience identifies with the subject. Moving the horizon down below a person makes them more dominant because the viewer is forced to adopt a lower eyeline viewpoint. We are in the size relationship of children looking up to adults. A low lens height may also de-emphasize floor or ground level detail because we are looking along at ground level and reducing or eliminating indications of ground space between objects. This concentrates the viewer's interest on the vertical subjects. A high position lens height has the reverse effect. The many planes of the scene are emphasized like a scale model.

Usually it is better to divide the frame into unequal parts by positioning the horizon line above or below the mid-point of the frame. Many camera operators intuitively use the Rule of Thirds (see Fig. 6.35) to position the horizon. A composition can evoke space by panning up and placing the line low in frame. Placing a high horizon in the frame can balance a darker foreground land mass or subject with the more attention-grabbing detail of a high key sky. It also helps with contrast range and exposure.

  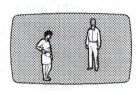

Low angle	Lens at eye height	High angle

Figure 6.29 Lens height. On a flat surface, the horizon line cuts similar size figures at the same point. The height of that point is the height of the lens.

6.17 Picture-making skills

6.17.1 Form and content

One of the skills required in picture-making is the ability to interest and hold the attention of the audience. Although the content of the shot such as a house, animal or personality may be the initial reason why a viewer's interest is captured by an image, the method of presentation is also a vital factor in sustaining that interest.

A television image is a two-dimensional picture but most shots will contain depth indicators that allow the audience to understand the two-dimensional representation of the three dimensions depicted. Text on a blank background has no depth indicators but the text is still perceptually seen as 'in front' of the page.

There are therefore two aspects of the composition. The content – house, animal or face – and the front surface arrangements of lines, shapes, contrasts, etc. which form the recognizable images. The majority of the audience may only remember the content of the shot – the specific house, animal or face – but they will also be affected by the series of lines, shapes, brightness points and contrasts, colour, etc. which constructs the front surface plane of the image. This 'abstract' element of the shot may be crucial to the way the viewer responds to the image.

(a) (b)

Figure 6.30

Each visual element in a shot can therefore serve two functions:

- as **content** – that part of the composition that provides depth indicators and information about the physical subject of the shot;
- as **form** – that part of the design that lies on the surface plane of the screen and forms an overall abstract design which can produce a reaction in the viewer independent of any response to the content of the shot.

The reduction of this aspect of the shot, its form, to a simplified diagram of line and shape has been termed the structural skeleton of the image. It reveals the perceptual elements that potentially can hold the viewer's attention over and above the interest in the content of the shot.

The structural skeleton of the shot is only partially formed by content. For example, every camera operator knows that a shot of an object can be made more interesting if the camera is moved from a square-on, symmetrical viewpoint to an angle of view favouring more than one side or surface and/or the height of the lens is varied. Repositioning the camera is altering the structural skeleton, for while the content of the shot remains and is recognizable as 'a car' or 'a building', converging lines of rooftop, windows, doors, etc. have been altered and restructured to provide a more pleasing 'front surface' design.

The degree to which these convergences can be controlled by lens height, lens position and lens angle requires an understanding of perspective.

6.17.2 Wide-angle effect

Working with the camera close to the subject produces an increase in the size ratio between foreground and background figures. The foreground object appears unnaturally large and the background appears unnaturally small. It is a perspective of mass relationship of which we are usually unaware. A wide-angle lens allows more of the foreground subject to be in frame and it is this combination that produces distortion when used too close to the face (a 'Pinocchio' nose). A wide-angle zoom is very useful in confined surroundings, especially if attempting to interview someone in a crowd of journalists and photographers. By being close to the interviewee, masking by other people (such as fellow photographers) is prevented as there is insufficient room between lens and subject.

6.17.3 Narrow-angle effect

A part of our perception of depth depends on judging size relationships. The smaller we perceive a known object, the further we judge it to be from us. The size relationships produced by a very narrow-angle lens at a distance from the subject produce the illusion of squeezing the space between equal-size figures. The camera distance from the subject produces the size relationships whilst the long focal length lens provides the magnification of the foreground and background. The space between the subjects in frame appears to be condensed. A common example is shooting a crowded pavement from a great distance on a long lens. The effect is that all people moving towards camera appear to be equal size and the time taken for them to change size, as they appear to be approaching the lens, appears to be abnormal.

6.17.4 The wide-angle/narrow-angle effect

Size relationships or the perspective of mass can be confused with the wide-angle effect and the narrow-angle effect. To increase the size of a background figure to a foreground figure it is common practice to reposition the camera back and zoom in to return to the original framing. The size relationships have now altered. It is not the narrower angle that produced this effect but the increased distance from the camera.

By tracking away from the two figures we have altered the ratio between lens and first figure and lens and second figure. It is a much smaller ratio and therefore the difference in size between the two of them is now not so great. When we zoom in and revert to the original full frame for foreground figure we keep the new size relationships that have been formed by camera distance. The two figures appear to be closer in size.

As part of our perception of depth depends on judging size relationships – the further away, the smaller they are – our perception of this new size relationship produced by tracking out and zooming in leads us to believe that the distance between equal height figures is not so great as the first framing.

Possibly, the narrow-angle and the wide-angle effect should be renamed the 'distant viewing effect'. The important point to remember is that subject size relationship is a product of camera distance. How the subject fills the frame is a product of lens angle. This, of course, is the crucial distinction between tracking and zooming. Tracking the camera towards or away from the subject alters size relationships – the perspective of mass. Zooming the lens preserves the existing relative size relationships and magnifies or diminishes a portion of the shot.

6.17.5 Movement within the shot and lens angle

A two-dimensional television image of three-dimensional space can involve a compromise between action and the requirements of the camera. A common adjustment is the speed of the actor movement to the size of the shot or the lens angle in use.

A small movement in a close-up can be the equivalent of a big movement in long shot. A full figure, three-pace walk towards a wide-angle lens will create a much bigger change in size than the equivalent full figure walk towards a 25° lens. The 'internal space' of the lens in use becomes a critical consideration when staging action for the camera.

One of the most common adjustments is the speed of a rise from a chair, which may need to be covered in close-up. A normal rise will often appear frantic contained in a tight shot (head and shoulders) and is often slowed down. This also helps with the problem of achieving good framing when covering a fast-moving subject on a narrow-angle lens.

6.18 Visual design

6.18.1 Internal space

Camera movement must have visual elements that change their relationship depending on camera position. A crab around a subject set against a featureless background will provide slight indication of change of viewpoint. The same movement with the subject set against a varied and broken background now has markers to indicate the change of viewpoint. If foreground features sweep across the frame there are even more indicators that the viewpoint is changing and the movement (if that is what is required) becomes more dominant and visual.

Camera movement using a narrow lens angle has a distinct visual quality but requires greater operational precision than with a wide angle lens movement which is easier to achieve and where there is greater

(a)

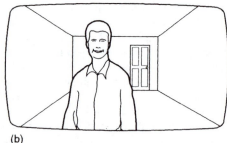

(b)

Figure 6.31
Changing the 'space' of a shot with lens angle and camera distance. The same size of foreground subject achieved with a narrow angle lens (a) and a wide angle lens (b) and repositioning the camera.

apparent movement in the frame for the distance covered.

The internal space of a shot often underlines the emotional quality of the scene. 'Normal' perspective for establishing shots is often used where the intention is to describe the locale plainly and straightforwardly. A condensed or an expanded space on the other hand may help to suggest the mood or atmosphere of the action.

The choice of lens angle and resulting composition should not be accidental unless, as is too often the case, camera position and angle is a *fait accompli* created by a multicamera compromise.

6.18.2 Control of background

A small area of background can be controlled by lighting or by limiting the depth of field by ND (neutral density) filter or shutter, but the greatest control is by choice of camera position, lens angle, camera distance and foreground subject position. Consideration must also be given to how the shot will be intercut, and often a matching background of similar tonal range, colour and contrast has to be chosen to avoid a mismatch when intercutting.

Too large a tonal difference between intercut backgrounds will result in obtrusive and very visible cuts. Visual continuity of elements such as direction of light, similar zones of focus and the continuity of background movement (e.g. crowds, traffic) in intercut shots have also to be checked.

6.18.3 Lens angle

The choice of lens angle and camera distance from the subject is the controlling factor in the way that depth is depicted in the image, but the 'internal' space of a shot often plays a crucial part in setting up the atmosphere of a shot.

A long lens positioned at a distance from a cramped interior will heighten the claustrophobia of the setting. Subject size ratios will be evened out from foreground to background and movement to and away from camera will show no significant change in size and therefore give a subjective impression that no distance has been traversed.

A wide angle lens close to the subject will increase space, emphasize movement and depending on shot content, emphasize convergence of line and accentuate the relative size of same size figures at different distances from the lens.

6.19 Composition

6.19.1 What is composition?

Composition is commonly defined as arranging all the visual elements in the frame in a way that makes the image a satisfactory and complete whole. Integration of the image is obtained by the positioning of line, mass, colour and light in the most pleasing arrangement.

This definition is a start in the examination of composition but it does prompt further questions. What counts as 'satisfactory and complete' and is 'pleasing arrangement' an objective or subjective judgement?

Many television camera operators know, through many years of experience, exactly how to position the lens in space or choose a different lens angle in order to improve the appearance of the shot. They are either working to inherited craft values of what is 'good' composition or they are repositioning and juggling with the camera until they intuitively feel that they have solved that particular visual problem.

Spatial organization

Sp ati l org anizati on isthe vit alfacto rin a noptic alm essage
Spatial organization is the vital factor in an optical message

- Understanding the nature of an image is initially accomplished by the perceptual grouping of significant structural patterns.
- Grouping objects together because they are near to each other in the frame is the simplest method of visual organization.
- Same size objects in a frame will be grouped together to form one shape or pattern.
- Searching for coherent shapes in a complex image, human perception will look for, and if necessary create, simple shapes.
- Objects grouped by colour is another effective method of compositional organization.

Figure 6.32

Frequently there is no time to analyse a situation and the only thing to fall back on is experience. Compositional experience is the result of many years of solving visual problems. Good visual communication is not a gift from heaven but is learnt from finding out in practice what does and does not work.

6.19.2 Visual communication

Effective communication can be carried out in many languages. The very basic requirement for communication between individuals is their need to speak in the same language. Using a visual medium is choosing to communicate through pictures and ultimately the visual language used must be compatible with human perception. Although aesthetic fashion influences composition, good visual communication rests on an understanding of the psychology of perception.

Man has specific ways of visually understanding the world. If a composition is arranged to work in accord with those underlying visual principles, then there is more chance of the visual information being understood and enjoyed. If the composition conflicts with the pattern of visual expectation, then confusion and rejection of the message may occur.

These perceptual phenomena have been intuitively understood and employed by painters of great works of art for centuries. Their work engages our attention and is visually satisfying. These masterpieces still communicate and satisfy because they are structured for visual understanding and their viewers respond intuitively to the underlying reinforcement of the visual system.

Visual coherence is related to the inherent characteristics of perception. 'Seeing' is not simply a mechanical recording by the eye. Understanding the nature of an image is initially accomplished by the perceptual grouping of significant structural patterns. One of the aims of good composition is to find and emphasize structural patterns that the mind/eye can easily grasp.

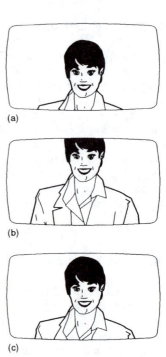

(a)

(b)

(c)

Figure 6.34 There is a strong perceptual awareness of the invisible reference points of the frame. (a) If the camera is panned up, a point is reached, with a large amount of headroom, where the subject appears to be slipping out of the bottom of the frame. (b) Panning down to create a shot with no headroom produces the feeling that the subject is leaving through the top of the frame. (c) There is a point of equilibrium where the subject is balanced against the invisible forces of the frame.

Seeing an image as the camera sees it requires training of the eye and brain. Understanding how we see is the first step in controlling visual communication.

6.19.3 Picture-making skills

Central to the craft of camerawork are the skills required to create arresting and informative images. Having discussed how to move the camera on and off shot smoothly, where should the lens be positioned to provide the most effective shot? What rules govern the craft of picture making?

'I see what you mean!'

There is usually a reason why a shot is recorded on tape or film. The purpose may be simply to record an event or the image may play an important part in expressing a complex idea. Whatever the reasons that initiate the shot, the camera operator should have a clear understanding of the purpose behind the shot.

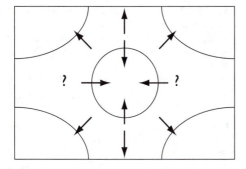

Figure 6.33 A field of forces can be plotted which plots the position of rest or balance (centre and midpoint on the diagonal between corner and centre) and positions of ambiguity (?) where the observer cannot predict the potential motion of the object and therefore an element of perceptual unease is created. Whether the object is passively attracted by centre or edge or whether the object actively moves on its own volition depends on content. The awareness of motion of a static visual element with relation to the frame is an intrinsic part of perception. It is not an intellectual judgement tacked on to the content of an image based on previous experience, but an integral part of perception.

After establishing why the shot is required, and usually this will be deduced purely from experience of the shot structure of the programme format, the camera operator will position the camera and adjust the lens angle, framing and focus. All four activities (including knowledge of programme formats) rely on an understanding of the visual design elements available to compose a shot within the standard television framing conventions. Effective picture-making is the ability to manipulate the lens position and the lens angle within a particular programme context.

Primary decisions

The seven primary decisions to be made when setting up a shot and their effect on the image are related to:

- camera angle;
- lens angle;
- camera distance;
- camera height;
- frame;
- subject in focus;
- depth of field.

Positioning the lens

Whether in a complex studio production where each shot has a pre-planned position and shot size (e.g. drama) or at an OB location where the siting of fixed camera positions will be crucial in achieving comprehensive coverage (e.g. the camera coverage of an eighteen hole golf course), positioning the camera lens in space is central to multicamera production technique.

Physically changing the lens position and altering the lens angle controls the appearance and the information contained in a shot. One essential skill required by a camera operator is the ability to visualize a shot from a lens angle in any position in space without the need to move the camera to that position in order to discover its visual potential.

If a shot on a camera is unsatisfactory, the camera operator should be able to assess how much movement and/or change of lens angle is required to improve its composition. This is doubly important when a camera has to be rigged and from a static position provide a variety of shots. Anticipating the visual potential between different camera positions is part of the craft of television camerawork.

6.19.4 Summary

Composition is the principal way of making clear the priorities of a shot. It emphasizes the main subject and eliminates or subdues competing elements of visual interest. There must be a reason for framing up any shot; good composition enables that reason to be transmitted to the viewer. Good visual communication is achieved by good composition. Here is a partial checklist of the 'do's and don'ts' of composition:

- The camera converts three dimensions into two dimensions. Try to compensate for the loss of the third dimension by looking for ways to represent depth in the composition.
- Avoid dividing the frame into separated areas by strong vertical and horizontal elements unless this is a specific required effect.
- Check the overall image, particularly background details (e.g. no chimneys/posts growing out of foreground subjects' heads).
- Keep important action away from the edge of the frame, but avoid repeating square on, symmetrical eye-level centre-of-frame shots.
- Offset the dominant interest and balance this with a less important element.
- Fill the frame if possible with interest and avoid large plain areas that are there simply because of the aspect ratio of the screen. If necessary, mask off part of the frame with a feature in the shot to give a more interesting composition.
- Emphasize the most important element in the frame by its position using control of background, lens angle, height, focus, shot size, movement, etc. Make certain that the eye is attracted to the part of the frame that is significant and avoid conflict with other elements in the frame.
- Selective focus can control the composition. Pulling focus from one plane to another directs attention without reframing.
- Attempt some visual mystery or surprise – but the stronger the visual impact the more sparingly it should be used. Repeated zooming results in loss of impact and interest.
- The Rule of Thirds proposes that an attractive balance can be achieved by placing the main subject on one of the intersections of two equally spaced lines horizontally in the frame and two lines equally spaced in the vertical.
- With profile shots, where people are looking out of frame, give additional space in the direction of their gaze for 'looking room'. Similarly, when someone is walking across frame, give more space in front of them than behind.
- Give consistent headroom for the same sized shots, decreasing the amount with CUs and BCUs (see Section 6.20.7). Always cut the top of the head rather than the chin in extreme close up.

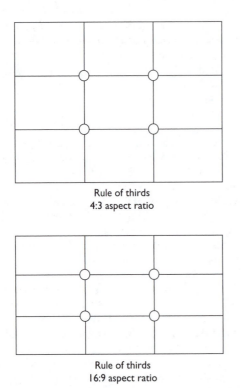

Rule of thirds
4:3 aspect ratio

Rule of thirds
16:9 aspect ratio

Figure 6.35 The rule of thirds proposes that a useful starting point for any compositional grouping is to place the main subject on any one of the four intersections made by two equally spaced horizontal and vertical lines.

- The eyes are the centre of attention in shots of faces. A good rule-of-thumb is to place them one-third of the way from the top of frame.

6.20 Intercutting

6.20.1 Invisible cuts

Continuous camera coverage of an event using a number of cameras relies on a stream of invisible shot changes – invisible in the sense that the transition between each shot does not distract the audience. The aim is to make the shot change unobtrusive to prevent the audience's attention switching from programme content to the programme production technique. Although individual camera operators frame up their own shots, the pictures they produce must fit the context of the programme and match what other camera operators are providing. No shot can be composed in isolation – its effect on the viewer will be related to the preceding and succeeding shot. The camera operator is directly involved in edit point decisions.

6.20.2 Why use more than one camera?

If intercutting between cameras is potentially distracting to the viewer why change the shot? Many football matches, for example, are covered by a single camera for news and sports reports, but there are inherent problems with this technique. Close shots capture the excitement and personalities in the match whereas wide shots reveal tactics and the flow of the game. A single camera has to resort to zooming in and out continuously in order to provide both types of shots. If the game is shot continuously wide then it lacks excitement. If it is shot too close then there is the risk of missing vital action (like goals!). It is around the goal area that the single-camera operator has to chance their arm. Zoom in for the expected goalkeeper save and the camera operator may miss the ball rebounding out to another player who scores from outside the frame.

6.20.3 Choice of shot

Multicamera coverage of sport allows a TV director the option of choosing the size of shot and camera angle to match the action. With a 5–6 camera coverage of football, for example, as the action moves towards the goal area each of the six cameras will have a designated role providing a range of close and wide shots which can be instantly cut to depending on the outcome of the attack. Many of the cameras will be isoed (their individual output continuously recorded) to provide instant replay in slow motion.

In general a change of shot will be unobtrusive:
- if there is a significant change in shot size or camera angle when intercutting on the same subject;
- if there is a significant change in content (e.g. a cut from a tractor to someone opening a farm gate);
- when cutting on action – the flow of movement in the frame is carried over into the succeeding shot (e.g. a man in medium shot sitting behind a desk stands up and, on his rise, a longer shot of the man and the desk is cut to);
- when intercutting between people if their individual shots are matched in size, have the same amount of headroom, have the same amount of looking space if in semi-profile, if the lens angle is similar (i.e. internal perspective is similar) and if the lens height is the same;
- if the intercut picture's are colour matched (e.g. skin tones, background brightness) and if in succeeding shots the same subject has a consistent colour (e.g. grass in a stadium);
- if there is continuity in action (e.g. body posture, attitude);
- if there is continuity in lighting, in sound, props and setting and continuity in performance or presentation.

Figure 6.36

6.20.4 Editing decisions

Particularly in as-directed situations such as sport, discussion and many forms of music, the camera operator must anticipate the shot structure and provide the right composition and choice of shot to satisfy standard editing requirements. Intercutting between cameras in multicamera coverage occurs in 'real' time without the benefit of the more extended decision-making time about edit points enjoyed in post-production. The timescale of the event covered dictates intercutting decisions and the shot rate (e.g. a 100 metres race is covered in under 10 seconds; a 5000 metre race in approximately thirteen minutes).

6.20.5 Matched shots on an interview

Multicamera coverage of an interview is about the most widespread format on television after the straight-to-camera shot of a presenter. The staging of an interview usually involves placing the chairs for good camera angles, lighting, sound and for the ease and comfort of the guests and the anchor person. The space between people should be a comfortable talking distance.

6.20.6 Eyeline

Eyeline is an imaginary line between an observer and the subject of their observation. In a discussion, the participants are usually reacting to each other and will switch their eyeline to whoever is speaking. The audience, in a sense, is a silent participant and they will have a greater involvement in the discussion if they feel that the speaker is including them in the conversation. This is achieved if both eyes of the speaker can be seen by the viewer rather than profile or semi-profile shots. The cameras should be able to take up positions in and around the set to achieve good eyeline shots of all the participants – that is, both eyes of each speaker, when talking, can be seen on camera.

In addition, the relationship of the participants should enable a variety of shots to be obtained in order to provide visual variety during a long interview (e.g. over-the-shoulder two-shots, alternative singles and two-shots and group shots). The staging should also provide for a good establishment shot or relational shot of the participants and for opening or closing shots.

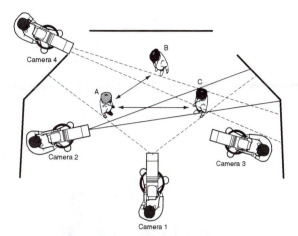

Figure 6.37 Because of the unrehearsed nature of a discussion, each camera takes up a position where it can match its shots to other cameras plus have the flexibility to offer more than one size of shot without repositioning. Constant camera repositioning during an interview can result in gaps in the camera coverage leading to participants talking in long shot because the camera that should be providing their closer shot is on the move. Camera 4, looking for 'interesting shots', has gone upstage of the imaginary line(s) that connects the participants' eyelines. When intercut with camera 3, two people who, in the studio, are looking at each other (and therefore in opposite directions) will appear on screen to be both looking in the same direction. If cameras on both side of the line are continually intercut, the viewer quickly loses the geographic relationship of the participants. Also, camera 4 has created a problem for camera 3 who is very close to being in cameras 4's shot. By taking up such a position, camera 4 has also pushed camera 3 downstage to keep out of shot and forced cameras 2 and 3 off their optimum eyeline position on the guests. Multicamera camerawork is a team effort and any individual camera move or shot usually affects the work of the rest of the camera crew.

6.20.7 Standard shot sizes

Because so much of television programming involves people talking, a number of standard shot sizes have evolved centred on the human body. In general, these shot sizes avoid cutting people at natural joints of the body such as neck, elbows and knees. Normal interview shots include:

- **CU** (Close Up). Bottom of frame cuts where the knot of a tie would be.
- **MCU** (Medium Close Up). Bottom of frame cuts where the top of a breast pocket of a jacket would be.
- **MS** (Medium Shot) Bottom of frame cuts at the waist.

BCU (close-up)
Whole face fills screen. Top of frame cuts
forehead. Bottom of frame cuts chin

CU (close-up)
Bottom of frame cuts where
knot of tie would be

MCU (medium close-up)
Bottom of frame cuts where
top of breast pocket of a jacket would be

MS (medium shot)
Bottom of frame cuts at
the waist

LS (long shot)
Long shot includes whole
figure

WS (wide shot)
Wide shot includes figure in
a landscape or setting

Standard shot sizes

Figure 6.38

Other standard shot descriptions are:

- **BCU** (Big Close Up). The whole face fills the screen. Top of the frame cuts the forehead. Bottom of the frame cuts the edge of chin avoiding any part of the mouth going out of frame (rarely used in interviews).
- **LS** (Long Shot). The long shot includes the whole figure.
- **WS** (Wide Shot) A wide shot includes the figure in a landscape or setting.
- **O/S 2s** (Over-the-shoulder 2-shot). Looking over the shoulder of a foreground figure framing part of the head and shoulders to another participant.
- **2-shot**, **3-shot**, etc. Identifies the number of people in frame composed in different configurations.

Note: Precise framing conventions for these standard shot descriptions vary with directors and camera operators. One person's MCU is another person's MS. Check that your understanding of the position of the bottom frame line on any of these shots shares the same size convention for each description as the director with whom you are working.

6.20.8 Cross-shooting

A standard cross-shooting arrangement is for the participants to be seated facing each other and for cameras to take up positions close to the shoulders of the participants. The usual method of finding the optimum camera position is to position the camera to provide a well composed over-the-shoulder 2-shot then zoom in to check that a clean single can be obtained of the participant facing camera.

A tight over-the-shoulder 2-shot always risks masking or being a poorly composed shot if the foreground figure should lean left or right. To compensate instantly, if this should occur, set the pedestal steering wheel in a position to allow crabbing left or right for rapid repositioning on or off shot.

Figure 6.39

6.20.9 Crossing the line

There may be a number of variations in shots available, depending on the number of participants and the method of staging the discussion/interview. All of these shot variations need to be one side of an imaginary line drawn between the participants.

To intercut between individual shots of two people to create the appearance of a normal conversation between them, three simple rules have to be observed. Firstly, if a speaker in a single is looking from left to right in the frame then the single of the listener must look right to left. Secondly, the shot size and eyeline should match (i.e. they should individually be looking out of the frame at a point where the viewer anticipates the other speaker is standing). Finally, every shot of a sequence should stay the same side of an imaginary line drawn between the speakers unless a shot is taken exactly on this imaginary line or a camera move crosses the line and allows a reorientation (and a repositioning of all cameras) on the opposite side of the old 'line'.

6.20.10 Matching to other cameras

In addition to setting up the optimum position for singles, 2-shots, etc., camera operators in a multicamera

intercutting situation need to match their shots with the other cameras. The medium close-ups (MCU) etc. should be the same size with the same amount of headroom. All cameras intercutting on singles should be the same height and if possible roughly the same lens angle (therefore the same distance from their respective subjects), especially when intercutting on over-the-shoulder 2-shots. This avoids a mismatch of the perspective of mass (i.e. the background figure is smaller or larger than the shot it is matching to).

Other matching points are the same amount of looking room with semi-profile shots by placing the centre of the eyes (depending on size of shot) in the centre of frame.

The best method of matching shots is to use the mixed viewfinder facility or check with a monitor displaying studio out.

6.20.11 Ability to assess a shot

Intercutting between different cameras provides an effective method of presenting information, telling a story or structuring an event. The pace, excitement and variety induced by a change of shot can potentially engage and hold the attention of the audience, but shot change requires an underlying coherent structure if it is not to collapse into a succession of fleeting images. That overall structure is imposed by the director, assisted in an 'as-directed' situation, by the input from the camera crew.

Camera operators therefore need to have a grasp of the editorial priorities of the programme format they are involved in. In an interview situation involving a number of people, for example, they must be aware of the flow of the discussion to be able to respond and provide the appropriate shot of a participant at the moment they begin to speak. In sports coverage, they must follow the commentary, the flow of the game, as well as direction in order that the appropriate shot is framed and ready moments before it is required.

Looking room

Eyes positioned at approx. half frame

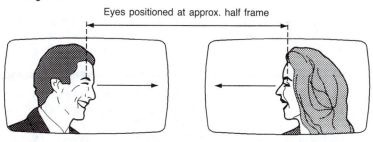

Balanced 'looking room' on intercut shots

Figure 6.40

The ability to assess what shots are required and a feeling for the production style is the product of experience and concentration. Keeping up with the programme content allows time for the camera operator to anticipate what shots are needed and the speed of reflex to provide them. The camera operators in many situations are the eyes of the director, but unless they share the same production values (i.e. they assume a certain shot structure is appropriate for the specific situation) a scrappy and often confusing treatment may result.

6.20.12 Variation in programme formats

Shot structure and production requirements will vary with programme format. As we have already discussed, programmes that are tightly camera scripted (e.g. drama or orchestral music) will require little or no additional shots except when resolving production problems discovered during rehearsal. Other programme formats such as discussion, sports coverage, game shows and many live events require a constant flow of 'as-directed' shots. These shots have to be appropriate to the specific programme and not simply a 'pretty' shot.

6.20.13 When to offer shots

One of the hardest techniques for camera operators to master in multicamera camerawork on a fast-moving show is when to offer shots or when to wait for direction. A camera operator, for example, will often spot during a discussion a participant not on camera bursting to get their word in and may be tempted to offer up a shot of them. Many directors appreciate this contribution and, providing there is the trust and experience developed in a long working relationship between camera crew, vision mixer and director, a variety of reaction shots can be offered and taken whilst still keeping up with the flow of the discussion.

Alternatively, many directors dislike being left without a cover shot and prefer to decide on all camera movement. In these circumstances the camera operator must stick on their last directed shot until directed to do otherwise. Whilst this avoids any misunderstandings or the mistake of cutting to a camera just as it moves to a new shot, it can also limit the opportunity for visual variety and spontaneity in the coverage.

6.20.14 What shots are required?

A 'cut-in' shot will give more information or detail directly connected with the main content of the

programme. A close-up of a golf ball going into the hole completes a sequence of shots starting with the golfer lining up his putt.

In the same golf coverage, 'a cutaway' to a seagull perched on a flag in an unplayed hole does not provide additional information about the match but it does provide variety and humour. This type of shot can only be offered when the tempo of the match allows. It is inappropriate, for example, at the moment of a critical putt.

Variation in camera angle and shot size are needed in most 'as-directed' situations to give variety and pace to the presentation. The director will ask for a string of requirements and coordinate each camera, but by listening to talkback, and with the occasional use of the mixed viewfinder facility to see what shot has been selected, a camera operator will often be able to find an appropriate shot that matches the needs of the programme at that point. The judgement and the ability to assess what shot is relevant is part of the skill needed to be developed by a camera operator. What shot is 'editorially' significant is part of the director's concept of the programme. Often, a camera operator will interpret that concept from experience or from deductions based on the production preferences of the director.

6.21 First show on a camera

6.21.1 Basic skills

When the day arrives for a trainee to operate their first camera on transmission or recording they may have already acquired the habits of preparation, anticipation and concentration.

The basic skills required for multicamera camerawork are:

- the skills needed to control smoothly the camera and mounting;
- the skills needed to prepare for a recording/transmission and to repeat what was rehearsed or agreed at a specific time in the programme;
- the skills needed to match the tempo of the camerawork to the timescale of the programme. In practice this means that every shot has to be delivered precisely when it is required with no opportunity for the camera operator to hold the action whilst last-minute preparations are made;
- the ability to work as part of a camera crew.

It is obviously not possible to acquire all the techniques associated with multicamerawork on Day

Pre-rehearsal check list
The following basic preparations should be followed when operating a camera for the first time.

- Check over camera, mount, remove chains if fitted and unlock pan/tilt head.
- Check that the cable is 'eighted' and free to follow any camera movement.
- Look through the camera cards if supplied and check opening position on floor plan.
- Check that you can clearly hear production and engineering talkback on your headset.
- Get the feel of the camera movement and adjust friction.
- Adjust pan bar and position of the zoom demand unit according to personal preference. Position of pan bar may need to be altered to accommodate very high or low shots during rehearsal.
- Check focus and the varying zone of focus depending on zoom angle.
- Reduce the headset cable loop to the minimum operational requirements and tie off to the camera. A long loop can easily get snagged.

Figure 6.41

One. These will only be mastered after exposure to a wide range of programme-making. What can be practised by the trainee when not involved in rehearsal is the control of camera movement, focusing and pedestal technique.

6.21.2 In rehearsal

At the start of rehearsal, remember that you are part of a camera crew and your work must match their shots. Despite the concentration required to master the steep learning curve before transmission/recording, keep in touch with what other members of the production team are doing. You need to display individual initiative plus the ability to be aware of what is happening around you. Do not bury your head in the viewfinder all the time. On many shows a camera operator will often be looking around the camera more than in the viewfinder.

Listen to talkback and mark up any information that concerns your shots and watch the cue lights in the viewfinder to check when you are 'off-shot' and 'on-shot'. If you are asked a question on recording or transmission, provided you are not on shot, 'nod' the camera in the tilt mode to communicate 'yes' and move the camera in the pan mode to communicate 'no'.

6.21.3 Coping with change

If there is a major change during the programme, anticipate how it will affect your shots and be prepared to adjust to a new and unrehearsed situation.

Never underestimate the importance of anticipation in making time for yourself. Do not allow the excitement and confusion of a situation to get in the way of thinking clearly in order to act decisively.

Hold rather than grip the pan bar. White knuckles and a sweaty palm will not improve your ability to control the camera. Nerves are natural and often a stimulus to concentration, but ignore how many hundreds of thousands of viewers may be watching your work and put your attention on the next shot. If you do make a mistake forget about it until after the show, and then consider how you can avoid making the same mistake again. Look for comment about your work after the programme has finished and mentally make a note of any advice after your first day as a camera operator has ended.

6.22 Pre-rehearsal checklist

Before rehearsal commences check that all the operational controls of the camera, pedestal and pan/tilt head are functioning and set up correctly, and that they are adjusted to suit your operational technique.

Check that movement of the camera, mounting and pan/tilt head is silent and that you have the means to mark up camera position and to mark up camera cards if supplied.

6.22.1 Camera

- Check that zoom drive cables are clamped and will not snag when the camera is in use.
- Check that the pan bar and zoom control/shot box are positioned to your operational requirements and that the crib card holder is conveniently positioned.
- Check the range of viewfinder movement and adjust if necessary.
- Set up viewfinder – contrast/brightness/peaking/edge of frame – and check that all cue lights are switched on and working.
- Check and adjust the back focus of the zoom if the lens has just been rigged.
- Check that the camera channel and viewfinder definition is adequate for you to be the first to see loss of optical focus.
- Check talkback and tie off headset cable for minimum loop.

- Set up shot box angles if this is your preferred method of working.
- Check zoom and focus control setting and check the smoothness of their operation.
- Check the setting of the zoom extender.
- Check the lens front element and clean with lens tissue if necessary.

6.22.2 Pan/tilt head

- Unlock the pan/tilt head.
- Adjust the balance of the camera and check correct size cams are fitted for lens/camera/viewfinder configuration.
- Adjust the degree of pan and tilt friction required for the programme format.

6.22.3 Pedestal

- Remove safety locking pin or bar if fitted.
- Check that the balance of the column is correct by raising the column to its highest point and check if the camera stays in this position. Reverse the procedure by depressing to the lowest point and check if the camera rises. Add or subtract trim weights to balance the pedestal.
- Check that there are sufficient trim weights in their storage tray to accommodate any change of temperature during rehearsal/recording.
- Check that the camera cable is clamped and there is sufficient loop of cable to allow nearly 360° movement on the head.
- Check that cable guards are correctly set to avoid riding over the camera cable.
- Check that the camera cable is 'eighted' and will provide an unimpeded flow of cable when the camera moves.

6.23 Camera rehearsal/recording/transmission

(See Chapter 2.)

Customary technique

The nature of many programmes (e.g. sport, discussion), does not allow precise information about shots either to be rehearsed or confirmed. What should be clear in the mind of each camera operator is the range of shots they will be involved with.

Rehearsal

- Use the rehearsal period to establish what your specific contribution will be. Ask questions if you are unsure.
- Make notes on your camera card or running order and mark up camera position (see crib cards).
- Make yourself aware of the role of other cameras.
- Plan for the unexpected and have contingency plans for any eventuality.
- Do not over-commit yourself with numerous camera repositions if you are unsure of the time available to implement them.
- Check the cable routing of the camera and any potential object on which it could get snagged (e.g. rostrum corners, stage weights, boom wheels).

Figure 6.42

Multicamera production technique relies on the assumption that every member of the production crew is equipped with a knowledge of the conventions of the specific programme format and has a thorough mastery of the basic skills in their particular craft. Information about shots will be supplied during rehearsal and/or during transmission/recording, but it will be assumed by the director that the camera crew will respond with customary technique to the specific programme requirements (for example matched shots for interviews – see Section 6.20.10).

6.24 Working in a camera crew

6.24.1 Crew reputation

A feature of multicamera productions since the earliest days of television production has been the contribution made by television camera operators working regularly together as a crew. The number of camera operators forming a crew varies depending on production requirements, but it is generally agreed that the continuity of working regularly as a team has a positive influence on the quality of the combined effort.

Working many years together on a range of top quality programmes, a number of outstanding camera crews have not only a taken a pride in their crew identity, but have amassed a breadth of collective experience that is often used by the director to the benefit of the production.

Working as part of a camera crew on multicamera productions requires a keen awareness of teamwork and a willingness to contribute. Apart from rehearsal/transmission, multicamerawork also requires cooperation with other members of the crew when rigging and de-rigging, in the care and handling of equipment and in the sense of responsibility, if equipment is shared, to check that equipment is never passed on (even to an unknown camera operator or crew) that is faulty or has parts that are missing. The golden rule is that you always return with everything you took to a location.

6.24.2 Production team

Live and recorded 'as-live' production methods rely on every member of the production team perfecting their input into the programme at the moment of transmission. All the different skills employed – performance, lighting, sound, vision control, vision mixing, etc. – interact and the quality of the production is only as good as the weakest contribution. If one member of the team is badly prepared or lacks sufficient experience to resolve production problems, their incompetence will eventually affect the rest of the production team. The speed of multicamera productions relies on everyone getting it right first time.

Working as a team
Your contribution to the team effort is by:

- being competent in your own job. This helps other craft skills to do theirs because they are not wrong-footed by your operational errors and misjudgements;
- being consistent in framing and shot structure and reproducing on transmission any part of the programme that was pre-rehearsed;
- having an understanding and a respect for other people's skills and being willing to adjust your work to help resolve their production problems;
- having a willingness to compromise from the ideal coupled with the judgement to assess the minimum standard that is acceptable.

Figure 6.43

Everyone wants to work and achieve the highest possible standards in their particular craft area, but television production is a group effort and good television techniques are working practices that enable other crafts as well as the individual to achieve a high standard of performance.

Perfect sound may be provided by a boom position that inhibits camera movement or a microphone position that casts shadows and intrudes into shot. This may be perfect sound but it is bad television production sound. A shot that is composed with so much headroom that there is no space for the boom

microphone to get close to the performers may be a great shot in isolation, but it is also bad television production practice.

An awareness of the day-to-day problems of the other skills within the production team and a willingness to reach a compromise on one's own production demands will improve the quality of the whole programme. Monopolizing rehearsal time to get your particular problems sorted out may possibly prevent someone else resolving their difficulties, resulting in a scrappy recording/transmission.

6.24.3 Working to cue lights

All television cameras designed for multicamera working are fitted with red lamps on the camera and in the viewfinder, called cue lights or tally lamps. These are switched on when the camera is selected on the vision mixing panel. The cue light system is an essential part of multicamera production technique as it identifies to the camera operator and all other production staff working alongside the cameras which camera is 'live' during rehearsal, recording or transmission.

Cue light position
A cue light is usually positioned on top of the camera and housed in a red cover that often displays the camera number. In this position, it can be seen by most people working on the production although it is often obscured when viewed from the front of the camera. As performers often have to be aware which camera is 'on', a duplicate of the light is positioned on the front of the camera and/or on the front of the lens housing. A prompter, if fitted, masks these lamps and therefore the front of the prompter is fitted with an additional cue light.

A cue light is also needed at the control point if the camera is remotely operated via a control panel in the studio/location or in a control room. When a camera is rigged on a crane or dolly, an additional cue light is often positioned in the eyeline of the trackers/riggers.

Viewfinder cue lights
A red cue light displayed in the viewfinder reminds the camera operator when his camera is 'on air'. The operator should be aware from the director's instructions on talkback when his or her camera is going to be used (e.g. 'Coming to 2. Cut to 2'), but sometimes on an ad-lib, fast-cutting sequence the shot they are providing may be taken without prior warning.

With experience, the cue light is used instinctively. There will be an automatic response to the cue light just as there will be instant adjustment in framing to compensate for subject movement. The tempo of intercutting between cameras requires the camera operator to develop the ability to work at two speeds. Off shot, there is often the need to find the required shot almost instantaneously. Once the framing is settled on and the camera has been cut to, there may be the need to develop the shot (zoom in or out, pan, track, etc.) at a tempo controlled by the subject matter. Frequently this will be a slow, unobtrusive movement. When the cue light goes off, the camera operator is again released to find the next shot in the fastest possible time.

The cue light is therefore a visual indicator that separates the two speeds of work. If, inadvertently, the camera is cut to whilst rapidly moving to a new shot, the cue light coming on should instantly change the camera movement to freeze on whatever composition is in the frame (if it is usable) or, as unobtrusively as possible, to adjust to an acceptable framing.

Control of cue light

As soon as the fader on the vision mixing panel controlling a camera's output is moved off the end stop, the cue light on that camera comes on even though the output of that camera may not yet be visible on the transmission output monitor in the control room. When the cue light comes on at the beginning of a mix, any camera movement that may be required should be delayed until the mix has ended unless there is a production requirement to carry a movement through a mix.

Depending on the design of the vision mixing panel, a camera's cue lights may come on (even if not on transmission or recording) if the camera is previewed and selected for a digital effect. Conversely, some mixer designs allow a camera to be cut to 'line' through an effects bank without switching on the camera cue light. This can happen with some types of chroma key compositing and a check should be made during rehearsal (if available) if the camera is 'live' without showing a cue light and informing anyone who may be affected.

Green cue light working

With the growth of productions where a camera's output is fed to more than one production control room (e.g. golf coverage by two or more independent broadcasters), the red cue light in the viewfinder is lit when the master control room is using the shot and a second green cue light comes on when another

control room has selected the camera's output for transmission. The camera operator can only work to one set of directions and therefore the red cue light takes precedence whenever there is a conflict of use.

Switchable cue lights

It is sometimes advantageous on location (or, for example, with a studio audience discussion) to switch off the external cue lights on the camera to avoid drawing attention to the use of the camera. The ability to switch off the cue lights can also help if unwanted reflections arise from glossy or polished surfaces. Alternatively, the cue lights are often blanked off using gaffer tape.

Other production staff's use of cue lights

Although the camera operator is continuously responding to the cue lights on the camera, other members of the production staff on the studio floor or location frequently need to know which camera is on air. The floor manager needs to be in a position alongside the taking camera to cue artistes, etc. Boom operators not only need to know which camera is on shot, but also the size of shot they are taking. Other floor staff making scenery and props changes work to cue lights or, if graphic material is being used, use them to decide when a caption can be replaced with succeeding material.

6.24.4 A mixed viewfinder

The camera operator can usually switch the viewfinder feed from the camera output to a mixed feed of camera output and a designated source (e.g. another camera). The viewfinder feed can be switched either by a button on the pan bar or by a switch on or near the viewfinder. A 'mixed viewfinder' feed is also the common term applied to switching the viewfinder picture to a single (unmixed) video feed such as 'studio out' – the visual source that is currently being selected at the vision mixing panel as opposed to 'station out' which is the programme currently being transmitted. 'Studio out' is useful when matching shots or identifying what other cameras are offering in an 'as-directed' situation.

The mixed viewfinder facility is an invaluable aid in many production situations such as in motor racing coverage where a specific car or group of cars may have to be picked up immediately they come into the field of view of a camera. By monitoring the OB output via mixed viewfinder, a camera operator can identify lead cars or cars in shot on other cameras before they reach the operator's position on the track. The speed of the event precludes identifying the cars in precise detail but, for example, the outline shape of two or three leading cars can be memorized and picked up and panned with as soon as they come into view.

The mixed output available at the viewfinder is usually selected in vision control although some models of cameras have a number of video sources that can be selected at the camera. Any video source can be mixed (depending on synchronization) with a camera output such as special effects and colour separation, but a check should be made that both video sources are combined at the viewfinder with correct timing. That is, one image is not displaced horizontally from the other due to taking a longer video path and therefore arriving later. This can cause problems when lining up a precise match between the camera's picture and, for example, an electronic graphic.

The balance of the mix between the two sources can be adjusted to make one image brighter than another, which sometimes helps when matching up the camera's output to another source (e.g. seeing the edge of a chroma key panel).

Another facility that is sometimes useful with mixed viewfinder working is a grid or a cursor that can be selected at the camera and superimposed over the camera's output to check horizontal lines. Although electronic generated text has superseded caption cards on cameras, occasionally there are situations when a visual element requires checking to see if it is horizontal or vertical.

6.24.5 Linear picture

The size of the scanned area in the viewfinder can be adjusted and it is obviously important that the whole of the picture area can be seen. It is also important that the viewfinder picture is free from geometric distortion. Check the linearity of the viewfinder by framing up on a grid or a circle. If the squares of a grid vary in size across the frame (providing the camera is square to the caption) then there will be errors in framing and composition. Sometimes one side of the picture is non-linear, which causes errors in framing.

6.24.6 Visual memory and cue cards

The ability to remember the precise framing of a shot comes with practice and experience. There are no visual memory rules or procedures to be learnt as visual memory appears to operate at the instinctive level. At the speed at which some shots are required, the reflex selection of lens angle and framing are completed in an instant. There is no time, for example, to leisurely check if the left-hand frame was exactly in line with a prominent edge. The shot is framed, focused and cut to. In these circumstances, visual memory is coordinating hand and eye to provide precisely the frame that is required. In general, however, it is always a good idea to make notes on the camera card as a reminder of a shot.

6.24.7 Camera cards

Many studio-based programmes and some OB programmes will have a pre-planned script which identifies which cameras will cover specific action, dialogue or narration. Each shot is numbered in sequence with a relevant shot description if known. The shots applicable to each camera are then listed on individual camera cards (commonly called crib cards) and attached to each camera.

The function of the shot cards on rehearsal is to provide sufficient information to set up each shot. The shot description needs to be abbreviated otherwise the cards would be unreadable when working at speed.

Camera cards therefore have two functions, which are sometimes in conflict:

- During rehearsal, adequate information needs to be on the card in order that the camera operator can understand what shot is required plus any special requirement relating to the shot.
- During transmission/recording the camera card provides a reminder of essential information and needs to be read at a glance whilst operating the camera. Anything superfluous to essentials or poor layout makes it difficult to 'snatch' information quickly from the card.

A camera card is an abbreviated script for the camera operator and the information is usually laid out in three columns:

Shot number   Camera position   Shot description

with plenty of space for camera operators to add notes and alterations during rehearsal.

Shot number
Normally a script is divided into segments and itemized as shots. Any other change of visual source

including VTR and electronic graphics is also assigned a shot number. The shot numbers are continuous and if during rehearsal an extra shot is added then it is given the previous shot number with an alphabet suffix. For example, 32 then new shot 32a followed by a second new shot 32b and so forth. This avoids renumbering the whole script.

If the programme contains 'as-directed' sequences such as a discussion then each camera will be given an indication on their individual cards such as 2-shot, MS, MCU, etc., followed by 'intercut' or 'as-directed'.

Camera position

If a programme has pre-planned camera positions marked on a floor plan, then each camera position will be lettered and this letter will appear against the appropriate shot number. Sometimes parts of the studio area or location will be identified by a name to indicate where a particular sequence will be staged For example, 'Cyc', which is the standard abbreviation for cyclorama, is the backcloth which is stretched in an arc around two or more sides of the studio.

Shot description

Shot descriptions are abbreviated as much as possible so that the information can be quickly scanned. In a complex show with many shot changes in a fast-cutting sequence, the camera operator may have only the briefest of time to look away from the viewfinder to check the next shot and camera position.

6.24.8 Marking up

Most camera operators prefer to scribble a few words against a complex shot description as additional information noted at rehearsal. These abbreviated reminders (which may be incomprehensible to anyone else) replace the typed shot description. The aim of any alteration to the card by the camera operator is to make instantly legible any essential camera movement and to link it to the action that cues it. During rehearsal, the camera operator will be marking up the card and marking the camera position, if necessary.

For example, if the camera is craned down on a tight shot of a performer and the shot requires the camera to hold the close shot as the artiste stands, the camera operator will have to crane up and keep a good framing, in focus, on the artiste. The essential point in this action is to know precisely when the stand occurs.

Watching during rehearsal, the operator may note that the performer will make one or two 'false' body movements as if they were going to stand, but only actually make the move at the third indication. Although most performers rehearse and reproduce movement to dialogue, scribbling key words down does help, particularly if a number of camera movements are linked to actor movement during a scene. But there is a limit to this method. The camera card quickly fills up with dialogue lines that are difficult if not impossible to read at speed. As the camera operator is using a viewfinder it is often best to use visually observed movement as a cue to camera movement.

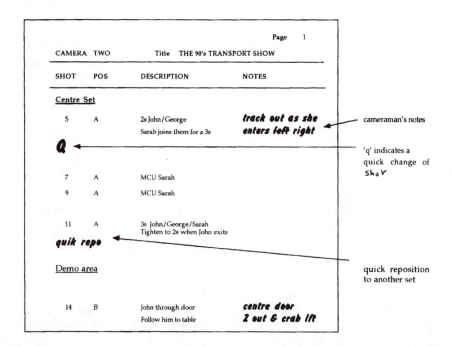

Figure 6.44 After rehearsal has finished, the camera card should provide the camera operator with all the information (plus the operator's visual memory) that is required to complete the show. It is not unknown for camera operators to spend time before transmission/recording re-marking their cards or even completely rewriting a card in order to make the information instantly legible and able to be read at speed. A crib card should contain only essential information that can be read at a glance.

For example, a camera card may have the scribble '2 lean fwd stands' which translated by the camera operator means 'when he leans forward for the second time he will stand and I will need to crane up and focus fwd'. A well laid out camera card will always have plenty of space for this type of rehearsal note. It is also important that the changeover between two cards occurs during a sequence of slow shot change to avoid hastily scrabbling to get the top card flipped over while looking for the next shot.

6.24.9 Reproduction

Many programmes require shots that have been set up in a rehearsal period to be accurately reproduced on transmission/recording. Marking up a camera card and marking up camera positions gives one set of parameters. The other essential component is the lens angle. Many zoom lenses can be controlled (in addition to the zoom demand control on the pan bar or lens) by a shot box (see Section 6.13).

If precise framing is required, either the shot box can be adjusted to give the required lens angle or the camera operator will have to rely on their visual memory to find the necessary framing.

6.24.10 Talkback

New to talkback

A camera operator new to wearing a headset and working with talkback might be overwhelmed by the amount of information received. With experience it is possible to ignore all but the information that affects camerawork. This is not simply camera direction. Any information that may affect future shots or shots that will be needed should be 'logged' by the camera operator and used when required.

Talkback discipline

With nearly all communication channelled through the control room, it is obviously important to choose the right time to talk to the director or control room. Do not interrupt an existing discussion or a briefing that will be addressed to the whole crew. Wait for a pause (and close to transmission or recording this never seems to occur) before opening your microphone and calling the control room. Keep the conversation brief and if questions from the director can be answered with a simple yes or no, nod the camera in the vertical direction for 'yes' and pan the camera in the horizontal direction for 'no'.

Programme sound

It is often important to listen to programme sound. During a discussion, sports commentary, etc. the camera shots offered will be directly related to the information supplied by programme sound. On OBs, 'clean commentary' is available that excludes the output of the effects microphones so that the commentary can be clearly heard. On other programmes, the spill from the sound monitor in the control room onto the director's microphone is usually adequate.

Many camera operators prefer to work with one of the headset earpieces on one ear and the other earpiece off the ear. Programme sound can then be heard directly and the uncovered ear is available in case of *sotto-voce* messages from other people such as floor managers during transmission.

Talkback spillage

Another simple discipline connected with talkback is to always unplug your headset when you are not wearing it. If you hang the headset on the pan bar and leave the studio when an item is being recorded which does not involve your camera, the talkback spillage could easily cause a retake. If you are working on the live side of microphone make certain you are working with the lowest talkback level that is required.

If you are new to wearing a headset, be careful that the reduction in local sound from wearing it does not cause you to raise your voice when talking on talkback and disturb the rehearsal. Remember that the artistes cannot hear the director and it may be necessary when pointing out a problem caused by an artiste position or movement to choose your words with discretion. Ill-chosen comments can imply a performer is at fault when it is simply a small detail that requires attention.

High levels of ambient noise such as rock concerts or motor racing require special noise cancelling headsets otherwise talkback will be inaudible.

6.24.11 Working with talkback

The lifeblood of multicamera camerawork is talkback. Without talkback, a camera operator is cut off from the production process and can make little or no contribution unless a clearly rehearsed plan of action has been prearranged.

There are a number of working areas involved in a multicamera programme and at some time in the production process they may individually need to speak to one or other of the team. Collectively they need the coordination of the director's talkback which knits the group effort together.

Director's talkback

The director organizes and directs the activity of the production team and coordinates changes or transitions during transmission or recording and keeps everyone informed about the progress of the production. He or she will give direct commands across a range of production decisions such as cueing of performers, intercutting between vision sources, shot size, details of up-coming action, etc. A number of other production decisions are the responsibility of individuals such as, for example, the control of audio levels by the sound supervisor, the control of the lighting balance by the lighting director, the adjustment of framing and focus by the camera operator, and the resetting of props or scenery by the floor manager.

Talkback on headset

The camera operator hears talkback on a headset plugged into the camera (or by radio talkback) and usually has the facility to communicate via a switched microphone attached to the headset. The director's talkback channel is usually shared by the production assistant (speaking on a separate microphone) working alongside the director in the control room. Both talkback levels are adjusted by the same volume control on the camera.

As well as the talkback from the director, most camera channels have an engineering talkback facility which is often shared by vision control and lighting. Their audio level is regulated by another volume control on the camera.

A direct feed of programme sound is usually provided and adjusted by a third volume control. These three basic talkback facilities are often augmented by omnibus talkback which allows other members of the production team (e.g. sound supervisor, technical manager), to 'switch in' and be heard on general talkback.

Some talkback systems also provide for inter-camera talkback, which allows camera operators to talk to each other and to trackers/grips.

6.25 Robotic camerawork

As we have discussed in this chapter, television camerawork is the integration of manual dexterity in order to control the camera mounting and camera

with quick and flexible reactions to precisely frame and focus a shot, plus harmonizing camera movement and shot size in accordance with the conventions of 'invisible technique', and developing the programme judgement to seek and find the appropriate shot in ad-lib or 'as-directed' formats.

These requirements have been discussed in the context of manually operating the camera (i.e. the camera operator stands behind the camera using the pan bar, camera mounting controls and viewfinder). But most of these operations can be carried out by remoting the camera controls to an operating position away from the studio floor.

6.25.1 Remote control

There are a number of camera remote control systems which attempt to mimic how a camera is manually operated. Usually they have three components: on-camera servo motors that enable the camera to be panned and tilted, lens controls that allow focus and zoom to be adjusted, and an elevation unit which can remotely alter the lens height. In more complex robotic operations there is also the ability to reposition the pedestal (x-y operation).

At the remote operating position the facilities include:

- the control of camera functions through a joystick, and/or rotating switch which allows control of pan, tilt, zoom and focus discretely on shot;
- the ability to remotely control the above functions on a number of cameras (often up to eight cameras), and to precisely set the time of a specific camera movement (e.g. a zoom in/out);
- the facility to set up a number of shots on each camera, to label and store each set-up and the capability of rapidly recalling a specific shot. Sometimes this memorized data is recorded on a computer floppy disk which can be removed from the memory system (e.g. the settings for a weekly programme);
- recall of the stored parameters of each shot memorized by button, mouse or using a touch-screen visual presentation.

6.25.2 Robotic control

Basic requirements for any robotic system of camera control are:

- silent operation;
- remote control of pan, tilt, zoom, and focus;

- rapid repositioning – fast acceleration – swift motor responses;
- tight damping without oscillation or overshoot;
- imperceptible control of movement on-shot;
- movement on-shot using pivot points;
- storage of a number of pre-set positions of pan/tilt settings, zoom and focus setting with a designated code or description;
- preview facilities of each camera's output – these can be displayed on the same screen;
- cue/tally light indicating which camera is currently selected at the vision mixing panel.

6.25.3 Setting up a shot

A shot can be framed up by means of a joystick, and by adjusting the camera height by way of the elevation unit. Once framed up, the shot can be stored and the speed of any zoom in/out can be adjusted and pre-set so that when the shot is recalled, the rehearsed position of panning head and lens angle/focus is quickly obtained. There is always the need to preview a stored camera position because whereas the camera parameters may be precise, presenters are human and their body position or chair position may have shifted (see Section 6.25.6). Trimming the shot to adjust headroom and composition may be necessary on preview or on-shot. The sensitivity of the controls will dictate if 'on-shot' adjustment can be achieved imperceptibly.

The servos have to be designed to match how an experienced camera operator will normally operate a camera. This includes non-linear speed of movement (e.g. panning, zooming and camera movement to match the action) and ensuring that zoom movement and the repositioning of the frame coincide at the end of the movement. The response of the servos can be adjusted, but there are certain rates of change of movement which are programmed in the software. For example, joystick sensitivity can be adjusted to customize the feel of the control to the operator's requirements. The ratio of change between zoom/focus, pan and tilt is determined by software factory pre-set to duplicate the manual use of pivot points.

6.25.4 Storing a shot

A number of shots can be programmed and quickly accessed either through a keypad recalling alphanumeric code for each shot, or by a touch screen displaying a mosaic of freeze frame of shots available. Whatever the system in use, there is always the essential requirement of maintaining an up-to-date index describing each shot stored so that it can be accurately recalled.

With touch-screen control up to eight cameras can be controlled; or, on a busy programme, there is the ability to split the operational control into two operating positions. The display screen can either display the output of any of the remotely controlled cameras, or show a mosaic of freeze frames of previously stored shots. When the image of the stored shot is touched, that camera/lens position immediately reverts to the recorded settings.

6.25.5 Movement on shot

Camera movement set up on a joystick can be accurately reproduced. Motion memory stores the start and end frame, and the speed selected for the movement. The pan, tilt and zoom rates (and adjustment of height if required) are contoured to arrive at the end frame in unison.

6.25.6 Recalling a shot

The accuracy of the robotic system's repeatability (i.e. returning to the same shot) is measured either in arcsecs or degrees (60 arcsec = 0.01°). Most systems are accurate enough to accommodate shots of presenters, who are unlikely to be absolutely immobile as they are usually paid to be animated and vivacious. A more important consideration is the speed of repositioning between shots. The robotic speed is unlikely to match a manual operator because of the servo motor's design requirement to avoid overshoot and oscillation at maximum speed, and the need to provide imperceptible movement at the slowest speed.

6.25.7 Safety

The safe operation of unmanned cameras requires a prominent sign informing studio production staff, or programme guests, that the camera may move without warning. When x-y servo pedestals are installed (pedestals that are powered to be remotely repositioned), collision avoidance programmes need to be built into the remote control software to prevent damage to people, equipment or studio sets. No-go areas or the operational zones of other remote cameras can be set for each remotely controlled pedestal. Each pedestal needs to be fitted with an auto-facility to stop when making contact with another object.

6.25.8 x-y servo pedestals

With x-y function fitted, the pedestal can be remotely repositioned or remotely moved on-shot. Over time, if a pedestal is moved around a studio, there may be a tendency for the base to move out of its original alignment and to twist, causing errors when recalling a stored pedestal position. One method of correcting this is to lay black and white squares on the studio floor, and then store their position in the remote control memory. When this position is recalled, the pedestal moves to the squares and uses their alignment to reorientate the base of the pedestal.

6.25.9 Elevation units

Remotely controlled elevation units can be fitted to most pedestals and can either reposition the camera height off-shot or smoothly crane the camera to a new lens height on-shot. One disadvantage of customizing a presenter position lens height as well as lens angle and pan/tilt is that presenters vary in height and each presenter may have to have their own set of parameters memorized. In general, shots can be set-up for a specific presenter, or a presenter position, with some trimming of the framing as required. Swivel chairs for interviews may not return to a pre-set position and close shots will need to be trimmed for optimum composition.

6.25.10 Dual operation – robotic designs for remote and manual operation

Camera mounting/lens controls can be designed for dual use and be manually or remotely operated. It is essential that when manually controlling the camera, the pan/tilt remote servo geared motors are completely disengaged and the operator has the facility to adjust the friction controls.

6.25.11 Visual memory and virtual reality

Chroma key virtual reality set-ups often require precise alignment of the foreground subject (e.g. lens position, lens angle, lens height, camera position) and the background keyed-in subject in order to achieve a believable composite perspective (see Section 8.5.16). This may require the foreground camera position to be returned to a precise pre-rehearsed framing. If the camera is manually operated, this precise framing may rely on good visual memory although viewfinder cursors (if available) are sometimes used as an aid to framing. Robotic cameras with stored parameters can usually exceed the precision achieved by manual operation.

The other advantage of robotic operation is that on news bulletins scattered throughout the day, manual operation can lead to boredom and inattention because of the lack of challenging camerawork. Remote control provides accurate, fast repeatability and variety of shot.

6.25.12 Location and adverse weather provision

A remote camera mounted in an exterior location can be weatherproofed and fitted with remotely controlled lens wipers, heaters and lighting.

6.25.13 Coverage of national assemblies and conferences

Shot control of robotic cameras installed in national assemblies or conferences can be controlled by a touch screen. When a member of the assembly rises to speak, the operator touches the image of the speaker in a wide shot and another robotic camera automatically covers the speaker in a closer shot.

Automatic control of robotic cameras providing close shots of a large number of people can also be achieved in those assemblies where a member is chosen to speak by the chairperson or speaker by means of switching a microphone to the next speaker position. The selection of the microphone position automatically selects the appropriate shots and repositions a camera such as a wide shot containing the new speaker which is cut to automatically. A closer shot can be trimmed for optimum framing before it is cut to.

7 Single-camera camerawork

7.1 Basic camerawork skills

Despite the drift from analogue to digital, linear tape editing to non-linear storage, the majority of single-camera camerawork remains a hybrid of TV and film technique. It requires a thorough understanding of the camera technology, the ability to choose the appropriate camera technique for the production, an understanding of the conventions and customary practice of the programme format, and always to shoot with editing in mind.

There is a standard technique which is employed in nearly all types of camerawork whatever the recording medium or the technology employed. A full description of this perennial technique is given in Chapter 6 (see invisible technique; the zoom lens; operational skills; camera movement; depiction of depth; visual design and composition).

But technology does influence technique. For example, digital video acquisition allows more detailed control of the image recorded via menus accessed through the viewfinder. Disk recording enables a new set of techniques to be practised. The common trend is for video cameras to become more like computers in their ability to store and index shots, and to customize the image.

The most common programme format that the multiskiller may be involved in is magazine and news coverage. The conventions and requirements for these production are described in later chapters (see Chapters 9 and 11). Each production type requires some specialist technique and possibly a specific format.

7.2 Digital tape formats

Analogue acquisition has the least control of signal processing. Digital tape cameras provide more control of the signal *before* it is recorded. Disk recording has the same control of the signal before recording, but in addition has the facility to control shot order, shot length, etc. *after* recording. Technology does affect technique, but depending on the recording medium, only about 20–30% of the complete shoot.

7.2.1 The camera as a computer

Data manipulation before recording is similar to the action of a computer, and can be applied to video because the signal is in a digital form. Digital manipulation of the image allows customizing the image through the camera menu. Digital acquisition allows an expansion of automatic facilities such as exposure zones, speed of iris response, precise control of face tone, the removal of blemishes and picture zones. Digital manipulation also allows selective contouring, and softer transitions between auto functions. Digital cameras are becoming computers with the same ability to manipulate data before the editing stage. We can also expect the development of specialized software that can be loaded into the camera for specific needs or to expand the camera's facilities.

7.2.2 Camerawork and budget

The price of equipment is an overriding factor in an industry that is forced to become more competitive, chasing fewer viewers scattered across a greater number of channels. This requires smaller programme budgets and cheaper equipment, and has generated interest in DVCPRO, Digital-S, DVCam and DV cameras.

The cost of equipment, and, in news production, speed of turn-around, influences which format is selected. Shooting timescales and editing in the field are also important factors. Increasingly, there is concern that tape libraries are rapidly becoming obsolete and inaccessible as old formats and replay machines disappear. It is not practical or economic to annually dub these libraries on to the latest format. Production companies do not want a proliferation of formats which involve them in duplicating editing systems and playback systems. There is also the debate about the pros and cons of linear or non-linear editing. All these changes affect how the material is shot.

7.2.3 Shooting for editing

Providing a story structure, and shot variety, to enable flexibility in editing are basic standard techniques required from the ENG/EFP camera operator. Editing in the field based on the low-cost DV format is a useful time-saver for news bulletins; as is SNG.

The material acquired by a portable camera/recorder can be edited or it can be used live via satellite or terrestrial links. Although the recording format may alter, standard camerawork practices remain largely unchanged. To competently employ the video/film hybrid technique, a basic knowledge of video recording, sound, lighting, video editing and TV journalism needs to be added to the primary role of the camera operator. This chapter mainly deals with the technology of video acquisition (see also Chapter 9 and Section 11.6).

7.2.4 Manual v auto

Most cameras have a range of automatic features. Auto-exposure, auto-gain, etc. can enable adequate pictures to be recorded when, as in news gathering, there is little or no time, or opportunity, to set the controls manually. Nevertheless, the trainee should aim to understand all the controls on the camera in order to intelligently override the average results an auto facility can provide. Despite the sophistication and computing power of a modern video camera, they can at times be remarkably obtuse, and arrive at the wrong conclusion about an image they are assessing. Only the camera operator will know what is the significant part of the image and how it should be presented on screen.

7.3 Viewfinder

7.3.1 Viewfinder: brightness and contrast

The monocular viewfinder is the first and often the only method of checking picture quality for the

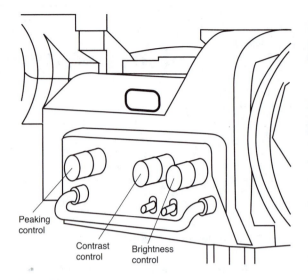

Peaking control

Contrast control　　Brightness control

Figure 7.1

camcorder camera operator. The small black and white image has to be used to check framing, focusing, exposure, contrast and lighting. It is essential, as the viewfinder is the main guide to what is being recorded, to ensure that it is correctly set up. This means aligning the brightness and contrast of the viewfinder display.

Neither control directly affects the camera output signal. Indirectly, however, if the brightness control is incorrectly set, manual adjustment of exposure based on the viewfinder picture can lead to under- or over-exposed pictures. The action of the brightness and contrast controls therefore needs to be clearly understood.

Brightness

This control alters the viewfinder tube bias control and unless it is correctly set up the viewfinder image cannot be used to judge exposure. The brightness control must be set so that any true black produced by the camera is just not seen in the viewfinder.

If, after a lens cap is placed over the lens and the aperture is fully closed, the brightness is turned up, the viewfinder display will appear increasingly grey and then white. This obviously does not represent the black image produced by the camera. If the brightness is now turned down, the image will gradually darken until the line structure of the picture is no longer visible. The correct setting of the brightness control is at the point when the line structure just disappears and there is no visible distinction between the outside edge of the display and the surrounding tube face. If the brightness control is decreased beyond this point, the viewfinder will be unable to display the darker tones just above black and will distort the tonal range of the image. There is therefore only one correct setting of the brightness control which, once set, should not be altered.

Contrast

The contrast control is in effect a gain control. As the contrast is increased the black level of the display remains unchanged (set by the brightness control) whilst the rest of the tones become brighter. This is where confusion over the function of the two viewfinder controls may arise. Increasing the contrast of the image increases the brightness of the image to a point where the electron beam increases in diameter and the resolution of the display is reduced. Unlike the brightness control, there is no one correct setting for the contrast control other than that an 'over-contrasted' image may lack definition and appear subjectively over-exposed. Contrast is therefore adjusted for an optimum displayed image which will depend on picture content and the amount of ambient light falling on the viewfinder display.

Peaking

This control adds edge enhancement to the viewfinder picture as an aid in focusing and has no effect on the camera output signal.

7.3.2 Setting up the viewfinder

(1) Select the aspect ratio if using a switchable format camera. Check that the viewfinder image is in the selected aspect ratio.
(2) Switch CAMERA to BARS or place a lens cap on the lens.
(3) Check the picture in the viewfinder and then reduce contrast and brightness to minimum.
(4) Increase brightness until just before the raster (line structure) appears in the right-hand (black) segment of the bars.
(5) Adjust the contrast until all divisions of the bars can be seen.
(6) Use the bars to check the viewfinder focus and adjust the focus of the viewfinder eyepiece to produce the sharpest picture possible.
(7) With CAMERA switched to ON recheck CONTRAST with the correctly exposed picture. Although CONTRAST control may occasionally need to be adjusted depending on picture content and ambient light change, avoid altering the BRIGHTNESS control.

(8) Set the PEAKING control to provide the minimum edge-enhancement that you require to find focus and adjust the eyepiece focus to achieve maximum sharpness of the viewfinder image. Adjust the position of the viewfinder for optimum operating comfort.

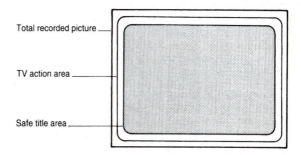

Figure 7.2 Most television receivers have a certain amount of overscan which results in a proportion of the image at the edge of the recorded picture not being visible on the TV screen. That part of the picture which is certain to be seen is termed the safety zone or TV Safe Action Area and is approximately 90% of the total picture area. When framing a shot, keep any vital information within this action area to guarantee it being seen by the majority of 4:3 set viewers. On some cameras, a border can be selected on the zebra/marker switch and inserted into the viewfinder picture to give an indication of the average loss. This safety zone marker has two positions set by an internal switch to provide a box of either 80% or 90% of total picture area.

7.3.3 Aspect ratios and safety zones

With the introduction of widescreen digital TV and the use of dual format cameras (see Section 7.14), programme productions may be shot in 16:9 aspect ratio but transmitted and viewed on 4:3 television receivers. To ease the transition between the two aspect ratios, many broadcasters use a compromise 14:9 aspect ratio for nominally 4:3 sets, but transmit the whole of the 16:9 frame to widescreen sets.

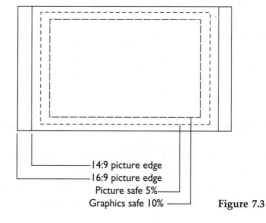

Figure 7.3

This requires the camera operator to frame up a 16:9 picture with these competing requirements in mind. Any essential information is included in the 14:9 picture area although the whole of the 16:9 frame may be transmitted in the future. A 14:9 graticule superimposed on the 16:9 viewfinder picture reminds the camera operator of this requirement. For the foreseeable future, actuality events such as sport may be covered for dual transmission – 16:9 and 14:9 – and therefore framing has to accommodate the smaller format if some viewers are not to be deprived of vital action.

7.3.4 Viewfinder indicators

On some models of analogue cameras the viewfinder indicators are selected from one of three modes of operation. With the OUTPUT/DCC selector to BARS push the AUTO W/B BAL switch to WHT. Each time you push the switch the viewfinder display mode changes. Mode three provides the greatest number of indicators including amount of gain, dynamic contrast on or off, selected filter, white balance pre-set (A or B) and, if audio indicator is set to ON, the channel-1 audio level is displayed. Tape remaining time is also indicated with the 5–0 figure blinking when remaining tape is less than 2 minutes. Battery indicator will also warn a few minutes before the battery voltage drops below the minimum level needed to operate the camera/recorder and will remain continually lit when battery voltage is inadequate. On digital cameras, adjustment of these variables is accomplished by selecting a menu of options.

7.4 White balance

Because the colour temperature of different light sources and mixture of light sources varies (see Section 4.3.2, Colour temperature), it is essential to select the correct filter and white balance the camera whenever you suspect a change has occurred.

Conditions for white balance
- Zero gain or as low as possible for exposure.
- Select auto exposure.
- White object must be illuminated by the same lighting conditions as the subject to be recorded.
- The reference white must be near the centre of the frame and not less than 20% of the frame area. It should be evenly lit with respect to colour and shading and contain no bright highlights.
- Select the appropriate filter to match the colour temperature of the light illuminating the white object.

Figure 7.4

7.4.1 To white balance

To white balance, select the appropriate filter according to the lighting condition and fill the frame with a white object lit by the predominant subject illumination. Check that the gain is at 0 or as low as possible and that any contrast control facility is switched out. On some cameras the white balance cannot be adjusted while the set-up menu is displayed on the viewfinder screen.

There are two memory buttons associated with each filter. Select A or B on the White Balance selector and set the IRIS to automatic iris control. Push up the AUTO W/B BAL switch to WHT. The adjustment will be completed in about one second and the adjusted value will be stored in the A or B memory selected. Depending on the camera model and viewfinder display setting, the viewfinder will display either a double figure with a decimal point which when multiplied by a 1000 will give an approximate colour temperature in Kelvin or will display the colour temperature in Kelvin complete.

If the white balance was unsuccessful the viewfinder may display a message such as 'WHITE:NG' – white balance no good – and a explanatory message. If you set the WHITE BAL selector to the PRST (pre-set) the white balance will be set to the factory pre-set value of 3200 K if the filter position is set to the 3200 K filter position.

7.4.2 In-camera filters

Many cameras are fitted with two filter wheels which are controlled either mechanically, by turning the filter wheel on the left-hand side at the front of the camera, or by selecting the required filter position from a menu displayed in the viewfinder. The filter wheels contain colour correction and neutral density filters and possibly an effects filter. The position of the various filters varies with camera model.

Filter selection

Set the FILTER selectors to match the colour correction filter appropriate to the light source and light intensity. The following combinations of colour correction and neutral density filters will be dependent on the sensitivity of the camera in use:

(1) 3200 K sunrise/sunset/tungsten/studio.
(2) 5600 K + ¼ ND (neutral density) exterior – clear sky.
(3) 5600 K exterior/cloud/rain.
(4) 5600 K + ¹⁄₁₆ ND (neutral density) exterior exceptionally bright.

Neutral density filters are used when there is a need to reduce the depth of field or in circumstances of a brightly lit location.

Cameras could be normalized to the colour temperature of tungsten or daylight. Because of the greater light levels of daylight, most cameras are designed to be operated with no colour correction under tungsten. The 3200 K is a clear glass filter whereas a 5600 K filter (with no ND) is a minus blue filter to cut out the additional blue found in daylight. All colour correction filters decrease the transmission of light and therefore the minus blue filter cuts down the light (by approximately one stop) where most light is available – in daylight. A white balance is required after changing filter position.

3200 K filter

When this filter position is selected, an optical plain glass filter is placed between the lens and the prism block to maintain back focus.

Although the position is marked as 3200 K, no colour correction filter is used because the circuitry of the camera is designed to reproduce as 'white' the proportion of red, green and blue reflected from a known white object lit by tungsten light with a colour temperature of 3200 K.

If there is a change in the colour temperature of the light illuminating the object, for example daylight at midday, which may have a colour temperature of 5600 K, and it is significantly more blue than tungsten light, then a correction filter is required to remove this additional blue and return the light collected by the CCDs to the colour temperature the camera circuitry was designed for, i.e. 3200 K.

7.5 Black balance

Black balance sets the black levels of the R, G, and B channels so that black has no colourcast. It is normally only required:

- when the camera is first used or if the camera has not been in use for some time;
- if the camera has been moved between radically different temperatures or the surrounding temperature has significantly altered;
- when the gain selector values have been changed.

First, white balance to equalize the gains and then black balance; then white balance again. In automatic black balance, the black balance is adjusted after the black set is adjusted. The black shading will then be adjusted if the automatic black balance switch is held

down during the black balance adjustment. Alternatively, manual black balance adjustments can be selected from the set-up menu.

7.5.1 Auto-black balance

The automatic black set/black balance adjustment consists of five phases starting with black set adjustment for Red, then Blue, Green, Red and ending with Blue. Messages will report the progress and results of the auto-black balance depending on the viewfinder display mode selected. Typical black balance procedure would be:

- Select camera output; gain to 0; push down the AUTO W/B BAL to the BLK position.
- Messages may appear in the viewfinder reporting the progress of the black balance, which will take a few seconds.
- During the balance, the iris will close automatically and if it was set to Manual Iris will need to be opened again after completion. The GAIN will also be changed but will return to its zero setting.
- On some cameras, the black balance cannot be adjusted while the set-up menu is displayed on the viewfinder.
- If successful, the adjusted black balance value will be stored in memory, otherwise a message will appear in the viewfinder.
- For many cameras, values stored in memory are saved for about one week when the camera/recorder is turned off. If when the camera is turned on an error message 'MEMORY:NG' is displayed in the viewfinder, the black balance content has been lost. The above black balance procedure will need to be activated.

7.5.2 Camera output selector

There are usually one of three signals that can be selected on the camera which are routed to the VTR and displayed in the viewfinder. They are colour bars, the vision output of the camera (any exposed subject in the field of view of the lens), or the vision output of the camera as above but modified by a variable contrast control circuit (see Section 7.6.4).

7.6 Contrast range

Every shot recorded by the camera/recorder has a variation of brightness contained within it. This variation of brightness is the contrast range of the scene. The relationship between the brightest part of the subject and the darkest part is the contrast ratio. The average exterior contrast ratio is approximately 150:1 but it can be as high as 1000:1.

Normally, exposure is adjusted to allow the contrast range of the scene to be accurately reproduced on the recording. The aim is to avoid losing any variation between shades and at the same time maintaining the overall scene brightness relationships.

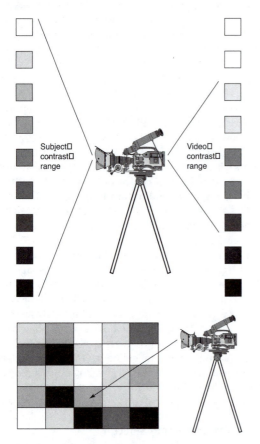

Figure 7.5 The auto exposure system measures the range of subject brightness and sets an *f*-number which will produce a mid-tone grey at 50% of peak white. 50% of peak white is equivalent to the light from a subject with 18% reflectance.

Achieving the correct exposure for any specific shot therefore requires reproducing the detail in the highlights as well as in the shadows of the scene. Additionally, if a face is the subject of the picture then the skin tones need to be set between 70% and 75% of peak white (there may be a wider variation depending on country and skin tones).

It sounds deceptively simple, especially when there is a specific control on the camera to do the job for

you (auto-iris), but like many other descriptions of television technique a simple statement can gloss over a multitude of practical problems.

7.6.1 Video contrast range

Whereas the contrast ratios of everyday location and interiors can range from 20:1 to 1000:1, a video camera can only record a scene range of approximately 32:1. Peak white (100%) to black level (3.125%) is equivalent to 5 stops. The contrast range can be extended by compressing the highlights using a non-linear transfer characteristic when translating light into the television signal (see below). The amount of compression on the highlights can be further increased by switching in contrast control circuits. The result of recording a contrast range greater than the camera can handle is that highlights of the scene will appear a uniform white – details in them will be burnt-out and the darker tones of the scene will be a uniform black. The limiting factor for highlight detail in high contrast scenes is the peak white clipper circuits and the 'knee' of signal amplification in the camera.

Peak white clippers
There are three peak white clippers, one in each colour channel, and their function is to limit any part of the scene that would produce a signal greater than a pre-set value. Their effect is to render all gradations in brightness above the 'clip' level as white – to burn-out any overexposed parts of the picture. This can be difficult for the camera operator to see if the viewfinder is not correctly adjusted (see Section 7.3.2).

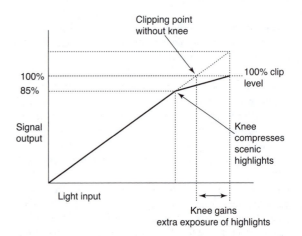

Figure 7.6

Knee

The 'knee', which is introduced into the camera head amplifiers, progressively compresses highlights which otherwise would be lost in the peak white clipper. It extends the camera's response to a high contrast range but with some loss of linearity.

7.6.2 Auto-exposure

There are various methods for determining exposure: manually; by using a light meter and the viewfinder picture, or alternatively, the zebra indicator in the viewfinder; or by using the auto iris-exposure circuit built into the camera. Many camera operators use a combination of all three.

The camera as light meter

A television camera has been called the most expensive light meter produced. If auto-exposure is selected, the feedback to the iris can be instantaneous and the auto circuit will immediately stop down the lens if any significant increase of scene brightness is detected.

Auto-exposure works by averaging the picture brightness and therefore needs to be used intelligently. In some cameras, different portions of the frame can be monitored and the response rate to the change of exposure can be selected. In general, expose for the main subject of the shot and check that the auto-iris is not compensating for large areas of peak brightness (e.g. overcast sky) in the scene.

The lens iris is controlled by the highest reading from the red, green or blue channel and therefore the auto circuit reacts whenever any colour combination approaches peak signal. This auto decision making about exposure may have disadvantages as well as advantages.

Auto-exposure problems

The most common disadvantage occurs when an interview is being recorded and auto-exposure has been selected and left on. The interviewee may be correctly exposed at the start of the interview but if any highly reflective object enters the background of the frame then the auto-exposure circuit may be triggered and will stop down the iris to expose for detail. The interviewee's face will be under-exposed. Additionally, there may be a problem with changing light conditions such as intermittent sunlight requiring significant and rapid changes in face exposure.

Using auto-exposure requires the application of common sense and judgement about the specific lighting conditions and location. Will auto-exposure switched in cause more problems than it solves? Only experience and an intelligent appraisal of the location conditions will produce consistent results.

Auto-iris response

The rate of response of the auto-iris system needs to be fast enough to keep up with a camera panning from a bright to a dark scene, but not so responsive that it instantly over- or under-exposes the picture for a momentary highlight brightness (e.g. a sudden background reflection). If using auto-iris, check that the rate of pan is in step with the auto-iris's ability to change exposure. Some cameras have switchable auto-iris response rates to suit the changing requirements of camera movement.

Zebra exposure indicator

The zebra pattern is a visual indicator in the viewfinder when areas of the picture have reached a certain signal level. If the zebra exposure indicator is switched on, those elements of the image that are above this pre-set level are replaced by diagonal stripes in the picture. The camera operator can respond by closing the iris to adjust the exposure until part or all of the zebra diagonals have been removed.

Onset of zebra level

The level at which the zebra indicator is triggered is obviously a critical factor in this method of assessing exposure and can be adjusted to suit particular operational preferences. Some camera designs have their zebra stripe indicator driven by the luminance signal. The zebra stripe warning is then only valid for nearly-white subjects and exposure of strongly coloured areas may go into over-exposure without warning. Other systems use any of the red, green or blue outputs which exceed the selected signal level to trigger the zebra indicator.

Selecting zebra level

The exposure point at which the zebra indicator is triggered can be a personal operational preference, but criteria to consider when setting that point are:

- If there is a 'pool' of cameras in use then that point should be standard on all cameras.
- The onset point should be close to full exposure but should warn before full burn-out occurs.
- The zebra strip indicator should not obscure important picture information such as the face but it should indicate when flesh tones are in danger of going into over-exposure.

Some UK zebra onset levels are 90–95% for RGB-driven systems and 68% for luminance systems, but the final limiting factor on exposure level is loss of detail, either to noise in the blacks or burn-out in the peak white clipper. Both losses are irrecoverable.

7.6.3 Adjusting the *f*-number

Controlling the light through the lens can be by aperture or ND filter. The *f*-number is defined as a ratio between focal length and the effective diameter of the lens aperture. The *f*-number is not an accurate indication of the speed of the lens because the *f*-number formula is based on the assumption that the lens transmits 100% of the incident light. Because of the variation in the number of elements in the lens and the variation in lens design, different lenses may have different transmittance. Two lenses with the same *f*-number may transmit different amounts of light to the prism block.

7.6.4 Dynamic contrast control

Another way of accommodating a high contrast scene is to alter the camera's transfer characteristics by using the dynamic contrast control (DCC) circuit. This compresses highlights to allow a greater contrast range than normal.

7.6.5 Peak white and black

A camera's contrast range is determined by the noise level which limits the darkest area of the scene which can be reproduced and the video peak level of maximum signal which clips the highlight detail.

When a high contrast scene such as an exterior in bright sunlight is recorded, most of the detail in the highlights will be reproduced as solid white. If a highlight compression circuit is used (DCC), the highlight part of the signal is non-linear amplified. As the magnitude and the size of the highlight areas increase, a 'knee' circuit compresses the highlight to keep it within the normal peak video level. Increasing the highlight will reduce the knee threshold still further.

7.6.6 Exposing for highlights

A highlight part of the shot (e.g. white sheets on a washing line in bright sun) which may produce a signal five times peak white level can be compressed into the normal video dynamic range. With the above example this means that the darker areas of the picture can be correctly exposed whilst at the same time maintaining some detail in the sheets.

If someone was standing in a room against a window and it was necessary to expose for exterior detail and the face, without additional lighting or filtering the windows, it would not be possible to reproduce detail in both face and exterior. Using highlight compression, the highlights outside the window would be squashed by the DCC circuit and although their relative brightness to each other would not be faithfully reproduced, the compression would allow the reproduction of detail across a greater range to be recorded.

7.6.7 Transient highlights

DCC uses average feedback and avoids unnecessary compression by not responding to transient high intensity light such as car headlamps.

If DCC is used with a normal contrast range scene (below 40:1) there is the risk that highlights will be distorted and the compression may result in a lower contrast reproduction than the original.

7.6.8 Avoiding high contrast

The rule of thumb that claims you should expose for the highlights and let the shadows look after themselves may give bright colourful landscapes but becomes very limited advice when shooting a face lit by sunlight under a cloudless summer sky. There may be more than three to four stops difference between the lit and the unlit side of the face.

Ways of controlling the contrast in a shot need to be found if there is to be no loss of detail in highlights or shadows. A simple but effective method is to frame the shot to avoid areas of high contrast. Stage people against buildings or trees rather than the sky if there is bright sunlight. Avoid direct sunlight on faces unless you can lighten shadows. With interiors, use curtains or blinds to reduce the amount of light entering windows and position people to avoid a high-contrast situation.

The problem of a bright sky can be controlled by an ND graduated filter if the horizon allows and other important elements of the shot are not in the top of frame. Low contrast filters and soft contrast filters may also help.

Avoid staging people, if possible, against an even white cloud base. Either the overcast sky is burnt out or the face is in semi-silhouette if exposure for detail in the clouds is attempted.

7.7 Face tones

A 'talking head' is probably the most common shot on television. Whether news, drama, sport or entertainment, people like watching people. Before the talking head can be recorded it needs to be staged, framed, lit and exposed. The first three requirements are dealt with elsewhere; here we will concentrate on exposure and face tones.

Video pictures of faces are the most demanding in achieving correct exposure and usually require exposure levels that are high but are free from burnout in highlight areas. The reflectivity of the human face varies enormously by reason of different skin pigments and make-up (see Section 4.19.1). An important consideration when shooting the same face in different locations or lighting situations is to achieve some measure of continuity in face tones.

7.7.1 Detail enhancement and skin tone detail

In most camera/recorder formats, image enhancement is used to improve picture quality. One technique is to raise the contrast at the dark-to-light and light-to-dark transitions, to make the edges of objects appear sharper, both horizontally and vertically. This is done electronically by overshooting the signal at the transition between different tones to improve the rendering of detail.

The degree of electronic manipulation of edge detail is variable but one limiting factor in the amount of enhancement that can be used is the adverse effect on faces. When pictures are 'over-contoured' skin detail can appear intrusive and unnatural; every imperfection is enhanced and becomes noticeable.

To overcome this problem, some cameras provide for selective reduction in skin detail to soften the appearance of faces. While variable electronic 'sharpening' or image enhancement may be applied to the overall shot, skin tone detail control allows for the separate handling of the specific degree of enhancement on any selected facial tones within that scene.

This is achieved by a circuit that separates facial skin colour from all other colours in a given shot, and its electronic detail level can be reduced without affecting other areas of the picture. The specific skin colour to be treated in this way is selectable and can be memorized to follow movement or recalled for subsequent shots.

7.7.2 Camera sensitivity

Camera sensitivity is usually quoted by camera manufacturers with reference to four interlinking factors:

- a subject with peak white reflectivity;
- scene illumination;
- f-number;
- signal-to-noise ratio for a stated signal.

It is usually quoted as being the resulting f-number when exposed to a peak white subject with 89.9% reflectance lit by 2000 lux and also quoting the signal-to-noise ratio (see Section 4.3.1).

7.7.3 Noise

The sensitivity of the camera could be increased by simply greater and greater amplification of weak signals but this degrades the picture by adding 'noise' generated by the camera circuits. The signal-to-noise ratio is usually measured without contour or gamma correction. As manufacturers vary in the way they state camera sensitivity, comparison between different models often requires a conversion of the specification figures. In general, with the same f-number, the higher the signal-to-noise ratio and the lower the scene illumination (lux), the more sensitive the camera.

7.8 Gain

The gain of the head amplifiers can be increased if insufficient light is available to adequately expose the picture. The amount of additional gain is calibrated in dB. For example, switching in +6 dB of gain is the equivalent of opening one stop of the lens, which would double the amount of light available to the sensors. The precise amounts of switched gain available differ from camera to camera. A camera may have a +9 dB and +18 dB switch with an additional +24 dB available from a pre-set inside the camera.

The extra gain in amplification is achieved by a corresponding decrease in the signal-to-noise ratio and therefore will increase the noise in the picture. For an important news story shot with insufficient light, this may be an acceptable trade-off, but if the item being recorded will be subject to much post-production work (particularly analogue format), then one should aim for a good noise-free first generation master (see also Chapter 1).

7.9 Electronic shutters

The electronic shutter varies the length of the pulse that reads out the charge on the CCD (see Section 1.5). With the electronic shutter switched out, the PAL 'picture' exposure time is 1/50 s. The electronic shutter reduces this exposure time by switched steps, improving reproduction of motion but reducing sensitivity.

7.9.1 Movement blur

The standard shutter speed (PAL) is set to 1/50 s. A fast-moving subject in front of the camera at this shutter speed will result in a blurred image due to the movement of the subject during the 1/50 of a second exposure. Reducing the time interval of exposure by increasing the electronic shutter speed improves the image definition of moving subjects and is therefore particularly useful when slow motion replay of sporting events is required. But reducing the time interval also reduces the amount of light captured by the CCD and therefore increasing shutter speed requires the aperture to be opened to compensate for the reduction in light (see Section 1.5).

7.9.2 Shutter speeds

The shutter speed can be altered in discrete steps such as 1/60–1/125–1/500–1/1000–1/2000 of a second or, on some cameras, continuously varied in 0.5 Hz steps.

Often, when shooting computer displays, black or white horizontal bands appear across the computer display. This is because the scanning frequencies of most computer displays differ from the (50 Hz) frequency of the TV system (PAL). Altering the shutter speed in discrete steps allows the camera exposure interval to precisely match the computer display scanning frequency and reduce or even eliminate the horizontal streaking.

7.9.3 Pulsed light sources

Fluorescent tubes, HMI discharge lamps and neon signs do not produce a constant light output but give short pulses of light at a frequency depending on the mains supply (see Section 4.4.4).

7.10 Time code

Time code enables every recorded frame of video to be numbered. This allows precise identification when editing.

There are two methods of recording the identification number:

- **Longitudinal time code.** Longitudinal time code (LTC) is recorded with a fixed head on a track reserved for time code. It can be decoded at normal playback speed and at fast forward or

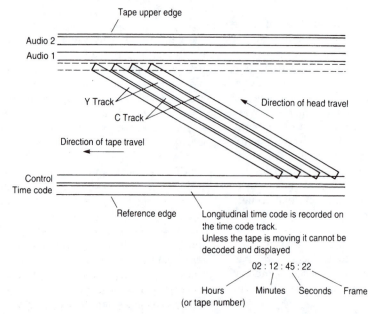

Time code tracks on Beta tape

Figure 7.7

rewind but it cannot be read unless the tape is moving as there is no replayed signal to be decoded. It is recorded once every frame as a series of pulses (binary digits) whose repetition rate changes according to whether it is recording 0 s or 1 s.

- **Vertical interval time code.** Vertical interval timecode (VITC) numbers are time-compressed to fit the duration of one TV line and recorded as a pseudo video signal on one of the unused lines between frames. It is recorded as a variation in signal amplitude once per frame as binary digits. 0 equals black and 1 equals peak white.

Many cameras have the ability to insert VITC twice on two non-consecutive lines. They are factory-set to insert the VITC signal, but there is often provision for another choice of line position for VITC insertion independent of the first choice.

7.10.1 Code word

Every frame contains an 80 bit code word which contains 'time bits' (8 decimal numbers) recording hours, minutes, seconds, frames and other digital synchronizing information. All this is updated every frame but there is room for additional 'user bit' information.

7.10.2 User bit

User bit allows up to 9 numbers and an A to F code to be programmed into the code word which is recorded every frame. Unlike the 'time bits', the user bits remain unchanged until reprogrammed. They can be used to identify production, camera operator, etc.

There are two ways of starting time code – Record Run and Free Run.

7.10.3 Record run

Record run only records a frame identification when the camera is recording. The time code is set to zero at the start of the day's operation and a continuous record is produced on each tape covering all takes. It is customary practice to record the tape number in place of the hour section on the time code. For example, the first cassette of the day would start 01.00.00.00 and the second cassette would start 02.00.00.00. Record run is the preferred method of recording time code on most productions.

7.10.4 Time code setting

If you are using time code and user bits, set user bits first. If you set time code first, the time code value will not be correct because the time code generator stops while the user bits are being programmed.

7.10.5 Setting the user bits for a typical camera

Do not reset the user bit data until the camera has been switched on for more than twenty seconds:

(1) Set the DISPLAY switch to U-BIT
(2) Set the F-RUN/R-RUN switch to SET.
(3) Set the REAL TIME switch to OFF.
(4) Set the user bits with the SHIFT button – press to make the desired hexadecimal number blink; press ADVANCE button to increase the value of the blinking number by one unit.
(5) Set the F-RUN/R-RUN switch to F-RUN or R-RUN.

7.10.6 Time code slave-lock

The time code can be locked to an external time code (e.g. provided by another camera) by connecting a reference time code to TIME CODE IN and a video reference signal to GENLOCK VIDEO IN. This allows accurate editing when for example, two cameras are working independently on the same subject:

(1) Set the POWER switch of this unit to ON.
(2) Set the F-RUN/R-RUN switch to F-RUN.
(3) Set the DISPLAY switch to TC.
(4) Connect the external master time code and the video reference signal to TIME CODE IN and GENLOCK VIDEO IN.
(5) The camera time code will be locked to the external time code after about 10 seconds and the connectors can be removed. Wait for ten seconds before recording.

7.10.7 Slave lock operation

(1) In the slave lock mode only the time code is locked to the external source. User bit information is still programmed in the camera.
(2) To cancel the external lock switch to R-RUN.
(3) The built-in time code generator cannot continue to generate the slave-locked time code correctly if the battery is removed (i.e. no power). To maintain the slave-lock connect external power source to DC IN before removing the battery pack.

Menu checklist when sharing a camera
Each camera is supplied with one card but additional cards can be obtained. A useful procedure is:

(1) The supplied card should be used to store the factory settings of the camera's operational parameters before the first operational use of the camera. This card should be labelled STANDARD or DEFAULT settings.
(2) First menu page reads the set-up card.
(3) Each regular user should have his/her personal set-up card with their preferred operational settings.
(4) Once a camera has been programmed by a set-up card the settings remain in force until overridden either by the menu or another set-up card.
(5) A camera with many users can obtain default settings with the original card.
(6) Usually the card can be inserted with power on or off.
(7) Frequently the card is inserted with the company logo facing outwards.
(8) The pins of the cards should not be touched.
(9) The card should be stored and safeguarded against the normal hazards that computer files are protected against.

Figure 7.8

7.11 Menus and scene files

In nearly all digital camera/recorder formats, all the electronic variables on the camera can be stored as digital values in a memory. These values can be recalled as required or saved on a removable storage file.

Access to the current settings of the electronic values is by way of menus which are displayed, when required, on the viewfinder screen. These menus are accessed by using the menu switch on the camera. Movement around the menus is by button or toggle switch that identifies which camera variable is currently selected. When the menu system is first accessed, the operation menu pages are usually displayed. A special combination of the menu controls allows access to the user menu which, in turn, provides access to the other menus depending on whether or not they have been unlocked for adjustment. Normally only those variables associated with routine recording (gain, shutter, etc.) are instantly available. Seldom used items can be deleted from the user menu to leave only those menu pages essential to the required set-up procedure. Menu pages are also available on the video outputs.

The values that can be adjusted are grouped under appropriate headings listed in a master menu. A typical set of sub-menus would provide adjustment to:

- **Operational values.** The items in this set of menus are used to change the camera settings to suit differing shooting conditions under normal camera operations. They would normally include menu pages which can alter viewfinder display, viewfinder marker aids such as safety zone and centre mark, etc., gain, shutter selection, iris, format switching, monitor out, auto-iris, auto-knee, auto set-up, diagnosis.
- **Scene file.** These can be programmed to memorize a set of operational values customized for a specific camera set-up and read to a removable file.
- **Video signal processing.** This menu contains items for defining adjustments to the image (e.g. gamma, master black level, contour correction) and requires the aid of a waveform monitor or other output device to monitor the change in settings.
- **Engineering.** The engineering menu provides access to all of the camera set-up parameters, but only selected parameters can be accessed in the master menu to avoid accidental changes to the settings.
- **Maintenance.** This menu is mainly for initial set-up and periodic maintenance, and normally not available via the master menu.
- **Reference file (or system configuration).** This file contains factory settings or initial customization of reference settings to meet the requirements of different users. It is the status quo setting for a standard operational condition. This menu is not usually accessible via the master menu and should never be adjusted on location except by qualified service personnel. Never try to adjust camera controls if you are unsure of their effect and if you have no way of returning the camera set-up to a standard operational condition.

7.12 Gamma

After all the image manipulation discussed on the previous pages, the picture the viewer will finally see is dependent on the characteristics of their TV set. The cathode ray display tube, however, has certain limitations. The television image is created by a stream of electrons bombarding a phosphor coating on the inside face of the display tube. The rate of change of this beam, and therefore the change in picture brightness, does not rise linearly in step with changes in the signal level corresponding to the changes in the original image brightness variations (see Section 1.4).

7.13 Matrix

All hues in the visible spectrum can be matched by the mixture of the three primary colours, red, green and blue. In the ideal spectrum characteristics of the three primary colours, blue contains a small proportion of red and a small negative proportion of green. Green contains a spectral response of negative proportions of both blue and red. It is not optically possible to produce negative light in the camera but these negative light values cannot be ignored if faithful colour reproduction is to be achieved. The linear matrix circuit in the camera compensates for these values by electronically generating and adding signals corresponding to the negative spectral response to the *R*, *G* and *B* video signals. This circuit is placed before the gamma correction so that compensation does not vary due to the amount of gamma correction (see Section 1.8).

7.14 Widescreen

The last few years have seen a move to replace the 4:3 aspect ratio TV picture with a 16:9 ratio. Originally the change accompanied the proposed introduction of a high-definition television system but the difficulties in agreeing a worldwide standard, and the economics of running a parallel service to the existing national TV systems, has resulted in a shift to the promotion of 'widescreen' digital TV.

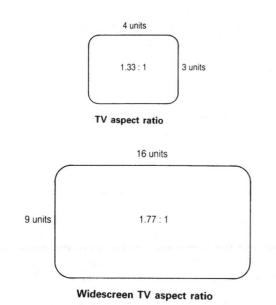

TV aspect ratio

Widescreen TV aspect ratio

Figure 7.9

7.14.1 Dual format

From a camera operator's point of view, the biggest difficulty during the transition period is attempting to find a compositional compromise between the two aspect ratios. If a 16:9 image is transmitted in a letter-box format (i.e. a black band at the top and bottom of the frame when viewed on a 4:3 TV set) then all shots can be framed with respect to the 16:9 border. Some companies, however, have adopted a half-way stage of transmitting the 16:9 format in a cropped format of 14:9 in an effort to make the letter-box effect less intrusive for 4:3 viewers. This technique loses a portion of the left and right hand edge of the frame and may destroy the balance of a 16:9 image. It is an experience that viewers watching widescreen films shown on TV have been subject to for many years modified by the limited remedial efforts of the widescreen image being panned and reframed via telecine on transmission. There is very little satisfactory compromise that can be made in an attempt to compose for both formats at the same time if they are viewed full screen on different aspect ratio screens.

7.14.2 Composition for 16:9

The growth of the cinema widescreen format in the 1950s provoked discussion on what changes were required in the standard 4:3 visual framing conventions that had developed in cinema since its beginnings. One problem often identified was that if artistes were staged at either side of the screen, the intervening setting became more prominent. Compositional solutions were found but the same learning curve is being experienced in television as the move is made to widescreen images. If anything, television is more of a 'talking heads' medium than cinema but the advent of a large, wider aspect screen has tended to emphasize the improvement in depicting place and setting. This can create its own problems in editing. Wide shots need to be sufficiently different in their distribution of similar objects to avoid jump cuts in editing. A cut that relies on action on the edge of a 16:9 frame may not be seen by viewers watching a 14:9 picture on a 4:3 screen and therefore the edit may jump (see Chapter 11). The same 'jump' can happen with some types of landscape shots.

7.15 Tape v disk

At present, tape remains a more economic and universal way of acquiring broadcast material. As the cost of disk storage falls, the advantages of instant non-linear access to recorded material will allow operational benefits. Digital tape acquisition formats use metal particle tape housed in a cassette with an anti-static lid. The Betacam and the Digital S format use half-inch tape and the DV formats use quarter-inch tape.

Tape formats	
Betacam	12.65 mm (0.5 inch) width oxide tape
Betacam SP	12.65 mm (0.5 inch) width metal particle
Digital Betacam	12.65 mm (0.5 inch) width metal particle
Betacam SX	12.65 mm (0.5 inch) width metal particle
Digital S	12.65 mm (0.5 inch) width metal particle
DVCPRO	6.35 mm (0.25 inch) width metal particle
DVCAM	6.35 mm (0.25 inch) width metal evaporated tape
DV	6.35 mm (0.25 inch) width metal evaporated tape

Figure 7.10

Tape problems

The tape is manufactured to a high tolerance and requires care in handling. Check for tape slack and tighten reels before loading. Do not force the cassette into the VTR. When battery voltage is almost below the level required to operate, the cassette can be removed. With some formats, when the voltage falls below this point, the cassette cannot be ejected or the cassette holder closed. Problems that can occur include:

- Head clogging caused by a build-up of invisible metal particles. You must use a cleaning cassette to maintain tape path performance but do not exceed the recommended timetable of cleaning as excessive cleaning can shorten the life of the head.
- Tape dropout caused by imperfections in the coating and by worn heads with insufficient contact between tape and head. After considerable use, the head may need replacing. Also, any part of the recorder that the tape comes into contact with (guides, rollers, etc.) should be periodically checked and cleaned.
- Problems resulting from excessive humidity or low humidity. Although the tape is manufactured with a built-in lubricant to reduce tape wear, high humidity causes stiction and increases the risk of head clogging. At lower humidities electrostatic charging will be more pronounced, resulting in greater attraction of dust and an increase in dropout. Allow tapes to acclimatize if they have been subject to extremes of temperature or humidity.

- Moisture condensation on the drum assembly if the camera is moved from a cold to a warm location or if the unit is used in a very humid place (e.g. an enclosed swimming pool). This may cause the tape to stick to the head and damage head and tape. Avoid this occurring by removing the cassette when changing from cold to hot locations and with the power on check that the HUMID indicator in the display window does not light. Do not insert the cassette until the HUMID indicator light goes off.
- Cinching of the tape caused by badly adjusted playback recorders which abruptly stop and cause several layers of tape to slip and bunch between themselves. Remember that the tape from the camera is the master tape and is irreplaceable. It should not be used to repeatedly view the day's shooting. Transfer to VHS for production viewing and guard the use of the master tape until it arrives in post-production.

7.16 Camera mounts

Because lightweight cameras were the first generation of video cameras that could be operated from the shoulder they were, and still are, frequently referred to as hand-held cameras. Although shoulder operation is suitable for fast-breaking news stories or where the camera needs to be frequently repositioned at speed, the great majority of lightweight camerawork benefits from the camera being mounted on a pan/tilt head and tripod. Shaky and unsteady pictures are not only difficult to edit, but are also a distraction from the content of the shot. They are, however, very fashionable with some types of production seeking to imitate the rawness of 'reality' news coverage.

7.16.1 Pan and tilt heads

(See Section 6.7.2)

7.16.2 Tripods

If a tripod is to be of any value it must be quick to set up, rigid, with no tendency for the legs either to twist or flex. These essential design features need to be achieved with the lightest possible construction. It must have a good range of easily adjustable heights with an infallible locking clamp on each leg section. The feet of the tripod can be spikes which also fit into a spreader – a device to prevent the tripod legs from spreading out. The head-to-tripod connection can be a bowl fitting (100 mm or 150 mm), allowing the camera to be levelled using the built-in level bubble in the head, or a flat plate fixing which requires levelling to be carried out by adjusting one or more legs. A set of wheels can be exchanged for the spreader if the camera has flat level ground to reposition on.

7.17 Batteries

For many years nickel cadmium (NiCd) batteries have been the standard power for portable video cameras. With the growth of portable computers and mobile phones, new battery technologies using nickel metal hydride (NiMH) and rechargeable lithium have been developed but at present nicad batteries form the main proportion of professional video batteries in use. The camera/recorder is normally powered by a 13.2 V or 14.4 V nickel cadmium rechargeable battery which is clipped to the back of the recorder. There are a range of different capacity batteries available to give extended running times or several batteries can be grouped together and worn on a belt.

Battery checklist
- Identify each battery with a conspicuous number so that an accurate record can be kept of its charging cycles.
- Match charger to battery. Use battery manufacturer's recommended charger.
- Ensure that batteries are rotated and a set pattern of charging and usage is employed. With older type batteries/chargers, give a slow overnight charge every 10 charging cycles.
- Try to keep all batteries at room temperature. Avoid extreme temperatures on location by thermal insulation or shade.
- Keep batteries away from intense heat.
- Allow battery to cool after heavy discharge before charging.
- Do not try to charge batteries that have been in extreme temperatures. Nickel cadmium batteries must not be fast-charged when they are colder than 0°C. Wait until they are close to room temperature (18°C)
- The voltage of the battery is not a reliable way of assessing the state of charge of a battery.
- Battery lamps have no power 'cut off' and could discharge a battery beyond a safe limit. Cells may be damaged if battery is discharged below 75% of its nominal voltage.
- Protect batteries from severe shock, vibration, high humidity, steam and rain. If battery should get very wet, shake out excess water and dry naturally in a warm place. Do not charge or use battery until it has fully dried.
- Try to slow-charge batteries before a shoot and, with older style batteries, at least every 10 usages.

- Take sufficient batteries to service a day's shoot. You may not be able to find suitable mains for recharging.
- Don't subject batteries to rough usage. Any dents in the battery case may penetrate and ruin a cell.
- Conserve battery power by reverting to standby as often as possible; use manual zoom to set up shots; use separate battery for on camera battery lamp.

Figure 7.11

7.17.1 Construction

The battery is made up of separate cells. The cell consists of a positive plate, a negative plate and two separators which are interleaved and wound around and around in a cylindrical case like four lengths of carpet in one roll. The plates are surface coated with the chemicals which form the active plate materials. The nickel-plated steel case is tightly sealed so that all gases and chemicals are contained within the cell but there is a safety provision to allow the cell to 'vent' if an emergency arises. The 13.2 V battery consists of 10 matched cells so that, when new, they will all uniformly charge and discharge at the same rate.

7.17.2 Capacity

The capacity of a battery is often rated in ampere-hours, which is the maximum current flow (amps) in one hour before the battery is completely discharged. A more useful measure is how long a specific battery will run a specific make of camera. The nominal run time is calculated by multiplying the battery voltage by its ampere-hour rating to determine a watt-hour figure which is then divided by the power rating of the camera/recorder.

For example, a 12 volt/5 AH battery = 12 (volts) $\times$ 5 (AH) = 60 watt-hours which will give a 2.5 hour run time for a camera drawing 24 W (60÷24). For the same camera, a 14.4 volt/5 AH battery = 14.4 (volts) $\times$ 5 (AH) = 72 watt-hours will give a 3 hour run time (72÷24).

Camcorder power consumption
Most camera/VTR units draw between 15 and 30 watts and are usually powered by a 4 amp-hour battery which will on average provide 1–2 hours of continuous use depending on camera power consumption. As well as battery cell design, the method of charging and discharging and the temperature crucially affect the performance and life of the battery.

Battery voltage range

Another crucial camera specification is the operating voltage range. Most cameras will specify a minimum voltage below which the camera will not operate and an upper voltage beyond which operating the equipment will cause damage or trigger the power breaker. The value of this power figure is stated, for example, as 12 V (–1 +5) which means that the camera will function over the voltage supply range of 11 V through to 17 V.

7.18 Battery charge

7.18.1 Constant current charge

Slow charging (the C10 rate) is a constant current charge equal to one-tenth of the ampere-hour rating of the battery. For a 4 AH battery the slow charge current would be 400 milliamps. The battery would be fully charged in 14–16 hours.

When the battery is fully charged the charging current produces heat and oxygen within the cell. The heat building up in the cell will prematurely age the cell – it will be cooked to death! Providing the charging current does not exceed the C10 rate the cell can absorb all the oxygen but if the charge rate is exceeded the cell will eventually 'vent', releasing the build-up of oxygen and the cell will be destroyed.

Safety hazards when charging a battery

Cold temperature charging
The fast charging of a cold battery is one of the most dangerous hazards associated with NiCd batteries and can result in a violent explosion. When a NiCd is fast charged at temperatures below +5°C (+41°F), the internal charging reaction cannot proceed normally and a significant portion of the charge current can be diverted into producing highly explosive hydrogen gas. A spark can ignite this gas causing an explosion that can turn the battery into a grenade. *Cold batteries must be allowed to reach room temperature before being placed on a charger.*

Fire hazards
NiCd batteries and chargers have been identified as the source of several fires and toxic smoke incidents over the years. One major TV network instructed their cameramen that batteries must not be charged in their hotel bedrooms. Most of these incidents are connected to fast chargers that failed to recognize when a battery reached full charge. The continuing current produces heat and eventually smoke or fire. This can be avoided by the use of a thermal fuse in the power circuit which will disconnect the battery from the charger if dangerous temperatures are detected. A similar fire hazard can also occur if there is a mismatch between

---

the charger and battery on a slow charge. Always provide for air circulation around batteries and do not charge batteries in a bag or flight case.

Physical shock
If a battery is internally damaged by physical impact or being accidentally dropped, internal wires can be short-circuited and become red-hot elements causing the battery to burst into flames. Take every precaution to avoid subjecting batteries to violent physical impact.

Interactive battery charger
Most of the above hazards can be avoided or eliminated by using an interactive charger that continuously interrogates the battery while charging.

Figure 7.12

Although most chargers are designed to cut off after full charge has been reached, the major drawback of slow charging is the 14–16 hours it takes. Modern high performance cells are often designed for fast charging only.

7.18.2 Fast charge/quick charge

Modern chargers therefore provide for a fast charge and a quick charge. A fast charge aims to recharge the battery in less than an hour, provided that all the cells charge at the same rate. A quick charge aims to recharge the battery in any time between 1 hour and 14 hours but usually 8 hours (overnight charge).

With ageing, individual cells in the battery charge and discharge at different rates. With a fast charge, the charger needs to assess when any cell has reached full charge and then drop the charging rate to the slow charge rate to prevent venting and overheating. The slow charge rate will continue until all cells are fully charged. The charger will then terminate the charge but monitor the condition of the cells over time to detect any discharge and apply the slow charge rate accordingly.

7.18.3 Shelf life

A battery that has been charged and not used for a few days may not remain fully charged. Because cells can self-discharge at different rates, the battery can become unequalized. Some cells will be at full capacity, others may be partially discharged and there may even be individual cells which are completely flat.

With older designed chargers and batteries, if this battery was put on fast charge, the charger would detect the fully charged cell and stop the fast charge rate. The completely discharged cell would remain uncharged. The only way to bring all ten cells up to charge would be to use the slow charge rate, which cannot harm the fully charged cells. Modern 'pulse' chargers can fast-charge interactive batteries and equalize all cells in approximately 1 hour.

7.18.4 Temperature

The nicad battery is affected by temperature. Temperatures below freezing (0°C) will not damage the cell but during discharge will seriously reduce the available capacity. If possible, try to keep batteries at room temperature (18°C/65°F) in a warm car or wrapped in thermal covering until needed.

A nicad battery must be above +5°C (about 45°F) before charging. Always allow a battery to approach room temperature before putting it on charge.

Avoid fast charging at temperatures above 20°C (70°F). A battery charged at higher temperatures will receive a reduced charge.

As a general rule, batteries should be stored in a cool area for charge retention. Below freezing, the batteries will retain 90% of their charge for three months or more depending on their age – but remember to bring nicad batteries up to room temperature before running them on the camera.

7.18.5 Battery memory

It is often claimed that if a battery is repeatedly discharged to the same point and then charged it will develop a memory of this point and will only be able to accept a partial charge. This can only occur if there is a precisely repetitive partial discharge rate and this degree of repeated precision has only been reliably confirmed with a battery powering a satellite which was precisely charging and discharging in orbit according to the position of the sun.

It is possible that the memory effect may be being confused with a condition that occurs when unequal cells discharge in older type battery design.

After a battery has been exhausted some cells will have reached zero voltage while others will still have some charge and these will then discharge through the flat ones. This reverse charging leads to the formation of hydrogen in the flat cell which is not designed to absorb hydrogen as it is for oxygen. Each time this occurs the hydrogen pressure increases until the cell vents and electrolyte is lost, reducing the cell's capacity to accept charge.

The solution is to make certain the battery is given an overnight slow charge rate at least every ten charging cycles in order to equalize the charge in each cell.

7.19 Operational checks

This section is for those people who have little or no experience of camerawork. They usually have a double disability. Firstly they are not proficient with the camera controls and need time to remember what to do and in what order. Secondly, they are probably operating with a camera that is shared with others.

7.19.1 Pool equipment

Many users of portable cameras are able to use the same camera each day and every day. They are attentive to its performance and are immediately aware of any electronic or mechanical malfunction with the associated equipment. If there is a fault, they make certain it is fully serviceable before the next shoot.

Other camera users work or study with organizations where there is a pool of shared or hired-in equipment. They may be less experienced and may operate with several different cameras of unknown serviceability.

To work with an unfamiliar camera each day is much more exacting than to work with a predictable and familiar camera. A start-of-day check on pool cameras and mounts is vital to eliminate problems with the equipment *before* arriving at the location.

Inventory check
Check that every item of equipment is there. Location work can be rushed and it is not unknown on a quick 'wrap' for a small item to be overlooked and left behind. Check for the obvious (external mics, in-line batteries, cables, etc.) and then the smaller items such as power and connecting cables for mains adaptor, wet weather cover, dichroic filter on battery lamp, etc. And remember to check over the equipment you brought to a location when you leave the location.

Battery check
Check the state of charge of the batteries. Find out when they were on charge and in what condition they were before the charge. A battery that has been charged and not used for several days may not remain fully charged. Individual cells discharge at different rates and the battery may have become

unequalized. It may not respond to a fast charge before you leave.

Mechanical checks

Check all mechanical parts for security and stability. A common problem is the interface between tripod adaptor and the pan/tilt head. Check that the tripod adaptor on the pan/tilt head is suitable for the camera and that the locking mechanism will hold the camera secure. Make certain the friction clamps on the legs lock the tripod at any height required.

Electronic adjustments

Run the camera up and carry out a quick check of all the main controls. Make certain that each switch is set to the mode you wish to operate in.

Menu

Most digital camera functions and parameters such as gain, shutter, viewfinder indicator display etc. can be programmed from a computer menu displayed in the viewfinder or external monitor. Each set of memorized variables is called a scene file and is stored either on a removable memory card or in a memory system integral to the camera. There are usually four or five different categories of file available:

(1) A default scene file containing values which have been pre-set by the manufacturer. This should be selected when using a camera following on from other users. Alternatively there may be a scene file which has been customized by an organization for a group of users such as students. This may have a standard zebra value for example, programmed for consistency in operation by a number of people or maybe a stored automatic adjustment to auto exposure to correct error readings on that specific camera/lens.
(2) A blank scene file which can save any adjustment to the camera variables displayed on the menu. It is advisable to name the file to indicate its application (e.g. J. Smith File or Pre-set Studio).
(3) Programmable camera variables, which may be split into two sections – camera operations and engineering. The engineering file may be locked to prevent accidental adjustment to crucial camera settings (e.g. Matrix Table).
(4) A self-diagnostic programme which checks the camera/recorder electronics and reports on the status of each section.

Select user and check the set-up card identification

Check the menu settings and select *default* or *factory setting* if another user of the camera has reprogrammed the set-up card.

Check the settings for the following and refer to the appropriate topic page if you are uncertain what should be selected for the intended shot/lighting conditions:

- shutter (1/50) and gain (0 dB);
- skin tone detail and variable detail frequency;
- gamma and matrix;
- contrast control and auto-exposure settings;
- level dependence and crispening setting;
- aspect ratio mode (if using switchable camera);
- viewfinder indicator graticules (e.g. centre screen mark, 4:3 indication).

If in any doubt of what setting should be used, restore the default setting.

7.19.2 Complete checklist

Here is a start-of-day checklist when working with a camera which someone else has been using.

Battery

Clip on the battery and turn the POWER switch to ON. Check the state of charge of the battery indicated in the display window.

Lens

Remove the lens and inspect the rear element and filter wheel for finger marks or scratches. Refit the lens if clean. Check that auto-iris and auto-zoom are set to the AUTO position if you wish to operate in this mode.

How to clean the lens

A front of lens screw-in filter such as an ultraviolet (UV) is the best protection for the front element of a zoom. The cost of replacement if damaged is insignificant compared with the cost of repairing or replacing a zoom front element.

Lens tissue and breathing on the front of the lens filter is the most common and the simplest method of removing rain marks or dust.

Dirt and dust can be removed with an air blower or wiped off gently with a lens brush. Never vigorously rub the lens surface or damage to the lens coating may result.

Oil, fingerprints or water stains may be removed by applying a small amount of commercial lens cleaner to a lens tissue and cleaning in a circular movement from the centre to the edge of the lens.

Protect the lens from driving rain. Dry off the lens casing with a cloth and the front element with lens tissue. Place the lens in a plastic bag overnight, with a desiccant such as silica gel.

Humidity

Check that the HUMID indicator is off in the display window before inserting a tape cassette.

Viewfinder

Adjust the physical position of the viewfinder for individual preference and then electronically set up the picture display (see Section 7.3.2).

On-camera mic

To check the microphone attached to front of camera via Ch-1 (*note*: some cameras have a microphone fitted to the camera which is permanently connected):

- Set AUDIO IN CH-1/CH-2 switches to their FRONT position.
- Set the AUDIO INDICATOR switch to ON.
- Set AUDIO CH-1 MANU/AUTO to MANUAL.
- Set the AUDIO CHANNEL 1 control on the viewfinder to maximum. Point the camera mic at a sound source (e.g. someone talking six feet from camera) and adjust the AUDIO CHANNEL 1 control on the side panel to read 6 dB (the colon (:) at the end of the audio indication in the viewfinder in series 300 cameras). Adjust the AUDIO CHANNEL 1 control on the viewfinder to bring the level down to 0 dB (3 dashes lit in the viewfinder display).

External mic

To check a microphone plugged into the rear of the camera, plug the microphone into the camera (CH-1 connector) and SW 48 V to ON if required. Switch AUDIO IN CH-1 to MIC position. Point the externally connected mic to a sound source as above. Check the level adjustment on the side display panel in AUTO and MANUAL mode. Using the external or on-camera mic, repeat the above procedure for Channel 2. (*Note*: Often Channel 2 can only be controlled via the side panel.)

Auto-iris

Select CAMERA ON – DCC OFF and with AUTO IRIS ON, frame up a well-lit subject and note the auto-iris setting. Reframe to a low light subject and check that the auto-iris compensates. (Switch in additional steps of GAIN and check that the iris stops down each time.)

Instant auto-iris

Select MANUAL IRIS and check INSTANT AUTO IRIS by under-exposing on MANUAL and check that INSTANT AUTO IRIS opens the iris to the correct exposure.

Set white balance

Select a filter appropriate to the colour temperature of the light source. Set GAIN to 0 and OUTPUT/DCC selector to CAM. Frame up the white card lit (without colour temperature variation) by the main light source. Expose the card using auto-iris. Set WHITE BAL to either pos A or B. Push the AUTO W/B BAL switch up to the WHT and hold it there for one second. Check in the viewfinder that white balance has been completed and release the button. Eight white balance values can be memorized – two (A or B) for each filter position. Switch between PRESET/A/B to check the white balance memory values.

Set black balance

Push the AUTO W/B BAL switch down to the BLK position and hold it there until the set/black adjustment is complete (2–15 seconds). Check in the viewfinder that the cycle is complete. (*Note*: During the set black level operation, the iris is closed completely and if in MANUAL mode, it will need to be opened before operation.)

Electronic shutter (series 300/400 cameras)

Select auto-iris and CAM/DCC OFF and frame up on an exposed picture. Select display mode 3 and the AUDIO IND switch to OFF. Push the SHUTTER selector to SEL. The shutter selected will be displayed in the viewfinder for about three seconds (e.g. SS:1/125).

When the colon to the left of 'SS' is on, push the selector again to SEL and the shutter will move to the next value. Each time the shutter selector is moved to SEL the shutter speed will increase if the colon is on (1/60–1/125–1/250–1/500–1/1000–1/2000). After 1/2000, it will start the cycle again. Check that the auto iris opens for each increase in shutter speed.

Filter

Set the FILTER selector to match the filter appropriate to the light source:

3200 K	sunrise/sunset/tungsten/studio
5600 K + ¼ ND	exterior – clear sky
5600 K	exterior – cloud/rain
5600 K + ¹⁄₁₆ ND	exterior exceptionally bright.

Zebra

Frame up on a grey scale if available and adjust for correct exposure (i.e. all divisions in the grey scale should be displayed in the viewfinder). Switch ZEBRA on and check the division at which ZEBRA patterning occurs.

Lens

Check MACRO is in its detent position and the range extender is out.

Flange-back (back focus)

Check the back focus (see Fig. 6.6 in Chapter 6), including zoom tracking with the range extender selected.

Time code

Depending on editing requirements, set up time code.

Record run (Sony 300/400 series cameras as an example)
(1) DISPLAY switch to TC   (1 – see Fig. 7.13)
(2) REAL TIME switch to OFF   (3 – see Fig. 7.13)
(3) SET F-RUN/R-RUNSET   (2 – see Fig. 7.13)
(4) Press RESET to zero counter.
(5) The time code will increase each time the camera records.
(6) If you wish to use the hour digit to identify each tape (e.g. 1 hour equals first tape, 2 hours equals second tape, etc.), set the hour time code with the SHIFT & ADVANCE buttons (4 – see Fig. 7.13):
SHIFT: Press to make the hour digit blink.
ADVANCE: Press to increase the value of the blinking digit by one unit to equal the cassette tape in use.

Real time (300/400 series cameras as an example)
(1) DISPLAY switch to TC   (1 – see Fig. 7.13)
(2) REAL TIME switch to OFF   (3 – see Fig. 7.13)
(3) SET F-RUN/R-RUNSET   (2 – see Fig. 7.13)
(4) Press RESET to zero counter.
(5) Set the time of day with the SHIFT & ADVANCE buttons until the time code reads a minute or so ahead of actual time:

SHIFT: Press to make the desired digit blink.
ADVANCE: Press to increase the value of the blinking digit by one unit.
(6) When real time equals time code 'time' switch to F-RUN and check that time code counter is increasing in sync with real time.

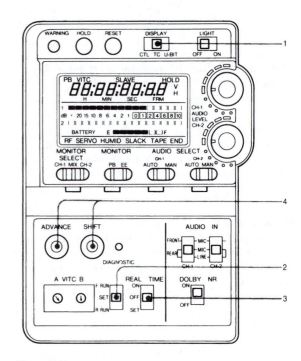

Figure 7.13

User bit

If any USER BIT information is required then always set up user bit information first. Wait approximately 20 seconds after the camera is turned on.

Time of day and user bit (300/400 series cameras as an example)

(1) Select display switch to U-BIT.
(2) Select F-RUN/R-RUN switch to SET.
(3) REAL TIME switch to OFF.
(4) Using the ADVANCE and SHIFT buttons insert user bit information (A to F letters are available and 0–9 numerals).
(5) Select display switch to TC.
(6) Using ADVANCE and SHIFT buttons adjust for time of day as above.
(7) Select F-RUN/R-RUN switch to F-RUN.
(8) The camera now records continuous time of day as the main display as well as the user-bit information selected.

7.20 Pre-recording checklist

Get into the habit of carrying out a routine check before each recording. All of the following checks may not be necessary on each shot and you may prefer to carry out your review in a different order:

(1) If the camera is mounted on a tripod, check that the camera is level and the required friction adjusted. Check the condition of the front element of the lens.
(2) Switch the power on and check the state of the battery charge and humidity warning indicator.
(3) Check whether there is a tape cassette loaded and, if the tape is unused, record 30 seconds of bars.
(4) Select a colour correction filter according to the colour temperature of the light source.
(5) Check and set the time code to the editing mode required.
(6) Frame and focus the shot required and check exposure and lighting.
(7) Check white balance.
(8) Select and plug-up the required microphone and obtain a test sound level and adjust the recording level.
(9) Switch the camera to standby – i.e. tape laced and ready to record instantly.
(10) Press the RECORD button and wait at least six seconds (or the recommended run-up time of the camera model) before starting the shot.

7.21 General operational notes

- Avoid recording from any 'power save' mode – this usually means that the tape is not laced up and in contact with the head drum, to conserve power. If the record button is pressed in this 'save' mode, there will be a small delay while the tape is laced and the recording achieves stability. This may result in a second or more of unusable picture. Always allow some run-up time before significant action to make certain that a stable edit can be achieved. Some formats require at least 5 seconds.
- Tape over any controls that are likely to be accidentally switched during operation (e.g. viewfinder brightness/contrast controls on the viewfinder if they are likely to be knocked during lens operation).
- On some formats, camera power must be on to load or eject tape.
- A portion of the last shot can be previewed by using the RET button. The VTR will park after review, awaiting next recording.
- Analogue Beta recorders require an adaptor to play back via a monitor. Digital formats provide a direct feed.
- The BREAKER BUTTON is designed to 'trip' out on a voltage overload to protect the camera. This seldom occurs and if it needs resetting more than once for no obvious reason, have the camera serviced.
- Cue lights on the front and back of the camera (which can be switched OFF) will light or blink while recording and will also light in sync with display panel warning lamps.
- The ALARM CONTROL can be adjusted for minimum audible warning.

8 Vision mixing

8.1 Introduction

8.1.1 Studio control and master control rooms

Vision mixing equipment is used in production control rooms, continuity and master control suites. Although there is some overlap between the different operating techniques employed, this chapter mainly deals with vision mixing in programme production.

8.1.2 Button pushing

The operational aspects of a vision mixing control panel can be mastered in a matter of hours. The ability to switch visual sources either by a cut, mix or through the digital effects bank is relatively simple to master. It would be a mistake to conclude (and this applies to all television production craft operations) that knowing which button to push will convert you into a vision mixer.

There are a number of essential skills that separate a vision mixer from someone who knows how a vision mixing panel works. A competent vision mixer is someone who can work with split-second timing so that a cut is taken precisely at the point the action requires, but who is constantly monitoring the previews to see if it will conflict with the mechanics of collecting the shot. They will have the ability to divide their attention between script, director's instructions, preview monitors and audio.

Good vision mixing, like good multicamera camerawork, is often a question of instant decision-making, fast reflexes and complete operational integration with the rest of the production crew. In high-speed cutting on a complex show there is almost a telepathic link between director, vision mixer and camera crew.

Camerawork and vision mixing are so interdependent that at times it would seem that telepathy is at work. Excluding those directors where telepathy is the only communication between gallery and floor, it is unnecessary to invoke extra-sensory explanations for the coordination needed between camera operator and vision mixer. In ad-lib situations when cutting between cameras constantly changing shot, the vision mixer and the camera crew know, from a knowledge of the programme format, what shots should be offered and taken. There is no more frustrating television than missing the right shot at the right moment. One of the skills developed by a vision mixer is knowing when to wait for directions to cut, and when to take the cut before the moment is lost.

8.1.3 Working in real time

One of the fundamental distinctions that exists between multicamera and single-camera techniques is that 'film-style' production splits its production decisions between acquiring the basic material and then editing the material in an extended timescale depending on budget and genre. Live, and much of recorded, television requires all the options closed at the time of transmission/recording. Editing decisions on the precise moment of a cut have to be taken in real time, unlike the more considered decision-making in an edit suite where a cut can be rehearsed, trimmed, rethought and then executed.

With iso working and rehearse/record production styles, a lot of the editing decisions have moved away from the gallery to the post-production edit suite, but the limitations of continuous, real time television is stylistically its true strength. Live television provides a sense of immediacy and spontaneity that is often missing from an overworked, edited product. The perennial advice for vision mixing still holds good – always have a reason for a change of shot.

8.1.4 Vision mixer's role in production

The basic vision mixing activity is switching visual sources when directed. With a scripted show, the cuts will be rehearsed and often the director will not call them on transmission. On an ad-lib show, where the precise nature of the content is not known, the director will call most of the cuts but at moments of high activity when they are fully engaged, they may leave an experienced vision mixer to follow the action and cut as appropriate.

As split-second timing is often involved, the vision mixer must have a good sense of the programme format conventions and the customary technique used in order to stay with the director's requirements. For example, they must know the rules of the sport being covered, or have a feel for rhythm and mood when covering music, or roughly know the possible attitudes or opinions of participants in a debate. So often in live television, the speed of the technique is controlled by the content of the programme, and there is no time 'on-air' to be precisely directed through all the vision mixing operations required. The director, vision mixer and camera crew activities are linked by the tempo of the event and must all be attentive to the immediate action and anticipate future events.

8.1.5 Vision mixing and video editing

Vision mixing and video editing share many common techniques. Whereas a vision mixer makes an edit decision in real time with little or no opportunity to adjust the point of edit, a video editor can rehearse and find a precise edit point before laying down the edit. They both, however, follow the standard, perennial conventions of shot transition. Although some of these conventions are dealt with in this chapter, a discussion in greater detail of the requirements of shot transition is to be found in Chapter 11. There is some overlap of content.

8.2 Technology

8.2.1 Vision mixing technology

Vision mixing a multicamera production requires an understanding of how to use effectively all the facilities available on the desk, in conjunction with the preview, effects and transmission monitors, and the ability to work in a team.

Although not appearing at first sight to be an important element of vision mixing, the physical relationship between the desk, script, monitors and control room lighting can be crucial. Every visual source required for the production should have a preview monitor or, if there are more incoming visual sources than monitors, control of the switching matrix should be easily accessible to the mixer.

The height and distance of the monitors should allow a rapid preview by the mixer without moving their body. Ideally this distance should be about six times the picture height from the viewer. There should be adequate space in front of the mixer for the script, which should be directionally lit to avoid spillage onto the preview monitors. The ambient lighting in the control room should be designed to avoid reflections on the monitor display screens.

8.2.2 Synchronization and timing

In order that all incoming visual sources can be mixed, wiped, superimposed and processed through the vision mixing desk, it is essential that certain conditions relating to signal timing are met otherwise it is impossible for the mixer to perform correctly. These conditions require a timing accuracy of less than 50 ns for the syncs and a phase difference of less than 5° between the sub-carrier reference bursts when transmitting PAL or NTSC. Every video signal passing through the desk must be aligned to achieve these conditions if it is intended to combine it with another visual source (see Chapter 1).

8.2.3 Analogue and digital vision mixing

Originally, all vision mixing was accomplished using analogue signals. Either the incoming sources were physically switched at the mixing panel or control voltages were activated when cutting and mixing to control the electronic mixing unit housed in the vision bays of the studio apparatus room. This avoided the need to run vision cables to the vision mixing desk.

Once an analogue signal has been converted to digital or the signal originates as a digital signal then a considerable number of effects can be produced via the vision mixing panel. Digital video effects such as picture in picture, freeze frames and picture manipulation have become a staple part of programme production.

The next step on from digital mixing has been the development of computer software to control visual transitions using graphical interface units controlled by a computer mouse. Although these add enormously to the flexibility in post-production work, 'real time' vision mixers on live or recorded-as-live productions usually prefer the security of buttons, faders and source selectors provided by the traditional vision mixing panel.

8.3 The vision mixing console

The controls on the mixing panel allow several basic visual transitions. These include:

- **Cut** – the simplest switch between shots. One image is instantaneously replaced by another image.
- **Dissolve** or **mix** (also known as a **crossfade**) – allows the incoming shot to emerge from the outgoing shot until it replaces it on screen. Sometimes both images are held on screen (a half-mix) before completing the transition. The time taken for the dissolve to make the transition from one image to the next can vary depending on content and the dramatic point the dissolve is making (e.g. a slow mix on slow music). The proportion of each image present at any point in the mix can be varied, with one image being held as a dominant image for most of the dissolve.
- **Fade** – similar to a mix except only one image is involved and either appears from a blank/black screen (fade-in) or dissolves into a blank/black screen (fade-out). A fade-in is often used to begin a sequence whilst a fade-out marks a natural end to a sequence.
- **Superimposition** – when one image (often text, such as the name of the speaker in shot) is superimposed on top of another image. Name-super text is usually faded-in or wiped-in, held so that it can be read, and then faded-out, cut-out or wiped-out.
- **Wipes** and **pattern wipes** – these provide an edge that moves across the screen between the outgoing image and the incoming image. The edge may be soft or bordered (a soft-wipe or a border-wipe) to add to the transition visually. The speed of a wipe can be controlled manually or programmed to move at a specified speed. Check with the director during rehearsal when setting up and memorizing the speed that is required.
- **Split screen** – when two different images are held on screen separated by a hard or soft edge wipe.
- **Digital video effect (DVE)** – When a picture is digitalized the image is formed by millions of separate parts called pixels. These pixels can be endlessly rearranged to produce a variety of random and mathematically defined transitions such as geometric wipes, spins, tumbles, squeezes, squashing, and transitions from one image to another simulating the page of a book, for example, being turned to introduce the next image.
- **Colour synthesizers** – a method of producing coloured captions and other effects from a monochrome source. The synthesizers rely on an adjustable pre-set video level to operate a switch, and usually two or three levels can be separated and used to operate colour generators and produce different colours. The switching signal is usually derived from a caption generator.
- **Chroma key** – a method of combining two images to achieve the appearance of a single image. This technique requires a switch to be inserted in the signal chain which will electronically select the appropriate image. Blue is commonly chosen as the colour to be used as the separation key but other colours can be employed (see Section 4.12).

8.3.1 The basic vision mixing panel

The output of the mixing panel is via a master fader although additional visual inputs can be added by a downstream keyer (see below). A basic mixer has two selection banks, normally termed A and B, and mixing or effects is performed between the two banks. Normally, each camera in use in the production has a dedicated button numbered in sequence from left to right as 1, 2, 3, 4, 5, 6, or however many cameras there are. Selection of other video sources can usually be switched to the required button with both banks duplicating the visual sources. Cutting between video sources is achieved by selecting one of the banks and then depressing the appropriate button on that bank.

Mixing between video sources is achieved by selecting the incoming video source on one bank and the outgoing source on the other bank. A pattern wipe on the transition can be achieved by routing the mix through the effects generator.

As well as an A and B bank, a C and D bank allows previewing of pictures prior to selection on the operational banks plus the ability to mix to a combination of two visual sources. For example, an image selected on the C bank with a superimposed caption selected from bank D can be mixed to the output of banks A and B.

A black input is available so that a correct waveform is transmitted when the pictures are faded down.

Figure 8.1

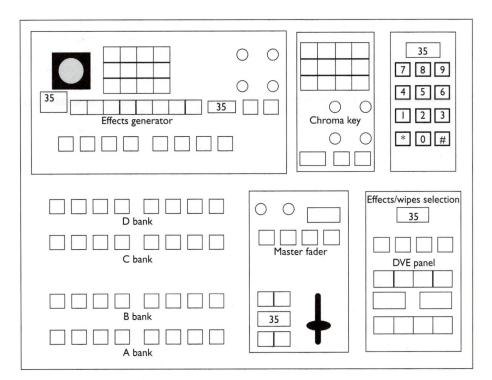

Effects generator

Chroma key

D bank

C bank

Master fader

Effects/wipes selection

DVE panel

B bank

A bank

A downstream keyer is a facility in-line with the output of a vision mixing panel which allows a superimposition on the output of a mixer panel which is unaffected by any changes on the mixer panel, e.g. a caption can be superimposed over changing shots selected at the mixer.

8.3.2 The importance of monitoring

All preview and effects previewing should be available on high-grade colour monitors. The phosphors should match so that skin-tones of any individual face or object colour are the same on each monitor. Each monitor should be set up for correct contrast and brightness. Every shot requires previewing for content, composition and exposure before it is cut to line (i.e. transmitted or recorded). Any large differences between monitors will prompt a visual 'jump' each time they are previewed, inducing inefficient hesitation before selection.

8.3.3 The importance of communications

The vision mixer needs to confirm incoming video signals availability and where they will appear on the switching matrix before transmission/recording, and often needs to query the availability of lines and their

source on transmission. Good communications between the control room and the operational point controlling switching and lines checks are therefore essential.

8.4 Editing skills

8.4.1 Limitations of technology

A digital vision mixing panel enables the most complex and sophisticated transitions between video sources that may be required in programme production. However, the vision mixing activity that is not available on any desk, and is crucial to programme production, is which vision source should be selected, and at what precise moment that transition should occur. Technology cannot help with these production decisions, and anyone new to vision mixing will have to learn the underlying principles of why to change shot and when to change shot.

As we have discussed in Chapter 2, continuous camera coverage of an event using a number of cameras relies on a stream of invisible shot changes – invisible in the sense that the transition between each shot does not distract the audience. The aim is to make the shot change unobtrusive to prevent the audience's attention switching from programme content to the programme production technique. No shot can be viewed in isolation – its effect on the viewer will be related to the preceding and succeeding shot. Standard conventions are employed, when cutting between shots, to ensure a smooth flow of images to guide the viewer unobtrusively to a new viewpoint.

8.4.2 Basic conventions

After mastering the operational controls on the vision mixing desk, the next stage is to fully understand these editing conventions. For a shot change to be unobtrusive:

- there must be an appropriate production reason to change the shot;
- the shots either side of the visual transition (cut, wipe, mix) must satisfy the editing requirements that link them.

8.4.3 Visual perception

Moving images in film or television are created by a succession of individual static frames. It is human perception that combines the separate images into a simulation of movement. One reason this succeeds is that the adjacent images in a shot are very similar. If the shot is changed and new information appears within the frame (e.g. what was an image of a face is now an aeroplane) the eye/brain takes a little time to understand the new image. The greater the visual discrepancy between the two shots the more likely it is that the viewer will consciously notice the change of shot.

A basic technique of vision mixing is to find ways of reducing the visual mismatch between two adjacent images. In general, a change of shot will be unobtrusive:

- if the individual shots (when intercutting between people) are matched in size, have the same amount of headroom, and have the same amount of looking space if in semi-profile; if the lens angle is similar (i.e. internal perspective is similar); and if the lens height is the same;
- if the intercut pictures are colour matched (e.g. skin tones, background brightness) and if in succeeding shots the same subject has a consistent colour (e.g. grass in a stadium);
- if there is continuity in action (e.g. body posture, attitude);
- if when cutting on action the flow of movement in the frame is carried over into the succeeding shot

(e.g. a man in medium shot sitting behind a desk stands up and, on his rise, a longer shot of the man and the desk is cut to);

- if there is a significant change in shot size or camera angle when intercutting on the same subject;
- if there is a significant change in content (e.g. a cut from a tractor to someone opening a farm gate);
- if there is continuity in lighting, sound, props and setting, and in performance or presentation.

Matching the visual design of shots is discussed in more detail in Chapter 11. The majority of studio work that the technical operator may be vision mixing will concern shots of people in discussion, and the transition from live to recorded items. Most of the following topics have been dealt with in Chapter 6, but the important points for vision mixing are repeated here.

8.4.4 Matched shots on an interview

Eyeline is an imaginary line between an observer and the subject of their observation. In a discussion, the participants are usually reacting to each other and will switch their eyeline to whoever is speaking. The audience, in a sense, is a silent participant and they will have a greater involvement in the discussion if they feel that the speaker is including them in the conversation. This is achieved if both eyes of the speaker can be seen by the viewer rather than profile or semi-profile shots. The cameras should be able to take up positions in and around the set to achieve good eyeline shots of all the participants. That is, both eyes of each speaker, when talking, can be seen on camera.

In addition, the relationship of the participants should enable a variety of shots to be obtained in order to provide visual variety during a long interview (e.g. over-the-shoulder 2-shots, alternative singles and 2-shots and group shots). The staging should also provide for a good establishment shot or relational shot of the participants and for opening or closing shots.

8.4.5 Standard shot sizes

Because so much of television programming involves people talking, a number of standard shot sizes have evolved centred on the human body. In general, these shot sizes avoid cutting people at natural joints of the body such as neck, elbows and knees. See Chapter 6 for illustration of standard shot sizes.

Standard shot descriptions

- **CU (Close Up).** Bottom of frame cuts where the knot of the tie would be.
- **MCU (Medium Close Up).** Bottom of the frame cuts where the top of a breast pocket of a jacket would be.
- **MS (Medium Shot).** Bottom of frame cuts at the waist.
- **BCU (Big Close Up).** The whole face fills the screen. Top of frame cuts the forehead. Bottom of the frame cuts the edge of chin, avoiding any part of the mouth going out of frame (rarely used in interviews).
- **LS (Long Shot).** Includes the whole figure.
- **WS (Wide Shot).** Includes the figure in a landscape or setting.
- **O/S 2s (Over-the-shoulder 2-shot).** Looking over the shoulder of a foreground figure framing part of the head and shoulders to another participant.
- **2-shot, 3-shot, etc.** Identifies the number of people in frame composed in different configurations.

Figure 8.2

Precise framing conventions for these standard shot descriptions vary between studios, broadcast organizations and country. One director's MCU may be another director's MS. The reason abbreviations are used is to speed up communication on live broadcasts. Make certain that you understand how the abbreviation is being used by the production team that you are working with.

8.4.6 Cross-shooting

A standard cross shooting arrangement is for the participants to be seated facing each other and for cameras to take up positions close to the shoulders of the participants. The usual method of finding the optimum camera position is to position the camera to provide a well composed over-the-shoulder 2-shot, then zoom in to check that a clean single can be obtained of the participant facing camera. A tight over-the-shoulder 2-shot always risks masking or a poorly composed shot if the foreground figure should lean left or right.

8.4.7 Crossing the line

There may be a number of variations in shots available depending on the number of participants and the method of staging the discussion/interview. All of these shot variations need to be one side of an imaginary line drawn between the participants (see Chapter 6).

To intercut between individual shots of two people to create the appearance of a normal conversation between them, three simple rules have to be observed. Firstly, if a speaker in a single is looking from left to right in the frame then the single of the listener must look right to left. Secondly, the shot size and eyeline should match (i.e. they should individually be looking out of the frame at a point where the viewer anticipates the other speaker is standing). Finally, every shot of a sequence should stay the same side of an imaginary line drawn between the speakers unless a shot is taken exactly on this imaginary line or a camera move crosses the line in vision, and allows a reorientation (and a repositioning of all cameras) on the opposite side of the old 'line'.

8.4.8 Matching to other cameras

In addition to setting up the optimum position for singles, 2-shots, etc., shots in a multicamera intercutting situation need to match. The medium close-ups (MCU) etc. should be the same size with the same amount of headroom. All cameras intercutting on singles should be the same height and if possible roughly the same lens angle (therefore the same distance from their respective subjects) especially when intercutting on over-the-shoulder 2-shots. This avoids a mismatch of the perspective of mass (i.e. the background figure is smaller or larger than the shot it is matching to). Other matching points are the same amount of looking room with semi-profile shots by placing the centre of the eyes (depending on size of shot) in the centre of frame.

Intercutting between different cameras provides an effective method of presenting information, telling a

Why change the shot?
The standard production reasons for a shot change are:

- To follow the action (e.g. coverage of horse racing. As the horses go out of range of one camera, they can be picked up by another and so forth).
- To present new information (e.g. a wide shot of an event shows the general disposition. A close-up shows detail).
- To emphasize an element of the event (e.g. a close-up shot revealing tension in the face of a sports participant).
- To tell a story (e.g. succeeding shots in a drama).
- To provide pace, excitement and variety in order to engage and hold the attention of the audience (e.g. changing the camera angle and size of shot on a singer).
- To visually structure an event in order to explain (e.g. a variety of shots of a cooking demonstration that show close-ups of ingredients and information shots of the cooking method.)

Figure 8.3

story or structuring an event. The pace, excitement and variety induced by a change of shot can potentially engage and hold the attention of the audience but shot change requires an underlying coherent structure if it is not to collapse into a succession of fleeting images. That overall structure is imposed by the director, assisted in an 'as-directed' situation by the input from the vision mixer and camera crew.

8.4.9 Continuity cutting

Any subject covered by multicameras must follow standard basic space/time visual conventions if the resultant flow of images is to be intelligible to the viewer. These shot change conventions ensure that:

- shots are structured to allow the audience to understand the space, time and logic of the action;
- each shot follows the line of action to maintain consistent screen direction so that the geography of the action is completely intelligible;
- unobtrusive camera movement and shot change directs the audience to the content of the production rather than the mechanics of production;
- continuity cutting creates the illusion that distinct, separate shots (possibly recorded out of sequence and at different times) form part of a continuous event being witnessed by the audience.

8.4.10 Vision mixing and video editing

See Chapter 11 for a more detailed description of methods of shot transition, rearranging time and space, basic editing principles, types of edit, matching visual design between shots, matching spatial relationships between shots, matching temporal relationships between shot, cutting on dialogue, etc.

8.5 Production methods

Different programme genres have different production techniques. Sports coverage has different shot patterns and camera coverage conventions, for example, from the conventions used in the continuous coverage of music. Knowledge of these customary techniques is an essential part of the vision mixing skills that need to be acquired. There is usually no time for a director to spell out his or her precise requirements during a fast, live transmission. They assume that the production team is experienced and understand the conventions of the programme being transmitted.

8.5.1 Programme formats

For a vision mixer, a basic distinction is whether the production is scripted (e.g. cuts to dialogue or narration are pre-planned and marked up in the camera script) or whether the majority of the programme speech is unscripted. With this type of ad-lib production, the vision mixer will need to follow direction and, at times, make edit decisions when the director is otherwise involved. At an early stage in rehearsal, establish with the director whether they wish to call every cut or if they are happy for the vision mixer to take the appropriate cuts in an interview when needed.

'As-directed' procedures
'As-directed' procedures require fast reflexes and an awareness of the development in programme content. Sometimes a programme will have sections which have a rehearsed shot structure interspersed with 'as-directed' sequences. The danger point is the junction between the two. It is easy to be caught in the 'as-directed' mode of operation and unable to find the correct place in the script when the programme moves into the scripted, numbered shot sequence.

Scripted programmes
A production that has been precisely camera scripted would seem an easier option than continuously keeping up with unexpected dialogue and discussion, but this is not necessarily the case. The scripted shots and cutting points need to be proved with a rehearsal. Those that do not work need altering, and in a very fast cutting sequence each shot has to be taken at its appointed place otherwise everyone, from the PA calling shot numbers to the camera crew working precisely to their listed shots, loses their place. A tightly scripted production requires the vision mixer to clearly mark-up all the changes during the rehearsal, and to be satisfied that all the vision mixing requirements (DVEs, chrome key set-ups, etc.) can be achieved in the time available as the production progresses in the timescale of the event being covered.

8.5.2 Camera positions

One production technique that sometimes helps the director and vision mixer in a complex ad-lib show is to position the cameras in the studio so that the preview monitors mimic the actual seated position of the participants. If the preview monitors are arranged to display cameras 1 to 4 from left to right, the cameras in the studio are placed so that camera one is looking at the person who is looking left to right. Likewise camera 4 is looking at the person who is looking right to left. The pictures displayed in the gallery are now a replica of what would be seen on the studio floor and make instant decisions of 'which camera when' easier than ad-hoc arrangement of camera position.

8.5.3 Standard openings

The opening of a programme is often deliberately designed to be fast and engaging to hook the audience. It will often follow a standard pattern that establishes the programme's identity (e.g. upcoming items in the programme). Often the director will rehearse the opening even if the main part of the programme will be 'as-directed'. As a vision mixer, it is worth marking up your script in detail and snatching some time for yourself to go through all the effects, routines and desk set-ups that are needed. Do not rely on memory. Put it in writing on your script even if you never read it. Make certain that you are technically clear on what you have to do and can cope with last-minute changes if they happen. A common problem is the non-appearance of a contributor at an outside source who is to be featured in a scene-setter at the beginning of the programme. Anticipate that this may not happen and have a fall-back plan of what you will do if they fail to arrive.

It is particularly important to get the show off to a good start in order to grab the viewers' attention, and also because mistakes at the start can lead to a 'domino' effect that will ripple all around the production team so that it will take time for everyone to return to competent operation.

8.5.4 Standard close

Many programmes also have a standard close. Three things often happen in quick succession. The presenter will wind-up the show, there may be a closing wide shot, sometimes with a lighting change, then closing graphics or credits to be supered over. The perennial problem with a live programme is time. If an interview precedes the close, the vision mixer will have been involved in a close and concentrated cutting sequence and may neither have anticipated nor set up the desk for the final sequence. At some time before the end you must anticipate what is required. A programme often crashes out because a contributor will not take a wind-up, and there is

inadequate time remaining for the pre-timed music and end credits. Arranging for the credits and music to end together is the usual professional aim for the end of a show. Be prepared with the end sequence before it is required.

8.5.5 Magazine format

In order for a topical daily magazine/news programme to be prepared, there is usually a well defined format with standard items and methods of presentation. Before working on such a programme, get to know the basic items which are going to appear on the daily running order and, most importantly, understand the specific abbreviations or slang descriptions that are used by the programme production staff. Get someone to explain any jargon that is new to you because on transmission there will not be time to question the implications of an unintelligible piece of information about changes to the running order that is thrown from the back of the control room to the director. You may be astute enough, for example, to work out that when the editor shouts out 'Kill the heads' that instead of going to presenter A on camera 2 to read the closing headlines, the next shot will be presenter B on camera 1 who will then link to the weather report. The production team may have been working on the same programme format for many years and know instantly the rearrangement necessary when the headlines item is dropped. If it takes you five to ten seconds to decipher the insider jargon, you could be completely wrong-footed and cut to the wrong camera. People who are in daily contact in the production of a programme have a habit of inventing shorthand descriptions of the daily items which only insiders are privy to.

The running order, although brief, is the key to what you as a vision mixer will need to know. Mark up any scripted links (which often arrive very late and sometimes while you are 'on-air') indicating camera and visual source in large letters (see Section 8.6.2). Check the end words coming out of a recorded item as you will be listening for them to cut out of and back to the presenter. Some presenters will ad-lib into an item and the cue to go the new item must be given by the director in order that both vision and sound can cut/mix at the same time. The director should always control any programme transition that requires coordination between sound and vision so that there is no misunderstanding causing sound or vision to lead or lag.

Keep up to date with changes, especially those last-minute changes that occur in the few moments before transmission when everyone is checking sources, levels and setting the desk for the opening routine. Try to look ahead on transmission to any complicated set-ups that are upcoming such as chroma key weather set-ups (see Section 8.5.16). On-air, watch out for the invariable jokey interchange between programme presenter and weather presenter or specialist sports reporter. Watch your previews to check that you can cut back to a programme presenter after going to the weather presenter if the repartee continues because sometimes a camera will clear immediately a link has finished. Check also that your desk set-up allows you to intercut between weather presenter/chroma key background and programme presenter. This type of ad-lib cutting can be visually very messy because of its spontaneous content and indecision about when it has ended.

Name supers on recorded items need to be checked for accuracy and whether there is sufficient time for the super to be put up, read, and taken out before the shot changes. A timed list of supers and when they occur should be available from editing; but be warned, if they have not been rehearsed the timings could be wrong.

8.5.6 Early morning and late night news bulletins

Local news inserts into a network programme or regional opt-outs can often be pre-rehearsed and accurately timed, but from a mixing point of view there is often the need to be flexible and adapt to the time actually allocated. If a network programme is over-running, the squeeze is often on the opt-out in order to catch up on the overall running time.

8.5.7 Interview format

The main points about cutting an interview have already been discussed, but the following additional points should be noted:

- The director should establish in rehearsal on which camera the presenter will make their introduction.
- The camera coverage and the order in which the participants will be introduced should also be established so that the vision mixer can mark up. A frequent problem in this part of the interview format is the presenter naming the participants too quickly, giving little or no chance for the cameras and the vision mixer to get the appropriate shot up as the person is named.
- Try and establish who the first question will be addressed to if it is known before recording/transmission.

- Establish with the director if they will call for reaction shots, although the best reactions are so quick that if the cut is not taken immediately the 'reaction' is lost.
- A popular convention is to cut to the participant who is being asked a question before the presenter has finished the question in order to observe their reaction to the point being put to them. Check with the director if they intend to follow this convention.
- It is not a good idea for cameras to make large repositions during an interview as the speed of question and answer may result in a camera being on the move when it is required to be on a participant. An experienced camera crew will inform the director in rehearsal if they are repeatedly having to make large off-shot movement to provide the camera coverage he or she requires. The vision mixer can only watch the preview monitors and hope that the required shot will be steady, focused, and with a matched frame when it is required.
- If the presenter does not name the person they are coming to, watch the preview monitor of the wide shot or the presenter shot to check their eyeline to establish who he or she is addressing before making the cut. It is better to be a beat behind the answer than cut to the wrong person.

8.5.8 The television demonstration

A television demonstration can have as its subject anything from a DIY item to cooking a Christmas pudding. It is often conducted by a presenter and an 'expert' who will do the demonstration. The camera coverage will require shots of the two participants and close-ups of the demonstrated items. If the items can be positioned for clean CUs in rehearsal the demonstration will be that much more intelligible to the viewer. Be quick to cut away from a small item that is held in big close-up and is being waved around by the participant. It is almost impossible to hold it in sharp focus and if it is waved around the viewer will not be able to understand the content of the shot. If tight close-ups are being picked up on a surface such as a table, be certain that the item is the one that is being referred to before cutting to it. Too often an interviewee will rest their hand on one item before discussing another item at the far end of the table. If in doubt, watch the 2-shot on the preview monitor to check the direction of the eyeline.

8.5.9 Audience show

Vision mixing on an audience show is similar to an enlarged interview. It helps if the anchor person is always on the same camera, and that there is a safety shot showing a wide shot of the audience. When a group of experts are gathered there may even be a seating plan with an order of speaking. Frequently, however, an audience discussion is a free-for-all with a need for the camera crew to rapidly find the speaker or even anticipate who the next speaker will be. The director must coordinate and communicate when duplicate shots turn up. The usual guidelines for mixing an ad-lib spontaneous event is to watch the previews, cut away quickly to allow cameras to reposition, and trust that an experienced director and camera crew will provide the appropriate shot. Establish with the director the opening and closing routines and make certain the anchor camera is released to go to the presenter for the wind-up.

8.5.10 Music coverage

Multicamera music coverage on television covers a wide range of musical performances, production styles and visual preferences. At one end of the spectrum there are relays from concert halls of orchestral performances that are often tightly scripted and in general have an unobtrusive technique where the emphasis is on matching picture to content with the minimum of visual interpretation. In extreme contrast to this 'invisible' technique, there is multicamera coverage of rock groups where an attempt is made to capture the atmosphere and excitement of a live event. Cutting rate and shots seek to reproduce the liveliness and frenzy of the rave.

Most of the following points are generalized and all are not applicable to the individual ways of presenting music on television within the wide range of production styles practised. They are an attempt to make the vision mixer new to multicamera music coverage aware of some aspects of production technique that he or she should consider when working on a continuous musical event.

The different methods of covering music continuously with multicameras without recording breaks or post-production can be grouped under the following headings:

- **Pre-scripted.** The whole performance is structured and shots assigned to each camera using a score or a breakdown of the number (e.g. the Prom concerts or production numbers in variety shows). With complex music (e.g. an orchestral piece), the director, vision mixer and PA will be following the score with the PA calling shot numbers and bar numbers to allow camera moves such as pans, zooms and tracks to be precisely timed. This

complex event is usually well outside the experience of a technical operator.
- **Camera scripted during rehearsal.** After looking on camera at the performance, shots are structured by the director and each shot numbered. This shot sequence is then exactly reproduced on the recording or transmission.
- **Top and tail.** The start and end of a musical piece are decided, leaving the middle section to be as-directed.
- **Assigned roles.** Each camera is assigned one or two performers or instruments and offers a variety of shots connected with them. This gives the director a guaranteed appropriate shot at any time.
- **As-directed.** No shot structure is assigned and each camera operator is directed and/or offers a variety of shots, checking that the shot they are offering is an alternative to the shot currently cut to line.

8.5.11 Cutting to music

It helps when cutting music to have a knowledge of music form, but the minimum skill that is required to be developed by a vision mixer is a feel for pace and tempo, and an understanding of bar structure. Most popular music is created around a 16 or 32 bar structure and the cutting rate and time of the cut happening will relate to this bar structure. Listen to a wide range of music and practise cutting on the beat.

Mixes are often used on slower tempo numbers. Remember that the camera operator will hold a static frame while the cue light is on. Sometimes the fader can be almost at its end stop with no hint of its image on the transmission monitor. The cue light will still be on, however, and the camera cannot clear until the fader is taken to the end stop and the cue light goes out. Match the speed of the mix to the music and attempt to imitate a sound technique which often uses a non-linear fade-up or fade-down. This technique fades the sound away so that the listener is not really aware when the music has gone. Something similar can be done with visual cross-mixes and combination shots when images are brought in and taken out.

8.5.12 Cutting on movement

The correct point at which to take a cut midway through a movement (e.g. someone standing up, walking to another chair, and then sitting in to a close-up) is discussed fully in Chapter 11. On multi-camera cutting it is sometimes possible to make a cut on action which appears to make the movement repeat itself. For example, a cut to a different camera angle as someone turns can give the impression that the turn has been extended and repeated, a visual effect often exploited in dance coverage. It is possible on multicamera mixing to disrupt the continuity of an action if care is not taken to time the cut and the size of shot.

8.5.13 Working in a production crew

Obviously the director/vision mixer wants the appropriate shot ready, in focus and steady when it is required, but for the camera operator there are a number of obstacles to achieving this. If all camera repositions in the studio were able to be rehearsed, and if all scripted words were delivered perfectly, in their correct order and fluff-free, then there would no problem and any tight 'repos' would be anticipated. But television production is far from being a precise science and it is surprising that any cup gets to any lip without a slip. As a vision mixer, try to understand why the shot is not ready. It may be the camera operator's fault, but more likely there is a cable or scenery problem or a dozen other reasons why the shot is not steady, in focus and on the correct subject. The preview monitors are a useful communication tool in these situations, and an experienced camera crew will show what the problem is (e.g. the floor manager has lost talkback) if they are not otherwise engaged 'on-air'. Be consistent, on scripted shows, to cut as rehearsed as the camera operator may be relying on the rehearsed time to make a reposition or adjust framing. Likewise the camera operator must deliver the shot that was agreed and rehearsed to ensure the cutting is appropriate.

8.5.14 Last-moment tweaks to the shot just as the mixer cuts

A recurring problem facing vision mixers is when, at the moment they are going to cut, the camera operator reframes or makes a slight 'twitch' to the framing. There are a number of reason why this happens. The most common one is that the presenter/participant alters their body position before they speak, forcing the camera operator to reframe just when the cut is required. With some professionals, the camera operator may know from their experience of that performer that they will straighten up from a slouched posture just before they are cued, and will make an allowance in the head room etc. to avoid last minute 'tweaks'. Other reasons are that the camera operator has only just arrived at the framing and having found focus

will reframe for the best composition, or the camera operator becomes aware of, for example, a distracting highlight in the background and attempts to lose it. The vision mixer can only watch the preview monitor and think the same way as the camera operator and anticipate, for example, that the operator will recompose the shot when someone straightens up and hold the cut until the shot settles.

8.5.15 Customary technique

It is crucial in a fast ad-lib spontaneous programme that the vision mixer and camera crew are on the same 'wavelength' as the director. This means everyone understanding the customary technique for the programme and all thinking in the same way. In practice this means that when everyone anticipates a cut, it happens. Or when everyone anticipates a specific shot, it is taken. If a camera crew or vision mixer are puzzled by the cutting preferences of the director and these do not follow customary conventions then the director, in a fast moving ad-lib production, will have to call every shot, and every cut, and this can be time-consuming and inefficient. If everyone can keep in step, then the production team can up its shot rate and still keep together.

For example, when a camera is 'on-shot' on a interviewee and a neighbouring speaker out of shot starts to speak, the camera operator could pan in vision to the speaker, although this is usually not customary technique, or the mixer can cut away to a quick reaction shot of the anchor or a group shot, allowing the camera to quickly reposition ready for a cut back with hardly a word being lost on screen. When trust is built up between director, vision mixer and camera crew many more shots are possible because repositions are faster. A camera operator may spot a person bursting to get into the debate and swing to them, which usually prompts the speaker to speak. If the director wants to call every move and every cut and every shot they may miss a number of useful shots and, unless they are very lucky, be left several shots behind the flow of the discussion. Tying up several cameras solely as wide 'belt and braces' covering shots leads to a camera coverage that is too loose and does not engage and involve the viewer in the personalities of the debate.

8.5.16 Chroma key technique

Invisible keying of one image into another requires the application of a perfect electronic switch obtained by appropriate lighting of foreground and background, correct setting up and operation of the keying equipment, a match between foreground and background mood and atmosphere which is achieved by lighting and design, appropriate costume and make-up of foreground artistes, and a match between foreground artiste's size, position and movement and background perspective achieved by camera position, lens and staging.

The control that selects the precise point where the colour key will operate is often situated on the vision mixing panel. This clip level control needs to be adjusted so that there is a clean switch between foreground and background images (see Fig. 4.150). Small detail in the foreground subject, such as hair, can 'confuse' the keying equipment so that there is not a clean switch between foreground and background. This usually appears in the combined image as fringing around the hair. The clip level control needs to be adjusted to provide a perfect key. Problems also arise when clothing or other items closely match the background keying colour or there is colour spill onto the foreground subject from the background chroma key area.

Smoke or glass items are difficult to chroma key with standard colour switching but linear keying eliminates the problems connected with transparency. It does not switch between foreground and background but suppresses the unwanted colour of the foreground (e.g. blue) and turns on the background image in proportion (linearly) to the brightness of the blue of the foreground image. Shadows cast by foreground objects can therefore be semi-transparent rather than black silhouettes.

A simple application would involve an artiste appearing against a blue background on one camera and a second camera looking at a picture or slide of a street scene. When these two pictures are used with chroma key the artist will appear on the screen as if he is in a street. The blue background can be produced by either blue-painted scenery or a blue-lighted cyclorama. In a long shot within a studio, the blue backing is usually insufficiently wide or high enough. A box wipe can be set up on the mixer with the background scene outside the box and the combination of foreground/background through chroma key inside the box (see also Chapter 4).

To provide the illusion of artistes appearing behind objects which are in the picture into which the artist is to be inserted, objects or flats painted in the keying colour are placed in front of the artiste to coincide with the foreground object's position in the picture. All cameras must be locked-off and alignment is performed by using a mixed feed viewfinder on the camera which shows both pictures.

There are technological methods of allowing the foreground and background cameras to move in synchronization, but in general if either camera moves the two images will be become misaligned, and the combined image will lose its visual credibility.

8.5.17 Picture manipulation

Another method of inserting one image into another is via the digital video effects bank on the mixing panel. The inserted image is reduced to the required size and then positioned by joystick control. The position can then be memorized and recalled during recording or transmission. Remember that some adjustment may be necessary of the memorized position because although the electronic memory is infallible, the camera operator has to rely on shot box setting (if available), a marked position for the camera mounting on the studio floor and perfect visual memory of what the combined shot looked like at rehearsal. Computers are better than people in repeating perfect positioning within the frame. The same problem can exist with combinations of computer graphics and camera shots.

8.5.18 The split screen

A split screen is another method of combining two images. Although the term is often applied to the method of combining two images separated by a vertical or horizontal wipe, it can also be applied to a composite involving box, circle, etc. shapes.

8.5.19 Caption key

A caption key facility provides for sharper separation between lettering and background image. This improvement in legibility can be enhanced by a black edge generator. A colour synthesizer can be used to colour captions or backgrounds for captions.

8.5.20 Floor monitors

Frequently floor monitor feeds are switched at the vision mixing panel. A typical production requirement is for an 'in-vision' monitor to be switched at a specific point in the production. The monitor, for example, may be displaying a contributor for an outside location who will be interviewed by the studio presenter. When the interview is finished, the monitor, if it is still in vision, will require to be switched to possibly the programme logo or a similar graphic.

Floor monitors may also require switching during the production of programme formats such as game shows or slung monitors for audience etc.

8.6 Rehearsal

8.6.1 Pre-rehearsal checks

There are a number of checks the vision mixer should carry out prior to rehearsal:

- Check the script or running order and establish the origin of all visual sources and where they will appear on the mixer, and on what preview monitor.
- Check source identification for incoming lines, and check if there are sufficient previews and sources on the mixer without the need to switch during transmission/recording.
- Make certain you have a method of identifying, and a written record of the origin of, a source on the matrix if switching is required.
- Check over the mixer and set up the facilities that will be required by the production.
- Check that you understand how to use all the facilities available rapidly.
- If it is the job function of the vision mixer, line up the monitors with a test signal (e.g. PLUGE) if available and check for consistency in brightness, contrast, colour rendering and sharpness between previews and transmission monitors.
- Check the cue lights on preview and transmission monitors, and with the camera crew/vision control, check the camera cue lights. If you are unfamiliar with the mixing panel check that cue lights still function when using the DVE facility.

8.6.2 Marking up a script

Vision mixing information on the script needs to be read at speed during transmission/recording. The size of the typescript is often inadequate to check the next visual change accurately when quickly looking between panel, monitor bank and script. The usual method of improving this is to write in large letters the camera number, instructions to cut, mix or fade and any other mixer facility to be used (chroma key etc.). Identify key dialogue connected with visual transitions (e.g. changing graphic material in vision to match spoken commentary) or 'in' or 'out' words on insert material.

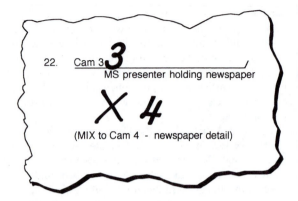

Figure 8.4

8.6.3 Why have a rehearsal?

Multicamera television production is a group activity. A live transmission requires the coordination and contribution of many different crafts and skills, each perfecting their input into the production at the precise time that it is required. A recorded item may have the luxury of retakes to eliminate imperfections if the programme content is under the control of the director (e.g. it is not an actuality event that cannot be repeated). To ensure that everyone is clear about their contribution to a transmission, the director/producer/editor must either brief each individual or arrange to run the item before transmission. A rehearsal provides the opportunity for everyone involved to check that the planned structure and detail of the programme is practical and achievable.

8.6.4 What a vision mixer needs from the rehearsal

As we have discussed, a camera-scripted programme needs to be run in its actual running time to establish if the cameras can get the required shots and the cuts, mixes and effects can be implemented at the dialogue point required by the director. It is usual to block the shots, altering and adjusting the shots and cuts as necessary. Because this is a stop/start activity it is very easy to overlook the time available to carry out complex mixer set-ups or for cameras to readjust the frame. A non-stop run of each complete section establishes the true timescale of the production. Make certain that you keep up-to-date with any changes and pay particular attention to fast-cutting sequences to ensure that you, and the camera crew, have sufficient time to provide the shots and cuts on time.

If you are working from a running order, the director should try to ensure that everyone has at least a look at each set-up and sequence, even if the shots are rehearsed with the floor manager standing in for absent presenters or interviewees. The running order should indicate visual and audio source, duration and any scripted intros or pieces to camera.

8.6.5 Talkback discipline

Remember that a number of people are on talkback with some wearing headsets for the whole of the rehearsal and transmission period. Avoid chattering in the control room about your holidays etc. or making comments about a transmitted programme that other people cannot see. It becomes very tiring for other members of the production crew to be forced to listen to chatter and gossip while waiting for vital information that is pertinent to the production. Imagine phoning up for a train time and being forced to listen to an inconsequential conversation between operators before the relevant facts came through.

8.6.6 Working with the director

At some time during the rehearsal, if you have not worked with the director previously, check on what cut decisions will be called and which mixing decision you should take from the script or programme content. The rehearsal period is also the time for you to assess the form of words with which the director will instruct you when he or she requires the edit points.

It is not being pedantic to require good clear communication from the director to avoid, in the heat of a live production, misunderstandings and confusion. Someone snapping their fingers in front of your face is not communication unless they have preceded the signal with words such as, 'Coming to 1. Cut to 1'.

It is necessary for the director to be as brief as possible on transmission, but not to the point of unintelligibility. Shouting one word 'Cut!' when there may be choice of cameras to go to can only lead to the vision mixer making the decision and then being blasted for not being telepathic and going to the camera the director was thinking about.

There is often a need for the director to alert the vision mixer or camera operator before an instruction. This can be as simple as preceding the instruction with 'coming to'. With experience, a vision mixer can react very quickly to content and the director's instructions if there is some warning of their intention

before the command is made. It helps if the director precedes an instruction, for example, 'Camera 2. Give me a 2-shot.' For a vision mixer: 'Coming to 2. Cut' or 'Mix to four next ... (pause) ... and mix.' Be careful, when new to vision mixing, that you do not confuse a direction to a camera operator with a command to cut to that camera. This can easily happen if the director does not choose the instruction carefully.

On recording or on transmission there is no need for the director to call everything. The camera rehearsal period should have established the main structure of the show and the vision mixer should be confident of the flow of shots. On a fast-cutting, scripted section, the less the director says the better. The director must, however, coordinate those transitions as, for example, coming out of a video insert, when both the vision mixer and sound need the command to make the cut coincide. The director should cue the artistes so that by the time the cut happens, the artiste is animated. The usual command is 'Cue and cut.' Mixing to a presenter takes longer than a cut and it is usual to use the command 'Mix and cue' to allow the mix to be fully complete by the time the artiste starts to talk.

By the end of the rehearsal the vision mixer should know as much about the shot sequence and cutting points as the director. The director's instructions during transmission or recording are merely an indication of when to do something.

8.6.7 VT clock

One final item to check on rehearsal for a recorded programme is the source of the ident clock and who is responsible for programming the correct details of the production. Make yourself aware of local custom and practice of when you should fade to black before the top of the clock is reached.

8.6.8 Solving problems

A rehearsal exists to solve problems. What was a paper planning exercise has now to be converted into a three-dimensional activity for everyone concerned all working against the hardest task master – the clock. Problems will arise, and sometimes sitting in your vision mixing chair you will feel you have the perfect solution. Depending on the moment, you can offer your suggestion, but make certain you have thought through all the implications and are not creating new problems elsewhere. Be cautious that one successful suggestion does not lead to a second and a third and so on. This is a diplomatic way of advising against trying to direct the show. There is only one director and all production communication should flow through the director's chair. It is a slippery slope to anarchy once everyone starts offering their viewpoint, and like the famous committee that set out to design a horse, your production team could end up transmitting a camel.

8.7 Transmission/recording

8.7.1 Transmission/recording procedure

With a good rehearsal, by the time transmission or recording begins, the vision mixer should be fairly confident of what their contribution is to the production. Unfortunately the unpredictable nature of television is such that most experienced practitioners subscribe to the belief that a good rehearsal often presages a chaotic transmission. This pessimism is frequently unfounded and you should always attempt to get as much information about your production role before you go 'on-air'. If you are not told, ask, as the process of briefing everyone on the production crew can sometimes be less than perfect.

8.7.2 Anticipate the unexpected

Television programme production is unpredictable, but its unpredictability often falls within a pattern.

Summary of vision mixing operational technique

Preparation
- Know how the mixer operates.
- Check over all the facilities and sources that are required.
- Check and mark up the script.
- Find out how the director will communicate with you.

Concentration
- Keep your attention on the transmitted content even if every one else around you in the control room is concerned with items yet to arrive or unobtainable.
- Do not try to do other people's jobs (such as directing).

Anticipation
- Look ahead.
- Anticipate what can go wrong.
- Have a mental plan of what to do when it does go wrong.

Figure 8.5

With experience, you can anticipate the unexpected and make appropriate alternative arrangements. Anticipation allows you to find time to do what is required. Being suddenly faced with a set of unrehearsed events without pre-thought eliminates any time to sort out the desk and make the correct operational decisions. Part of your preparation for the show is to mentally plan what you will do if the rehearsed sequences are changed.

8.7.3 Make time

Set up complex effects before they are needed to make time for yourself. Keep with the flow of the production but constantly look ahead to what is upcoming.

8.7.4 Problems during the show

No live or 'recorded as live' programme will be without its problems or unexpected emergencies. Artistes missing their marks or cameras prevented from getting to a prearranged position will require instant adjustment to the shot structure. Watch the previews for alternative shots.

If you miss a shot or cut to a wrong camera, forget about it and make certain the next shot is there. Too often, the number of operational errors escalate because people spend time agonizing over their mistakes. If a shot is not ready and the director is unaware, bring it to their attention so that action can be quickly taken. If there is a production mistake on transmission, never spend time deciding on the cause. Get on with the next item and leave the post mortems until after the programme has finished.

Remember to follow up any equipment malfunction that affected your work and check that it will not occur next time.

8.7.5 Making mistakes

Everyone makes mistakes, including the director. Sometimes he or she will call for a cut to a shot that is obviously wrong. The vision mixer in such circumstances will have to use their own individual initiative and a knowledge of the production either to cut to the right shot or, if they feel this will cause greater confusion, to go to the directed shot.

9 Television journalism and camerawork

9.1 Introduction

Video news journalism covers a wide spectrum of visual/sound reports which use a number of camerawork conventions. A loose classification separates hard news stories, which aim to transmit an objective, detached account of an event (e.g. a plane crash), from those soft news stories which incline more towards accounts of lifestyle, personality interviews and consumer reports.

Acceptable camera technique and style of shooting will depend on content and the aim of the report. For example, a politician arriving to make a policy statement at a conference will be shot in a fairly straightforward camera style with the intention of simply 'showing the facts'. An item about a fashion show could use any of the styles of feature film presentation (e.g. wide angle distortion, subjective camerawork, canted camera). The political item has to be presented in an objective manner to avoid colouring the viewers' response. The fashion item can be more interpretative in technique and presentation in an attempt to entertain, engage and visually tease the audience. A basic skill of news/magazine camerawork is matching the appropriate camerawork style to the story content.

The basic points of news/topical magazine camerawork to consider are:

- producing a technically acceptable picture;
- an understanding of news values;
- matching camerawork style to the aims of objective news coverage;
- structuring the story for news editing and the requirements of news bulletins/magazine programmes;
- access to the story and getting the story back to base.

The technical requirements of producing a picture are approximately the same as any other styles of camerawork although there is often less time to set up the shot and record (see Chapter 7).

9.2 What makes a story news?

There is no universally acceptable definition of news. A wide diversity of stories can be seen every day as the front page lead in newspapers. There appears to be little consensus as to what is the main news story of the day. The only generalization that can be made in television is that news is usually considered to be those topical events that need to be transmitted in the next immediate news broadcast. Access, rapid working methods, a good appreciation of news values and the ability to get the material back, edited and on the air are the main ingredients of 'hard news' camerawork. There is no specific agreed technique in camera/recorder news coverage although there are a number of conventions that are widely accepted.

9.2.1 Human interest

People almost always take precedence over scenery as the principal subject of news stories. Faces make good television if they are seen in context with the crisis. Where to position the camera to get the shot that will summarize the event is a product of experience and luck, although good news technique will often provide its own opportunities. A news story can quickly lose the interest of its potential audience if it does not, at some point in the report, feature a person.

9.2.2 Record or interpretation

One basic convention is the distinction between news camerawork as a record of an event and camerawork as an interpretation of an event.

As the **record of an event**, information shots are specific. They refer to a unique event – the wreckage of a car crash, someone scoring a goal, a political speech. They are often non-repeatable. The crashed car is towed away, the politician moves on. They are the guts of a news story and if the crucial shot is missing, the story will lose impact and significance. The item will deteriorate into an account of what has happened, but can no longer be seen.

Interpretative or decorative shots are non-specific. They are often shot simply to give visual padding to the story. A typical example is a shot of an interviewee walking in a location before an interview. This shot allows the dubbed voice-over to identify who the interviewee is and possibly their attitude to the subject. The shot needs to be long enough to allow information that is not featured in the interview to be added as a voice-over. The interviewee leaves frame at the end of the shot to provide a cutting point to the interview. Have the interviewee medium close-up facing in the same direction as the preceding walk to the interview.

There is a basic dilemma in news bulletins between objectivity and the need to engage and hold the attention of the audience. As the popularity of cinema films has shown, an audience enjoys a strong story that involves them in suspense and moves them through the action through wanting to know 'what happens next'. This is often incompatible with the need for news to be objective and factual.

9.2.3 Fact and fiction

The production techniques used for shooting and cutting fiction and factual material are almost the same. These visual storytelling techniques have been learned by the audiences from a lifetime of watching fictional accounts of life. The twin aims of communication and engaging the attention of the audience apply to news as they do to entertainment programmes.

9.3 Fact and opinion

A television news report has an obligation to separate fact from opinion, to be objective in its reporting, and, by selection, to emphasize that which is significant to its potential audience. These considerations therefore need to be borne in mind by a potential news camera operator as well as the standard camera technique associated with visual storytelling. Although news aims to be objective and free from the entertainment values of standard television storytelling (suspense, excitement, etc.) it must also aim to engage the audience's attention and keep them watching. The trade-off between the need to visually hold the attention of the audience and the need to be objective when covering news centres on structure, pace and shot selection.

Communication and audience involvement
- Communicate in an objective style without unduly 'colouring' the item.
- Identify the main 'teaching' points the audience should understand. What is this item about? What is the crucial point (or points) the audience should grasp?
- Find the appropriate method of presentation (shots, structure, narrative) to hold the audience's attention.
- Involve the viewer by pace, brevity (e.g. no redundant footage) and relevance (e.g. How does it affect me? Can I empathize with this situation?).
- Capture the attention by arresting images supported by lucid and appropriate narration and exposition.
- Although news is often an unplanned, impromptu shoot, the transmitted item should end up as a seamless flow of relevant shots spliced together to meet the standard conventions of continuity editing.
- Balance the shooting ratio (too much footage, and it cannot be edited in the timescale available) against sufficient coverage to provide flexibility as the story develops over time, to allow the editor to cut the item down to the required running time.

Figure 9.1

9.3.1 What increases subjectivity?

Subjectivity is increased by restaging the event to serve the needs of television (e.g. re-enacting significant action which occurred before the camera arrived), and by selecting only 'action' events to record. For example, violent demonstrations as opposed to discussion about the subject, or a police car chase rather than routine police work of computer checks through a database. Also the use of standard 'invisible' technique editing can distort an objective report (e.g. the compression of time, selecting only action aspects of the story). Editing is selection and can produce a partial account of an event. For example, a football match can be cut down to a thirty second 'highlights' report of the match and make it a great deal more exciting than the match witnessed by the crowd at the stadium. All these 'entertainment' aspects of storytelling are usually avoided when shooting a news story.

9.3.2 Topical magazine items

Like news, magazine items often attempt to capture spontaneous action and present an event objectively. But whereas news is generally topical information of the day, shot on the day, magazine themes and issues are shot over a period of time. A news item may have a duration of less than thirty seconds while a 'feature' report can run for 3 to 5 minutes. All these factors have a bearing on the camera techniques that are used on the different genres.

News attempts to emphasize fact rather than opinion, although journalistic values cannot escape subjective judgements. Feature items can use fact, feeling and atmosphere, argument, opinion, dramatic reconstruction and subjective impressions, which can be very similar to standard feature film storytelling. Non-topical items can be filmed and edited, and shelved as stand-by or used to balance the programme when required. Without the immediate pressure to transmit, they can have more considered post-production (e.g. the addition of music and effects).

9.3.3 Diary events

Many topics that are featured in news and magazine programmes are known about a long time before the event occurs. These 'diary' events allow forward planning and efficient allocation of people and time. They also provide the opportunity for advanced research so that a location shoot can be structured and more considered.

Even if a 'diary' item is considered to be predictable and straightforward, be flexible on the day and be prepared for the unexpected (e.g. an unexpected demonstration by protesters in the middle of a VIP tour).

9.4 News – condensing time

A news bulletin has a limited transmission time to present the news of the day. There is always constant pressure to reduce the running time of a topic. This should be borne in mind when shooting an item. Provide cutaway shots to allow the journalist/editor to compress the actual time of an item to fit the duration allocated in the programme (see Chapter 11).

The editor only has a certain amount of time to cut the item. The camera operator can help by remembering:

- Shoot with editing in mind and for hard news keep shooting ratios low for a fast turnaround in the edit suite.
- It is important to be brief and provide only significant shots for news as tape has to be reviewed in real time before being cut.
- With a hard news story, help to reduce the amount of shuttling the editor will be involved in and, wherever possible, shoot in sequence and shoot interviews on one tape and cutaways on a second tape.
- Record each story on a separate tape to allow a separate editor (if required) to work on each story.

- Record only those shots that are significant and best sum up the essence of the story. Each shot must serve a purpose in telling the story.
- The viewer will require a longer on-screen time to assimilate the information in a long shot than the detail in a close shot. Provide more detail than geography shots or scene setting.
- Avoid long panning or zooming shots. News stories are cut down to the essentials and need the flexibility of editing at any point in the shot.
- It is more difficult to edit moving shots than static shots.
- Provide a higher proportion of static shots to camera movement. It is difficult to cut between pans and zooms until they steady to a static frame and hold.
- Use short pans (no more than two seconds long) to inject pace into the story.
- Moving shots require more perceptual effort to understand than static shots, therefore include more close, static shots than ones with camera movement.
- Use the 5 second module for news which is:
  10 second hold at the start of the pan or zoom;
  5/10 second camera movement;
  5/10 second hold at the end of the pan or zoom.
  This provides the editor with three different shots.
- Check continuity and avoid shooting interviews against a moving background which could 'jump' when edited (e.g. a background to a ten-minute interview of a crowd leaving a stadium after a match, which when edited may use comment from the start and the end of the interview and produce a mismatch with the background).
- A substantial change in shot size or camera angle/camera position is needed for shots intending to be intercut.
- Provide relevant but non-specific shots so that voice-over information (to set the scene or the report) can be dubbed on after the script has been prepared (see also Chapter 7).
- Remember to provide adequate run-up time before significant action to allow for a stable shot/syncs for editing.
- Use 'record run' time code rather than 'time of day' wherever possible.
- Provide accurate information on cassette or add v/o on tape to identify specific people or events (e.g. on a courtroom exit, identify any significant people in the shot).
- Remember that a casual title given to the item at the morning editorial meeting may change by transmission. Provide a brief description of content on the cassette.
- Have in mind a structure for the shots you provide to allow the editor to create pace, shot variety and fluid continuity.

9.4.1 The nucleus of a structure

Hard news by its nature is seldom, if ever, pre-scripted and therefore material is recorded without a written plan. The camera operator, with the journalist, needs to shoot with editing in mind and think in terms of a structure for the shots provided. A series of shots have to be meaningfully edited together and this relies on the camera operator anticipating edit points. As has been emphasized, nothing is more time-consuming than an attempt to edit a pile of cassettes of ill-considered footage into some intelligent and intelligible form. To avoid this, the editor requires from the camera operator maximum flexibility with the material supplied, and the nucleus of a structure.

> **A useful shot**
> An appropriate shot will fulfil one of the following functions in the structure of the piece:
>
> - It emphasizes the essence of the principal subject.
> - It provides variation in shot size.
> - It gives added prominence to the selected subject.
> - It provides more information about the subject.
> - It provides for a change of angle/size of shot to allow unobtrusive intercutting.
> - It allows for variety of shot and shot emphasis.
> - It allows variety of pace by camera or artiste movement.

Figure 9.2

> **Unusable shots**
> Many shots are immediately eliminated because:
>
> - they are not relevant to the story;
> - they are too short;
> - significant action has begun before recording is stable;
> - camera movement is too slow resulting in the duration of the shot becoming too long for the news item (see the ten-second news module in Section 9.4 above);
> - the speed of the camera movement conflicts with the pace of the story;
> - there is continuity mismatch;
> - there is size mismatch;
> - there are technical imperfections;
> - they are out of focus;
> - they are shaky;
> - they are badly framed;
> - there are conflicts with background;
> - there is difficulty with time code (e.g. edit controller using 'time-of-day' timecode cannot find anticipated code on a rollback for a run-up to an edit – see Section 11.2.10).

Figure 9.3

9.4.2 An appropriate shot

Every shot is recorded for a purpose; that purpose should fit the outline of a possible structure. No shot can exist in isolation. A shot must have a connection with the aim of the item and its surrounding shots. It must be shot with editing in mind. This purpose could be related to the item's brief, script, outline, or decided at the location. It could follow on from an interview comment or reference. It could be shot to help condense time or it could be offered as a 'safety' shot to allow flexibility in cutting the material.

9.4.3 'Invisible' editing

Standard tape editing technique avoids reminding the audience that they are watching an edited version. The politician steps off the plane, followed by a cutaway shot of camera operators, followed by the politician in the airport being interviewed. The news item ostensibly deals with fact, while the technique is derived from film fiction. Screen time and space has been manipulated and the technique employed is invisible to the audience.

9.5 Visual communication and structure

A well composed shot directs the viewer to the principal subject. If the camera operator is unclear what is the main subject in the frame, or even what is the purpose of the shot, then it is highly unlikely that the viewer will receive an undistorted message.

Visual communication (as well as communication with language) is identifying what is to be communicated and finding an appropriate method of transmitting that idea. The camera operator/journalist/editor must find methods of structuring the material and be clear why they are using that particular pattern.

Creating a structure out of the available material will tell a story, present an argument or provide a factual account of an event (or all three). It starts with a series of unconnected shots which are built into small sequences. These are then grouped into a pattern which logically advances the account either to persuade or to provide sufficient information leaving the viewer to draw their own conclusion. Usually the competing points-of view are underlined by the voice-over but a sequence of strong images will make a greater impact than words.

9.5.1 Definition of structure

Structure is arranging the building blocks – the individual unconnected shots – into a stream of small visual messages that combine into a coherent whole. Before a shot is recorded, three basic questions need (approximate) answers:

- What is the proposed running time of the item in the programme?
- When will it be broadcast (i.e. how much time is available for shooting, returning the material to base, and then editing/sound dub)?
- Given this timescale, how many locations can be realistically used?

Most news items will not be scripted. There may be a rough treatment outlined by the presenter or a written brief on what the item should cover, but an interview may open up new aspects of the story. Without pre-planning or a shot list, the shots provided will often revert to tried and trusted formulas. A safe rule-of-thumb is to move from the general to the particular – from wide shot to close-up. A general view (GV) to show relationships and to set the scene and then make the important points with the detail of close-ups. The camera operator has to provide a diversity of material to provide a cutting point.

Lastly, the structure of a television magazine item is often unplanned; but a location shoot for a two-minute item that results in ten twenty-minute cassettes with no thought to its eventual structure other than a misguided belief that it can all be sorted out in editing will usually mean that the time saved on location by not structuring the treatment will be more than quadrupled and lost when the editor attempts to bring order to the chaos he or she is presented with.

9.5.2 Engaging the audience's attention

The strongest way of engaging the audience's attention is to tell them a story. In fact, because film and television images are displayed in a linear way, shot following shot, it is almost impossible for the audience not to construct connections between succeeding images whatever the real or perceived relationship between them. Structuring a report is determining what to tell the audience, and when. Cause and effect or question and answer are convenient ways of holding the viewer's interest over time.

A factual story can be created by building up a series of details rather than broad generalizations. The crucial decision by the journalist and the camera operator is to determine which details are chosen to best illustrate the main theme.

Story structure
A story about the proposed introduction of a minimum wage may start with a brief to provide the following uncut shot order:

Factory
- interview with the owner of a small business that may go bust when the minimum wage is introduced or he may not be able to take on new staff
- reverse noddies of interviewer and establishing shots of interview
- pick-up shots of anything mentioned in the interview
- shots of owner walking through factory and talking to workers
- shots of workers
- shots of factory
- interview with a low-pay employee
- shots of the employee at work
- reporter with factory as background doing a piece to camera for the set-up at the top of the item (may use voice-over only which will be dubbed back at base)

Exterior church location
- interview with church/social services groups that have been studying the effect of a minimum wage on people's lives
- reverse noddies of interviewer and establishing shots of interview
- pick-up shots of anything mentioned in the interview

Job Centre
- shots of Job Centre showing jobs available at current rates

Supermarket
- wives shopping (if time)
- reporter supermarket background – piece to camera for the wind-up

These shots are recorded with a structure that will allow a piece by the journalist to set up the story either as a voice-over or on camera. Followed by the owner interview with enough cutaway shots to allow it to be edited down to run the required time. Then the low-pay worker, the effect of a minimum wage and job prospects, etc. A potential structure has been provided but with enough flexibility for the item to be cut to any rearranged time depending on the quality of the comments and the importance of the story in the context of the final running order.

Figure 9.4

A necessary element to link the selected details is some kind of thread or motif which is easily followed and guides the viewer through the sequence of shots. For example, an item on the widespread colonization of the English countryside by Japanese knotweed could be structured by walking the reporter and 'expert' along the bank of an infested stream. The walk could be shot starting at a point with a clear stretch of stream, then passing a stretch of weed, and then ending on remedial work being done to clear the stream. Each stage of the walk could be accompanied by actuality sound or voice-over dubbed in editing plus the required cut-in to close-ups relating to the interview comments. The walk is the thread that links the item together.

9.5.3 Beginning, middle and end

Although this a fairly straightforward treatment, it does need some thought and preparation by the camera operator when constructing the shots (i.e. shoot with a structure in mind) so that normal continuity editing technique can be applied (see Chapter 11).

This type of structure is similar to the old advice when doing your English essay homework – plan for a beginning, development and a conclusion. To inject interest, and to avoid a predictable pattern to an item, not all structures need to lay the events of a story out in simple chronological order (see Section 11.4.9).

9.6 Shooting for continuity

Any activity must be filmed to provide a sufficient variety of shots that are able to be cut together following standard editing conventions (avoidance of jump cuts, not crossing the line, etc.) and with enough variety of shot to allow some flexibility in editing.

Just as no shot can be considered in isolation (what precedes and what follows always has an effect), every sequence must be considered in context with the overall aims of the production.

9.7 Interviews

The interview is an essential element of news and magazine reporting. It provides for a factual testimony from a participant or witness to an event. Interviews can be shot in a location that reinforces the story and possibly gives more information to the viewer about the speaker (e.g. office, kitchen, garden).

9.7.1 Location interview

Exterior interviews are easier to stage when there is a continuity of lighting conditions such as an overcast day or where there is consistent sunshine. The natural lighting will have to cater for three shots and possibly three camera positions – an MCU of the interviewee, a similar sized shot of the interviewer and some kind of two-shot or 'establishing' shot of them both.

If it is decided to shoot the interview in direct sunlight, then the interview needs to be positioned with the sun lighting both 'upstage' faces (i.e. the camera is looking at the shaded side of the face) using a reflector to bounce light into the unlit side of the face. The position of the participants can be 'cheated' for their individual close shots to allow a good position for modelling of the face by the sun.

Because of the intensity of sunlight, and sometimes because of its inconsistency, it is often preferable to shoot the interview in shade, avoiding backgrounds which are in the full brightness of the sun.

The background is often the main decider of position because of either its relevance to the story or the wish to establish the location. Frequently a position is chosen to avoid a high contrast background (large area of sky in frame) or to avoid wind noise or other background noise.

9.7.2 Staging an interview

An interview is usually shot using a combination of basic shots:

- an MS, MCU or CU of the interviewee;
- a matched shot of the interviewer asking questions or reacting to the answers (usually shot after the interview has ended);
- a 2-shot which establishes location and relationship between the participants or an over-the-shoulder 2-shot looking from interviewer to interviewee.

After the interview has been shot, there is often the need to pick-up shots of points raised in the interview (e.g. references to objects, places or activity). In order for normal 'invisible' editing to be applied, the shots should match in size and lens angle between interviewee and interviewer (see Section 8.4.3) and the camera operator should also bear the following points in mind:

- Agree with the journalist that he or she will start the interview when cued (or take a count of 5) when the camera is up to speed.
- It is useful for editing purposes to precede the interview with details of name and title of the interviewee.
- Remind the reporter and interviewee not to speak over the end of an answer.
- Do not allow interviewee to speak over a question.

- Change shot size of the interviewee during a question from the interviewer.
- Do cutaways immediately after the interview to avoid changes in light level.
- Always provide cutaways to avoid jump cuts when shortening answers.
- Watch that the background to an establishing two-shot is shot from a different angle to any cutaway shot of the subject. For example, a similar wide shot of the ruins of a fire is not used later as the background to an interview about the fire. This causes a continuity 'jump' if they are cut together.
- Think about sound as well as picture – e.g. avoid wind noise, a ticking clock or repetitive mechanical sound in the background.
- Depending on the custom and practice of the commissioning organization that will cut the material, use track 1 for v/o and interview, and use track 2 for effects.
- Indicate audio track arrangements on the cassette and put your name/story title on the tape.

9.7.3 Vox pops

'Vox pops', random street interviews, are shot to reveal the mood and opinions of the public. Alternate the 'cons' people to look in a different frame direction to the 'pros' so that when the shots are intercut they have the feeling of a conversation.

9.7.4 Eyewitness report

Sometimes it is necessary for the camera operator, who may be first on the scene of a civil disaster, to get eyewitness statements if a journalist has yet to arrive and there is the possibility that people may leave the scene of the incident.

People respond and give more information if they are asked an 'open' question. This is usually an invitation to give an account or description of an event or what happened to them. It can be in the form of 'Tell us what happened to you' or 'What did you see?' Some questions such as 'Did you see the crash' can be answered in a single word, 'yes' or 'no'. These are called 'closed' questions. They close down possible responses from the interviewee. Look for questions that will provoke the fullest response from the witness or participant.

9.7.5 Abstract items

Many issues dealt with by factual programmes are often of an abstract nature which at first is thought have

little or no obvious visual equivalent. Images to illustrate such topics as inflation can be difficult to find when searching for visual representations. Often the solution, with the above example, is to fall back on clichéd shots of shoppers and cash tills with a great deal of voice-over narration providing the explanations.

Whatever the nature of a news story there must be an on-screen image, and whatever is chosen, that picture will be invested by the viewer with significance. That significance may not match the main thrust of the item and may lead the viewer away from the topic. For example, a story about rising house prices may feature a couple looking at a house for sale. To the viewer, the couple can easily, inadvertently, become the subject of the story. Consider the relevance of all details in the shot, and have a clear idea of the shape of the item, its structure, and what it is communicating.

9.7.6 Access

One crucial requirement for news coverage is to get to where the story is. This relies on contacts and the determination to get where the action is. Civil emergencies and crisis are the mainstay of hard news. Floods, air/sea rescue, transport crashes, riots, fire and crime are news events that arise at any time and just as quickly die away. They require a rapid response by the camera operator who has to be at the scene and begin recording immediately before events move on. Equipment must be ready for instantaneous use and the camera operator must work swiftly to keep up with a developing story.

In some countries or regions, access may be denied unless you are in possession of a Certified Police Pass, Press Pass and, in the case of some civil disasters, the appropriate safety clothing (see Chapter 3). Inform the police and/or the appropriate authority for any extensive use of a street or public place for location recording. Security clearance is almost always required in order to enter military, naval and other restricted access sites.

9.7.7 Piece to camera

Probably the most frequent location shot in news, magazine and other topical programmes is the journalist/presenter speaking straight to camera. It is usually staged so that the keynote image of the item (Houses of Parliament, White House, etc.) is the background to the shot.

If it is shot during the day, then care must be taken to find a camera position that allows the reporter to speak to camera comfortably whilst allowing an exposure balanced between face and background 'topic'. This can often be achieved with the sun at the three-quarter back position doubling as backlight and 'side kicker' to the face to provide some modelling. A reflector may be needed to lift the unlit side of the face, depending on the intensity of the sun.

At night the exposure balance is between the background floodlit building and the foreground presenter. A battery light needs to be filtered or the camera distance adjusted so that a good overall exposure is achieved between face and building.

The other point to consider is background traffic noise and, in a public place, freedom from the occasional eccentric passer-by who decides to stand in the background and divert attention from the presenter. With most public buildings, there is usually one favoured viewpoint marked out by 'tripod marks' from countless camera crews that have been there before.

9.8 Going live

The ability to broadcast live considerably increases the usefulness of the camera/recorder format. As well as providing recorded news coverage of an event, a single-camera unit with portable links can provide live 'updates' from the location.

As the camera will be non-synchronous with the studio production, its incoming signal will pass through a digital field and frame synchronizer and the reconstituted signal timed to the station's sync pulse generator. One advantage of this digital conversion is that any loss of signal from the location produces a freeze frame from the frame store of the last usable picture rather than picture break-up.

9.8.1 Equipment

Cameras with a dockable VTR can attach a portable transmitter/receiver powered by the camera battery in place of the VTR. The camera output is transmitted 'line of sight' to a base antenna (up to 1000 m) which relays the signal on by land line, RF link or by a satellite uplink.

Other portable 'line of sight' transmitters are designed to be carried by a second operator and are connected to the camera by cable.

When feeding into an OB scanner on site, the camera/recorder operator can receive a return feed of talkback and cue lights, whilst control of its picture can be remoted to the OB control truck to allow vision control matching to other cameras. It can therefore be used as an additional camera to an outside broadcast unit. In this mode of operation it can supply recorded inserts from remote parts of the location prior to transmission. During transmission the camera reverts to being part of a multicamera shoot. Unless there is very rapid and/or continuous repositioning, mount the camera on a tripod.

9.8.2 Communications

Good communications are essential for a single-camera operator feeding a live insert into a programme. Information prior to transmission is required of 'in and out' times, of duration of item and when to cue a front-of-camera presenter. A small battery-driven 'off-air' portable receiver is usually a valuable addition to the standard camera/recorder unit, as is a mobile phone.

A single camera insert can be a very useful programme item in a fast-breaking news story, providing location atmosphere and immediacy; but because it is a single camera any change of view must be achieved 'on shot'. This may involve an uncomfortable mixture of panning and zooming in order to change shot. If the story is strong enough, then absorbing content will mask awkward camera moves. Alternatively, a cut-back to the studio can allow quick reframing at the location.

9.9 Satellite news gathering

Satellite news gathering (SNG) is a camera/recorder feeding into a small portable dish aerial transmitting a signal up to a satellite in geosynchronous orbit which relays the signal back to a base station. This allows live coverage of events from locations inaccessible to normal land line or terrestrial links equipment.

9.9.1 Geosynchronous location

In order that an SNG unit can continuously transmit an unbroken signal without constantly realigning its dish aerial, the satellite must be placed in an orbit stationary above the earth. This is achieved by placing the satellite in an orbit 22 300 miles from the earth where it is held in place by the balance between the opposing forces of the gravity pull of earth and the centrifugal force pulling it out into space. Geosynchronous orbit

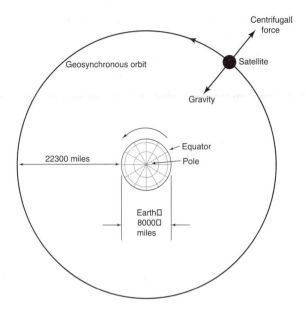

Figure 9.5

(GEO) satellites revolve at the same rotational speed as the earth and appear stationary from the earth's surface. Signals can be transmitted to and from them with highly directional antennas pointed in a fixed direction. It is the satellite's fixed position in relation to earth that has allowed the growth of small, portable dish transmitters.

9.9.2 Orbital arcs

The number and position of the satellites located in this orbital arc 22 300 miles above the earth are regulated by a number of worldwide authorities. The satellites are positioned, after the initial launch, by a gas thruster which ensures they keep their position 2° from adjacent satellites. Frequencies used for communications transmission are grouped into Ku band (10.7–18 GHz) and C band (3.7–4.2 GHz). The Ku band is almost universally used for portable SNG service because the antennas are smaller for a given beam width due to the shorter wavelength, and the freedom from interference to and from microwave systems.

There are problems with transmission paths to satellites positioned close to the horizon and therefore some orbital slots are more favourable than others. A minimum elevation angle of 10–20° for Ku band is required to avoid difficulty in clearing buildings, trees and other terrestrial objects, atmospheric attenuation, and electrical noise generated by heat near the earth's surface.

9.9.3 Frequency sharing

Whilst C-band satellite uplinks and downlinks share frequency bands allocated to common carrier microwave systems, Ku-band satellite systems have exclusive use of their allocated frequency band and therefore are not restricted by sharing considerations. C-band satellites are limited to lower, downlink power levels to avoid interference with terrestrial microwave systems. Ku-band satellites have no such limitation and can operate at higher power within the limitations of the power source of the satellite. This generally permits the use of smaller downlink antennas in the Ku band.

Ku-band signal transmissions are subject to degradation from heavy rainfall, particularly in the tropics where cloudbursts occur frequently; C-band transmissions, however, suffer negligible attenuation when passing through belts of high rainfall.

9.9.4 Elevation angle

The elevation of the path to the satellite above the horizontal (the look angle) is critical to establishing an SNG link. A low elevation angle of the satellite just above the horizon can cause the following problems:

- Difficulty in clearing trees, buildings, pylons and other terrestrial objects results in the attenuation of the signal by absorption or multipath reflection distortion.
- A low elevation path through the atmosphere before it emerges into space is much longer and this increases rain attenuation.
- Electrical noise is generated by heat near the earth's surface, and can be picked up by the side lobes of the receiving antenna.

Careful site selection is therefore important to ensure a clear line-of-sight to the designated satellite. The antenna requires protection against strong winds, which could shift the antenna's precise alignment to the satellite.

9.9.5 SNG set-up

The process involved in establishing an SNG link from location to a base station involves aligning the antenna onto the correct satellite using compass and azimuth bearings and, if available, the transmitted beacon identification. Polarization is checked and the correct vision transmission frequency and communication transmission frequency is selected. The antenna signal radiation can damage electronic equipment (including camera/recorders!) and people, if they are in direct line of sight of the beam. Check for clearance before switching on the high-powered amplifier (HPA) to warm-up and then to stand-by. Contact the satellite operation centre (SOC) to confirm channel and booked time and seek permission to 'come up' for line-up. Permission is given to transmit a clean carrier followed by a gradual increase in transmission power of colour bars and identification. Instant full power can damage the satellite transponder. Finally, check with base station that it is receiving a good strength signal.

10 Video recording formats

10.1 From analogue to digital recording

The mid-1990s saw the introduction of digital recording techniques followed by digital acquisition. There was an expansion in the number of digital recording formats on tape. Each format, such as Digi-Beta, DVCPRO, Digital-S, DVCam and DV, offered different advantages at different prices. The price of equipment became an overriding factor in an industry that was forced to become more competitive chasing fewer viewers scattered across a greater number of channels. This required smaller programme budgets, and cheaper equipment. The manufacturer's battle was to ensure that their format was the one to replace Betacam SP, the dominant acquisition format of the 1980s. However, the existing format competition may be a false battle as all the present competing formats are tape. The eventual winner, to replace the universal Betacam SP, may be a disk camera.

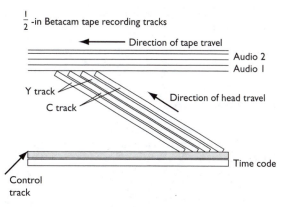

$\frac{1}{2}$ -in Betacam tape recording tracks

Figure 10.1 A control track is recorded onto the video tape at frame frequency as a reference for the speed of replay VTR to position the reading of the video tracks and to drive a tape counter. One of the main purposes of striping tapes before editing (see Chapter 11 on video editing) is to record a control track.

10.2 Analogue Betacam format

The picture is recorded on a ½" Beta tape cassette using two adjacent video heads. The luminance signal (Y) is recorded on one track and on the other track the chroma consists of a compressed time division multiplex of the colour difference signals (Red – Y) and (Blue – Y). Two audio longitudinal tracks are recorded at the top of the tape with longitudinal Control and Time Code tracks at the bottom of the tape. Betacam SP recording on metal particle tape provides two additional audio FM channels recorded with the chrominance signal. They allow improved sound quality but cannot be edited

independently of the video and must be laid-off to be edited.

With the introduction of digital processing and recording of the video and audio signal, additional operational controls were made available. Many of the digital design features were intended to help with faster acquisition and more compatible digital editing although no format was considered ideal for universal programme production. There are two digital versions of the Betacam format. The Betacam SX format is designed to replace the ENG analogue cameras whilst the Digital Betacam format with 2:1 DCT compression and an 85 Mbps video data rate has a higher specification to meet more complex programme-making requirements.

10.3 Digital Betacam

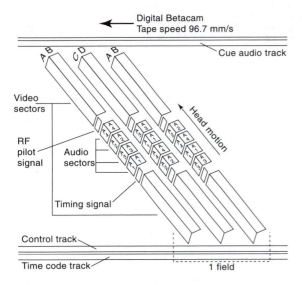

Figure 10.2

10.4 Betacam SX

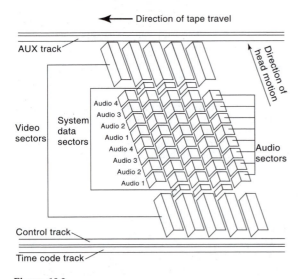

Figure 10.3

10.5 The DV format

In the early 1990s, a consortium of camera manufacturers collaborated on the development of a new, small, digital tape format. The intention was to reach agreement on a single international format. This was achieved with a consumer digital video (DV) format which had a compression standard, a mechanism and

tape format, a chip set and a standard family of cassettes.

Originally intended for the domestic camcorder market, the DV format cameras did not meet the basic ENG requirements of operational features and ruggedness. The picture quality, however, was good enough for broadcasters to use the format in productions that required small, inexpensive lightweight kit that could be operated by journalists.

Broadcast operational weaknesses

There are a number of inherent weaknesses in the format when the cameras are used for standard broadcast production but the cameras are cheap, small and increasingly being used for documentary work.

DV can be edited by transferring straight onto disk for non-linear editing or to analogue or digital Beta for Beta transmission. The initial transfer across to another format adds to the editing time but this is often preferred by picture editors because the DV format records sound on the FM tracks combined with the pictures. There is no longitudinal sound track and therefore editors cannot hear the digital sound as they shuttle through the tape. There is no regen facility on DV and placing a cassette into the camera resets the time code to zero. This could possibly result in several shots on the same tape having the same time code. This can be avoided by either recording 'black and burst' (continuous time code and black tape) on tapes prior to use or, prior to editing, replacing the original time code with a continuous edit code for the edit machine. The DV cameras are designed for occasional domestic use by one careful owner and lack the rugged design necessary for hard ENG usage on location. To overcome some of these production limitations, a 'professional' version of the DV format was developed.

10.6 DVCPRO and DVCAM formats

DVCPRO and DVCAM are upgrades of the DV format primarily designed for news acquisition. The two formats have improved recording specification and a number of broadcast operational facilities not found on consumer DV cameras.

The camera/recorders are smaller, lighter and cheaper; and with less power consumption than previous ENG formats, coupled with smaller cassettes, allow longer recording times. The lightweight cameras allow easier handling in ENG work and have the ability to provide colour playback. With low power consumption, a two-machine editor can

Figure 10.4

	DV	DVCPRO
Video coding	Component Digital	Component Digital
	13.5 MHz, 8 bit	13.5 MHz, 8 bit
Compression	5:1 intraframe	5:1 intraframe
	DCT-based standard	DCT-based standard
Track layout	12 tracks/frame	12 tracks/frame
	10 microns track pitch	18 microns track pitch
Tape speed	18.8 mm/s	33.8 mm/s
Tape	6.35 mm	6.35 mm
	metal evaporated	metal particle
Max recording time	270 minutes	123 minutes
for cassette		
Video data rate	24.948 Mbits/s	24.948 Mbits/s
Audio channels	48 kHz, 16 bits, 2 channel	48 kHz, 16 bits, 2 channel
		1 analogue cue channel
Recorded data rate	41.85 Mbits/s	41.85 Mbits/s
		[also 50 Mbps]

provide rapid, portable editing on location and stories can be put to air more quickly.

Outline specification of DV and DVCPRO is shown in Fig. 10.4.

10.7 DVCPRO format

A major difference between DVCAM and DV is the increase in track pitch from 10 microns to 18 microns which is wider for frame-accurate editing on the 6.35 mm/quarter inch metal particle tape. The first generation of cameras provided for 5:1 DCT compression with 25 Mbps video data rate, 4:1:1 resolution. The maximum tape length allowed 63 minutes of recording on location, increased to 123 minutes on studio machines. DVCPRO cameras can be obtained with ⅓″, ½″ and ⅔″ CCDs and with switchable 4:3/16:9 aspect ratio.

There are two uncompressed audio channels and two longitudinal audio tracks to give audio access when editing as the digital audio is of limited use in shuttle. This linear audio cue channel is also available as a third, lower quality, audio channel.

4:1:1 systems can exhibit errors on chroma edges when applying special effects (e.g. keying, digital effects), or when recording computer-generated graphics, but DVCPRO 50 format camera/recorders have 4:2:2 sampling, 3.3:1 DCT compression, a 50 Mbps video data rate using a larger 123 minute (max.) cassette recording at twice the tape speed of the 4:1:1 cameras, and with interchangeable lenses.

The DV format has auto-tracking mechanisms that eliminate the need for a control track whereas the DVCPRO, with a control track, provides for a faster lock-up and a shorter pre-roll when editing. DVCPRO incorporates both VITC and LTC in the helical scan. This enables the tape size to be kept small and both time codes to be read at any tape speed. The higher DVCPRO specification cameras have 10-bit A/D conversion, 16-bit processing, scene file memory with memory card.

DVCPRO and Betacam cassette sizes are shown in Fig. 10.5.

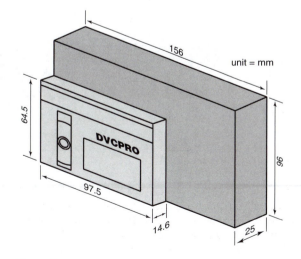

156

unit = mm

64.5

DVCPRO

96

97.5

14.6

25

Figure 10.5

10.8 DVCAM format

DV-based systems use compression in the most cost-effective way to increase tape usage. DVCAM has a 4:1:1 compression, 25 Mbps data rate recorded on metal evaporated tape and 4 channels of uncompressed audio to achieve a 40 minute recording on DVCAM camera mini-cassette or 184 minutes on a standard cassette. A single DV compression system is used throughout the production process. Non-linear editing is facilitated by high speed transfer at 4 times the normal speed to a disk recorder.

10.9 Digital-S (D9 format)

In the transition from analogue to digital acquisition many camera/recorder manufacturers, when introducing new digital formats, have attempted to provide backward compatibility with existing equipment. In many parts of the world, S-VHS has been used not only for ENG purposes but also for a broad range of local broadcasting productions. Digital-S uses the same size half-inch tape and cassette as S-VHS and records on metal particle tape.

Certain Digital-S studio VTRs can replay standard analogue S-VHS tapes allowing continuing access to previous S-VHS tape libraries. Digital-S uses 4:2:2 processing with a video data rate of 50 Mbps per second with a 3.3:1 compression. The half-inch width tape allows 2 linear audio cue-tracks for audio access in edit shuttle and 4 digital audio (16 bit, 48 kHz)

tracks and for 2 lines for uncompressed video for closed captioning. Up to 104 minutes of material can be recorded. (See Fig. 10.6.)

10.10 Disk camera

The Camcutter format records direct to disk in the camera/recorder. This allows certain edit functions to be performed in the camera. Whereas the previous digital formats discussed require downloading from tape to disk, the Camcutter's FieldPak (a disk drive in the camera) can be removed and inserted into the desktop FieldPak adaptor and non-linear edited. Each FieldPak can be re-used many thousands of times. The disk recording unit is available in two configurations: as an add-on to a suitable existing Ikegami camera or as an integrated single-piece camera/recorder unit.

10.11 VT recording areas

The usual function of a VT recording area is:

- to record programmes or programme inserts;
- to replay recorded inserts into a studio/OB production;
- to replay recorded programmes to air;
- to record material transferred from another region or source;

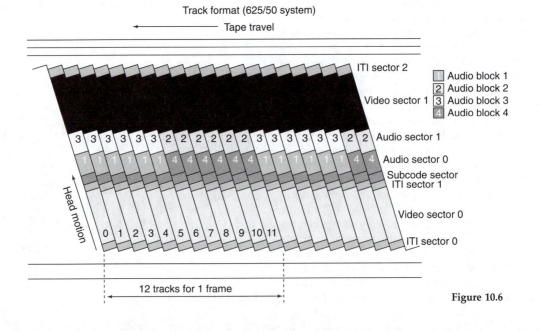

Figure 10.6

- to record off-air material from any transmitted channel (e.g. for news purposes, sports reports);
- to transfer archive material from one format to the current format in use;
- to transfer material to an off-line format (such as VHS) and add a burnt-in time code;
- to transfer from 'sub-broadcast' formats (such as Hi8) to Beta etc.

10.11.1 Programme production

The VT area is an operational area fed with talkback and is part of the programme production chain. As well as feeding material into live and recorded programmes, it frequently services transmission requirements such as programmes, promotions and commercials.

VT machines are allocated for rehearsal and transmission as well as being available for transfers and down-the-line recordings. Each record/playback operational position needs to be equipped for communication with other areas such as the studio control room which has preview monitors displaying the allocated VT machines or a master control or continuity control room.

10.11.2 Transfer facilities

Equipment and facilities may include:

- VT machines that can either record or playback;
- a matrix to provide for a number of sources to be fed to any machine (studio, SNG, outside sources, 'off-air', VHS, Hi8, U-matic for archive purposes, etc.) plus a patch panel for incoming video and audio sources;
- audio sources which can be monitored and levels checked and adjusted if required;
- line-up with bars and tone from the matrix selector;
- provision for off-line editing by transferring from Beta to VHS with burnt-in time code to allow material to be previewed off-line.

11 Video editing

11.1 Introduction to editing

11.1.1 'A good cutter'

There is an old Hollywood saying which claims that 'a good cutter cuts his own throat'. Cutter meaning a film editor. What does this mean?

Well, simply that the skills and craft employed by the film editor to stitch together a sequence of separate shots persuades the audience that they are watching a continuous event. They are unaware of the hundreds of subtle decisions that have been made during the course of the film. The action flows from shot to shot and appears natural and obvious. The editing skills and techniques that have achieved this are rendered invisible to the audience, and therefore the unenlightened may claim, 'But what has the editor done? What is the editor's contribution to the production?'

The editor has become anonymous and apparently his or her skills are redundant. As we have seen, nearly all TV craft skills employ invisible technique. The control and quality of programme sound only becomes apparent to the viewer when a fade-up is missed, when the recorded quality of a location interview is marred by background noise, when a sound balance makes a top-selling group sound like they are performing in the Village Hall.

Exactly like the Hollywood film editor, if the technique is competent and there are no operational mistakes, the viewer is unaware of production skills. Nearly every viewer will become aware of really bad technique in camerawork, sound, lighting, and all the other craft skills even though individually they may be unable to analyse exactly what is wrong.

A technical operator who is required to edit will usually be assigned to news or news feature items. This chapter examines the technique required for this type of programme format. Obviously the craft of editing covers a wide range of genres up to, and

including, the sophisticated creative decisions that are required to cut feature films. However, there is not such a wide gap between different editing techniques as would first appear.

11.1.2 What is editing?

Essentially editing is selecting and coordinating one shot with the next to construct a sequence of shots which form a coherent and logical narrative. There are a number of standard editing conventions and techniques that can be employed to achieve a flow of images that guide the viewer through a visual journey. A programme's aim may be to provide a set of factual arguments that allows the viewer to decide on the competing points of view; it may be a dramatic entertainment utilizing editing technique to prompt the viewer to experience a series of highs and lows on the journey from conflict to resolution; or a news item's intention may be to accurately report an event for the audience's information or curiosity.

The manipulation of video, sound and picture can only be achieved electronically, and an editor who aims to fully exploit the potential of television must master the basic technology of the medium.

To the knowledge of technique and technology must be added the essential requirement of a supply of appropriate video and audio material. As we have seen in Chapter 7, the camera operator, director and journalist need to shoot with editing in mind. Unless the necessary shots are available for the item, an editor cannot cut a cohesive and structured story. A random collection of shots is not a story, and although an editor may be able to salvage a usable item from a series of 'snapshots', essentially editing is exactly like the well known computer equation which states that 'garbage in equals garbage out'.

11.2 The technology of news editing

11.2.1 The recording format

Video and audio can be recorded on a number of media such as tape, optical disk, hard disk or high density memory chips (integrated circuits). Tape has been the preferred method of acquisition because of its storage capacity and cost. An edit suite will be defined by the format of its principal VTR machines, but will often be equipped with other VTR machine formats to allow transfer of acquisition material to the main editing format, or to provide lower quality copies for off-line editing or previewing.

The other defining technology of the edit suite is whether the edited tape has been recorded in analogue or digital format (see Chapter 10), and the format of the finished master tape.

11.2.2 Archive material

When editing news and factual programmes, there is often a requirement to use library material that may have been recorded in an older, and possibly obsolete, video format (e.g. 2″ Quadruplex, U-matic). Most news material before the 1980s was shot on film, and facilities may be required to transfer film or video material to the current editing format when needed.

11.2.3 Video editing

Recorded video material from the camera almost always requires rearrangement and selection before it can be transmitted. Selective copying from this material onto a new recording is the basis of the video editing craft. Selecting the required shots, finding ways to unobtrusively cut them together to make up a coherent, logical, narrative progression takes time. Using a linear editing technique (i.e. tape-to-tape transfer) and repeatedly re-recording the material exposes the signal to possible distortions and generation losses. Some digital VTR formats very much reduce these distortions. An alternative to this system is to store all the recorded shots on disk or integrated circuits to make up an edit list detailing shot order and source origin (cassette number etc.) which can then be used to instruct VTR machines to automatically dub across the required material, or to instruct storage devices to play out shots in the prescribed edit list order.

On tape, an edit is performed by dubbing across the new shot from the originating tape onto the out point of the last shot on the master tape. Simple non-linear disk systems may need to shuffle their recorded data

in order to achieve the required frame-to-frame, whereas there is no re-recording required in random access editing – simply an instruction to read frames in a new order from the storage device.

11.2.4 On-line editing

An edit suite is where the final edit is performed in full programme quality. Each shot transition and audio will be selected and dubbed onto the master tape. The alternative to the high cost of making all edit decisions using broadcast equipment is to log and preview all the material, and choose edit points on lower quality replay/edit facilities. These edit decision lists can then be used to carry out an auto-transfer dub in the on-line edit suite (see Section 11.2.7). Preparation in an off-line suite will help save time and money in the on-line facility.

11.2.5 Linear editing

Cameras recording on tape are recording in a linear manner. When the tape is edited, it has to be spooled backwards and forwards to access the required shot. This is time-consuming with up to 40% of the editing session spent spooling, jogging and previewing edits. Although modern VTRs have a very quick lock-up, usually less than a second, which allows relatively short pre-rolls, normally all edits are previewed. This involves performing everything connected with the edit except allowing the record machine to record. The finished edited master has limited flexibility for later readjustment, and requires a return to an edit session with the originating tapes if a different order of shots is required. Nevertheless, this method of editing video has been in use since the 1950s, and has only been challenged as the standard technique in the late 1980s when technology became available to transfer, store and edit video material in a non-linear way. Tape-to-tape editing then became known as linear editing. There are two types of linear editing:

- **Insert editing** records new video and audio over existing recorded material (often black and colour burst) on a 'striped' tape.
  Striped tape is prepared (often referred to as blacking up a tape) before the editing session by recording a continuous control track and time code along its complete length. This is similar to the need to format a disk before its use in a computer. This pre-recording also ensures that the tape tension is reasonably stable across the length of the tape. During the editing session, only new video and

audio is inserted onto the striped tape, leaving the existing control track and time code already recorded on the tape undisturbed. This minimizes the chance of any discontinuity in the edited result. It ensures that it is possible to come 'out' of an edit cleanly, and return to the recorded material without any visual disturbance. This is the most common method of video tape editing and is the preferred alternative to assemble editing.

- **Assemble editing** is a method of editing onto blank (unstriped) tape in a linear fashion. The control track, time code, video and audio are all recorded simultaneously and joined to the end of the previously recorded material. This can lead to discontinuities in the recorded time code and especially with the control track if the master tape is recorded on more than one VTR.

The **master tape** is the result of the editing session. It can also exist as an edit playout list for shots stored on disk.

11.2.6 Limitation of analogue signal

The analogue signal can suffer degradation during processing through the signal chain, particularly in multigeneration editing where impairment to the signal is cumulative.

This loss of quality over succeeding generations places a limit on the amount of process work that can be achieved in analogue linear editing (e.g. multipass build-ups of special effects). This limitation can be reduced by coding the video signal into a digital form (see Chapter 1).

11.2.7 Off-line editing

Off-line editing allows editing decisions to be made using low-cost equipment to produce an edit decision list (EDL – see below) or a rough cut which can then be conformed or referred to in a high quality on-line suite. A high quality/high cost edit suite is not required for such decision-making, although very few off-line edit facilities allow settings for DVEs, colour correctors or keyers. Low cost off-line editing allows a range of story structure and edit alternatives to be tried out before tying up a high-cost on-line edit suite to produce the final master tape.

11.2.8 The digital signal

Whereas an analogue signal is an unbroken voltage variation, a pulse coded modulated (PCM) digital signal is a series of numbers each representing the analogue signal voltage at a specific moment in time. The number of times the analogue signal is measured is called the sampling rate or sampling frequency. The value of each measured voltage is converted to a whole number by a process called quantizing. These series of whole numbers are recorded or transmitted rather than the waveform itself. The advantage of using whole numbers is that they are not prone to drift, and the original information in whole numbers is better able to resist unwanted change. The method of quantizing to whole numbers will have an effect on the accuracy of the conversion of the analogue signal to digital. Any sampling rate which is high enough could be used for video, but it is common practice to make the sampling rate a whole number of the line rate.

Video editing terms [1]

Burnt-in time code. In order for edit decisions to be made in a limited off-line preview facility, time code is superimposed on each picture of a copy of the original for easy identification of material.

Logging. Making a list of shots of the recorded material speeds up the selection and location (which cassette) of shots. When this is compiled on a computer it can be used as a reference to control which sections of the recorded images are to be digitized.

Edit decision list (EDL). The off-line edit decisions can be recorded on a floppy disk giving the tape source of the shot, its in and out time code or duration. In order to work across a range of equipment there are some widely adopted standards such as CMX, Sony, SMPTE and Avid.

Conform. The set of instructions contained in the EDL can be used to directly control conforming in an on-line edit suite dubbing from source tape to master tape adding any effects or special transitions between shots as required.

Auto assemble. Editing process using an edit controller programmed with the required edit point identified by time code, which automatically runs the source tape back for the requisite run-up time and then runs both source and master VTRs to make a perfect edit transition.

Figure 11.1

11.2.9 Compression

Compression, data reduction or bit-rate reduction, is the technique of filtering out some of the information that is contained in a digital video signal. By eliminating selected data, the signal can be passed through a channel that has a lower bit rate. The ratio between the source and the channel bit rates is called the compression factor. At the receiving end of the channel an expander or decoder will attempt to restore the compressed signal to near its original range of values. A compressor is designed to recognize and pass on the useful part of the input signal known as the entropy. The remaining part of the input signal is called the redundancy. It is redundant because the filtered-out information can be predicted from what has already been received by the decoder. If the decoder cannot reconstruct the withheld data, then the signal is incomplete, and the compression has degraded the original signal. This may or may not be acceptable when viewing the received image.

What is redundant?

Portions of an image may contain elements that are unchanging from frame to frame (e.g. the background set behind a newsreader). Considerable saving in the amount of data transmitted can be achieved if, on a shot change, all of the image is transmitted and then with each successive frame only that which alters from frame to frame is transmitted. The image can then be reconstructed by the decoder by adding the changing elements of the image to the static or unvarying parts of the image. The degree of compression cannot be so severe that information is lost. For example, even if the newsreader background set is static in the frame, a shadow of the newsreader moving on the background must be preserved even if the shadow is undesirable. Compression also allows a greater amount of information to be stored on disk or integrated circuits.

Motion compensation

Passing on only the difference between one picture and the next means that at any instant in time an image can only be reconstructed by reference to a previous 'complete' picture. *Editing such compressed pictures can only occur on a complete frame.* If there is significant movement in the frame there will be very little redundancy, and therefore very little compression possible. To overcome this problem, motion compensation compression attempts to make even movement information 'redundant' by measuring successive areas of pictures which contain movement and producing motion vectors. These are applied to the object and its predicted new position reconstructed. Any errors are eliminated by comparing the reconstructed movement with the actual movement of the original image. The coder sends the motion vectors and the discrepancies along the channel to the decoder which shifts the previous picture by the vectors, and adds the discrepancies to reproduce the

next picture. This allows a saving in the amount of data that needs to be transmitted along a channel even with movement.

Provided the digital signal is uncompressed, there is no limit to how many generations of the original are 're-recorded' as each new digital generation of the original material is a clone rather than a copy. Imperfections introduced in the editing chain are not accentuated. But care must be taken when editing compressed video to make certain that the edit point of an incoming shot is a complete frame, and does not rely (during compression decoding) on information from a preceding frame.

Video editing terms [2]

Uncommitted editing. This technique can only be achieved in a true random access edit suite where the source material has been digitized and stored on high density memory chips (integrated circuits). Hard disk video storage systems require more than one TV interval (1.6 ms or less) to reposition their read/write heads (typically 10 ms) to access any part of the disk so replay is limited to accessing the next track, rather than any track and therefore any picture. Uncommitted editing allows any shot to be played out in any order in real time under the control of the EDL. Because the playout is not re-recorded in a fixed form, it is uncommitted and trimming any cut or recutting the material for a different purpose is relatively simple.

Timebase corrector (TBC). Most VTRs have a TBC to correct the timing inaccuracies of the pictures coming from tape.

Tracking. Tracking is adjusting the video heads of the VTR over the picture information recorded on tape to give the strongest signal. The position of the heads should also be in a constant relationship with the control track.

Pre-roll. The pre-roll is the time needed by a VTR to reach the operating speed to produce a stable picture. With some VTRs this can be as little as a single frame. When two or more transports are running up together, it is highly unlikely that they will all play, lock and colour frame within a few frames as they each chase and jockey to lock up correctly. For this reason, virtually all transport based editing systems provide for an adjustable pre-roll duration. This cues the machine to a pre-defined distance from the required in-point in order that, with a suitable cue, all synchronized devices can reliably lock in time for the required event. VTRs also have to achieve a pre-determined time code off-set to each other – so lengthening the overall lock-up time.

Figure 11.2

11.2.10 Time code and control track

Video editing can only be achieved with precision if there is a method of uniquely identifying each frame. Usually at the point of origination in the camera (see

Chapter 7, a time code number identifying hour, minute, second and frame is recorded on the tape against every frame of video. This number can be used when the material is edited, or a new series of numbers can be generated and added before editing. A common standard is the SMPTE/EBU which is an 80 bit code defined to contain sufficient information for most video editing tasks:

- **Code word.** Every frame contains an 80 bit code word which contains 'time bits' (8 decimal numbers) recording hours, minutes, seconds, frames and other digital synchronizing information. All this is updated every frame but there is room for additional 'user bit' information.
- **User bit.** User bit allows up to 9 numbers and an A to F code to be programmed into the code word which is recorded every frame. Unlike the 'time bits', the user bits remain unchanged until re-programmed. They can be used to identify production, camera operator etc.

There are two types of time code, record run and free run:

- **Record run.** Record run only records a frame identification when the camera is recording. The time code is set to zero at the start of the day's operation, and a continuous record is produced on each tape covering all takes. It is customary practice to record the tape number in place of the hour section on the time code. For example, the first cassette of the day would start 01.00.00.00, and the second cassette would start 02.00.00.00. Record run is the preferred method of recording time code on most productions.
- **Free run.** In free run, the time code is set to the actual time-of-day, and when synchronized is set to run continuously. Whether the camera is recording or not, the internal clock will continue to operate. When the camera is recording, the actual time-of-day will be recorded on each frame. This mode of operation is useful in editing when covering day-long events such as conferences or sport. Any significant action can be logged by time as it occurs and can subsequently be quickly found by reference to the time-of-day code on the recording. In free run (time-of-day) a change in shot will produce a gap in time code proportional to the amount of time that elapsed between actual recordings. These missing time code numbers can cause problems with the edit controller when it rolls back from an intended edit point, and is unable to find the time code number it expects there (i.e. the time code of the frame to cut on, minus the pre-roll time).

There are two types of recorded time code:

- **Vertical interval time code (VITC).** Numbers are time-compressed to fit the duration of one TV line and recorded as a pseudo video signal on one of the unused lines between frames. It is recorded as a variation in signal amplitude once per frame as binary digits; 0 equals black and 1 equals peak white. Most broadcast cameras have the ability to insert VITC twice on two non-consecutive lines. The VITC signal line position is factory-set in the camera, but there may be another choice of line position for VITC insertion independent of the first choice. VITC time code can be read by the video heads from tape at any time pictures are displayed except when spooling.

Video editing terms [3]

Preview. Previewing an edit involves rehearsing the point of a transition between two shots without switching the master VTR to record to check that it is editorially and technically acceptable.

Split edit. An edit where the audio and video tracks are edited at different points.

Digital video effect (DVE). This is the manipulation of a digitized video signal such as squeezing, picture bending, rotations, flipping, etc. These effects can be used as an alternative to a cut or a dissolve transition between two images (see Chapter 8).

Video graphics. Electronically created visual material is usually provided for an editing session from a graphics facility although character generators for simple name-supers are sometimes installed in edit suites.

Frame store. Solid-state storage of individual frames of video. Frames can be grabbed from any video source, filed and later recovered, for production purposes.

Jam/slave time code. Sometimes time code needs to be copied or regenerated on a re-recording. Slave and jam sync generators provide for the replication of time code signals.

Crash record/crash edit. This is the crudest form of editing by simply recording over an existing recording without reference to time code, visual or audio continuity.

Colour framing. It is necessary when editing in composite video to maintain the correct field colour phase sequencing. In PAL, it is possible to edit different shots on every second frame (4 fields) without the relocking being visible. Analogue and digital component formats have no sub-carrier and so the problem does not exist.

Figure 11.3

- **Longitudinal time code (LTC).** This is recorded with a fixed head on a track reserved for time code. It can be read on playback by a static head, decoded at normal playback speed, and at fast forward or rewind, but it cannot be read unless the tape is moving as there is no replayed signal to be decoded. It is recorded once every frame as a series of pulses (binary digits) whose repetition rate changes according to whether it is recording 0s or 1s. LTC complements the VITC time code (which is displayed on a freeze frame or during jogging), ensuring time code can be read at any time.

11.2.11 The importance of audio

Audio plays a crucial part in editing and requires as much attention as video. See Chapter 12.

11.2.12 On line – description of a typical edit suite

The basic facilities found in a news/factual programme edit suite could include:

* 2 video play and 1 record analogue or digital format VTRs;
* transfer machine format availability;
* audio replay machine;
* edit controller and monitor;
* vision mixing and DVE panel;
* audio mixer with the facility of a lip mic for adding v/o;
* time code reader;
* identification clock generator;
* character generator;
* video monitors;
* audio monitors;
* video scope;
* audio metering.

11.2.13 Line-up

A start-of-day check in an edit suite would include:

* switch on all equipment;
* select machine source on edit controller;
* check routing of video and audio;
* line-up video monitors with PLUGE or bars;
* check bars and tone from replay to record machine;
* check playback of video/audio from playback and record machine;
* if available, check the operation of the video and audio mixing panels;
* black-up tape: record on a complete tape a colour TV signal (without picture information) plus sync pulses, colour burst, and black level for use for insert editing.

11.2.14 Preparation for editing

* Check script or brief for tape numbers.
* Select and check tape cassette for correct material.
* If time allows, preview all material with reference to any shot list or running order that has been prepared.
* Check the anticipated running time of the piece.
* Transfer bars and tone and then the ident clock onto the front of the final edit cassette (master tape).

Video editing terms [4]

Match frame (edit) is an invisible join within a shot. This is only possible if there is no movement or difference between the frames – the frames have to match in every particular.
A and B rolls. Two cassettes of original footage either with different source material are used to eliminate constant cassette change (e.g. interviews on one tape A, cutaways on tape B) or the original and a copy of the original to allow dissolves, wipes or DVEs between material originally recorded on the same cassette.
Cutting copy. An edited, low quality version used as a guide and reference in cutting the final, full quality editing master.
Trim (edit). A film editing term for cutting a few frames of an in or out point. It is possible to trim the current edit point in linear editing, but becomes difficult to attempt this on a previous edit. This is not a problem with random access editing.

Figure 11.4

11.2.15 Technical requirements for an edit

* Enter the replay time code in and out points into the edit controller.
* Enter the record tape time code in-point.
* Preview the edit.
* Check sync stability for the pre-roll time when using time-of-day time code.
* Make the edit.
* Check that the edit is technically correct in sound and vision and the edit occurs at the required place.
* When two shots are cut together, check that there is continuity across the cut and the transition (to an innocent eye) is unobtrusive.

11.3 Perennial editing technique

11.3.1 Historical need for editing

Film began with recording images of actuality events such as a train arriving at a station, or workers leaving a factory. These were viewed by the audience as a single shot lasting as long as the amount of film that was wound through the camera. Shots of different 'views' in different locations were later spliced together by the exhibitor. Within a few years, the audiences developed a taste for a story, a continuity element connecting the separate shots, and so narrative film techniques began to be developed. The visual storytelling methods chosen ensured that the audience understood the action. Shooting and editing had to develop ways of presenting the causal, spatial and temporal relationship between shots. This was a completely new craft, and other storytelling disciplines such as theatre or literature were of little help in providing solutions to the basic visual problems faced by these early pioneers.

One typical editing dilemma, for example, was later called the doorway problem. In *The Life of an American Fireman* (1903), two people are seen to exit from inside a burning room through a window. The next shot shows the window from outside with the two people coming through the window, repeating action already seen by the audience in the previous shot. The shot transition is noticeable to a modern audience because of this repeated action. Film-makers soon learnt how to make a cut on action in order to provide a smoother transition between two shots, and invented a number of other continuity editing techniques. The classical grammar of film editing was invented and understood not only by the film-makers, but also by the film audience. It is the basis of most types of programme-making to this day.

11.3.2 Continuity editing

As we have discussed in Chapter 8, continuity editing ensures that:

- shots are structured to allow the audience to understand the space, time and logic of the action;
- each shot follows the line of action to maintain consistent screen direction so that the geography of the action is completely intelligible;
- unobtrusive camera movement and shot change directs the audience to the content of the production rather than the mechanics of production;
- continuity editing creates the illusion that distinct, separate shots (possibly recorded out of sequence and at different times) form part of a continuous event being witnessed by the audience.

11.3.3 The birth of 'invisible technique'

As the early film pioneers discovered, it is not possible, without distracting the audience, to simply cut

one shot to another unless certain basic continuity rules are followed. The aim is to ensure that the spectator understands the story or argument by being shown a variety of shots, without being aware that in fact the shots are changing. Visual storytelling has two objectives – to communicate the required message, and to sustain the interest of the audience. Changing shot would appear to interrupt the viewer's flow of attention, and yet it is an essential part of editing technique in structuring a sequence of shots and controlling the audience's understanding of the intended message.

The technique used to achieve these aims is invisible to the audience. Once the audience becomes aware of shot change, camera movement, etc., or the lack of visual continuity, their attention drifts away from the content of the story and focuses on the methods employed to present the story. Continuity editing virtually dominates programme production and anyone working in television or film-making around the world is expected to be thoroughly familiar with it.

11.3.4 Methods of shot transition

There are a number of ways to make the transition from one shot to the next. See Section 8.3 for a full description.

11.3.5 Perception and shot transition

Film and television screens display a series of single images for a very short period of time. Due to the nature of human perception (persistence of vision), if these images are displayed at an effective rate of 48/50 times a second, flicker is reduced and there is the illusion of continuous motion of any subject that changes position in succeeding frames.

It takes time for a change of shot to be registered, and with large discrepancies between shot transitions, it becomes more apparent to the viewer when the composition of both shots is dissimilar. If the programme-maker aims to make the transition between shots to be as imperceptible as possible in order to avoid visually distracting the viewer, the amount of eye movement between cuts needs to be at a minimum. If the incoming shot is sufficiently similar in design (e.g. matching the principal subject position and size in both shots), the movement of the eye will be minimized and the change of shot will hardly be noticeable. There is, however, a critical point in matching identical shots to achieve an unobtrusive cut (e.g. cutting together the same size shot of the same individual where possibly there is only the smallest difference in the angle of the head), where the jump between almost identical shots becomes noticeable.

Narrative motivation for changing the shot (What happens next? What is this person doing? etc.) will also smooth the transition. A large mismatch between two shots, for example action on the left of frame being cut to when the previous shot has significant action on extreme right of frame, may take the viewer four or five frames to catch up with the change, and trigger a 'What happened then?' response. If a number of these 'jump' cuts (i.e. shot transitions that are noticeable to the audience) are strung together, the viewer becomes very aware of the mechanics of the production process, and the smooth flow of images is disrupted. This 'visual' disruption, of course, may sometimes be a production objective.

11.3.6 Matching visual design between shots

When two shots are cut together, the visual design, that is the composition of each shot, can be matched to achieve smooth continuity. Alternatively, if the production requirement is for the cut to impact on the viewer, the juxtaposition of the two shots can be so arranged as to provide an abrupt contrast in their graphic design.

The cut between two shots can be made invisible if the incoming shot has one or more similar compositional elements as the preceding shot. The relationships between the two shots may relate to similar shape, similar position of dominant subject in the frame, colours, lighting, setting, overall composition, etc. Any similar aspects of visual design that are present in both shots will help the smooth transition from one shot to the next.

With intercut dialogue shots (especially noticeable in widescreen format), often the protagonists are framed in separate shots on either side of the screen to indicate they are spatially linked. The empty space on one side of the frame indicates the presence of the other. On each cut the incoming image fills the space left in the outgoing image.

A popular use of this in news/current affairs programmes is the vox pop sequence where members of the public are asked their opinion on a subject, and their answers intercut with those positive about the subject on one side of the frame, and those negative about the subject being framed in their individual shots on the other side of the frame. Depending on the questions and answers, the cut sequence has the appearance of a dialogue between the participants even though they have never met and conversed amongst themselves.

11.3.7 Matching rhythm relationships between shots

The editor needs to consider two types of rhythm when cutting together shots: the rhythm created by the rate of shot change, and the internal rhythm of the depicted action.

Each shot will have a measurable time on screen. The rate at which shots are cut creates a rhythm which affects the viewer's response to the sequence. For example, in a feature film action sequence, a common way of increasing the excitement and pace of the action is to increase the cutting rate by decreasing the duration of each shot on screen as the action approaches a climax. The rhythms introduced by editing are in addition to the other rhythms created by artiste movement, camera movement and the rhythm of sound. The editor can therefore adjust shot duration and shot rate independently of the need to match continuity of action between shots; this controls an acceleration or deceleration in the pace of the item.

By controlling the editing rhythm, the editor controls the amount of time the viewer has to grasp and understand the selected shots. Many productions exploit this fact in order to create an atmosphere of mystery and confusion by ambiguous framing and rapid cutting which deliberately undermines the viewer's attempt to make sense of the images they are shown.

Another editing consideration is maintaining the rhythm of action carried over into succeeding shots. Most people have a strong sense of rhythm as expressed in walking, marching, dancing, etc. If this rhythm is destroyed, as for example cutting together a number of shots of a marching band so that their step becomes irregular, viewers will sense the discrepancies, and the sequence will appear disjointed and awkward. When cutting from a shot of a person walking, for example, care must be taken that the person's foot hits the ground with the same rhythm as in the preceding shot, and that it is the appropriate foot (e.g. after a left foot comes a right foot). The rhythm of a person's walk may still be detected even if the incoming shot does not include the feet. The beat of the movement must not be disrupted. Sustaining rhythms of action may well override the need for a narrative 'ideal' cut at an earlier or later point.

11.3.8 Matching spatial relationships between shots

Editing creates spatial relationships between subjects which need never exist in reality. A common example is a passenger getting into a train at a station. The following shot shows a train pulling out of the station. The audience infers that the passenger is in the train when they are more probably on an entirely different train or even no train at all. Cause and effect patterns occur continuously in editing. A shot of an apple falling off a tree followed by a shot of Isaac Newton rubbing his head must inevitably lead the viewer to conclude that Newton has been hit by the very same apple. This assumption is a combination of what the viewer knows (an apple apocryphally fell on Newton) and what is shown, and then mentally connecting the two shots in a cause/effect relationship. For example, a reporter in medium close-up nods their interest in what the interviewee is saying. The viewer's assumption is that the reporter at that moment is listening to the interviewee when in fact the 'noddies' were shot some time after the interviewee had left the location.

Any two subjects or events can be linked by a cut if there is an apparent graphic continuity between shots framing them, and if there is an absence of an establishing shot showing their physical relationship. Portions of space can be cut together to create a convincing screen space provided no shot is wide enough to show that the edited relationship is not possible. For example, a shot of a person leaning against a signpost can be cut with a shot of a person sitting on a wall; these shots can be intercut and, to the viewer, hold a believable conversation together provided there is no shot which either reveals that there is no wall by the signpost, or no signpost by the wall.

11.3.9 Matching temporal relationships between shot

The position of a shot in relation to other shots (preceding or following) will control the viewer's understanding of its time relationship to surrounding shots. Usually a factual event is cut in a linear time line unless indicators are built in to signal flashbacks or, very rarely, flash-forwards. The viewer assumes that the order of depicted events is linked to the passing of time.

The duration of an event can be considerably shortened to a fraction of its actual running time by editing if the viewer's concept of time passing is not violated. For example, a politician enters a conference centre (see Fig. 11.5), and delivers a speech to an audience. This whole event, possibly lasting thirty minutes or more, can be reduced to 15 seconds of screen time by cutting between the appropriate shots.

In the first shot (Fig. 11.5(a)), the politician is seen entering the building with a voice-over giving details of the purpose of the visit. A cutaway to an audience shot with a pan to the politician on the platform (Figs 11.5(b), (c)) allows all the intervening time to be collapsed without a jump cut, and also allows the voice-over to paraphrase what the politician is saying. A third, closer, profile shot of the politician (Fig. 11.5(d)), followed by a shot of the listening audience (Fig. 11.5(e)), continues with the voice-over paraphrase, ending with an MCU of the politician (Fig. 11.5(f)), with his actuality sound, delivering the key 'sound bite' sentence of his speech. A combination of voice-over and six shots that can be cut together maintaining continuity of time and place allows a thirty minute event to be delivered in 15/20 seconds.

The standard formula for compressing space and time is to allow the main subject to leave frame, or to provide appropriate cutaways to shorten the actual time taken to complete the activity. While they are out of shot, the viewer will accept that greater distance has been travelled than is realistically possible.

Provided the main subject does not leap in vision from location one immediately to location two, and then to three and four, there will be no jump in continuity between shots. The empty frames and cutaways allow the editing-out of space and time to remain invisible. News editing frequently requires a reduction in screen time of the actual duration of a real event. For example, a ninety-minute football match recording will be edited down to thirty seconds to run as a 'highlights' report in a news bulletin.

Screen time is seldom made greater than the event time, but there are instances, for example, in reconstructions of a crime in a documentary, where time is expanded by editing. This stylistic mannerism is often accompanied by slow-motion sequences.

11.3.10 Matching tone, colour or background

Cutting between shots of speakers with different background tones, colour or texture will sometimes result in an obtrusive cut. A cut between a speaker with a bright background and a speaker with a dark background will result in a 'jump' in the flow of images each time it occurs. Colour temperature matching and background brightness rely on the camera operator making the right exposure and artiste positioning decisions. Particular problems can occur, for example, with the colour of grass which changes its colour between shots. Face tones of a presenter or interviewee need to be consistent across a range of shots when cut together in a sequence. Also, cutting between shots with in-focus and defocused backgrounds to speakers can produce a

(a) Politician enters building – v/o describes the event

(b) Pan from audience . . .

(c) To politician speaking (v/o continues)

(d) Profile shot of politician (v/o continues)

(e) Cutaway to audience

(f) MCU of politician – actuality sound of speech

Figure 11.5

mismatch on a cut. Continuity of colour, tone, texture, skin tones and depth of field will improve the seamless flow of images.

11.3.11 Rearranging time and space

When two shots are cut together, the audience attempts to make a connection between them. Expanding the example given above: a man on a station platform boards a train. A wide shot shows a train pulling out of a station. The audience makes the connection that the man is in the train. A cut to a close shot of the seated man follows, and it is assumed that he is travelling on the train. We see a wide shot of a train crossing the Forth Bridge, and the audience assumes that the man is travelling in Scotland. Adding a few more shots would allow a shot of the man leaving the train at his destination with the audience experiencing no violent discontinuity in the depiction of time or space. And yet a journey that may take two hours is collapsed to thirty seconds of screen time, and a variety of shots of trains and a man at different locations have been strung together in a manner that convinces the audience they have followed the same train and man throughout a journey.

11.3.12 Basic editing principles

This way of arranging shots is fundamental to editing. Space and time are rearranged in the most efficient way to present the information that the viewer requires to follow the argument presented. The transition between shots must not violate the audience's sense of continuity between the actions presented. This can be achieved by:

- **Continuity of action.** Action is carried over from one shot to another without an apparent break in speed or direction of movement. In a medium shot, for example (Fig. 11.6(a)), someone places a book on a table out of shot. A cut to a closer shot of the book (Figure 11.6(b)) shows the book just before it is laid on the table. Provided the book's position relative to the table and the speed of the book's movement in both shots is similar, and there is continuity in the table surface, lighting, hand position, etc., then the cut will not be obtrusive. A close shot that crosses the line (Fig. 11.6(c)) will not cut.
- **Screen direction.** If the book is travelling left to right in the medium shot, the closer shot of the book will need roughly to follow the same direction. A shot of the book moving right to left will

a)

b)
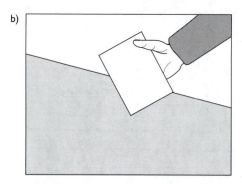

c)
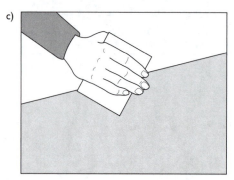

Figure 11.6

produce a visual 'jump' which may be apparent to the viewer.
- **Eyeline match.** The eyeline of someone looking down at the book should be in the direction the audience believes the book to be. If they look out of frame with their eyeline levelled at their own height, the implication is that they are looking at something at that height. Whereas if they were looking down, the assumption would be that they are looking at the book. An interviewer and an interview in separate shots must be eyeline matched in order to cut between them. Their eyeline out of frame must match with the audience's expectation of where the person they are talking to is positioned.

There is a need to cement the spatial relationship between shots. A subject speaking and looking out of the left of frame will be assumed by the viewer to be speaking to someone off camera to the left. A cut to another person looking out of frame to the right will confirm this audience expectation. Eyeline matches are decided by position (see 'Crossing the line', Section 6.20.9), and there is very little that can be done at the editing stage to correct shooting mismatches except flipping the frame to reverse the eyeline – which alters the continuity of the symmetry of the face and other left/right continuity elements in the composition, such as hair partings.

- **Shot size.** Another essential editing factor is the size of shots that form an intercut sequence of faces. A cut from a medium close-up to another medium close-up of another person will be unobtrusive provided the eyeline match is as above. A number of cuts between a long shot of one person and a medium close-up of another will jump and be obtrusive.

11.3.13 Types of edit

There are a number of standard editing techniques that are used across a wide range of programme-making. These include:

- **Intercutting editing** can be applied to locations or people. The technique of intercutting between different actions that are happening simultaneously at different locations was discovered as early as 1906 to inject pace and tension into a story. Intercutting on faces in the same location presents the viewer with changing viewpoints on action and reaction.
- **Analytical editing** breaks a space down into separate framings. The classic sequence begins with a long shot to show relationships and the 'geography' of the setting followed by closer shots to show detail, and to focus on important action.
- **Contiguity editing** follows action through different frames of changing locations. The classic

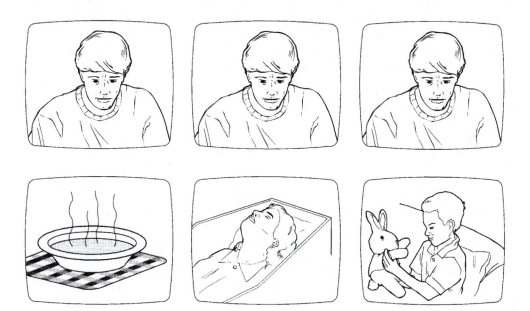

Figure 11.7 Kuleshov and I made an interesting experiment. We took from some film or other several close-ups of the well-known Russian actor Mosjukhin. We chose close-ups which were static and which did not express any feeling at all – quiet close-ups. We joined these close-ups, which were all similar, with other bits of film in three different combinations.

In the first combination the close-up of Mosjukhin was looking at the soup. In the second combination the face of Mosjukhin was joined in shots showing a coffin in which lay a dead woman. In the third the close-up was followed by a shot of a little girl playing with a funny toy bear. When we showed the three combinations to an audience which had not been let into the secret the result was terrific. The public raved about the acting of the artist. They pointed out the heavy pensiveness of his mood over the forgotten soup, were touched and moved by the deep sorrow which looked on the dead woman, and admired the light, happy smile with which he surveyed the girl at play. But we knew that in all three cases the face was exactly the same.

Film Technique and Film Acting
V. I. Pudovkin.

pattern of shots in a western chase sequence is where one group of horsemen ride through the frame past a distinctive tree to be followed later, in the same framing, by the pursuers riding through shot past the same distinctive tree. The tree acts as a 'signpost' for the audience to establish location, and as a marker of the duration of elapsed time between the pursued and the pursuer.

- **Point-of-view shot.** A variant of contiguity editing, which establishes the relationship between different spaces, is the point-of-view shot. Someone on-screen looks out of one side of the frame. The following shot reveals what the person is looking at. This can also be applied to anyone moving and looking out of frame, followed by their moving point-of-view shot.

11.3.14 Summary of perennial technique

These editing techniques form the basics of an invisible craft which has been developed over nearly a hundred years of film and video productions. There are innovation and variation on these basic tenets, but the majority of television programme productions use these standard editing conventions to keep the viewer's attention on the content of the programme rather than its method of production. These standard conventions are a response to the need to provide a variety of ways of presenting visual information coupled with the need for them to be unobtrusive in their transition from shot to shot. Expertly used, they are invisible and yet provide the narrative with pace, excitement and variety.

An alternative editing technique, such as, for example, pop promotions, uses hundreds of cuts, disrupted continuity, ambiguous imagery, etc., to deliberately visually tease the audience, and to avoid clear visual communication. The aim is often to re-create the 'rave' experience of a club or concert. The production intention is to be interpretative rather than informative.

11.4 Telling a story

11.4.1 Fact and fiction

The editing techniques used for cutting fiction and factual material are almost the same. When switching on a television programme mid-way, it is sometimes impossible to assess from the editing alone if the programme is fact or fiction. Documentary makers use storytelling techniques learned by audiences from a lifetime of watching drama. Usually, the indicator of what genre the production falls into is gained from the participants. Even the most realistic acting appears stilted or stylized when placed alongside people talking in their own environment. Another visual convention is to allow 'factual' presenters to address the lens and the viewer directly, whereas actors and the 'public' are usually instructed not to look at camera.

11.4.2 Communication and holding attention

The primary aims of editing are to provide the right structure and selection of shots to communicate to the audience the programme-maker's motives for making the programme, and to hold the audience's attention so that they listen and remain watching.

Communication with the audience

Good editing technique structures the material and identifies the main 'teaching' points the audience should understand. A crucial role of the editor is to be audience 'number one'. The editor will start fresh to the material and he or she must understand the story in order for the audience to understand the story. The editor needs to be objective and bring a dispassionate eye to the material. The director/reporter may have been very close to the story for hours/days/weeks but the audience comes to it new and may not pick up the relevance of the setting or set-up if this is spelt out rapidly in the first opening sentence. It is surprising how often, with professional communicators, that what is obvious to them about the background detail of a story is unknown or its importance unappreciated by their potential audience. Beware of the 'I think that is so obvious we needn't mention it' statement. As an editor, if you do not understand the relevance of the material, say so. You will not be alone.

Holding the audience's attention

The edited package needs to hold the audience's attention by its method of presentation (e.g. method of storytelling – what happens next, camera technique, editing technique, etc.). Pace and brevity (e.g. no redundant footage) are often the key factors in increasing the viewer's involvement in the item. Be aware that visuals can fight voice-over narration. Arresting images capture the attention first. The viewer would probably prefer to 'see it' rather than 'hear it'. A successful visual demonstration is always more convincing than a verbal argument – as every successful salesperson knows.

11.4.3 Selection

Editing, in a literal sense, is the activity of selecting from all the available material and choosing what is relevant. Film and video editing requires the additional consideration that selected shots spliced together must meet the requirements of the standard conventions of continuity editing.

A clear idea of the aims of the piece that is being cut must be understood. Choosing what is relevant is the first set of decisions to be faced. Sometimes this is completely controlled by the shots available.

In the golden age of the Hollywood studio production system, most studios did not allow their directors to supervise the editing. It is said that John Ford circumvented this restriction by simply making one take of each shot whenever possible, and making certain that there was very little overlap of action from shot to shot. This virtually forced the editor to cut the film as planned by the director. Alfred Hitchcock storyboarded each shot and rarely looked through the camera viewfinder. The film was already 'cut' in his head before the shooting started.

Providing the editor with only the bare essential footage may work with film craftsmen of the quality of Ford and Hitchcock, but in the everyday activity of news and feature items it is simply not possible. News by definition is often an unplanned, impromptu shoot with a series of information shots which can only be structured and pulled together in the edit suite. Selecting what is relevant is therefore one of the first priorities when editing.

11.4.4 Previewing

The restraints of cutting a story to a specific running time, and having it ready for a broadcast transmission deadline, are a constant pressure on the television editor. Often there is simply not enough time to preview all the material in 'real' time. Usually material is shuttled though at a fast forward speed, stopping only to check vital interview content. The editor has to develop a visual memory of the content of a shot and its position in the reel. One of the major contributions an editor can make is the ability to remember a shot that solves some particular visual dilemma. If two crucial shots will not cut together because of continuity problems, is there a suitable 'buffer' shot that could be used? The ability to identify and remember the location of a specific shot,

even when spooling and shuttling, is a skill that has to be learnt in order to speed up editing.

Solving continuity problems is one reason why the location production unit needs to provide additional material to help in the edit. It is a developed professional skill to find the happy medium between too much material that cannot be previewed in the editing time available, and too little material that gives the edit no flexibility if structure, running time or story development changes between shooting and editing the material.

11.4.5 Story

As we have discussed in Chapter 9, the strongest way of engaging the audience's attention is to tell them a story. In fact, because film and television images are displayed in a linear way, shot follows shot, it is almost impossible for the audience not to construct connections between succeeding images whatever the real or perceived relationships between them. Image follows image in an endless flow over time and inevitably the viewer will construct a story out of each succeeding piece of information.

The task of the director/journalist and editor is to determine what the audience needs to know, and at what point in the 'story' they are told. This is the structure of the item or feature and usually takes the form of question and answer or cause and effect. Seeking answers to questions posed, for example, 'What are the authorities going to do about traffic jams?' or 'What causes traffic jams?' involves the viewer and draws them into the 'story' that is unfolding. Many items can still be cut following the classical structure of exposition, tension, climax and release.

The storytelling of factual items is probably better served by the presentation of detail rather than broad generalizations. Which details are chosen to explain a topic is crucial both in explanation and engagement. Many issues dealt with by factual programmes are often of an abstract nature which, at first thought, have little or no obvious visual representation. Images to illustrate topics such as inflation can be difficult to find when searching for precise representations of the diminishing value of money. Newsreels of the 1920s showing Berliners pushing prams filled with banknotes going shopping graphically demonstrated inflation, but this was a rare and extreme visual example. The camera must provide an image of something, and whatever it may be, that something will be invested by the viewer with significance. That significance may not match the main thrust of the item and may lead the viewer away from the topic.

Significant detail requires careful observation at location, and a clear idea of the shape of the item when it is being shot. The editor then has to find ways of cutting together a series of shots so the transitions are seamless, and the images logically advance the story. Remember that the viewer will not necessarily have the same impression or meaning from an image that you have invested in it. A shot of a doctor on an emergency call having difficulty in parking, chosen, for example, to illustrate the problems of traffic congestion, may be seen by some viewers as simply an illustration of bad driving.

11.4.6 A linking theme

Because the story is told over time, there is a need for a central motif or thread which is easily followed and guides the viewer through the item. A report, for example, on traffic congestion may have a car driver on a journey through rush-hour traffic. Each point about the causes of traffic congestion can be illustrated and picked up as they occur – such as out-of-town shoppers, the school run, commuters, traffic black spots, road layout. The frustrations of the journey throughout the topic will naturally link the 'teaching' points, and the viewer can easily identify and speculate about the story's outcome.

11.4.7 Time

With the above example, as the story progresses over time, the attitude of the driver will probably change. He or she may display bad-temper, irritation with other road users, etc. There will be a difference over time and without time there is no story. Finding ways of registering change over time is one of the key activities of editing. Choosing shots that register the temperament of the driver by using small observational details (providing the camera operator has shot the detail) reveals the story to the viewer. If the main topic of the item is traffic congestion and its wear and tear on everyday life, it can be effectively revealed by focusing on one drive through a narrated journey rather than generalizations by a presenter standing alongside a traffic queue.

11.4.8 Real time and compressed time

The editor can shape and manipulate time by the editing methods we have discussed, but any action continuously shown within a shot will run its actual time. Apart from slightly speeding up or slowing

down the replay of the image, there is no way to reorganize the actual time of an action shown in full. Slightly adjusting the speed of the replay machine can sometimes allow an over-long action to fit the required time slot, but the time adjusted must be small otherwise the wrong tempo of a shot will become obvious to the viewer. Another method of extending the length of a shot is to freeze the last frame of the shot. This technique again is dependent on shot content.

11.4.9 Structuring a sequence

The chosen structure of a section or sequence will usually have a beginning, a development and a conclusion. Editing patterns and the narrative context do not necessarily lay the events of a story out in simple chronological order. For example, there can be a 'tease' sequence which seeks to engage the audience's attention with a question or a mystery. It may be some time into the material before the solution is revealed and the audience's curiosity is satisfied.

Whatever the shape of the structure, it usually contains one or more of the following methods of sequence construction:

- A **narrative sequence** is a record of an event, such as a child's first day at school, an Olympic athlete training in the early morning. Narrative sequences tell a strong story and are used to engage the audience's interest.
- A **descriptive sequence** simply sets the atmosphere or provides background information. For example, an item featuring the retirement of a watchmaker may have an introductory sequence of shots featuring the watches and clocks in his workshop before the participant is introduced or interviewed. Essentially, a descriptive sequence is a scene setter, an overture to the main point of the story, although sometimes it may be used as an interlude to break up the texture of the story, or act as a transitional visual bridge to a new topic.
- An **explanatory sequence** is, as the name implies, a sequence which explains the context of the story, facts about the participants or event, or an idea. As mentioned before, abstract concepts like inflation, land erosion or a rise in unemployment usually need a verbal explanatory section backed by 'visual wallpaper' – images which are not specific or important in themselves, but are needed to accompany the important narration. Explanatory sequences are likely to lose the viewer's interest, and need to be supported by narrative and

description. Explanatory exposition is often essential when winding-up an item in order to draw conclusions or make explicit the relevance of the events depicted.

11.4.10 The shape of a sequence

The tempo and shape of a sequence, and of a number of sequences that may make up a longer item, will depend on how these methods of structuring are cut and arranged. Whether shooting news or documentaries, the transmitted item will be shaped by the editor to connect a sequence of shots either visually, by voice-over, atmosphere, music, or by a combination of any of them. Essentially the camera operator or director must organize the shooting of separate shots with some structure in mind. Any activity must be filmed to provide a sufficient variety of shots that are able to be cut together following standard editing conventions (i.e. avoidance of jump cuts, not crossing the line, etc.), and there should be enough variety of shot to allow some flexibility in editing. Just as no shot can be considered in isolation (what precedes and what follows always has an effect), every sequence must be considered in context with the overall aims of the production.

The available material that arrives in the edit suite has to be structured to achieve the clearest exposition of the subject. Also, the edited material has to be arranged to find ways of involving the viewer in order to hold their interest and attention. Structure is arranging the building blocks – the individual unconnected shots – into a stream of small visual messages that combine into a coherent whole. For example, a government report on traffic pollution is published which claims that chest ailments have increased and that many work hours are lost though traffic delay, and urges car owners to use their vehicles only for essential journeys.

A possible treatment for this kind of report would be an outline of the main points as a voice-over or text graphic, interviews with health experts and a motorist pressure group spokesperson, a piece to camera by the reporter, and possibly comments from motorists. The camera operator would provide shots of traffic jams, close-ups of car exhausts, pedestrians, interviews, etc. The journalist would decide the order of the material whilst writing his or her voice-over script, whilst the editor would need to cut bridging sequences which could be used on the more 'abstract' statistics (e.g. increase in asthma in children). Essentially these montages help to hold the viewer's attention and provide visual interest on what would otherwise be a dry delivery of facts. A close-up of a baby's face in a pram followed by a cut to a shot of a lorry exhaust belching diesel fumes makes a strong, quick, visual point that requires no additional narrative to explain. The juxtaposition of shots, the context and how the viewer reads the connections is what structures the item, and allows the report to have impact. The production team in the field must provide appropriate material, but the editor can find new relationships and impose an order to fit the running time.

11.4.11 Unscripted shot structure

Most news and magazine items will not be scripted. There may be a rough treatment outlined by the presenter or a written brief on what the item should cover, but an interview may open up new aspects of the story. Without pre-planning or a shot list, the shots provided will often revert to tried and trusted formulas. A safe rule-of-thumb is to move from the general to the particular – from wide shot to close-up. A general view (GV) to show relationships, and to set the scene, and then to make the important points with the detail of close-ups. The camera operator has to provide a diversity of material to provide cutting points. The editor will hope that the camera operator/journalist has provided:

- a substantial change in shot size or camera angle/camera position for shots intended to be intercut;
- a higher proportion of static shots to camera movement. It is difficult to cut between pans and zooms until they steady to a static frame and hold;
- relevant but non-specific shots so that voice-over information (to set the scene or the report) can be dubbed on after the script has been prepared (see Section 9.2.2).

11.4.12 Emphasis, tempo and syntax

Just as a written report of an event will use a structure of sentence, paragraph and chapter, a visual report can structure the elements of the storytelling in a similar way. By adjusting the shot length and fine tuning the rate and rhythm of the cuts, and the juxtaposition of the shots, the editor can create emphasis and significance.

A piece can be cut to relate a number of connected ideas. When the report moves on to a new idea there is often a requirement to indicate visually – 'new topic'. This can be achieved by a very visible cut – a mismatch perhaps, or an abrupt change of sound

Figure 11.8

(a)

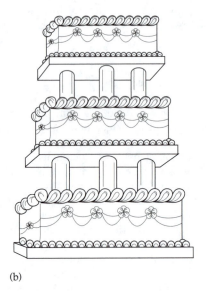

(b)

level or content (e.g. quiet interior followed by a cut to a parade marching band) – to call attention to a transitional moment.

Attention can also be captured by a very strong graphic match usually in a dissolve, where the outgoing shot, for example the strong shape of the architecture of a church (Fig. 11.8(a)) which has substantial columns converging up to towers, is mixed to a shot of a similar shaped wedding cake (Fig. 11.8(b)), matched in the same frame position and lens angle. The audience registers the visual connection because the connection has been overstated. The visual design match is so strong it becomes visible, and signals a change of time, place or a new scene or topic.

11.4.13 Teasing the audience

A linear, logical progression of the story is not the only way to hold the viewer's attention. Often, a puzzle is set up or a question is posed to draw the audience into the story. Like a mystery novel, clues are given before the dénouement at the end. This is obviously a fairly lightweight treatment and would be inappropriate in many hard-news stories.

Be sparing with editing structures that visually tease the audience with sequences that are ambiguous and mystifying. The technique of withholding the connection between succeeding shots, until the link shot is shown, risks losing the audience's attention and interest. Too complicated a clue to a crossword puzzle may alienate the solver's interest. However, a

montage that puzzles the viewer may also engage their interest

The viewer will always believe that the programme-maker has some reason for putting a shot on the screen – unless a production continually misleads them.

11.4.14 Sort it out in the edit

Lastly, as we have already stressed, a location shoot for a two-minute item that results in ten twenty-minute cassettes, with no thought to its eventual structure other than a misguided belief that it can all be sorted out in editing, can end in a long and inefficient trawl through inappropriate material. Transcribing the random letters produced by a monkey and a keyboard into meaningful words, then sentences, then an article is probably easier. TV production requires planning, thought and structure from shooting right through to the master tape.

11.5 Sound and picture

The importance of audio may be overlooked in acquisition but any shortcomings will become increasingly obvious in editing. In nearly every type of production, sound and picture interweave and are mutually dependent. It is vital that the range of audio recorded (apart from being technically perfect) matches the visual coverage in providing the editor with flexibility and creative choice.

Audio in editing and post-production is covered in Chapter 12.

11.6 News and factual editing

11.6.1 News editing requirements

Hard news is by its nature seldom, if ever, pre-scripted, and therefore material is recorded without a written plan. The editor, sometimes with a journalist, needs to shape and structure the raw material supplied as a sequence of unconnected shots.

It is essential for the news unit to shoot with editing in mind. A series of shots have to be meaningfully edited together and this relies on the camera operator anticipating edit points. As we have emphasized before, nothing is more time-consuming than an attempt to edit a pile of cassettes of ill-considered footage into some intelligent and intelligible form. To avoid this, the editor requires from the camera operator maximum flexibility with the material supplied, and the nucleus of a structure.

News reportage attempts to emphasize fact rather than opinion, but journalistic values cannot escape subjective judgements. What is newsworthy? What are news values? These questions are answered and shaped by the prevailing custom and practices of broadcasting organizations. Magazine items can use fact, feeling, atmosphere, argument, opinion, dramatic reconstruction and subjective impressions. These editing techniques differ very little from feature film storytelling. For a more detailed account of objective and subjective reporting, see Section 11.9.

11.6.2 News – condensing time

A news bulletin will have a number of news items which are arranged in importance from the top story down through the running order to less important stories. This running order, compiled by the news editor, will usually allow more time to the main stories, and therefore the editor and journalist will often face the task of cutting an item to a predetermined time to fit the news agenda.

There are a number of ways of chopping time out of an item. If a voice-over script has been prepared to the running time allocated, the editor can use this as a 'clock' to time the insertion of various images throughout the piece. The task then is to slim down the selection from the available material to a few essential images that will tell the story. It is a news camera operator's complaint that when the editor is

(a)

Master shot showing bridge and damaged bus

(b)

Close-up of damage

(c)

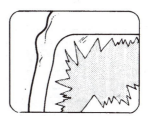

Close-up of damage

(d)

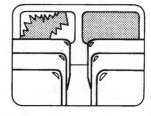

Wide shot interior top deck
Hold for 10 seconds
Zoom into front seats of bus...

(e)

...hold for 5 seconds

Figure 11.9 'Bus Hits Bridge' news story, unedited footage[1].

(a) Under bridge looking at front of bus

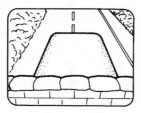

(b) From top of bridge looking down on to bus

(c) From top of bridge looking along rail track

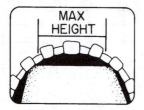

(d) Close up of 'height of bridge' sign

(e) Close up of cracks in bridge brickwork

Figure 11.10 'Bus Hits Bridge' news story, unedited footage[2].

up against a transmission deadline, he or she will only quickly preview the first part of any cassette, often missing the better shots towards the end of the tape. If there is time, try to spin through and review all the material. The camera operator can help the editor, wherever possible, by putting interviews on one tape and cutaways and supporting material on another cassette. This allows the editor to quickly find material without shuttling backwards and forwards on the same tape.

Reducing time on screen can be achieved by the standard methods of cutting away from a shot of an activity after it has been established, and then returning to the shot of an event to see its completion. In the example already illustrated, a politician's speech which may have taken twenty minutes to deliver can be reduced to ten seconds by a voice-over paraphrasing the main points under a shot of the politician speaking, and then, after a cutaway to the appreciative audience, cutting back to hear the politician deliver the short essential 'sound bite' that sums up the policy being advocated.

11.6.3 News – brevity and significance

The pressure of cutting an item down to a short duration will impose its own discipline of selecting only what is significant and the shots that best sum up the essence of the story. The viewer will require longer on-screen time to assimilate the information in a long shot than the detail in a close shot. Moving shots require more perceptual effort to understand than static shots. The skill in news cutting can be summed up as:

- Each shot must serve a purpose in telling the story.
- Use more detail than geography shots or scene setting.
- Use more close, static shots than ones with camera movement.
- Use short pans (no more than two seconds long) to inject pace into a story.
- Use a structure containing pace, shot variety, and dynamic relevant images.

11.7 What the editor requires from the camera operator

11.7.1 An appropriate shot

Every shot should be recorded for a purpose. That purpose is at its weakest if it simply seemed a good idea at the time to the camera operator or director to record a shot 'just in case' without considering its potential context. No shot can exist in isolation. A shot must have a connection with the aim of the item and its surrounding shots. It must be shot with editing in mind. This purpose could be related to the item's brief, script, outline, or decided at the location. It could follow on from an interview comment or reference. It could be shot to help condense time or it could be offered as a 'safety' shot to allow flexibility in cutting the material (see also Section 9.4).

'Bus Hits Bridge' news story, unedited footage[3]

(a) Interview with eyewitness

(b) Piece to camera by reporter with bus/ bridge in background

'Bus Hits Bridge' news story after editing

Vision	Sound
WS of bus stuck under bridge (Fig. 11.10(a))	V/O reporter describing circumstances
CU damage (Fig. 11.9(b)) CU damage (Fig. 11.9(c)) CU sign – 'Max height' (Fig. 11.10(d)) WS of bus (Fig. 11.9(a))	
MCU eyewitness (bus background) (Fig. 11.11(a))	Eyewitness description
WS interior of bus (Fig. 11.9(d)) CU interior of bus (Fig. 11.9(e)) Front of bus (Fig. 11.10(a)) MCU eyewitness (Fig. 11.11(a)) From top of bridge looking down on bus (Fig. 11.10(b))	
Rail track on bridge (Fig. 11.10(c)) WS of bus under bridge (Fig. 11.10(a))	V/O reporter
Reporter to camera, bridge and bus background (Fig. 11.11(b))	Reporter

Figure 11.11

11.7.2 Cutting a simple news item

- The journalist previews the material (if there is time).
- Decide whether the item will be cut to picture or audio.
- **Cutting to audio**
  The journalist writes the script identifying where interviews and essential visuals will occur.
  The journalist records the voice-over (v/o) in the dub studio or, if time is short or the dub studio is in use, records off a lip mic in the edit suite.
  The VT editor then lays down as much audio as is available – v/o, interviews, etc. – and then cuts pictures to the sound.
  Atmos or music may be added after this cut.
- **Cutting to picture**
  Load the correct cassette and jog and shuttle to find the start of the first shot.

11.7.3 Interviews

The interview is an essential element of news and magazine reporting. It provides for a factual testimony from an active participant similar to a witness's court statement; that is, direct evidence of their own understanding, not rumour or hearsay. They can speak about what they feel, what they think, what they know, from their own experience. An interviewee can introduce into the report opinion, beliefs and emotion – as opposed to the reporter who traditionally sticks to the facts. An interviewee therefore brings colour and emotion into an objective assessment of an event and captures the audience's attention. A first-hand account by people involved in an incident provides facts in themselves. It is often spontaneous and vivid in its description and delivery. Because of the nature of some personal testament, its emotional impact can overwhelm other factual comments. The structure of such an item needs careful consideration to avoid distortion when using interviews that contain strong emotional appeals if these are balanced against more low-key reasoned argument.

'Vox pops', random street interviews, is another method of providing the mood and opinions of the public. Its weakness is that to some extent the participants are self-selecting, and the method favours only those willing to talk to a reporter and a camera on a street corner. These people's opinions may be eccentric and not an accurate representation of the majority view.

11.7.4 Cutting an interview

A standard interview convention is to establish who the interviewee is by superimposing their name and possibly some other identification (farmer, market street trader, etc.) in text across an MCU of them. The interview is often cut using a combination of basic shots such as:

- an MS, MCU or CU of the interviewee;
- a matched shot of the interviewer asking questions or reacting to the answers (usually shot after the interview has ended);
- a two-shot which establishes location and relationship between the participants or an over-the-shoulder two-shot looking from interviewer to interviewee;
- staging the interviewee so that their background is relevant to their comments.

The interview can follow straightforward intercutting between question and answer of the participants; but more usually, after a few words from the interviewee establishing their presence, a series of cutaways are used to illustrate the points the interviewees are making. A basic interview technique requires the appropriate basic shots:

- matched shots in size and lens angle (see Chapter 7);
- over-the-shoulder (o/s) shots;
- intercutting on question and answer;
- cutaways to referred items in the interview;
- 'noddies' and reaction shots (reaction shots should be reactions – that is, a response to the main subject);
- cutaways to avoid jump cuts when shortening answers.

11.7.5 How long should a shot be held?

The simple answer to this question is as long as the viewer needs to extract the required information, or until the action depicted requires a wider or closer framing to satisfy the viewer's curiosity or a different shot (e.g. someone exiting the frame) to follow the action. The on-screen length is also dependent on many more subtle considerations than the specific content of the shot.

As discussed above, the rhythm of the editing produced by rate of shot change, and the shaping of the rate of shot change to produce an appropriate shape to a sequence, will have a bearing on how long a shot is held on screen. Rhythm relies on variation of shot length, but should not be arbitrarily imposed simply to add interest. As always with editing, there is a balance to be struck between clear communication and the need to hold the viewer's interest with

visual variety. The aim is to clarify and emphasize the topic, and not confuse the viewer with shots that are snatched off the screen before they are visually understood.

The critical factor controlling on-screen duration is often the shot size. A long shot may have a great deal more information than a close shot. Also, a long shot is often used to introduce a new location or to set the 'geography' of the action. These features will be new to the audience, and therefore they will take longer to understand and absorb the information. Shifting visual information produced by moving shots will also need longer screen time.

A closer shot will usually yield its content fairly quickly, particularly if the content has been seen before (e.g. a well known 'screen' face). There are other psychological aspects of perception which also have a bearing on how quickly an audience can recognize images which are flashed on to a screen. These factors are exploited in those commercials which have a very high cutting rate, but are not part of standard news/magazine editing technique.

Although news/magazine editing is always paring an item down to essential shots, due consideration should always be given to the subject of the item. For example, a news item about the funeral of a victim of a civil disaster or crime has to have pauses and 'quiet' on-screen time to reflect the feelings and emotion of the event. Just as there is a need to have changes of pace and rhythm in editing a piece to give a particular overall shape, so a news bulletin or magazine running order will have an overall requirement for changes of tempo between hard and soft items to provide balance and variety.

11.7.6 Time is of the essence

As we have mentioned, the editor is often (and always when cutting news) under pressure to cut an item to a prescribed running time and to meet a transmission deadline. Resist any panic around you and work in an orderly, logical way. Develop a structure to your working methods so that errors and oversights are guarded against.

11.8 Cutting points

11.8.1 Cutting on movement

A change of shot requires a measurable time for the audience to adjust to the incoming shot. If the shot is part of a series of shots showing an event or action, the viewer will be able to follow the flow of action across the cut if the editor has selected an appropriate point to cut on movement. This will move the viewer into the next part of the action without them consciously realizing a cut has occurred. An edit point in the middle of an action disguises the edit point.

Cutting on movement is the bedrock of editing. It is the preferred option in cutting, compared with most other editing methods, provided the sequence has been shot to include action edit points. When breaking down a sequence of shots depicting a continuous action there are usually five questions faced by the editor:

- What is visually interesting?
- What part of a shot is necessary to advance the 'story' of the topic?
- How long can the sequence last?
- Has the activity been adequately covered on camera?
- Is there a sufficient variety of shots to serve the above requirements?

For example, a story to be edited concerns the difficulties disabled people have with normal everyday domestic appliances. A sequence where the subject of the report was making a cup of tea was shot to illustrate these problems (see Fig. 11.12). The intention was for the reporter, on a voice-over commentary, to identify each hazard.

The editor has a guide to the length of the sequence, which equals the running time of the relevant voice-over. Next he has a guide to what is significant – what will advance the story. The voice-over may mention, for example, difficulties in turning on a tap, pouring boiling water into a tea pot, pouring out the tea, opening a milk carton. The vital factor, of course, is whether shots covering these activities have been provided by the location crew, and, crucially, whether they can be cut together.

With this kind of sequence, the editor needs to be economic with the use of screen time, using only so much of a specific action (e.g. turning on a tap) to provide the viewer with the necessary visual information whilst advancing the point of the 'story'. The total running time of the recorded event has to be pared down by selecting only essential parts of necessary shots to fit the voice-over. Cutting on movement, such as hands coming in and out of frame, will allow the whole activity to be collapsed into half-a-dozen close shots, wasting no screen time on irrelevant action (for example, searching the kitchen for the tea pot). Cutting on action such as movement in the frame will provide the motivation for the cuts and allow compression of the activity without the viewer being aware that the event has been considerably speeded up.

11.8.2 Cutting on exits and entrances

One of the basic tenets of perennial editing technique is that each shot follows the line of action to maintain consistent screen direction so that the geography of the action is completely intelligible. A sequence of shots following someone walking down a street can be cut so that they enter and leave frame in suitable changing size of shot, or different camera angle, following their walk from one frame into the next frame, always moving across the frame in the same direction until an appropriate shot shows the audience that they have changed direction (e.g. walked around a corner and into a new street). For the novice editor, the problem is to decide at what point in each shot they should make the cut to the next shot.

Cutting on exits and entrances into a frame is a standard way of reducing the amount of screen time taken to traverse distance. The usual convention is to make the cut when the subject has nearly left the frame. It is natural for the viewer, if the subject is disappearing out of the side of the frame, to wish to be shown where they are going. If the cut comes after they have left the frame then the viewer is left with an empty frame and either their interest switches to whatever is left in the frame or they feel frustrated because the subject of their interest has gone. Conversely, the incoming frame can have the subject just appearing, but the match on action has to be good otherwise there will be an obtrusive jump in their walking cadence or some other posture mismatch.

Allowing the subject to clear the frame in the outgoing shot and not be present in the incoming shot is usually the lazy way of avoiding continuity mismatches. An empty frame at the end of a shot is already 'stale' to the viewer. If it is necessary, because there is no possibility in the shots provided of matching up the action across the cut, try to use the empty frame of the incoming shot (which is new to the viewer) before the action begins to avoid continuity problems. This convention can be applied to any movement across a cut. In general, choose an empty frame on an incoming shot rather than the outgoing shot unless there is the need for a 'visual' full stop to end a sequence. Ending on an empty frame is usually followed by a fade-down or mix across to the new scene.

(a)

Crossing the line

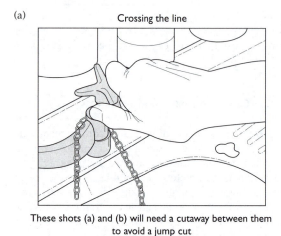

(b)

Making a cup of tea

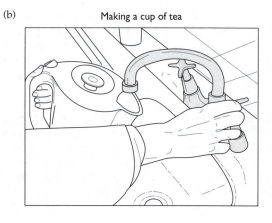

These shots (a) and (b) will need a cutaway between them
to avoid a jump cut

(c)

Staging action

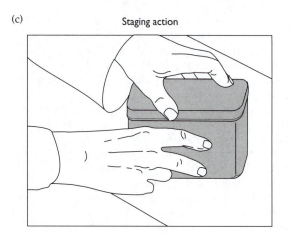

(d)

Making a cup of tea

Action can be staged to avoid continuous cutting. The shot demonstrating the difficulty of opening the tea caddy (c) can be developed to demonstrate the difficulty of picking up the tea bag (d) and left to form a continuous shot unless there is a need to condense time.

(e)

Check continuity

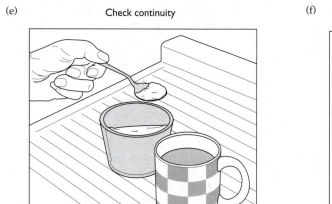

(f)

Watch for continuity mismatch. There is milk in the mug in Figure 11.12(e) (figure demonstrates difficulty in handling a teaspoon) which may be picked up if the shot showing the problems opening a milk container (Figure 11.12(f)) follows.

Figure 11.12

11.8.3 Cutting on sound

In Martin Scorsese's *Raging Bull* (1980), there is a cut from a shot of Robert de Niro closing a fridge door to a shot of him sitting down on a sofa (Fig. 11.13(a), (b)). There is no continuity match between the two shots although it forms part of continuous action. If the cut had not come on the loud clunk of the fridge door closing, the cut would have produced a visual 'jump'. The cut on the loud sound of the fridge door acted like a magician's misdirection when they distract their audience by waving their left hand in the air while the right hand is producing a rabbit from their sleeve. A loud sound can act as a similar distraction and allow an acceptable cut between two shots that are not continuity matched. The sound used to disguise the cut is usually part of the action and not an unseen background event.

Cutting to sound is an extremely effective method of creating a seamless flow of images that moves the viewer though the storyline. The most obvious use of sound is in an interview where shots are cut to dialogue following a question and answer pattern. A more subtle use in matching sound to visual is, for example, on a voice-over narration where the shots to illustrate the content of a report are cut on the ending of a sentence or a paragraph. A similar integration of vision and sound is employed in editing music. Cutting to the beat of accompanying music allows rhythm and fluency to a string of images that may in themselves have no continuity connections. The strong rhythm of the music sweeps across the cuts and integrates the visual sequence. When shooting a musical group the camera operator can help the editor by providing, first, a continuous shot of the musical item and then additional shots of the musicians (possibly playing another, similar tempo number), which avoids seeing synchronized hand or arm movement. These can be used to break up the long take, and add variety and pace to the cut item. The same requirement is needed in dance coverage.

Another technique often used in news reports is to match a voice-over narration comment with an equivalent visual metaphor. For example, the voice-over text may be something like, 'The Prime Minister will try to close the door on more leaks from the Cabinet.' If it is provided, the editor will insert a shot of the door of 10 Downing Street being firmly closed at the point of the voice-over narration's mention of 'close the door'. Actuality sound and speech can weave in and out of the visuals and combine to form an evocative and atmospheric impression on the viewer.

What must be avoided, if possible, is the prosaic 'slide show' and commentary repetition, where words simply explain what can be clearly seen on the screen, and follow in a regular series of shot–comment–shot–comment. A feel for the creative possibilities of sound is one of the strongest skills an editor can develop. For example, the sound of an incoming shot can precede the visual cut and give a forward lift and momentum to the storytelling. Look for ways of using music and actuality sound to create 'space' around the visuals.

11.8.4 The montage

Montage is a sequence of brief shots created to compress action and often to indicate a change of time or location. It is a visual convention that people have learnt to understand from films where, for example, images of calendars or falling leaves are used to indicate the passing of time. Although the format has fallen out of favour because it became an overworked and clichéd technique, it can still be reinvigorated if the right choice of images and subject is chosen. Usually music is used to bridge the shots which may be continuity matched

(a)

Cutting on sound

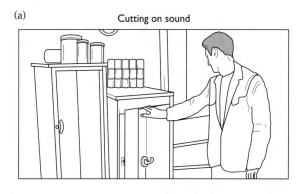

(b)

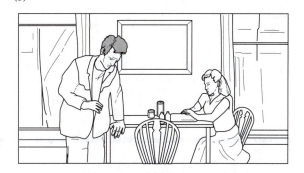

Figure 11.13 The cut from the shot of the closing of the fridge door (a) to the shot of sitting down in a two shot (b) would be a jump cut if the loud noise of the fridge door closing did not distract from the cut.

(a)

(b)

(c)

(d)

but tightly compressed in action to succinctly make the required point in a very short time.

11.8.5 Cutaway and cut-in

A cutaway literally means a cut away from the main subject or topic either as a reaction to the event (e.g. cutting to a listener reacting to what a speaker is saying) or to support the point being made (e.g. a speaker discussing slum property is cutaway from to see the type of building they are talking about).

A cut-in usually means going tighter on an aspect of the main subject. For example, an antiques expert talking in mid-shot about the manufacturer's mark on a piece of pottery she is holding would require a cut-in close shot of the pottery for the item to make sense to the viewer.

11.8.6 Stings and bridges

Sometimes there is a requirement for a visual and sound bridge between two distinct sequences that nevertheless need to be connected. For example, a round-up of all sporting activity that has taken place over a weekend may have several different sports activities that are to be shown together in one package. Between each separate sporting activity, a bridging graphic or visual with a sound 'sting' (a short self-contained piece of music lasting no more than five seconds) will be spliced in. The bridging visual can be repeated on each change of report, and can be, for example, the tumbling last frame of the end of one activity introducing the next activity or possibly a customized digital video effect.

11.8.7 Clichéd visual metaphor

Just as there are stale and worn-out verbal metaphors, so there are visual clichés that have been over-used.

Figure 11.14 Montage: Six scenes of a marriage (32 shots) (*Citizen Kane*, 1940) over time starting with 'honeymoon bliss' ending with indifference. Screen running time 2 minutes 5 seconds. Each scene after the first track-in is linked with a whip pan (Figure 11.14(f)).

a) Track into a close 2 shot – staged to provide a small amount of space between them indicating the intimacy of the relationship.
b) Kane in first scene. Each scene is an intercut between wife and Kane. Note the barrier of flowers (Figure 11.14(c)) absent in the first 'marriage bliss' MCU.
c) The hostilities begin in scene 3.
d)

(e)

(f)

(g)

(h)

These include weak attempts at copying mainstream feature film genres and techniques such as humour, suspense or shock effects. Attempt visual connections that are original and fresh. Rethink first, obvious thoughts, and attempt to find fresh visual or audio relationships. Avoid using superimposed text to describe what is visually plainly obvious (e.g. a shot of a village signpost identifying the location has the village name supered over the signpost).

11.9 Documentary

11.9.1 News and documentary

Like news, documentary often attempts to capture spontaneous action, and present a slice of life avoiding influencing the subject material with the presence of the camera. But there is also the investigative form of documentary – an exposé of social ills.

Whereas news is generally topical information of the day, shot on the day, to be transmitted on that day, documentary themes and issues are shot over a period of time. The documentary format is often used to take a more considered look at social concerns that may have occurred in the form of a quick, specific event in a news bulletin. For example, a news report on a drug's trial could be expanded into a documentary on the influence of drugs on young people. A news item may have a duration of less than thirty seconds while a documentary programme often exceeds 30 minutes. All these factors have a bearing on the editing techniques that are used on the different genres.

News attempts to emphasize fact rather than opinion, but journalistic values cannot escape subjective judgements. Documentary can use fact, feeling and atmosphere, argument, opinion, dramatic reconstruction and subjective impressions which can be very similar to standard feature film storytelling. Should the documentary-maker present the facts and let the audience make up their own minds, or should the way the evidence is presented in a documentary reach an arguable conclusion? Objectivity is often a key issue in factual programmes, but is treated in a

Figure 11.14 *continued*
e) The whip pan is always from left to right as if from Kane to wife ending on wife.
f) In this scene (scene 6) there is no dialogue from wife behind newspaper.
g) Matching MS of Kane with newspaper also silent.
h) Track from MS Kane (Figure 11.14(g)) ending on wide shot, couple separated by the large space of the length of the table without any communication.

different way to news reportage. The way the material is cut touches on all these concerns.

11.9.2 What is documentary?

Like a fiction film, documentary is another form of representation of reality which is structured and presents a point of view which is neither 'innocent' or neutral. A popular viewer's conception of documentary is that it is a recording of 'actuality' – raw footage of real events as they happen, real people as they speak, real life as it occurs, spontaneous and unmediated; this is rarely the case.

Similarly to feature films, documentaries present a visual description or story using a variety of standard techniques such as the invisible authority of the voice-over, archival footage, interviews, facts or commentary 'truths', and often staged action of the participants. Interview is the mainstay of many television documentaries using 'off-screen' questions often edited out, scenes shot on the fly, compilation footage glued together by commentary, music, and a structure that attempts to set the subject in a social context. There is a claim that this standard 'factual' documentary style with its authoritative voice-over etc. is misleading; that this 'sober' style is as much a fabrication as the obvious 'feature' film style; that, in effect, style does not guarantee truth.

A shot is a record of an event. How much the production team have influenced that event will vary. In what context the shot is presented will add another layer of choice or subjectivity to the production. In effect, as we discussed above, to structure a series of shots is to decide how the story is to be told, how the evidence is to be presented to the viewer. When preparing a documentary, among the initial questions is, 'What scenes should be recorded?' Even with the 'direct' style of documentary-making, where a small production unit arrives at a venue and records whatever is happening there, the material has to be edited. At some stage in the production process, decisions of what is relevant to the topic are made even if these subjective preferences are made with the sole intention of making the material coherent and understandable. Any editing shape that is put to the material will influence the audience in its understanding of the programme. Either in an obvious way or in a disguised way, most documentaries end up by saying to their audience – look at the evidence in this way. It is almost impossible for any visual product not to reflect the decision-making processes of its maker. Even the image from a security camera is the product of the decisions on its chosen position and lens angle needed to cover a particular view. It has

been said that making a documentary is a powerful way of confronting ourselves with our own, often unexamined, attitudes and prejudices.

11.9.3 Is objectivity required?

Even if a record of an aspect of reality cannot be prepared without being filtered through the presuppositions of its creator, documentary-makers still attempt to achieve the ideal of an objective viewpoint in order to allow the audience to observe an event neutrally without influence. Other practitioners reject this approach and suggest that as subjectivity is inescapable, a documentary should offer a proposition or feeling about an event; in the words of the founder of the documentary movement, John Grierson, documentary should be 'the creative treatment of actuality'.

What increases subjectivity
- restaging
- selecting events to be recorded
- attempting invisible technique
- manipulation of the material in editing

Figure 11.15

11.9.4 Minimum subjectivity

In the search for the minimum subjectivity that can be achieved, small unobtrusive camera equipment is used, and a minimum crew shoot in available light attempting the least interference to the event or people. Because this technique avoids any control of subject or events there is inevitably a very high shooting ratio in order to capture 'relevant' material. The major subjective influence is in editing when selection and structure shape the material.

11.9.5 Three influences on documentary

- **Technological.** Lightweight sensitive sound video cameras allow access to any situation with minimum intrusion affecting the event. The use of 'cheap' video cartridges allows extended recording to capture the crucial significant event.
- **Sociological.** The programme maker's social influences, concerns and political attitudes will be reflected in the choice and treatment of the documentary.

- **Aesthetic.** The aesthetic approach adopted (e.g. the individual programme maker's answer to what is a documentary) will manipulate the material and form the creative treatment of actuality.

11.9.6 Standard documentary technique

Feature production is concerned with the development of the plot. Documentary production is concerned with the exposition of a theme. In documentaries, the camera position may be a matter of convenience rather than the planned intention of a fiction film set-up. Unobtrusive lighting or available lighting is used. Shots are 'found', then structured in editing.

Like feature films, documentaries present a description or story using a variety of standard techniques such as the invisible authority of the voice-over, archival footage and interviews' facts or truths, but how much 'reality' must a documentary ignore? How much attention should be paid to the usual 'Hollywood' priorities of pace, excitement, human interest, audience attention in the production? In a factual account of police procedure, should the boring, tedious, painstaking days of conventional police work be suppressed to allow the occasional car chase, house raid or suspect interrogation form the body of the documentary? Many documentary subjects are based on the journalistic search for the exceptional – man walks on ice skates to the North Pole – not on the mundane, the ordinary, the uneventful. Scheduled evening programmes require pace, excitement, novelty, even in documentaries, to hold the audience's interest.

Edward Dmytryk's basic editing rule
- Never make a cut without a positive reason.
- When undecided about the exact frame to cut on, cut long rather than short.
- Whenever possible, cut 'in movement'.
- The 'fresh' is preferable to the 'stale'
- All scenes should begin and end with continuing action (i.e. have something happening in the frame before the 'start' of the shot – be certain the journalist is walking before talking).
- Cut for proper *values* rather than for proper 'matches'. For example, if the scene demands a cut at that point from an MS to an MCU make the cut even if there is a continuity mismatch. The alternative of finding a continuity match, but the cut happening too early or too late for the scene, makes the cut more obvious.

extracted from 'On Film Editing'

Figure 11.16

Perennial editing technique avoids reminding the audience that they are watching an edited version. The politician steps off the plane, followed by a cutaway shot of camera operators covering their arrival (the camera operators have nothing to do with the political story, but are shown simply for editing purposes to avoid a jump cut), followed by the politician in the airport being interviewed. The item ostensibly deals with a record of fact while the technique is derived from fiction. Screen time and space has been manipulated, and the technique employed is invisible to the audience.

11.9.7 Realism and expressionism

What is considered 'realistic' in a documentary has changed over the years. One suggestion is to contrast it with 'expressionism', which is a very subjective view by an individual of a subject. In contrast realism emphasizes the subject and attempts to keep some detachment between the subject and the methods of production.

Documentary expressionism allows any form of image, sound, narration, dramatic reconstructions or straightforward invented sequences to move, affect or provoke its audience. An expressionist director imposes no restraint or limits to creative freedom. Realism attempts to be objective even though, as we have discussed above, objectivity is difficult if not impossible to achieve. Even the presence of a camera may influence the event.

Advocates of expressionism therefore accept that the film-maker's influence will always be present in the finished product and attempt to maximize their creative input. By the use of atmospheric sound, abstracted close-ups for emphasis of special points, cross-cutting and cutaways to make novel connections, and technological effects such as stop frame action, for example, to speed up urban traffic in order to visually comment on city life, the expressionistic documentary attempts to influence by feeling and emotion rather than by a doomed attempt at presenting impartial evidence.

11.9.8 Conventional documentary style

A standard documentary structure, popular for many years, involves an unseen presenter (often the producer/director) interviewing the principal subject(s) in the film. From the interview (the questions are edited out), appropriate visuals are recorded to match the interviewee comments which then becomes the voice-over. A professional actor is often used to deliver an impersonal narration on scientific or academic subjects. The choice of the quality of the voice is often based on the aim to avoid an overt personality or 'identity' in the voice-over whilst still keeping a lively delivery.

The camera can follow the documentary subject without production intervention, but often the individual is asked to follow some typical activity in order for the camera to catch the event, and to match up with comments made in previous interviews.

11.9.9 Style and truth

Errol Morris, an American documentary film-maker, claimed that this type of standard 'factual' documentary style with authoritative voice-over etc. does not guarantee truth. The sober style is as much a fabrication as the obvious 'feature' film style he created for an investigative film into a murder case. The 'Thin Blue Line' is an examination of an actual murder using 'film noir' style reconstructions. The documentary looks like a feature film in its shooting and editing techniques, but it stuck with the facts and succeeded in gaining the acquittal of the man unjustly convicted of the crime. It is worth remembering that styles borrowed from news footage, such as the camera surprised by events resulting in uncertain and shaky pictures, can be fabricated and that the 'look' of a documentary is no guarantee of the authenticity or truth of the information being presented.

11.9.10 'Verité' as a style

The 'verité' style attempts to be a fly-on-the-wall, simply observing events without influence. It over-relies on chance and the coincidence of being in the right place at the right time to capture an event which will reveal (subjectively judged by the film-maker at the editing stage) the nature of the subject. With this style, the main objective of being in the right place at the right time becomes the major creative task. There is often an emphasis on a highly charged atmosphere to inject drama into the story. It may use minimum scripting and research other than to get 'inside' where the action is estimated to be. The style often incorporates more traditional techniques of commentary, interviews, graphics, and reconstruction, using hand-held camerawork and available light technique.

A variant of this approach is to use very high shooting ratios, but spend time researching subjects in order to find structures in editing. 'Verité' has lower shooting ratios, structuring work to the requirements

---

Questions of documentary ethics, politics and aesthetics

- Is the recorded event a truthful representation?
- Does it agree with how the participants feel about the event?
- Have the participants of the documentary been truthfully briefed on the purpose and motives of the production?
- Does a 'release form' (a document signed by people appearing in the documentary giving their permission for the recorded material to be used) give the director of that programme unlimited freedom to use the recorded material in any way that he or she wishes?
- What exploitative techniques should the production use or not use (e.g. secret filming, impersonation and deception to obtain information, etc.)?
- As camera equipment becomes less intrusive, what is able to be filmed becomes more intrusive and can invade the most private of situations. Should the privacy of the public be respected?
- Should reconstructions or any 'agent provocateur' activity be identified on screen?
- How much distortion is introduced by editing techniques to keep the audience interested in the subject? Should the use of standard 'Hollywood' production values of pace, excitement, dramatic 'storyline' be fully exploited?
- Does an imposed filmic 'dramatic' time distort the event (e.g. all boredom and non-events are cut out)?
- What influence has the programme's commissioning agent had on the treatment/content?

Figure 11.17

of the television evening schedules (e.g. six thirty-minute episodes), but spends less time *in situ* studying the subject.

11.9.11 Letting it all hang out

This section on documentary editing has said very little about the process of editing because, in general, documentary technique follows most of the perennial techniques already discussed. As there are so many opinions as to what documentary is and what its aims are, a novice editor will be opening a can of worms if guidance is not provided by the director/journalist at the outset of the post-production stage of what 'style' they wish to follow. The style of editing is the major shaping force, especially for the type of production where a large amount of material has been shot with no prepared structure.

For most documentary programme-makers, the invisible technique of standard continuity editing will achieve their aim of providing a compelling piece of television that holds the audience's attention but provides new information or arranges an argument about a social issue in an original and dynamic way.

They seek for technique that hides the methods of production to create the standard seamless flow of images familiar to the audience. Some programme-makers, however, have a different agenda, and wish to remind the audience that they are watching a 'construct' – an artificial fabrication which has arrived on their screen after careful choice from amongst a number of possible options. They want their audience to stand back from the material and make objective judgements about its causes.

The audience is in effect reminded to query the documentary's 'message' and ask the familiar questions: 'Who is saying this?', 'How do they know? and 'For what purpose are they saying it?'

Revealing the mechanics of the production can take many forms, including occasionally seeing the camera in shot, reminding the viewer of the presence of the location unit in the same room as the subject(s), letting the subject(s) talk to people behind the camera, hearing the questions as well as the answers; and, in editing, making obvious the clips of answers that have been cut out by either fading down and up again on the same shot of the interviewee, or by obtrusive jump cuts on the same shot to remind the viewer that the film has been edited and that editorial judgements have been made in the creation of the programme.

12 Audio post-production

Introduction

Audio post-production, audio sweetening or dubbing are the names given to the process of enhancing original sound by adding new, processing the original and carefully mixing all this material into a new and composite sound track that will complement and enhance the picture.

Unfortunately, post-production is often regarded as a quick fix for poorly planned sound, where a few extra effects are added and some music used to cover up any discontinuities. These techniques will never produce really good programmes that have a close relationship between sound and pictures.

The correct approach will depend on the type of programme and the facilities available for both the original acquisition and those in dubbing.

This chapter on audio post-production discusses:

(1) **Sound in editing**
    – linear suites
    – non-linear suites
(2) **Audio dubbing suites**
    – simple news dubbing
    – multitrack dubbing
    – non-linear dubbing suites
(3) **The art of dubbing**
    The second half of the chapter considers the artistic process of dubbing. It discusses all of the considerations from dialogue to effects and their relationship to the pictures with which they are associated. Note that there are general artistic discussions on sound recording and mixing in Section 5.6.8. The topics covered include mixes and fades and these techniques should be considered along with the issues discussed here.
(4) **Transmission**
    There are many factors related to the transmission system that affect the way in which programmes are produced. This short section describes the operation of the transmission department and the systems by which the programmes will be transmitted.

When performing any sound mixing process it is important to understand the way in which the human ear will interpret the sound and its relation with the picture. Monitoring sound requires a particular understanding of the effects of audio level, dynamic range and home viewing conditions. These issues are fully discussed in Section 5.4.

Planning

Like all stages of making television programmes, planning the sound requirements and establishing the techniques to be employed must be carried out before anything is committed to tape. The type of programme, and the way in which the material is to be presented, should be the driving force. Of course there will be limitations imposed by the resources available, but the techniques to be employed should be driven by the artistic requirements, not purely by the technical facilities.

For a simple documentary, if care is taken to record sound that is consistent and matches the pictures, the audio post-production may be fairly straightforward. The requirement will be to ensure smooth transitions from one sequence to another, adding voice-overs and music where this helps the pace of the programme. In some cases the transmission sound might be achieved in an edit suite, but care is needed here as many edit suites are designed around pictures and may not provide clear audio monitoring.

For a more complex documentary or drama the requirement is quite different. Each sound take will need careful equalization and the addition of acoustic effects in order to ensure a good match between the takes and the correct sound-to-picture perspective. There may be stereo or surround positioning to consider. There will certainly be many separate tracks to produce for the dialogue, sound effects and music and the careful recording of voice-overs. Only when each component part has been meticulously prepared will the mixing process take place. This complexity of work demands a well-equipped dubbing theatre, with a competent operator.

12.1 Sound in editing

12.1.1 The linear suite

A linear edit suite is the traditional operation where the editing takes place using the original camera tapes and transfers the material onto another tape in real time.

The way in which the audio can be handled here will depend on the equipment available. A normal suite will comprise two or three video machines, each with a number of audio tracks which will vary with the format in use. Most formats have two tracks with some, especially the digital systems, allowing four independent audio tracks to be recorded with the picture. For example, in a Betacam SP suite each machine has four audio tracks, but not all of them are available all the time.

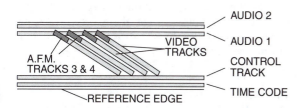

Figure 12.1 Track configuration on Beta SP tape.

On the tapes from the camera (called the rushes), tracks one and two are conventional longitudinal (LNG) tracks. These are like the two tracks on a domestic cassette recorder. As well as these, tracks three and four are audio frequency modulated (AFM) tracks. The AFM tracks are special recordings made in the same area of the tape as the video signal, and can only be recorded with the vision in the Assemble mode. These tracks will have been recorded on the location or in the studio and a log (written details of how the tracks have been used) should be provided with the tapes. On some cameras the AFM tracks cannot be recorded separately and so automatically

will carry the same audio information as the LNG tracks. Track one will be repeated on track three with track two repeated on track four.

In the edit suite the AFM tracks from the original tapes can be replayed, but new AFM tracks cannot be made on the record machine as this is not possible in the Insert mode. The Insert mode is used in editing to enable the selection of recording on video, audio one or audio two or time code recording.

With the digital formats, in editing, all of the tracks are available for recording or replay at any time.

A properly configured edit suite will have all the machine audio outputs connected to a sound mixing desk. This allows a selection of the appropriate source to be made and its level and quality controlled on the mixing desk. The alternative would mean the appropriate sound being switched or plugged to the record machine as required, which would be a lengthy process.

Figure 12.2 Edit suite sound desk.

As well as the video tape machines there will be access to other sound sources, which may include all or some of the following:

- Voice recording booth for voice-overs.
- Compact disc machine to provide music and sometimes sound effects.
- Cartridge machine (digital or analogue) for sound effects. These are capable of providing short 'spot effects' or looped effects like background traffic, running continuously. This means that the effect can be faded up whenever it is required.

- Tape machine (digital or analogue). Useful for moving sound from one part of the programme to another. This machine may also be used during the mixing process if it is a time code machine and can be locked and controlled by the edit controller.

Other equipment may include:

- Equalization (usually part of the sound console).
- Audio compression to reduce the dynamic range of the audio.

Monitoring

Sound monitors need to be mounted near to the picture monitor so the audio appears to come from the screen. This is important, as the brain does not interpret the relation between sound and pictures properly if the sound comes from a position that has no real relationship to the picture. Audio metering should be near the eyeline as well – all too often sound levels on tape are ignored as the meters are not easy to see.

12.1.2 The linear editing process

System checks

The first job to be done at the start of each session will be a check of all the equipment to ensure no non-standard settings have been left from the previous use. One common example of not making proper checks is the use of equalization on the sound-mixing console. If a frequency correction has been left in place, everything routed through the particular channel will have an inappropriate equalization applied to it. To correct this could mean a major re-edit!

Line-up

Before commencing the edit, the machines are aligned using test signals of colour bars and tone. This ensures that the mixing desk and the machines are all set to replay and record the signals at the correct level. The camera tapes can then be placed in the players and the test signal at the start of each tape checked to ensure that these signals are also at the correct level. Anything other than small adjustments made at this stage may point to faults in the recording camera or video tape machine.

Preparing the record tape

The final job is to ensure that the tape in the record VTR is 'blacked up'. This process entails recording, in real time, a colour black picture signal, control track, and time code throughout the tape. This produces a time code and control track which is continuous

throughout the master recording tape and ensures that the edit controller can properly control the machines. It also means that no confusing frames of picture remain from any previous use of the tape.

Control track and time code

It is worth noting here the importance of the time code and control track information. The control track must be continuous throughout the tape as it is this information that provides the video machine with the precise place on the tape that each new video field starts. Loss of this track will cause break-up of the picture as the machine will be unable to properly decode the video information.

The time code provides the reference as to the exact time of each individual frame. This is vital information to the edit controller which needs to know exactly where it is on every tape. As the time code is a longitudinal track it can only be read when the tape is moving at near normal speeds. So that the edit controller can obtain a reference when stationary a copy of the time code is recorded in the video signal in a form called vertical interval time code (VITC). During the edit, each newly inserted picture must include a copy of the correct time code to ensure that this reference is continuous. To achieve this the record video machine must be set to 'regenerate'; in this condition it will use the existing longitudinal time code to produce a replacement of the VITC.

If the time code is not continuous, or the VITC and LNG codes are not the same, the edit controller will have difficulty in finding the correct in and out points during the edit session.

The edit

During the edit process the editor records the pictures in the order that they are required for the final programme. The master takes of audio are transferred at the same time and this is recorded onto tracks one and two on the record machine (in the case of some tape formats up to four tracks of audio are available). Care must be taken to check the audio level of each shot. Even though a line-up has been done, there may be errors in level recorded onto the camera tapes. This must be put right now or the final mix will be very difficult, and unnecessary noise may be generated.

The exact use of the tracks will depend on how, and where, the final audio is to be finished. If the mix is to take place in the edit suite there are a number of ways to proceed:

- It is possible to use the tracks, recording from one to the other and back again, adding extra sounds at each pass. This is called 'track bouncing'. The main problem here is one of generations – at each pass the sound quality will reduce. Too many passes and system noise, mainly in the form of tape hiss, will become more and more noticeable.

- Track bouncing can also be used to enable a mix at the edit. The first shot is recorded onto both tracks, allowing extra sound at the end of the shot. When the next shot is inserted, only track one is record enabled with track two faded up and the new sound mixed in, with the outgoing sound faded out as required. As soon as the outgoing sound is finished with track two is switched back to the record mode, ready for the next edit.

- The simplest method is to record all the original, or sync, sound onto track two and when the edit is complete, record this back onto track one along with any music or extra sound effects added during this mixing process. This version of track bouncing only degrades the signal by one generation but is very limiting in the complexity of sound available. Note that track one is always used as the master transmission track. This leaves track two containing the unmixed sync material, useful if the material is required for future work as the sync effects and dialogue remain unmodified.

- A further method is to use both tracks to assemble the different sounds required. In order to mix this material, the tape will require to be dubbed, both sound and pictures, to another tape (with the possible loss of both sound and picture quality). Alternatively the sound can be transferred off the master video tape to a separate time code locked machine. It is then mixed back, along with any extra sounds required. If analogue equipment is used, care must be taken with equipment line-up and levels to ensure that the extra generations in the audio do not significantly degrade the sound.

- This last method can be used to produce 'chequer-boarded' tracks. Each consecutive shot is recorded onto alternate tracks. This is done with the start and end of each shot overlapping the picture by a few seconds. When this material is mixed, the sound for each shot can be faded up under the sound of the outgoing shot; also the outgoing sound can be allowed to carry on into the next shot. This technique helps soften any large changes in sound level – particularly useful in sport where the sound of the cheering crowd can be allowed to die away after the vision has cut to the next piece of action.

In some linear edit suites the audio is recorded onto a separate multitrack sound machine. This can be analogue or digital and is locked to the video machine using the time code to control its operation. In practice the edit controller is fed with information on the status (stop, play, wind and rewind) of each machine. This allows the edit controller to make allowances for the different times the various machines take to run up to speed; this is the machine ballistics.

More complex sound, especially stereo, is really outside the scope of most edit suites. This material is best handled in a purpose-built dubbing area. The stereo that has been recorded on the original camera tapes will need to be transferred to some other, time code locked medium, in order to pass it through to the dubbing area.

12.1.3 Non-linear editing

This is a very different way of working and a vast number of studios use non-linear systems. In these suites the sound and pictures are transferred to a computer-based editor and all the work takes place within the computer. It is still possible to add sound from outside the computer, for example a voice-over can be recorded from the voice booth, using an analogue-to-digital converter to record directly to the computer disk.

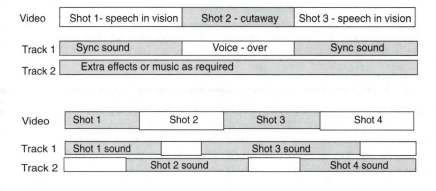

Figure 12.3 Laying simple sound tracks corresponding to the pictures.

Figure 12.4 Chequer-boarding sound tracks to achieve sound overlaps.

The non-linear systems vary considerably in the way in which they are configured, but most have many tracks of audio built into their software. By this method separate tracks can be used for each source allowing original sync material, voice-overs, effects, and music tracks to be built up with the operation. The software may also have the ability to alter the equalization and even compress the material.

Preparation

The first part of the process is to digitize the material. This involves taking the master tapes and transferring the pictures, sound and the relevant time code onto the computer storage system, usually the hard disks within the machine. If analogue source tapes are to be used this is a time-consuming exercise, as it has to be done in real time. Some digital systems allow the material to be downloaded in faster time to reduce this delay. It is possible that real-time transfer is helpful as it may provide the first opportunity for the editor to see the material to be edited.

The edit

The actual edit can be a much faster operation than linear editing as it is only necessary to mark the in and out points of each shot, give it a name and then tell the editor to assemble all these cuts in a selected order. The time taken for this process will depend upon the complexity of the artistic work to be carried out. Each picture cut can have sound included from any of the original tracks and the sound is laid on a virtual track within the editor. By this method audio tracks are built up as required and these can have their levels or equalization and other parameters controlled within the editor. The operation for the sound is rather like making a multitrack recording where each track can be used exactly as required.

How effective the audio processing is will depend on how well designed the system is. It is reasonably easy to use these systems to compile the tracks, but the mixing process and the use of equalization and making dynamic adjustments may be quite difficult. When changing a parameter like frequency, the human mind works most effectively when the ear can hear the change at the same time as the adjustment is made. This allows the brain to work like a servo loop and achieves results very quickly. Some non-linear systems require the operator to put in the frequency changes either on a graphical display or by putting real values of frequency and gain onto the screen. These changes are then applied to the sound sample and replayed to see if the result is suitable. The servo loop between hand and ear is broken and it may take

many attempts to achieve the required result. The effect would be much more simple on the control surface of a conventionally presented sound desk. Some manufacturers have recognized this problem and supply a control panel which mimics the conventional systems, whilst still controlling the effect digitally within the editor.

The final process is to mix down the assembled tracks, which can then be replayed along with the picture, to whatever format is required for transmission. Many of the audio processes are much quicker with the non-linear system. Crossfades can be defined to take place over a number of frames and the effect applied to as many edits as required; this can be carried out in just a few seconds and altered, at will, after the track laying and editing has finished. In an analogue linear system this would be impossible.

12.1.4 In editing or dubbing?

The operational methods, skill of the operator and complexity of the sound will dictate how much sound work is to be done in the editing suite. It may be better to carry out more detailed audio adjustments in a purpose-designed area where the equipment is more suited to difficult audio adjustments. Monitoring may also be a problem in video edit suites. Quite often the video machines are not contained in soundproof units, so there may be a lot of background machine noise that will mask out some of the detail of the audio being monitored.

It is also worth considering that video edit suites are very costly areas. Time wasted here is expensive, whereas sound suites are generally less expensive as well as being specifically designed to achieve the required result.

12.2 Sound in dubbing

Audio dubbing areas come in many forms. They are targeted at specific programme types so it is important to know exactly what audio work is to be done, before deciding on the form the dubbing area should take.

12.2.1 Simple dubbing for news

The simplest operation has the ability to lock the picture to a two- or four-track sound machine (analogue or digital). The sound tracks from the videotape are recorded onto the sound machine and then extra sound can be added to the other tracks, with the whole mixed back to the original video tape. Access to music, sound effects machines and voice-overs, all connected to a small sound desk, makes this area suitable for news or simple documentary work.

12.2.2 Multitrack dubbing

A more flexible system is to use a high quality, digital multitrack audio recorder, locked to the video; in this way a large number of audio tracks can be generated. The video machine can be a non-transmission format so that the master video tape cannot be damaged during the dubbing process.

The tracks that are compiled can be equalized and adjustments to the dynamics made as required, prior to mixing and finally laying the sound back onto the transmission tape. Dynamics and compression techniques are described in Section 5.6.

This area allows for the generation of a complex final mix and many special effects like echo and other processing. This kind of suite is also capable of producing music and effects tracks (M & E). Where a programme is to be sold in other countries, or the material may be required for further programmes, M & E tracks are mixed with the new language tracks and thus retain the original sound effects and background music of each sequence.

12.2.3 Non-linear digital dubbing

The most flexible dubbing areas use non-linear sound editing systems like those found in video editing. These computer-based machines can be linked to a sound desk enabling the most flexible of operations.

The approach to the audio is rather different in operation to conventional sound operations in that the audio, once transferred to a hard disk, is manipulated by a **software operation**. In fact the process is altering the audio to achieve the same end result as if the system were analogue but all the controls are 'on-screen'. Menus allow access to the various parameters with controls that resemble analogue systems. The best, and most costly, of these systems have 'real' controls that allow the operator to adjust the parameters exactly as they would with analogue equipment whilst maintaining the benefits of the software-based systems. These controls are usually multi-functional and thus the desk can be more compact with fewer knobs. One great advantage is that the audio waveforms can be seen, scrolling across the screen, which allows very accurate marking of in and out points. The software further makes the operation

quicker by the ability of the systems to copy fades and effects to any part of the tracks.

Software systems like this are used in non-linear edit suites as well as dubbing. The big advance is the addition of a tangible sound desk. Where this associated sound desk is digital it can become part of the editor and a highly flexible and very fast system is produced. The controls on the sound desk may look conventional but actually control software within the computer and their adjustments are recorded against the time code so that the operation can automatically be repeated by the computer. In fact these desks have more facilities than would at first appear as they use a layering technique. This allows each control to have different applications in each layer of control.

Figure 12.5 An AMS Neve digital dubbing desk (courtesy of Paul Roberts Sound).

Digital sound suites are operated using time code and an edit controller, which may be built in or a separate device, to lock the control desk to the picture source, which can be virtually any format.

In some dubbing suites a compressed version of the picture is recorded into the system. With no analogue tapes running, it is possible to move almost instantly from one part of the programme to another. This speeds up the process as the system can 'rewind' to the start point virtually instantaneously for retakes of any sequence that may be required.

Digital dubbing areas are a very effective way of post-producing the audio. The whole environment is designed around seeing and clearly hearing the images, which helps considerably in the appreciation of the programme material.

The most efficient are able to take digital sound and other information from the original edit to help speed up the process. The sound can be quickly downloaded from the original digital editor and the 'in and out' points of the cuts are passed on via the Edit Decision List (EDL) generated during the edit.

This list of cues is usually recorded onto a floppy disk and can be used in any compatible area.

The most efficient use of time comes with studios that employ fully digital operations and have central digital storage. These operations allow the digital information to be accessed by many different areas, studio, video edit suite, dubbing and transmission, all accessing the sound from the centralized store, sometimes called a silo.

A digital dubbing suite can accept both digital and analogue sources. The area is therefore equally suitable for edits that have taken place in a more conventional linear edit suite as well as the non-linear ones, providing that the picture format is available in the dubbing area. The sound from a linear edit will have to be downloaded in real time so this will take longer.

The associated sound desk provides all the normal controls, equalization and dynamics, and echo and other special effects are usually built in to the software. The desk faders can be motorized, so they move without being touched, and all the control surface adjustments are recorded against the programme time code.

This complex design means the operator can perform the dub in steps, building up the adjustments and the subsequent mix in small stages. The dialogue tracks might be processed first and the effects tracks later. The faders for the tracks already completed will move on their own in subsequent passes, thus allowing the whole operation to be broken down into small manageable operations.

One significant advantage of planning a programme to utilize a digital dubbing suite is that if the correct system of recording the sound on location is used, it is possible to transfer the audio directly from the master, unedited source material, into the dubbing editor. This may be in the form of digital sound tapes or field recorders using removable hard disks or solid state storage on removable cards. These hard disks or storage cards can be plugged directly into the dubbing editor, removing the need for downloading time entirely.

12.3 The art of dubbing

In Chapter 5, much reference was made to the importance of matching sound and pictures. The need for recorded sound to be consistent cannot be over-emphasized. The human brain is very sensitive to changes in both sound level and quality. Small changes in quality are very distracting unless the changes are in sympathy with the picture or would otherwise be expected in real life. The dubbing process is there to take the raw material and translate it into a sound image that matches and enhances the picture.

Audio dubbing chart

Programme Title	*The Flight*					Director:		*C.D.M.*		
Date	*20/01/99*					Dubbing mixer		*P.R.*		

	Time Code	Track 1	Track 2	Track 3	Track 4	Track 5	Track 6	Track 7	Track 8	Notes
	00:00:00			Music						
								Aircraft		
	00:01:35	Dialogue						take-off		
						Airport				
						interior				
						effects				
			Dialogue					Aircraft	Aircraft	
	00:02:21							interior	ann.	
	00:04:57			Music	Voice-over	Airport exterior effects				
	00:05:48	Dialogue						Aircraft interior		
	00:06:49								Aircraft announce	

Figure 12.6 Dubbing sheet, showing audio track usage.

The actual dubbing work follows the same principle whatever system is to be employed. A series of tracks is built up to cover a number of separate areas. These will include the location or studio sound, effects tracks, music tracks, and voice-overs. Some of this material will be provided by the editor, the rest is generated in dubbing.

12.3.1 Voice quality

Even when great care is used in the original recording, there will always be small changes taking place where voice sounds are recorded in different locations, at different times. Microphone placement, background sounds, nearby buildings, various room acoustics and the mood of the performer are some of the factors that will affect the end result. The dubbing operator will spend time, and a great deal of skill, reducing these variations to a minimum.

This process is carried out using complex equalization and compression to make the sound as consistent as is possible.

12.3.2 Voice-overs

Not all the sound can be recorded on location or in the studio. It is often necessary to write some of the script after the vision recording has finished. For this reason a good dubbing suite will have the facility to record voices. Where the suite is used for drama, or even for some documentary programmes, these mini-studios will be used for the recording of sound effects as well.

The recording of voice-overs can be very difficult. The first requirement is an acoustically quiet area in order to record a sound that can be matched to that already recorded. Voice-over booths are usually equipped with high quality microphones and the sound is cleverly equalized to match the studio or location sound that already exists. It may be valuable to use the same microphone as on the location, as this should produce the sound quality of the original recording.

In any programme, every artist should sound consistent throughout their performance. Even in a news programme it can be very confusing if the reporter on camera does not sound the same when speaking out of vision. For this reason the use of close-talking microphones, like lip-microphones, are not really desirable. They may be of value where editing is done on location, but a well designed voice-over booth is vital to good sound dubbing.

The final variation is the performance of the artiste. When on location it is quite natural to speak up and project the voice well, keeping the level reasonably consistent. Sit the artiste down, in a quiet comfortable studio, and the voice will drop; there is nothing to compete with and the voice projection goes altogether. An experienced performer will be able to 'pretend' to be on location and the resultant voice may be acceptable. If they are less experienced it will be helpful to feed the sound effects or the relevant music to their talkback headphones. Mixed with this sound is their voice at a lower level. The effect of competition to the voice is to force them to speak up in order to hear themselves properly. The result should be much better. In any case people perform better when standing up so that they breathe and project their voice properly.

12.3.3 Acoustic effects

Matching the sound to the pictures is quite a difficult matter. The acoustics of the room in which the recording was made will have added to the sound, modifying its characteristics. Hopefully, at the original shoot, the locations were chosen and microphone techniques employed to keep these effects to a minimum and match the expectations of the shots.

The size of the shot, the angle of the lens, how close the camera is to the speaker as well as the background that is visible in the shot all have an effect on the sound the viewer expects to hear. For this reason it is usually better to match the sound as part of the dubbing process, which can only be done if the original sound is reasonably clean of background and acoustic effects.

Modern multi-effects processors are able to reproduce room acoustics with great realism. It is therefore possible to add acoustic effects to match with the edited pictures.

12.3.4 Ambient effects

Ambient effects can present problems that are similar to those of acoustics. Provided the causes of the background sounds are clear in either the shot or the context of the action, there is no problem if they are recorded on the master material. Keeping these effects at a suitable level will be difficult as this too will depend on the shot. Ensuring that the effects remain consistent may be very difficult indeed and variations here will show up very clearly when the different shots are edited together. On all but the most simple programmes, here too it is better to add the effects in dubbing.

Good long effects tracks (sometimes called buzz-tracks or wild-tracks) shot on the original location will be very useful here. There are many libraries of these effects that can be used and all dubbing mixers have their favourites that they have compiled over the years.

The dub is often the best place to add both acoustic and ambient effects, as the location recordist may not know which pictures the sound will be used with. There are many occasions when voices from an interview, recorded at an interior location, are used against a sequence of exterior shots. This will always be distracting and cannot be effectively corrected at the dubbing stage as the removal of acoustic effects is virtually impossible.

It is therefore important to know how the location sound is to be used, or it should be recorded without unnecessary effects, enabling the dubbing mixer to put them in place later, as is appropriate to the shot.

It is always better to err this way – it can be quite acceptable to have sound with little or no acoustic and use it over pictures that are either exterior or interior without causing a noticeable distraction. On the other hand, an inappropriate acoustic or ambient effect will always be unacceptable and in a documentary will cause loss of concentration. Worse still, in a drama, it may result in a loss of dramatic reality.

12.3.5 Sound effects

This topic has been discussed as part of ambient effects above. The primary concern is the principle of ensuring that the viewer can hear what the pictures lead them to expect.

Some extra sound effects may be required by the context of the programme rather than the pictures alone. A drama action taking place in a house in a town will need to have some town effects – distant cars, people walking, wind or rain noise – added to complete the 'picture'.

Spot effects, telephones, door bells, explosions will also have to be added if they were not included in the original recording. Indeed, quite often the 'real' sound on location may sound wrong when recorded and is better added at the dub.

Occasionally it will be necessary to plan these effects very carefully. A good example is a recording to be made in a loud disco. If the original recording included the sound of the music at the levels that are normally experienced in the disco, it would be impossible to record the dialogue over the sound of the music. It will also make the editing of this sequence completely impossible due to having to keep the continuity of the music. More practical will be to record the dialogue sequences without any music at all – the actors will have to remember the music rhythm. Recordings of dancing and other action can be done with the music, but this will only be used as a guide track, the final programme mix being produced almost entirely at the dubbing stage.

Other sound effects can be recorded on location, perhaps as wild tracks, and these can be used as appropriate at the dubbing stage.

12.3.6 Music

In the example above, the music is intended to appear as part of the actual location sound. The type of music to be used is probably dictated by the writer. The mix of voice and music will be difficult; in reality it is almost impossible to hear dialogue at a disco – the dubbing mixer will have to cheat and make the music compete so it is quite difficult to hear the words but the music is not so loud as to overpower the dialogue completely.

Music added to a sequence as a mood-giving layer must be chosen and used with care. Music can add a lot – it can provide mood, emotion and change considerably the impact of the sequence. It is very important that it is chosen early and not just added as an afterthought.

The beginning and end of any music must be motivated by the action or the editing. The action itself, and certainly any movement of the camera shots, should relate to the pace of the music. To achieve this it will help to play the music at the time of the recording, although it may be better not to actually record it, except as a guide. The editing must be in sympathy with the music, perhaps cutting on the beat, or the off-beat, of the music as the pace and mood of the item dictates.

If these criteria are fulfilled, the music will become part of the whole experience, helping to create the mood. If the placement of music is inappropriate, it will simply be an annoyance, making it difficult for the viewer to follow the plot; worse, the dialogue may be lost altogether.

12.3.7 Reality

The example of the disco illustrates that real sound is not always the most effective way to ensure that the sound and picture become one experience. There are many cases where thought has to be given to creating the appropriate illusion.

An example of 'cheating' is action visible through a glass partition or window. Would any intelligible dialogue be heard from the other side? With a closed window probably not. Yet if the dialogue is altered in quality, removing some of the higher frequencies to make the sound appear muffled and taking care with the level, the viewer will be quite happy that hearing it is quite real.

Another example of this is distant people being observed from inside a car. The camera point of view stays inside the car whilst the dialogue of the distant people can be clearly heard by the television audience. The audience know from the build-up to this sequence that they are privileged to hear the dialogue when the observers inside the car cannot hear it. The result can accentuate the frustration of the observers, as they do not know what is going on, even though the audience does.

Rules regarding reality can be broken providing it is done with care and consideration as to how the result will affect the viewer.

Very large changes in sound levels are another big problem. Some detail has already been given about the wide 'dynamic range' of real life and the fact that this range cannot be transmitted, nor would it be desirable even if it could. Loud sounds must be only slightly louder than normal ones and quiet sounds only slightly quieter. There is a range, but it is very much smaller than reality. This 'compression' of the sounds experienced in everyday life will work as a suitable illusion. Occasionally, even the rule of keeping things in loudness order will need to be broken. In the disco example the dialogue was probably a little bit louder than the music, rather than the other way around. This is the same when recording voices and loud aircraft. In reality the aircraft would completely drown out the voice, but if the aircraft sound is balanced to compete with the voice the effect will be believable.

Sometimes, to tell a particular story, the final mix may need to contain effects that were not recorded, and cannot be seen in the shot. An example might be the condemned man being pushed into a prison cell when the camera does not follow, so the viewer cannot see the cell. Only his back is seen, as he shouts his protests. The sound quality of his voice changes as he enters the cell, becoming very echoey and the high frequencies more predominant. Just this sound quality change will give us the impression of a cold, unwelcoming place, with hard walls and floors, no soft furnishings or comforts. All this from the sound and the powerful images produced in the viewer's mind.

12.3.8 Summary

Good dubbing needs good raw material. Sound quality must be consistent, with acoustics and background effects kept to a minimum – extras can always be added. Most importantly, the background effects must not vary in level between the takes or the editing will be impossible. It is better to allow the dialogue to vary slightly and keep the backgrounds

the same. A common error is the rotating of fish poles fitted with directional microphones.

As the microphone rotates, the backgrounds will vary, depending on what is included in its pick-up pattern. Swinging the pole between the artistes, keeping the microphone pointing in the same direction, will balance the voices and keep the effects at a constant level.

Sound dubbing is a powerful part of programme making. It requires care to ensure that facilities are appropriate to the material to be produced. A clear understanding of how the viewer will perceive the complete image is vital to this operation. It is very important to plan what is required as an end result, and the crew who are going to record the original material need to know how their material will be used.

12.4 Transmission

The final stage of all television programmes is the actual transmission. This link in the chain has three areas: the transmission or presentation suite at the programme company studio; the routing of the signal to the transmission system; and the actual transmission system itself.

12.4.1 Signals

The signals to be transmitted comprise the video information and its associated sound channels. The audio information can be routed to the transmitter with separate lines, but more commonly it is digitally encoded and inserted into part of the video signal, using a system called 'sound in syncs'.

As has been shown in Chapter 1 of this book, connection of all video devices requires their outputs to be synchronized. This can be achieved by using one piece of equipment to provide a pulse to the others – this is known as 'slaving'. A much more satisfactory solution is for each studio, or whole television station, to have a centrally generated sync pulse and all equipment connected to it. This allows video signals to be routed from any area to any other without problems. When the station has to connect to an external signal this problem still has to be overcome. Whilst it is possible to slave to the external signal the ability to store picture information has changed this practice. These 'frame stores' take the external signal and hold the information until a complete picture can be released in time with the station. Frame stores are in common use and can cause problems. When many are used, the picture can be slightly time-delayed with respect to the sound. Sound delays may be required to bring the sound back in sync with the picture.

12.4.2 The transmission suite

The transmission suite, or master control area, is the final stage of programme control at most television stations. Whilst its primary function is to produce a smooth output, as it combines all the various sources of material, it has complex technical operations to perform and is often responsible for the accurate time and quality logging of all the transmitted material. This log may be required for legal reasons, and is particularly important at commercial stations where the exact timing and quality checking of advertisements will be vital to the financial income of the station.

Transmission suites are small production control areas that have switching and mixing consoles with combined sound and vision capabilities. They have digital video effects generators and caption equipment as well as sound equipment to insert short stings and music backgrounds. With these suites there is normally a small television studio, used for the continuity announcer. Some of these studios are large enough to accommodate simple interviews, containing two television cameras. The presentation engineer operates the cameras remotely, utilizing computer-controlled systems that can produce pre-programmed shot changes on command.

Whilst the presentation engineer has to operate all of this equipment to produce a seamless programme output, there is a large amount of planning and communication that has to take place. If the next programme is from a remote studio or outside broadcast, the engineer will want to check the sound and pictures from this source, using talkback systems installed to allow this communication. There may be two-way conversations between the studio and the continuity announcer, requiring checks that the systems are in place that allow them to hear each other. In commercial stations the 'breaks' containing the advertisements will need to be viewed before the transmission time. In countries where there is a network of broadcasters, considerable communication takes place throughout the network to keep all the contributors informed about news bulletins and programme or advertisement changes, which may occur only a few minutes prior to their transmission.

12.4.3 Programming

The operation in the transmission suite is run according to a schedule provided by the presentation department. This department provides a daily schedule that identifies to the second the order of material to be transmitted.

This includes the programme, commercial breaks, local announcements from the small presentation

National Television			Transmission Schedule for Week 26		Monday 1st July 1999	Issued - 26/05/99 (jwsmith)
Time	Vision	Audio	Duration	Item details		Tape Details
22:13:49	CART2		3'0"	1 OPTICAL IDENT		NTVOPT
				60 THE DRINKER		HIC/DRI1234/060
				30 CARS GTV		CAR/RTW546/030
				30 NATIONAL AIRWAYS		FLY/8765/030
				20 HOME DIY		DIY/6540/020
				10 BEST CHOCOLATE		YUM/2745/010
				29 CARS GTV2		CAR/RTW547/020
22:16:49	CART1		0'10"	LISTEN TO ME PROMO		LTM/456
22:16:59	VTR4		11'51"	CHRIS ON TV part 2		NTV215678
22:28:50	CART1		0'30"	WONDERFUL WORLD		WW/98765
22:29:20	CART1	ANN	0'10"	NATIONAL IDENT		NTV/I1
22:29:30	REM1		10'30"	NATIONAL NEWS		LIVE
22:40:00	VTR1		2'00"	NATIONAL WEATHER		WET/456

Figure 12.7 Transmission schedule.

studio, and switching to remote studios as required. The presentation studio is staffed by an announcer who will be given scripts to promote other programmes and given details of the programmes that they have to announce. This job requires a good understanding of the material to be transmitted as well as an ability to ad-lib, as there are occasions when the timings are inaccurate or a piece of equipment fails, and the announcer will have to fill the time to allow the problem to be rectified. In many cases an experienced announcer will be able to fill the extra time required without the viewer knowing that any problem has occurred.

Figure 12.8 A typical transmission suite.

12.4.4 Transmission methods

Terrestrial

For conventional land-based, or terrestrial, broadcasting systems, the route starts at the studio where the output is commonly connected to a national telecom land line. The alternative is the station using a microwave link, via a dish aerial, to connect to the telecom system. Further land lines or microwave links will route the signal to the transmission sites where the final processing and the actual transmission takes place.

The video signals are transmitted using a video carrier with the audio on a separate carrier alongside. For stereo transmission a Near Instantaneous Companded Audio Multiplex (NICAM) system was developed that added a second sound carrier for the digitally encoded stereo sound. The sound is compressed for transmission (the audio is expanded in the receiver) and digitally sampled at 32 kHz for the NICAM 728 system.

For an analogue transmission system the signal can suffer degradation due to a number of effects. Theoretically the transmitters require 'line of sight' to the receiving aerial. Long distances or wooded areas may cause a loss of signal strength, resulting in noise on the picture. Hills and tall buildings can produce reflected signals, which, due to small time delays in the reception of the reflected signal, will produce 'ghost' images on the screen.

Some terrestrial transmitters also relay digital versions of the signals. These allow for more channels to be relayed and keep the sound and picture quality high, as the decoded signals do not suffer from the noise and ghosting problems.

Satellite

For satellite systems the signals are digitally encoded and fed to a microwave uplink. This large transmitting dish may be at the site of the broadcaster or there may be a requirement for landlines or intermediate links to reach the uplink. The signals are received and re-broadcast to the chosen geographic regions using directional aerials on the satellite. This system provides large numbers of very high quality signals, where sound and pictures can be viewed by the subscriber at almost studio quality.

These systems are very sophisticated as they allow the broadcasters to interrogate the receiver decoder. It means that the broadcasters can control the channels that each viewer can see as each decoder carries a smart card that identifies the individual customer.

Cable

In areas of high density population there can be special cables laid to each home allowing the subscriber to be directly connected to the distribution system. This system is especially useful in that whilst the systems will be provided with all the available normal programmes it can also allow very small local low-cost studios to be set up. These can provide community programming as an extra to the national and international channels. Cable systems can be used for both analogue and digital systems and should be very high quality.

13 Television graphics

13.1 Computer-generated imagery

The majority of television pictures are created by a camera, but electronic graphics have increasingly provided a method of creating complex images to supplement the standard method of picture acquisition.

The widespread use of powerful digital, computer graphic equipment has enabled graphic designers to design, manipulate and animate any conceivable image in two or three dimensions. These designs can be commissioned for title sequences, programme identification logos, explanatory maps, or charts to illustrate or explain news stories. It is news and current affairs programming that has seen the biggest growth in the use of computer graphics.

This technological development has created images which are unique to television, existing without dimension, but able to move from a surface design to images that have apparent depth.

The source images can be electronically generated or grabbed from film, video or conventional artwork. They can then be reworked and integrated to provide a single seamless composite image.

Essentially the imagery relies on the creative potential of the individual who creates arresting and dynamic images. Technology can never be a substitute for design flair, and sometimes the enormous range and power of computer graphic equipment can inhibit and prevent the execution of good, simple design ideas.

13.2 Graphic design

The graphic design department is often split into two operations:

- Designers create original art work to a programme brief. The designers and design assistants are trained in visual and computer-generated techniques, and their finished work will either be pre-recorded to be played or edited into the programme, or exist as a series of frame stores that are played-out in sequence by a graphics operator.
- Operators may originate text on a character generator for subsequent insertion into a programme, or form part of a production team to play-out the graphics created by a designer. Other operational equipment can be effects equipment and stills stores. Usually, a technical operator will only be involved in an operational role, but a strong visual awareness, and an understanding of the technology involved, is essential. Operators are frequently cued by the director, or it should be clear from the script at what point the graphics require changes or animation.

Figure 13.1

Work flow

Producers, editors or directors will create the initial brief for a graphics requirement. Sometimes this will be for a programme series that may require a complete set of graphics from titles to name supers. Other briefs may be for a one-off map, or a politician's quote over a suitable background visual. Station identification logos, style of promotions, etc. are important to a broadcast company as it is their corporate brand image, and establishes their 'identity' as a broadcasting channel with the watching public.

Depending on the complexity of the graphics, the brief may be discussed and commissioned many weeks before it is required for transmission or recording. News and current affairs programmes have a much shorter lead-in time and therefore cannot match the complexity of animated graphics that may take a considerable time to render (see Section 13.13).

Computer graphic technology is complex and developing continuously. The graphic designer is the best person to advise the production staff on how the originating brief should be executed. The second part of the work flow chart is deciding what technique/equipment is to be employed to realize the original idea. This choice must fit in with the allocation of equipment to service other commissions.

The final graphic has to be recorded in some medium to be accessible and easily played out when required. The choice of the recording medium becomes the third decision.

13.3 Visual communication

Communication using graphical material shares the same requirements as film or video storytelling. There is a need to attract and hold the attention of the viewer before information can be absorbed. Sometimes the viewer can be overloaded with detail. For example, a weather forecaster standing in front of a weather chart with animated graphics and text presents the viewer with three sets of competing data. The weather forecaster is one 'message', and every time they move, wave their arms at the chart, or speak, they claim the viewer's attention. The chart also needs to be deciphered by the viewer, and the information absorbed. Moving weather symbols compete for attention and need to be decoded. It is hardly surprising, with attention split three ways, that some people, after a weather forecast, have little or no idea what tomorrow's weather is going to be.

At the other end of visual communication is the use of international symbols or icons. The fragility of a wine glass is immediately understood when the symbol is displayed on the side of a parcel. The function of a lever attached to a car steering wheel imprinted with a windscreen wiper symbol is transparently obvious. Good graphics should have the same clarity and intensity as traffic signs or international symbols. They should immediately command attention, be decoded, and understood with little or no supporting text.

Good visual communication contains:

- simplicity – unnecessary detail is eliminated with not more than three or four competing subjects for attention;
- accessibility – the main subject/topic is quickly understood as the message may be on the screen for a limited time;
- clarity – television screens vary in size, technical quality and viewing conditions therefore the message must be legible even in imperfect viewing conditions;
- impact – a visually dynamic design to compete, but not conflict, with surrounding visuals;
- no ambiguity – the observer's eye must be guided with unmistakable certainty to the principal message displayed.

The visual design elements that can be used to create these characteristics include:

- movement;
- colour, texture, pattern, tone;
- grouping and organization;
- visual weight and balance;
- a balance or contrast between figure and background;
- line, curve, rhythm, direction;
- compositional emphasis of the main subject.

Effective computer graphics depends on a clear production brief in order that the image supports the script.

13.4 Different types of graphics

Graphics are used in a number of different ways in television production. Each format has its individual technique and conventions:

Figure 13.2 Name super strapline.

- **Straplines.** A strapline is a line of text supered over live action, usually at the bottom of the frame. It can be static or crawled across the frame (see Section 13.9). It can be used to reinforce the main image and audio, or it can be used to add completely new information with the risk (and sometimes the intention) of conflicting with the background information. Name supers are frequently designed with the programme logo included.
- **Supered text.** Any text that is required to be supered over moving images should be checked for legibility. If the background image varies in contrast and tone, a grey toned strap or edge enhancement can make the text more distinct.
- **Stacks, maps and charts.** Specially designed maps are frequently used in news bulletins to show the location of the story. If it is a story about an unfamiliar country or city, a common convention is to establish neighbouring countries (or even continent) before focusing in on the designated area. Maps are designed to be easily read with the minimum amount of geographical information, cities and towns that are required by the story.
- **Words or pictures.** Full frame graphics can be made up of text, pictures, symbols or any combination of these. The information can be animated by building up the complete frame using a background image and movement appropriate to the subject. The graphic presentation should be simple and uncluttered to allow the viewer to understand the main points being communicated.
- **Headings.** Sometimes a story or a documentary uses stand-alone graphics to identify new subjects or themes. These can be accompanied by musical 'stings' (short musical phrases), all repeated in a similar style.
- **Quotes.** Graphical text that is displayed to reinforce a voice-over should usually be identical to the words spoken. The viewer will read along with the spoken words and any difference between what is read and what is heard can be obtrusive and jarring.
- **Insets and over-the-shoulders.** Most news bulletins use a chroma key window or DVE window sharing the newsreader's frame. The graphic displayed in the window can either be a generic logo (e.g. a football image for match reports) or a specific graphic to match the subject of the story (e.g. a politician's image). Many programmes other than news and current affairs use over-the-shoulder graphics to support a piece to camera.
- **Outline points.** With news stories, such as proposed new legislation, budget proposals, etc., the main points of the report are frequently built up, point by point, in the frame to form a summary of the changes. If each point is to be synchronized

Figure 13.3 Over-the-shoulder inset achieved by a full frame graphic via a monitor.

with voice-over replication make certain that the text is identical to the text read out or, if the summary is a 'headline' list, the spoken text enlarges on the keyword.

13.5 The computer graphics suite

In general, there are three functions required to be performed in a graphics suite:

- creation, modelling, animation, rendering or acquisition of images and text;
- manipulation and effects performed on the created images;
- recording, sequence editing, storing, and play-out or transfer of the graphics.

13.6 Picture acquisition

Images can be created solely by painting programmes by the manipulation of pen and tablet, or mouse.

These original designs can be based on:

- images recorded from photographs, illustrations or artwork via a rostrum camera or other type of camera;
- a video frame from a frame store, or an 'off-air' screen grab;
- single frames captured from VTR, telecine or a slide scanner.

13.7 Picture manipulation

There is almost unlimited flexibility in image manipulation using a digital video effects unit. A digitalized image consists of millions of separate pixels that can be rearranged in virtually any order, controlled by available software.

13.8 Image storage

As well as performing the basic function of storing the completed graphic, a frame store can be used for a variety of animation effects. For example, a map used for a weather forecast bulletin can be built up by adding to the base weather map a number of weather symbols. Each frame can have a weather symbol in a different place, and when the frame store is programmed to play out at a pre-determined speed, the weather symbol will move across the frame in a simple simulated movement.

Off-line editing of moving graphics can achieve the same sophistication of movement using the same techniques as standard animation.

13.9 Character generators (CG)

A character generator originally began as a facility that allowed text to be entered via a keyboard.

Various visual manipulations could then be carried out on the text and stored, ready to be accessed when required. The main requirement was speed and reliability for on-air work. As the cost of digital computing power decreased, many more facilities were added and character generators can now include:

- a vast range of font styles and size with the ability to incorporate new and unique typefaces;
- manipulation of the text in its on-screen presentation such as real time dynamic titling effects, dissolve, roll, crawl, zipping, reveal in or out, etc., and flying text in 3D space. Three standard text movements are known as **zipping** – words or phrases appear on the screen letter by letter; **roll** – the text runs up the screen to a preset time, often matched to music in an end credit sequence; and **crawl** – a horizontal movement of text, often from right to left.
- text set in any colour with effects like a drop shadow, surround, or strapline added to make the type more legible against its background;
- shapes and areas of colour such as backings, charts, straplines, boxes, etc.;
- the design and storage of symbols or logos that can be recalled and positioned with text;

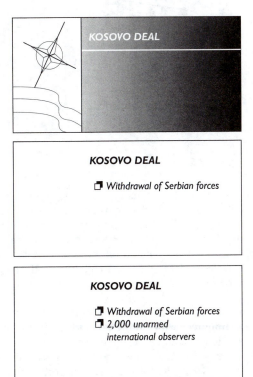
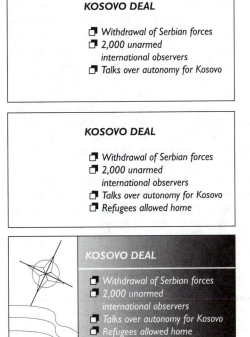

Figure 13.4

- a built-in still store;
- painting with pen and tablet;
- video capture;
- video clip management to import external video clips to incorporate with captions or graphics, and allow shrinking, repositioning and zooming the external clip. A typical use is to squeeze down video clips and play them in the corner of the screen to promote up-coming items;
- spellchecker;
- dual/multichannel output;
- removable hard disks so that a specific programme's stings and animated graphics can be instantly available when loaded;
- the ability to import from a PC a text file which, when loaded, is formatted into the current production style template of appropriate font, size, etc.;
- the ability to integrate with newsroom workstation systems so that graphics can be created at the same time as a news script is compiled;
- the ability to move files from different production areas, avoiding retyping and allowing the production team to directly compile lists of credits, titles and name-super graphics.

Alongside the stand-alone character generators there has been developed CG software able to be run on PC platforms. These software systems can be quickly updated by new versions of the original program, or replaced with new software without the need to replace hardware. Another advantage is that graphics workstations can use different software systems depending on the job in hand. In general, the dedicated character generator boxes are faster than using software through a workstation, and are therefore often preferred for on-air presentations.

A prime function of a CG is still to prepare text for the screen, but the added facilities allow a greatly expanded range of graphic treatment. For example, an animated programme logo can be added to each name super in the 'house' style of the specific programme. At a time of ever-increasing programme channels, programme identification has a high priority in the quest for audiences. Many programmes have therefore created their own typeface digitized as part of its house style in order to remind their audience of the programme they are watching.

The accuracy of text

The spelling and accuracy of text and graphics should be checked by a member of the programme production team before it is transmitted or edited. The spelling of unusual surnames, their correct title or official position can easily be misread, especially from a handwritten list of graphic requirements. This type of error can cause offence to the participant. As detailed above, many character generator and software applications now allow direct input from journalist workstations or PC files produced by a programme production office. This may reduce the risk of a mistake, but accuracy should still be checked prior to transmission.

13.10 Still store

In its original basic form, a still store was a digital piece of equipment that allowed a frame of video to be stored and accessed when required. One frame of video in a standard 625/50 picture includes 720 pixel groups, each made up of full resolution luminance pixel plus two half-resolution colour difference pixels – a total of 829 440 pixels. Sampled at 8-bit resolution, this creates over 6.6 million bits of data (6.6 Mb). Each uncompressed stored frame therefore requires 6.6 Mb of memory.

Figure 13.5

As the cost of memory has plunged, there has been a huge increase in the storage and computing ability of still stores, allowing many more programme production techniques to be executed to augment the original function of storage and retrieval of television images.

Dedicated (and open architecture) still stores can provide:

- a high capacity of still images (e.g. up to 56 minutes of uncompressed video);
- file management using databases that classify each image by title, category, original acquisition date, keyword, etc. for rapid search, sort and fast selection. As each picture is recorded it is given a number and can easily be recalled;

- manipulation of the image size and position on screen for over-the-shoulder use;
- arrangement and storage of selected images into stacks to match the running order of the production;
- forming of images into stacks for animation;
- preview facilities to check the next image to be accessed on-air;
- acquisition of visual material from dedicated graphics machines, and input graphic files from many different computer formats;
- frame grabs from moving images with the ability to process and eliminate interfield flicker etc. on the image;
- duplicate outputs to allow more than one 'client' to have access to the stored material and facilities;
- remote control of access (e.g. an operational panel in a production studio or OB control room), plus the ability to network to many different users;
- on-air control providing speed, accuracy and reliability;
- drag and drop selection of required image;
- a range of DVEs including wipes, transition and dissolves;
- storage and replay of video clips;
- keying of signals to allow on-air semi-transparent graphics;
- ... and many more facilities depending on equipment design.

Storing picture information digitally allows individual images to be recorded from many sources such as graphics machine, still store or character generator one at a time. Material can be built up, adding elements from a number of different sources until the sequences of images form an animated clip when played-out. Individual frames can be easily edited into a new order and the playback speed can be altered or made into a loop.

Figure 13.6 Full frame over-the-shoulder graphic.

Dedicated frame store equipment has developed to overlap the function of computer graphics, vision mixing, video editing, animation, etc. but the ability to acquire, store, index and replay a still, or a sequence of images, remains at the heart of its value to most productions.

13.11 Digital video effects (DVE)

A 625/50 picture is composed of 720 pixel groups (829 440 pixels in total). Individual pixels can be programmed and repositioned within one frame to alter the appearance of the image or successively changed in adjacent frames to control a shot transition (e.g. a circle wipe from the centre of an outgoing shot to be replaced by the new shot). This ability to manipulate the picture elements can create movement and visual diversity in a series of graphic images. Images can be flown around the screen, stacked and revealed, flipped over to reveal new graphics/text, etc. Movement through space of a three-dimensional graphic requires considerable computing power plus time to render; two-dimensional movement using DVEs can be quick and very effective.

13.12 Two-dimensional graphics

The creation of television graphics is now centred on dedicated hardware/software paint systems that allow freehand drawing and painting, complex manipulation of the image and the creation of shapes and effects.

Freehand drawing/painting is controlled through an electronic pen and tablet with the ability to simulate any thickness of line or quality, air brush, watercolour, line drawing and any combination of mixed media. Original work can start with a blank screen, or any image can be acquired and reprocessed to serve the graphic requirements.

The flexibility of technique and facilities available is enormous, and is being added to each year. Typefaces can be of any size or colour, and can be enhanced with pattern, filter, drop shadow or a three-dimensional edge. Parts of an image can be cut out and enlarged, reduced, inverted, repeated, reversed and positioned anywhere in the frame. Two-dimensional animation is produced by recording each frame after the required adjustment of section or image position.

Most paint systems provide storage for the finished art work, or more complex stacks can be saved in a dedicated still store or digital tape recorder. The potential for manipulating images is enormous, and this is sometimes inhibiting to the newcomer because of the sheer amount of design choice available.

13.13 Three-dimensional movement

A computer graphic design system allows three-dimensional objects to be created and moved with the same degree of realism as any 'real-life' subject recorded and displayed on a two-dimensional screen.

The newly created object begins as a wire frame image or simple polygons. These can be rotated to display a new viewpoint or moved to a new location. After the appearance of these simplified objects is acceptable, the designer will then add information about the surface of the objects (colour, texture, reflectivity, etc.) to transform the wire frame into an image with a substantial form. Information about light source and direction, shadows, etc. is now required to fully bed the three-dimensional image into its environment.

The creation of wire frames is time-consuming, and the application of surface, movement, different viewpoints, different distances and light requires the computer to make many calculations for each frame. This rendering takes a considerable amount of time depending on the computer power employed. Finally, the completed frames are recorded and can be played out in real time to simulate movement and action.

Rostrum camerawork

One of the oldest methods of creating movement with two-dimensional graphics was placing the material in front of a camera and either moving the material, the camera, or zooming the lens. This perennial technique

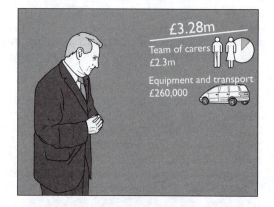

Figure 13.7 A 'reveal graphic' keyed into the background of the presenter. Usually the presenter (e.g. weather forecaster) cannot see the information on their 'blue screen' background and uses an off-screen monitor in their eyeline to find the approximate place to point.

has been adapted to take advantage of computer power, and a vertical camera looking down on a movable base where the graphic material is placed is servo-controlled by a programmable computer to allow many complex movements.

Further reading

Audio

Audio for Television, John Watkinson (Focal Press)
Introduction to Digital Audio, John Watkinson (Focal Press)
Stereo Sound for Television, Francis Rumsey (Focal Press)
The Digital Interface Handbook, Francis Rumsey and John Watkinson (Focal Press)
Microphones – Technology and Technique, John Borwick (Focal Press)
Sound and Recording, Francis Rumsey and Tim McCormick (Focal Press)
Audio Post-Production in Video and Film, Tim Amyes (Focal Press)

Camerawork

Applied Photographic Optics, Sidney F. Ray (Focal Press, 1994)
Basic Betacam and DVCPRO Camerawork, Peter Ward (Focal Press, 1998)
Batteries, Anton/Bauer Inc.
Composition for Film & TV, Peter Ward (Focal Press, 1996)
Multi-Camera Camerawork, Peter Ward (Focal Press, 1997)
Satellite Communications, James Wood (Newnes, 1994)
Satellite Technology, Andrew F. Inglis and Arch C. Luther (Focal Press, 1997)
The Reproduction of Colour in Photography, Printing and Television, Dr R. W. G. Hunt (Fountain Press, 1989)
The Technique of Film & Video Editing, Ken Dancyger (Focal Press, 1997)
TV Fundamentals, John Watkinson (Focal Press, 1996)
TV Optics 11, Broadcast Equipment Group, Canon Inc., 1992
Video Techniques, Gordon White (Focal Press, 1988)

Editing

In the Blink of an Eye, Walter Murch (Silman-James Press, 1995)
Non-linear Editing, Patrick Morris (Focal Press, 1999)
Video Editing Basics, Steven Browne (Focal Press, 1998)

Engineering

The Video Studio, Alan Bermingham *et al.* (Focal Press)
Broadcasting Television Fundamentals, Michael Tancock (Pentech Press)
Television Fundamentals, John Watkinson (Focal Press)
An Introduction to Digital Video, John Watkinson (Focal Press)
Your Essential Guide to Digital, John Watkinson (Focal Press)
The Engineer's Guide to Compression, John Watkinson (Focal Press)
Video Standards, Victor Steinberg (Snell & Willcox)
MIDI Systems & Control, Francis Rumsey (Focal Press)
An Introduction to Video Measurement, Peter Hodges (Focal Press)
The Video Camera Operator's Handbook, Peter Hodges (Focal Press)
The Digital Fact Book, Quantel
The Digital Interface Handbook, Francis Rumsey & John Watkinson (Focal Press)

Lighting

Concert Lighting Techniques, James L. Moody (Focal Press)
TV Lighting Methods, Millerson (Focal Press)
The Techniques of Lighting for TV and Motion Pictures, Millerson (Focal Press)

Professional Lighting Handbook, V. & S. E. Carlson (Focal Press)

Film Lighting, K. Malkiewicz (Prentice Hall)

Stage Lighting, Pilbrow (Studio Vista)

Eye and the Brain (The Psychology of Seeing), Gregory (World University Library)

Electronic Cinematography: Achieving photographic control over the video image, Matias & Patterson (Wadsworth)

The Photographer's Guide to Using Light, Schwarz & Stoppee (Watson-Guptill)

Professional Portrait Techniques, Kodak

The Art of Seeing, Kodak

Light – Science & Magic, Hunter & Fuqua (Focal Press)

Light (Collins' Photographic Workshop), Michael Freeman (Collins)

Lighting for Film & Electronic Cinematography, Dave Viera (Wadsworth Publishing Co.)

The Gaffer's Handbook, Box & Fitt (Focal Press)

Control Systems for Live Entertainment, John Huntington (Focal Press)

Motion Picture and Video Lighting, Blain Brown (Focal Press)

Stage Lighting Handbook, Francis Reid (A. & C. Black)

Stage Lighting Controls, Ulf Sandstrom (Focal Press)

Lighting Technology, Fitt & Thornley (Focal Press)

Colour Temperature (Colour Temperature Correction & Neutral Density Filter in TV Lighting), Alan Bermingham (The Society of TV Lighting Directors)

Safety

Camera Operations on Location (Safety), Health & Safety Executive (Crown Copyright, 1997)

See also Bibliography at end of Chapter 3, 'Safety'

Glossary

A/D conversion Converting an analogue signal into a digital signal.

Actuality event Any event that is not specifically staged for television that exists in its own timescale.

Ad-lib shooting Impromptu and unrehearsed camera coverage.

AES/EBU American Engineering Society/European Broadcasting Union – standards organizations who, amongst other specifications, have both defined the interface to connect digital audio signals.

Alarm control Control of audible warning through speaker of camera/recorder of a fault condition in camera or VTR fault.

Aliasing Incorrect sampling due to input frequencies exceeding one-half of the sampling rate.

Amplitude Maximum height of a waveform or signal.

Analogue signal A varying voltage signal.

Angle of view The horizontal angle of view of a specific focal length lens. Angle of view varies with a zoom lens.

ASA American Standards Association. A method of rating the speed of film. Replaced by International Standard Organization, ISO, or Exposure Index, EI.

As-directed Unrehearsed camera coverage controlled at any moment by the director.

Aspect ratio The proportion of the picture width to its height.

Assembly edit Recording process where the video, audio and time code are recorded, in sequence, to a blank tape.

Aston A collective name for any text generator (equivalent to 'hoover' for a vacuum cleaner, 'biro' for a ball point pen).

Attenuation Reduction of signal level.

Auto-gain An electronic circuit which automatically adjusts audio recording level to keep within prescribed limits.

Auto-iris Automatic adjustment of the iris depending on main subject luminance.

Azimuth The azimuth on an audio tape machine is correct when the record head is at a right angle to the tape.

Back focus *See* **Flange-back**.

Backlight Lamp used to separate subject from the background by rim lighting the subject from upstage.

Balance The relative level between sound sources or light sources.

Balanced line Connection of audio signals where the two signal paths are kept separate from earth.

Bandwidth The range of frequencies required for successful transmission of audio (20 kHz) or television (PAL – 5.5 MHz).

Barndoors Hinged metal flaps on the front of a lamp used to control the spread of light.

Bars   *See* **Colour bars**.

Bass   Lower end of the frequency spectrum.

Battery lamp   Small battery-powered lamp often mounted on top of the camera.

Betacam format   12.5 mm tape cassette video format recording, on two adjacent video heads, the luminance signal (Y) and a chroma signal consisting of a compressed time division multiplex of the colour difference signals ($R - Y$) and ($B - Y$).

Bias   High frequency signal added to the audio during the magnetic recording process.

Big close-up (BCU)   A description of the size of a shot. When applied to the face, the frame only includes the point of the chin to mid-forehead.

Bit   A unit of binary code.

Bitstream   A series of binary digits.

Black balance   Automatic adjustment of the black level of the camera.

Black level   The amplitude of the television video signal representing the darkest part of the picture.

Black wrap   Black anodized aluminium foil used to control spill light or shaping a light beam.

Blonde   A 2000 W portable lamp.

BNC   A twist-lock cable connector often used on monitor video cables.

Bouncing   A method of transferring audio from one track to another. Also a method of obtaining a soft light source from a hard source.

Breaker button   Automatic cut-out of power supply to electronic equipment if overload is detected.

Brightness   A term often incorrectly used to mean luminance. Brightness is a subjective effect – it is how brightly we see an object.

Bus   A connection point in a sound desk for a number of signals.

Butterfly   A large frame to hold nets, silks or blacks measuring 6′ × 6′ or 12′ × 12′ or 20′ × 20′.

C10 rate   A slow charge of constant current equal to one-tenth of the ampere-hour rating of the battery. A safe extended charge rate that will not produce a build-up of oxygen.

Camera angle   The position of the camera relative to the main subject in the shot.

Camera left   Left of frame as opposed to the artiste's left when facing camera.

Camera right   Right of frame as opposed to the artiste's right when facing camera.

Camera sensitivity   Quoted in relation to a subject with peak white sensitivity, scene illuminance (lux), *f*-number of lens and signal-to-noise ratio for a stated signal.

Candela   The unit of measurement of the luminous intensity of a lamp.

Canting the camera   Angling the camera so that the horizon is not parallel to the bottom of the frame.

Caption generator   Electronic equipment that allows text to be created and manipulated on screen via a keyboard.

CCD   A charge-coupled device; it converts light into electrical impulses which are compiled into the TV picture format.

Chroma key   An electronic process for inserting an artiste (foreground) into a background picture; also known as Colour Separation Overlay (CSO) in the BBC.

Chroma   Another name for saturation, a control usually found on monitors.

Clean feed   An audio source providing a programme participant with all audio signals but excluding their own audio contribution.

Clear (*or* Clearance)   The instruction to a cameraman to move to the next position.

Close-up (CU)   Shot size. When applied to the face, the top of the frame rests on the top of the head and the bottom of the frame cuts at the position of a knotted tie if worn.

C-mount   Standard broadcast video lens mount.

Coaxial cable Cable with a central conductor surrounded by a sheath of screening.

Coincident pair Two microphones that are effectively in the same position.

Coloration Unpleasant effect where sound is repeated with a small time delay. This may occur where two microphones pick up the same sound.

Colour balance *See* **White balance.**

Colour bars A special test signal used in colour television.

Colour temperature A convenient way to describe the colour of a light source by relating it to a black body radiator, e.g. heated poker, measured in Kelvins (K) after Lord Kelvin (physicist).

Component The individual or difference signals from the red, blue and green channels and luminance signal.

Composite The colour signals encoded (combined) with the luminance signal. Also, old definition for luminance signal plus synchronizing pulses.

Compression The process of reducing the amount of signal data that is required to be passed through a finite channel whilst endeavouring to maintain the quality of the originating signal. Also a method of reducing the range of audio levels.

Condenser A type of microphone using charged plates to transfer sound pressure changes into electrical signals.

Console Audio mixing device with many inputs.

Contrast ratio The ratio between the brightest part of the subject and the darkest part.

Control track A regular pulse recorded on video tape to identify the position of the video signal and tape speed.

Convergence In a monitor, the ability to converge all three television rasters to make a single raster.

Cookie (*or* Cucoloris) A perforated plate used in front of a luminaire to break up the light beam producing a dapple effect.

Cosine law A law which follows the cosine 0–90°. (See page 51.)

Crash zoom Either an intentionally maximum speed zoom or an 'emergency' fast zoom to recompose 'on-shot'.

Crib card Camera card attached to the side of the camera describing the planned shots and production information connected with that camera.

Cross talk Unwanted signal picked up between adjacent signal cables or from one audio track to another.

Crossing the line Moving the camera to the opposite side of an imaginary line drawn between two or more subjects after recording a shot of one of the subjects. This results in intercut faces looking out of the same side of frame and the impression that they are not in conversation with each other.

CSO Colour separation overlay. *See* **Chroma key.**

CTDM Compressed time division multiplexed chrominance recording; part of the Betacam method of recording.

Cue A particular lighting condition or an indication for action to start, e.g. actor to start performing or lighting change to start.

Cursor A vertical or horizontal line that can be positioned by the cameraman in the viewfinder as a reminder of a precise frame position or to check a vertical or horizontal visual element.

Cut to line The video source selected as the output of the vision mixing panel.

Cutaway Cutting away from the main subject or master shot to a related shot.

Cutter As **Flag** but long and narrow, usually used to darken off the top of a set.

Cyclorama A general purpose background curtain, usually off-white.

DAT Digital audio tape.

DCC Dynamic contrast control. Compresses highlights of the picture to allow a greater contrast range to be recorded.

Decibels (dB) A logarithmic ratio of changes in sound intensity similar to the ear's logarithmic response to changes in sound intensity.

Density A measure of the light transmitted by a film or filter:

$$\text{Density} = \log_{10} \frac{1}{\text{transmission}} = \log_{10} \text{opacity}$$

Depth of field The zone of acceptable focus in the field of view.

Dichroic filter A mixture of glass layers with different refractive indices, designed to reflect one colour whilst passing other colours through. Commonly used on battery lamps to convert the colour temperature of tungsten to daylight, and in light-splitting blocks.

Diffuser Material which scatters the light to create a softer light source.

Digital injection (DI) A method of directly connecting an audio output from a musical instrument or other audio equipment to a balanced audio input.

Digital manipulation Rearranging and recombining small elements (pixels) of an image.

Digital A data stream of individual binary numbers representing an unbroken variable value.

Dimmer An electronic device for controlling the light output from a light source. Usually a thyristor or silicon controller rectifier (SCR) but recent developments have included the transistor dimmer.

Dingle Branches placed in front of a luminaire to create a dapple effect or in front of a lens to create a foreground feature.

Discharge light source Lamps which produce light by ionizing a gas contained in a bulb.

Display mode Selecting particular information about the camera to be displayed in the viewfinder.

Distortion Unwanted damage to an analogue signal that results in the output of a system being different from the original.

DMX 512 Digital multiplex system for sending dimmer/moving light information down one pair of wires.

Dolby A noise reduction process used in audio recording and playback.

Downlink The signal path between satellite and receiver.

Downstage Towards the camera or audience.

Dropout The short loss of a recorded signal due to faulty head-to-tape contact or tape imperfections.

Dry Describes the inability of a performer either to remember or to continue with their presentation.

Dynamic range The relationship of the highest value to the lowest value of sound intensity or picture brightness that can be reproduced.

EBU European Broadcasting Union. Advisory and regulatory body for broadcasting in Europe.

Edited master The final version of edited material that will be seen by the viewer.

EDL Edit decision list. Created to define the in and out points of an edit sequence.

E-E Electronics to electronics; a VTR facility switch which enables the signal to bypass the recording head.

Effects (Fx) Visual or audio effects.

EFP Electronic field production. The term used to describe single-camera location video programme-making other than news.

Electronic shutter An electronic method of varying the length of exposure time of the CCD. Can be used to improve the slow motion reproduction of motion.

Encode The technique of combining colour information with a luminance (monochrome) signal.

ENG Electronic news gathering. Describes the single-camera video recording of news events.

Entropy The unpredictable part of a signal which has to be transmitted by a compression system if quality is not to be lost.

Equalization Increase or decrease in the level of chosen audio frequencies.

Establishing shot The master shot which gives the maximum information about the subject.

EVDS Enhanced Vertical Definition System. A method of reducing motion blur.

Extender An additional lens which can be switched internally in the zoom lens to extend the zoom range of focal lengths.

Eyeline The direction the subject is looking in the frame.

Face tones Signal derived from face tones, typically (average European face) about 0.5 V.

Fader A control for varying the level of an audio or video signal.

Feed Either a video signal or the cable that carries the signal.

Field integration A technique connected with the read-out of a CCD where adjacent lines are averaged.

Field One top-to-bottom scanning of an image. Two fields interlaced make up one frame.

Fill light A light source used to make shadows transparent, i.e. reduce the contrast.

Filter wheels Filter holders of colour correction, neutral density or effects filters that are arranged within the camera to allow for the quick selection, by rotating the wheel, of the required filter combination.

First generation The acquisition medium on which the video signal was first recorded.

Flag A solid rectangle of black card/board or a rectangular wire frame covered with a black serge cloth. Used to block the light or shape a light beam. Usually used with a griphead, grip arms and a flag stand.

Flange-back The distance from the flange surface of the lens mount to the image plane of the pick-up sensor. Commonly known as the back focus.

Flight kit A portable set of location lamps and stands able to be packed in a compact container for easy transportation.

***f*-number** A method of indicating how much light is being allowed to pass through the aperture of the lens.

Focal length of a compound lens The distance from the principal point of a compound lens (e.g. a zoom lens) to the point at which rays from an object at infinity form the most sharply defined image.

Focus pull Moving the zone of sharpest focus to another subject.

Foldback A feed to allow artistes to hear selected sound sources on loudspeakers or headphones.

Foot candle Unit of illuminance in imperial units, 1 $lumen/ft^2$ = 1 foot candle.

Format The method of recording the image (DVCPRO, S-VHS, Betacam, etc.).

Frame integration A technique connected with the read-out of a CCD where vertical resolution is improved at the expense of motion blur.

Frame interline transfer (FIT) A method of transferring the CCD charge to eliminate vertical smear.

Frame store An electronic device for storing individual video frames.

Frame transfer (FT) The method of transferring the charge vertically from the CCD pixels exposed to the subject, to a duplicate set of pixels.

Frame One complete television picture comprising two interlaced fields or a single film image.

Free run Frame identification by time code which is set to the actual time of day when the frame was recorded.

Frequency response The range of frequencies that a particular system can reproduce without distortion.

Frequency The number of complete cycles per second.

Fresnel Stepped lens used in the fresnel spotlight.

Fundamental The original or lowest frequency of a complex signal.

Gaffer The chief lighting electrician.

Gain The amplification of a video or audio signal calibrated in dB (e.g. +6 dB of video gain is the equivalent of opening the lens iris by 1 stop).

Gallery Production control room.

Gamma The law of the transfer characteristic of a system, i.e. the relationship between input and output signals.

GEO Geosynchronous orbit satellite. Revolves at the same rotational speed as the earth and appears stationary from the earth's surface.

Gobo Stainless steel stencil used in profile projectors to create effects, e.g. windows, abstract pattern, moon.

Grads An abbreviation of 'graduated'. Applied to front of lens filters which progressively filter or colour the picture vertically.

Graticule Engraved calibration scale on the front of waveform monitors and vectorscopes.

Grid area The structure above a studio floor.

Grip Supporting equipment for lighting or camera equipment. Also the name of the technicians responsible for handling grip equipment, e.g. camera trucks and dollies.

GV General view. A long shot of the subject.

HAD Hole accumulated diode. A CCD sensor which increases the proportion of the sensor that can collect light without decreasing resolution.

Hand-held Operating a portable camera without a camera mounting.

Hard light Any light source that casts a well defined shadow.

Harmonic A range of frequencies that are multiples of the fundamental that make up a complex waveform.

Hertz Unit of frequency. 1 Hertz = 1 cycle/second.

High angle Any lens height above eye height.

High key Picture with predominance of light tones and thin shadows.

HMI A discharge lamp producing light by ionizing a gas contained in the bulb.

Hot head A remotely controlled camera pan/tilt head often on the end of a jib arm.

Hue The dominant wavelength, colour describing what we see, e.g. red.

Hyper HAD Increasing the sensitivity of the HAD CCD by the use of a micro lens with each pixel.

Illuminance (*or* Illumination) (E) A unit of light measurement for incident light, lumens/m² = lux.

Image size The image formed by the lens on the face of the CCD.

Insert edit The adding of video, audio or time code, out of sequence, to a pre-recorded tape.

Insert point An input/output in a system allowing the connection of other equipment.

Interlace A method of scanning separate parts of an image in two passes (fields) in order to reduce the bandwidth required for transmission.

Interline transfer (IT) A method of transferring a charge from the pixels exposed to the subject to an adjacent duplicate set of pixels.

Inverse square law A fundamental law in lighting and sound where the intensity of light and sound falls off as the inverse of the distance squared.

Invisible technique Production method which emphasizes the content of the shot rather than the production technique.

Iris Variable circular aperture in the camera used to control exposure, calculated in f_{stops}.

ISDN Integrated Services Digital Network. A system that allows the transfer of audio or other data via a telephone line.

Isoed Recording the (isolated) output of an individual camera or cameras in a multicamera shoot in addition to the main recording.

JPEG Joint Photographic Experts Group. Identifies a standard for the data compression of still pictures.

Kelvin (K) A unit of measurement of heat used to describe colour temperature.

Key Keying signal for chroma key operations.

Key Mood of a picture, i.e. high key/low key.

Keylight (*or* Key) The main source of light illuminating the subject.

Kicker Light used at eye level from upstage to 'kick' the side of the artiste's head.

Knee Modified part of the transfer characteristic of a camera designed to progressively compress highlights.

Ku-band The frequency spectrum between 10.7 GHz and 18 GHz.

Level The volume of an audio or video signal.

Line level A reference audio level measured at 1000 Hz.

Linear matrix Involves cross-coupling between *R*, *G* and *B* to help obtain the desirable analysis characteristics essential for faithful colour reproduction.

Live The transmission of an event as it takes place.

Locked-off Applying the locks on a pan and tilt head to ensure that the camera setting remains in a pre-selected position. Can also be applied to an unmanned camera.

Long lens A lens with a large focal length or using a zoom at or near its narrowest angle of view.

Look angle The angle of elevation of the signal path above the horizon to a satellite.

Low angle A lens height below eye height.

Low key Picture with a predominance of dark tones and strong shadows.

LS (Long shot) A description of a shot when the full length human figure fills the frame.

LTC Longitudinal time code. Recorded with a fixed head on a designated track on the tape.

Lumen Unit of quantity of light flow per second, 'weighted' by the photopic curve.

Luminaire Name given to a complete lighting unit, i.e. light source or lamp plus its casing.

Luminance (L) A measure of the light reflected from a surface. A total flux reflected of 1 lumen/m^2 has a luminance of 1 Apostilb. (Imperial measurement: 1 lumen/ft^2 = 1 foot lambert.)

Luminance signal That part of the video signal which represents the relative brightness points of an image.

Luminous intensity A measure of a lamp's ability to radiate light, measured in candelas (old term – Candlepower).

Lux A unit for illuminance. 1 lumen/m^2 = 1 lux.

Macro A switchable facility on a lens that allows focusing on an object placed closer to the lens than the normal minimum object distance. *See* **MOD**.

Matrix Electrical circuit for deriving 'mixtures' of signals, e.g. colour difference signals and luminance signals from RGB signals.

Matte box A filter holder and bellows extension for the control of flare, fitted to the front of the lens.

Medium close-up shot (MCU) A shot description usually describing a framing of a person with the bottom of the frame cutting where a suit breast pocket would normally be.

Medium shot (MS) A description of shot size with the bottom of the frame cutting at the waist when applied to the human figure.

Megahertz (MHz) One million cycles per second.

Metal particle A video tape coating allowing a wider frequency response to be recorded and an improved signal-to-noise ratio compared with oxide tape coating.

Millisecond One thousandth of a second.

Mired Micro reciprocal degree value. Allows the relationship between a correction filter and the colour temperature shift to be calculated.

MOD Minimum object distance. The closest distance a subject in acceptable focus can be to the lens.

Modelling The action of light revealing contour and texture of a subject.

Monitor termination A switchable electronic 'load' (usually 75 ohms) on the back of a monitor inserted at the end of a video cable feed to prevent the signal 'bouncing back'. If several monitors are looped together, termination only occurs at the last monitor.

Monochrome Reproduction of a single colour such as a black and white image.

Movement blur The degradation of the image related to the speed of subject movement during the exposure time of a single picture.

MPEG2 Moving Picture Experts Group 2. A series of benchmark values specifying different degrees of compression.

Multi-generation Numerous re-recordings of the original recording.

Narrow end of the lens The longest focal length of the zoom that can be selected.

Neutral density filter A filter which reduces the amount of light transmitted without altering the colour temperature.

Nicad Nickel cadmium. The constituent of rechargeable batteries widely used to power broadcast camcorders and cameras.

Noddies Television jargon for cutaway shots recorded for editing purposes after an interview showing the interviewer listening and 'nodding' at the interviewee's comments.

Noise reduction A method of reducing the noise on recorded or transmitted analogue audio.

NTSC National Television System Committee. Usually signifies an American method of encoding colour.

OB Outside Broadcast. Usually a multicamera production from a non-studio venue using a mobile control room.

Off-line editing Low quality images that are used to produce edit lists or a non-transmittable edited guide tape.

Off-shot Describes the camera when its output is not selected at the vision mixing panel to be fed 'to line'.

On-line editing Any system that produces a final edited broadcast-quality programme.

On-shot Describes the camera when its output is selected at the vision mixing panel to be fed 'to line'.

Opacity The reciprocal of transmission of light through a film or filter.

Oscillator Equipment to produce pure tone (sine wave) used for lining-up and calibrating systems.

Oscilloscope Cathode ray oscilloscope used to provide a visual display of video signals.

Oxide tape Tape coating used in the first generation of the Beta format cameras.

Pad A circuit used to reduce or attenuate the signal level.

PAL Phase Alternating Line. A European development of the American NTSC system of encoding colour.

Pan-pot Pan(oramic) pot(entiometer). This adjusts the apparent position of a sound source in a stereo image.

Peak programme meter (PPM) Meter which measures sound by averaging the peaks of intensity over a specified period and rapidly responds to high level transients.

Peak white clipper A 'gain limiting' circuit set to the same level in each colour channel of the camera that restricts any signal to a maximum level.

Peak white Either 100% video signal level or 60% reflectance neutral grey surface.

Ped Pedestal. A camera mounting.

Perspective The apparent position of closeness of sound in an image. Also the optical methods used to assess or construct image depth.

Phantom power The DC supply to some types of condenser microphone using the signal cable.

Phase A time delay between two signals. It is expressed in degrees as the actual time will vary with frequency.

Picture monitor Good quality viewing monitor, similar to a receiver but without RF and sound sections.

Pink noise A random signal that appears to the human ear to contain an equal level of frequencies.

Pistol grip Hand grip controlling zoom movement that may be attached to a lightweight lens when operating the camera 'hand-held' or attached to a pan bar.

Pixel Picture cell. A single point in an electronic image.

Planning meetings A meeting of some members of the production staff held for the exchange of information and planning decisions concerning a future programme.

Playback Replaying a recorded shot or sequence of shots or audio.

PLUGE Picture Line-up Generating Equipment. Test signal used for alignment of monitor contrast and brightness.

Point-of-view shot A shot from a lens position that seeks to duplicate the viewpoint of a subject depicted on screen.

Polecat Adjustable spring-loaded aluminium tubes with rubber feet that can be used vertically or horizontally to support lightweight luminaires.

Pole-operation System for remotely adjusting pan/tilt, spot/flood, etc. of luminaires from the studio floor using an operating pole.

Post-production Editing and other work carried out on pre-recorded material.

Practical An in-shot light source, e.g. wall light.

Prime lens A fixed focal length lens.

Print-through The transfer of magnetic information from one layer of tape to another when stored on a reel.

Production control rooms Production areas on outside broadcasts (*see* **Scanner**), or adjacent to studios, used by production staff, lighting and audio.

Prompters A coated piece of glass positioned in front of the lens to reflect text displayed on a TV monitor below the lens.

PSC The production method of recording material on a portable single video camera.

Pulse coded modulated (PCM) Digital transmission system.

Purity In a monitor, the ability of the red gun only to hit red phosphors, etc.

Quantize In a digital system, allocation of 'sample' level prior to coding.

Real time The actual running time of an event as opposed to 'screen time' – the compression of time achievable by editing.

Real time Time code which changes in step with the actual time of day.

Recce The inspection of a location by production staff to assess the practicalities involved in its use as a setting for a programme or programme insert.

Record run Time code which increases only when a recording is made. Record run only records a frame identification when the camera is recording.

Recorded-as-live A continuous recording with no recording breaks.

Redhead An 800 W portable lightweight lamp.

Redundancy When compressing a signal, the part which can be predicted from the signal already received and therefore need not be sent. It is redundant.

Reflector Any white or silvered surface that can be used to reflect a light source.

Reverberation The gradual decay of reflected sound.

Reverse angle When applied to a standard two-person interview, a camera repositioned at 180° to the immediate shot being recorded to provide a complementary shot of the opposite subject.

RMS Root mean square. Used in the calculation of the effective value of an alternating voltage or current.

Robotic camera A camera with a remotely controlled camera head, e.g. pan/tilt, zoom and focus. May also include camera position and height.

Rocking focus Moving the focus zone in front of and behind the selected subject in order to determine sharpest focus.

S/PDIF   A consumer version of the AES/EBU digital interface.

Sampling rate   The number of measurement points over time that describes a continuously variable voltage.

Saturation   A measure of the purity of a colour, e.g. pale red or deep red.

Scanner   The production control rooms of an outside broadcast production.

Scene file   A removable data storage chip from the camera that contains memorized settings.

SECAM (Sequential Couleur à Memoire)   A French-developed method of encoding colour.

Shooting off   Including in the shot more than the planned setting or scenery.

Shot number   A number assigned to a specific shot as detailed in a camera script or camera rehearsal.

Shuttling   Rapidly reviewing video tape to determine content or edit point.

Signal-to-noise   The level difference, in dB, between the wanted signal and the unwanted background system noise.

Simple PAL   Monitor mode which enables the eye to average out colour errors, i.e. no delay line used. Also enables phase errors to be seen.

Single shot technique   The single-camera discontinuous recording of a number of shots that are later edited in post-production.

Sitcom   Situation comedy. A mini-drama (usually approximately thirty minutes duration) performed before an audience.

Slo-mo replay   Replaying a pre-recording at a slower speed than normal transmission.

SNG (Satellite News Gathering)   The technique of relaying video location news reports or news material via a satellite to a base station.

SOC (Satellite operation centre)   The control centre of the owner/operator of a satellite.

Soft light   A light source that produces a soft-edged shadow.

SPL   Sound pressure level. Expressed in dB where the reference is the threshold of human hearing.

Spot effects   Sounds that relate to short actions, usually in vision.

Star quad   A four-core sound cable designed to reduce unwanted interference pick-up.

Station out   The programme output being fed to a transmitter, satellite or for cable distribution.

Stereo   Usually understood to mean a system of reproducing a wide sound image using two channels.

Stop   Either the f-number the lens is set to or the unit change between two standard f-numbers.

Studio out   The output of the vision mixing panel.

Switcher   *See* **Vision mixer**. Note that job titles vary from country to country.

Talkback   Inter-communication by microphone and headset between a television control room and other operational areas and technicians.

Termination   75 Ω resistor included across the video cable at the end of a transmission chain. Inclusion of 75 Ω termination ensures no reflection of energy, and ensures the signal level is correct.

Tight lens   A long focal length primary lens or zoom lens setting.

Time code   Enables every recorded frame of video to be numbered.

T-number   Indicates the amount of light transmitted by a lens at a specific iris setting. Unlike f-numbers, identical T-numbers on lenses will transmit the same amount of light independent of lens design.

T-piece   Small BNC connectors to allow teeing of video connectors, e.g. to connect two video cables to one video socket.

Transformer   A device made with two coils wound around a magnetizable core to isolate a signal or to change its voltage.

Transient response   The ability of equipment to follow fast changes in level.

Transient A fast-changing signal.

Translucent Semi-transparent; usually some form of light diffuser.

Tungsten The filament material in a lamp producing light by heat.

Turtle Very low lighting stand for rigging luminaires at floor level.

Tweak Term used for small adjustments to a lighting rig or operational settings, e.g. black level or iris setting.

Tx Transmission.

Uplink The signal path from an earth station to a satellite.

Upstage Further away from the camera or audience.

User-bit A programmable identification code compiled by the 'user' of the camera which is recorded as part of the time code on each video frame. User-bit allows up to 9 numbers and an A to F code to be programmed into the code word which is recorded on every frame.

VCA Voltage controlled amplifier.

Vectorscope Special oscilloscope designed to display the chrominance information in an easily recognizable way, i.e. hue and saturation.

Video barrel A small in-line adaptor designed to connect two BNC video cables together.

Video contrast range The relationship between the brightest part of the scene and the darkest part.

Video wall A number of individual TV screens often stacked in a rectangle displaying multiple, individual or composite images.

Vignette The shading of the edges of the picture area.

Virtual reality System of chroma key where the background is computer-generated. The size and positioning of the background is controlled by the foreground camera movements.

Vision control The person who adjusts camera exposure, colour, gamma, etc. in a multicamera production. Also applied to the area where they perform this function.

Vision mixer The person who switches between video sources. Also applied to the equipment they use to perform this function.

VITC (Vertical Interval Time Code) Time code numbers recorded in one or more of the unused lines in the TV signal and which can be read when the tape is in still frame.

Voice-over A commentary mixed with effects or music as part of a sound track.

Vox pops (Vox populi) The voice of the people, usually consisting of a series of impromptu interviews recorded in the street with members of the public.

VTR Video tape recorder.

VU meter Volume meter. Indicates average level of sound.

Waveform monitor Oscilloscope with appropriate time-base for displaying the television waveform. Usually includes a face-plate graticule to indicate sync level, black level, peak white and percentage signal level.

Wavelength The length between adjacent peaks of a signal.

White balance The electronic process of defining a reference white lit by a light source of a specific colour temperature.

White noise Random noise containing an equal level of the audio frequency spectrum

Wide angle The horizontal field of view of a lens greater than approximately 40°.

Wide shot (WS) A description of shot size which includes objects greater than the size of the human figure.

Working behind the camera Operating the camera using remoted lens controls attached to pan bars and a non-monocular viewfinder.

Working-as-live Continuous recording with no opportunity for recording breaks or retakes.

Wow and flutter Variations in speed of a mechanical system, audible as frequency variations in an analogue recording.

Zebra exposure indicator A black and white striped pattern that appears in the viewfinder at points in the picture corresponding to a pre-set video level. Used as an aid to manual exposure.

Zero level voltage A standard reference audio signal of 0.775 V at 1000 Hz used for audio equipment line-up.

Zoom ratio The ratio of the longest focal length to the shortest focal length a specific zoom lens can achieve.

Zoom tracking A lens pre-focused on a distant subject will stay in focus for the whole of its zoom movement towards (or away from) that subject providing the back focus (flange-back) has been correctly aligned.

Zoom A variable focal length lens achieved by internally moving elements of the lens.

Index

Focal Press

http://www.focalpress.com

Visit our web site for:

- ❏ The latest information on new and forthcoming Focal Press titles
- ❏ Technical articles from industry experts
- ❏ Special offers
- ❏ Our email news service

Join our Focal Press Bookbuyers' Club

As a member, you will enjoy the following benefits:

- ❏ Special discounts on new and best-selling titles
- ❏ Advance information on forthcoming Focal Press books
- ❏ A quarterly newsletter highlighting special offers
- ❏ A 30-day guarantee on purchased titles

Membership is FREE. To join, supply your name, company, address, phone/fax numbers and email address to:

USA
Christine Degon, Product Manager
Email: christine.degon@bhusa.com
Fax: +1 781 904 2620
Address: Focal Press,
225 Wildwood Ave, Woburn,
MA 01801, USA

Europe and rest of World
Elaine Hill, Promotions Controller
Email: elaine.hill@repp.co.uk
Fax: +44 (0)1865 314572
Address: Focal Press, Linacre House,
Jordan Hill, Oxford,
UK, OX2 8DP

Catalogue

For information on all Focal Press titles, we will be happy to send you a free copy of the Focal Press catalogue:

USA
Email: christine.degon@bhusa.com

Europe and rest of World
Email: carol.burgess@repp.co.uk
Tel: +1(0)1865 314693

Potential authors

If you have an idea for a book, please get in touch:

USA
Terri Jadick, Associate Editor
Email: terri.jadick@bhusa.com
Tel: +1 781 904 2646
Fax: +1 781 904 2640

Europe and rest of World
Beth Howard, Editorial Assistant
Email: beth.howard@repp.co.uk
Tel: +44 (0)1865 314365
Fax: +44 (0)1865 314572